D1523406

FUZZY INFORMATION ENGINEERING

A Guided Tour of Applications

EDITED BY

Didier Dubois, Henri Prade, and Ronald R. Yager

WILEY COMPUTER PUBLISHING

JOHN WILEY & SONS, INC.

New York • Chichester • Brisbane • Toronto • Singapore • Weinheim

Executive Publisher: Katherine Schowalter
Editor: Marjorie Spencer
Text Design & Composition: North Market Street Graphics

This text is printed on acid-free paper.

Library of Congress Cataloging-in-Publication Data:
Fuzzy information engineering: a guided tour of applications/edited
    by Didier Dubois, Henri Prade, and Ronald R. Yager.
        p.   cm.
    Includes bibliographical references.
    ISBN 0-471-14766-4 (cloth : alk. paper)
    1. Information technology.   2. Fuzzy sets.   I. Dubois, Didier.
 II. Prade, Henri M.   III. Yager, Ronald R., 1941–
 T58.5.F89   1996
 511.3′22—dc20   96-18036
                                                                      CIP

Printed in the United States of America
10 9 8 7 6 5 4 3 2 1

Contents

Retrieving Information
Part 1: Querying

Preface

This book provides a representative sampling of the use of a range of fuzzy set techniques in different engineering problems aimed at clarifying, retrieving, and exploiting information. Contributors were invited on the basis of what they accomplished in showing the practical interest of these techniques. For this reason, most of the chapters are revised and updated versions of papers scattered in the literature rather than research papers presenting the newest theoretical advances on the various topics. In some cases, the previous versions of these works appeared more than five years ago. However, because those papers provided suggestive illustrations of the applicability of fuzzy sets to a new class of problems, still unsufficiently exploited, their updated version has a natural place in this guided tour.

The recent impressive success of fuzzy sets in control and systems engineering, in coordination with neural net approaches and stochastic optimization methods, often dubbed "soft computing," has created a new generation of researchers who often have a limited knowledge of all that has been done with fuzzy sets since its inception. Because of this there is a risk that the tree of soft computing will mask the forest of results, algorithms, and applications of fuzzy sets. The range of fuzzy set tools that are described in this book is much greater than the fuzzy rule-based technique, which has been popularized with the success of fuzzy controllers. These tools include the panoply of fuzzy set aggregation connectives, the representation of fuzzy similarity relations and fuzzy orderings, the calculus of fuzzy relations, the modelling of uncertainty in terms of possibility and necessity measures, and the calculus of fuzzy numbers among others. This book intends to give a comprehensive introduction to the whole range of fuzzy set tools and to show in what types of applications they can be successfully used. To help the reader, guiding notes introduce each section devoted to a given class of applications and point out what kind of fuzzy tools are used in the section.

Although many chapters exhibit complete applications in realistic settings, some other chapters only provide examples that aim to suggest potential applications for the future. In spite of the huge development of both the methodology and the applications of fuzzy logic in the last 10 years, this tool is still a young, although fruitful, addition to the general corpus of engineering methods. It is clear that there are still open problems that require deeper investigation in order to facilitate still a larger variety of applications. Among these problems, although not limited to them, we mention the proper scaling of membership grades, which call for a better understanding of measurement issues, and the development of algorithms specifically suitable for use in fuzzy environments.

We hope that this book will help to contribute to a better understanding of what use can be made of fuzzy sets. We want to thank all the contributors and the publisher for their kind cooperation in this project.

The Editors

Introduction

A Manifesto: Fuzzy Information Engineering

Didier Dubois
Henri Prade
I.R.I.T., University of Toulouse III, France

Ronald R. Yager
Machine Intelligence Institute, Iona College, New Rochelle, New York

I.1. A View of Information Engineering

At this time in history, *information* is a very important matter of scientific investigation, with a potentially enormous economical, industrial, and social impact. This interest is in part strongly motivated by the confluence of computer and communication technologies which allows for the collection and storage of large amounts of information and its subsequent dissemination in a very efficient way. The future promises even greater advances in this direction. By information, we mean any collection of symbols or signs, produced either by the observation of natural or artificial phenomena, or by the cognitive activity of human beings, which can be used to understand the world around us, help in decision making, or to communicate with one another.

The last 20 years have seen the development of a large number of techniques whose purpose is to take advantage of the great potential of the symbiotic relationship between the human and the computer for using all the available types of information needed to solve problems of interest. In introducing the concept of information engineering we are attempting to bring together under one umbrella many of these methods. Informally, we can tentatively see information engineering as consisting of three main components, namely *clarifying, retrieving,* and *exploiting information,* although time will possibly extend and refine this initial categorization.

By clarifying information we mean the process of elaborating primary information, or raw data, into more useful and comprehensible forms. This task ranges from enhancing information via smoothing or eliminating redundant or erroneous data, completing information via interpolation, to higher cognitive activities such as abstracting and modeling. Some clarification tasks can be performed at the level of a sensor itself. Clarification appears as a transformation process that turns primary information into a more structured information, clarified information, that is more understandable and useful. In some cases, especially when abstracting is in order, it necessitates the use of linguistic labels to communicate the main features of the information. Alternatively, clarification may also come down to a kind of data compression by laying bare an underlying mathematical model. Clarified information then can be appropriately stored and be further exploited in reasoning and decision processes.

Typical of clarification are techniques such as clustering, other data analysis methods such as regression, identification, inductive learning, and, more generally, any method aimed at abstracting and structuring information. A particularly extensive family of clarification methods is the arsenal of techniques used in computer vision, whose purposes are the reduction of uncertainty, the recognition of relevant patterns, and the labelling of scenes. In addition, many of the operations used in data fusion for synthesizing and combining pieces of data fall in the category of clarification methods, since more often than not, information is supplied by several, possibly conflicting sources and not in an homogeneous format.

When retrieving information we are trying to extract, based on certain requirements and specifications, already existing, possibly hidden, pieces of information. This component of information engineering includes many of the methodologies used in databases, information retrieval, and the emerging field of multimedia. It is strongly dependent on the storage technology and the knowledge representation framework used.

In its most elementary form, which we may call querying, the retrieval of information does not involve a modification of existing information, as in the clarifying task. A large body of information is stored in some format and a query is entered. As a result of a query-matching process a class of objects satisfying the query are provided. An important objective in the construction of these types of systems with respect to the querying task is the facilitation, for the user, of the expression of their goals regarding the information to be retrieved.

This objective requires allowing for rather sophisticated forms of queries. It is also worth noting that a basic distinction between the database and information retrieval technologies is related to the use in information retrieval of intermediary descriptions of the information in terms of keywords, whereas in databases, information is described directly in terms of attributes values.

Some modes of storing information do not allow the retrieval process to be reduced to one of simply locating items in a file. For instance, in deductive databases, information is encoded in a declarative way via some kind of logic-based language. The retrieval process requires that the information system be equipped with inferential power. In this environment, retrieving information involves a reasoning task, whereby hidden information is made explicit for the user. This type of concern is present in so-called intelligent information systems, which lie at the boundary between database research and artificial intelligence.

In the exploiting information component we are encompassing a large range of activities including decision making, optimization, and design. Generally, in this task, the information plays a supportive role to some sort of paradigm or model. In order to make the best use of the knowledge embedded in the model, the ability to represent and manipulate different types of information becomes very important here. The development of technologies that allow us to combine numerical, logical, linguistic, and visual information is an important part of the agenda of this aspect of information engineering. All pieces of information are used in the problem-solving task, whose solution is presented to the users in order to guide their course of action. Several prototypical situations can be distinguished; the number of potential solutions is very small but the choice is made difficult due to many conflicting goals and/or the presence of several decision makers, or on the contrary the computation of a solution is a highly combinatorial task but the preference modeling is very clear and simple. In other cases, the solution is itself a complex entity that is built in several steps.

In each of these three components of information engineering, we want to emphasize the importance of the communication of information between human and machine. This communication goes in both directions: information generated by the machine should be in a form easily comprehensible by human beings, while information provided by human beings should be in a format exploitable by the computer. One conclusion that emerges from considering the collection of papers in this book is that fuzzy sets play an important role in providing this bridge.

I.2. The Role of Fuzzy Sets in Information Engineering

Historically, fuzzy sets have been mostly noted for their ability to model linguistic categories. This situation is due to their ability to represent gradedness of concepts, a reality that is pervasive both in the mental as well as the physical worlds. This idea has perhaps been most succinctly captured in Zadeh's [4] recent view of fuzzy sets as "computing with words." This view highlights the importance of the interface between the data emanating from the physical world and the categories with which human beings are most comfortable in comprehending and using information. In addition, many of the basic notions used in the measurement and manipulation of information, such as *uncertainty, preference,* and *similarity,* are naturally graded.

A number of different semantics can be associated with the use of fuzzy sets. A first semantics (and historically the oldest one) is the expression of closeness, proximity, similarity, indiscernibility, indistinguishability and the like. Under this semantics elements with membership one are viewed as prototypical elements of the fuzzy set, while the other membership grades estimate the closeness of elements to the prototypical ones. This view is most commonly used in pattern classification where objects that are judged to be sufficiently similar are gathered in the same (fuzzy) class (Bellman, Kalaba, and Zadeh [1]). Moreover, the idea of similarity can be naturally graded by means of fuzzy relations, thus refining the idea of equivalence classes. The idea of proximity is also central in interpolation processes. This is the usual understanding of fuzzy sets in clarification tasks.

A second semantics associated with fuzzy sets is related to the representation of incomplete or vague states of information under the form of possibility distributions (Zadeh [3]). This view of fuzzy sets enables imperfect, imprecise, or uncertain information to be stored. Uncertain information expressed in terms of possibility and necessity measures can be propagated through inference patterns.

A third semantics for a fuzzy set useful when modelling a flexible constraint, specification, or goal expresses preferences between more or less acceptable solutions with respect to the constraint (Bellman and Zadeh [2]). The gradedness introduced by the use of fuzzy sets refines the simple binary distinction made by ordinary constraints, crisp specifications, or all-or-nothing goals between completely acceptable values and completely forbidden ones. This is especially important for exploiting information in decision making. More generally classical constraint satisfaction algorithms, optimization techniques, and multifactorial evaluation tasks can be extended in order to deal both with flexible requirements and uncertain data using a fuzzy set representation. In addition, flexible queries addressed to a database storing uncertain or imprecise pieces of information provides another example of a situation where both the preference and the uncertainty semantics are encountered. The similarity semantics may be also present in this context for modelling the approximate synonymy of terms, or the interchangeability of close values from a user point of view.

In this framework, the grades of membership of a fuzzy set such as *tall* may be understood in three different manners depending upon the context. First, tall may describe a fuzzy class of sizes more or less close to prototypical values. Second, it may represent an incomplete state of information, such as, we only know that "John is tall" without knowing his height more precisely. Lastly, it may express a flexible constraint, such as, we are looking for somebody who is tall.

We should note at this point two important aspects of fuzzy sets that are not always sufficiently emphasized:

- First, fuzzy sets are always context-dependent. For instance, there cannot be any universal agreement on the membership function of a fuzzy set like tall, even when we have indicated if we are speaking of elephants, butterflies, or humans. Even if we are restricted to speaking of humans, the meaning of the concept tall will be different when considering children or basketball players. Moreover, for a definite domain, the view of tallness will also depend upon the user and the intended use. Thus, if a Rockefeller tells a Kennedy about a meal being expensive, the concept of expensive used by the Rockefeller may be different from the one when he is telling a professor that it is an expensive meal.

- Second, when aggregating fuzzy sets, an implicit commensurability assumption on the membership grades is made. The use of a unique membership scale underlies the hypothesis that the membership degree to a fuzzy set is turned into a universal quantity that can be somehow measured. It can be interpreted in several ways as pointed out: level of satisfaction with respect to some ideal, or to a level of similarity to prototypes, or yet to a level of uncertainty. The membership scale is usually the interval [0,1], but it can be any ordinal scale as well. Thus, when using a grade of membership to indicate to what extent a house belongs to the class of beautiful houses, which is a matter of subjective preference, we mean to what extent the house meets the expectation of a user with respect to his or her own goal. In some situations, it is natural to use numerical membership grades: this is when the universe of discourse is described by means of numerical parameters (size, age, temperature, and so on). In other situations, it is not clear how to come up with numerical membership grades. This is when the fuzziness seems to be induced by exceptions in a class (what is the degree of birdness of a penguin?) or when the fuzzy category is so complex that its underlying dimensions are hard to grasp (terms like beautiful, for instance). In such situations, it is often enough to consider a finite lattice of qualitative membership levels.

Let us look at the three components of information engineering and summarize the role fuzzy sets can play in each of them. In clarification techniques such as clustering, recognition, and classification, obvious use is made of fuzzy sets for providing linguistic labels to sets of objects; however at a deeper level, we are also taking advantage of the similarity naturally embedded in the membership functions and the proximity or possible overlap between classes. In classification techniques such as image processing, again, though less obvious, use is also made of fuzzy sets for the representation of tentativeness in precisiation and disambiguation processes. Fuzzy sets, in some sense, provide a porous interface between numerical and linguistic/logical representations of information. Although displaying a strong logical flavor, fuzzy sets leave room for typically numerical processing methods such as interpolation, as exemplified in fuzzy control and fuzzy modeling.

When retrieving information, it is often desirable to allow for flexible requests in order to more faithfully express the desires of the user of the information system. An important issue in this task is the aggregation of the satisfaction levels to the individual objectives involved in the request. Here considerable use is made of the vast array of aggregation operators available in fuzzy set theory to model the different relationships between the objectives (are they compensatory or not). Here again considerable use is made of the porous interface fuzzy sets provide between numerical and logical methods. At the heart of the use of the aggregation operators is the commensurability assumption. Another aspect, in this task, of the use of fuzzy sets might be the representation of the uncertainty pervading the data or their descriptions. The ability of fuzzy sets to represent various types of information (precise, imprecise, partially conflicting, linguistic) is of great benefit in this task. At an operational level the facility to use arithmetic and logical operations for propagating this information through the model or reasoning from uncertain or vague premises is required. The theories of fuzzy logic-based approximate reasoning and fuzzy arithmetics play a fundamental role in accomplishment of this task.

When exploiting information, the use of fuzzy sets may appear in the representation of uncertainty (when making decisions in uncertain environments), in the expression of preferences (in formulating objectives in optimization problems), or in the capturing of similarities (as in case-based reasoning). An important asset of fuzzy sets in decision making lies in the very general framework it provides that allows us to cope with the presence of multiple criteria, including the representation of complex relationships between criteria (using techniques such as OWA operators and fuzzy integrals for instance), the notion of flexible constraints in design and scheduling problems, the presence of uncertainty in the data (using possibility theory). It can bridge the gap between value functions that insist on numerical, totally ordered preference models, and relational approaches that handle nontransitive notions of preference and indifference and capture notions of incomparability.

It should be noted that in advocating the use of fuzzy sets in information engineering we are not doing this at the expense of probability theory. As we see it, fuzzy set theory and probability theory are complementary. Probability methods are also used in all the three components of information engineering. A point of tangency between fuzzy sets used as a basis for possibility theory and probability theory is the modelling of uncertainty. However, it seems wrong to claim that the realm of subjective uncertainty is fuzzy logic while probability theory is devoted to random phenomena only. This is getting rid of subjective probability, which has acquired a prominent place in the additive modeling of uncertainty. In that respect, possibility theory may basically offer the option of a more qualitative treatment of uncertainty, especially when information is poor. It means either an ordinal view of uncertainty that comes close to modal logic, or the presence of incomplete or imprecise statistical information. It is important to remember that while probability is naturally accounting for precise but dissonant pieces of information, possibility theory captures imprecise but coherent information (through the level-cuts of the underlying possibility distribution). For instance, fuzzy sets can be viewed as the compressed representation of ill-observed, thus imprecise, data that take the form of random sets. As a matter of fact, we envision information engineering as encompassing both probabilistic and fuzzy set methods. However, this volume only focuses on the contributions of fuzzy sets to information engineering.

I.3. Fuzzy Information Engineering: Aims and Scope

The aim of this volume is to somewhat resist a current trend in fuzzy logic applications whereby the emphasis of research is put on purely data-driven concerns that seem to gradually dispose of the knowledge representation capabilities of fuzzy sets. Systems of fuzzy rules are in some communities more and more viewed as tools for the approximation of numerical functions that compete with neural networks and other mathematical methods of function approximation. As a consequence, the linguistic aspect of fuzzy rules is no longer the main point. The term "soft computing" is sometimes used to name this trend, especially for works that use systems of fuzzy rules only as a variant of neural nets or a means of encoding a nonlinear function. Originally, a fuzzy controller had been understood as a "quick and dirty" (but very useful) way of building up a control law from expert knowledge, which can cope with the lack of a numerical model of a physical process. As such, fuzzy control could be considered at the crossroads between artificial intelligence and information engineering. However, we feel that works that use fuzzy rules only as an artful surrogate for approximating functions (such as control laws) and modifying them locally, regardless of the semantics of the underlying concepts, adopt a very narrow view of soft computing, and move away from the essence of fuzzy logic, which, to quote Zadeh again, aims at computing with words [4]. It should be clear that in data analysis and modelling, the quality of approximation of a method is incompatible with its linguistic interpretability. In other words, when learning from data, one must choose between a numerical model that achieves good performance, and a linguistic representation that explains what is going on to a user. This is another example of Zadeh's principle of incompatibility between precision and meaning.

In light of this observation, we have deemphasized in this volume the importance of data-driven fuzzy logic control in information engineering and viewed it rather as a separate discipline that has its own objectives and formal tools and that looks less and less related to the issue of computing with words. On the contrary, we should emphasize the diversity of past and potential applications of fuzzy sets in areas such as intelligent sensing, pattern classification and symbolic learning, computer vision, information systems (including information retrieval and databases), expert systems and automated reasoning under uncertainty and preference, decision analysis with one or several agents, engineering design, and operations research. In each case, the introduction of fuzzy sets is motivated by the need for more human-friendly computerized devices that help a user input pieces of information, queries or preferences, understand a set of data or observations, extract information, get advice to cope with a problem. This book has the ambition of showing that nice applications of genuine fuzzy set research were done in the past, and that this tradition is alive, with a potentially appealing future.

I.4. References

[1] Bellman, R.E., et al. "Abstraction and Pattern Classification." *Journal of Mathematical Analysis and Applications,* Vol. 13 (1966), pp. 1–7.
[2] Bellman, R.E., and L.A. Zadeh. "Decision Making in a Fuzzy Environment." *Management Sciences,* Vol. 17 (1970), pp. 141–164.
[3] Zadeh, L.A. "Fuzzy Sets as a Basis for a Theory of Possibility." *Fuzzy Sets and Systems,* Vol. 1 (1978), pp. 3–28.
[4] ———. "Fuzzy Logic = Computing with Words." IEEE *Transactions on Fuzzy Systems.* 4, 103–111, 1996.

Clarifying Information

PART 1
Sensing and Enhancing

GUIDING NOTE

Raw or noisy data are not easily interpreted by humans and should be enhanced. Providing sensors with an interface making use of labels meaningful for the users certainly helps them to have a better understanding of the sensor output. Fuzzy sets offer then an appropriate and flexible format for expressing these labels, as well as for representing clusters to be extracted from data. Basically two approaches can be used, sometimes in combination, to enhance information in order to facilitate its interpretation. The first is a knowledge-based approach where the available knowledge about the environment, expressed under the form of fuzzy rules, is used to reduce the uncertainty. The second approach takes advantage of multiple sources of information for clarifying the information by using the redundancy to help in reinforcement. Image processing is a natural field of applications for all these techniques.

In this part, we present a number of applications that use fuzzy methodologies to help in the problem of information clarification enhancement. In the first chapter by Mauris, Benoit, and Foulloy, the authors investigate the use of fuzzy sensors. Fuzzy sensors allow for the interpretation of sensor data in linguistic terms. The authors provide a number of applications, such as color detection, temperature and humidity detection, and the use of ultrasonic information in robotics. The second chapter by Chen and Xie describes a novel application of fuzzy methods to a freehand drawing system. They make use of fuzzy filtering rules to help smooth freehand drawings. This system is able to clearly detect intended geometric shapes inputted by a user. The chapter by Gader,

Keller, and Cai describes an application of fuzzy sets to automated recognition of addresses on mail. The authors use a fuzzy rule knowledge base to generate information about the location of the street number in a handwritten address. The system provides as an output multiple hypothesis along with confidences for this location. The next chapter by Bezdek, Hall, et. al. concentrates on a fuzzy set application to medical imaging. They are particularly interested in the issue of enhancement and are particularly concerned with the problem of segmentation and edge detection in medical images. The chapter by Bloch, Pellot, et. al. is also an application of fuzzy techniques to medical imaging. They use fuzzy mathematical morphology to help in the problem of 3D reconstruction of blood vessels. Use is made of fuzzy numbers to help in the representation of uncertain geometric parameters. The chapter by Roux and Desachy makes use of multiple sources of information to help in the clarification of images. The authors use possibility distributions to describe the imprecise information. They discuss methods for fusing multiple possibility distributions. The chapter by Sandri also provides an application of the use of multiple sources to help clarify information. In this chapter the author is interested in combining information from multiple experts. Again, possibility distributions are used for the representation of the uncertain information. However, the author also discusses methods for converting probabilistic information into possibilistic information. Various methods are described for pooling of the information from the different experts.

1 Fuzzy Sensors: An Overview

G. Mauris, E. Benoit, and L. Foulloy
Laboratoire d'Automatique et de MicroInformatique Industrielle
LAMII/CESALP, Université de Savoie,
41 Avenue de la Plaine, BP 806
74016 ANNECY FRANCE

ABSTRACT: This chapter deals with sensors that compute and report linguistic assessments of numerical acquired values by means of the fuzzy subset theory. Such sensors, called fuzzy sensors, are particularly adapted when working with intelligent control systems. After having detailed the formal representation of numeric and symbolic information, the design of fuzzy sensors by operators and by interpolation is presented. Then the applications of the proposed methods in color detection, in qualification of the feeling of comfort, and in ultrasonic range finding are described.

1.1. Introduction

The control of operations in a view of improving the performances or the production quality of an industrial system is becoming more and more complex. The conventional sensors and controllers, conceived for operating in well-known environmental conditions are no longer adapted to the complexity of the situations considered. To face this complexity, new components or techniques have been introduced either in measurement or in control.

In the measurement domain, the progress of electronics and computer science has led to adding new functionalities to the sensors. These new sensors have been called smart sensors [1],[2],[3]. It is generally admitted that the functionalities of smart sensors are communication, the validation of measurements, and the adaptation to the variations of the measurement context. Today, most smart sensors are microprocessor-based. As the performance of such processors is increasing, one can consider the introduction of artificial intelligence techniques in measurement [4],[5].

Artificial intelligence techniques have also been introduced in control. Expert control, fuzzy control, qualitative control, neural control, rule-based control, intelligent control have all been used to design alternative control techniques (see among many others [6],[7],[8],[9]). Except for neural control, a common feature of these techniques is their reliance on symbolic coding and manipulation instead of algebraic relations. They only differ in the level at which symbolic coding is employed: from reasoning for supervision in most expert controllers to low-level inference in fuzzy controllers. Therefore rather than "intelligent control," these control techniques are more accurately termed "symbolic control" [10].

Symbolic sensors were developed to perform some symbolic processing in order to provide a symbolic-to-numeric interface for symbolic controllers [11]. A special case is obtained when a fuzzy numeric-to-symbolic interface is used, leading to fuzzy symbolic sensors or simply fuzzy sensors [12]. In the following, after having described their formal aspects, the designs and applications of fuzzy sensors in color detection [13], in qualification of the feeling of comfort [14], and in ultrasonic range finding [15] are presented.

1.2. Foundations of Fuzzy Symbolic Sensors

1.2.1. Typology of Fuzzy Information Handling

The aim of this paragraph is to provide general but nevertheless clear definitions of the three general stages involved generally in fuzzy information handling [16].

- Fuzzification is an interface that produces a fuzzy subset from the measurement; that is, it is a mapping from the set of measurements X to a set of fuzzy subsets associated with the input, denoted $\mathcal{F}(Y)$.

- The inference is an interface that produces a new fuzzy subset from the result of the fuzzification using for example a set of rules. The result of the inference is a fuzzy subset associated with the output. It can be represented by a mapping from the set $\mathcal{F}(Y)$, associated with the input, to a set of fuzzy subsets associated with the output and denoted $\mathcal{F}(Z)$.

- The defuzzification is an interface that produces a crisp output from the result of the inference; that is, it is a mapping from the set $\mathcal{F}(Z)$, associated with the output, to the set U.

The set Y related to the input can either be the set of numerical values, X, or the set of linguistic values, $\mathcal{L}(X)$. In the same way, the set Z related to the output can either be the set of numerical values, U, or the set of linguistic values, $L(U)$. Therefore, the previous definitions can be used to provide an efficient classification, a typology of fuzzy information handling in four classes as shown in Figure 1.1.

From the preceding typology, three types of components can be introduced:

- Fuzzy sensors provide a representation of the measurements by means of fuzzy subsets; they perform the fuzzification.

- Fuzzy actuators are components that are able to act on the physical world depending on the fuzzy subset they receive; they perform the defuzzification.

- Fuzzy inference components produce new fuzzy subsets from fuzzy subsets they have received, thus performing fuzzy reasoning.

This chapter focuses on fuzzy symbolic sensors, which deal with fuzzy subsets of symbols. Such sensors can be represented directly by means of the φ_2 mapping, as for example in the comfort sensor and in the color sensor described in sections 1.4 and 1.5. They can also be represented indirectly by means of the composition of several mappings as long as the resulting information is a fuzzy subset of linguistic terms. For example, the ultrasonic telemeter described in section 1.6 uses the $g_4 o \varphi_2$ mapping.

1.2.2. Symbolic Fuzzification

We propose to call the fuzzification defined by the mapping $\varphi_2: X \rightarrow \mathcal{F}(L(X))$, a *symbolic fuzzification* because it provides a fuzzy subset of a set of symbolic values (the universe of discourse is the set of linguistic values associated with the input).

1.2.2.1. Meaning and Description. Let X be the universe of discourse associated with the measurement of a particular physical quantity. Denote x any element of X. In order to symbolically characterize any measurement over X, let $L(X)$ be a set of words, representative of the physical phenomenon. For example, the set $L(X)$ = {**cold, cool, mild, warm, hot**} could be used to represent the symbolic values of a temperature.

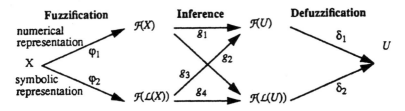

Figure 1.1 Typology of fuzzy information handling.

Let us introduce the injective mapping $M_X: L(X) \to P(X)$, called the *meaning* of a symbol over X[17]. It associates any symbol L of $L(X)$ with a subset of X. Injectivity guarantees that two different symbols must not have the same meaning. In other words, two synonymous symbols have the same meaning. Let $X = [0, 40]$ be the universe of discourse for the measurement of temperature in Celsius degree. The meaning of the linguistic value **mild** could be the interval M_X (**mild**) $= [17, 22]$.

Let us introduce a new mapping $D_{L(X)}: X \to P(L(X))$, called the *description* of a measurement over $L(X)$ [17]. It associates any measurement of X with a subset of symbols of $L(X)$. Any measurement that belongs to the meaning of a symbol, can obviously be symbolically described at least by this symbol. Therefore, the description of a measurement is linked to the meaning of a symbol by the following relation:

$$L \in D_{L(X)}(x) \Leftrightarrow x \in M_X(L) \tag{1}$$

Assume the meaning of the elements of $L(X)$ are:

$$M_X \text{ (cold)} = [0, 10], M_X \text{ (cool)} = [9, 17], M_X \text{ (mild)} = [17, 22]$$

$$M_X \text{ (warm)} = [20, 25], M_X \text{ (hot)} = [24, 40].$$

The description of a measurement $x_0 = 22$ is the subset $D_{L(X)}(x_0) = \{$**mild**, **warm**$\}$ because $x_0 = 22$ belongs to the meaning of both symbols.

1.2.2.2. Fuzzy Meanings and Fuzzy Descriptions. The *fuzzy meaning* over X of a symbol is defined as a mapping from $L(X)$ to $F(X)$. The fuzzy meaning over X of a symbol L is characterized, for all $x \in X$, by its membership function denoted $\mu_{M_X(L)}$. The *fuzzy description* of a measurement is defined as a mapping from X to $F(L(X))$. The fuzzy description of a measurement is characterized, for all $L \in L(X)$, by its membership function $\mu_{D_{L(X)}(x)}$. The fundamental relation linking the meaning and the description, given by Eq. (1), becomes in the fuzzy case:

$$\mu_{D_{L(X)}(x)}(L) = \mu_{M_X(L)}(x) \tag{2}$$

It means that if a symbol belongs to the description of a measurement at the grade of membership $\mu_{D_{L(X)}(x)}(L)$, then the measurement belongs to the meaning of the symbol for the same grade of membership. The fuzzy meanings of **cold**, **cool**, **mild**, **warm**, and **hot** are respectively represented by the membership functions labelled 1, 2, 3, 4 and 5 in Figure 1.2. The fuzzy description of the measurement $x_0 = 22°C$ is obtained according to equation (2).

1.3. Design of Fuzzy Sensors

1.3.1 Fuzzy Sensors Based on Operators

Obviously, it is a tedious task to specify the meaning of each symbol. Moreover, in this case, one can say that a sensor based on such an approach is no

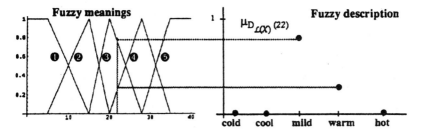

Figure 1.2 Fuzzy meanings and fuzzy description.

longer smart. Defining a new symbol and its meaning can be done using modifiers, usually called linguistic hedges. Each operation on the symbolic domain is linked to an operation on the numerical one. Links between these functions are represented in Figure 1.3.

Let us begin with crisp sets, the function $F\colon L(X) \to L(X)$ operates on the symbolic domain such that:

$$L_2 = F(L_1) \tag{3}$$

Now the function $f_F\colon \mathcal{P}(X) \to \mathcal{P}(X)$ operates on the numerical domain such that:

$$M(L_2) = M(F(L_1)) = f_F(M(L_1)) \tag{4}$$

The crisp case can be easily extended to the fuzzy one. The definition domain of f_F becomes the set of fuzzy subsets of X with the following relation on membership functions:

$$\mu_{M(L_2)}(x) = \mu_{M(F(L_1))}(x) = f_F(\mu_{M(L_1)}(x)) \tag{5}$$

A more general definition has been proposed by Novak [18]:

$$\mu_{M(L_2)}(x) = \mu_{M(F(L_1))}(x) = m_F(\mu_{M(L_1)}(q_F(x))) \tag{6}$$

$m_F\colon [0,1] \to [0,1]$ is a *modifier* for the hedge F while q_F is a *translator*.

Many operators are well known; most of them have been introduced by Zadeh [19] (see also [20], [21], [22]). To simplify the reading, $\mu_{M(L_2)}$ will be written μ_{L_2}. Let C be a symbol and μ_C its meaning; the new generated symbol and its meaning will be respectively noted $C1$ and μ_{C1}. Several classical operators are recalled here:

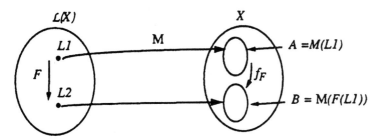

Figure 1.3 Creating a new symbol.

Symbolic domain	Numerical domain
$C1$ = **very** (C)	$\mu_{C1}(x) = \mu^2{}_C(x)$
$C1$ = **not** (C)	$\mu_{C1}(x) = 1 - \mu_C(x)$
$C1$ = **more_or_less**(C)	$\mu_{C1}(x) = \mu^{1/2}{}_C(x)$

Operators defined by Zadeh act on the left-hand side composition of functions. To define a translation of meanings using Novak's definition, one will now have the identity as *modifier* and $x \to x \pm \Delta$ as *translator*. This operation can also be seen as the convolution of the initial concept by a delayed Dirac's distribution. Just as composition, convolution could be taken as a general mechanism to define new hedges. Using previous writing conventions, new operators can be introduced; two of them are given next (δ is the Dirac's distribution and * the convolution operation).

Symbolic domain	Numerical domain
$C1$ = **more_than** (C)	$\mu_{C1}(x) = \mu_C(x) * \delta(x - \Delta)$
$C1$ = **less_than**(C)	$\mu_{C1}(x) = \mu_C(x) * \delta(x + \Delta)$

Let us give an example for a fuzzy sensor where the generic meaning is defined by a normalized gaussian function.

$$\mu_C(x) = gaussian\left(m_C, \sigma_C, x\right) = e^{-\frac{(x - m_c)^2}{2\sigma_c^2}} \tag{7}$$

Obviously, operators **more_than** and **less_than** give new gaussian functions defined by:

$$\mu_{\text{more\_than}(C)}(x) = gaussian(m_c + \Delta, \sigma_c, x)$$

$$\mu_{\text{less\_than}(C)}(x) = gaussian(m_c - \Delta, \sigma_c, x) \tag{8}$$

The translation value can be chosen so that the initial and the new concepts have intersecting points where the grade of membership is 0.5.

Once this information has been sent, the sensor generates membership functions for all the measurement domains and then is able to provide symbolic measurements. Therefore, for a given measurement, it can return either the symbolic value (based on the description) or the grade of membership for each symbol in the lexical domain (the numerical value and further information such as identification, installation date, revision date can also be obtained).

N-ary operators have been also defined (see for example [23], [24]); in particular binary operators such as $C1$ **and** $C2$, $C1$ **or** $C2$ are commonly defined by means of triangular norms and triangular conorms. These n-ary operators provide a way to build multidimensional fuzzy meanings by composing basic monodimensional fuzzy meanings. For example, a multidimensional variable Y could be defined on the monodimensional variable Xi's by rules such as: Y is B when $X1$ is $C1$ and $X2$ is $C2$ or $X3$

is *C3*. In this approach, first the decomposition of *B* along the basic features is made by the expert, and then the recombining is made by the fuzzy operators to obtain the description of the variable *Y* on *B* knowing the *Xi*'s.

1.3.2. Fuzzy Sensors Based on Interpolation

In particular situations, the decomposability of the multidimensional variable is difficult to express, or it leads to a large number of rules resulting in very large computations. For example, in a sorting out problem based on a human color criteria, we could define the class of the orange color from the basic red-green-blue components. This definition of the term orange is very difficult to express by operators, and thus requires an expert having a deep knowledge of the color phenomenon. Moreover, due to the complexity of this phenomenon, the expert will use a lot of rules to express his or her knowledge of the orange color from the basic components RGB. For such cases, we propose an interpolation method based on initial characteristic points for building the multidimensional fuzzy meanings directly on the cartesian product of the elementary measurements.

Let us consider an initial knowledge about the measurements. This knowledge is characterized by the meaning of symbols on a small *crisp* (usual) subset *V* of the measurement set. Then the measurement set is partitioned in n-simplexes with the Delaunay triangulation method. An n-simplex in an n-dimensional space is a polyhedra with n + 1 vertices. For example, a 2-simplex is a triangle and a 3-simplex is a tetrahedron. The points used to perform the triangulation are the elements of the *V* set.

The membership function of the meaning of each symbol is defined on each n-simplex by a multidimensional interpolation [13], [14]. We suppose the restriction on an n-simplex of the membership function of the meaning of a symbol *s* is:

$$\mu_{M(s)}(v) = \mu_{M(s)}(x_1, x_2, \ldots, x_n) = a_1 x_1 + a_2 x_2 + \cdots + a_n x_n + a_{n+1} \qquad (9)$$

The value of this function is known for the *n* + 1 vertices of the n-simplex. So the *n* + 1 factors a_i can be calculated by the following equation system:

$$A = M^{-1}B \quad M = \begin{bmatrix} x_{1_1} & \cdots & x_{1_n} & 1 \\ \cdots & \cdots & \cdots & \cdots \\ x_{n+1_1} & \cdots & x_{n+1_n} & 1 \end{bmatrix} \quad A = \begin{bmatrix} a_1 \\ \cdots \\ a_{n+1} \end{bmatrix} \quad B = \begin{bmatrix} \mu_{M(s)}(v_1) \\ \mu_{M(s)}(v_2) \\ \cdots \\ \mu_{M(s)}(v_{n+1}) \end{bmatrix} \qquad (10)$$

where v_i is the ith vertex of the n-simplex, and x_{ij} is its jth component. This process is performed on each n-simplex and for each symbol.

With this method, the knowledge needed to configure the sensor is very compact. It can be acquired during a learning phase by a communication with a system, called the *supervisor*, which can be a human or an expert system. During the learning phase, the supervisor and the sensor analyze the same phenomenon. The supervisor gives its description to the sensor. The sensor increases its knowledge with its own measurement and the supervisor's description. After each learning point, the new fuzzy partition is built. Hereafter, this method will be applied to the perception of colors.

1.4. A Fuzzy Sensor for the Perception of Comfort

In this part, we apply the building of multidimensional fuzzy meanings by n-ary operators to the perception of comfort. We consider that the description of comfort requires the knowledge of the relative humidity and of the temperature. Then a linguistic definition of the comfort can be modelized by a set of rules.

The temperature and humidity measurements take their respective values in the sets denoted T and H. The temperature is described by symbols in the set $\mathcal{L}(T)$ = {**cold, cool, mild, warm, hot**}. The humidity is described by symbols in the set $\mathcal{L}(H)$ = {**very_low, low, medium, high**}. It is also assumed that the meanings of the symbols generate a partition of the respective numerical sets. The problem is now to aggregate both measurements to obtain information about the feeling of comfort. Such a feeling could be symbolically defined as follows:

> the atmosphere is *comfortable* when the temperature is *mild* **and** the humidity is *medium*,
>
> the atmosphere is *acceptable* when the temperature is *cool* **or** *mild* **or** *warm* **and** the humidity is *low* **or** the temperature is *cool* **or** *warm* **and** the humidity is *medium*,
>
> the atmosphere is *uncomfortable* when atmosphere is **not** (*comfortable* **or** *acceptable*).

One solution is to consider that two symbols connected by the **and** operator are in fact one symbol whose meaning is defined on the Cartesian product of the numerical sets. For example, "the temperature is *mild* **and** humidity is *medium*" should be no more considered as the two expressions connected by the operator **and**, but as one expression such as "the temperature_humidity is *mild_medium*." The new symbolic variable temperature_humidity takes its value in a new set of symbols; for example denoted $\mathcal{L}(TH)$. The symbol *mild_medium* belongs to $\mathcal{L}(TH)$, and its meaning is defined on the cartesian product $T \times H$. Then the meaning of *comfortable* is defined by:

$$M(comfortable) = M(mild\_medium) = M(mild) \times M(medium) \qquad (11)$$

The meanings of the **or** and the **not** operators are respectively defined by the union operator and by the negation operator. All of this is graphically shown in Figure 1.4.

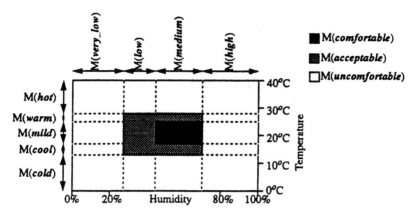

Figure 1.4 Graph of the meanings of **comfortable**, **acceptable** and **uncomfortable**.

Let t and h be the temperature and humidity measurements. The fuzzy description of the couple (t, h) can be expressed in terms of the fuzzy descriptions of t and h by means of a triangular norm $\top$.

$$\mu_{D(t, h)}(a\_b) = \mu_{D(t)}(a) \top \mu_{D(h)}(b) \qquad (12)$$

As a fuzzy partitioning was chosen for the temperature and the humidity, we have:

$$\Sigma_{a \in L(T)} \, \mu_{D(t)}(a) = 1 \text{ and } \Sigma_{b \in L(H)} \, \mu_{D(h)}(b) = 1 \qquad (13)$$

Therefore, if we want to obtain a fuzzy partition for the new symbolic set $L(TH)$, the triangular norm has to be distributive with respect to the addition (for example, the product). Now we have to define the fuzzy meaning of the **or** operator. Let E be a set of measurements and $L(E)$ its associated set of symbols. Let L_1 and L_2 be two symbols of $L(E)$. Let $\perp$ be the triangular conorm which defines the fuzzy meaning of **or**:

$$\mu_{M(L1\_or\_L2)}(x) = \mu_{M(L1)}(x) \perp \mu_{M(L2)}(x) = \mu_{D(x)}(L_1) \perp \mu_{D(x)}(L_2) \qquad (14)$$

It can be shown that to preserve the fuzzy partition, the triangular conorm should verify:

$$x \perp y = x + y \text{ if } x + y \leq 1 \qquad (15)$$

For example: $x \perp y = \min(x + y, 1)$. This is the triangular conorm chosen to define the **or** operator. The meaning of the negation operator **not** is defined by: $\mu_{M(\text{not } L)}(x) = 1 - \mu_{M(L)}(x)$. The fuzzy meanings of **comfortable** and **acceptable** are shown in Figure 1.6 based on the fuzzy partitions given in Figure 1.5.

The fuzzy sensor is now able to describe the temperature and humidity for the symbol **comfortable** by a grade of membership that qualifies the comfort feeling. Three results are given here for three different values of the temperature in Celcius and humidity in percentages.

$$\mu_{D(23, 50)}(\textit{comfortable}) = 1, \mu_{D(25, 60)}(\textit{comfortable}) = 0.5, \mu_{D(5, 80)}(\textit{comfortable}) = 0 \qquad (16)$$

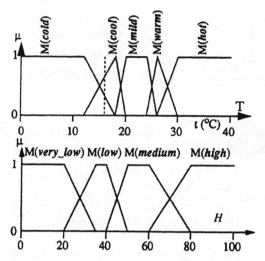

Figure 1.5   Fuzzy partitions for the temperature and the humidity.

1.5. A Fuzzy Sensor for the Perception of Colors

In this part, we apply the building of multidimensional fuzzy meanings by means of the interpolation method to the perception of colors. Human beings perceive electromagnetic light beams by four types of photo-chemical transducers: three cones for the day vision and one rod for the night vision. The photometric sensors give back information in relation to the received energy. The sensation of color is generated by the different spectral sensitivities of the cones. The blue cones detect short wavelength, whereas the green and red cones detect respectively medium and long wavelengths.

The artificial sensing (for example, the video camera) is based on three photometric transducers that re-create the effects of red, green and blue cones. Their respective sensitivities are denoted $R(\lambda)$, $G(\lambda)$, $B(\lambda)$ where λ is the wavelength. The responses of the detectors are given in equation 17 where $s(\lambda)$ denotes the spectrum of the light to be analyzed. When the

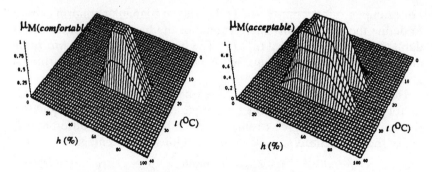

Figure 1.6   Fuzzy meaning of **comfortable** and **acceptable**.

responses are normalized between 0 and 1, the color space is simply a unit cube called the RGB cube.

$$r = \int_{\lambda_1}^{\lambda_2} s(\lambda)R(\lambda)d\lambda$$

$$v = \int_{\lambda_1}^{\lambda_2} s(\lambda)V(\lambda)d\lambda \qquad \left(with \quad \begin{matrix} \lambda_1 = 400nm \\ \lambda_2 = 700nm \end{matrix} \right) \qquad (17)$$

$$b = \int_{\lambda_1}^{\lambda_2} s(\lambda)B(\lambda)d\lambda$$

When describing a color in the common language, the luminosity is usually separated. For example we say pale blue or dark red. In order to introduce this knowledge into the sensor, a nonlinear mapping is applied to the RGB cube. This mapping has been chosen in order to obtain a color information that does not depend on the luminosity. This information (C'_1, C'_2) is called the chrominance. The RGB cube and its transformation are seen in Figure 1.7.

A way to build a fuzzy description of colors is to describe the luminance and the chrominance separately. The measurements set of the luminance is monodimensional, and its description is not developed in this paper. The measurement set of the chrominance is two-dimensional. It is called the chrominance plane of colors, and it is used as the measurement set (see Figure 1.8). Initially, seven colors are used for the configuration of the sensor:

$$S = \{Neutral, Red, Magenta, Blue, Cyan, Green, Yellow\} \qquad (18)$$

$$D(0,0) = \{Neutral\}, D(-1/2, \sqrt{3}/2) = \{Blue\}, D(1/2, \sqrt{3}/2) = \{Magenta\}, \qquad (19)$$

$$D(-1/2, -\sqrt{3}/2) = \{Green\}, D(1/2, -\sqrt{3}/2) = \{Yellow\}, D(1,0) = \{Red\},$$
$$D(-1,0) = \{Cyan\} \qquad (20)$$

Experiments show that only one or two characteristic colors are needed to perform the configuration of the sensor. The small number of

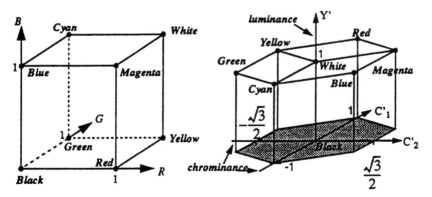

Figure 1.7 The RGB cube and its transformation.

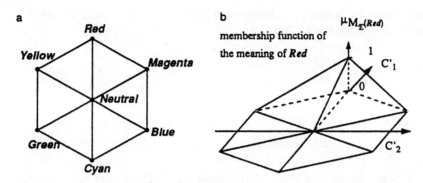

Figure 1.8   Triangulation of the chrominance plane and the fuzzy meaning of **red**.

configuration points can be explained by the choice of the mapping used
to obtain the chrominance plane. Indeed, if two colors differ only by their
darkness, then they have the same coordinates in the chrominance plane.
Figure 1.9 shows the result of the configuration performed to adapt the
sensor to return a description of colors close to the human perception in
a classification task of colored objects. We have here four types of colored objects: red, yellow, green, and blue objects. Each class is represented by a characteristic color that is used for the configuration. In
general, any number of classes and any number of colors per class can be
used to perform the configuration. The only condition is to define one
symbol per class. Figure 1.9 shows Delaunay's triangulation when learning four new characteristic points, one red, one yellow, one green, and
one blue. A new interpolation is built, which leads to a fuzzy partition.
The symbols have a new fuzzy meaning; see for example the fuzzy meaning of red given below.

The previous methods were also applied to implement a fuzzy sensor
that performs the fuzzy description of the colored surfaces. The measurement is based on the analysis of the light reflected by an illuminated surface. The reflection phenomenon can be modelized by the combination

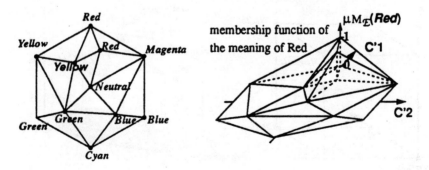

Figure 1.9   New triangulation and new fuzzy meaning of red.

of two cases: the diffused reflection that is predominant for dull surfaces, and the specular reflection that is predominant for polished surfaces. In general, the light coming from the specular reflection depends only on the color of the emitted light while the color of the surface can be acquired by analyzing the diffused light. The sensor has three components: a light source, a sensing unit, and a measurement head (Figure 1.10). The measurement head is designed to illuminate the surface and to integrate the light coming from the diffused reflection. The spatial integration reduces the effect of surface texture. The light source is a thermic one. It was chosen to have an illumination close to the sun light.

The sensing unit includes three transducers, a signal conditioner, and a computation device that performs the signal processing, the fuzzy descriptions, and the learning. The transducers are phototransistors with optical filters. The computational device is based on a 80C196KB microcontroller, with 32Kbytes of RAM and an I2C interface for network communication. The computational device performs the configuration process and generates the fuzzy description of the analyzed surface. The I2C network interface is used for the communication with the fuzzy control system, fuzzy actuators, or other fuzzy sensors.

1.6. An Ultrasonic Range-Finding Sensor

In this part, we present an intelligent ultrasonic telemeter dedicated to the navigation of mobile robots. The sensor uses an original method based on a frequency-modulated emission [15], which proposes many configuration parameters, thus allowing an adaptation to different measurement situations. But the problem of the management of the configuration according to the maximization of the validity defined is not very simple at the mathematical level. The approach described here consists in representing the physical and experimental knowledge of the configuration by fuzzy rules. Therefore, in this application, the fuzzy ultrasonic sensor realized handles, in addition to φ_2, the symbolic inference g_4 in order to carry out the dynamic configuration.

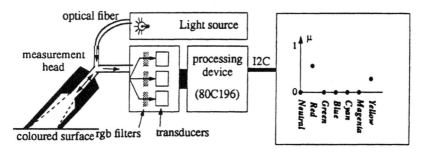

Figure 1.10   Description of the fuzzy color sensor.

1.6.1. Frequency-Modulated Method

In the proposed method, two transducers are in use respectively for emission and reception. Both modules are placed close to each other for obstacle echo detection. The emitter is linearly modulated in frequency with a frequency sweep rate of $\alpha = \Delta F/T_r$, with $\Delta F = fmax - fmin$ span of frequency and T_r repetition period (see figure 1.11). As sound travels through the air between the receiver at a speed of $v = 340 m/s$, the receiving transducer collects a frequency modulated signal delayed by a time $t_0 = 2d/v$ (d: distance to the obstacle). The two signals (emission and reception) are made to beat together in a nonlinear device (a multiplier) and thus the low beat note, isolated by a low pass filter with a cut frequency f_c, is found to contain two distinct tones f_a and f_b. Then, for the final detection, the signal is compared to a threshold K.

We have the following relationships:

$$f_a = \alpha \times t_0 = 2 \times \frac{\Delta F}{T_r} \times \frac{d}{v} \qquad \text{with} \qquad \alpha = \frac{\Delta F}{T_r} \tag{19}$$

$$N = f_a \times \left(T_r - t_0 \right) = 2 \times \frac{\Delta F}{T_r} \times \frac{d}{v} \times \left(T_r - \frac{2d}{v} \right)$$

$$N \text{ is the number of cycles of } f_a \quad (20)$$

The measurement of the distance d could be obtained by the measure (during a period T_r) of f_a or N, by inhibiting the acquisition during a time t_0' in order not to take the frequency f_b into account. In summary, for this measurement principle, we have:

- two measurement parameters f_a and N
- six configuration parameters $\Delta F = fmax - fmin, fmin, T_r, t_0', K, f_c$
- one reference parameter v

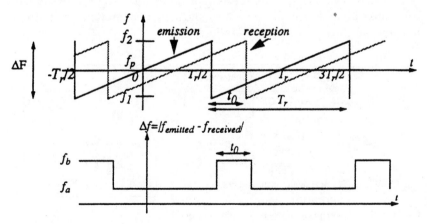

Figure 1.11 Principle of a linearly modulated range-finding sensor.

The other intervening parameters, which are not controlled, are the temperature and the characteristics of the obstacle (nature, orientation, shape). The interest of this measurement method in comparison to the conventional pulse method lies, on the one hand, in the redundancy of the measure, and on the other hand, in the diverse configuration capabilities. As we will show hereafter, these aspects could be used for the profit of adjusting the sensor according to the measurement context and its final aim.

1.6.2. Definition of the Validity

To define the validity for the considered telemeter, we propose to use the redundancy between the two measurement parameters linked to the distance: f_a and N. In fact, during a period T_r, we measure N_{exp} cycles of period f_{ai}. We will denote N_{exp} the number of measured pulses, N_b the number of pulses considered as good, that is, corresponding to a frequency close to f_a, and N the theoretical number of pulses corresponding to the distance measured. We propose to use the first parameter type, the values f_{ai}, to define the distance, and to use the second parameter type, N_b, to validate the preceding distance measurement. At the experimental level, to obtain f_a and N_b, a treatment of the N_{exp} measurements must be done. To extract good measurements, we have taken the median of all the values, because this filter is not very sensitive to extreme values. Then we compare every measurement to this median, and we consider it as good if it is close to this median value. Experiments for a plane obstacle perpendicular to the beam have led to adopting a tolerance of 15 percent for the f_{ai} measurements. Finally, the distance is computed by taking the mean value of all the good values of f_{ai}.

Then, to define the validity function f_v, we propose to take: $f_v = N_b/N$, N being deducted from f_a by the equation 20. In fact, this ratio is a coherence index between the distance measurements from f_a and from N_b. This index is comprised between 0 and 1: 0 corresponding to null coherence and 1 corresponding to ideal coherence. When the obstacle-sensor configuration is coherent with the model, that is, obstacle perpendicular to the ultrasonic beam and sensor configuration parameters ($\Delta F = fmax - fmin, fmin, T_r, t_0', K, f_c$) adjusted to the distance to the obstacle, then $N_b = N$ and $f_v = 1$, otherwise $N_b < N$ and f_v decreases. Indeed, a bad choice of the values of the configuration parameters leads to a lowering of the number N_b. For example, if we take $t_0' \gg t_0$, many cycles of f_a, which are present in the reception signal, are not taken into account for the distance acquisition. In the same way, values of ΔF and $fmin$ not adapted to the bandwidth of the transducers, produce a low level of the reception signal, and this time lead to the absence of cycles of frequency f_a. Except for a bad configuration, another case, where we have $N_{exp} < N_{th}$, occurs with situations where we have frequency selective fadings. In particular, these fadings could be due to the characteristics of the obstacle, such as its inclination. Indeed, a plane-inclined obstacle with dimensions larger than the wavelength induces diffraction phenomena, which cancel the reception signal for particular frequencies in the bandwidth. This effect leads to a diminution of N_b and so of the validity function f_v.

1.6.3. Fuzzy Rule-Based Configuration of the Sensor

The problem of a good configuration of the parameters intervening on the validity is not a simple problem because:

- There is no simple mathematical solution optimizing all the constraints (in particular the acquisition time-validity compromise).
- In practice, there is a lot of phenomena difficult to modelize, such as complex reverberation, which strongly intervene on the measurement acquired.

Moreover, the configuration depends on the distance, which is not known *a priori*. A solution consists in configuring dynamically the parameters by a set of rules based on the fuzzy subset theory. This set of fuzzy rules has for objective to account for the equations linking the parameters, but also for the expertise acquired during experiments. For example, the theoretical study of the influence of ΔF on the validity shows that we have a non-linear decreasing law, which could be represented by:

- If the distance is small, then ΔF is high.
- If the distance is medium, then ΔF is medium.
- If the distance is high, then ΔF is small.

At the equipment level, the implementation in the sensor itself of such a knowledge base, as well as the handling of fuzzy linguistic information for the configuration parameters, require a specific structure. In Figure 1.12, we present the results recorded during a robot sweep over a plane supporting a stairstep obstacle.

1.7. Conclusion

The final aim of any measurement process remains the acquisition of evidence that enables us to understand and possibly formulate decisions upon a topic. Therefore, numerical data about the measured quantities are ultimately turned into a qualitative response to the requirements that started the measurement process. This decision is generally made by a natural intelligent entity (an operator) or by an artificial intelligent entity (an expert system). The approach developed in this article is to implement these intelligent capabilities directly in a new type of sensors called

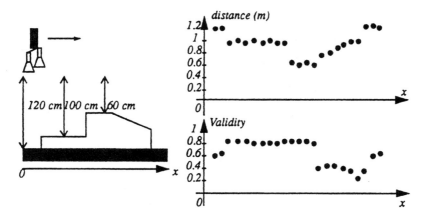

Figure 1.12   Distance and validity results for a robot sweep over the plane.

fuzzy sensors by means of the fuzzy subset theory. As examples, a color matching sensor, a comfort sensor, and an ultrasonic sensor have been successfully implemented.

As a conclusion, the proposed structure for the fuzzy symbolic sensors allows conventional sensing, interpretation, adaptation to the measurement context and treatment of errors. Hence, we can consider cases where measurement systems involve a lot of sensors. In such situations, we are faced with new problems: the concept level assessment and organization, the choice of the appropriate constituent devices, the optimal configuration of the sensors, and the validation of data from the point of view of the global system. For all these aspects, the new ways opened by symbolic representations seem promising, and they are being developed in our laboratory.

1.8. References

[1] Burd, N.C., and A.P. Dorey. "Intelligent Transducers." *Journal of Microcomputer Applications,* Vol. 7 (1984), pp. 87–97.

[2] Middelhoek, S. and A.C. Hoogerwerf. "Smart Sensors: When and Where?" *International Conference on Solid State Sensors and Actuators Transducers,* Vol. 85, pp. 2–7. Philadelphia, U.S.A.: 1985.

[3] Giachino, J.M. "Smart Sensors." *Sensors and Actuators,* Vol. 10 (1986), pp. 239–248.

[4] Finkelstein, L. "Theoretical basis of Intelligent and Knowledge Instrumentation." Proceedings, *IMEKO TC7, International Symposium on Artificial Intelligence-based Measurement and Control.* pp. 43–50. Kyoto, Japan: 1991.

[5] Zingales, G. and C. Narduzzi. "The Role of Artificial Intelligence in Measurement." *8th International Symposium on Artificial Intelligence-based Measurement and Control.* pp. 3–12. Ritsumeikan University. Kyoto, Japan: September, 1991.

[6] Astrom, K.J. and J.J. Anton. "Expert Control." *Proceedings, IFAC 9th Triennial World Congress.* pp. 2579–2584. Budapest, Hungary: 1984.

[7] Clocksin, W.F., and A.J. Morgan. "Qualitative Control." *Advances in Artificial Intelligence II.* pp. 473–479. North Holland: 1987.

[8] Mamdani, E.H. "Application of Fuzzy Algorithms for Control of Simple Dynamic Plant." *Proceedings, Institution of Electrical Engineers, Control and Science.* Vol. 121, No. 12, pp. 1585–1588. 1974.

[9] Psaltis, D., et al. "Neural Controllers." *Proceedings, 1st IEEE International Conference on Neural Networks.* pp. 551–558. San Diego, U.S.A.: 1987.

[10] Foulloy, L., and B. Zavidovique. "Towards Symbolic Process Control." *Automatica.* Vol. 30. No. 3. (1994), pp. 379–390.

[11] Benoit, E., and L. Foulloy. "Symbolic Sensors." *Proceedings, International Symposium on Artificial Intelligence-based Measurement and Control.* pp. 131–136. Kyoto, Japan: September, 1991.

[12] Mauris, G., et al. "Fuzzy Symbolic Sensors: From Concept to Applications." *International Journal of Measurement.* Vol. 12 (1994), pp. 357–384.

[13] Benoit, E., et al. "A Fuzzy Colour Sensor." *Proceedings, IMEKO XIII World Congress.* pp. 1015–1020. Torino, Italy: September 5–9, 1994.

[14] ———. "Fuzzy Sensors Aggregation: Application to Comfort Measurement." *5th International Conference, IPMU.* pp. 721–726. Paris, France: July, 1994.

[15] Mauris, G., et al. "Ultrasonic Smart Sensors: The Importance of the Measurement Principle." *Proceedings, IEEE/SMC International Conference on Systems Engineering in the Service of Humans.* Vol. III, pp. 55–60. Le Touquet, France: October, 1993.

[16] Foulloy, L., and S. Galichet. "Typology of Fuzzy Controllers," in *Theoretical Aspects of Fuzzy Control.* Eds. H.T. Nguyen, et al. New York: John Wiley and Sons, Inc. 1995.

[17] Novak, V. *Fuzzy Sets and their Applications.* Bristol & Philadelphia: Adam Hilger, 1989.

[18] Zadeh, L.A. "Quantitative Fuzzy Semantics." *Information Services,* Vol. 3, (1971), pp. 159–176.

[19] Zadeh, L.A. "The Concept of a Linguistic Variable and its Application to Approximate Reasoning." *Information Services,* Part 1, Vol. 8, No. 3, pp. 199–249; Part 2, Vol. 8, pp. 301–357; Part 3, Vol. 9, pp. 43–80. 1975.

[20] Bouchon-Meuneir, B., and J. Yao. "Linguistic Modifiers and Imprecise Categories." *International Journal of Intelligent Systems,* Vol. 7 (1992), pp. 25–36.

[21] Dubois, D., and H. Prade. "Fuzzy Sets in Approximate Reasoning. Part I: Inference with Possibility Distributions." *Fuzzy Sets and Systems,* 25th Anniversary Memorial, Vol. 40, No. 1 (1991), pp. 143–202.

[22] Eshragh, F., and E.H. Mamdani. "A General Approach to Linguistic Approximation." *International Journal of Man-Machine Studies* (1979), pp. 501–519.

[23] Pedrycz, W. *Fuzzy Control and Fuzzy Systems.* New York: John Wiley & Sons Inc., 1989.

[24] Yager, R.R. "Connectives and Quantifiers in Fuzzy Systems." *Fuzzy Sets and Systems,* Vol. 40, No. 1, (1991), pp. 39–75.

2 A Fuzzy Freehand Drawing System

C. L. Philip Chen, Sen Xie
Department of Computer Science and Engineering
Wright State University, Dayton, Ohio

ABSTRACT: A pen-based drawing system using fuzzy logic concept has been developed. The Fuzzy Freehand Drawing System (FFDS) can infer human drawing intention and generate the corresponding geometric primitives and smooth B-spline curves. FFDS is a pen-based real-time drawing system. Based on drawing position, speed, and acceleration information, FFDS establishes geometric primitives. Unintentional points are eliminated using fuzzy filtering rules. FFDS analyzes the drawn curve with reference models and obtains the corresponding possibility. Fuzzy inference rules are used to recognize the correct model. Finally, the correct geometric primitives are automatically drawn.

2.1. Introduction

Fuzzy Freehand Drawing System (FFDS) is designed as a pen-based drawing program. It is a real-time shape recognizer and generator. It can interpret the spatial and time information of hand drawing, recognize a drawer's intention, and generate the smooth and precise geometric primitives that the drawer really wants to draw. More specifically, based on obtained information, FFDS filters out the points that are not intentionally drawn, detects the point that is the starting point of one geometric basic curve and the end point of another geometric basic curve, divides the hand drawing into some subcurves, recognizes each of them and generates the corresponding precise geometric primitive or B-spline curve. We introduce α-level to reflect the fuzziness of the drawing intention, which can be selected among $[0.0 - 1.0]$. If α-level is low, FFDS tends to recognize hand drawing as one of the standardized geometric primitives even though it is drawn very roughly. If α-level is high, FFDS tends to recognize hand drawing as a free curve even though it is drawn very carefully.

In the FFDS, the hand drawing is essentially a sequence of points, with each two consecutive points connected by a line. A 32-bit unsigned integer time stamp value increased by every millisecond is recorded. The time stamp is used to measure elapsed time between two consecutive events, which are actually two consecutive points. So the distance and time between consecutive points (events) depend on drawing speed. Figure 2.1 illustrates the procedure of FFDS. FFDS is a real-time system; each complete hand drawing is processed by a fuzzy processing engine. Fuzzification is the first procedure that fuzzifies each point. It calculates degrees of membership functions of speed, acceleration, change of angle, and change of vector for each point. The fuzzy filter checks each point and filters out unintentional points with fuzzy inference rules. Since a hand drawing may consist of more than one basic class and free curves, the fuzzy separator finds the turning point and divides the drawing into some subcurves. The Fuzzy Identifier checks all possible points for each possible reference model, obtains the value of possibility for the model, and uses a set of fuzzy inference rules to decide which model it belongs to. It may not belong to any model if it is just a free curve. The fuzzy generator finds the corresponding geometric representation of the curve and draws it on canvas. Of course, the original freehand drawing is erased. Fuzzy generation also requires fuzzy information in order to generate the curve that matches most precisely with the drawer's intention.

Different with FSCI [1], the FFDS identifies geometric primitives based on the drawer's intention not only from drawing speed, but also from drawing acceleration, change of angles, and change of vectors at each point. The FFDS also meets real-time performance requirements and avoids the loss of information of drawer's intention. If a user draws slowly, the freehand curve may consist of some points that do not represent his or her intention and are created because of hand vibration. The fuzzy filter in FFDS will eliminate such points. In addition, FFDS also generates precise geometric primitives or B-spline curves. The geometric primitives discussed in this chapter include line, circle, circular arc, ellipse, elliptic arc, and free curve. A free curve is a subcurve that does not belong to any geometric primitives. Figure 2.2 shows the flowchart of the FFDS.

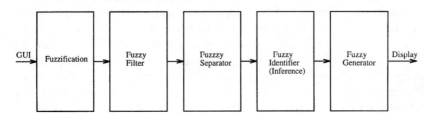

Figure 2.1   Procedure of FFDS.

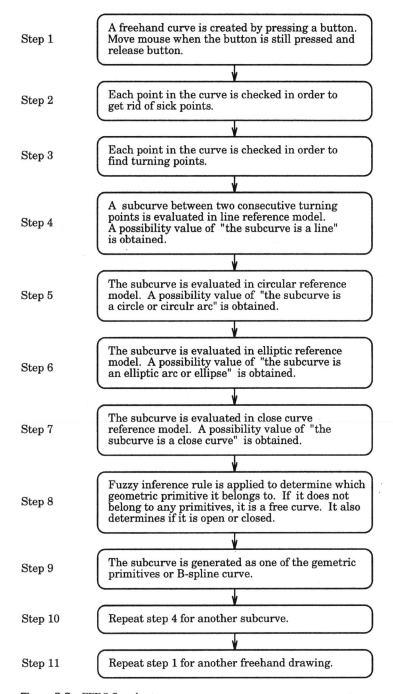

Step 1 — A freehand curve is created by pressing a button. Move mouse when the button is still pressed and release button.

Step 2 — Each point in the curve is checked in order to get rid of sick points.

Step 3 — Each point in the curve is checked in order to find turning points.

Step 4 — A subcurve between two consecutive turning points is evaluated in line reference model. A possibility value of "the subcurve is a line" is obtained.

Step 5 — The subcurve is evaluated in circular reference model. A possibility value of "the subcurve is a circle or circulr arc" is obtained.

Step 6 — The subcurve is evaluated in elliptic reference model. A possibility value of "the subcurve is an elliptic arc or ellipse" is obtained.

Step 7 — The subcurve is evaluated in close curve reference model. A possibility value of "the subcurve is a close curve" is obtained.

Step 8 — Fuzzy inference rule is applied to determine which geometric primitive it belongs to. If it does not belong to any primitives, it is a free curve. It also determines if it is open or closed.

Step 9 — The subcurve is generated as one of the gemetric primitives or B-spline curve.

Step 10 — Repeat step 4 for another subcurve.

Step 11 — Repeat step 1 for another freehand drawing.

Figure 2.2   FFDS flowchart.

It is clear that fuzzy logic, as a mathematical method, has advantages over conventional mathematical methods in dealing with vague, imprecise, and uncertain information, with which human beings are always involved. Systems designed and developed utilizing fuzzy logic methods have been shown more effective than those based on conventional approaches. Basic fuzzy logic concepts and definitions are listed in section 2.5. More details of fuzzy logic and systems can be found [2,3].

2.2. Freedhand Drawing Using Fuzzy Logic Concept

Since the information from the observance of a drawing is always vague, imprecise, and uncertain, fuzzy logic becomes the choice to model the drawing behavior. Our FFDS is a real-time system. When a person draws a curve, a sequence of points can be obtained. Each point contains the coordinate and the time at which this point is drawn. Based on this observance, we can use fuzzy logic to interpret the drawing intention.

It is very important to select membership functions that can reflect the intention correctly and precisely. Another criterion for selecting membership functions is computational efficiency. Having considered these two criteria, we choose a triangular membership function. The membership functions considered here are drawing speed, drawing acceleration, change of drawing vector, and change of drawing angles. Membership functions for vector changed and angles are shown in Figure 2.3. The acceleration membership function is defined as follows; other membership functions can be defined similarly.

$$
\mu_{AcceDown}(x) = \begin{cases} \dfrac{AcceAve - x}{AcceAve - AcceMin} & \text{if } AcceMin < x \leq AcceAve \\[2ex] 1 & \text{if } x \leq AcceMin \\[1ex] 0 & \text{otherwise} \end{cases}
$$

$$
\mu_{AcceNormal}(x) = \begin{cases} \dfrac{x - AcceMin}{AcceAve - AcceMin} & \text{if } AcceMin < x \leq AcceAve \\[2ex] \dfrac{AcceMax - x}{AcceMax - AcceAve} & \text{if } AcceAve < x < AcceMax \\[2ex] 0 & \text{otherwise} \end{cases}
$$

$$
\mu_{AcceUp}(x) = \begin{cases} \dfrac{x - AcceAve}{AcceMax - AcceAve} & \text{if } AcceAve < x \leq AcceMax \\[2ex] 1 & \text{if } x > AcceMax \\[1ex] 0 & \text{otherwise} \end{cases}
$$

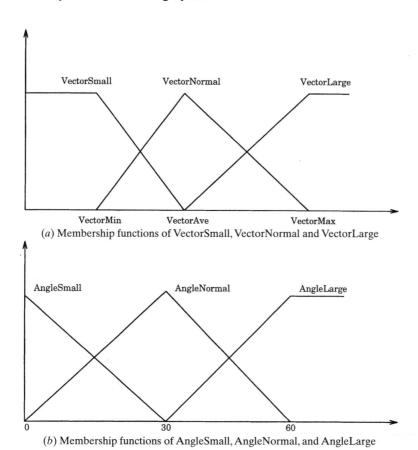

(a) Membership functions of VectorSmall, VectorNormal and VectorLarge

(b) Membership functions of AngleSmall, AngleNormal, and AngleLarge

Figure 2.3   Membership function.

2.2.1. Fuzzy Filter

Fuzzy inference is applied in three areas in FFDS. One of them is fuzzy filter. Fuzzy filter uses fuzzy inference rules to preprocess freehand drawing in order to eliminate undesirable points. When a person draws slowly and carefully, the freehand drawing will reflect what he or she wants to draw if we look at it from a distance. However, if we look at it closely, the curve is not as smooth as it should be. This is because of vibration when the user draws. We call the points, which are created due to hand's vibration instead of drawing intention, *sick points,* as shown in Figure 2.4.

2.2.1.1. Rule for Fuzzy Filter.   We use the following rule to identify sick points.

> **Rule:** If speed is slow, change of angles at current point is large, change of angles at next point is large, and change of vectors is small, then the current point is a *sick point.*

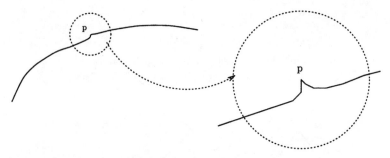

Figure 2.4   Illustration of a sick point.

2.2.2. Rule for Fuzzy Separator

If a curve that consists of more than one geometric primitive is drawn, we must identify each of them and generate the corresponding precise geometric primitive. The fuzzy separator is to identify the turning points and determine the subcurves. Figure 2.5 shows the turning points. If a person draws a freehand curve, which consists of more than one subcurve, he or she will slow down when he or she reaches the point connecting two subcurves and then speed up when he or she just passes the point. Another observation is that the change of angles is large. Hence, the rule is derived as follows:

> **Rule:** If acceleration is slow or normal, speed is down or normal, change of angles at current point is normal or small, and change of angles at next point is large, then the current point is a *turning point.*

2.3. Identification of Freehand Drawing

2.3.1 Evaluation of Predicted Points

After dividing a freehand drawing into several segments, in which each segment is supposed to be a geometric primitive or a simple free curve, we

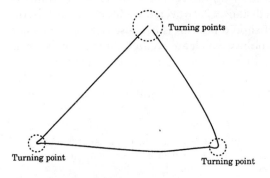

Figure 2.5   Turning points.

have to recognize each individual curve. Let C be the freehand drawing, $C = \{S_i \mid i = 1,2,3, \dots\}$. Each S_i represents a basic curve, which is a sequence of points, $S_i = \{q_j \mid j = 1,2,3, \dots, m_i\}$. It is also denoted as $\{q_j\}$ for convenience. Each q_j contains the coordinates of this point and a time stamp at which this point is drawn. If we assume $\{q_j\}$ forms a specific geometric primitive, a point in $\{q_j\}$ may not fit in the geometric primitive. However, we want to know how near this point is to the supposed place; that is, the degree to which this point is near the supposed point. Another problem is that we actually do not know where the specific geometric primitive is.

In our FFDS, we construct a reference model for each geometric primitive and calculate the possibilities that each $\{q_j\}$ belongs to the reference models. For instance, when we use some points to construct the reference model for a specific geometric primitive, the number of points is determined by the type of the primitive. If the reference model is a line, we need two points; if it is a circle, we need three points; if it is an ellipse, we need five points. We then select another point q from $\{q_j\}$ except the points already used. From the relationship between q and the points that are used to construct the reference model, in the freehand drawing, we can calculate the supposed place that q would locate in the model. We denote that point as q'. We compare these two points and obtain the degree to which q is near the supposed point q'. The degree implies the truth value of the assumption that q fits in the supposed geometric primitive.

Zadeh has pointed out the relationship between possibility measure and fuzzy set [7], so we evaluate the possibility or the truth degree of "point q' is point q" in the following $p = sup_{v \in V}(\mu_{q'}(v) \wedge \mu_q(v))$. Figure 2.6 illustrates the possibility of "point q' is point q"; the dotted circles around q and q' are the drawing speed at point q and point q'. Select other points, calculate p in the same way, and obtain a sequence of $p_i, i = 1, 2, 3, \dots$, which will be used to calculate the final possibility of the curve as the supposed model.

2.3.2. Reference Model of Line

Given a curve, a sequence of points $\{q_j \mid j = 1,2, \dots, m\}$, we want to fit them to all models and find the best fitness. The first reference model is line. We divide the curve $\{q_j\}$ into three segments evenly:

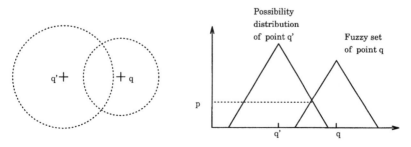

Figure 2.6   The possibility of "point q' is point q."

$$g_1 = \{q_1, q_2, \ldots, q_n\},$$
$$g_2 = \{q_{n+1}, q_{n+2}, \ldots, q_{2n}\},$$
$$g_3 = \{q_{2n+1}, q_{2n+2}, \ldots, q_{3n}, \ldots, q_m\}.$$

We choose a point from each segment, say a_0, a_1, a_2. The line reference model is:

$$b(t) = (1 - t)a_0 + ta_1, \tag{1}$$

where t is the ratio of the arc length between a_0 and a_2 to the arc length between a_0 and a_1. According to equation (4.1), the ratio, t, and a predicted point, b, can be obtained. The possibility of "point b is point a_2" is evaluated by the following:

$$p_i(b, a_2) = sup_v(\mu_b(v) \wedge \mu_{a_2}(v)), \tag{2}$$

where μ_{a_k} is the fuzzy set of *SpeedSlow* at point a_k, $k = 0, 1, 2$, and μ_b is the fuzzy set of *SpeedSlow* at point b. The *Speed* at b can be obtained similarly. Figure 2.7 illustrates the reference model, where $a0, a1, a2$ are points from $\{q_i\}$ and b is the point obtained by equation (4). In this figure, the dotted circle represents the fuzzy measure around each point. The faster the speed is when the line is drawn, the larger the circle is and the more imprecise, more uncertain and vaguer the location of this point is. Point b is the predicted point of a_2 if $\{q_j\}$ forms a line. Equation (5) indicates the possibility of the prediction.

In this way we get a sequence of $p_i, i = 1, 2, \ldots, n$. The possibility of "The curve is a line" is $P_{line} = \sum_{i=1}^{n} p_i / n$, where n is the number of line reference models constructed.

2.3.3. Reference Model of Circle and Circular Arc

Similar to the line model, a circle or circular arc reference model can be constructed. We divide the sequence of points, which forms a basic curve, into four groups:

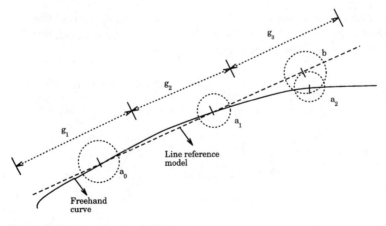

Figure 2.7   Line reference model.

$$g_1 = \{q_1, q_2, \ldots, q_n\},$$
$$g_2 = \{q_{n+1}, q_{n+2}, \ldots, q_{2n}\},$$
$$g_3 = \{q_{2n+1}, q_{2n+2}, \ldots, q_{3n}\},$$
$$g_4 = \{q_{3n+1}, q_{3n+2}, \ldots, q_{4n}, \ldots, q_m\}.$$

We then select a point from each group of g_1, g_3, and g_4, say a_0, a_1, a_e for the model as shown in Figure 2.8. Choose another point f from $\{q_j\}$ between a_0, a_1, so that the distance between f and a_0 is equal to the distance between f and a_1. It is most likely that f falls into g_2, but not necessarily. If we cannot find such a point from $\{q_j\}$, we find two consecutive points from $\{q_j\}$, so that a point in the line formed by these two points will have the equal distance to a_0 and a_1; we also denote this point as f.

Refer to Figure 2.8, in order to determine if an arc is a circle or a circular arc; the rational quadratic Bezier curve [8] is used. Let $b_0 = a_0$, $b_2 = a_1$, and define $m = (a_0 + a_1)/2$, $h = |f - m|$, and $l = |a_0 - m|$. We want to find a point b_1 such that $b_1 b_0$ and $b_1 b_2$ are tangent to the circle determined by b_0, f, and b_2 at points b_0, and b_2, respectively.

The rational quadratic Bezier curve is expressed as:

$$b(t) = \frac{b_0 B_0^2(t) + (-w) b_1 B_1^2(t) + b_2 B_2^2(t)}{B_0^2(t) + (-w) B_1^2(t) + B_2^2(t)} \tag{3}$$

where $B_i^2(t), i = 0,1,2$ are Bernstein polynomials and defined as:

$$B_i^2(t) = \binom{2}{i}(1 - t)^{2-i} t^i,$$

and w is called the weight of the corresponding control polygon vertices, b_0, b_1 and b_2; and t will be a value such that the ratio of the arc length between a_0 and a_1 to the arc length between a_1 and a_e is equal to the arc length between b_0 and b_2 to the arc length between b_2 and b_e along the circle reference model. Figure 2.9 shows the Bezier curve model. Equation (3) represents a circle when $w = mf/fb_1$. From Figure 2.9, w can be found and equals to $(l^2 - h^2)/(l^2 + h^2)$. The point b_1 that satisfies the condition $f = (wb_1 + m)/(1 + w)$ can be found.

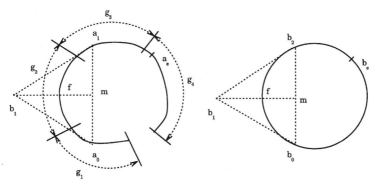

Figure 2.8   The circular reference model.

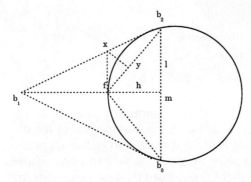

Figure 2.9   Point b_1 in circular reference model.

The point b_e will be obtained from equation (3) with the found t, w, b_0, b_1, and b_2. The possibility of "point b_e is point a_e" is evaluated by:

$$p_i(b_e, a_e) = \sup{}_v(\mu_{b_e}(v) \wedge \mu_{a_e}(v))].$$

Pick all possible points from $\{q_j\}$, and finally we get a sequence of p_i, $i = 1, 2, \ldots, n$. The final possibility of "the curve is a circle" is $P_{circle} = \sum_{i=1}^{n} p_i/n$, where n is the number of circle reference models constructed.

2.3.4. Reference Model of Ellipse and Elliptic Arc

Since an ellipse can be determined uniquely by five points, we divide the sequence of points, which forms a basic curve, into five groups:

$$g_1 = \{q_1, q_2, \ldots, q_n\},$$

$$g_2 = \{q_{n+1}, q_{n+2}, \ldots, q_{2n}\},$$

$$g_3 = \{q_{2n+1}, q_{2n+2}, \ldots, q_{3n}\},$$

$$g_4 = \{q_{3n+1}, q_{3n} + 2, \ldots, q_{4n}\},$$

$$g_5 = \{q_{4n} + 1, q_{4n} + 2, \ldots, q_{5n}, \ldots, q_m\}$$

Choose two points a_0 and a_1 from g_1 and g_3. Choose a point f on the curve between a_0 and a_1 so that f is the farthest point from line a_0a_1. It is most likely that f falls into g_2, but not necessarily. Find the middle point of a_0 and a_1 by $m = (a_0 + a_1)/2$; choose a point a_2 from the third group. The point t is the intersection of line fm and the line that passes through p and is parallel to line a_0a_1, as shown in Figure 2.10.

The weight w of the controlling polygon vertices, b_0, b_1, b_2, and p is also the ratio of mf and fb_1, which is finally evaluated by:

$$w = \frac{(\alpha + \beta)^2 c^2 - \alpha(\alpha + 2\beta)d^2}{\alpha^2 d^2 - (\alpha + \beta)^2 c^2},$$

where α, and β are barycentric coordinates of t with respect to f and m, c is the distance between p and t, d is the distance between a_1 and m. Figure 2.11 shows the elliptic reference model constructed in the form of a

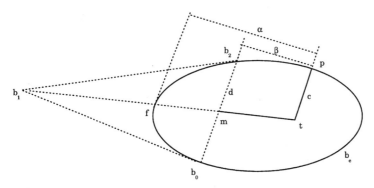

Figure 2.10   The detailed elliptic reference model.

rational *Bezier* curve. Similarly, b_e is calculated by equation (3) when t is a value so that the ratio of the arc length between a_0 and a_1 to the arc length between a_1 and a_e is equal to the ratio of the arc length between b_0 and b_2 to the arc length between b_2 and b_e.

Checking all possible points, we get a sequence of possibilities $p_i, i = 1,$ $2, \ldots, n$. Finally, the possibility of "the curve is an ellipse or elliptic arc" is $P_{ellipse} = \sum_{i=1}^{n} p_i / n,$ where n is the number of ellipse reference models constructed.

2.3.5. Reference Model of a Closed Curve

If a person draws a closed curve fast, the end point(s) may not be closed to the start point(s), as shown in Figure 2.12. However, a person, who observes such a curve, is more likely to claim that this is a closed curve. This is because the observer thinks that the curve was drawn roughly and therefore should give more tolerance to the distance between start points and end points. In such a case, drawer's intention will be interpreted as a closed curve. On the other hand, if the drawer draws a curve carefully and slowly, the curve may be interpreted as an open curve. This is because drawing speed is slow, which implies the fuzzy measure (degree) at each point is high, and, hence, each point has more accurate geometric meaning.

In order to recognize such intention, we have to model the fuzzy information to interpret the drawer's intention accurately. It is obvious that

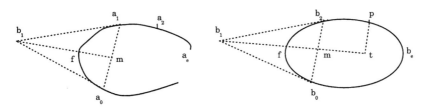

Figure 2.11   The elliptic reference model.

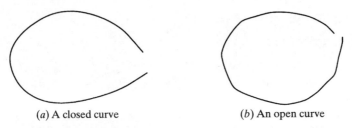

(a) A closed curve   (b) An open curve

Figure 2.12   Closed and open curve.

drawing speed is the most proper indicator of the degree of the drawer's carefulness (also roughness when the degree is small). In our system, we compare each of the first five points with each of the last five points by the following measurement:

$$p_i(q_{start}, q_{end}) = \sup_v(\mu_{start}(v) \wedge \mu_{end}(v)), i = 1, 2, \ldots, 25$$

The possibility of "the curve is a closed curve" is $P_{closed} = \sum_{i=1}^{25} p_i / 25$.

If there are less than 15 points in the $\{q_j\}$, we divide them into three groups and compare each point in the first group with each point in the third group in the same way as explained above.

2.3.6. Inference and Identification

After we obtain the values of possibilities for possible reference models, we can use fuzzy inference rules to determine the closed or open form of the curve and the type of the geometric primitive; α-level is used to determine the truth of conditions. The following are the fuzzy inference rules to identify it:

Rule 1: If P_{line}, then the subcurve is a *line*.

Rule 2: If *not* P_{line} and P_{circle}, then the subcurve is a *circular arc*.

Rule 3: If *not* P_{line} and *not* P_{circle} and $P_{ellipse}$, then the subcurve is an *elliptic arc*.

Rule 4: If *not* P_{line} and *not* P_{circle} and *not* $P_{ellipse}$, then the subcurve is a *free curve*.

The following are the fuzzy inference rules to identify openness or closeness of a curve:

Rule 5: If P_{closed} and *not* P_{line}, then the subcurve is *closed*.

Rule 6: If *not* P_{closed} and *not* P_{line}, then the subcurve is *open*.

After drawing geometric primitives have been identified, the least square method is used to generate the standard geometric primitives.

2.4. Generation of Primitives and B-Spline Curves

2.4.1 Generation of Line

When we have identified that the curve is a line, we need to generate a straight line from the sequence of points. In other words, we want to find a line that best approximates the scattered data. The least square method is used to generate it [9].

Suppose the representation of the line is:

$$y = ax + b \tag{4}$$

The sum of the squares of the deviation is given by:

$$S(a,b) = \Sigma w_i(y_i - ax_i - b)^2, i = 1, 2, \ldots, m \tag{5}$$

where w_i is the weight, which is the degree of membership function for *SpeedSlow* at point (x_i, y_i), and is explained in the following.

Since the intention represented at each point is different, the contribution of each point to the formation of the line is also different. The best measure of the difference is the membership function of speed at a point. This is why we use the degree of membership function for *SpeedSlow* at point (x_i, y_i) as the weight. More specifically, the less the degree of the membership function, the slower the drawing speed is, and, hence, the more the intention the point contributes to the formation of the line. We define $w = \mu_{SpeedSlow}(q_i)$, where $q_i = (x_i, y_i)$.

The function $S(a,b)$ is minimum when:

$$\frac{\partial S}{\partial a} = \sum_{i=1}^{m} 2w_i(y - ax - b)(-x) = 0 \tag{6}$$

$$\frac{\partial S}{\partial b} = \sum_{i=1}^{m} 2w_i(y - ax - b)(-1) = 0 \tag{7}$$

Simplifying equations 6 and 7, we can get the following:

$$a\sum_{i=1}^{m} w_i x_i^2 + b\sum_{i=1}^{m} w_i x_i = \sum_{i=1}^{m} x_i y_i \tag{8}$$

$$a\sum_{i=1}^{m} w_i x_i + b\sum_{i=1}^{m} w_i = \sum_{i=1}^{m} y_i. \tag{9}$$

Variables a and b can be easily solved from equations (8) and (9), so the representation of line is determined.

The generated line may not interpolate the first and the last points of $\{q_i\}$, so we have to determine the starting and end points of the straight line. Figure 2.13 shows the method to determine the start and end points. The intersection of the generated line and the line, which passes q_0 and is perpendicular to the generated line, is the start point of the generated line. The end point is determined in the same way.

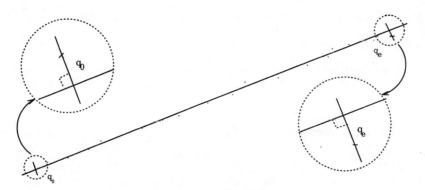

Figure 2.13   Generation of line at its start and end points.

2.4.2. Generation of Circle and Circular Arc

If the result of fuzzy inference has determined that the curve is a circle or a circular arc, we must find the representation of a circle, which approximates the curve best. Since a circle can be determined by three points that are not collinear, we can choose three points from $\{q_j\}$ each time and obtain the representation of the circle. Since we are only interested in the center and radius of the circle, we use the three points to find them.

In addition to obtaining the center and radius of a circle, we also need fuzzy information about the circle; the fuzzy information and the weight can be measured by:

$$w_i = \mu_{SpeedSlow}(c) = \min \{\mu_{SpeedSlow}(q_{i_1}), \mu_{SpeedSlow}(q_{i_2}), \mu_{SpeedSlow}(q_{i_3})\}$$

where $c_i = (x_i, y_i)$ is the center of the circle determined by q_{i_1}, q_{i_2} and q_{i_3}. After we have chosen all possible triple points from $\{q_j\}$, we can obtain a sequence of centers and radiuses and their weights.

The final representation of the circle can be found by the following:

$$x = \frac{\Sigma w_i x_i}{\Sigma w_i}, y = \frac{\Sigma w_i y_i}{\Sigma w_i}, z = \frac{\Sigma w_i z_i}{\Sigma w_i}.$$

If the curve forms a closed circle, we just draw the circle. If the curve is an arc, we have to find the start and end points.

Based on the representation of the circle and $\{q_j\}$, we can find the start and end points. In Figure 2.14, the circle is obtained by the preceding method; q_1 is the first point in $\{q_i\}$, q_m is the last point in $\{q_i\}$, and q_j is an arbitrary point in $\{q_i\}$, except q_1 and q_m, θ_1 are determined by q_1 and the circle; so are θ_j and θ_m.

The start angle of the arc is θ_1 and the end angle is θ_m. The drawing direction is determined by the position of θ_j. The drawing direction is clockwise if θ_j is between θ_1 and θ_m; counterclockwise if between 0_m and θ_1.

The angles θ_1, θ_j and θ_m can be obtained by the following:

$$\theta_i = \cos^{-1} \frac{y_i - y_c}{x_i - x_c}.$$

It is very easy to find the drawing direction by looking at the positions of three angles. However, it is not so easy for FFDS to determine the drawing direction because the arithmetic comparison does not indicate the correct drawing direction.

In order to determine the drawing direction, we normalize three angles such that the value represents the angle between $X - axis$ and the corresponding line, as shown in Figure 2.14. Then, use the following scheme to determine the drawing direction.

The drawing direction is clockwise if it satisfies the following conditions:

$$((\theta_j \geq \theta_1) \text{ and } (\theta_j \leq \theta_m))$$

or

$$((\theta_j \geq \theta_1) \text{ and } (\theta_j \geq \theta_m) \text{ and } (\theta_1 \geq \theta_m))$$

or

$$((\theta_j \leq \theta_1) \text{ and } (\theta_j \leq \theta_m) \text{ and } (\theta_1 \geq \theta_m))$$

The drawing direction is counterclockwise if it satisfies the following conditions:

$$((\theta_j \leq \theta_1) \text{ and } (\theta_j \geq \theta_m))$$

or

$$((\theta_j \geq \theta_1) \text{ and } (\theta_j \geq \theta_m) \text{ and } (\theta_1 \leq \theta_m))$$

2.4.3. Generation of Ellipse and Elliptic Arc

2.4.3.1. General Implicit Quadratic Equations. The implicit representation of an ellipse can be written as following quadratic equation:

$$ax^2 + 2hxy + by^2 + 2gx + 2fy + c = 0$$

Such general quadratics are called *conic sections* because they actually represent all the shapes that it is possible to get by cutting a cone with a plane. The three shapes that can be obtained in this way are ellipse (of

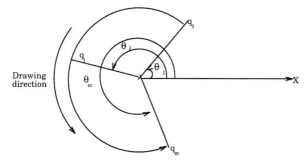

Figure 2.14 Generation of a circle and its start and end angles.

which circle is a special case), parabola, and hyperbola. If we calculate three values from the coefficients as follows:

$$\delta = a\,(cf - e)^2 + b\,(bf - de) + d\,(be - dc)$$

$$\Delta = ac - b^2, S = a + c$$

then, no matter how the quadratic is moved about in the plane using translation and rotation, these three values will stay the same as long as the shape of the quadratic stays the same.

If δ is 0, then the quadratic is degenerated and represents two straight lines (which may not always exit); otherwise:

Quadratic is a hyperbola, if $\delta < 0$.

Quadratic is a parabola, if $\delta = 0$.

Quadratic is an ellipse, if $\delta > 0$.

In the latter case, the ellipse only exists if δ is negative.

2.4.3.2. Interpolation Using General Implicit Quadratics. Reconstructing an ellipse from scattered data is a research area that has attracted a lot of attention. Many methods have been developed. In FFDS, we use five points to construct the ellipse [10,11]. Figure 2.15 shows the scheme. Suppose we have five points $a_1, a_2, a_3, a_4,$ and a_5, a line l_1 determined by a_1 and a_4, l_2 by a_2 and a_3, l_3 by a_1 and a_2, and l_4 by a_3 and a_4, where $l_i = a_i x + b_i y + c_i, i = 1, 2, 3, 4$.

We multiply these line equations together with a factor λ, which is known as *liming multiplier*:

$$(1 - \lambda)l_1 l_2 + \lambda l_3 l_4 = 0$$

We will generate a family of implicit quadratic equations. Each different λ value is a different quadratic. All the quadratics will have the prop-

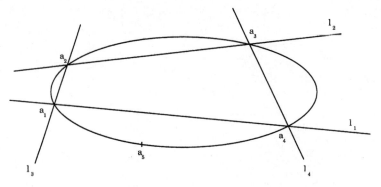

Figure 2.15 Generation of an ellipse.

erty that they will pass through the intersection points of the pairs of lines, a_1, a_2, a_3, and a_4. To specify one quadratic, we need a value for λ. This can be found by specifying the fifth point, through which the quadratic must pass and then substituting the value of (x_{a^5}, y_{a^5}) into the quadratic to find λ. Finally, we find the representation of an ellipse in the following form:

$$ax^2 + 2hxy + by^2 + 2gx + 2fy + c = 0 \qquad (10)$$

The ellipse can be rotated by θ, which is obtained by the following:

$$\theta = \frac{1}{2} \tan^{-1} \frac{h}{a - b}$$

so that the term $2hxy$ in equation (10) can be deleted, which implies the ellipse is parallel to the X or Y axis. The representation of the rotated ellipse now becomes:

$$a'x^2 + b'y^2 + 2g'x + 2f'y + c' = 0 \qquad (11)$$

where $\begin{aligned} a' &= a\cos^2\theta + b\sin^2\theta + 2h\sin\theta\cos\theta \\ b' &= a\sin^2\theta + b\cos^2\theta - 2h\sin\theta\cos\theta \\ g' &= g\cos\theta + f\sin\theta \\ f' &= -2g\sin\theta + 2f\cos\theta \\ c' &= c \end{aligned}$

Equation (11) can be rewritten in the following form:

$$\frac{(x - x_c)^2}{a_e^2} + \frac{(y - y_c)^2}{b_e^2} = 1, \qquad (12)$$

where $x_c = -g'/a'$, $y_c = -f'/b'$, $a_e = \sqrt{(g'^2/a' + f'^2/b' - c')/a'}$, and $b_e = \sqrt{(g'^2/a' + f'^2/b' - c')/b'}$, (x_c, y_c) is the center point of the ellipse determined by equation (12); a_e and b_e are its radiuses.

In addition, to obtain x_c, y_c, a_e, and b_e of an ellipse, we also need fuzzy information about the ellipse; the fuzzy information and the weight can be measured by:

$$w_i = \mu_{SpeedSlow}(c) = \min\{\mu_{SpeedSlow}(q_{i_k}) \mid k = 1, 2, 3, 4, 5\},$$

where $c = (x_c, y_c)$ is the center of the ellipse determined by $q_{i_1}, q_{i_2}, q_{i_3}, q_{i_4}$, and q_{i_5}. After we have chosen all possible points from $\{q_j\}$, we can obtain a sequence of centers, radiuses, and their weights.

The final representation of the ellipse can be found by the following:

$$x = \frac{\Sigma w_i x_{c_i}}{\Sigma w_i}, y = \frac{\Sigma w_i y_{c_i}}{\Sigma w_i}, a_e = \frac{\Sigma w_i a_{e_i}}{\Sigma w_i}, b_e = \frac{\Sigma w_i b_{e_i}}{\Sigma w_i}.$$

If the curve is an open elliptic arc, the start and end angles have to be determined. Similar to circular arc, they can be determined in the same way.

2.4.4. Generation of B-Spline Curve

Each B-spline function is based on polynomials of a certain order m. If $m = 3$, the polynomials will be of order 3 and thus of degree 2, and so they will be quadratic B-splines. If the order is $m = 4$, the underlying polynomials will be of degree 3, *cubic*. They are the two most important cases, although the formulation allows us to construct B-splines of any order. Cubic B-splines [8] are used in our FFDS.

We derive the k-th B-spline blending function of order 3 by $N_{k,3}(t)$. Hence, a *B*-spline curve equation will be:

$$P(t) = \sum_{k=0}^{l} p_k N_{k,3}(t)$$

Summarizing the ingredients to this point, we have:

- A knot vector $T = (t_0, t_1, t_2, \ldots)$,
- $(l + 1)$ control points p_k, and
- the order m of the *B*-spline functions.

The fundamental formula for the B-spline function $N_{k,m}(t)$ is:

$$N_{k,m}(t) = \left(\frac{t - t_k}{t_{k+m-1} - t_k}\right) N_{k,2}(t) + \left(\frac{t_{k+m-1} - t}{t_{k+m} - t_{k+1}}\right) N_{k+1,2}(t), k = 0,1,\ldots,l$$

This is a recursive definition, specifying how to construct the *mth*-order function from two B-spline functions of order $(m - 1)$. To get things started, the first order function must be defined. It is simply the constant function 1 with its span:

$$N_{k,1}(t) = \begin{cases} 1 & \text{if } t_k < t \leq t_{k+1} \\ 0 & otherwise \end{cases}$$

In order to generate B-spline curve, we need to know a knot vector, control points, and *mth*-order B-spline functions. However, parameter values such as knot vector are not given in practice and therefore must be made up somehow. The easiest way to determine the u_i is simply to set $u_i = i$. This is called uniform or equidistant parameterization. This method is the simplest to cope with most practical situations. It would clearly be more reasonable to adjust the distance between consecutive knots to the distribution of the data points.

One way of achieving this is to have the knots spanning proportional to the distances of the data points:

$$\frac{\Delta_i}{\Delta_{i+1}} \triangleq \frac{\|\Delta x_i\|}{\|\Delta x_{i+1}\|} \tag{13}$$

A parameterization of equation (13) is called *chord length* parameterization. This equation does not uniquely define a knot sequence. Rather, it defines a whole family of parameterizations that are related to each other by affine parameter transformations. In practice, the choices $u_0 = 0$ and $u_l = 1$ or $u_0 = 0$ and $u_l = l$ are reasonable options.

Another parameterization is called *centripetal,* which is:

$$\frac{\Delta_i}{\Delta_{i+1}} \triangleq \sqrt{\frac{\|\Delta x_i\|}{\|\Delta x_{i+1}\|}}$$

The resulting motion of a point on the curve will smooth out variations in the centripetal force action on it.

In our FFDS, the curve is q and $q_i = (x_i, y_i), i = 0, 1, 2, \ldots, l+2$, then

$$knot[0] = 0.0$$
$$knot[1] = \sqrt{(x_2 - x_0)^2 + (y_2 - y_0)^2}$$
$$knot[i] = knot\,[i-1] + \sqrt{(x_{i+1} - x_i)^2 + (y_{i+1} - y_0)^2}, i = 2, 3, \ldots, l-1$$
$$knot[l] = knot[l-1] + \sqrt{(x_{l+2} - x_l)^2 + (y_{l+2} - y_0)^2}$$

A curve based on B-spline blending functions does not automatically interpolate all of its control points. Hence, a preprocessing step is carried out on the given control points so that the B-spline curve will in fact interpolate all of the control points. During preprocessing, a new set of control points is carefully fashioned out of the set. This new set has the property that when a B-spline curve is formed from it, the curve passes through all of the points in the original set. Cubic spline interpolation is used to approximate $\{q_j\}$.

We have interpolated open curves with B-spline curves. If we want to approximate a closed curve, the construction can be done with uniform B-spline of any order and we use the uniform B-spline formula. The only difference from open curves is the way in which the control points enter the formula. The sequence of control points also must be extended on both ends in a cyclic way.

2.5. Experiment and Conclusion

FFDS has been implemented on a UNIX platform in the X Windows environment. Figure 2.16 a, b, and c show sampled experiments. The results show that fuzzy logic can interpret drawer's intention correctly, especially when a user draws lines and circles. The drawer's intention to draw an ellipse is hard to capture sometimes. It is especially hard to interpret correctly when the user draws an elliptic arc. This is reasonable because when the user draws an elliptic arc, he or she might actually draw a part of hyperbola or parabola, which can all be represented by quadratic sections. In such a situation, FFDS will not be able to find the correct representation of the curve as an elliptic arc. If the curve is a free curve, a B-spline curve is generated to interpolate all points in the sequence. Since we have filtered out unintentional points, the generated B-spline curve can reflect drawer's intention more accurately.

In this chapter, we have applied fuzzy logic to freehand drawing. It shows that fuzzy logic is an effective method to deal with vague, imprecise, and uncertain information from the user's drawing manner.

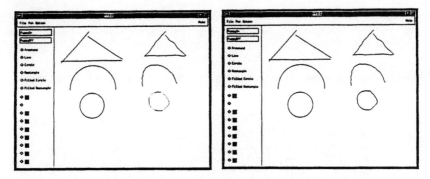

Figure 2.16a Examples of curves before drawing (left) and after drawing (right).

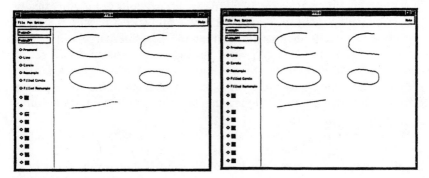

Figure 2.16b Example for low α-level.

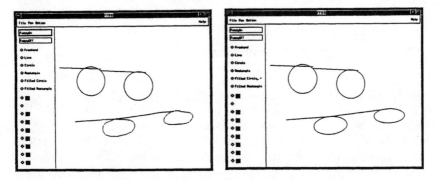

Figure 2.16c Lines and ellipses before and after they are drawn quickly (low α-level).

2.5. Fuzzy Logic Concepts

In this chapter, the following fuzzy logic terminologies are used. A classical (crisp) set is normally defined as a collection of elements or objects, $x \in X$, which can be finite, countable, or uncountable. Each single element can either belongs to or does not belong to a set $A, A \subset X$.

Definition 1: If X is a collection of objects, which is always called *universe of discourse,* and each object is always denoted by x, then a fuzzy set $A \subset X$ is a set of ordered pairs: $A = \{(x, \mu_A(x)) | x \in X\}$, where $\mu(x)$ is the membership function that maps x to the membership space M and $\mu_A(x)$ is the grade of membership (also degree of compatibility or degree of truth) of $x \in A$.

Definition 2: If $sup_{x \in X} \mu_A(x) = 1$, then the fuzzy set A is called normal. In this chapter, we assume all fuzzy sets are normalized; that is, the range of the membership function is $[0,1]$.

Definition 3: The support of a fuzzy set A, $S(A)$, is the crisp set of all $x \in X$ such that $\mu_A(x) > 0$.

Definition 4: The crisp set of elements that belong to fuzzy set A, at least to the degree α is called the α-level set, which is $A_\alpha = \{x \in X | \mu_A(x) \geq \alpha\}$. The set $\{x \in X | \mu_A(x) > \alpha\}$ is called *strong α-level set* or *strong α-cut.* The membership function is the most important concept of a fuzzy set. The operations on fuzzy set are defined via their membership functions.

Definition 5: The membership function $\mu_C(x)$ of the intersection $C = A \cap B$ is defined for all $x \in X$ by $\mu_C(x) = \min\{\mu_A(x), \mu_B(x)\}$.

Definition 6: The membership function of the union $D = A \cup B$ is defined by $\mu_D(x) = \max\{\mu_A(x), \mu_B(x)\}$.

Definition 7: The membership function of the complement of a fuzzy set A, $\overline{A}$, is defined by $\mu_{\overline{A}}(x) = 1 - \mu_A(x), x \in X$.

The most widely used implication inference fuzzy rules in fuzzy logic and approximate reasoning are *generalized Modus Ponens* and *generalized Modus Tollens* [4,5]. The generalized Modus Ponens is used in this chapter, which is defined as follows:

premise 1 : x is A',

premise 2: if x is A then y is B,

---

consequence: y is B',

where A, A', B and B' are fuzzy predicates. The fuzzy implication inference is based on the compositional rule of inference for approximate reasoning. The consequence result can be obtained by the following:

$$\mu_{B'}(v) = sup_{u \in U} \min\{\mu_{A'}(u)\mu_B(v)\},$$

where U and V are precise information input and output domains, respectively, and $u \in U, v \in V$.

Another simple fuzzy inference rule [1, 6], which is also used in this chapter, is in the following:

If x is A and y is B, then z is C

The truth value of the rule is evaluated as:

$$\mu = \min\{\mu_A(x), \mu_B(y)\},$$

where μ is the degree to which "x is A and y is B" implies "z is C."

2.6. References

[1] Saga, S., and H. Makino. "Fuzzy Spline Interpolation and its Application to Online Freehand Curve Identification." *Proceedings, 2nd IEEE International Conference on Fuzzy Systems*, pp. 1183–1190. 1993.

[2] Yager, R., and L. Zadeh. *An Introduction to Fuzzy Logic Applications in Intelligent Systems*. Boston: Kluwer Academic Publishers, 1992.

[3] Zimmerman, H.J. *Fuzzy Sets, Decision Making and Expert Systems*. Boston: Kluwer Academic Publishers, 1987.

[4] Lee, C.C. "Fuzzy Logic in Control Systems: Fuzzy Logic Controller—Part I." *IEEE Transactions on Systems, Man, and Cybernetics*, Vol. 20, No. 2 (1990), pp. 404–418.

[5] ———. "Fuzzy Logic in Control Systems: Fuzzy Logic Controller—Part I." *IEEE Transactions on Systems, Man, and Cybernetics*, Vol. 20, No. 2 (1990), pp. 419–435.

[6] Langari, R. "Synthesis of Nonlinear Controllers via Fuzzy Logic." *Proceedings, 2nd IEEE International Conference on Fuzzy Systems*, pp. 1397–1399. 1993.

[7] Zadeh, L.A. "Fuzzy Sets as a Basis for a Theory of Possibility." *Fuzzy Sets and Systems*, Vol. 1, No. 1, (1978), pp. 3–28.

[8] Farin, G. *Curves and Surfaces for Computer Aided Geometric Design, A Practical Guide*. San Diego: Academic Press Inc., 1990.

[9] Mathews, J. *Numerical Methods for Mathematics, Science, and Engineering*. Englewood Cliffs: Prentice Hall, 1992.

[10] Faux, I.D., and M.J. Pratt. *Computational Geometry for Design and Manufacture*. Chichester: Ellis Horwood Limited, 1979.

[11] Gasson, P. *Geometry of Spatial Forms*. Chichester: Ellis Horwood Limited, 1983.

3 Handwritten Numeric Field Location via Fuzzy Logic

Paul Gader, James M. Keller, and Juliet Cai
Computer Engineering and Computer Science Department
University of Missouri-Columbia, Columbia, Missouri

ABSTRACT: Fuzzy logic has gained widespread attention in the solution of automated control tasks. Here, fuzzy logic is applied to the problem of locating street numbers in digital images of handwritten mail. A fuzzy rule-based system is defined that uses uncertain information provided by image processing and neural network-based character recognition modules to generate multiple hypotheses with associated confidence values for the location of the street number in an image of a handwritten address. The results of a blind test are presented to demonstrate the value of this new approach. The results are compared to those obtained using a neural network trained with backpropagation. The fuzzy logic system achieves higher performance rates, and reasons for this improvement are suggested.

3.1. Introduction

Handwritten address interpretation by a computer system is important for automatic mail processing. The numeric fields in an address—the street number and the zip code—can play a crucial role in reducing the complexity of address interpretation [1–5]. If these numeric fields are correctly detected and identified, then the number of possible addresses is significantly reduced.

Figure 3.1 shows a common control structure for an address interpretation system. The written matter from the address image is first located, and then each text line is located and separated into image blocks. Each image block should contain at least one word from the address. The search for numeric fields is confined to either the first image block on a

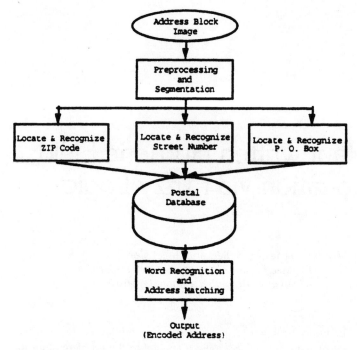

Figure 3.1   Control structure for a typical handwritten address interpretation system.

subset of the address lines (street numbers) or the last image block on a subset of the lines (zip codes).

Figure 3.2 displays a typical address image with image blocks indicated (the name has been removed). Zip code, street number, and post office box number candidates are determined from these blocks. If a street number is present, the hypothesized zip codes and the street numbers are used to query a database to obtain a lexicon of street names. Lexicon-based word recognition is used to generate entire address hypotheses that are matched against full records in the postal database to determine the delivery point of the mail [3, 4].

Word recognition rates range from 85 percent to 95 percent using lexicons of size 1000 or less [6–9]. There are over 100,000 unique street names in the United States, so an algorithm cannot read the street name directly without reducing the number of possibilities. This is why the sys-

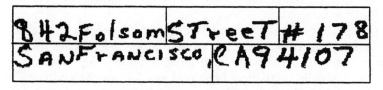

Figure 3.2   Typical address images and image block.

tem should generate small lexicons of street names using hypothesized zip codes and street numbers.

Locating and reading street numbers is difficult. There are a variable number of digits in a street number and there is ambiguity between certain numerals and alphabetic characters. For example, the J in the word Johnson in Figure 3.3 can be easily misidentified as a 9, and the o as a 0 (zero). The ambiguity can be resolved by reading the word, but this is currently beyond the capabilities of any program. Other ambiguous examples are shown in Figure 3.3.

There are many factors that can indicate the presence of a street number. There is usually a gap between a street number and the street name. A street name usually starts with a capital letter, and capital letters are usually "big." Furthermore, if we run a character recognition algorithm on the first letter, we should get a high score. If we run a numeric field recognition algorithm on a street number, then we should get a high score, whereas if we run a numeric field recognition algorithm on a word that is not a street number, then we should get a low score. Unfortunately, each of these heuristics can fail. Sometimes street numbers are not even separated from street names. Sometimes alphabetic character recognition algorithms get low scores on alphabetic characters and high scores on numerals. Sometimes numeric field recognition algorithms get high scores on non-numeric fields and low scores on numeric fields. The ambiguity in the input data and the inherently imperfect nature of the image processing and pattern recognition algorithms implies that a method that can gracefully aggregate disparate, partial information is required for high-performance street number location.

In this chapter we present the incorporation of fuzzy logic into the process of detecting street number fields in handwritten addresses. We show

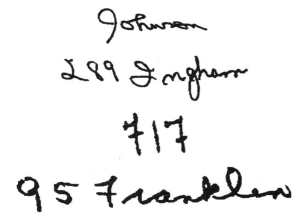

Figure 3.3 Examples of confusing street numbers: a J that looks like a 9, an I that looks like a 2, 7s that look like Fs, and an F that looks like a 7.

how fuzzy logic provides a natural mechanism to increase or decrease confidence in "street number" as a handwritten image block is processed by the computer vision modules. The fuzzy logic system uses the uncertain results obtained from segmentation and recognition modules to form hypotheses concerning the locations of street numbers. The focus of this chapter is on the use of fuzzy logic; the segmentation and recognition modules have been independently described elsewhere [8, 10, 11]. The rules and membership functions were initially designed based on our experience, and were modified using the results obtained on training images. The resultant system was then tested with several data sets taken from the real address images.

For comparison, we also trained a neural network to locate street numbers. We used the same training and testing sets and the same numerical features. The neural network did not perform as well as the fuzzy logic system, although it did not perform badly.

3.2. System Description

The street number location system takes an image block as input. An image block is a subimage of an address line. The output of the system is a set of possible locations of the street number field. A confidence value is associated with each possible location. The system is comprised of two major components, a feature extraction module and a fuzzy rule-based module. We briefly describe the feature extraction process and then we describe the fuzzy logic system in detail.

3.2.1. Feature Extraction

The feature extraction module is a complex system that extracts numerical features using image processing, neural networks, and dynamic programming. These features are inputs to the fuzzy logic system. The control structure is shown in Figure 3.4. During segmentation, each image block is divided into primitives. Several neural networks are activated to obtain character and numeral confidence measurements from the primitives. Dynamic programming is used to obtain numeric field recognition confidence measurements and to compute confidence that the image block contains the string PO, a part of P.O. Box.

The segmentation algorithm is described in [8, 10]. The input is an image block. The output is a sequence of subimages of the image block, called primitives. Each primitive should consist of either a single character or a piece of a single character. If so, the correct segmentation of the image block into characters can be assembled from the primitives. This process, called "oversegmentation," is useful in handwriting recognition and computer vision.

For example, Figure 3.5 shows an image block and the associated primitives. These images illustrate the necessity for segmentation (since the A

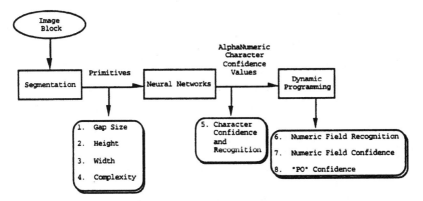

Figure 3.4 Control structure for the feature extraction system.

and p are touching) and the uncertainty introduced by the process (e.g., the A is segmented into primitives that look like 14).

There are six recognition neural networks: two for numerals and four for alphabetic characters. Two types of feature vectors are used as inputs, the transition and bar feature vectors. They are described in [8, 11]. The neural networks were trained using backpropagation, and use class-coded outputs (one output unit per class). They contain a class named "garbage" to represent segments that do not represent characters, such as multiple characters or pieces of characters.

The dynamic programming algorithms find the best match between sequences of unions of primitives and sequences of characters or digits. The best match depends upon the character or digit confidence for each of the primitives obtained from the neural networks. The dynamic programming algorithm is used for word recognition or for numeric field recognition.

For word recognition, it takes an image of a handwritten word, a string, and a list of the primitives from the image as input and returns a value between 0 and 1 indicating the confidence that the word represents the string. This algorithm is described in [8, 12]. We use it to compute the confidence that a sequence of primitives represents the string PO. In the case of numeric field recognition, no string is used as input. The output is a string of digits with a confidence value. The confidence value represents

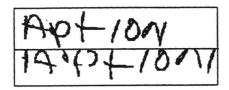

Figure 3.5 An image block and the primitives computed by the segmentation algorithm.

the confidence that the image is a numeric field and the string represents the system's best guess at the identity of the field.

The dynamic programming algorithms produce one set of outputs for each subsequence of primitives $P_k = \{p_1, p_2, \ldots, p_k\}$, $k \leq n$, where n is number of primitives in an image block. The output consists of the confidence that P_k represents a numeric field, the hypothesized identity of the numeric field, and the confidence that the subimage block contains the character string PO.

We describe the numeric field dynamic programming algorithm in detail. The input is a sequence of k primitives. The output is the confidence that the sequence represents a numeric field and the hypothesized identity of the field. The field can have any length between 1 and k. For example, if $k = 3$ then 1, 53, and 864 are all possible hypothesized identities.

The algorithm constructs a k × k array called dparray. The columns of the array correspond to primitives. The rows of the array correspond to digits in the hypothesized identity. The (i, j) element of the array is the value of the best match between all possible digit strings of length i and the first j primitives. The match values come from the digit recognition neural networks. We match sequences of different lengths by forming unions of primitive segments as illustrated in Figure 3.6. For each pair of integers i, j between 1 and k with $i \leq j$, we let $p_{ij} = \cup_{h=i}^{j} P_h$ denote the union of primitives i through j.

We define a function, match(s), that takes a segment s (either a primitive or a union of primitives) as input and computes the highest digit recognition confidence for any class. That is, if bf(s, c) and tf(s, c) denote the output activation values for the bar and transition feature digit recognition networks for classes $c = 0, 1, \ldots, 9$, then:

$$match(s) = \max \{ bf(s,c) + tf(s, c) \mid c = 0, 1, \ldots, 9 \}.$$

Let legalp(s) be a Boolean function that returns TRUE if s is not too complex to segment, and FALSE otherwise. The elements of dparray are first initialized to $-\infty$. The (i,j) element of dparray is then computed as follows:

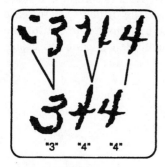

Figure 3.6 Matching a sequence of primitive segments to digit strings of different lengths.

```
IF i = 1 (matching against the first digit in the string) THEN
   IF legalp(p_ij) THEN
      dparray(1, j) = match(p_1j)
ELSEIF legalp (p_ij) THEN
      dparray(i,j) = MAX {dparray(i-1,k) + match(p_ij) | i ≤ k < j
               k
      and legalp(p_kj) }
```

The best match is found by computing the maximum value in column k (the last column) after normalizing by length. That is, the output confidence is given by:

$$\text{num\_field\_conf} = \underset{i}{\text{MAX}} \left\{ \frac{\text{dparray}(i, k)}{i} \mid 1 \le i < k \right\}.$$

This formula produces the best match since [dparray(i, k)]/i is the value of the best match between all digit strings of length i and all unions of primitives. Note that we must keep track of the classes for which the best matches occur if we want to return the most confident digit string.

3.2.2. Fuzzy Rule-Based System

The fuzzy rule base developed for the street number location system contains 48 rules and is implemented using the software package, CubiCalc. We used correlation-min inference and centroid based defuzzification [13].

The input to the fuzzy rule base is a set of features associated with primitives $p_1, p_2, \ldots, p_k$. The output of the rule base is a number representing the confidence that the subimage block $p_1 \cup p_2 \cup \ldots \cup p_k$ is a street number field. Three assumptions are made:

1. A street number always starts from the beginning of an address line.

2. No street number starts with a zero.

3. No street number is longer than five digits.

There are eight input variables and one output variable for each subimage block $p_1 \cup p_2 \cup \ldots \cup p_k$. The input variables are gap_k, height_k, width_k, too_comp_to_recog (complex_k), character confidence reading (conf_k), numeric field reading, numeric field confidence measurement (n_k), and PO confidence (po_k), while the output variable is called adjconf. For example, one of the input variables is height, the normalized height of a union of primitives. The terms used to describe gap are large, medium, small, and tiny. Their membership functions are shown in Figure 3.7. All membership functions used in our system are completely described in [14].

All the input variables computed from the feature extraction system for the fuzzy rule-based system are shown in Table 3.1.

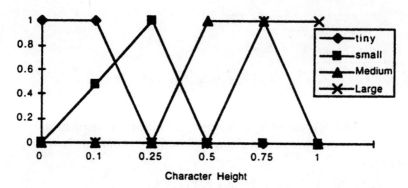

Figure 3.7 Membership functions for the terms of the linguistic variable character height.

In addition to the preceding variables, a variable

po-set$_k$ = MAX{confidence that $p_1 \cup p_2 \cup \ldots \cup p_j$

represents the string "PO" | $j \leq k$ }

is computed internally and used by the system.

The output variable, called adjconf, indicates the adjustment of the confidence value for a street number field. It is initialized to zero at the beginning of each image block. The range of adjconf is [–1.0, 1.0]. The final output is linearly mapped between 0 and 1. The terms are neglarge, negsmall, negtiny, nearzero, postiny, possmall, and poslarge.

There are 48 rules. The complete rule set can be found in Appendix A of [14]. Each rule consists of one or more antecedent and one consequence. There are three types of rules for the street number location system:

- Rules using numeric field confidence readings and gap size;
- Rules using PO confidence, width, and character confidence readings;
- Rules for the last primitive in an image block.

Thirty-five rules relate numeric field and gap size. Most possess one of the two basic structures:

IF complex$_{k+1}$ is **large** AND n_k is **A** AND gap$_k$ is **B**
THEN adjconf is **C**

IF complex$_{k+1}$ is **small** AND n_k is **A** AND n_k + 1 is **B** and gap$_k$ is **C**
THEN adjconf is **D**.

An example is the rule:

Table 3.1 Input Variable Definitions

Input variable	Description	Value range	Terms
gap_k	The distance between p_k and p_{k+1}. It is normalized using an image-dependent value C, where C is calculated as: $$C = \frac{1}{p+q}\left(\sum_{i=1}^{p} width_i + \sum_{[i=1\,\&\,gap_i >= 5]}^{p} gap_i\right)$$ p is the number of primitives in the image block, q is the number of gaps with size no less than 5 pixels, $width_i$ is the width of the ith primitive, and gap_i is the distance in pixels between the ith and $(i+1)$th primitive. It is set to 1 if the normalized result is larger than 1.	[0, 1]	{huge, large, medium, small}
$height_k$	The height of the primitive p_k. It is normalized by the fixed height of an address line, 64 pixels.	[0, 1]	{large, medium, small, tiny}
$width_k$	The width of the subimage block $p_1 \cup p_2 \cup \ldots \cup p_k$. It is normalized by the constant 7×60. If the subimage width is bigger than 7×60 pixels, the value is set to 1.	[0, 1]	{large, medium, small}
$complex_k$	The flag set for primitives that are too complex to be digits. It is used as a fuzzy variable that has only two terms, high and small, corresponding to the values 1 and 0.	[0, 1]	{large, small}
$conf_k$ character confidence reading	The maximum value of the character confidence. The character that corresponds to the value is also used to determine the weighting factors of some of the rules.	[0, 1]	{large, medium, small}
numeric field reading k	The highest confidence digit string returned by the dynamic programming algorithm given the primitives $p_1, p_2, \ldots, p_k$ as input. This variable is not directly used in the fuzzy rules, but is used to determine the input of some rules.	N/A	N/A
n_k numeric field confidence	This confidence that $p_1 \cup p_2 \cup \ldots \cup p_k$ is a numeric field.	[0, 1]	{large, medium, small}
"PO" confidence	The dynamic programming match value between $p_1, p_2, \ldots, p_k$ and the string "PO".	[0, 1]	{large, medium, small}

IF complex_n is **large** AND n is **large** AND gap is **medium**
THEN adjconf is **poslarge**;

which can be interpreted as:

If the next primitive is too complex to be recognized as digits
and the numeric field confidence, n, is large

and the gap size between this primitive and next primitive, gap, is medium

then the street number confidence should be adjusted to positive and large.

There are also rules involving PO confidence, width, and character confidence. One rule in this category is:

IF po-set is large THEN adjconf is neglarge;

where po-set is the largest PO confidence value read from the image block. This rule implies that if the subimage block has high confidence of containing the string PO, then the overall confidence on street number is adjusted to be negative large.

A weighting factor preceding a rule alters the relative importance of rules. Weights span the range 0 through 1. If a rule weight is zero, that rule is disabled. The default weight factor is 1, indicating full activation. The weighting factor is applied to the result fuzzy set by scaling the set proportional to the weight prior to the summation process in the rule activation phase. Some rules have binary weights, such as:

(w2) IF width is **large** then adjconf is **neglarge**;

where   w2 = 1.0   if reading = 0;

     w2 = 0   otherwise;

reading is the street number read by the neural nets. It is set to 0 if the street number is longer than five digits. This rule implies that if the width of the subimage is large and the street number reading is longer than five digits, then the street number confidence is adjusted to negative large.

Another rule regarding character confidence is:

(w1) IF n is **medium** AND c is **large**

THEN adjconf is **negsmall**;

where   w1 = 0   if the character is one of {'O', 'Z', 'S', 'I', 'Z', 'o', 'z', 's', 'I', 'g', 'b'};

     w1 = 1   otherwise;

and c is a character confidence. In this case, the rule is activated only when the character read is other than any of these characters, 'O', 'Z', 'S', 'I', 'o', 'z', 's', 'I', 'g', 'b'; avoiding the ambiguity between those characters and the digits '0', '2', '5', '1', '6', '3' and '9' in handwriting. If the character read is one of these, w1 is set to 0, and the rule is disabled. This rule states that if the numeric field confidence is medium and the character confidence on the characters other than the above is large; then the street number confidence is adjusted to be negative small.

Two rules are used for processing the last primitive in an image. The variable size_n is used to determine whether the end of a image block is reached. Size_n is the height of next primitive, and it is set to zero at the last primitive of an image block. The rules are:

IF complex_n is small AND size_n is **tiny** AND n is large

AND n_n is small AND gap is small

THEN adjconf is poslarge;

and

IF complex_n is small AND size_n is **tiny** AND n is medium

AND n_n is small AND gap is small

THEN adjconf is possmall.

The fuzzy rule base produces a confidence value for each sequence of primitives in the image block beginning with the leftmost primitive, indicating the degree of confidence that the subimage block is a street number field. The final procedure of the street number location system is thresholding of the final confidence. Locations that have confidence values above a threshold are interpreted as ending positions of street number fields. Image blocks for which all confidence values are below the threshold are interpreted as nonstreet number blocks.

3.3. Experiments

The data were binary image blocks, supplied by the Environmental Research Institute of Michigan. We selected the first block in each address line except the first and last lines in an address block. Initially, 71 image blocks were used for training, with 41 having street numbers. Another 78 image blocks were used as an initial test set; 40 of them contained street numbers. These images were then combined into a single training set that was used to train the final system. A blind test of the final system was conducted using another 155 image blocks containing 79 street numbers. The training and initial test sets are referred to as train1 and test1. The combination of the train1 and test1 is referred to as btrain, and the blind test set is referred to as btest. The feature extraction processes were all trained on completely different data.

The development of the fuzzy rule base followed the usual development path of rule-based systems: an iterative cycle of rule definition, testing, and refinement. The fuzzy rules were initially formulated using pictures of addresses. The system was trained with the train1 set. The training process was iterated until the results were satisfactory. Upon completion of training, initial testing was performed with the test1 set. A few adjustments were performed based on the test results. The final system was applied to the btest set once, constituting the blind test.

Final decisions concerning the street number locations were made by thresholding the output confidence, which is between 0 and 1. Those locations for which the confidence was above the threshold were labeled as locations of street numbers by the system. The threshold used on the blind test set, btest, was selected by choosing the threshold that gave the best success rate on the training set, btrain. The best threshold was defined as the threshold that produced the best success rate and was found using exhaustive search (which is very quick for this problem).

3.4. Results

We evaluate the performance of the system using the success rate, which is defined as the number of correct responses divided by the number of possible responses. The response is either that there is a street number at a particular location in the block or that there is no street number in the block. A response is correct if there is actually a street number in a block and the system indicates the correct location, or if there is no street number in a block and the system indicates that there is not a street number.

The best threshold found using the btrain set was 0.535. For comparison, results for thresholds 0.5 and 0.75 are also shown in Table 3.2. Figure 3.8 compares the success rate of training and testing for various threshold levels. This figure illustrates the robustness of the fuzzy system.

3.5. Street Number Location Using Neural Networks

We trained several multilayer feedforward networks for locating the street numbers. We used the numeric input variables used in the fuzzy logic system as given in Table 3.1. The street number location neural networks used features from the blocks $B = p_1 \cup p_2 \cup \ldots \cup p_k$ and $B' = p_1 \cup p_2 \cup \ldots \cup p_k \cup p_{k+1}$. The 16 input features are: gap_k, $height_k$, $width_k$, $complex_k$, $conf_k$, n_k, po_k, $po\text{-}set_k$, gap_{k+1}, $height_{k+1}$, $width_{k+1}$, $complex_{k+1}$, $conf_{k+1}$, n_{k+1}, po_{k+1}, $po\text{-}set_{k+1}$. The network has one output: the confidence that block B contains only a complete street number.

We used exactly the same data sets for training and testing as for the fuzzy logic system. Using the set train1, we varied the learning rate and number of hidden units. We also trained with and without balancing the

Table 3.2 Success Rate for the Blind Test

thresh = 0.5		thresh = 0.535		thresh = 0.75	
train	test	train	test	train	test
85%	81%	91%	86%	77%	81%

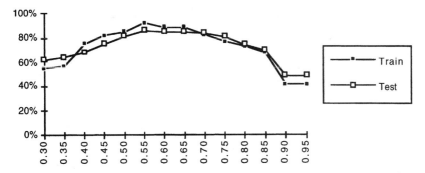

Figure 3.8 Comparison of training and testing levels on blind test set.

training set. A balanced training set is one that contains the same number of samples per class. If a training set is not balanced, then a least squares error criteria can lead to a classifier, which ignores a class with few training samples. For each variation, we evaluated the performance of the network on both the training set, train1, and the initial testing set, test1. Table 3.3 shows the results on obtained with different numbers of hidden units and with and without balanced training. These results represent the best that we could obtain by varying the learning rate and are lower than those obtained using the fuzzy logic system, which were 93 percent for train1 and 90 percent for test1.

We then trained 15 different networks using the combined training set, btrain. We balanced the combined training set before training. Each network had a different number of hidden units. The networks were trained for 1500 epochs. Every 25 epochs, the performance of the network was evaluated on the blind test set, btest. If the success rate of the network was better than the previous best success rate achieved by that network, the weights were saved. Thus, the performance results achieved were essentially the best achievable *on the blind test set* in 1500 epochs of training. This is in contrast to the fuzzy logic system experiment. In that experiment, the blind test set was actually used as a blind test set. The performance of the networks on the blind test set always either remained

Table 3.3 Best Neural Network Street
Number Location Performance Results
on the Initial Training and Test Sets

# Hidden Units	Training Success Rate	Testing Success Rate
4	85%	83%
4 (bal)	89%	86%
14	86%	83%
14 (bal)	89%	86%
16	83%	85%
20	83%	82%
21	85%	83%

constant or deteriorated for the last several hundred epochs of training, indicating that no further increases in performance were likely to occur.

The results of training on the balanced combined training set and evaluating on the blind test set are shown in Table 3.4. It is interesting to note that the networks trained to exactly or about the same rates, regardless of the number of hidden units.

The fuzzy rule base achieved a testing success rate of 86 percent, which is significantly better than the 79 percent achieved by the neural network. One may argue that if we tried 100 or 150 hidden units we may get a better success rate. We may not however. This, of course, is a problem with neural networks; it is very difficult to know what the correct parameters are.

There are several possible interpretations of these results: (1) The knowledge required to assign street number location confidence is not at the microstructure level; it is more coarsely grained and therefore more suitable for fuzzy logic. (2) There is not enough training data for the neural network. A fuzzy rule-based approach can incorporate human knowledge that is not statistically well represented in the data. Actually, (1) and (2) are not disjoint. It is difficult to incorporate human knowledge into a problem such as character recognition since the information (the shape of the characters) is on such a fine level, cf. [15, 16]. On the other hand, it is relatively easy to define a neural network to perform character recognition, and the results are usually good. It is natural to think of rules for locating street numbers (if one thinks about such things) and, as our results show, it is not so easy to train a network that will perform as well as a fuzzy logic system.

We had a similar experience with fusion of handwritten word classifiers [9]. In those experiments, we devised a novel method of fusing the outputs of handwritten word classifiers using fuzzy integrals. We also tried to train neural networks to fuse the outputs of the classifiers using the same input features. We tried several methods, but were unable to train the networks to perform nearly as well (The fuzzy integral testing rate was 88.0 percent, whereas the best neural network rate was 83.9 percent).

In summary, although we performed numerous experiments and used the same numeric features, we were unable to train the multilayer feedforward neural networks to perform as well as the fuzzy logic system. We

Table 3.4 Best Neural Network Street Number Location Performance Results on the Combined Training and Blind Test Sets

# Hidden Units	Training Success Rate	Testing Success Rate
2	85%	78%
4, 6, 8, 10, 12, 14, 16	83%	79%
18	84%	78%
20, 22, 24, 30, 32, 50	83%	79%

conjecture that the reason is that the granularity of knowledge required to locate street numbers is "coarser" than that required to perform tasks such as character recognition. Tasks that require knowledge about the world that is not statistically represented in the data are difficult or impossible for neural networks to learn, but the knowledge can be encoded into rules.

3.5. Conclusion

We developed a fuzzy rule-based system for locating street number fields. The performance of this system illustrates the capacity for locating street number fields using a fuzzy rule-based system. The fuzzy rule base outperformed a neural network approach based on the same features. Although rule-based systems in computer vision are often too rigid to provide robust results, our results on blind test data suggest that if care is given not to make rules too specific, then a robust, fuzzy rule-based system can be developed for this computer vision application.

3.6. References

[1] Shridhar, M., and F. Kimura. "Handwritten Address Interpretation using Word Recognition with and without Lexicon." *Proceedings, IEEE Conference on Systems, Man, and Cybernetics.* pp. 2341–2346. Vancouver, Canada: October, 1995.

[2] Srihari, S.N., et al. "Name and Address Block Reader System for Tax Form Processing." *Proceedings, International Conference Document Analysis and Recognition.* pp. 5–11. Montreal, Canada: August, 1995.

[3] Ganzberger, M.J., et al. "Matching Database Records to Handwritten Text." *Proceedings, SPIE Conference Document Recognition, IS&T/SPIE International Symposium on Electronic Imaging: Science and Technology.* San Jose, California: 1994.

[4] ———. "A System for Handwritten Address Interpretation." *Proceedings, United States Postal Service Advanced Technology Conference,* (1992), pp. 337–351.

[5] Govindaraju, V., et al. "Interpretation of Handwritten Addresses in U.S. Main Stream." *Proceedings, 3rd International Workshop on Frontiers of Handwriting Recognition,* (1993), pp. 207–217.

[6] Kim, G., and V. Govindaraju. "Handwritten Word Recognition for Real-Time Applications." *Proceedings, International Conference Document Analysis Recognition,* pp. 24–28. Montreal, Canada: August, 1995.

[7] Kimura, F., et al. "Lexicon Directed Segmentation—Recognition Procedure for Unconstrained Handwritten Words." *Proceedings, 3rd International Workshop on Frontiers in Handwriting Recognition,* pp. 122–132. Buffalo, New York: 1993.

[8] Gader, P.D., et al. "Handwritten Word Recognition with Character and Inter-Character Neural Networks." *IEEE Transactions on Systems, Man, and Cybernetics,* no. accepted, 1995.

[9] Gader, P.D., et al. "Fusion of Handwritten Word Classifiers." *Pattern Recognition Letters,* accepted for publication, 1995.

[10] Gader, P.D., et al. "Handprinted Word Recognition on a NIST Data Set." *Machine Vision and its Applications,* Vol. 8 (1995), pp. 31–40.

[11] Gader, P.D., et al. "Comparison of Crisp and Fuzzy Character Neural Networks in Handwritten Word Recognition." *IEEE Transactions on Fuzzy Systems,* Vol. 3, No. 3 (1995), pp. 357–364.

[12] Gader, P.D., and M.A. Mohamed. "Multiple Classifier Fusion for Handwritten Word Recognition." *Proceedings, IEEE Conference on Systems, Man, and Cybernetics.* Vancouver, Canada: 1995.

[13] Kosko, B. *Neural Networks and Fuzzy Systems.* Englewood Cliffs: Prentice Hall, 1992.

[14] Gader, P.D., et al. "A Fuzzy Logic System for the Detection and Recognition of Street Number Fields on Handwritten Postal Addresses." *IEEE Transactions on Fuzzy Systems,* Vol. 3, No. 1 (1995), pp. 83–95.

[15] Gillies, A.M., and B.T. Mitchell. "A Model-based Approach to Handwritten Digit Recognition." *Machine Vision and Applications,* Vol. 2 (1989), pp. 231–243.

[16] Gader, P.D., et al. "Recognition of Handwritten Digits using Template and Model Matching." *Pattern Recognition,* Vol. 24, No. 5 (1991), pp. 421–432.

4 Segmenting Medical Images with Fuzzy Models: An Update

J. C. Bezdek
Department of Computer Science
University of West Florida, Pensacola, Florida

L.O. Hall, Matt Clark, and Dmitri Goldgof
Department of Computer Science and Engineering
University of South Florida, Tampa, Florida

L.P. Clarke
Department of Radiology
University of South Florida, Tampa, Florida

ABSTRACT: This chapter has two objectives. First, it updates several recent surveys by Bezdek et. al and Hall et. al on the use of fuzzy models for segmentation and edge detection in medical image data. Second, we also present some previously unpublished results on the use of a knowledge-based system to upgrade the results of segmentation of magnetic resonance images for the purpose of tumor volume estimation. Our survey is divided into methods based on supervised and unsupervised learning, and is organized first and foremost by groups that are active in this area. There is a further subdivision into methods for two- and three-dimensional data and/or problems. We do *not* cover methods based on fuzzy neural-like networks, fuzzy morphology, or fuzzy reasoning systems. These topics are covered by other authors in this volume, or in a companion survey recently published by Keller et. al.

4.1. Introduction

Figure 4.1 depicts an overall architecture for the segmentation of images, and gives us a reference map for the discussion to follow.

Medical imaging systems use various sensors to collect spatial distributions of tissue-related parameters. The leading example, *magnetic resonance images* (MRIs), comprise several relaxation times as well as proton density at each spatial location. These raw data support pixel, edge, and region-based segmentation, the distinction being which numerical features extracted from the image are used as the basis for processing. This is illustrated at the top of Figure 4.1, which shows the extraction of a vec-

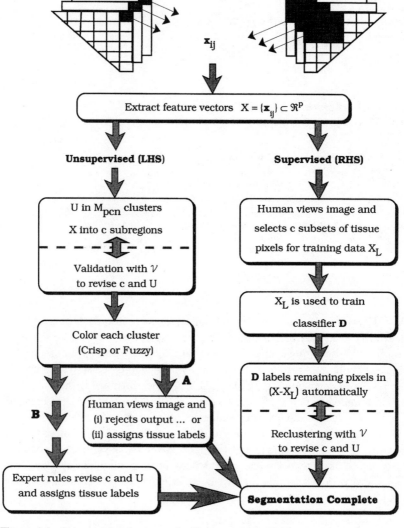

Figure 4.1 Supervised and unsupervised image segmentation.

tor $\mathbf{x}_{ij}$ from just the ij-th pixel on the *left-hand side* (LHS); and from a region (window) surrounding the ij-th pixel on the *right-hand side* (RHS). The LHS thus illustrates pixel-based features, while the RHS illustrates either edge or region-based features. In either case, we say features are extracted from the image.

Image data are represented here as sets of vectors $X = \{\mathbf{x}_1, \mathbf{x}_2, \ldots, \mathbf{x}_n\}$ in *feature space* $\mathfrak{R}^p$, where p is the number of measurements associated with each spatial location in the image. As an example, let $T1_{ij}$, $T2_{ij}$, and ρ_{ij} denote the spin lattice relaxation, transverse relaxation, and proton density of pixel (i,j) in an MR slice of overall dimensions (m × n). We can aggregate these three measurements into *pixel vector* $\mathbf{x}_{ij} = (T1_{ij}, T2_{ij}, \rho_{ij})$ in $\mathfrak{R}^3$; and the pixel vectors so constructed comprise a data set X that supports *pixel-based* methods. On the other hand, if we estimated the horizontal and vertical gradients, say $g_{v,ij}$ and $g_{h,ij}$ of the intensity function at pixel (i,j) from intensities in some neighborhood of pixel (i,j) in each of the three MR slices, there would be either three sets of features in $\mathfrak{R}^2$ or one set of features in $\mathfrak{R}^6$ to support *edge-based* segmentation of X^1. Finally, we might instead extract and order the nine intensities from a 3 × 3 window centered at pixel (i,j) in each of the three slices. This would result in either three sets of features in $\mathfrak{R}^9$ or one set of features in $\mathfrak{R}^{27}$ to support *region-based* segmentation of X.

Many studies of nonfuzzy segmentation methods of all three types have been published [1–8]. This article concentrates on—but is not limited to—pixel-based fuzzy methods for the segmentation of medical images that are sometimes augmented by higher-level processing via knowledge-based systems. Most of our survey concerns MRI, but we will also review the use of fuzzy models for segmentation of several other types of medical images. We will also discuss the emergent use of fuzzy models for applications to 3D segmentation and volume estimation. Another chapter in this volume (Bloch) discusses image processing with fuzzy mathematical morphology, so this topic is not covered by our review.

4.2. Fuzzy Numerical Pattern Recognition: The Basic Ideas

There are four types of *class labels:* crisp, fuzzy, probabilistic, and possibilistic. Let integer c denote the number of classes, $1 < c < n$, and define three sets of *label vectors* in $\mathfrak{R}^c$ as follows:

$$N_{pc} = \{\mathbf{y} \in \mathfrak{R}^c : y_i \in [0, 1] \; \forall \; i, \; y_i > 0 \; \exists \; i\}; \tag{1a}$$

$$N_{fc} = \left\{ \mathbf{y} \in N_{pc} : \sum_{i=1}^{c} y_i = 1 \right\}; \tag{1b}$$

$$N_{hc} = \left\{ \mathbf{y} \in N_{fc} : \sum_{i=1}^{c} y_i = 1, y_i \in \{0, 1\} \forall i \right\}. \tag{1c}$$

---

[1] Some writers call gradients *texture* features; however, we will reserve this term for more refined measures of texture.

N_{hc} is the canonical (unit vector) basis of $\mathfrak{R}^c$; N_{fc}, a piece of a hyperplane, is its convex hull; and N_{pc} is a hypercube in $\mathfrak{R}^c$, *excluding the origin*. The i-th vertex of N_{hc},

$$\mathbf{e}_i = (0, 0, \cdots, \underset{i}{1}, \cdots, 0)^T,$$

is the crisp label for class i, $1 \leq i \leq c$. The vector $\mathbf{y} = (0.1, 0.6, 0.3)^T$ is a constrained label vector; its entries lie between 0 and 1, and sum to 1. If $\mathbf{y}$ is a label vector for some $\mathbf{x} \in \mathfrak{R}^p$ generated by, say, the fuzzy c-means model, we call $\mathbf{y}$ a fuzzy label for $\mathbf{x}$. If $\mathbf{y}$ came from a method such as maximum likelihood estimation in mixture decomposition, $\mathbf{y}$ would be a probabilistic label. Vectors such as $\mathbf{z} = (0.7, 0.2, 0.7)^T$ in $N_{pc} = [0, 1]^3 - \{\mathbf{O}\}$ are called *possibilistic* label vectors. Labels in N_{pc} are produced, such as, by possibilistic clustering algorithms [9]. Note that $N_{hc} \subset N_{fc} \subset N_{pc}$.

When X is unlabeled, the assignment of label vectors to its elements is *clustering* (or unsupervised learning). If the labels are crisp, we hope they identify c natural subgroups (tissue classes) in X. The *c-partitions* of X are sets of (cn) values $\{u_{ik}\}$ that are arrayed as a (cxn) matrix $U = [\mathbf{U}_1 \ldots \mathbf{U}_k \ldots \mathbf{U}_n] = [u_{ik}]$, where $\mathbf{U}_k$ denotes the k-th column of U:

$$M_{pcn} = \left\{ U \in \mathfrak{R}^{cn} : \mathbf{U}_k \in N_{pc} \ \forall \ k; 0 < \sum_{k=1}^{n} u_{ik} < n \ \forall \ i \right\}; \quad (2a)$$

$$M_{fcn} = \{ U \in M_{pcn} : \mathbf{U}_k \in N_{fc} \ \forall \ k \}. \quad (2b)$$

$$M_{hcn} = \{ U \in M_{fcn} : \mathbf{U}_k \in N_{hc} \ \forall \ k \}. \quad (2c)$$

Equations (2a–c) define, respectively, the sets of possibilistic, fuzzy (or probabilistic), and crisp *c-partitions* of X. Each column of U in M_{pcn} (M_{fcn}, M_{hcn}) is a label vector from N_{pc} (N_{fc}, N_{hc}). Note that $M_{hcn} \subset M_{fcn} \subset M_{pcn}$. If U is fuzzy, u_{ik} is the *membership* of $\mathbf{x}_k$ in the i-th fuzzy cluster of X. Fuzzy clustering, including early work in fuzzy image processing and segmentation is discussed in Bezdek and Pal [10]. Underlying ideas about fuzzy models are covered well by Ross [11].

Clustering algorithms are functions $\mathbf{C}:X \mapsto \mathcal{R}_c$, where $\mathcal{R}_c$ is the range of $\mathbf{C}$. When the output of $\mathbf{C}$ is *just* a partition, $\mathcal{R}_c = M_{pcn}$. Some clustering algorithms produce outputs besides partitions. The most common example is a second set of parameters called point prototypes (or cluster centers) $\mathbf{V} = \{\mathbf{v}_1, \ldots, \mathbf{v}_c\}$, $\mathbf{v}_i \in \mathfrak{R}^p \ \forall \ i$. In this case, $\mathcal{R}_c = M_{pcn} \times \mathfrak{R}^{cp}$.

Since definite class assignments for each pixel are the usual goal in image segmentation, labels in N_{pc} are often transformed into crisp labels. Noncrisp labels $\mathbf{y}$ are usually converted to crisp ones using the conversion function $\mathbf{H}:N_{pc} \mapsto N_{hc}$:

$$\mathbf{H}(\mathbf{y}) = \mathbf{e}_i \Leftrightarrow \| \mathbf{y} - \mathbf{e}_i \| \leq \| \mathbf{y} - \mathbf{e}_j \| \Leftrightarrow y_i \geq y_j; j \neq i. \quad (3)$$

In (3), $\|*\|$ is the Euclidean norm, $\delta_E(\mathbf{y} - \mathbf{e}_i) = \| \mathbf{y} - \mathbf{e}_i \| = \sqrt{(\mathbf{y} - \mathbf{e}_i)^T(\mathbf{y} - \mathbf{e}_i)}$ on $\mathfrak{R}^c$. $\mathbf{H}$ finds the crisp label vector $\mathbf{e}_i$ in N_{hc} closest to $\mathbf{y}$. Alternatively, $\mathbf{H}$ finds the *maximum coordinate* of $\mathbf{y}$, and assigns the corresponding crisp label to the object z that y labels. The rationale for using H depends on the algorithm that produces y. For example, the justification for y from the k-nearest neighbor rule is simple majority voting. If y is gotten from mixture decomposition, using H is Bayes rule—label z by its class of maximum posterior probability. And if the labels are fuzzy, this step is called defuzzification of U by the maximum membership rule. We call this operation the *hardening* of y by H. Partitions of X are hardened by applying H to each column of U in M_{pcn}.

Let $\rho = \{U_i \mid 1 \le i \le N\}$ denote N different partitions (with or without extra parameters such as V) of a fixed data set X that may arise as a result of:

1. clustering X with one algorithm C at various values of c; or
2. clustering X over other algorithmic parameters of C; or
3. applying different $\{C_j\}$ to X, each with various parameters; or
4. all of the above.

Cluster validity is the study (selection or rejection) of which $U_i \in \rho$ is best. There are two ways to view C, and hence, two ways to approach this problem. First, C finds substructure in X as represented by U—this is the *partitioning for substructure* viewpoint. Examination of the algorithmically suggested, artificially colored structure as in LHS(A) of Figure 4.1 is human validation. The operator inspects the segmentation and either rejects it or accepts it, and assigns a physical label to each region (cluster). LHS(A) can be successful only if the operator can imagine tissue structure as it must be in the data in order to label the segmented regions correctly. Since X is not labeled, the "true" substructure in the data is unknown. Thus, human validation is subjective and to some extent non-repeatable.

The other possibility is to instead follow LHS(B), rule-based validation, in which the human's knowledge is encapsulated in the form of a rule-based system. This circumvents the need for a human on-line, and probably represents the best hope at present to realize a truly unsupervised image segmentation scheme.

It is also possible to regard C as a *parametric estimation method*—U (and perhaps V) are being estimated by C using X. This view enables us to introduce *validity functionals* $\mathcal{V}:\mathcal{D}_\mathcal{V} \mapsto \mathfrak{R}$, which are essentially measures of goodness of fit of the estimated parameters (to an unknown optimal set!). Validity functionals are used to mathematically rank $U_i \in \rho$, as shown in the LHS of Figure 4.1. The domain of $\mathcal{V}$, $\mathcal{D}_\mathcal{V}$, is usually (but not necessarily) chosen to match the range of C, $\mathcal{D}_\mathcal{V} = \mathcal{R}_c$. When $\mathcal{D}_\mathcal{V} = M_{hcn}$, we call $\mathcal{V}$ a *direct measure;* because it assesses properties of crisp (real) clusters in X; otherwise, it is *indirect*. When $\mathcal{D}_\mathcal{V} = M_{hcn} \times \mathfrak{R}^{cp}$, the test $\mathcal{V}$ performs is still direct; and otherwise, it is still indirect.

The dashed horizontal line in the clustering box indicates that some users don't bother with $\mathcal{V}$ (preferring to rely on either a human (LHS(A)) or a knowledge base (LHS(B)) to decide how good the segmentation is. At the other extreme, some investigators not only use $\mathcal{V}$, but try to incorporate it into the control of $\mathbf{C}$, in which case, the resultant algorithm is said to possess *dynamic* (direct or indirect) cluster validity—the automatic adjustment of c and therefore U during the operation of $\mathbf{C}$. When X is not labeled, the true parameters of any model attempting to represent substructure in it are unknown. Consequently, validity functionals have little chance of being generally useful for identifying the "best" solution. More typically, they are relied upon instead to eliminate *badly wrong* solutions, so they are usually used as part of the processing done *prior* to validation by humans or rule bases.

After clustering on the LHS of Figure 4.1 is complete, a crisp color is assigned to each tissue class. If U is already crisp, this is straightforward. Otherwise, the simplest way to do this is to harden U with equation (3). Another possibility is to assign "fuzzy" colors to each pixel by mixing the c basic colors in proportion to their memberships. Lighter shades are usually assigned to the pixels with high membership values, and darker shades are used for lower membership values. This has the effect of outlining borders where classes are intermixed, and has been preferred by physicians [12]. The choice of which color to use for which region, and how to shade regions in images is a seemingly trivial part of segmentation. However, visual display issues greatly affect the utility of computed outputs, so this issue deserves careful attention.

The other major approach to image segmentation—the RHS in Figure 4.1—is by classifier design. A *classifier* is any function $\mathbf{D} : \mathfrak{R}^p \mapsto N_{pc}$. The value of $\mathbf{D}$ at $\mathbf{z} \in \mathfrak{R}^p$ is $\mathbf{y} = \mathbf{D}(\mathbf{z})$, the label vector for $\mathbf{z}$ in N_{pc}. $\mathbf{D}$ is a *crisp classifier* if and only if the image of $\mathfrak{R}^p$ under $\mathbf{D}$ is N_{hc} (that is, $\mathbf{D}(\mathbf{z}) = \mathbf{e}_i =$ some vertex in N_{hc} for all $\mathbf{z} \in \mathfrak{R}^p$). Training $\mathbf{D}$ means finding its parameters, and is sometimes called supervised learning. Usually (but not always), $\mathbf{D}$ is trained with labeled data. Classifiers represented by computational neural networks (CNNs) are included in this definition, but we will not review the use of fuzzy CNNs for image segmentation in this article.

Supervised methods for *image segmentation* need (usually crisp) labels for some of the pixel vectors in each subclass of X, so X is crisply partitioned into a *training set* X_L, $n_L = \sum_{i=1}^{c} n_i = |X_L|$ and a *test set* X_T, $n_T = |X_T|$, so that $X = X_L \cup X_T$; $X_L \cap X_T = \varnothing$, and $n = |X| = n_L + n_T$. When the data in X_T have crisp labels, X has the following form:

$$X = \left\{ \underbrace{\mathbf{x}_1^1, \ldots, \mathbf{x}_{n_1}^1}_{\text{labeled 1}}, \underbrace{\mathbf{x}_1^2, \ldots, \mathbf{x}_{n_2}^2}_{\text{labeled 2}}, \ldots, \underbrace{\mathbf{x}_1^c, \ldots, \mathbf{x}_{n_c}^c}_{\text{labeled c}} \mid \underbrace{\mathbf{x}_1^u, \ldots, \mathbf{x}_{n_T}^u}_{\text{unlabeled}} \right\} = X_L \cup X_T. \qquad (4)$$

where superscripts show the class label, and n_i is the number of data having label vector $\mathbf{e}_i$ for $i = 1, 2, \ldots c$. In this clash of notations, u stands for both the designation *unlabeled* when it is a superscript, as well as for the name of a membership function or value otherwise.

In the conventional approach to classifier design for image segmentation, X_L is used to train **D** (find its parameters); and then **D** is used to label X_T (the rest of the image). In this approach, which is depicted on the RHS of Figure 4.1, X_L is constructed by judicious selection of training pixels by an operator who is familiar with the substructure in the data. For each observed tissue class, the operator assigns every pixel in the chosen subregion a (crisp) physical label (color). Since each patient has different anatomical structure, it is necessary at present to obtain labeled data for algorithmic training for each subject. This is an expensive and time-consuming procedure, and is thus not the preferred technique for automated segmentation of medical imagery. The most desirable situation is that the evolution of some form of LHS(B) will eventually lead to a library of prelabeled prototypical images that can be used to train a generic classifier, thereby eliminating this costly step. However, variations in real images make this possibility rather remote at present.

Now we can define the scope of the present review. Fuzzy approaches to the tracks LHS(A) and RHS in Figure 4.1 have been recently reviewed by Bezdek et al. [12]. Fuzzy models for track LHS(B) were recently surveyed by Clark et al. [13]. A first purpose of the present chapter is to update and supplement these two reviews. One of the most striking features of much of the new work in the LHS tracks is the use of two stage hybrid models that combine more than one technique and style of processing. For readers interested in image processing based on the reasoning paradigm that has emerged from fuzzy control, we highly recommend the survey by Keller et al. [14] as a companion to this article.

Fuzzy models have the further potential to improve boundary definition for therapy treatment planning and electronic surgery simulation. The use of segmentation methods for data fusion from multiple sensors such as MRI, PET, and SPECT is also currently being considered as a means of improved differentiation of tumor and normal tissues [15, 16]. Our second objective is to describe some new fuzzy approaches for volume estimation and segmentation of 3D spatial image data.

4.3. Unsupervised Methods I: Track LHS(A) of Figure 4.1

The basic ingredients of most of the papers we review here are: the hard, fuzzy, and possibilistic c-means (HCM, FCM, PCM) clustering algorithms and their variants; the hard and fuzzy k-nearest neighbor (k-nn) rules; and various cluster validity functionals for these. Mathematical details for these methods are available in the works referenced.

The earliest LHS(A) fuzzy segmentation of *medical* images seems to be the work of a group at Stanford and IBM/Palo Alto headed by De La Paz, Chang, Bernstein, and others [17]. Their work concentrated exclusively on pixel-based MR features such as just described. This group published perhaps a dozen papers that compared MR segmentation by FCM to other approaches, most notably unsupervised decomposition of normal mixtures with the expectation-maximization (EM) algorithm. Di Gesu et al. [18] summarize and update much of this work. The studies were based on a large number of cases (upwards of 300 patients), and the basic conclusion was that FCM provided the best segmentations (as validated by humans, track LHS(A)), but that it was too slow. Thus, they eventually recommended an approximate version of FCM known as AFCM, the first technique studied to speed up FCM [19]. Improved implementation schemes [20–23] and computational platforms for FCM have probably relegated AFCM to the (scientific) graveyard. On the other hand, several aspects of automated analysis of medical imagery were pioneered by this group, and we feel that their papers deserve close attention.

A group at the New York State Department of Health led by Carazo, Frank, and others spearheaded studies of electron microscopy images with a variety of fuzzy clustering methods [24]. FCM, Gustafson-Kessel's modification of FCM [10], and a clustering algorithm due to Roubens [25] were the fuzzy clustering methods used. This study also investigated the use of a large number of direct and indirect indices for mathematical validation of fuzzy clusters in the images. Validity indices included: the partition coefficient and entropy [10], the proportion exponent and uniform data functionals [10], the nonfuzziness index [25], and the M-J function [26]. Moreover, Carazo et al. also introduced several new validity measures of their own. In this study, n = 100 (64 × 64) images were created by slicing a 3D reconstruction of the 50S ribosomal subunit of E coli 25 times, followed by projection compression, filtering, scaling, and the addition of white noise. Correspondence analysis was then used to extract one 8D vector from each image. Thus, X comprises 100 region-based feature vectors in $\Re^8$, where only one region (the whole image) is used per image. This is a good, wide ranging paper, and this group was one of the first to discuss all the important aspects of clustering for image segmentation (feature extraction, clustering, and validation) for track LHS(A) in an integrated fashion.

de Oliveira and Kitney [27] used 5D features extracted from 64 MR images (single feature slices) as the basis of their LHS(A) segmentation studies. We mention this work mainly to exhibit the wide variety of features that can be and are extracted from medical images to support segmentation studies. The five features were the pixel intensity and four measures of neighborhood texture (including the mean and two gradients). The texture features were smoothed twice with two measures of neighborhood energy before submission to the FCM clustering algorithm with c fixed at 8. Thus, the important issue of validity was laid aside. This investigation used hardening of fuzzy label vectors as shown at (3) to produce black and white images. They concluded that the method advocated could support 3D volume estimation, but we are unaware of subsequent work that shows this to be the case.

A team at the biophysics laboratory at UFR Alexis CARREL has recently performed a very thorough study of segmentation of digital cardiographic scintigraphic images for quantitative analysis of cardiac function. Boudraa et al. [28, 29] combined the elements of LHS(A) as follows. The basic image data were 64×64 single intensity (Gamma camera) images collected over 16 equispaced times for 105 patients. The raw data from each image was linearly filtered and median-normalized. Then, each temporal sequence was compacted into a single phase image Φ using Fourier analysis and the 16 intensities in each spatial location. Three *weighted* features were then extracted, resulting in the feature vector $\mathbf{x}_{ij} = (\alpha x_{ij}, \beta y_{ij}, \gamma \varphi_{ij})$ in $\mathfrak{R}^3$, where (x, y) are the spatial coordinates of pixel (i,j), and (α, β, γ) are coefficients that determine the relative importance of each feature for the segmentation.

FCM was applied to the 3D data, and the Xie-Beni validity index [30, 31] was used—*not* to choose c, the proper number of clusters, which was known and fixed at $c = 3$—but to find optimal values for (α, β, γ). This interesting use of an indirect validity index (domain $\mathcal{D}_V = M_{fcn} \times \mathfrak{R}^{cp}$) falls within the clustering module shown in the LHS of Figure 4.1, but in a very different way. After choosing (α, β, γ), the ventricle cluster was identified and isolated, a new reduced image with 2D features was generated, and FCM was applied to recluster it into left and right ventricles. (The idea of successively finer reclustering on reduced images takes other forms that we will meet later in this chapter.) Finally, the left ventricle boundary was isolated, and the ejection fraction was estimated.

These results were evaluated two ways. First, a team of trained clinicians performed human validation, and deemed the results on all 105 images as quite satisfactory. And second, they were compared with two commercially available semi-automatic gamma camera systems (Philips and SOPHA). Correlation coefficients between estimates of the ejection fraction from the fuzzy scheme and the two commercial methods were 0.91 and 0.94. These studies make novel use of several ideas, and are worth careful reading.

Another French group based at INRIA has also studied two-stage segmentation of both MR and cardiographic images with fuzzy models. Boujeema et al. [32, 33] use FCM as the first processing step in a two-stage algorithm for edge detection in cardiographic images. The second step is a fuzzy k-nn type algorithm [34, 35] that is used to refine the boundaries at pixels in the image that have weak FCM memberships from first-stage processing. In [36], FCM is used as the first step in a segmentation scheme that sharpens ambiguous pixels (as found by FCM) using minimization of an energy functional. The application is to segmentation of X-ray images for ventricular endocardiogram detection. The features used in these studies were pixel-based; the edge-finding methodology depends on using the k-nn rule on neighbors of pixels with very fuzzy label vectors. This is an interesting use of the fuzzy k-nn rule, and this idea should be pursued further as a method for edge detection that is very different from traditional approaches.

Di Gesu and Romeo [37] discuss MR segmentation using four crisp clustering algorithms operating on the data either in series or in parallel an architectural style that is currently called information fusion. The four algorithms were single linkage, histogram partitioning, sequential k-means, and a two-phase clumping procedure. In the parallel case, each of these produced a crisp c-partition U_i of X, which led to a fuzzy c-partition of X by computing $U = \sum_{i=1}^{4} \alpha_i U_i$, where $U_i \in M_{hcn}$; $\alpha_i \in (0,1)$; $\sum_{i=1}^{4} \alpha_i = 1$; $\Rightarrow U_i \in M_{fcn}$. The convex weights $\{\alpha_i\}$ were estimated algorithmically, and the segmented image was colored by applying (3) to the columns of U. In this study, c = 8 was fixed, and the data were slices of an MR image from a patient with a hemorrhage. The MR data were 4D (T1, T2, TI, ρ), augmented with the spatial coordinates (as integers) of each pixel, so the data were pixel-based feature vectors in $\mathfrak{R}^6$. Two measures of crisp validity were discussed, but were not used to alter c or U. Crisp ISODATA was used as a surrogate "expert," so this hybrid model is in the style of LHS(B), but we discuss it here because no rules from human experts were used. A somewhat different version of the same platform appears in [38]. Conclusions drawn by the authors about these models were mixed. We have included a discussion of these papers here to illustrate how pervasive the idea of mixed or hybrid models for image segmentation has become.

A group at the University of Houston (UH) medical center led by Brandt has also studied the use of FCM for completely unsupervised segmentation of MR images [39]. The paper referenced here is interesting because it is, to our knowledge, the first attempt to apply PCM—possibilistic c-means—to medical imagery. Brandt and Kharas compared the effectiveness of HCM, FCM, and PCM for separation of three simulated clusters as the amount of boundary overlap increases, and reported that FCM had a slight advantage in the study they made.

We conclude our discussion of new developments in track LHS(A) with an overview of recent work at the University of South Florida (USF) headed up by Hall, Goldgof, and Clarke [40]. The technique is called *validity-guided (re)clustering* (VGC). The aim of this modification of FCM is to enhance the quality of unsupervised partitions of X obtained with FCM by examining each cluster individually. Once FCM terminates at U for a fixed c, the general procedure begins by selecting a particular cluster in X (say $U_{(i)}$ = row i of U) for splitting. After hardening this row with **H**, FCM with c = 2 is applied to the points corresponding to $\mathbf{H}(U_{(k)})$. To preserve the chosen value of c, two other clusters in U are merged at the same step. The overall effect of this is to join tightly coupled clusters while splitting loosely coupled ones whilst preserving the chosen value for c. Hence, VGC is NOT a cluster validation scheme in the same sense as defined in section 4.2, since it is not applied to different partitions of X. However, it *is* driven by a validity functional, namely,

$$\mathcal{V}_{\mathrm{VGC},i}(\mathbf{U}_{(i)}, \mathbf{V}) = \sum_{k=1}^{n} u_{ik}^{m} \lVert \mathbf{x}_k - \mathbf{v}_i \rVert_A^2 \bigg/ \left(\sum_{k=1}^{n} u_{ik} \right)\left(\sum_{j=1}^{c} u_{ik} \lVert \mathbf{v}_i - \mathbf{v}_j \rVert_A^2 \right) \tag{5}$$

where $\mathcal{D}_\mathcal{V} = M_{hcn} \times \mathfrak{R}^{cp}$, $\mathbf{V} = \{\mathbf{v}_1, \cdots, \mathbf{v}_c\}$, $\mathbf{v}_i \in \mathfrak{R}^p \; \forall \, i$ are the terminal FCM cluster centers, $M > 1$, and $\lVert * \rVert$ is any inner product norm, $\delta_A(\mathbf{x} - \mathbf{v}) = \lVert \mathbf{x} - \mathbf{v} \rVert_A = \sqrt{(\mathbf{x} - \mathbf{v})^T A (\mathbf{x} - \mathbf{v})}$ on $\mathfrak{R}^p$. The measure in (5) assesses the i-th cluster, and summing this measure over i from 1 to c provides an overall validity function for U:

$$\mathcal{V}_{\mathrm{VGC}}(\mathbf{U}, \mathbf{V}) = \sum_{i=1}^{c} \mathcal{V}_{\mathrm{VGC},i}. \tag{6}$$

Low values of $\mathcal{V}_{\mathrm{VGC}}$ correspond to low numerators, which indicate compact clustering about the centers, and large denominators, which increase as the separation between cluster centers does. VGC continues reclustering until further improvement (decrease in $\mathcal{V}_{\mathrm{VGC}}$) cannot be realized. The end result is usually a greatly improved partition of X at the original value of c. The utility of (5) for the standard cluster validity problem has yet to be explored, but since this index is a generalization of the good Xie-Beni index [10], it is very possible that $\mathcal{V}_{\mathrm{VGC}}$ will be useful in the general context of validation as discussed in section 4.2.

Bensaid et al. used 30 MR images to determine whether VGC really improved outputs of FCM segmentation (cf. [40] for the computational protocols). For each image, an *optimized supervised* segmentation was constructed through an iterative process whereby the training set was repeatedly reselected in order to optimize the segmentation quality, as determined by two investigators, of segmentation using the k-nn rule [41] with $k = 7$ and the Euclidean norm. These investigators had substantial experience working, in collaboration with radiologists, on interactive selection of training pixels and visual evaluation of MRI segmentations. The k-nn rule was chosen as a way to construct supervised ground truth because it has been shown that this classifier is, for MR segmentations at USF, superior to various neural-like networks and probabilistic designs [42].

The optimized k-nn, FCM and VGC segmentations were subsequently evaluated by three expert radiologists in a blind study. Each radiologist was provided with three views (T1, T2, and ρ) of each raw image and the three segmentations, and was asked to fill out a survey form. Specifically, the individual panelists were asked to rate the quality of the first four performance indicators shown in Table 4.1 on a scale from 0 to 10, where 0 = very bad and 10 = excellent. Each radiologist was also asked to rate the last two items (5 and 6) on a percentage basis. That is, to rate the percentage of true positive tumor (correctly classified tumor pixels) and the percentage of false positive tumor (pixels incorrectly classified as tumor).

The results of the blind study are also given in Table 4.1. For each of the first four items, the scores corresponding to each algorithm are averages

Table 4.1   Results of a Blind Study for Three MR Segmentation Methods [40]

Item	Description	Supervised, Optimized k-nn rule	Unsupervised FCM	Reclustering FCM with VGC
1	White matter vs grey matter	7.8	7.4	7.5
2	Normal tissues vs. pathology	8.3	7.5	7.8
3	Tumor vs edema	8.6	6.7	8.3
4	CSF quality	8.5	7.3	7.8
6	True positive tumor (in %)	90.61	80.56	86.78
6	False positive tumor (in %)	12.44	17.61	5.17

on [0, 10] over all 30 segmentations and radiologists. The percentages of true and false positives reported for items 5 and 6 are simply averaged for each algorithm. Table 4.1 shows that VGC does enhance segmentations made by FCM. For example, VGC is better able to correctly recognize CSF and to differentiate between WM and GM on one hand, and between normal and pathological tissues on the other. Statistical hypothesis tests concerning these results show that, with 99 percent confidence, VGC outperforms FCM for distinguishing between normal tissue and pathology (row 2) and between tumor and edema (row 3); and VGC is superior to FCM for identifying CSF (row 4). Despite this improved performance, however, VGC segmentations are not quite as good as those obtained with the optimized, supervised k-nn rule. This is as expected, since supervision always (or at least should!) improves algorithmic outputs. VGC shows significant progress in differentiating between tumor and other tissues compared to FCM, and moreover, the ratio between its percentages of true positive and false positive tumor pixels is higher than the corresponding ratio for the supervised k-nn rule. With 99 percent confidence, VGC produces significantly less false positive tumor than k-nn. On the other hand, even with confidence as low as 90 percent, k-nn's true positive tumor percentage is not significantly better than VGC's. So, this model seems to be a positive step on the way to truly unsupervised designs.

4.4. Unsupervised Methods II: Track LHS(B) of Figure 4.1

One of the earliest (nonfuzzy) articles discussing the use of rules in the context of MR segmentation was by Menhardt and Schmidt [43]. The use of rule-based guidance for the segmentation process as shown in LHS(B) of Figure 4.1 within the context of fuzzy models was begun at USF [13]. FCM is used in this context as the first step in a *knowledge-based* (KB) clustering system that automatically segments and labels glioblastoma-multiform tumors in successive MR slices of the human brain and subsequently estimates total tumor volume [44]. We call this the USF-KB system.

Initial clustering of image sections in the USF-KB approach is performed by FCM with a strategy of overclustering; that is, the image is deliberately segmented into more clusters than are known to exist. Attempts at using the same number of clusters as (operator labeled) tissue classes show that FCM often has difficulty in separating tissue types correctly in feature space. Overclustering is based on the premise that multiple clusters containing the same tissue type are easier to merge than it is to separate tissues in undersegmented clusters. (This is in some sense the reverse of the VGC approach: a different method is used here because clusters will be merged using midlevel rules rather than low-level pixel-based processing.)

After initial FCM segmentation, the overclustered partition and the cluster center for each region are provided to a (crisp) rule-based expert system that contains knowledge gathered from a variety of sources such as radiologist expertise and empirical observations. The USF-KB includes heuristics concerning tissue characteristics in feature space (T1, T2, ρ) and anatomical information about the internal structure of the brain.

Using the KB and model-based recognition techniques, the system iteratively locates tissues of interest. These focus-of-attention tissues are analyzed by matching measured to expected characteristics. For the purposes of tumor segmentation, focus-of-attention is used with additional stages of fuzzy clustering to separate normal brain tissue from pathology, then to separate tumor from nontumor pathology. This cycle is important as it allows the results of applying FCM to the raw images to guide knowledge application, which in turns guides further clustering, making it possible to break down the more complex problem of tumor segmentation into smaller, more easily attainable goals.

Table 4.2 shows results from processed slices of a single patient with diagnosed glioblastoma-multiforme scanned over five repeat sessions. The slices in Table 4.2 were used to refine the rules in the KB system. Ground truth for these slices in the form of tumor pixel counts were made by a human operator. False positives (FP) are nontumor pixels that are mislabeled. The true positives and false negatives sum to the tumor size, TP + FN = TS.

Table 4.2 Numbers of Pixels for a Glioblastoma-Multiforme Patient Using the USF-KB System

Patient No. and Slice	FP = False Positive	TP = True Positive	FN = False Negative	TS = Tumor Size	CR = Corr. Ratio
p32s19	4	667	36	703	0.920
p32s20	33	1007	54	1061	0.908
p45s17	28	420	16	436	0.913
p50s21	131	1197	41	1238	0.897
p50s22	101	960	46	1006	0.881
p52s18	17	491	37	528	0.878
p52s19	82	1010	26	1036	0.922
p56s19	112	984	47	1031	0.877
p56s20	82	892	47	939	0.881

The correspondence ratio shown in Table 4.2 is computed with the formula $CR = (TP - (\frac{1}{2} * (FP + FN)))/TS$. This is one way to assess the overall quality of the segmentation. CR maximizes at the value 1.00 when there are no FPs or FNs. On the other hand, FPs not in the tumor can cause this number to be negative. Thus, values close to 1 indicate segmentations that closely match human estimates. Table 4.2 shows that the processed slices for this patient were very accurate.

A group at Texas A&M headed by Yen, Chang, Hillman, and others has reported on recent work that is in some ways diametrically opposite to the USF-KB model. This group introduced *fuzzy rules*[2] as a *preprocessing* stage followed by FCM clustering to segment rat and human brain MR images [45–47]. In agreement with USF, this group reported that using FCM alone was not sufficient to produce satisfactory segmentations of MR images. They noted again that the computational complexity of FCM was a problem, and that it had difficulty in directly utilizing spatial (nonfeature) information about the MR image. Furthermore, they reported that FCM sometimes mislabeled "easy" pixels of classes that did not have concave hulls in feature space.

The fuzzy rule-based system in [45] failed to completely segment images properly, so Chang and Hillman proposed a hybrid fuzzy system that combined the strengths of two methods. The technique was first discussed for segmenting stroke lesions in rat brain MR images. Fuzzy rules are used to segment and label pixels that are easily identifiable. Fuzzy rules allow greater flexibility than crisp rules, which often require adjustment between data sets. Morever, Chang and Hillman were able to use fewer rules than the crisp rule-based systems discussed previously.

In the Texas A&M approach, pixels that have distinct membership in a known class are labeled and used for FCM initialization, while others are set aside for labeling by FCM. Approximately 80 percent of the pixels are identified and labeled with the fuzzy rule-base *before clustering*. This significantly reduces the number of pixels FCM must label, and thus eases the computational burden of using it. The mean vector of each class of labeled pixels (after a hardening alpha-cut) provides FCM with initial prototypes. After FCM segmentation, the final rat brain segmentation reported was satisfactory. This technique has also been used to study HIV-positive lesions in human MR images. The results of this effort are promising, but so far the system has been tested on a very limited set of images.

To summarize, research teams at USF and Texas A&M both advocate hybrid models that fuse low-level, pixel-based processing with midlevel rules, facts, heuristics, and rules of thumb in knowledge-based systems. This is the trend in other image understanding efforts, and there is enough evidence to warrant the use of this approach in medical image analysis. Interestingly, the major difference between the two approaches

---

[2] Do not confuse fuzzy rules with crisp rules in a fuzzy model as discussed in [44]. Fuzzy rules lead to an entirely different paradigm that is well summarized by Keller et al. [14].

just reviewed are that they use the low- and midlevel processes in the reverse order of each other!

4.5. Supervised Methods: RHS of Figure 4.1

Non-neural network fuzzy methods for supervised medical image segmentation are, to our knowledge, confined at present to applications of the *semi-supervised FCM* (ssFCM) methods. Techniques of this kind in the context of c-Means clustering were first discussed by Pedrycz [48]. The development and use of ssFCM in the context of MRI segmentation was pioneered by Bensaid et al. at USF in a number of papers, of which [49] is representative. Algorithms in this category are (i) clustering algorithms that (ii) use a finite design set $X_L \subset \mathfrak{R}^p$ of *labeled* data to (iii) help clustering algorithms partition a finite set $X_T \subset \mathfrak{R}^p$ of *unlabeled* data, and then (iv) terminate without the capability to label other points in $\mathfrak{R}^p$. The methodology is most applicable in domains such as image segmentation, where users may have a small set of labeled data, and can use it to supervise classification of the remaining pixels in a single image. The word "semi" is used because ssFCM is not supervised in the sense that labeled training data are used to find the parameters of a classifier **D** which is subsequently used to complete segmentation of X_T as shown on the RHS of Figure 4.1. Partitions of X induced by data such as these, shown in (4), have the form

$$U = [\underbrace{\mathbf{U}_1^1 \ldots \mathbf{U}_{n_1}^1}_{\mathbf{e}_1} \ldots \underbrace{\mathbf{U}_1^1 \ldots \mathbf{U}_{n_c}^1}_{\mathbf{e}_c} \vdots \underbrace{\mathbf{U}_1^u \ldots \mathbf{U}_{1,n_T}^u}_{\text{unlabeled}}] = \underbrace{U}_{c \times n} = [\underbrace{U_L}_{c \times n_L} \mid \underbrace{U_T}_{c \times n_T}] \qquad (7)$$

In general, the n_is need not be equal, nor is it necessary that the column vectors shown in (7) be crisp. In this model, a modified version of FCM (i.e., ssFCM) is applied to X_T. The training data X_L is used to guide ssFCM toward improved clustering of the unlabeled pixels. The way this is done is to split the update conditions for U and **V** into labeled and unlabeled components. The labeled components of U are fixed, and can be weighted by class so that ssFCM effectively uses many copies of the relatively few training data in X_L. We give an example of the application of ssFCM to MR image data in section 4.6.

The USF-KB model has been augmented by the addition of fuzzy rules. Namasivayam and Hall have shown that over a large set of MR images from different patients, fuzzy rules perform most reliably when they are based on relative differences in pixel intensities for different tissue types [50]. Relative fuzzy rules and ssFCM applied to the unlabeled pixels in X_T, yield more accurate and much faster (than with FCM alone) segmentations of normal MR images. ssFCM has also been used in the reclustering stage of the USF-KB system. In this application, crisply labeled training pixels are chosen by a set of rules that identify tissue types with a high degree of confidence.

4.6. Three-Dimensional Problems: Supervised and Unsupervised

There has been much nonfuzzy work that attempts to extend 2D techniques such as segmentation and visualization into the 3D domain [15, 16]. A limited amount of research based on unsupervised and supervised fuzzy methods is available in this area. However, we are aware of only three groups that are currently engaged in either of these activities, so both approaches are discussed here.

The UH group has studied the estimation of volumes of tissue changes in three hydrocephalic children with FCM [51, 52]. Brandt et al. [52] used FCM on MR brain images of normal children and three children of the same age who had hydrocephalus. Proton density and T2 weighted images provided the features. The method is not fully automatic, but more in the spirit of ssFCM. An operator selected threshold (in T2) is used to set a "noise floor" to filter out low-intensity noise pixels as well as pixels that belong to the area between the cerebrum and the skull. In cases where CSF and gray matter were very close, a user set threshold was necessary to separate them.

Images for each of the six children were segmented into $c = 3$ classes: white matter, gray matter, and CSF. Three slices per subject were segmented. Each slice was clustered individually and a tissue volume was created by merging the results from individual slices. How clusters were labeled is not discussed. The results clearly showed what was expected—an increased amount of CSF in the hydrocephalus group as compared to the control group. The ratio of white matter to gray matter in the hydrocephalic children is much lower than for the normal children with the percentage of gray matter remaining stable. These results are both predictable and encouraging. This application of FCM was compared favorably with a standard morphometric measurement approach and confirms work reported in [13] that indicates FCM is effective in segmenting normal brain tissue. See [53] for a report on efforts by the Texas A&M group to use fuzzy logic for 3D volume estimation.

The USF KB system discussed in section 4.4 has also been used to estimate total tumor volume. Signal nonuniformity between slices makes clustering a set of MR slices as a volume problematic. Also, from a knowledge perspective, developing a model of the entire structure of the brain, even qualitatively, would be an extremely complex task. As with many other approaches to 3D MR segmentation, the fact that the USF KB system performs well on individual slices is exploited. A 3D segmentation can be constructed by combining labeled tumor areas from each processed slice (as long as there are no gaps) into a single volume. Qualitative models, called templates, were added to KB to model specific regions (in the axial plane) of the brain. These models capture changes in the brain's anatomical structure at different points in the volume. Also, slices were processed in contiguous order to allow knowledge gleaned from processing one slice to be propagated axially to assist in classification and labeling decisions in subsequent (and spatially adjacent) slices.

The graph in Figure 4.2 compares the total tumor volume estimated by the KB system with the tumor volume based on hand labeling by radiological experts at five times (weeks 0, 7 13, 16, and 20). The patient had diagnosed Glioblastoma multiforme, and was undergoing both chemo and radiation therapy during the 20-week period, as indicated in Figure 4.2. There were approximately nine slices per volume in the axial plane (each 5mm thick with no gaps between slices) at each of the five sampling periods. The graphs show that the unsupervised KB system very closely models physician generated ground truth.

Results from a series of experiments to measure tumor volume from MR brain images using ssFCM, the k-nn rule, and a seed growing approach called ISG are reported in [42]. The objective was to determine how sensitive these three methods were to training data chosen by observers (technicians with some medical physics training). It is difficult to choose training data from the raw images such that the measured tumor volume is consistent over multiple trials. Four patient cases were used in the study with repeat scans available for two patients (three for patient 1, and five for patient 2). The results reported are over the 10 tumor volumes obtained from the four patient cases. The tumors involved were either meningioma or glioblastoma multiforme. All patients were undergoing therapy during the course of repeat scans.

The experiments reported in [42] are summarized in Table 4.3, where tumor volume variability (in percent) resulting from the choice of the

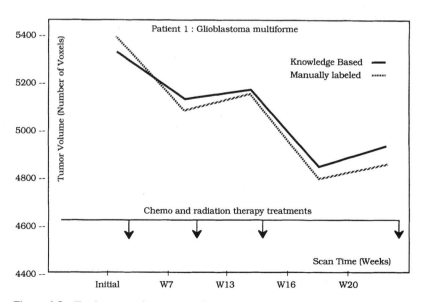

Figure 4.2 Total tumor volume comparison.

training data for each trial is reported. A value p = 100 was used in ssFCM to weight each vector in the training data. The differences in volume estimates for multiple training sets chosen by one observer are given in the first row of Table 4.3. For two observers, ssFCM and ISG had the lowest interobserver variability. The ssFCM algorithm had the lowest overall intraobserver variability as shown by the first column in Table 4.3. This experiment indicates that ssFCM is less sensitive to the choice of training data.

This article also demonstrated that ssFCM is an accurate predictor of the relative growth or shrinkage of a tumor over time. In particular, ssFCM appears to provide the most accurate assessment that is least affected by the particular choice of training data of the growth (or shrinkage) of a tumor.

We conclude by summarizing some of the methods discussed using an image that illustrates several of the models developed at USF. Figure 4.3 shows three views (T1, ρ, and T2) of one MR slice (with gadolinium enhancement) of a patient with an obvious tumor in the middle left section of the brain. The features extracted from this image are *pixel vector* $\mathbf{x}_{ij} = (T1_{ij}, T2_{ij}, \rho_{ij})$ in $\Re^3$ as described in section 4.1, and subsequent processing depicted in Figure 4.4 is based on these data, which we again call X for convenience.

Figure 4.4 is a set of seven black and white images made by various techniques, each of which is an estimate of the tumor pixels in X. Figure 4.4(a) shows the ground truth image for the tumor, hand labeled by an expert radiologist. Figure 4.4(b) shows a segmentation of X into c = 7 regions by the supervised, optimized k-nn rule (recall that this requires repeated submissions to the k-nn classifier of operator selected training data for each class to find, by trial and error, the best set of training data for this image). Figure 4.4(b) makes it clear that the k-nn rule does very poorly.

The remaining views in Figure 4.4 are based on the following steps. First, an initial segmentation of X is made by clustering it into c = 7 classes with unsupervised FCM under control by the KB system. The KB system removes the skull tissue and air classes using expert rules. At this stage, the KB system identifies the patient as abnormal and removes what it believes to be the CSF, white matter and gray matter pixels. This leaves the KB mask we call X_m^0 whose locations are shown in Figure 4.4(c), which is the set of (mostly) pathological (tumor, edema and necro-

Table 4.3 Inter- and Intraobserver Variability in Percent of Tumor Volumes Estimated with Three Supervised Segmentation Methods

	ssFCM	ISG	k-nn
Intraobserver	6	6	9
Interobserver	4	17	5

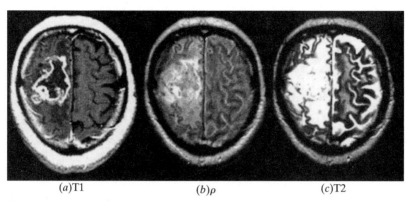

(a)T1   (b)ρ (c)T2

Figure 4.3   MR Data for the Tumor Estimates Shown in Figure 4.4.

sis) pixels. The vectors associated with X_m^0 are a reduced image that is reclustered into c = 5 classes using various techniques. In these views, "Seg" stands for "segmentation of."

View 4.4(d) shows the results of segmenting X_m^0 using unsupervised FCM with c = 5, followed by hand labeling of the pixels in the resultant segmentation by a human operator as in track LHS(A). You can see a number of islands in the southeastern quadrant of this output that are mistakes. Let X_m^1 denote the pixel vectors associated with the spatial locations in 4.4(d). View 4.4(e) shows the results of reclustering X_m^1 using VGC. It is pretty hard to see any improvement, but the number of false positives in 4.4(e)—as measured against the ground truth in 4.4(a)—is reduced by VGC. However, the island mistakes persist. Let X_m^2 denote the pixel vectors associated with the spatial locations in 4.4(e).

The last two views are created first by having the rules in the KB select training pixels from X_m^0. This training data is used with the ssFCM algorithm to create view 4.4(f), the pixels of which we call X_m^3. In view 4.4(f), the tumor pixels are identified by hand labeling of the top three memberships in the five clusters. Figure 4.4(g) is the output obtained by applying the KB to X_m^3. This view compares well with the ground truth in view 4.4(a) and was obtained with no human input for the image. Most of the southeastern islands are eliminated, but there are few new islands sprinkled around and closer to the tumor mainland. In summary, only the KB view 4.4(g) was created without operator intervention; none of the other methods are truly unsupervised. We think this example illustrates that fuzzy models can help us make real progress toward the ultimate goal.

4.7. Conclusion and Discussion

We have reviewed a number of (non-neural) fuzzy methods for segmentation and edge detection in medical images. The examples provided allow us to assert that fuzzy models are useful for this problem, but that

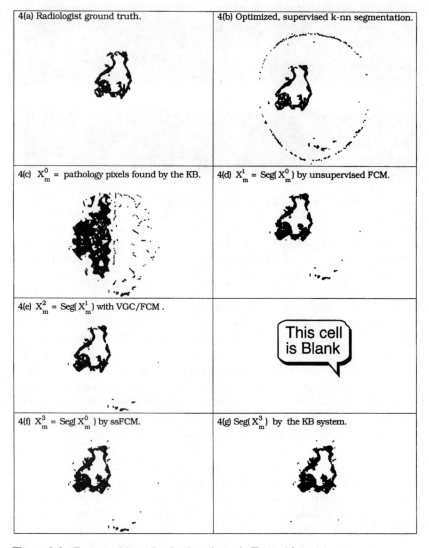

Figure 4.4   Tumor estimates for the data shown in Figure 4.3.

we still have a long way to go. To conclude, we offer some remarks about improving the techniques reviewed in this paper.

4.7.1. LHS(A)

1. The better unsupervised techniques are still too slow. Improving speed via parallelization and optimization will improve their competitiveness with, for example, neural networks, which are the fastest and most accurate nonfuzzy techniques in RHS. We have reviewed a number of methods for speeding up FCM. Of these, perhaps the

most promising is offered by reducing the image it is applied to, either by random sampling [23], or by parsing with fuzzy rules [47].

2. Another area for development is dynamic cluster validity. Unsupervised methods need better ways to specify and adjust c, the number of tissue classes found by the algorithm. The VGC method described here seems useful for a limited objective, but in general, the main problem persists: if c is unknown, is there an automatic way to deduce that your algorithm has found an interpretation of the image that humans will find agreeable? Our opinion is that much research needs to be done before much reliance can be placed on mathematical validition.

3. Initialization is a third important area of research. The USF group in particular has invested a lot of effort in ways to initialize unsupervised methods at points in the solution space that don't lead to local trap states. This is a pervasive problem for all hill-climbing techniques, and is very serious in the application domain discussed here. The error functions that are being optimized here have very large numbers of unknowns, so there will be a concomitant increase in local solutions that offer little to medical practitioners. One way to circumvent this problem is with optimization by genetic algorithms [54], but this class of techniques still carries too much computational overhead to be practical at this writing.

4.7.2. LHS(B)

1. Most of the active image understanding groups have long since recognized the need for fusion of low- and midlevel data and information. The papers reviewed here support this trend, and we believe that LHS(B) is the track that will ultimately yield a truly unsupervised design. Knowledge-based labeling with well-established rules can dramatically reduce the number of unlabeled pixels that need to be classified. We believe that research in this area will grow, as will the achievement of dynamic cluster validity using cluster merging and splitting rules. These rules will be both mathematically and teleologically based.

4.7.3. RHS

1. Experience and careful documentation of many MR case studies are needed to make progress in this area. The instability of supervised techniques with one training set across patients and MR slices might be improved by the generation of more globally representative training sets. However, without expert rules, we feel that classical supervised learning for segmentation of medical images is a dead end—small improvements will never lead to an automated system.

4.7.4. All Schemes

The general accuracy of techniques that perform well needs to be further investigated across different imaging devices, types of patient problems, and medical communities. Perhaps the largest single impediment to real success in this domain is the lack of a very large (e.g., 20,000 sets of patient slices for MR) well-documented database. The construction of such a database, one that could be shared worldwide, would be difficult and expensive. On the other hand, the reward—delivery by the health care industry of an economical means of vastly improved diagnosis, treatment, and recovery procedures—is well worth the cost.

4.8. References

[1] Morrison, M., and Y. Attikouzel. "An Introduction to the Segmentation of Magnetic Resonance Images." *Australian Computer Journal*, Vol. 26, No. 3 (1994), pp. 90–98.

[2] Gohagan, K., et al. "Multispectral Analysis of Magnetic Resonance Images of the Breast." *Radiology*, Vol. 163 (1987), pp. 703–707.

[3] Just, M., and M. Thelen. "Tissue Characterization with T1, T2 and Proton Density Values: Results in 160 Patients with Brain Tumors." *Radiology*, Vol. 169 (1988), pp. 779–785.

[4] Vannier, M.W., et al. "Validation of Magnetic Resonance Imaging (MRI) Multispectral Tissue Classification." *Computerized Medical Imaging and Graphics*, Vol. 15, No. 4 (1991), pp. 217–223.

[5] Liang, Z. "Tissue Classification and Segmentation of Magnetic Resonance Images." *IEEE EMB Magazine*, Vol. 12, No. 1 (1993), pp. 81–85.

[6] Raman, S.V., et al. "Tissue Boundary Refinement in Magnetic Resonance Images using Contour-based Scale Space Matching." *IEEE Transactions on Medical Imaging*, Vol. 10, No. 2 (1991), pp. 109–121.

[7] Hyman, T.J., et al. "Characterization of Normal Brain Tissue using Seven Calculated MRI Parameters and a Statistical Analysis System." *Magnetic Resonance in Medicine*, Vol. 11 (1989), pp. 22–34.

[8] Dellepiane, S. "Image Segmentation: Errors, Sensitivity and Uncertainty." *IEEE EMBS* (1991), pp. 253–254.

[9] Krishnapuram, R., and J. Keller. "A Possibilistic Approach to Clustering." *IEEE Transactions on Fuzzy Systems*, Vol. 1, No. 2 (1993), pp. 98–110.

[10] Bezdek, J.C., and S.K. Pal. *Fuzzy Models for Pattern Recognition*. Piscataway: IEEE Press, 1992.

[11] Ross, T.J. *Fuzzy Logic with Engineering Applications*. New York: McGraw-Hill, 1995.

[12] Bezdek, J.C., et al. "Review of MR Image Segmentation Techniques using Pattern Recognition." *Medical Physics*, Vol. 20 (1993), pp. 1033–1047.

[13] Clark, M., et al. "MRI Segmentation using Fuzzy Clustering Techniques: Integrating Knowledge." *IEEE Engineering in Medicine and Biology Magazine*, Vol. 13, No. 5 (1994), pp. 730–742.

[14] Keller, J., et al. "Fuzzy Rule-based Models in Computer Vision," in *Fuzzy Modeling: Paradigms and Practice*, ed. W. Pedrycz. Norwell: 1996.

[15] Xiaoping, H., et al. "Visualization of MR Angiographic Data with Segmentation and Volume Rendering Techniques." *Journal of Magnetic Resonance Imaging*, Vol. 1, No. 5 (1991), pp. 539.

[16] Levin, D.N., et al. "The Brain: Integrated Three-Dimensional Display of MR and PET Images." *Radiology*, Vol. 172 (1989), pp. 783–789.

[17] De La Paz, R., et al. "Approximate Fuzzy C-Means (ACFM) Cluster Analystis of Medical Magnetic Resonance Image (MRI) Data—A System for Medical Research and Education." *IEEE Transactions on Geoscience and Remote Sensing, GE25.* (1986), pp. 815–824.

[18] Di Gesu, V., et al. "Clustering Algorithms for MRI," in *Lecture Notes for Medical Informatics,* eds. Adlassing, K.P., et al. 1991, Springer-Verlag, pp. 534–539.

[19] Cannon, R.L., et al. "Efficient Implementation of the Fuzzy C-Means Clustering Algorithms." *IEEE Trans. PAMI,* Vol. 8, No. 2 (1986), pp. 248–255.

[20] Kamel, M.S., and S.Z. Selim. "A New Algorithm for Solving the Fuzzy Clustering Problem." *Pattern Recognition,* Vol. 27, No. 3 (1994), pp. 421–428.

[21] Shankar, B.U., and N.R. Pal. "FFCM: An Effective Approach for Large Data Sets." *Proceedings, 3rd International Conference on Fuzzy Logic, Neural Nets and Soft Computing, IIZUKA.* pp. 331–332. Fukuoka, Japan: 1994.

[22] Cheng, T.W., et al. "Fast Clustering with Application to Fuzzy Rule Generation." *Proceedings, International Conference on Fuzzy Systems IV.* pp. 1719–2342. Piscataway: IEEE Press, 1995.

[23] Shankar, B.U., et al. "An Efficient Implementation of Fuzzy C-Means for Large Data Sets." In review, *IEEE Trans. on Fuzzy Systems,* 1996.

[24] Carazo, J.M., et al. "Fuzzy Sets-based Classification of Electron Microscopy Images of Biological Macromolecules with an Application to Ribsomeal Particles." *Journal of Microscopy,* Vol. 157, No. 2 (1990), pp. 187–203.

[25] Roubens, M. "Fuzzy Clustering Algorithms and their Cluster Validity." *European Journal Operation Research,* Vol. 10 (1982), pp. 294–301.

[26] Moreau, J.V., and A.K. Jain. "How Many Clusters?" *Proceedings, IEEE CVPR.* pp. 634–636. Piscataway, N.J.: IEEE Press, 1985.

[27] de Oliveira, M.C., and R.I. Kitney. "Texture Analysis for Discrimination of Tissues in MRI Data." *Proceedings, Computers in Cardiology.* pp. 481–484. Piscataway: IEEE Press, 1992.

[28] Boudraa, A.E., et al. "Left Ventricle Automated Detection Method in Gated Isotropic Ventriculography using Fuzzy Clustering. *IEEE Transactions on Medical Imaging,* Vol. 12, No. 3 (1993), pp. 451–465.

[29] Boudraa, A.E., et al. "Automatic Left Ventricular Cavity Detection using Fuzzy ISO-DATA and Connected-Components labeling Algorithms." *Proceedings, 14th IEEE Conference in Medicine and Biology,* CH3207-8. Piscataway, 1992, pp. 1895–1899.

[30] Xie, X.L., and G.A. Beni. "Validity Measure for Fuzzy Clustering." *IEEE Transactions PAMI,* Vol. 3, No. 8 (1991), pp. 841–846.

[31] Pal, N.R., and J.C. Bezdek. "On Cluster Validity for the Fuzzy C-Means Model." *IEEE Transactions Fuzzy Systems,* Vol. 3, No. 3 (1995) pp. 370–379.

[32] Boujeema, N., et al. "Toward Fuzzy Models for Visual Perception." *SPIE Proceedings 1818, Visual Communication and Image Processing.* pp. 1271–1281. Bellingham: 1992.

[33] Boujeema, N., et al. "Fuzzy Ventricular Endocardium Detection with Gradual Focusing Decision." *Proceedings, International Conference of the IEEE EMBS,* Vol. 14, pp. 1893–1894. Piscataway: 1992.

[34] Keller, J., et al. "A Fuzzy k-nearest Neighbor Algorithm." *IEEE Trans. SMC,* Vol. 15. (1985), pp. 580–585.

[35] Bezdek, J.C., et al. "Generalized k-nearest Neighbor Rules." *Fuzzy Sets and Systems,* Vol. 8, No. 3 (1986) pp. 237–256.

[36] Boujemaa, N., and G. Stamon. "Fuzzy Modeling in Early Vision Application to Medical Image Segmentation." *Proceedings, 7th International Conference on Image Analysis and Processing,* ed. S. Impedovo. pp. 649–656. Singapore: World Scientific Press, 1994.

[37] Di Gesu, V., and L. Romeo. "An Application of Integrated Clustering to MRI Segmentation." *Pattern Recognition Letters,* (1994), pp. 731–738.

[38] Di Gesu, V. "Integrated Fuzzy Clustering." *Fuzzy Sets and Systems,* Vol. 68 (1994), pp. 293–308.

[39] Brandt, M.E., and Y.F. Kharas. "Simulation Studies of Fuzzy Clustering in the Context of Brain Magnetic Resonance Imaging." *Proceedings, 3rd International Conference on Industrial Fuzzy Control and Intelligent Systems.* pp. 197–203. Piscataway: IEEE Press, 1993.

[40] Bensaid, A., et al. "Validity-Guided (re) Clustering for Image Segmentation." In press, *IEEE Transactions on Fuzzy Systems,* Vol. 4, No. 2, 1996, pp. 112–113.

[41] Devijver, P., and J. Kittler. *Pattern Recognition: A Statistical Approach.* Englewood Cliffs, N.J.: Prentice Hall, 1982.

[42] Vaidyanathan, M., et al. "Comparison of Supervised MRI Segmentation Methods for Tumor Volume Determination during Therapy." *Magnetic Resonance Imaging,* Vol. 13, No. 5 (1995), pp. 719–728.

[43] Menhardt, W., and K.H. Schmidt. "Computer Vision on Magnetic Resonance Images." *Pattern Recognition Letters,* Vol. 8, (1988), pp. 73–85.

[44] Li, C., et al. "Knowledge-based Classification and Tissue Labeling of MR Images of Human Brains." *IEEE Transactions on Medical Imaging,* Vol. 12, No. 4 (1993), pp. 740–750.

[45] Chang, C., et al. "Segmentation of Rat Brain MR Images using a Hybrid Fuzzy System." *Proceedings, NAFIPS/IFIS/NASA '94.* pp. 55–59. 1994.

[46] Hillman, G.R., et al. "Automatic System for Brain MRI Analysis using a Novel Combination of Fuzzy Rule-based and Automatic Clustering Techniques," in *SPIE Proceedings, Medical Imaging 1995: Image Processing,* ed. M.H. Lowe. pp. 16–25. Bellingham, W.A.: 1995.

[47] Chang, C.W., et al. "A Two-Stage Human Brain MRI Segmentation Scheme using Fuzzy Logic." *Proceedings, FUZZ-IEEE.* pp. 649–654. 1995.

[48] Pedrycz, W. "Algorithms of Fuzzy Clustering with Partial Supervision." *Pattern Recognition Letters,* Vol. 3 (1985), pp. 13–20.

[49] Bensaid, A., et al. "Partially Supervised Clustering for Image Segmentation." In Press, *Pattern Recognition.* 1996, pp. 859–871.

[50] Namasivayam, A., and L.O. Hall. "The use of Fuzzy Rules in Classification of Normal Human Brain Tissues." *Proceedings, ISUMA-NAFIPS '95.* pp. 157–162. 1995.

[51] Brandt, M.E., et al. "Estimation of CSF, White and Gray Matter Volumes from MRI's of Hydrocephalic and HIV-positive Subjects." *Proceedings, SimTec/WNN.* pp. 643–650. 1992.

[52] Brandt, M.E., et al. "Estimation of CSF, White and Gray Matter Volumes in Hydrocephalic Children using Fuzzy Clustering of MR Images." *Computerized Medical Imaging and Graphics,* Vol. 18, No. 1 (1994), pp. 25–34.

[53] Chang, C.W., et al. "Automatic Labeling of Human Brain Structures in 3D MRI using Fuzzy Logic." *Proceedings, CFSA/IFIS/SOFT '95.* pp. 27–34. 1995.

[54] Hall, L.O., et al. "Genetic Algorithm-Guided Clustering." *Proceedings, 1st IEEE International Conference on Evolutionary Computation.* pp. 34–39. 1994.

5 Fuzzy Modelling and Fuzzy Mathematical Morphology Applied to 3D Reconstruction of Blood Vessels by Multimodality Data Fusion

Isabelle Bloch and Francisco Sureda*
*Ecole Nationale Supérieure des Télécommunications,
département Images
46 rue Barrault, 75634 Paris Cedex 13, France*

Claire Pellot and Alain Herment
*INSERM U66, CHU La Pitié Salpétrière
91 Bd de l'Hôpital, 75013 Paris*

ABSTRACT: We show in this chapter how fuzzy sets can be used in a real-world problem suffering from imprecision, using fuzzy modelling, mathematical morphology, and fusion. The application concerns 3D vessel reconstruction, which has a great medical interest for understanding and interpreting the morphology of atheromateous vascular lesions. To avoid the limitations of reconstruction methods based on angiographic images only, we propose an original approach for 3D reconstruction based on fusion of digital angiography and endovascular echography data, without any geometrical *a priori* of the vessel anatomy. A geometrical fusion step leads to the determination of the unknown rotation and translation parameters, which allow one to register all data in a common reference frame, leading to a binary reconstruction of the vascular lumen from the echographic slices. Another binary reconstruction is obtained from the angiographies using a probabilistic approach. Then a reconstruction integrating

* Now with General Electric Medical Systems, Buc, France.

both angiographic and echographic data is performed. Imprecision on the geo-metrical parameters is taken into account in an original process which associates fuzzy number modelling and fuzzy mathematical morphology for the reconstruc-tion. The obtained fuzzy reconstructions are combined by a fuzzy operator before a binary decision is taken. Taking into account all information about the problem, along with its imprecision, the method avoids ambiguities of a reconstruction based only on one modality and solves the possible contradictions between both imaging modalities. Note that this study has been carried out in the context of GdR CNRS 134 "Traitement du Signal et des Images" and has been partly sup-ported by the French Ministery MESR (DRED founding).

5.1. Introduction

The three-dimensional reconstruction of blood vessels by objective and reproducible methods aims at helping in the interpretation and under-standing of pathological vascular structures and at providing quantitative information about vessels and possible lesions. Such a precise and detailed morphological reconstruction (not available from MR images for instance, since they have a too large voxel size with respect to small vessels, in particular for coronary vessels) has several advantages from a medical point of view: for prognosis and diagnosis of atheromateous dis-eases, for choosing a suitable therapy (including angioplasty and sur-gery), for controlling therapeutic or angioplastic gesture, and for a better understanding of restenosis phenomena.

In order to provide a better 3D description of complex atheromateous lesions, we propose an original approach for reconstructing vascular seg-ments by data fusion, from two different imaging sources: two orthogonal X-ray angiographic projections (the actual reference technique), and a series of endovascular echographic slices (one other effective approach). Moreover, we introduce in the reconstruction process the imprecision on data and parameters, which is, to our knowledge, seldom taken into account.

Several methods have been developed for the 3D reconstruction from two digital angiographies (DA) (radiography of vessels opacified by injection of a iodinated agent): in most of these methods, the ill-posed reconstruction problem is solved by introducing strong geometrical hypotheses and a priori knowledge on the vascular structures (simple geometrical models for the shape of sections [13], [7], [14], or connectiv-ity and smoothness constraints [24]). However, due to physical factors (geometrical and densitometric distorsions, random and structural noise, heterogeneity of contrast medium), the obtained results are often unreli-able, and generally over regularized.

Since the apparition of endovascular echography (EE) (high-resolution images of the vascular section recorded from inside the vessel using a miniaturized echograph located at the catheter tip), 3D reconstruction methods from intravascular tomographic slices have been pro-posed. In this case, too, the reconstruction is limited by physical acquisi-tion factors (uncertainty on catheter orientation, nonperpendicularity of ultrasonic radiation with respect to the vessel wall, eccentric position of the catheter [12], [17]). The reconstruction methods consist mainly in stacking EE slices, without taking into account the translation and rota-tion of the catheter inside the vessel [15], [21]. More recently, a recon-struction method has been developed, where the motion of the catheter is controlled by a motor and the vessel curvature and EE slice positions are estimated from two angiographies (3D central axis of the vessel), acquired simultaneously [16]. This method, although less restrictive than the previous ones, assumes that the catheter follows exactly the vessel curvature, and this is seldom satisfied.

To avoid the limits inherent to the reconstruction from only one modality, we propose a reconstruction method relying on the fusion of both modalities. This is much more than a matching between the two sets of data. Indeed, the data are really combined, in order to obtain a more complete knowledge of the 3D vessel morphology by using complemen-tarity between both types of data (DA provides a correct longitudinal information and overall 3D geometry of the vessel, while high-resolution vessel cross-sections are obtained with EE), while reducing imprecision and uncertainty by using redundancy between these data. The method consists in modelling both acquisitions and related data in a common ref-erence frame (section 5.2), leading to a first binary reconstruction from the ultrasonic data in this frame (section 5.3). In the same time, a binary reconstruction is built from the angiographies, using a regularization approach based on Markov random fields [18], [19]. Then the fusion of both reconstructions is performed: imprecision about the acquisition, the geometrical parameters, and the binary reconstructions (from each modality) is modelled using fuzzy set theory and is taken into account by fuzzy mathematical morphology; then the two fuzzy reconstructions are fused by a conjunctive fusion operator (section 5.4). The entire method has been tested on a dog aorta and provides good results.

5.2. Geometry of Angiographic and Ultrasonic Acquisitions and Data

The experience in this study was performed on a dog aorta, with a well-defined protocol, near from routine acquisition (see Figure 5.1): two orthogonal contrast-injected angiographic projections are first acquired; then the echographic probe is introduced into the vessel and progres-sively withdrawn; at each probe position, an EE slice is acquired, together with a nonopacified X-ray radiography (with the same inci-dence than one of the angiographies), which allows the partial control of position and orientation of the probe through the vessel.

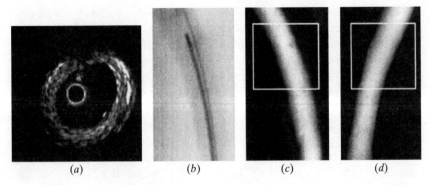

(a) (b) (c) (d)

Figure 5.1   Images used for the reconstruction. (a): Echographic slice. (b): Control radiography. (c) and (d): Digital angiographies after background subtraction (the reconstruction will be performed in the surrounded area).

The reference frame $(0, x, y, z)$ of the vessel to be reconstructed has been chosen such that the DA images correspond to the projections of the vessel on planes $(x0y)$ and $(x0z)$ respectively (see Figure 5.2). The EE images are more difficult to represent, since they are located in planes that depend on the position and orientation of the probe. Therefore we introduce a frame related to the probe, defined by a translation vector (x_t, y_t, z_t) and three rotation angles: φ measures the angular deviation of the probe with respect to the z axis, θ represents the angle between the probe projection on the plane $(x0y)$ and the x axis, and ω corresponds to the rotation angle of the probe on itself.

This geometrical modelling of the acquisitions leads to the derivation of equations relating the polar coordinates (τ, α) of an echographic point to its cartesian coordinates (x, y, z) in the reference frame [23]:

$$x = x_t + \tau \cdot [(\cos^2 \theta \cos \varphi + \sin^2 \theta) \cdot (\cos \xi \cos(\omega + \alpha))$$
$$+ (\cos \theta \cos \varphi \sin \theta - \sin \theta \cos \theta) \cdot (\cos \xi \sin(\omega + \alpha)) + \sin \varphi \cos \theta \sin \xi]$$

$$y = y_t + \tau \cdot [(\cos \theta \cos \varphi \sin \theta - \sin \theta \cos \theta) \cdot (\cos \xi \cos(\omega + \alpha))$$
$$+ (\cos \varphi \sin^2 \theta + \cos^2 \theta) \cdot (\cos \xi \sin(\omega + \alpha)) + \sin \varphi \sin \theta \sin \xi] \qquad (1)$$

$$z = z_t + \tau \cdot [-\cos \theta \sin \varphi \cos \xi \cos(\omega + \alpha)$$
$$- \sin \theta \sin \varphi \cos \xi \sin(\omega + \alpha) + \cos \varphi \sin \xi].$$

5.3. Geometrical Fusion: First Reconstruction from Echographies

A preliminary step consists in segmenting the contours of the echographic slices and of the two angiographic projections. This has been performed on the EE images by a fuzzy classification technique (derived from [1]), based mainly on gray-level information and made robust to noise, followed by mathematical morphology operators. For

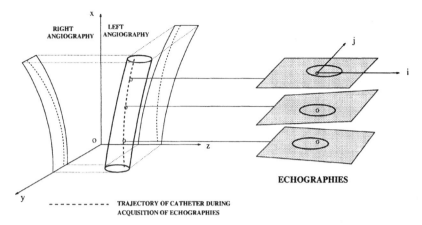

Figure 5.2   Acquisitions and reference frame.

the DA images, the segmentation process is based on dynamic tracking of vessel centerlines and contours [18]. The background component (contribution of underlying tissues) is then estimated and subtracted on each angiographic image in order to obtain the actual vessel density information. A densitometric normalization of the two angiographic projections is also achieved in order to evaluate the absolute value of the attenuation coefficient, which determines the shape of the reconstructed solution (two injections of contrast must generally be made to acquire the two angiographies) [18]. Results of the segmentation are shown on Figure 5.3.

The next step is the registration between DA images and control radiographies, in order to correct possible small motions of the vessel

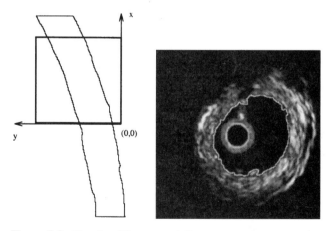

Figure 5.3   Results of the segmentation processes on one angiographic projection (with reference frame) and one echographic slice (overlaid on the initial image). Similar results are obtained on the other data.

during the acquisition. This global registration has been performed using external landmarks provided by the fixing support in our experiment.

The geometrical fusion step consists in determining the six parameters θ, φ, ω, x_t, y_t, and z_t. Parameters θ, φ, x_t and y_t can be directly determined on the control radiography (Figure 5.4). Indeed, this radiography is located in the $(x0y)$ plane, providing directly θ (angle between the probe and the x axis), x_t and y_t (coordinates of probe extremity). Moreover, φ is given on this image by the apparent length ρ of the probe, its real length L_{probe} being known: $\varphi = \arcsin(\rho/L_{probe})$.

The rotation of the probe on its own axis (angle ω) cannot be directly estimated. Considering the small length of the vascular segment to be reconstructed (about 2 cm), the continuity of the vessel and of the catheter trajectory, it is reasonable to assume that ω is constant along the segment to be reconstructed. This angle is estimated by minimizing iteratively and with a decreasing angular step the distance between EE contour points and DA contours. In the same way, the last translation parameter z_t is computed by minimizing the distance between the projection of EE contours onto the right DA and the contours of this angiography. This value could be obtained more simply if we would have a second control radiography, in the same plane as the right DA. However, only few systems exist that allow this acquisition (in France) and they impose to double the patient dose.

This geometrical fusion step allows to obtain a binary reconstruction (denoted by V_{bin}^{EE}) by interpolating the EE slices registered in the reference frame, in order to obtain a regularly sampled surface (with the same resolution as the DA data). More details about these steps can be found in [23]. This reconstruction provides an improvement over existing techniques, since it takes into account all the geometrical parameters of the

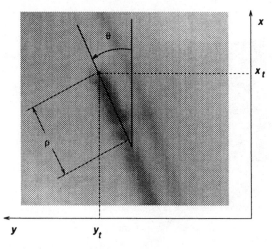

Figure 5.4 Determination of ρ (and therefore φ), θ, x_t, and y_t on the control radiography.

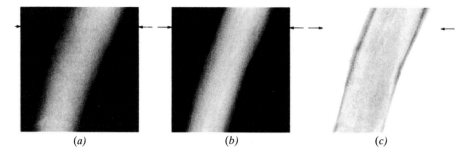

(a)   (b)   (c)

Figure 5.5 (a): Original right DA. (b): Right projection of the reconstruction of EE. (c): Absolute difference between (a) and (b) (white = 0, black = 255).

acquisitions. The comparison of the projections of this reconstruction with the angiographies shows quite satisfactory results, with a few differences (Figures 5.5, 5.6), which are partly due to the rough segmentation, which accounts for errors located at vessel walls. However, this reconstruction does not take into account the imprecision related to the acquisitions and the estimation of parameters, nor the densitometric information on vessel thickness provided by the gray levels of the DA images. These will be introduced in the next sections.

5.4. Fuzzy Fusion

Fuzzy modelization of variables, for instance using possibility distributions, is well suited for dealing with imprecise information (better than the classical error calculus). It allows to mathematically express propositions like "the value of parameter θ is approximately equal to the measure θ_0 obtained on a radiography" [26], [27], [9]. This kind of modelization has also the advantage to provide a generalization of operations on real val-

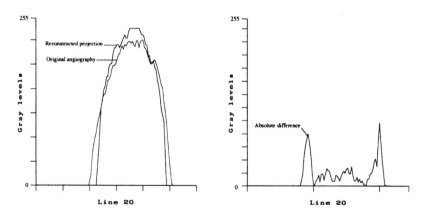

Figure 5.6 Density profiles of a line of the right projection (indicated by the arrow in Figure 5.5). Left: DA and reconstruction projection. Right: Absolute difference.

ues in operations on fuzzy values, following the extension principle. For a pixel of the echographies, imprecisions on the geometrical parameters lead to imprecision on the point position in the reference frame. This point may thus have several positions with different possibility grades. We propose to represent the set of these positions by a 3D geometrical imprecise set, called fuzzy structuring element, which will be exploited in the framework of fuzzy mathematical morphology.

5.4.1. Fuzzy Modelling of Variables and Measures

For representing a fuzzy number, we have chosen the following classical form:

$$\mu(a) = \frac{1 + \exp(-b)}{1 + \exp\left[b \cdot \left(\frac{|a - a_0|}{S} - 1\right)\right]}. \tag{2}$$

This expression is more flexible than the classically used trapezes or triangles, and has the advantage of providing an easy control of the form and extension of the fuzzy number, through the parameters S and b. S controls the width of the curve, while b controls its form (flattening, slope). The value $|a - a_0|$ corresponds to the distance between a and the measured value a_0. The parameters b and S are estimated as function of imprecision on the measured parameters.

We have set here $b = 5.54$ for all parameters, which corresponds to a possibility grad of $1/256$ for a distance equal to $2S$. Then for each parameter, the value that gives a possibility of 0.5 is estimated, providing the value of S. For instance, for θ, it can be considered that the value having possibility 0.5 corresponds to an error of 1 pixel at each extremity of the probe. For our experiment, this corresponds to an error of 3 degrees on θ. The possibility distributions obtained this way for θ, ρ, ω and translation parameters x_t, y_t, z_t are shown in Figure 5.7. This method is coarse but proved to be sufficient in our experiment.

5.4.2. Fuzzy Mathematical Morphology

The problem can now be stated as follows: how to introduce the imprecisions modelized in the previous section? Fuzzy mathematical morphology is a well-adapted tool, as it allows the propagation of a spatial imprecision around each point used in the reconstruction, in a controlled way, through the structuring element [3].

Several principles for constructing a fuzzy mathematical morphology have been proposed in the literature (see [4] for a comparative review). The most general principle relies on the translation of set equations defining morphological operations on binary sets into their functional (or fuzzy) equivalents. This principle guarantees that the definitions reduce to the classical case if the structuring element is binary (crisp). Intersection is

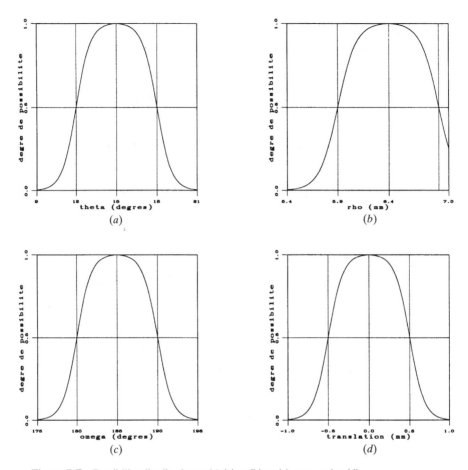

Figure 5.7   Possibility distributions of θ (a), ρ (b), ω (c), x_t, y_t and z_t (d).

thus replaced by a T-norm i and union by a T-conorm u ([8], [25]). This leads to the following definitions for the dilation $D_v(\mu)$ and erosion $E_v(\mu)$ of a fuzzy set μ by a fuzzy structuring element (SE) v of $\mathbb{R}^3$ (u is the T-conorm associated with i with respect to complementation c):

$$\forall x \in \mathbb{R}^3, D_v(\mu)(x) = \sup\{i[\mu(y),v(y-x)] \mid y \in \mathbb{R}^3\}, \qquad (3)$$

$$\forall x \in \mathbb{R}^3, E_v(\mu)(x) = \inf\{u[\mu(y),c(v(y-x))] \mid y \in \mathbb{R}^3\}. \qquad (4)$$

These definitions for the basic operators have excellent properties with respect to mathematical morphology and with respect to fuzzy sets [2]. At first, these operations are internal in [0,1] (as opposed to the classical definitions on functions). Secondly, all analytical and algebraic properties of mathematical morphology are satisfied (for the basic operations and for the ones derived by combination like opening and closing), at least for particular T-norms and T-conorms. Most of them are satisfied whatever the choice of i and u. At last, these definitions inherit the properties of T-norms and T-conorms in terms of data fusion, reasoning under uncertainty, and decision making [4].

For our problem, we have to replace a point, possibly fuzzy, by a fuzzy set v which represents all possible positions of this point. This is equivalent to dilating this point by the fuzzy structuring element defined by v. Fuzzy dilation is therefore perfectly adapted for introducing spatial imprecision in the detected contours. Moreover, the compatibility property of the dilation with fuzzy set union (expressed here by a "max" of the membership degrees), which is written as:

$$D_v[\max(\mu,\mu')] = \max[D_v(\mu), D_v(\mu')], \tag{5}$$

allows the direct computation of the dilation of a set of points by the same structuring element. At last, the iteration property of fuzzy dilation, expressed as:

$$D_{v'}[D_v(\mu)] = D_{D_{v'}(v)}(\mu), \tag{6}$$

allows the dilation of a fuzzy set successively by two fuzzy structuring elements or equivalently by their dilation. These two properties will be used for the fuzzy reconstruction.

5.4.3. Constructing the Fuzzy Structuring Elements

According to the geometrical modelization, the coordinates (x, y, z) of an echographic point (τ, α) are defined by a function g of θ, φ (or ρ), ω, x_t, y_t and z_t. Each variable v is modelized by a possibility distribution μ_v. The 3D fuzzy SE associated with point (τ, α) takes then the form $v = \Gamma(\theta, \varphi, \omega, x_t, y_t, z_t)$, where Γ is induced by g:

$$\forall p \in \mathbb{R}^3, v(p) = \begin{cases} \sup\{i[\mu_\theta(\theta),\mu_\varphi(\varphi),\mu_\omega(\omega),\mu_{x_t}(x_t),\mu_{y_t}(y_t),\mu_{z_t}(z_t)]/ \\ (\theta,\varphi,\omega,x_t,y_t,z_t) \in g^{-1}(p)\}, \\ 0 \text{ if } g^{-1}(p) = \varnothing. \end{cases} \tag{7}$$

The SE computation is performed directly in the discrete 3D space by determining, for each point of this space, the possibility associated with it following equation 7. The definition domain of the variables in $\mathbb{R}^6$ has been sampled accordingly to the sampling of $\mathbb{R}^3$ in order to obtain a connected SE: a variation of one sampling step of a variable must induce a displacement of the points smaller than a sampling step of $\mathbb{R}^3$.

5.4.4. Fuzzy Reconstruction from Echographic Slices

In this part, we make use of the nice formulation obtained during the geometric modelling. Indeed, it can be observed from equation 1 that the Cartesian coordinates of a point are expressed by quite simple formulae, which separate translation and rotation parameters. Also, the radius τ (in polar coordinates) appears only as a scaling factor in the second part of the equations (related to rotation). Therefore, the problem can be split in two parts, one concerning translation and the other one concerning rotation.

In a first step, imprecisions on θ, φ (or equivalently ρ), and ω are taken into account for each point $x = (\tau, \alpha)$ of the interpolated surface V_{bin}^{EE} under the form of a SE v_1^x. The possibility degree (or membership degree to the reconstructed vessel) of each point of the 3D space is obtained as the maximum of possibility degrees in this point issued from the different v_1^x's. Actually, the v_1's for identical values of α differ only by a scaling depending on τ, and the v_1's for similar values of α are only slightly different. These remarks allow one to reduce considerably the computation cost by computing only a small number of v_1's (we have computed 36 v_1's, each 10 degrees), and then by introducing the scaling factor τ. A first fuzzy volume V_f' is thus obtained:

$$V_f' = \cup \{D_{v_1^x}(\{x\}) \mid x \in V_{bin}^{EE}\} \tag{8}$$

whose membership function is:

$$\forall x \in \mathbb{R}^3, \mu_{V_f'}(x) = \sup\{v_1^y(x) \mid y \in V_{bin}^{EE}\}. \tag{9}$$

In the second step, the final fuzzy reconstruction is obtained by a fuzzy dilation with SE v_2, which takes into account imprecision on the translation parameters x_t, y_t, and z_t. Since v_2 is constant over the whole volume, the properties 5 and 6 avoid to dilate each v_1^x by v_2 and allow one to perform only one fuzzy dilation, directly on the fuzzy volume V_f':

$$V_f^{EE} = \cup\{D_{D_{v_2}(v_1^x)}(\{x\}) \mid x \in V_{bin}^{EE}\} = D_{v_2}(V_f'). \tag{10}$$

Figure 5.8 represents the 3D support of v_1 and three slices of this support orthogonal to the z axis (gray levels are proportional to possibility degrees), for $\alpha = 40$ degrees. In the same manner, Figure 5.9 represents the 3D support of v_2 and four slices orthogonal to the z axis.

Figure 5.10 presents an axial slice of the reconstructed vessel at different steps of the method: binary reconstruction by geometrical fusion (a), first fuzzy reconstruction including imprecision on the angles θ, ϕ (or ρ)

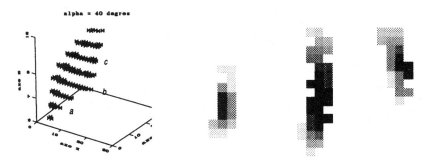

Figure 5.8   3D support and 3 slices of v_1 (black = 1, white = 0 for the membership degrees) for $\alpha = 40$ degrees.

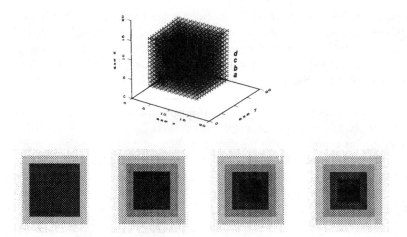

Figure 5.9   3D support of v_2 and 4 slices.

and ω (b), and second fuzzy reconstruction after the fuzzy dilation including imprecision on x_t, y_t, and z_t (c).

One of the advantages of the proposed method is that the fuzzy structuring elements that are used are determined directly from the data without any arbitrary choices.

5.4.5. Fuzzy Reconstruction from DA Data

The last available information is the vessel thickness provided by the DA data. The binary reconstruction obtained from the two DA projections using a regularization approach (see [19], [20]) has therefore to be combined with the previous reconstruction. However, this binary reconstruction does not include imprecisions on the DA data (due to acquisition, segmentation, etc.), and this may lead to contradictions with the reconstruction from EE data.

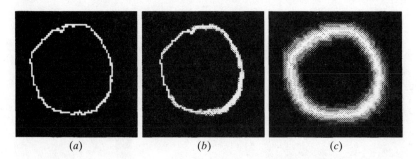

Figure 5.10   EE slice parallel to the $(y0z)$ plane of the reconstruction at different steps (the process is a 3D one, although only a 2D slice is presented). (a): Binary reconstruction. (b): Fuzzy reconstruction including imprecisions on θ, ρ and ω. (c): Fuzzy reconstruction after fuzzy dilation by v_2 (this reconstruction includes all imprecisions).

Imprecision is modelized, like for the EE data, by a fuzzy structuring element, which represents membership possibility degrees to the vessel surface of the points situated in a neighborhood of the reconstructed surface. The variation of vessel surface position corresponding to a possibility degree of 0.5 is estimated to 3 pixels (about 0.5 mm for the DA resolution of 0.1666 mm per pixel) along all three axes. The resulting structuring element is denoted by v_3 and is of the same type as the one used for translation parameters (v_2, see Figure 5.9). The introduction of imprecisions on the binary reconstruction, denoted V_{bin}^{DA}, is then obtained by a fuzzy dilation by v_3, providing a fuzzy volume V_f^{DA} (see Figure 5.11):

$$V_f^{DA} = D_{v_3}(V_{bin}^{DA}) \tag{11}$$

5.4.6. Fusion of Both Fuzzy Reconstructions

The last fusion step consists in introducing the densitometric information on vessel thickness provided by DA data in the reconstruction obtained from echographic slices, that is, in combining both fuzzy volumes V_f^{EE} and V_f^{DA} by a fusion operator F, resulting in a fuzzy volume V_f^F:

$$V_f^F = F(V_f^{EE}, V_f^{DA}). \tag{12}$$

The choice of F may be guided by following remarks. The fuzzy set framework provides the user with a large variety of operators, having various behaviors (ranging from strongly severe to highly indulgent, with all degrees of compromise). Therefore, they may be adapted to a large class of situations. The introduction of imprecisions in both reconstructions has led to fuzzy volumes V_f^{EE} and V_f^{DA} that have a large overlapping part (of course with more or less high degrees) and that do not present any more contradiction. So a conjunctive operator (with severe behavior) can be used [5], which has the advantage to reduce imprecision in the result. Among the most used T-norms, the "min" and product have been chosen, which lead to similar results after the decision. Figure 5.12 represents a few slices of the fusion with the "min" operator.

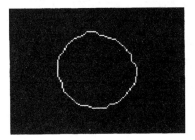

Figure 5.11 A slice of the reconstruction from DA and of its fuzzy dilation.

Figure 5.12   Fusion by "min" operator.

5.4.7. Binary Decision

Obtaining a binary volume necessitates a decision step. To overcome the topological problems in the resulting surface inherent to classical decision rules, we prefer to select the points of the "crest surface" of the fuzzy volume. This way, we obtain a unit thickness connected surface, going through the maximum membership points, and thus having the required properties. This surface is obtained by a morphological algorithm of 3D watershed [22]. The result is shown on Figure 5.13, superimposed to the fuzzy fusion.

This figure shows the good positioning of the watershed surface with respect to to the high membership values. Figure 5.14 presents the binary contours obtained (without taking imprecisions into account) from the angiographies and from the echographies, and the watershed. Ambiguities are solved in a satisfactory way: in nonconflictual areas, the watershed surface coincides with both contours, while in conflicting areas, an intermediary position is found, which is the only reasonable solution in absence of other information. These results can also be observed on the density profiles of the right projections along a line (Figure 5.15).

It should be noted that this decision process is pertinent since the fusion by a conjunctive operator results in a fuzzy volume having exactly one crest surface of cylindrical topology. This is due to the fact that the membership values of one of the fuzzy volumes through a diameter of a vessel section always present two maxima. If we compare the corre-

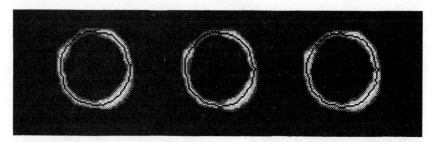

Figure 5.13   Superimposition of the fuzzy volume after fusion and of the watershed (in black) on a few slices of the vascular segment.

Figure 5.14 Comparison between V_{bin}^{EE} (black), V_{bin}^{DA} (dark gray), and the watershed of the fusion of V_f^{EE} and V_f^{DA} (light gray).

sponding diameters of the two volumes, they may be shifted with respect to each other in areas where ambiguities occur. This is illustrated on Figure 5.16. Therefore, a conjunctive operator is suitable and will result in a membership function again showing two maxima. The watershed algorithm applied on this fuzzy volume will thus extract exactly one surface, with the desired topology.

5.5. Conclusion

A complete original approach has been proposed for the reconstruction of vascular segments by DA and EE data fusion. It illustrates how fuzzy

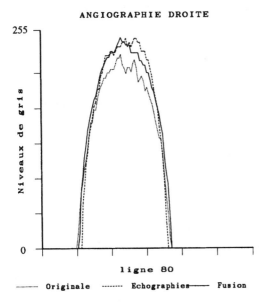

Figure 5.15 Comparison between density profiles along a line of the right projections of the original right angiography (dotted), of the binary reconstruction from echographies (dashed), and of the binary decision taken on the fusion of both fuzzy reconstructions (full line).

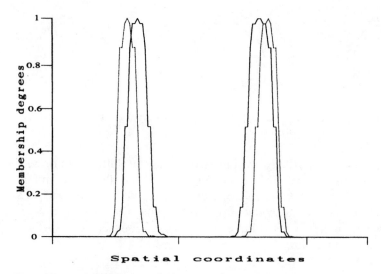

Figure 5.16 Comparison between membership degrees along a diameter of the fuzzy reconstructions obtained from the EE data (full line) and from the DA data (dotted line). Each curve presents two maxima. A cunjunctive operator (like the min) will also provide a curve with two maxima (i.e., one crest surface of cylindrical topology in the fuzzy volume resulting from the fusion).

sets can be used in a data fusion problem in medical imaging at four levels: for the segmentation of echographic images, for the modelling of imprecision, for the introduction of imprecision through fuzzy mathematical morphology with structuring elements derived from the data themselves, and for the information fusion. The main advantages of the method are the following: all geometrical parameters are estimated, and their introduction in a geometrical fusion step leads to a first reconstruction, which is already an improvement over existing approaches; fuzzy modelling and fuzzy mathematical morphology allow to take imprecision into account in an original approach, leading to a reconstruction by fuzzy fusion which takes all problem data into account and avoids ambiguities; decision by watershed provides a result that is consistent from a topological and geometrical point of view, while going through the maxima of the membership functions.

The first results clearly prove the feasibility of the method and the interest of combining several modalities for improving 3D vessel reconstruction, without any *a priori* geometrical model of the vessels.

Although the application presented here is quite specific, the proposed methodology and the use of fuzzy sets is much more generic, and similar approaches could be used for several problems in medical imaging. Indeed, for a number of medical applications, several modalities have to be used in conjunction, in order to improve the amount and quality of information, and therefore to improve the interpretation, the diagnosis, and the decision. Examples can be found:

- in computer-assisted surgery, where presurgical data (3D anatomical images, angiographies, etc.) have to be combined in order to find the best surgical planning, and then registered to observations during surgery,

- in several reconstruction problems (Single Photon Emission Tomography, Positron Emission Tomography, Electro-Encephalo-Graphy, Magneto-Encephalo-Graphy), where the ill-posed reconstruction problem can be regularized using anatomical data (like MRI),

- in functional brain imaging, where an activation related to a sensori-motor or cognitive task, detected in TEP or functional MRI, has to be correlated to brain anatomy, or where several functional imaging modalities are combined in order to confirm and improve the localization and spatial extent of an activation,

- in medical image interpretation and structure recognition using an atlas.

In all these domains, images and knowledge suffer from imprecision, which could be modelled in a way similar to the one proposed in this chapter.

5.6. References

[1] Bezdek, J.C. *Pattern Recognition with Fuzzy Objective Function Algorithms.* New York: Plenum, 1981.
[2] Bloch, I. "About Properties of Fuzzy Mathematical Morphologies: Proofs of Main Results." Technical Report, 93DO23, Telecom. Paris: 1993.
[3] Bloch, I., and H. Maitre. "Fuzzy Mathematical Morphology." *Annals of Mathematics and Artificial Intelligence,* Vol. 10, (1994), pp. 55–84.
[4] ———. "Fuzzy Mathematical Morphologies: A Comparative Study." *Pattern Recognition,* Vol. 28, No. 9 (1995), pp. 1341–1387.
[5] Bloch, I. "Information Combination Operators for Data Fusion: A Comparative Review with Classification." *IEEE SMC,* Vol. 26, No. 1, pp. 52-67, January 1996.
[6] Bloch, I., et al. "3D Reconstruction of Blood Vessels by Multi-Modality Data Fusion using Fuzzy and Markovian Modelling." *Computer Vision, Virtual Reality and Robotics in Medicine.* CVRMed '95, pp. 392–398. Nice, France: April, 1995.
[7] Bresler, Y., and A. Macovsky. "Estimation of the 3D Shape of Blood Vessels from X-ray Images." *Proceedings, IEEE Computer Soc. International Symposium Medical Images Icons.* pp. 251–258. Arlington, Texas: 1984.
[8] Dubois, D., and H. Prade. "A Review of Fuzzy Set Aggregation Connectives." *Information Sciences,* Vol. 36, (1985), pp. 85–121.
[9] ———. *Théorie des Possibilitiés, Applications à la Représentation des Connaissances en Informatique.* Masson, Paris: 1988.
[10] Geman, S., and D. Geman. "Stochastic Relaxation, Gibbs Distribution and the Bayesian Restoration of Images." *IEEE Transactions on Pattern Analysis and Machine Intelligence,* Vol. PAMI-6, pp. 721–741. 1984.
[11] Haneishi, H., et al. "Analysis of the Cost Function used in Simulated Annealing for CT Image Reconstruction." *Applied Optics,* Vol. 29, (1990), pp. 259–264.

[12] Hoff, H. "Imaging Artifacts in Mechanically Driven Ultrasound Catheters." *International Journal of Cardiac Imaging,* Vol. 4, No. 2–4 (1989), pp. 195–199.

[13] Hulzebosch, A.A., et al. "3D Reconstruction of Stenosed Coronary Artery Segments with Assessment of the Flow Impedance." *International Journal Cardiac Imaging,* Vol. 5 (1990), pp. 135–143.

[14] Kitamura, K., et al. "Estimating the 3D Skeletons and Transverse Areas of Coronary Arteries from Biplane Angiograms." *IEEE Transactions on Medical Imaging,* Vol. 7 (1998), pp. 173–187.

[15] Kitney, R.I., et al. "3D Visualization of Arterial Structures using Ultrasound and Voxel Modelling." *International Journal of Cardiac Imaging,* Vol. 4, No. 2–4 (1989), pp. 135–143.

[16] Klein, H.M., et al. "3D Surface Reconstruction of Intravascular Ultrasound Images using Personal Computer Hardware and a Motorized Catheter Control." *Cardiovascular Interventional Radiology,* Vol. 15 (1992), pp. 97–101.

[17] Maurincomme, E., et al. "Methodology for 3D Reconstruction of Intravascular Ultrasound Images." *SPIE, Vol. 1653, Medical Imaging IV: Image Capture, Formatting and Display,* pp. 26–34. 1992.

[18] Pellot, C., et al. "Segmentation, Modelisation and Reconstruction of Arterial Bifurcations in Digital Angiography." *Medical & Biological Engineering & Computing,* Vol. 30 (1992), pp. 576–783.

[19] ———. "A 3D Reconstruction of Vascular Structures from Two X-ray Angiograms using an Adapted Simulated Annealing Algorithm." *IEEE Transactions on Medical Imaging,* Vol. 13, No. 1. (1994), pp. 48–60.

[20] ———. "Data Fusion of X-ray Angiographic and Endovascular Echographic Images for the 3D Reconstruction of Vessels using a Probabilistic Approach." *SPIE Conference on Medical Imaging: Image Processing.* San Diego, Calif.: 1995.

[21] Rosenfield, K., et al. "3D Reconstruction of Human Coronary and Peripheral Arteries from Images Recorded During Two-Dimensional Intravascular Ultrasound Examination." *Circulation,* Vol. 84 (1991), pp. 1938–1956.

[22] Stanier, J., et al. "A Segmentation Scheme for Knowledge-based Construction of Individual Atlases from Slice-type Medical Images." *SPIE Conference on Medical Imaging VII,* pp. 14–18. Newport Beach, Calif.: February, 1993.

[23] Sureda, F., et al. "Reconstruction 3D de Vaisseaux Sanguins par Fusion de Donnés à partir d'Images Angiographiques et Échographiques." *Traitement du Signal,* Vol. 11, No. 6 (1994) pp. 525–540.

[24] van Tran, L., et al. "Reconstructing the Cross Sections of Coronary Arteries from Biplan Angiograms." *IEEE Transactions on Medical Imaging,* Vol. 11 (1992), pp. 517–529.

[25] Yager, R.R. "Connectives and Quantifiers in Fuzzy Sets." *Fuzzy Sets and Systems,* Vol. 40 (1991), pp. 39–75.

[26] Zadeh, L.A. "Fuzzy Sets." *Information and Control,* Vol. 8 (1965), pp. 338–353.

[27] ———. "Fuzzy Sets as a Basis for a Theory of Possibility." *Fuzzy Sets and Systems,* Vol. 1 (1978), pp. 3–28.

6 Multisources Information-Fusion Application for Satellite Image Classification

Ludovic Roux
Jacky Desachy
Université Paul Sabatier, IRIT
118, route de Narbonne
31062 Toulouse Cedex France

ABSTRACT: We present a multisources information-fusion method for satellite image classification. Main characteristics of this method are the use of possibility theory to handle imprecision due to pixel classification, and the ability to merge both numeric sources (satellite image spectral bands) and symbolic sources (expert knowledge about best localization of classes). Moreover, this information-fusion method has a linear time complexity. We applied successfully this method on a Landsat image in order to achieve a vegetation and crops classification from characteristic samples.

6.1. Introduction

We present a multisources information-fusion method for satellite image classification. Main characteristics of this method are the use of possibility theory to handle imprecision due to pixel classification, and the ability to merge numeric sources (satellite image spectral bands) and symbolic sources (expert knowledge about best localization of classes). Moreover, this information-fusion method has a linear complexity.

First we introduce briefly the possibility theory and the conjunctive fusion method used. Then we apply this fusion method to a satellite image classification problem. Classes are defined by their spectral response on the one hand, and by the description of their geographical context on the other hand. We compute the possibility distributions for both numeric sources and symbolic sources. At last, fusion handles possibility measures coming from numeric sources and from symbolic sources.

6.2. Possibility Theory

Possibility theory is based on fuzzy sets. L.A. Zadeh has proposed both fuzzy sets in the 1960s [15] and possibility theory in 1978 [16]. Several developments on possibility theory can be found in Dubois and Prade book [8]. Possibility measures allow to deal with imprecise and uncertain knowledge. The imprecision notion is represented by fuzzy sets, and the uncertainty is quantified by a couple of values (possibility and necessity values).

6.2.1. Histogram and Possibility Distribution

Dubois and Prade [8] suggest to define a fuzzy set from a histogram. A coherence condition between probability and possibility is:

$$\forall A \in \Omega, P(A) \le \Pi(A) \tag{1}$$

A histogram gives a probability distribution p for each element $\omega \in \Omega$. A possibility distribution π is computed from this probability distribution by:

$$\pi(\omega_i) = \sum_{k=1}^{n} \min(p(\omega_i), p(\omega_k)) \tag{2}$$

This transformation strengthens the weight of the most representative gray levels of each class, allowing to make classes more distinguishable from the others (Figure 6.1).

6.2.2 Fusion of Possibility Distributions

Several fusion operators having different fusion behaviors are available in possibility theory. The main basic behaviors are:

- *conjunctive* behavior designed for reliable and agreeing sources,
- *disjunctive* behavior designed for conflicting sources.

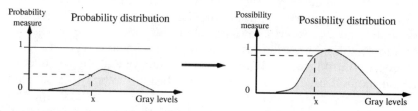

Figure 6.1   Converting a probability distribution into a possibility distribution.

A complete description of most fusion operators available in probability theory, evidence theory, and possibility theory has been achieved by Bloch [4].

In our application, we use a conjunctive operator because spectral bands of a satellite image are agreeing sources. Conjunctive fusion is designed for merging agreeing sources; that is sources for which possibility distributions overlap a lot [4] [8] [9]. Let π_i be the possibility distribution for source i. $(i = 1, \ldots, n)$. A conjunctive fusion is an intersection (noted $*$) of possibility distributions:

$$\forall x \in \Omega, \pi_{\text{conj}}(x) = *_{i=1}^{n} \pi_i(x) \qquad (3)$$

$*$ is a fuzzy-set intersection operation. When all sources are reliable, we take $* = \min$. This allows to make information more accurate by combination.

6.3. Application

Classification of a satellite image is improved when classification information of each image is merged. We make a classification of a Landsat satellite image. This image is a mountainous area located near Palni (southern India). We manage with heterogenous information sources for this classification: spectral bands of the Landsat image and out-image data defined by geographical information about the Palni area such as slopes, elevations, distance to rivers, and so on.

We compute possibility measures in a different way for these two kinds of information. First, we present how to compute a possibility distribution from a histogram for numeric sources (spectral bands). Then we compute a possibility distribution for symbolic sources (geographical contexts). At last we give results of the conjunctive fusion method

Landsat Mss4 image of Palni area.

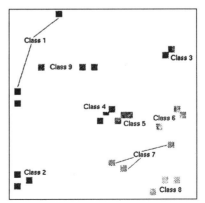

Characteristic samples of the nine classes in the image.

Figure 6.2 Landsat and samples images.

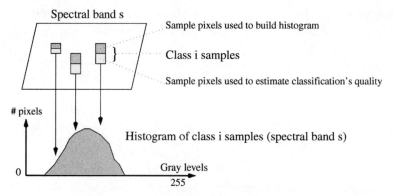

Figure 6.3   Making a gray-level histogram from class samples.

applied to possibility distributions coming from numeric sources and symbolic sources.

6.3.1. Possibility Distribution for Numeric Sources (Spectral Bands)

Our classification is supervised. Nine classes have been selected. We have characteristic samples of each of the nine classes (vegetation and cultivation classes). Figure 6.2 shows the Landsat Mss4 image of the Palni area and the localization of samples in this image.

We use the spectral response of class i samples to estimate the distribution function of that class i. We build the gray-level histogram for a class i from the gray level of each pixel of class i samples. There is one histogram per source for each class i. Half of the pixels of class i samples are used to build the class i histogram. The other half will be used at end of processing (when fusion is done) to estimate the quality of classification and information fusion (Figure 6.3).

We have four spectral bands (four images of the same area). So we build four histograms for each class i (one histogram per spectral band for class i).

These histograms give a probability distribution for a class i in spectral band s. The probability distribution is computed from a histogram by (Figure 6.4):

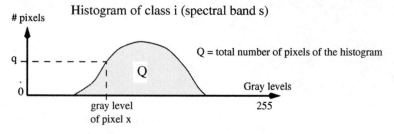

Figure 6.4   Using gray-level histogram to compute $p_s(x/C_i)$.

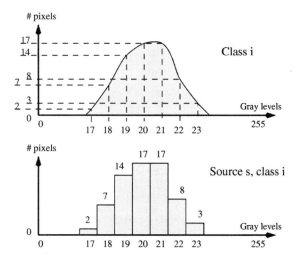

Figure 6.5 Gray-level histogram for class i in spectral band s.

$$p_s(x/C_i) = \frac{q}{Q} \ (x \text{ is a pixel}) \qquad (4)$$

where q is the number of pixels of class i samples that have the same gray level as pixel x, and Q is the total number of pixels that have been used to build class i histogram.

The last step consists in computing the possibility distribution from the probability distribution. A class i has a possibility distribution for each source s. We compute this possibility distribution as follows:

$$\pi_s(C_i/x) = \sum_{\substack{255 \\ \text{gray level } g = 0}} \min[p_s(\text{gray level of } x/C_i), p_s(g/C_i)] \qquad (5)$$

At this point, we have possibility distributions for each pixel x and class i on each spectral band.

For example, let us have a class i. Its histogram in spectral band s is showed in Figure 6.5. It is made up of 68 pixels $(2 + 7 + 14 + 17 + 17 + 8 + 3 = 68)$. Possibility distributions computed from this histogram are (Figure 6.6):

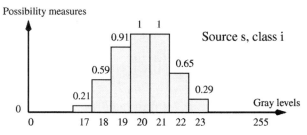

Figure 6.6 The possibility distribution computed from histogram of Figure 6.5.

$$\pi_s(C_i/17) = \frac{2+2+2+2+2+2+2}{68} = \frac{14}{68} = 0.21$$

$$\pi_s(C_i/18) = \frac{2+7+7+7+7+7+3}{68} = \frac{40}{68} = 0.59$$

$$\pi_s(C_i/19) = \frac{2+7+14+14+14+8+3}{68} = \frac{62}{68} = 0.91$$

$$\pi_s(C_i/20) = \frac{2+7+14+17+17+8+3}{68} = \frac{68}{68} = 1$$

$$\pi_s(C_i/21) = \frac{2+7+14+17+17+8+3}{68} = \frac{68}{68} = 1$$

$$\pi_s(C_i/22) = \frac{2+7+8+8+8+8+3}{68} = \frac{44}{68} = 0.65$$

$$\pi_s(C_i/23) = \frac{2+3+3+3+3+3+3}{68} = \frac{20}{68} = 0.29$$

6.3.2. Possibility Distributions for the Symbolic Source (Geographical Contexts)

We work with geographical contexts of each class. An expert in photo-interpretation gives us some rules to describe; according to him, the most favorable context for each class. We represent a context description by a rule made up of unions of intersections of basic contexts. A basic context can be slope, elevation, soil type, distance to roads, distance to urban areas, distance to rivers, and so on. We evaluate how much the geographical context of a pixel x satisfies rules that define the most favorable geographical context of a class i. The more the context of a pixel x satisfies to the context defined for class i, the higher the probability for this pixel x to be a member of class i.

For example, a rule that describes the favorable context for a class i might be:

the class i is

[(principally on south slopes) AND (often at elevation from 800 to 1500 m.)]

OR

[(never on north slopes) AND (rarely at elevation over 1200 m.)]

The adverbs *principally, often, never, rarely,* and so on are frequency degrees. These adverbs are a kind of weight. For example, "*principally on south slopes*" is translated by "*80 percent of time, class i is on south slopes*"; "*rarely at elevation over 1200 m.*" is translated by "*20 percent of time, class i is at elevation over 1200 m.*"

We use a set of fuzzy neural networks to represent the rules (Figure 6.7). There is one network per rule, that is, per class. The network i gives

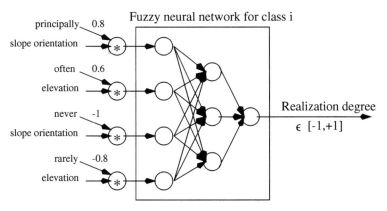

Figure 6.7 Fuzzy neural network for a class *i*.

a realization degree for each pixel evaluating how much the context of a pixel matches the context required for class *i*.

A network has as many inputs as the rule has basic contexts, and one output. A rule with *n* basic contexts has a corresponding network with *n* inputs. For the preceding class *i* example, the rule has four basic contexts (south slopes, elevation from 800 to 1500 m., north slopes and elevation over 1200 m.). So the corresponding network has four inputs.

The output of network *i* (for class *i*) is a realization degree; that is, how much a pixel context matches class *i* required context. This realization degree is a value belonging to the $[-1, +1]$ set.

Network inputs (such as elevation) are values varying in the $[-1, +1]$ set. For example, the realization degree of basic context "*elevation over 1200 m.*" is represented by Figure 6.8.

The output of network *i* (for class *i*) is almost a fuzzy set. We project the $[-1, +1]$ set to the $[0, +1]$ set in order to have a fuzzy set. The possibility measure for a pixel *x* to belong to class *i* comes from its membership degree to the set given by the network *i*.

6.3.3. Fusion of Possibility Distributions

Possibility measures of the geographical context sources and measures of the four numeric sources are available. We have to merge them now.

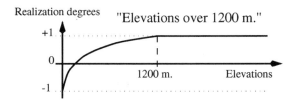

Figure 6.8 Realization degrees for a basic context "*elevation over 1200 m.*"

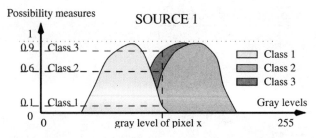

Figure 6.9   Source 1 possibility measures for a given pixel x.

We have presented the fusion formula in section 6.2.2. For our problem, this formula becomes:

$$\pi(C_i/x) = \frac{\min_{\text{source } s}[\pi_s(C_i/x)]}{\max_{\text{class } k}[\min_{\text{source } t}(\pi_t(C_k/x))]} \tag{6}$$

The fusion performs final possibility distributions for each class i. A pixel x is classified in the class that has the greatest possibility measure. Example: Let us have two sources and three classes. Possibility distributions are:

For source 1 (Figure 6.9):

$$\pi_1(C_1/x) = 0.1$$

$$\pi_1(C_2/x) = 0.6$$

$$\pi_1(C_3/x) = 0.9$$

For source 2 (Figure 6.10):

$$\pi_2(C_1/x) = 0.6$$

$$\pi_2(C_2/x) = 0.8$$

$$\pi_2(C_3/x) = 0.3$$

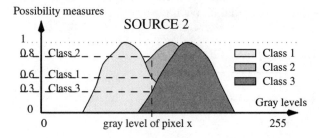

Figure 6.10   Source 2 possibility measures for a given pixel x.

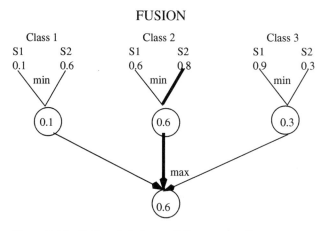

Figure 6.11   Fusion of pixel x possibility measure (for two sources and three classes).

The final measure comes from the 0.6 possibility measure given by source S_2 to class 2 (Figure 6.11). So the pixel x is assigned to class 2 after fusion.

6.3.4. Classification Results after Information Fusion

The nine classes of our study are vegetation and cultivation classes. The histogram of class i samples is largely overlapped by the other histograms, so it is quite difficult to distinguish that class i from the others. But by computing possibility distributions (which give more weight to the most representative gray levels of a class) and by adding geographical context information to a spectral information, we can improve distinction of a class from the other ones. The aim of information fusion is to give a unique final measure from all the information available represent-

Table 6.1   Classification of Each Spectral Band Separately, Then after Fusion without Geographic Contexts and with Geographic Contexts

Class	MSS4	MSS5	MSS6	MSS7	Fusion without geographic contexts	Fusion with geographic contexts
1	56.21%	23.75%	23.31%	19.83%	32.90%	69.93%
2	28.98%	31.81%	32.90%	48.15%	50.11%	67.97%
3	4.25%	27.12%	27.78%	16.34%	39.54%	68.30%
4	38.87%	40.66%	19.44%	10.23%	52.17%	91.56%
5	42.48%	42.27%	53.16%	44.44%	58.39%	87.15%
6	56.21%	27.23%	14.16%	29.85%	64.05%	85.62%
7	67.97%	45.97%	20.70%	50.33%	70.37%	76.47%
8	49.46%	61.22%	57.08%	0.00%	64.71%	79.96%
9	11.11%	46.41%	18.95%	0.00%	43.14%	41.83%
TOTAL	**40.90%**	**38.90%**	**29.97%**	**24.91%**	**53.35%**	**74.25%**

ing at best the whole initial informations. Conjunctive fusion has a severe behavior, considering all sources as being reliable. It selects the smallest value of each source that is the most reliable information.

Table 6.1 presents the results of classification. The classification of each spectral band separately gives a 41 percent successful classification rate for spectral band MSS4 (0.5 to 0.6 μm, green-yellow), and only a 25 percent rate for spectral band MSS7 (0.8 to 1.1 μm, near infrared). But merging classification information of the four spectral bands MSS4 to MSS7 gives a 53 percent successful classification rate.

The addition of geographical context information to spectral information improves a lot the classification with a 74 percent successful classification rate. Figure 6.12 presents classified image obtained after fusion and samples areas on this classified image.

6.4. Conclusion

We have presented a multisources information-fusion method using possibility theory. This method allows to merge heterogeneous sources such as numeric and symbolic sources. Classification results are improved both by information fusion and by use of spectral and geographical information. On our example, we have had 74 percent of pixels correctly classified after the fusion. Moreover, it is low computing-time consuming because the possibility theory operators are min and max.

To improve further the overall classification, adaptive fusion may be used. An adaptive fusion adapts its behavior to data to be merged, having a conjunctive behavior when sources are agreeing, and switching to a disjunctive behavior when sources are in conflict [9] [6] [12].

Result image after information fusion.

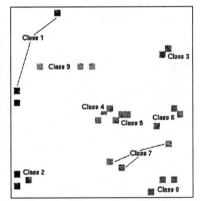

Characteristic samples of the nine classes in the classified image.

Figure 6.12 Classified and samples images.

6.5. References

[1] Berenstein, C., et al. "Consensus Rules," in *Uncertainty in Artificial Intelligence*, eds. L.N. Kanal and J.F. Lemmer. North Holland: Elsevier Science Publishers B.V., 1986.

[2] Bhatnagar, R.K., and L.N. Kanal. "Handling Uncertain Information: A Review of Numeric and Non-Numeric Methods," in *Uncertainty in Artificial Intelligence*, eds. L.N. Kanal and J.F. Lemmer. North Holland: Elsevier Science Publishers B.V., 1986.

[3] Bloch, I., and H. Maitre. "Fusion de Donnees en Traitement d'Images: Modeles d'Information et Decisions." *Traitement du Signal*, Vol. 11, No. 6 (1994), pp. 435–446.

[4] Bloch, I. "Information Combination Operators for Data Fusion: A Comparative Review with Classification." *IEEE Transactions on Systems, Man, and Cybernetics*. 1995.

[5] Bouchon-Meunier, B. "La Logique Floue." *Que Sais-Je?*, No. 2702. Presses Universitaires de France, January, 1993.

[6] Deveughele, S., and B. Dubuisson. "Estimation of Geometric Tokens: Possibility Theory Handles Severe Conflicts." SCIA '93, *Proceedings, 8th Scandinavian Conference on Image Analysis*, Vol. 2, pp. 1365–1372. Tromso University, Norway: May, 1993.

[7] Desachy, J. "Interpretation Automatique d'Images Satellite: Le Systeme ICARE." Ph.D. Dissertation, Paul Sabatier University, 1991.

[8] Dubois, D., and H. Prade. *Possibility Theory, an Approach to the Computerized Processing of Uncertainty*. New York: Plenum Press, 1988.

[9] ———. "Combination of Fuzzy Information in the Framework of Possibility Theory," in *Data Fusion in Robotics and Machine Intelligence*, eds. M.A. Abidi and R.C. Gonzalez. New York: Academic Press, 1992.

[10] ———. "Fuzzy Numbers: An Overview," in *Analysis of Fuzzy Information, Vol. 1, Mathematics and Logic*, ed. J.C. Bezdek. Boca Raton: CRC Press, 1994.

[11] Roux, L., and J. Desachy. "Information Fusion for Supervised Classification in a Satellite Image." *FUZZ-IEEE '95*, Vol. 3, pp. 1119–1124. Yokohama, Japan: March, 1995.

[12] Roux, L. "Auto-Adaptive Information-Fusion for Satellite Image Classification." To appear, *Satellite Remote Sensing*. Paris: September, 1995.

[13] Sandri, S. "La Combinaison d'Informations Incertaines et ses Aspects Algorithmiques." Ph.D. Dissertation, Paul Sabatier University, June, 1993.

[14] Yager, R.R. "A General Approach to Decision Making with Evidential Knowledge." *Uncertainty in Artificial Intelligence*, eds. L.N. Kanal and J.F. Lemmer. North Holland: Elsevier Science Publishers B.V., 1986.

[15] Zadeh, L.A. "Fuzzy Sets." *Information and Control*, Vol. 8 (1965), pp. 338–353.

[16] ———. "Fuzzy Sets as a Basis for a Theory of Possibility." *Fuzzy Sets and Systems*, Vol. 1 (1978), pp. 3–28.

[17] Zahzah, E.H. "Contribution a la Representation des Connaissances et a leur Utilisation pour l'Interpretation Automatique des Images Satellite, Ph.D. Dissertation, Paul Sabatier University, September, 1992.

7 Elicitation, Pooling, and Assessment of Expert Opinion in the Possibilistic Framework

Sandra A. Sandri
Brazilian National Institute for Space Research

ABSTRACT: We discuss here the use of possibility theory in the elicitation, assessment, and pooling of expert opinion. We also describe the main features of a possibilistic expert judgment system, and illustrate its use by means of a simple example. In this system, expert opinion is elicitated through possibility distributions or probability quantiles, which are then transformed into possibility distributions. Assessment evaluation is carried out in terms of calibration and level of precision. Several pooling modes are available in the system supported by formal models based on various assumptions concerning the experts.

7.1. Introduction

In the field of reliability and safety analysis of newly designed installations, statistical data are not always available, especially regarding rare or destructive events, or for devices whose novelty implies a scarcity of experimental data at the time when the safety analysis must be carried out. In such cases, the knowledge of experts is very useful to evaluate unknown parameters, typically the number of times a given event occurs within a given period, or the number of hours needed to repair some equipment, and so on. In order to get useful information from the experts, several problems must be solved. The first one is a proper modelling of the pieces of data supplied by a single expert about a given parameter. This type of data is almost never precise and reliable because the expert only possesses a rough idea of the value of quantitative parameters, due to limited precision of human assessments and to the variability of such values (e.g., failure rates). The second task to be solved is to assess the quality of the expert, namely his or her calibration, and the precision of his or her response. Lastly, when several expert responses are available, they must be combined so as to yield a unique, hopefully better response.

A procedure for processing expert opinion, in a given uncertainty model, can be divided as follows: i) establishment of the domain of expertise; determination of the set of experts and the seed (test) variables that will be used to calibrate them; ii) elicitation of variables values by experts; iii) assessment of experts calibration and precision; iv) pooling of the experts assessments; v) comparison of the performance of pooling methods on seed variables; vi) employement of the best method yielded by v) to produce the values for the variables of interest.

Items iii) and iv) are not used in some frameworks, notably on those adopting the Bayesian framework. In most systems the uncertainty model adopted is related to the probabilistic framework (see [1] for a survey). However, a pure probabilistic model of expert knowledge is not so satisfactory, since probabilistic information looks too rich to be currently supplied by individuals. For this reason, possibility theory is a more natural framework. Indeed, information supplied by individuals is often incomplete and imprecise, rather than tainted with randomness. Moreover, the possibilistic framework offers a robust assessment mechanism, and a large set of formally and intuitively sound pooling methods (see [2] for a comparison between the probabilistic and possibilistic framework).

In this chapter we discuss a possibilistic approach to expert judgment (see [2] for details). Section 7.2 brings an overview of possibilistic elicitation of information, section 7.3 describes a possibilistic assessment evaluation mechanism, and section 7.4 deals with the pooling of uncertain pieces of information. Section 7.5 illustrates the use of system PEAPS, which implements this approach, by means of a simple example. Section 7.6 brings the conclusion.

7.2. Possibilistic Elicitation

Let v be a variable defined on a given domain X. The simplest form of a possibility distribution [3] for v is given by $\pi(x) = 1$ if $v \in [s_1, s_u], 0$ otherwise, where $[s_1, s_u]$ is an interval of X. This type of possibility distribution is naturally obtained from experts claiming that "the value of v lies between s_1 and s_u." This way of expressing knowledge is more natural than giving a point-value x_0 for v right away, because it allows for some imprecision: the true value of v is more likely to lie between s_1 and s_u than to be equal to x_0.

However, this representation is not entirely satisfactory. Claiming that $\pi_v(x) = 0$ for some x means that $v = x$ is impossible, and that would tempt experts to give wide uninformative intervals (e.g. $s_1 = x_1, s_u = x_u$).

A natural way of eliciting information from experts consists in asking them to supply several intervals $A_1, \ldots, A_m$ directly, together with levels of confidence $\lambda_1, \ldots, \lambda_m$. The level of confidence λ_i can be conveniently interpreted as the least probability that the true value of v hits A_i (e.g., from the point of view of the experts, the proportion of cases he or she has observed where the realization of v lies in A_i). Having obtained the set of intervals A_i and levels of confidence λ_i it is then easy to construct a possibility distribution (see [8] for details). In practice, a limited number of intervals is already capable of providing a rich amount of information, for example, the three intervals: $A_1 = [c_1, c_u]$ with $\lambda_1 = 0.05$, $A_2 = [m_1, m_u]$ with $\lambda_2 = 0.5$, and $A_3 = [s_1, s_u]$ with $\lambda_3 = 0.95$.

7.3. Possibilistic Assessment

Experts can be deficient with regard to three aspects:

1. Inaccuracy: Values given by the expert are inconsistent with the actual information about the seed variables.

2. Imprecision: The expert is too cautious because the intervals he or she supplies are too large to be informative, although he or she is accurate.

3. Exaggerated precision: the value of the test variable is not precisely known to date but the expert supplies intervals that are too narrow (or point-values).

Most expert judgment systems try to detect and treat these deficiencies. In this case, two basic approaches are used: either the analyst knows the experts' deficiencies and is able to furnish coefficients that will modify the experts' estimates, or the experts are submitted to a battery of tests, and evaluated thereupon.

In the second case, in order to assess the quality of experts, the latter are asked questions whose answers are known, and are rated on the basis of these results. The questions pertain to the true values of a series v_1, $v_2, \ldots, v_n$ of "seed" (test) variables; the values of these parameters are either known by the analyst and not known by the experts, or more often can be determined afterwards by means of physical experiments or other means. In order to build a meaningful rating system, one must first identify the type of deficiencies experts may be prone to, and then define indices that enable the true answer and the expert answer to be compared and take these deficiencies into account. Note that the true value of a seed variable may be ill known itself, sometimes because the state-of-the-art in the field does not allow for its precise evaluation, or because the available information consists of some histogram.

Let v be a seed variable whose value x^* is precisely known. Let E be the fuzzy set supplied by an expert e, to describe his or her knowledge about

v. Let μ_E be the membership function of E (so that $\mu_E = \pi_v$). It is easy to see that the greater $\mu_E(x^*)$, the more calibrated is the expert. Indeed if $\mu_E(x^*) = 0$, E totally misses x^*, while if $\mu_E(x^*) = 1$, x^* is acknowledged as a usual value of v. Hence a natural measure of calibration is given by:

$$A(e, v) = \mu_E(x^*)$$

The larger is E, the more imprecise (hence under-confident) the expert. A reasonable specificity index is then:

$$Sp(e,v) = f(|E|) = (|X| - |E|) / |X|$$

where $|E| = \int_X \mu_E(v)\, dv$.

On the whole, the overall rating of the expert regarding a single seed variable can be defined as:

$$Q(e,v) = A(e,v) \cdot Sp(e,v)$$

that requires him or her to be both calibrated and informative in order to score high.

Using simple arithmetic mean over the individual scores of the seed variables, global measures can be obtained for an expert, regarding his or her overall accuracy $A(e)$, precision $Sp(e)$, and quality $Q(e)$. It is important to note that generally $Q(e) \neq A(e) \cdot Sp(e)$. The standard deviation is also useful to check the significance of the gaps between average ratings of experts. Based on these evaluations, a set K of experts can be divided into groups of unequal reliability.

7.4. Possibilistic Pooling

The basic principles of the possibilistic approach to the pooling of expert judgments are, first, that there is no unique combination mode, and, second, that the choice of the combination mode depends on an assumption about the reliability of experts, as formulated by the analyst. Basically, we can divide the combination modes in two classes: one in which the experts are viewed as a set of sources in parallel to be combined in a symmetric way, and another in which the opinion of an expert may be taken more into account in the determination of the result. Let π_i be the possibility distribution supplied by expert i, for $i \in K$. Some of the combination modes are as follows.

7.4.1. Conjunctive Mode

If the experts are considered to be reliable, then the response of the group of experts is given by a distribution π_c which can be defined by:

$$\pi_c(x) = \pi_{\min}(x) = \min_{i \in K} \pi_i(x)$$

This mode makes sense if all the π_i significantly overlap; if the degrees in $\pi_c(x)$ are very low, this mode of combination makes no sense. Other T-norms [4] could be used for π_c but it is interesting to note that when all experts perfectly agree ($\pi_i = \pi_c$, $\forall i$), min is the only T-norm that induces no reinforcement effect. Generally, agreement between experts is due to common background, and the idempotence of min deals with such a kind of redundancy.

7.4.2. Disjunctive Mode

The most careful optimistic assumption about a group of experts is that one of them is right, without specifying which one. This assumption corresponds to obtaining a distribution π_d as response, which can be defined by:

$$\pi_d(x) = \pi_{\max}(x) = \max_{i \in K} \pi_i(x)$$

This is a very conservative pooling mode that allows for contradiction between experts but may lead to a very poorly informative result, although not always a vacuous one. This effect is increased if other T-conorms are employed.

7.4.3. Trade-Off Mode

One type of consistency-based trade-off between the conjunctive and disjunctive modes of pooling is to use a measure κ of conflict between the experts and define:

$$\pi_{\text{trade}}(x) = \kappa \cdot \max(\pi_1, \pi_2) + (1 - \kappa) \cdot \min(\pi_1, \pi_2)$$

This index gives the conjunctive (respec. disjunctive) mode if $\kappa = 0$ (respec. $\kappa = 1$). Index κ can be for instance defined as:

$$\kappa_h = 1 - h(\pi_{\min}),$$

$$h(\pi) = \sup_x \pi(x).$$

We can also use the Jacquard index J defined by a quotient of fuzzy cardinalities yielding:

$$\kappa_J = 1 - J(\pi_1, \pi_2),$$

$$J(\pi_1, \pi_2) = | F_1 \cap F_2| / | F_1 \cup F_2|$$

where $\mu_{Fi} = \pi_i$.

An interesting class of trade-off methods is that of the symmetric sums [4]. An operator of this class is such that it gives high membership degrees to values on which both experts have high confidence, and low membership degrees to those on which both experts have small confidence. An idempotent parametrized and useful family that resembles this class of operators can be defined using dual triangular norms π_c and π_d and the arithmetic mean. Using $\pi_c = \pi_{\min}$ and $\pi_d = \pi_{\max}$, it is given by:

$$\pi_{\text{sum}-\alpha}(x) = \pi_{\max}(x), \text{if } \pi_{\min}(x) \geq \alpha$$

$$\pi_{\min}(x), \text{if } \pi_{\max}(x) \leq 1 - \alpha$$

$$\pi_m(x), \text{otherwise}$$

where $\alpha \in [0,1]$, and π_m stands for the arithmetic mean on the $\pi_i(x)$.

Another intermediary mode of pooling is based on numerical quantifiers and consists in assuming that j experts out of $k = |K|$ are reliable. The pooling method then consists in selecting a subset J, $K \supseteq J$, of experts such that $|J| = j$, assume that they are reliable and combine their opinions conjunctively. Then, considering that at least one of these subsets J contain reliable experts, combine the intermediary results disjunctively. The following formula is obtained [5]:

$$\pi_{(j)}(x) = \max_{J, K \supseteq J, |J| = j} \min_{i \in J} \pi_i(x)$$

Clearly, $\pi_{(k)} = \pi_{\min}$ and $\pi_{(1)} = \pi_{\max}$.

7.4.4. Discounting Experts

Let us suppose that the degree of certainty that a given expert e_i is reliable is known, say w_i. Then it is possible to account for this information by changing π_i into $\pi_i' = \max(\pi_i, 1 - w_i)$ (as suggested in [4]). When $w_i = 1$ (reliable expert), $\pi_i' = \pi_i$ and when $w_i = 0$ (unreliable expert), then $\pi_i' = 1$. Note that $w_i = 0$ does not mean that the expert lies, but that it is impossible to know whether his or her advice is good or not. Once discounted, expert opinions can be combined conjunctively. However, it is difficult to quantitatively relate w_i to the ratings $cr(e_i)$, where cr is either A, Sp, or Q, except that the higher $cr(e_i)$ the higher w_i. Moreover, the result of a conjunctive combination of discounted possibility distributions is rather difficult to interpret in the case of conflicting opinions of equally reliable experts.

7.4.5. Priority Aggregation of Expert Opinions

Let us suppose that we have determined a partition on the set K of experts into classes $K_1, K_2, \ldots, K_q$ of equally reliable ones, where K_j corresponds to a higher reliability level than K_{j+1}, for $j = 1,q$. Then the preceding symmetric aggregation schemes can be applied to each class K_j. The combination between results obtained from the K_j's can be performed upon the following principle: the response of K_2 is used to refine the response of K_1 insofar as it is consistent with it. If π_1 is obtained from K_1 and π_2 from K_2, the degree of consistency of π_1 and π_2 is $\text{cons}(\pi_1,\pi_2) = h(\pi_{\min}(\pi_1,\pi_2))$, and the following combination rule has been proposed [6], [7]:

$$\pi_{1-2} = \min(\pi_1, \max(\pi_2, 1 - \text{cons}(\pi_1,\pi_2))$$

Note that when $\text{cons}(\pi_1,\pi_2) = 0$, K_2 contradicts K_1 and only the opinion of K_1 is retained $(\pi_{1-2} = \pi_1)$, while if $\text{cons}(\pi_1,\pi_2) = 1$ then $\pi_{1-2} = \min(\pi_1,\pi_2)$. A similar behavior can be obtained if we replace $\text{cons}(\pi_1,\pi_2)$ by $J(\pi_1,\pi_2)$.

7.5. System PEAPS

PEAPS (Possibilistic Elicitation, Assessment, and Pooling System) runs in C++, using Openwindows interface facilities. The objects manipulated by this system are variables, experts, groups of selected experts, virtual experts represented by the application of a given pooling method on a given group, and the possibility distributions related to either the experts or the virtual experts. The system offers facilities for the creation of groups of selected experts, and the creation of virtual experts (i.e., application of pooling methods). All information available at any time of the use of the interfaces can be visualized using specific buttons.

7.5.1. Example

Let the true value and the domain of a seed variable v_j be respectively denoted by $x^*(v_j)$, and $[x_1, x_u](v_j)$. Let $\pi(e_i, v_j)$ denote the possibility distribution yielded by expert e_i for variable v_j.

In the example described next, we have a group of two experts $g = \{e_1, e_2\}$ giving their opinions about 10 variables. Each possibility distribution is given in the form of four intervals A_i, with $\alpha_1 = 1, \alpha_2 = .55, \alpha_3 = .1, \alpha_4 = .05$.

Variable domain: $[x_1, x_u](v_j) = [0, 10], 1 \leq j \leq 10$

Real value of variables:

$$x^*(v_1) = 2.5, x^*(v_2) = x^*(v_3) = x^*(v_4) = x^*(v_5) = 3.5$$

$$x^*(v_6) = x^*(v_7) = x^*(v_8) = x^*(v_9) = 4.5, x^*(v_{10}) = 7.5$$

Expert's input:

$$\pi(e_1, v_j) : A_1 = [1,4], A_2 = [1,8], A_3 = [0,8], A_4 = [0,10], 1 \leq j \leq 10$$

$$\pi(e_2, v_j) : A_1 = [3,4], A_2 = [3,7], A_3 = [0,10], A_4 = [0,10], 1 \leq j \leq 10$$

7.5.2. Elicitation

The system accepts as input either possibility distributions or quantiles of a probability distribution. In the latter case, the probabilistic information is immediately transformed into a possibility distribution (see [2] for details). Each possibility distribution is defined by a linear by parts function, represented in the form of a list of inflexion points $(x, \pi(x))$. Figure 7.1 brings the possibility distributions yielded by the experts in our example. The realizations of the variables are also represented in the figure.

7.5.3. Assessment

For each expert, the system calculates his or her precision, accuracy, and quality measures, and the standard deviation for these measures. The performance of the experts in our example can be found in Table 7.1.

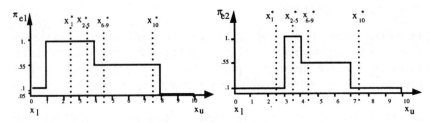

Figure 7.1 Possibility distributions yielded by experts e_1 and e_2.

We can see that, considering the whole set of seed variables, even if expert e_1 is more accurate than expert e_2, his or her low performance on precision makes him or her be considered less "good" than expert e_2. Note that here $Q(e_i) \neq A(e_i) \cdot Sp(e_i)$.

7.5.4. Pooling

Before giving the operators available in the system, let us define the two normalization methods the system employs:

$$\forall\, x \in X,\ \pi_{\text{norm1}}(x) = \pi(x)\,/\,h(\pi)$$

$$\forall\, x \in X,\ \pi_{\text{norm2}}(x) = \pi(x) + (1 - h(\pi))$$

In the present version of the system, two groups of combination methods are available. In the first group, we have the symmetric operations min, max, consistency-based trade-off and symmetric sum given previously (yielding π_{min}, π_{max}, π_{trade} and $\pi_{\text{sum}-\alpha}$ respectively). We use π_{norm1} to normalize π_{min}, and π_{norm1} to normalize π_{trade}. Also, in π_{trade} we use a global measure of conflict κ_J calculated as the arithmetic mean of the individual κ_J for each variable.

The basis of the second class of pooling methods is an asymmetric operation that favors the opinion of some of experts in relation to others. First of all, given a group of experts g, the system determines three orderings $\text{order}_{cr}(g)$ based solely on the experts global measures A, Sp, and Q. In our example, the orderings are: $\text{order}_A(g) = (e_1, e_2)$, $\text{order}_{Sp}(g) = (e_2, e_1)$, $\text{order}_Q(g) = (e_2, e_1)$.

Table 7.1 Assessment of Experts and Possibilistic Methods by PEAPS

Experts and Virtual Experts	A	Sp	Q
π_{min}	.64	.685	.4384
e_2, π_{Sp-0}, π_{Q-0}, π_{Sp-1}	.64	.675	.432
π_{A-0}	.7054	.5868	.4139
π_{trade}, π_{A-1}, π_{Q-1}	.6976	.5845	.4078
$\pi_{\text{sum}-.5}$	.6975	.5675	.3958
e_1	.775	.46	.3565
π_{max}	.775	.45	.3487

The orderings **order**$_{cr}(g)$ are then partitioned into a set of ranked homogeneous subgroups, using a parameter ρ, and the standard deviations $\sigma_{cr}(e_i)$ [2]. These new refined orderings are denoted by **order**$_{cr-\rho}(g)$. The experts inside a subgroup are considered to be equally reliable in relation to cr, and their opinions are combined using the symmetric operator π_{trade}. The resulting distributions constitute then the opinion of that subgroup in relation to a given variable v. These opinions are then combined using the asymmetric priority aggregation operator given previously, in such a way that the opinion of the best ranked subgroup is more favored in the final result than that of the second best ranked subgroup, in a pairwise manner (see [2] for details).

The first step on the mechanism implementing this asymmetric method yields a distribution that summarizes the collective opinion of a group of n closely ranked experts, none of whom is regarded as completely reliable. The second step comes down to discounting the information of the less reliable distribution by the degree of conflict with the more reliable one.

The details about the determination of the homogeneous subgroups can be found in [2]. Using ρ equal to 0 and 1 in group $g = \{e1, e2\}$ in our example, we obtain: order$_{A-0}$ = $(\{e_1\}, \{e_2\})$, order$_{A-1}$ = order$_{Q-1}$ = $(\{e_1, e_2\})$, order$_{Sp-0}$ = order$_{Sp-1}$ = order$_{Q-0}$ = $(\{e_2\}, \{e_1\})$.

The methods in this group are denoted by $\pi_{cr-\rho}$, where cr is either A, Sp, or Q, respectively, representing the accuracy, precision, and quality indices.

In our example, the pooling methods π_{Sp-0}, π_{Sp-1} and π_{Q-0} yield the same distributions as those furnished by expert e_2. Pooling methods π_{A-1} and π_{Q-1} yield the same distributions as π_{trade}. Figure 7.2 shows the application of rules $\pi_{\min}$, $\pi_{\max}$, π_{trade}, and π_{A-0}.

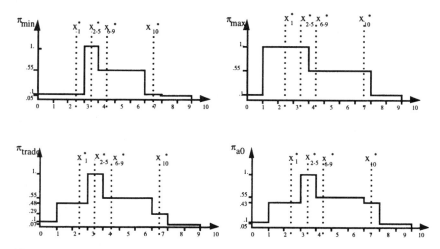

Figure 7.2 Application of rules $\pi_{\min}$, $\pi_{\max}$, π_{trade} and π_{A-0} to the distributions supplied by e_1 and e_2.

7.5.5. Model Assessment

When a series of estimations on test variables is available, the procedure allows for a quality assessment on the results of any of the described combination mechanisms, by treating the aggregated result as a "virtual" expert, and comparing it with the observed true values. The three average scores of the "model" are computed and may be compared with those of the participating experts, in order to see whether the aggregation results behave globally better than any of experts taken individually. By varying the composition of the expert pool and/or the combination mechanism, the analyst may search for some optimal processing, yielding results that are more reliable than the individual expert input data.

The measures obtained by the model assessment are given in Table 7.1. We can see that they behave well in practice. Since the normalization step is not used in this example, the accuracy coefficient increases from π_{min} to π_{max}, and the specificity coefficients vary in the inverse order. The experts agree most of the time what makes π_{min} have the best overall performance.

7.6. Conclusion

We presented here a procedure for processing human-originated information in the possibilistic framework, implemented in system PEAPS. We proposed mechanisms to elicit, assess, and pool expert opinions in the possibilistic framework.

The elicitation of information in the possibilistic framework is more user-friendly than that in the probabilistic one. The possibilistic evaluation does not overload the system analyst, it can be easily checked by the experts, and does not lead to incoherences. It presents advantages in relation to the probabilistic evaluation in a conceptual level, also confirmed in practice (see [2]).

In what concerns pooling, the possibilistic approach is much richer than the probabilistic one, and presents fewer problems in relation to an eventual dependance between the sources. In practice, with only a small set of methods, we can find satisfying ways of pooling expert opinions.

7.7. References

[1] Cooke, R.M. *Experts in Uncertainty.* The Netherlands: Department of Mathematics, TU Delft, 1989.

[2] Sandri, S., et al. "Elicitation, Assessment, and Pooling of Expert Judgements using Possibility Theory." *IEEE Transactions on Fuzzy Systems,* Vol. 3, No. 3 (1995), pp. 313–335.

[3] Zadeh, L.A. "Fuzzy Sets as a Basis for a Theory of Possibility." *Fuzzy Sets and Systems,* Vol. 3, No. 3 (1995), pp. 3–28.

[4] Dubois, D., and H. Prade. *Possibility Theory.* New York: Plenum Press, 1988.

[5] Dubois, D., et al. "Weighted Fuzzy Pattern Matching." *Fuzzy Sets and Systems,* Vol. 28 (1988), pp. 313–331.

[6] Dubois, D. and H. Prade. "Default Reasoning and Possibility Theory." *Artificial Intelligence,* Vol. 35 (1988), pp. 243–257.

[7] Yager, R.R. "Using Approximated Reasoning to Represent Default Knowledge." *Artificial Intelligence,* Vol. 31 (1987), pp. 99–112.

[8] Dubois, D., et al. "On Possibility/Probability Transformations." *Proceedings, IFSA '91.* Brussels, Belgium. 1991.

Clarifying Information

PART 2
Abstracting and Modelling

GUIDING NOTE

Fuzzy set methods have perhaps found their greatest success in the field of modelling. The technique of fuzzy systems modelling has been extensively used in the development of fuzzy logic controllers. The prototypical fuzzy model consists of a rule base made up of fuzzy if-then rules. A central component of these rules is the fuzzy set representation of linguistically specified antecedents and consequents. While fuzzy systems modelling of the type used in fuzzy logic control has been the most pervasive, other forms of fuzzy modelling, based on fuzzy numbers or fuzzy cognitive maps for instance, have been used in applications; these are illustrated by some of the applications in this section. The success of fuzzy modelling has raised to great prominence the problem of model construction, which requires the use of abstracting and learning techniques. In this section we present a number of fuzzy modelling techniques along with some applications to learning methodologies.

The chapter by Bouchon-Meunier, Marsala, and Ramdani focuses on the problem of learning in the spirit of decision trees where one is interested in classifying objects into different categories based on the attributes of the objects. Their approach uses linguistic classes/fuzzy sets to describe attribute values. They show how the use of fuzzy linguistic partitioning helps eliminate some of the problems faced by the standard classification techniques. Chui is concerned with the problem of extracting fuzzy rules from data for the construction of function approximation (fuzzy system models) and pattern classification. His approach is based upon the use of clustering techniques. In this approach, the centers of clusters, obtained from the observations, become the nucleus of fuzzy rules. The author uses the subtractive method of clustering, which is special case of the mountain clustering, a technique that has been incorporated with great success into the Math Lab fuzzy package. The chapter by Bergadano and Cutello also concerns itself with the problem of learning fuzzy rules from data. The authors concentrate on a special class of fuzzy rules, those with a crisp consequence. Probabilistic techniques are used to help in the validation of the model.

The next three chapters provide an illustration of different methods of fuzzy modelling. The chapter by Wang and Mendel provides a prototypical illustration of fuzzy systems modelling. However, rather than using it for fuzzy control, they apply the technology to the problem of adaptive filtering. The authors show how the incorporation of linguistic information about the channel, in terms of fuzzy rules, greatly improves the adaptive capabilities of the system over the classic neural net and polynomial adaptive filtering. Watada is concerned with the problem of modelling time series data using fuzzy numbers. He describes an algorithm for obtaining the fuzzy parameters in this type of model. He makes considerable use of possibility distributions and fuzzy arithmetic. He provides an application of his techniques to analyze data on alcohol consumption.

Dickerson and Kosko discuss the potential use of fuzzy techniques in the emerging field of virtual reality. The tool that they use for modelling are fuzzy cognitive maps. As described in this chapter these cognitive maps can be used to help model complex feedback systems in a relatively simple way. The authors illustrate their approach by describing its application to a virtual reality made up of a competitive underwater world.

8 Learning from Imperfect Data

Bernadette Bouchon-Meunier
Christophe Marsala
LAFORIA-IBP, Université Pierre et Marie Curie

Mohammed Ramdani
LAFORIA-IBP, Université Pierre et Marie Curie
Faculté des Sciences et Techniques de Mohammadia

ABSTRACT: Inductive learning has given rise to many developments and algorithms in the case of symbolic data and, up to a certain point, in the case of numerical data. In this chapter, we present several approaches to inductive learning dealing with mixed data (either symbolic or numerical) or imprecise data. These approaches also bring solutions to the case of numerical data. A first approach corresponds to situations where some expert knowledge is available; for instance, regarding possible partitions of the universes of attributes. A second approach consists in an automatic construction of such a partition from examples, when no expert knowledge is available.

8.1. Introduction

Acquisition of knowledge pertaining to a specific domain of expertise is an essential step to achieve an effective reasoning. In many cases, the knowledge is not general, but it consists in a list of particular cases that have been solved or situations that have occurred and can serve as examples. The examples constitute a training set. Each element of this set is represented by a description and a class, where a description is a set of pairs [attribute, value]. We focus on this case and we study inductive learning, with the aim of exhibiting general laws from the training set, and providing a means to assign a class to any new situation associated with a description. We consider two options: either some additional knowledge exists, concerning the attributes enabling to describe the examples, or the training set is the only available knowledge.

In the case where the attributes are symbolic, inductive learning has given rise to many developments and algorithms. They can be extended, up to a certain point, to the case of numerical data. In this chapter, we present several approaches to inductive learning dealing with mixed data (either symbolic or numerical), or imprecise data. These approaches also bring solutions to difficulties occurring in the case of numerical data. Inductive learning is generally based on the construction of a decision tree. Each vertex is associated with an attribute. The edges coming out of a vertex are associated with characterizations of the attributes. The choice of the attributes is based on their efficiency with regard to the identification of a class. Various methods fulfill this task, for instance Top Down Induction of Decision Trees (TDIDT)-based methods that use an evaluation function to arrange the attributes in the decision tree. For example, the ID3 algorithm [1][2] uses a measure of entropy, and the CART algorithm [3] is based on Gini's test of impurity. This kind of method is connected to the theory of questionnaires [4] and uses various tools from information theory [5]. Other methods are based on the theory of data analysis, for example C-means methods or ascending methods. However, all these methods do not fit very well the numerical nature of the data to deal with. Furthermore, they do not take into account the imprecision and the fuzziness of the data in the training set. Sometimes, numerical data are considered as symbolic [6]. This kind of method builds large trees, and it is difficult to rely on induction from a single numerical datum.

Most of the just-mentioned systems discretize the universe of continuous attributes and construct the characterizations as crisp intervals. However, in such a case, the continuous aspect of the attribute is completely ignored (for example, problems occur near the boundaries). To take into account this continuous aspect, other systems incorporate fuzzy sets in their methods [7] [8]. Fuzzy techniques are also interesting in the case of numerical-symbolic attributes. The training values for such attributes are either numerical or expressed in natural language as vague symbolic values, depending on the examples. There exist two kinds of systems that integrate fuzzy techniques. The first one integrates fuzzy techniques during the learning phase, for instance the system SAFI [9] [10] or Janikow's system [11]. Other systems use such techniques during the classification phase, for instance Catlett's and Jang's systems [12][13]. In this chapter, we present an algorithm that improves traditional inductive algorithms. In section 8.2, we propose a solution to the problems of numerical-symbolic data during the construction of decision trees. In section 8.3, we briefly explain how to use decision trees to classify new data. In section 8.4, we present an application exhibiting the interest of the approach to the learning phase presented in section 8.2. Finally, we conclude on interesting new developments that could be added.

8.2. A Way of Handling Numerical-Symbolic Data

We consider a list of attributes $A_1, \ldots, A_N$ and classes $C_1, \ldots, C_K$ that can be regarded as modalities of a decision attribute C. A training set contains examples that are associated with both values of the attributes and a class. The problem is to find a way of determining the class, given values of the attributes. From the training set, we determine an order of the attributes leading to the determination of a class, enabling us to associate a class with any new example only described by means of values of $A_1, \ldots, A_N$. In the case where the data are not homogeneous, numeric or symbolic values of the attributes are used, depending on the case. There are many difficulties to deal with numerical-symbolic training data. We propose two ways of handling such data. The first one is applicable when expert knowledge regarding the attributes is available. An expert (or many experts) gives some linguistic characterizations of the attributes. For instance, he or she provides a symbolic partition of a numerical attribute. This kind of expert knowledge is often difficult to obtain, or, sometimes, it does not exist. The second proposed way enables to infer a fuzzy partition if no expert knowledge is available.

8.2.1. Case Where Expert Knowledge Is Available

Let E be a training set with numerical-symbolic attributes. For example, we study the high jump specialty in the domain of athletics. We want to determine the relation of pertinence between the height somebody is able to jump (the class) and his or her age, size, and weight (values of the attributes) (Table 8.1). An expert is supposed to provide a list L_i of symbolic modalities for each attribute A_i, for instance {young, mature} for the attribute *age*. In order to take into account these symbolic values, we use an interface that translates numerical values into symbolic ones, with the help of fuzzy set theory. Symbolic values are represented by fuzzy sets of the universe of values of the numerical attribute (Figure 8.1). Thus, symbolic values of L_i will replace the specific values of attribute A_i given in Table 8.1, with the adjunction of a *degree of satisfiability* (Table 8.2). We need to determine these degrees of satisfiability. Let us consider the value w of attribute A_i (with universe of definition X) for a given example of the training set. We look for coefficients indicating to which extent each symbolic value v of L_i can replace w, or to which extent v is satisfi-

Table 8.1 Typical Training Set

case	age	size	weight	**height**
e1	20	1.85 m	80 kg	1.70 m
e2	25	1.60 m	80 kg	1.35 m
e3	35	1.70 m	60 kg	1.35 m
e4	40	1.75 m	75 kg	1.20 m
e5	29	1.65 m	90 kg	1.25 m

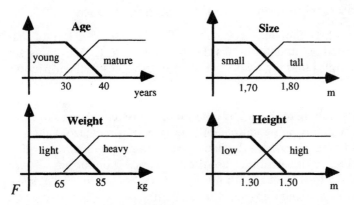

Figure 8.1 Typical fuzzy partitions.

able for w (Figure 8.2). We use the so-called degree of satisfiability [14], [15] defined as follows:

$$\text{Deg}(w \subset v) = \frac{\int_x f_{w \cap v} dx}{\int_x f_w dx} \qquad \text{if } w \neq \varnothing$$

$$= 0 \qquad \text{if } w = \varnothing$$

For the sake of simplicity, we suppose that all the values of a numerical attribute A are precise in the training set E. They can be either numerical or symbolic for a new example. Let $X = \{x_1, x_2, \ldots, x_n\}$ be this set of values. Let $v_1, \ldots, v_m$ be the modalities that define a fuzzy partition on the universe of the values of A. The *fuzzy probability* [16] of modality v_i is defined as:

$$P^*(v_i) = \sum_{1 \leq l \leq n} f_{v_i}(x_l) P(x_l)$$

where the probability $P(x_l)$ is approximated by the frequency of x_l in E, and f_{v_i} is the membership function of the fuzzy set representing v_i. Let $Y = \{y_1, y_2, \ldots, y_q\}$ be the set of numerical values of the decision attribute C in E. The *fuzzy conditional probability* of modality c_j of C, given v_i, is defined as:

$$P^*(c_j|v_i) = \frac{P^*(c_j, v_i)}{P^*(v_i)} \text{ with } P^*(c_j, v_i) = \sum_{1 \leq l \leq q} \sum_{1 \leq k \leq n} \min\Big(f_{c_j}(y_l), f_{v_i}(x_k)\Big) P(y_k, x_k)$$

Table 8.2 Training Set with Degree of Satisfiability for Each Attribute

case	age		size		weight		height	
	young	mature	small	tall	light	heavy	low	high
e1	1	0	0	1	0.25	0.75	0	1
e2	1	0	1	0	0.25	0.75	0.75	0.25
e3	0.5	0.5	1	0	1	0	0.75	0.25
e4	0	1	0.5	0.5	0.75	0.25	1	0
e5	1	0	1	0	0	1	1	0

We call *entropy-star* [8] the fuzzy entropy of the decision C related to the attribute A, defined as:

$$E^*_A = -\sum_i P^* (v_i) \sum_j P^* (c_j|v_i) \log P^* (c_j|v_i)$$

This entropy measures the uncertainty of the fuzzy decision when the modalities of the attribute A are known. This entropy is the criterion chosen to order the attributes during the construction of the decision tree. It generalizes the classical Shannon entropy [17].

The selection of the parameters for the membership functions is crucial. A good definition from the expert is very important for the whole system. When the expert is not sure of his or her definition, we have to adjust these parameters. Obviously, it seems convenient to adjust them with the values pertaining to the training set, by minimizing the entropy-star. However, usually the best partition minimizing the entropy-star is a crisp partition, which does not interest us in this case. To avoid this kind of limitation, we introduce the notion of *minimal spread degree*. This measure is the lower distance allowed between the kernels of two neighboring membership functions in the fuzzy partition of the universe (Figure 8.3). Another method would be to adjust the membership functions by means of genetic algorithms.

8.2.2. Case Where No Expert Knowledge Is Available

In some particular cases, there is no available knowledge from any expert of the domain we want to learn about. In other cases, we have no knowledge about a fuzzy partition of the universe X_j of an attribute A_j. Some existing methods adapt the ID3 algorithm to take into account the problem of such training sets of data. One possible way of improvement lies into the integration of fuzzy notions in order to smooth the boundaries found during the discretization stage when classifying a new example [8], [13], [18]. However, this kind of fuzzification can be enhanced by another type of discretization. We propose to use again the notion of fuzzy entropy in this kind of problem. To achieve this purpose, we introduce techniques derived from *mathematical morphology* [19], [20] to find a fuzzy partition on the universe of A_j. We formalize these techniques using

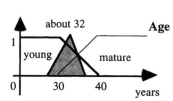

Figure 8.2 Example for the satisfiability degree.

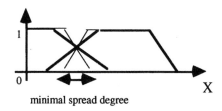

Figure 8.3 Minimal spread degree.

the formal language theory [21], [22] in order to respect the particular structures of our data. Such work, relating the formal language theory and pattern recognition techniques can be found in [23]. Our algorithm allows to find a fuzzy partition of X_j with respect to the distribution of the classes $c_1, c_2, \ldots, c_k$ on X_j in E. This will make possible the use of the fuzzy entropy to sort the attributes. In this chapter, we restrict ourselves to the case of crisp classes (nonfuzzy classes). In the following, we present our method to transform the universe of values of an attribute into fuzzy partitions. For more details, the reader should refer to [24] where all the algorithms are described.

In order to induce a fuzzy partition on the universe of the training data, we use operators of the mathematical morphology: *erosion, dilatation, closure, opening,* and *filter* [19]. Basically, the training set is considered as a word on the alphabet of the classes, each class is viewed as a letter of this alphabet. The two basic operators (*erosion* and *dilatation*) are represented as rewriting systems upon this alphabet, with a particular letter as structuring element. The *erosion* eliminates the very short sequences of letters in a word, the *dilatation* enables to merge two sequences of the same letter separated by a short sequence of different letters. The operators *closure* and *opening* are combinations of erosion and dilatation. A *filter* is n closures followed by n dilatations ($n > 0$). With these techniques, we are able to extract a significative *sequence* from the data (Figure 8.4). Such a sequence is a set of successive letters in the word induced by the training set. Each of these sequences is related to an interval of X_j. The lower boundary of this interval is the value of the attribute corresponding to the first letter of the sequence, and the higher boundary is the value corresponding to the last letter of the sequence. In order to generalize a fuzzy partition from the data in training set E to the whole universe X_j of the attribute A_j, we expand the extreme interval until the limits of the universe. When we apply a filter upon a training set considered as a word, we are able to eradicate uncertain sequences of classes in this word. The size of the sequences we want to keep determines the number of applied filters. Then, we have a word with large sequences. Let r be the number of fuzzy modalities we want for the attribute. We select the r largest sequences containing one class, for instance $[S_1^{min}, S_1^{max}]$ and

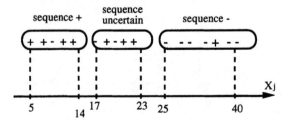

Figure 8.4 Sequences upon a training set with classes + and −.

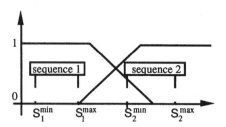

Figure 8.5 Induced fuzzy partition.

$[S_2^{min}, S_2^{max}]$ when $r = 2$. In the case where we cannot find r such sequences, we can either reduce the number of applied filters or select fewer sequences. We infer a fuzzy partition upon the universe of data with these r sequences: the considered intervals define the kernel of each fuzzy modality (Figure 8.5).

For instance, with the sequences given in Figure 8.4, we obtain the following intervals: $[5, 14], [17, 23]$, and $[25, 40]$. Thus, $[5, 14]$ becomes $[0, 14]$ and $[25, 40]$ becomes $[25, + \infty]$. Within such intervals, *most* examples belong to the same class c_i (for instance, in the example $c_i = +$ or $c_i = -$). We say that the class of this sequence is c_i. Some sequences, related to an interval where the classes of the data are highly mixed, are called *uncertain*. Therefore, we infer the partition given by $S_1^{min} = 0, S_1^{max} = 14, S_2^{min} = 25$ and $S_2^{max} = + \infty$.

8.2.3. Construction of Decision Trees

Now we have the elements to use an extended version of the ID3 algorithm, devoted to the case of numerical-symbolic data. This means that we build a decision tree with the ID3 algorithm but we use the entropy-star measure as a discrimination criterion.

8.3. Fuzzy Classification

When a new example needs to be classified, we have to take into account various kinds of values for the attributes. Given an attribute, the example can have either a numerical value or a symbolic modality. However, numerical values do not appear in the tree and the symbolic modality can differ from the modalities used in the training step. This new modality may come from other experts or be a training modality altered by linguistic modifiers. Therefore, we use the degree of satisfiability to match this new modality with the modalities occurring in the tree. Thus, the tree is used as usual. But, in spite of binary values as result of each test, we obtain a degree of satisfiability for each path of the tree. Finally, the example is associated with a final degree of satisfiability for each class [25].

8.4. Application in the Case of Lack of Expert Knowledge

This application has been implemented in the framework of the Numeric-symbolic Project of the French PRC-GDR of Artificial Intelligence [18]. Many tests have been conducted with the Breiman's waveform data [3]. A waveform is a vector with 21 numeric components. It is built from three basic waveforms. Each case is obtained by the combination of two basic waveforms. This combination defines the class of the case. Here, all attributes are numeric and the class is symbolic. The discretization is an essential step of the construction of the decision tree. Typically, it is difficult to obtain any expert knowledge for this kind of data. We use our method based on mathematical morphology and formal language theory to infer a fuzzy partition over all the attributes. Here, we give the results obtained when searching a fuzzy partition in two fuzzy subsets for the numeric universe of an attribute. We present one of such fuzzy trees (Figure 8.6). Each node is associated with the tested attribute and the medium value between the membership functions obtained in the fuzzy partition inference. This value is only indicative here. In the program, we use the membership functions as described previously for the construction of the tree and for the classification of new cases. At each leaf of the tree, we find the class 1, 2, or 3. Here, we could have more than one class in a leaf because we use a threshold for the entropy-star during the construction of the tree, as previously mentionned. The percentage for each class in a leaf is the frequency of the cases with such class in the terminal training set corresponding to the leaf. We compare this method with a traditional ID3-based method of decision trees con-

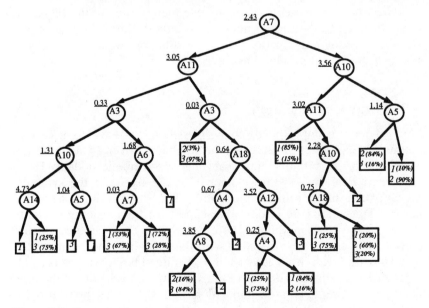

Figure 8.6 Fuzzy decision tree for the waveforms.

struction [3]. It appears that the results are more efficient with the fuzzy decision tree: fuzzy trees are shorter and generalize better for new cases. We use several training sets of 300 examples, and we test the method on a test set of 5000 cases. We obtain fuzzy trees with an average size of 21 paths and an average number of 4.8 nodes on each path. We obtain an average rate of 72.53 percent good classified examples, which can be compared to the average rate of 68.9 percent obtained with a CART-based nonfuzzy method [18].

8.5. Conclusion

In this chapter, we presented two methods to take into account numerical-symbolic data and problems derivated from this kind of values in induction learning systems. The first method works with additive knowledge from an expert that supports the usual training set. This knowledge is given as fuzzy partitions of the universes of the numerical attributes. Moreover, it makes possible to deal with fuzzy decisions. The second method is usable when no particular additive knowledge is available from experts. It is necessary to induce fuzzy partitions of the universes of the attributes to use the given algorithm. These methods are very close. They are based on the same algorithm and use a new measure, the entropy-star, that generalizes the classical Shannon's entropy. They handle particular knowledge in data that appears in a numerical-symbolic formalism. These methods have been tested on data. Some results are given in [10] for the first kind or in [8], [18] for the second one.

This kind of improvement will be enhanced with another type of expert knowledge. In future developments, we want to add more expert knowledge in such systems: knowledge to help building such trees and knowledge to use decision trees to classify objects.

8.6. References

[1] Quinlan, J.R. "Induction of Decision Trees." *Machine Learning*, Vol. 1, No. 1 (1986), pp. 86–106.

[2] ———. C4.5: Program for Machine Learning. San Mateo: Morgan Kaufmann, 1993.

[3] Breiman, L., et al. *Classification and Regression Trees.* New York: Chapman and Hall, 1984.

[4] Picard, C.F. *Graphes et Questionnaires.* France: Gauthier-Villars, 1972.

[5] Fu, K.S. "Sequential Methods in Pattern Recognition and Machine Learning." *Mathematical Science and Engineering*, Vol. 52. 1968.

[6] Maher, P.E., and D. Saint-Clair. "Uncertain Reasoning in an ID3 Machine Learning Framework." *Proceedings, 2nd IEEE International Conference on Fuzzy Systems*, pp. 7–12. 1993.

[7] Umano, M., et al. "Fuzzy Decision Trees by Fuzzy ID3 Algorithm and its Application to Diagnosis Systems." *Proceedings, 3rd IEEE Conference on Fuzzy Systems.* pp. 2113–2118. Orlando, Fla.: 1994.

[8] Marsala, C. Arbres de Decision et Sous-Ensembles Flous. *Rapport 94/21.* LAFORIA-IBP, 1994.

[9] Ramdani, M. "Une Approche Floue pour Traiter les Valeurs Numeriques en Appren-tissage." *Journees Francophones d'Apprentissage et d'Explication des Connaissances.* 1992.

[10] ———. "Systeme d'Induction Formelle a Base de Connaissances Imprecises." These de l'Universite P. et M. Curie. LAFORIA-IBP, 1994.

[11] Janikow, C.Z. "Fuzzy Decision Trees: FIDMV." *Proceedings of the Joint Conference on Information Science,* Pinehurst, N.J.: 1994.

[12] Catlett, J. "On Changing Continuous Attributes into Ordered Discrete Attributes." *Lecture notes in Artificial Intelligence,* Vol. 482 (1991), pp. 164–178.

[13] Jang, J.S.R. "Structure Determination in Fuzzy Modeling: A Fuzzy CART Approach." *Proceedings, 3rd International Conference on Fuzzy Systems.* pp. 480–485. 1994.

[14] Bouchon-Meunier, B., et al. "Towards General Measures of Comparison of Objects." To appear, *Fuzzy Sets and Systems.*

[15] Sanchez, E. "Inverses of Fuzzy Relations: Application to Possibility Distributions and Medical Diagnosis." *Fuzzy Sets and Systems,* Vol. 2, No. 1 (1979), pp. 75–86.

[16] Zadeh, L.A. "Probability Measure of Fuzzy Events." *Journal of Mathematical Analysis and Application,* Vol. 23 (1968), pp. 421–427.

[17] Shannon, C.E., and W. Weaver. *The Mathematical Theory of Communication.* Urbana: University of Illinois Press, 1949.

[18] Bouchon-Meunier, B., et al. "Arbres de Decision et Theorie des Sous-Ensembles Flous." *Actes des 5emes Journees du PRC-GDR d'Intelligence Artificielle.* pp. 50–53. 1995.

[19] Serra, J. *Image Analysis and Mathematical Morphology.* New York: Academic Press, 1982.

[20] Coster, M., and J.L. Chermant. *Precis d'Analyse d'Images.* Presses du CNRS, 1989.

[21] Ginsburg, S. *The Mathematical Theory of Context Free Languages.* New York: McGraw-Hill, 1966.

[22] Autebert, J.M. *Languages Algebriques.* Masson: 1987.

[23] Fu, K.S. "Syntactic Methods in Pattern Recognition." *Mathematics in Science and Engineering,* Vol. 112, 1974.

[24] Marsala, C. "Fuzzy Partition Inference over a Set of Numerical Values." *Rapports 95/22,* LAFORIA-IBP, 1995.

[25] Marsala, C., and R. Ramdani. "Connaissances Expertes Floues et System d'Appren-tissage Descendant." *Rencontres Francophones sur la Logique Floue et ses Applica-tions, LFA '95.* pp. 163–168. Paris: 1995.

9 Extracting Fuzzy Rules from Data for Function Approximation and Pattern Classification

Stephen L. Chiu
Rockwell Science Center

ABSTRACT: Extracting fuzzy rules from data allows relationships in the data to be modeled by if-then rules that are easy to understand, verify, and extend. This chapter presents methods for extracting fuzzy rules for both function approximation and pattern classification. The rule extraction methods are based on estimating clusters in the data; each cluster obtained corresponds to a fuzzy rule that relates a region in the input space to an output region (or, in the case of pattern classification, to an output class). After the number of rules and initial rule parameters are obtained by cluster estimation, the rule parameters are optimized by gradient descent. Applications to a function approximation problem and to a pattern classification problem are also illustrated.

9.1. Introduction

One of the hallmarks of fuzzy logic is that it allows nonlinear input/output relationships to be expressed by a set of qualitative if-then rules. Nonlinear control/decision surfaces, process models, and pattern classifiers may all be expressed in the form of fuzzy rules. Most fuzzy systems are handcrafted by a human expert to capture some desired input/output relationships that the expert has in mind. However, often an expert cannot express his or her knowledge explicitly, and, for many applications, an expert may not even exist. Hence, there is considerable interest in being able to automatically extract fuzzy rules from experimental input/output data. The key motivation for capturing data behavior in the form of fuzzy rules instead of, say, polynomials and neural networks, is that the fuzzy rules are easy to understand, verify, and extend. A system designer can check the automatically extracted rules against intuition, check the rules for completeness, and easily fine-tune or extend the system by editing the rulebase.

This paper presents methods for extracting fuzzy rules from input/output data for both function approximation and pattern classification applications. For function approximation, where the output data correspond to a continuous-valued variable, the extracted rules express continuous-valued relationships (e.g., "if input is small, then output is big"). For pattern classification, where the output data correspond to class assignments, the extracted rules have discrete-valued consequents (e.g., "if input is small, then output is class 1"). In both cases, fuzzy rules provide a powerful framework for capturing and, perhaps more importantly, explaining the input/output data behavior.

The problem of extracting fuzzy rules from data for function approximation has been studied for some time [1]. Several methods for extracting fuzzy rules for function approximation have used data clustering to determine the number of rules and initial rule parameters [2,3,4,5]. Each cluster essentially identifies a region in the data space that contains a sufficient mass of data to support the existence of a fuzzy input/output relationship. Because a rule is generated only where there is a cluster of data, the resultant rules are scattered in the input space rather than placed according to grid-like partitions in the input space. This fundamental feature of clustering-based rule extraction methods help avoid combinatorial explosion of rules with increasing dimension of the input space. Also, because the clustering step provides good initial rule parameter values, the subsequent rule parameter optimization process usually converges quickly and to a good solution.

Early works on fuzzy pattern classification were focused not so much on rule extraction but on extending classical, crisp clustering algorithms by allowing an object to have partial membership in multiple clusters/classes [6,7,8,9]. Recently, with increasing awareness of the advantages of representing a classifier in the form of fuzzy rules, attention has turned to rule extraction. Extracting fuzzy rules for pattern classification can be viewed as the problem of partitioning the input space into appropriate fuzzy cells that separate the classes. Methods for extracting fuzzy rules for pattern classification often incorporate neural network concepts for adaptive learning. For example, an extension of Kohonen's Self-Organizing Map method was used in [10] to learn the membership function centers; the backpropagation technique was used in [11] to optimize membership functions that define grid-like input partitions as well as optimize parameterized fuzzy operators. These methods typically require the user to prespecify the structure of the rulebase (i.e., number of rules per class [10] or number of membership functions per input feature [11]) along with initial values for the adjustable parameters. A method that can quickly determine the rulebase structure and good initial membership functions in one pass was proposed in [12]. This method employs nested fuzzy cells, which results in nested rules such as "if input is in region A and not in region A', then output is class 1," where region A' is an exception region nested *inside* region A; other rules would handle region A', which may contain its own nested exception regions. Rule extraction involves generating deeper nested rules for increasingly smaller subregions until all errors are eliminated. The nested fuzzy cell method is fast and produces compact rules that do not grow with the dimension of the data space; however, it is sensitive to noisy data.

Our work has been guided by the objective of developing a practical, easy-to-use software for extracting fuzzy rules from data for real-world, high-dimensional problems. Efficiency and robustness of the algorithm in dealing with high-dimensional and noisy data are primary factors driving our approach. Simplicity of the method from a user's perspective is also important (i.e., to minimize the number of parameters the user must specify and minimize the need for trial and error). A clustering method called *subtractive clustering* [5] forms the basis of our approach. Subtractive clustering is a fast and robust method for estimating the number and location of cluster centers present in a collection of data points. Initial fuzzy rules with rough estimates of membership functions are obtained from the cluster centers; the membership functions and other rule parameters are then optimized with respect to some output error criterion. This approach can be applied to extract rules for both function approximation and pattern classification, with some small differences in the detailed methods for these two types of applications.

In the following sections, we describe the rule extraction methods in detail. We also illustrate their use in a function approximation example and in a pattern classification example.

9.2. Cluster Estimation

Clustering of numerical data forms the basis of many modelling and pattern classification algorithms. The purpose of clustering is to find natural groupings of data in a large data set, thus revealing patterns in the data that can provide a concise representation of the data behavior. Clustering algorithms typically require the user to prespecify the number of cluster centers and their initial locations; the locations of the cluster centers are then adapted in a way such that the cluster centers can better represent a set of archetypical data points covering the range of data behavior. The Fuzzy C-Means algorithm [13] and Kohonen's Self-Organizing Map [14] method are well-known examples of such clustering algorithms. For these algorithms, the quality of the solution, like that of most nonlinear optimization problems, depends strongly on the choice of initial values (i.e., the number of cluster centers and their initial locations).

Yager and Filev [4] proposed a simple and effective algorithm, called the mountain method, for estimating the number and initial location of cluster centers. Their method is based on gridding the data space and computing a potential value for each grid point based on its distances to the actual data points; a grid point with many data points nearby will have a high potential value. The grid point with the highest potential value is chosen as the first cluster center. The key idea in their method is that once the first cluster center is chosen, the potential of all grid points is reduced according to their distance from the cluster center. Grid points near the first cluster center will have greatly reduced potential. The next cluster center is then placed at the grid point with the highest remaining potential value. This procedure of acquiring a new cluster center and reducing the potential of surrounding grid points repeats until the potential of all grid points falls below a threshold. Although this method is simple and effective, the computation grows exponentially with the dimension of the problem. For example, a clustering problem with 4 variables and each dimension having a resolution of 10 grid lines would result in 10^4 grid points that must be evaluated.

Chiu [5] proposed an extension of Yager and Filev's mountain method, called subtractive clustering, in which each data point, not a grid point, is considered as a potential cluster center. Using this method, the number of effective "grid points" to be evaluated is simply equal to the number of data points, independent of the dimension of the problem. Another advantage of this method is that it eliminates the need to specify a grid resolution, in which trade-offs between accuracy and computational complexity must be considered. The subtractive clustering method also extends the mountain method's criterion for accepting and rejecting cluster centers.

The subtractive clustering method works as follows. Consider a collection of n data points $\{x_1, x_2, \ldots, x_n\}$ in an M dimensional space. Without loss of generality, we assume that the data points have been normalized in each dimension so that they are bounded by a unit hypercube. We consider each data point as a potential cluster center and define a measure of the potential of data point x_i as:

$$P_i = \sum_{j=1}^{n} e^{-\alpha \| x_i - x_j \|^2} \qquad (1)$$

where

$$\alpha = 4/r_a^2, \qquad (2)$$

$\|.\|$ denotes the Euclidean distance, and r_a is a positive constant. Thus, the measure of the potential for a data point is a function of its distances to all other data points. A data point with many neighboring data points will have a high potential value. The constant r_a is effectively the radius defining a neighborhood; data points outside this radius have little influence on the potential.

After the potential of every data point has been computed, we select the data point with the highest potential as the first cluster center. Let x_1^* be the location of the first cluster center and P_1^* be its potential value. We then revise the potential of each data point x_i by the formula:

$$P_i \Leftarrow P_i - P_1^* e^{-\beta \| x_i - x_1^* \|^2} \tag{3}$$

where

$$\beta = 4/r_b^2$$

and r_b is a positive constant. Thus, we subtract an amount of potential from each data point as a function of its distance from the first cluster center. The data points near the first cluster center will have greatly reduced potential, and therefore will unlikely be selected as the next cluster center. The constant r_b is effectively the radius defining the neighborhood that will have measurable reductions in potential. To avoid obtaining closely spaced cluster centers, we set r_b to be somewhat greater than r_a; a good choice is $r_b = 1.25\, r_a$.

When the potential of all data points has been revised according to equation 3, we select the data point with the highest remaining potential as the second cluster center. We then further reduce the potential of each data point according to their distance to the second cluster center. In general, after the k'th cluster center has been obtained, the potential of each data point is revised by the formula:

$$P_i \Leftarrow P_i - P_k^* e^{-\beta \| x_i - x_k^* \|^2}$$

where x_k^* is the location of the k'th cluster center and P_k^* is its potential value.

The process of acquiring new cluster center and revising potentials repeats until the remaining potential of all data points falls below some fraction of the potential of the first cluster center P^*_1. In addition to this criterion for ending the clustering process are criteria for accepting and rejecting cluster centers that help avoid marginal cluster centers. The following criteria are used:

if $P_k^* > \bar{\varepsilon}\, P_1^*$

> Accept x_k^* as a cluster center and continue.

else if $P_k^* < \underline{\varepsilon}\, P_1^*$

> Reject x_k^* and end the clustering process.

else

> Let d_{min} = shortest of the distances between
>
> x_k^* and all previously found cluster centers.

if $\dfrac{d_{min}}{r_a} + \dfrac{P_k^*}{P_1^*} \geq 1$

> Accept x_k^* as a cluster center and continue.

else

> Reject x_k^* and set the potential at x_k^* to 0.
>
> Do not revise the potential of other data points.
>
> Select the data point with the next highest
>
> potential as the new x_k^* and re-test.

    end if

end if

Here $\bar{\varepsilon}$ specifies a threshold for the potential above which we will definitely accept the data point as a cluster center; ε specifies a threshold below which we will definitely reject the data point. Good default values are $\bar{\varepsilon} = 0.5$ and $\varepsilon = 0.15$. If the potential falls in the gray region, we check if the data point offers a good trade-off between having a sufficient potential and being sufficiently far from existing cluster centers.

9.3. Extracting Rules for Function Approximation

For function approximation applications, clustering is performed in the combined input/output space; that is, each data point x_i is a vector that contains both input and output values. Each cluster center found is in essence a prototypical data point that exemplifies a characteristic input/output behavior of the system.

Consider a set of m cluster centers $\{x_1^*, x_2^*, \cdots, x_m^*\}$ found in an M dimensional space. Let the first N dimensions correspond to input variables and the last M-N dimensions correspond to output variables. We decompose each vector x_i^* into two component vectors y_i^* and z_i^*, where y_i^* contains the first N elements of x_i^* (i.e., the coordinates of the cluster center in input space) and z_i^* contains the last M-N elements (i.e., the coordinates of the cluster center in output space).

We consider each cluster center x_i^* as a fuzzy rule that describes the system behavior. Intuitively, each cluster center represents the rule:

Rule i: If {input is near y_i^*} then output is near z_i^*.

Given an input vector y, the degree of fulfillment of rule i is defined as:

$$\mu_i = e^{-\alpha \| y - y_i^* \|^2} \tag{4}$$

where α is the constant defined by equation 2. We compute the resultant output vector z via:

$$z = \left[\sum_{i=1}^{m} \mu_i z_i^* \right] \div \left[\sum_{i=1}^{m} \mu_i \right]. \tag{5}$$

We can view this computational model in terms of a fuzzy inference system employing traditional fuzzy if-then rules. Each rule has the following form:

if Y_1 is A_{i1} & Y_2 is A_{i2} & ... then Z_1 is B_{i1} & Z_2 is B_{i2} ...

where Y_j is the j'th input variable and Z_j is the j'th output variable; A_{ij} is an exponential membership function in the i'th rule associated with the j'th input, and B_{ij} is a membership function in the i'th rule associated with the j'th output. For the i'th rule, which is represented by cluster center x_i^*, A_{ij} is given by:

$$A_{ij}(Y_j) = \exp\left\{-\frac{1}{2}\left(\frac{Y_j - y_{ij}^*}{\sigma_{ij}}\right)^2\right\} \tag{6}$$

and B_{ij} can be any symmetric membership function centered around z_{ij}^*, where y_{ij}^* is the j'th element of y_i^*, z_{ij}^* is the j'th element of z_i^*, and $\sigma_{ij}^2 = 1/(2\alpha)$. Our computational scheme is equivalent to an inference method that uses multiplication as the AND operator, weights the consequent of each rule by the rule's degree of fulfillment, and computes the final output value as a weighted average of all the consequents.

There are several approaches to optimize the rules. One approach is to apply a gradient descent method to optimize the parameters z_{ij}^*, y_{ij}^*, and σ_{ij} in equations 5 and 6 to reduce the root-mean-square (RMS) output error with respect to the training data. Gradient descent formulas to perform this optimization can be found in [15]. This is the approach adopted by Yager and Filev [4] to optimize the initial rules obtained from the mountain method.

Another approach is to let the consequent parameter z_{ij}^* be a linear function of the input variables, instead of a simple constant. That is, we let:

$$z_{ij}^* = G_{ij}\, y + h_{ij}$$

where G_{ij} is an N-element vector of coefficients and h_{ij} is a scalar constant. The if-then rules then become the Takagi-Sugeno type. As shown by Takagi and Sugeno [1], given a set of rules with fixed premise membership functions, optimizing G_{ij} and h_{ij} in all consequent equations is a simple linear least-squares estimation problem. Chiu [5] adopted this approach to optimize the rules obtained from the subtractive clustering method; optimizing only the coefficients in the consequent equations allows a significant degree of model optimization to be performed without adding much computational complexity.

A third approach also involves using the Takagi-Sugeno rule format, but it combines optimizing the premise membership functions by gradient descent with optimizing the consequent equations by linear least squares estimation. This is the ANFIS (Adaptive Network-Based Fuzzy Inference System) methodology developed by Jang [16]. When the ANFIS approach is used to optimize the same rules, the resultant model is generally more accurate than that obtained from either of the two preceding approaches. This is the preferred approach that we adopt here.

Although the number of clusters (or rules) is automatically determined by our method, we should note that the user-specified parameter

r_a (i.e., the radius of influence of a cluster center) strongly affects the number of clusters that will be generated. A large r_a generally results in fewer clusters and hence a coarser model, while a small r_a can produce excessive number of clusters and a model that does not generalize well (i.e., by overfitting the training data). Therefore, we may regard r_a as an approximate specification of the desired resolution of the model, which can be adjusted based on the resultant complexity and generalization ability of the model.

9.4. Extracting Rules for Pattern Classification

For pattern classification applications, we first separate the data into groups according to their respective classes; subtractive clustering is then applied to the input space of each group of data individually to extract the rules for identifying each class of data.

The clusters found in the data of a given group identify regions in the input space that map into the associated class. Hence, we can translate each cluster center into a fuzzy rule for identifying the class. For example, suppose subtractive clustering was applied to the group of data for class c1 and cluster center x_i^* was found, then this cluster center provides the rule:

Rule i: If {input is near x_i^*} then class is c1.

Given an input vector x, the degree of fulfillment of rule i is defined as:

$$\mu_i = e^{-\alpha \| x - x_i^* \|^2} \tag{7}$$

where α is the constant defined by equation 2. We can also write this rule in the more familiar form:

Rule i: If X_1 is A_{i1} & X_2 is A_{i2} & ... then class is c1.

where X_j is the j'th input variable and A_{ij} is the membership function in the i'th rule associated with the j'th input. The membership function A_{ij} is given by:

$$A_{ij}(X_j) = \exp\left\{-\frac{1}{2}\left(\frac{X_j - x_{ij}^*}{\sigma_{ij}}\right)^2\right\} \tag{8}$$

where x_{ij}^* is the j'th element of x_i^*, and $\sigma_{ij}^2 = 1/(2\alpha)$. The degree of fulfillment of each rule is computed by using multiplication as the AND operator, and, because the fuzzy system performs classification, we simply select the consequent of the rule with the highest degree of fulfillment to be the output of the fuzzy system. It would be erroneous to interpolate the output value from the different rule consequents because the class values usually have no numerical meaning; for example, a class 2 object is not necessarily "between" class 1 and class 3 in any sense.

After the initial rules have been obtained by subtractive clustering, we use gradient descent to tune the individual x^*_{ij} and σ_{ij} parameters in the membership functions (cf. equation 8) to minimize a classification error measure.

We define the following classification error measure for a data sample x that belongs to some class c:

$$E = \frac{1}{2}(1 - \mu_{c,\max}(x) + \mu_{\neg c,\max}(x))^2 \qquad (9)$$

where $\mu_{c,\max}(x)$ is the highest degree of fulfillment among all rules that assign x to class c, and $\mu_{\neg c,\max}(x)$ is the highest degree of fulfillment among all rules that do not assign x to class c. Note that this error measure is zero only if a rule that would correctly classify the sample has a degree of fulfillment of 1 and all rules that would misclassify the sample have a degree of fulfillment of 0. Gradient descent formulas to optimize the membership function parameters with respect to this error measure can be found in [17]. An important feature of this optimization process is that only the rules responsible for $\mu_{c,\max}$ and $\mu_{\neg c,\max}$ are updated, since all other rules do not affect the error measure. This gradient descent algorithm can be viewed as a type of competitive learning algorithm: a winner in the "good rule" category is reinforced and a winner in the "bad rule" category is punished. Because only two rules are updated each time, the algorithm is highly efficient.

We have found that a classifier can achieve higher accuracy and the resultant classification rules are easier to understand if the membership functions are allowed to be "two-sided" Gaussian functions. A two-sided Gaussian function may have a flat plateau region and different standard deviations on the left and right sides (see Figure 9.1). The two-sided Gaussian function is better suited than the standard Gaussian function for capturing the relations in pattern classification data.

For two-sided Gaussian functions, there are four adjustable parameters per membership function: the left and right side peak positions (left

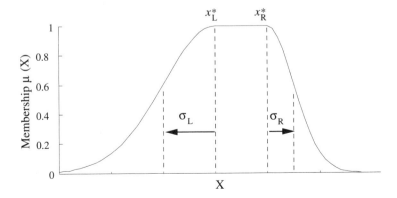

Figure 9.1   A "two-sided" Gaussian function.

and right x^*_{ij}), and the left and right side standard deviations (left and right σ_{ij}). The gradient descent equations derived for Standard Gaussian functions are mathematically valid for two-sided Gaussian functions when the input value X_j is outside the plateau region, but are no longer valid when X_j is inside the plateau region because the error gradient there is zero. A method for handling this special situation is also presented in [17].

9.5. Application Examples

To illustrate the rule extraction methods, we now apply them to a function approximation problem and to a pattern classification problem.

9.5.1. Automobile Trip Prediction

We consider a function approximation problem in which we wish to predict the number of automobile trips generated from an area based on the area's demographics. The data used for rule extraction consists of demographic and trip data for 100 traffic analysis zones in New Castle County, Delaware. The original data set provided in [18] contains five input variables: population, number of dwelling units, number of car ownerships, median household income, and total employment. However, to better graphically illustrate the rule extraction method, here we consider only two input variables: car ownership and employment. A discussion on how to select the most important input variables is beyond the scope of this chapter; the interested reader is referred to [19].

Of the 100 data points, we randomly selected 75 points as training data for generating the rules and 25 points as checking data for validating the rules. Using cluster radius $r_a = 0.5$, two cluster centers were found in the training data. Recall that the cluster radius is expressed relative to the normalized data space, hence $r_a = 0.5$ corresponds to half the width of the data space. The training data and the cluster centers are shown in Figure 9.2, where the cluster centers are marked by Xs. The two cluster centers were translated into two rules of the Takagi-Sugeno type, with initial premise membership functions obtained from the cluster center positions via equation 6. The ANFIS approach was then applied to optimize the model; that is, the rules' premise membership functions were optimized by gradient descent while the consequent equations were optimized by linear least squares estimation. The optimization process stops when the improvement in RMS error after a pass through the data becomes less than 0.1 percent of the previous RMS error. The resultant rules are shown in Figure 9.3. A comparison of the actual output versus the output predicted by the fuzzy model is shown in Figure 9.4. The fuzzy model has an RMS output error of 0.582 with respect to the training data and an error of 0.586 with respect to the checking data, indicating the model generalizes well. The computation time for generating this model was two seconds on a Macintosh computer with 68040 processor running at 25 MHz.

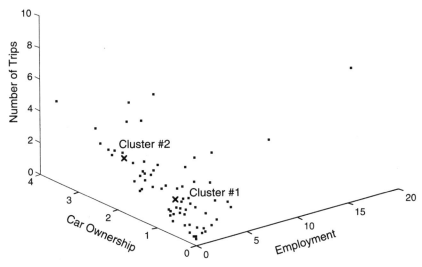

Figure 9.2 Training data for the automobile trip prediction problem; all numbers are expressed in units of a thousand. The two cluster centers found are marked by Xs.

9.5.2. Iris Classification

We now consider a classical benchmark problem in pattern classification—Fisher's iris flower data [20]. The iris data consists of a set of 150 data samples that maps four input feature values (sepal length, sepal width, petal length, petal width) into one of three species of iris flower. There are 50 samples for each species. We used 120 samples as training data (40 samples of each species) and 30 samples as checking data (10 samples of each species). To simplify the illustration, here we consider only two input variables: petal width and petal length (using an analysis method similar to that described in [19], we have determined the petal width and petal length to be the most important variables).

The training data were normalized and then separated into three groups according to their species. Using a cluster radius of 0.5, one clus-

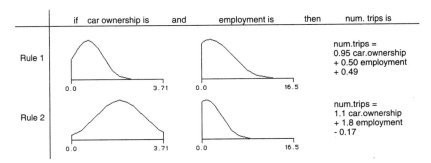

Figure 9.3 Rules extracted for the trip prediction model.

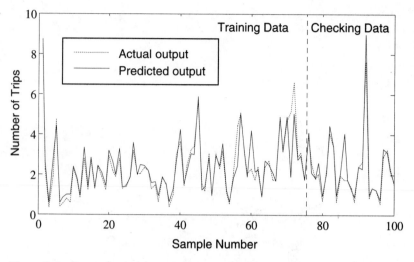

Figure 9.4 Comparison of actual output values with the predicted output values for the trip prediction model. The number of trips are expressed in units of a thousand.

ter was found in each group of data, resulting in one rule for classifying each species. The rules' membership functions were allowed to be two-sided Gaussians and were optimized by gradient descent. The optimization process stops when the improvement in the error measure after a pass through the data becomes less than 0.1 percent of the previous error measure (the error measure is defined as the average of the individual error measures given by equation 9). The resultant rules are shown in Figure 9.5. The fuzzy classifier misclassified three samples out of 120 samples in the training data and classified all samples correctly in the checking data. The computation time for generating this classifier was six seconds on the Macintosh computer.

Looking at the rules in Figure 9.5, the advantages of capturing data behavior in the form of fuzzy rules become clear. We can see that flowers in species 1 generally have small petals (short petal width and short petal length); flowers in species 2 generally have medium petals; and flowers in species 3 generally have large petals. Furthermore, we see that the petal shapes generally follow the same proportion; that is, there are no strange combinations such as a short petal width with a long petal length. Our ability to easily interpret fuzzy rules makes fuzzy rule-based models and classifiers easy to understand and debug.

9.6. Conclusion

We presented efficient methods for extracting fuzzy rules from data based on cluster estimation. Rules can be generated to solve both function approximation and pattern classification problems. These methods have been successfully applied to extract fuzzy rules for a variety of

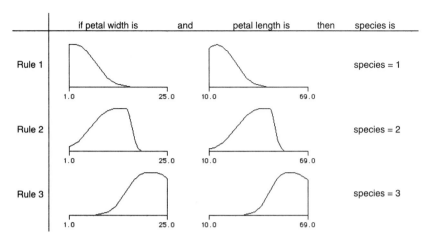

Figure 9.5   Rules extracted for the iris classifier.

applications, including the modelling of human operators, software quality prediction, selecting the best robot arm posture for performing a task, numeric character recognition [17], blood cell classification, underwater mine detection, and power generator leakage detection. Where comparison with neural network is available, the performance of the fuzzy rule-based model or classifier has been comparable to those based on neural network [5, 17]. However, our rule extraction method is generally more efficient and easier to use than neural network, typically producing good results without any trial and error. In addition, fuzzy rule-based models and classifiers are easy to understand, verify, and extend.

9.7. References

[1] Takagi, T., and M. Sugeno. "Fuzzy Identification of Systems and its Application to Modeling and Control." *IEEE Transactions on Systems, Man, and Cybernetics,* Vol. 15 (1985), pp. 116–132.

[2] Sugeno, M, and T. Yasukawa. "A Fuzzy Logic-based Approach to Qualitative Modeling." *IEEE Transactions on Fuzzy Systems,* Vol. 1 (1993), pp. 7–31.

[3] Wang, L.X. "Traning of Fuzzy Logic Systems using Nearest Neighborhood Clustering." *Proceedings; 2nd IEEE International Conference on Fuzzy Systems.* pp. 13–17. San Francisco, Calif.: 1993.

[4] Yager, R., and D. Filev. "Generation of Fuzzy Rules by Mountain Clustering." *Journal of Intelligent and Fuzzy Systems,* Vol. 2 (1994), 209–219.

[5] Chiu, S. "Fuzzy Model Identification based on Cluster Estimation." *Journal of Intelligent and Fuzzy Systems,* Vol. 2 (1994), pp. 267–278.

[6] Ruspini, E.H. "Numerical Methods for Fuzzy Clustering." *Information Science,* Vol. 2 (1970), pp. 319–350.

[7] Dunn, J. "A Fuzzy Relative of the ISODATA Process and its Use in Detecting Compact, Well-Separated Clusters." *Journal of Cybernetics,* Vol. 3 (1974), pp. 32–57.

[8] Bezdek, J. "Cluster Validity with Fuzzy Sets." *Journal of Cybernetics,* Vol. 3 (1974), pp. 58–71.

[9] Keller, J., et al. "A Fuzzy k-nearest Neighbor Algorithm." *IEEE Transactions on Systems, Man, and Cybernetics*, Vol. 15 (1985), pp. 580–585.

[10] Chung, F.L., and T. Lee. "A Fuzzy Learning Method for Membership Function Estimation and Pattern Classification." *Proceedings, 3rd International Conference on Fuzzy Systems.* pp. 426–431. Orlando, Fla.: 1994.

[11] Sun, C.T., and J.S.R. Jang. "A Neuro-Fuzzy Classifier and its Applications." *Proceedings, 2nd IEEE International Conference on Fuzzy Systems.* pp. 94–98. San Francisco, Calif.: 1993.

[12] Abe, S., and M.S. Lan. "A Classifier using Fuzzy Rules Extracted Directly from Numerical Data." *Proceedings, 2nd IEEE International Conference on Fuzzy Systems.* pp. 1191–1198. San Francisco, Calif.: 1993.

[13] Bezdek, J. *Pattern Recognition with Fuzzy Objective Function Algorithms.* New York: Plenum Press, 1981.

[14] Kohonen, T. "The Self-Organizing Map." *Proceedings of IEEE*, Vol. 78 (1990) pp. 1464–1480.

[15] Wang, L.X., and J.M. Mendel. "Back-Propagation Fuzzy System as Nonlinear Dynamic System Identifiers." *Proceedings, 1st International Conference on Fuzzy Systems.* pp. 1409–1418. San Diego, Calif.: 1992.

[16] Jang, J.S.R. "ANFIS: Adaptive Network-based Fuzzy Inference System." *IEEE Transactions on Systems, Man, and Cybernetics*, Vol. 23 (1993), pp. 665–685.

[17] Chiu, S. "Extracting Fuzzy Rules for Pattern Classification by Cluster Estimation." *Proceedings, 6th International Fuzzy Systems Association Congress*, Vol. 2, pp. 273–276. Sao Paulo, Brazil: July, 1995.

[18] Kikuchi, S., et al. "Estimation of Trip Generation using the Fuzzy Regression Method." *Proceedings, 1994 Annual Meeting of Transportation Research Board.* Washington, D.C.: January, 1994.

[19] Chiu, S. "Selecting input Variables for Fuzzy Models." To appear, *Journal of Intelligent & Fuzzy Systems*, 1996.

[20] Fisher, R.A. "The Use of Multiple Measurements in Taxonomic Problems." *Annals of Eugenics*, Vol. 7 (1936), pp. 179–188.

10 Probabilistic Validation of Fuzzy Rules with Nonfuzzy Conclusions

Francesco Bergadano
Universitá di Torino

Vincenzo Cutello
Universitá di Catania

ABSTRACT: We discuss a model for learning (trapezoidal) fuzzy membership functions from examples. Once a system of classification rules containing fuzzy sets is structurally given by an expert along with positive and negative examples, we will see how one can build (possibly in polynomial time) the membership functions for the sets occurring in the classification system. The learned membership functions can then be used to classify further examples. The obtained classification system is always approximately correct with high probability. As a consequence, we can use these results to probabilistically validate a given system of fuzzy rules by providing a particular answer to the classical question: "Who gave you the membership functions?"

10.1. Introduction and Preliminaries

Very often in life we are faced with the problem of making a decision based on some imprecise knowledge. Typical cases of this kind occur in the medical field. In an emergency room of a hospital, doctors have to decide (fast) whether to admit a patient to the hospital (see [7]). Their knowledge is what they have learned in medical school (enriched by the experience gained at work) and the symptoms they observe in the patient. For instance, they may see that the patient has a low fever, is sweating a lot, and feels a small pain in the chest. By introducing ad hoc membership functions, one can use standard fuzzy inference mechanisms to come up with a value of admissibility for the patient. Then based on this value (typically introducing a security threshold parameter) one can decide whether to admit the patient or not. However, since in this case we are dealing with human lives, we need to be reasonably sure that the used membership functions are well-tuned, and in turn that the system of fuzzy rules with a nonfuzzy conclusion we are working with has been validated (see [6]). How can we do that?

The theoretical framework for tuning membership functions inside a nonfuzzy classification system that we propose (see [1,2,3]) gives a possible answer to the question. In particular, it will give us the mathematical means to claim that the classification system is *probably, approximately correct* (in the sense of Valiant [12]); that is to say:

- the learned classification system is approximately correct with high probability, and
- the induction learning procedure is polynomial.

For performance-sensitive applications similar to the one described, such strong requirements are appropriate. However, only very simple classifiers are learnable in this sense [8,10,11]. We follow a more practical and useful approach. We assume that a system of linguistic classification rules is given by an expert. However, the expert does not provide any definition of the fuzzy sets being used. Common sense tells us that a medical student may be told that a patient with high fever and strong abdominal pain must be admitted to the hospital, though certainly he/she is not told that a body temperature of 38 centigrades has a degree of membership .4 to the fuzzy set high fever. Therefore, we require the induction system to learn the membership functions of the fuzzy predicates occurring in that system by observing positive and negative examples.

- We will show when and how this can be done in polynomial time.
- We notice in particular that for the classification systems we will consider the membership functions produced by the learning algorithm will always be trapezoidal.

10.2. Valiant's Model of Probabilistic Learning

Let us now briefly describe the probabilistic learning paradigm introduced by Valient in [12,10]. Let C be a class of concepts over a universe $\mathcal{U}$. Every element $C \in C$ can therefore be "seen" either as a subset of $\mathcal{U}$ or equivalently as a unary predicate (the *indicator function I_C of C*) defined over the universe. For sake of simplicity, in what follows we will use C to denote the set C and the indicator function I_C.

Let D be any probability distribution on $\mathcal{U}$. Given a concept $C \in \mathcal{C}$, for every $\epsilon > 0$ a concept C_1 is an ϵ-approximation (with respect to D) of C if

$$\sum_{C(x) \neq C_1(x)} D(x) < \epsilon.$$

Definition 1: Given a concept class $\mathcal{C}$ over a universe $\mathcal{U}$, we say that the class $\mathcal{C}$ is probably approximately correct (PAC) learnable if and only if there exists an algorithm $\mathcal{A}$ such that for every probability distribution D on $\mathcal{U}$, every $C \in \mathcal{C}$, every $\epsilon > 0$ (accuracy parameter), $\delta > 0$ (confidence parameter) with probability at least $1 - \delta$, the algorithm $\mathcal{A}$ produces an ϵ-approximation of C in time polynomial on $1/\epsilon$, $1/\delta$ and the size of C.

From the definition we have that a concept class is PAC-learnable if and only if there exists an algorithm $\mathcal{A}$ such that

- using $\mathcal{D}$ draws a number of examples that is bounded by some polynomial function in $1/\epsilon$, $1/\delta$ and the length of the concept (i.e. the *sample complexity* of the concept class is polynomial); and

- in polynomial time is able to produce a concept that is consistent with the set of examples seen.

If we concentrate on the sample complexity, very intuitive considerations let us conclude that a sufficient number of examples that we need to draw (see [8,10] for more details) is bounded by:

$$n \geq \frac{1}{\epsilon}(\ln |C| + \ln \frac{1}{\delta})$$

We have therefore found a bound on the sample complexity that depends on the cardinality of the concept class C.

Let us now introduce a measure of complexity for the concept class $\mathcal{C}$ defined over a nonempty universe $\mathcal{U}$, which will provide us with another and more useful (for our purposes) bound on the sample complexity.

Definition 2: Let $U \subseteq S \subseteq \mathcal{U}$. We say that U is selected by C in S if and only if there exists $C \in \mathcal{C}$ such that

$$U = C \cap S.$$

Definition 3: Let $S \subseteq \mathcal{U}$. We say that S is shattered by $\mathcal{C}$ if and only if for all $U \subseteq S$, U is selected by C in S.

We then define the Vapnik-Chervonenkis (VC) dimension of C as:

$$vc(C) = \max\{|S| : S \text{ is shattered by } C\}.$$

The Vapnik-Chervonenkis (VC) dimension was introduced in [13], and as proven in [5], the sample complexity—the number of examples needed by a consistent PAC-learning algorithm for the concept class C—is bounded by:

$$\max\left(\frac{4}{\epsilon} \ln \frac{2}{\delta}, \frac{8d}{\epsilon} \ln \frac{13}{\epsilon}\right),$$

where $d = vc(C)$.

10.3. Formalizing Our Learning Problem

Let C be a given concept class over a universe $\mathcal{U}$. For the time being, we will suppose that $\mathcal{U} \subseteq \mathcal{R}^k$ for some integer k. Therefore, each element of $\mathcal{U}$ is a k-tuple of real numbers whose intended meaning is to characterize specific subparts of the system under study.

Let $C \in \mathcal{C}$ and suppose a system S_m of classification rules for C is given in the following form:

$$Q_1^1(p_{Q_1^1}(x)) \wedge \ldots \wedge Q_{n_1}^1 (p_{Q_{n_1}^1} (x)) \to C(x)$$

$$\cdots \qquad \cdots \qquad\qquad \cdots \qquad\qquad (1)$$

$$Q_1^m(p_{Q_1^m}(x)) \wedge \ldots \wedge Q_{n_m}^m (p_{Q_{n_m}^m} (x)) \to C(x)$$

where

- the predicates Q_i^j are taken from a set $\mathcal{P} = \{Q_1, \cdots, Q_n\}$ of given unary predicates;
- for all Q_j, p_{Q_j} is a projection function that returns the parameter which is of significance for Q_j.
- for every component k, the predicates $Q_1, \cdots, Q_{m_k}$ corresponding to k (i.e. such that p_{Q_i} returns the value of the k-th component) define a linguistic order.

Notice that:

- it is possible that the same predicate occurs in different rules;
- the unknown membership functions we are trying to learn are *convex* (see [9], p. 17). Thus, they do not have local maxima. Moreover, for what concerns the linguistic order, the convexity hypothesis implies that for every predicate Q the set $\{x|Q(x) > \alpha\}$ is an interval of the real line for every α. So, we can suppose that if $j > i$ then for every $0 \le \alpha \le 1$ we have $\{x|Q_i(x) > \alpha\} < \{x|Q_j(x) > \alpha\}$, where $<$ is the standard order relation on real intervals:

$$[a, b] < [c, d] \text{ iff } a \le c \text{ and } b \le d.$$

The intuitive meaning of the rule system is that a given individual x is classified as a positive example for the concept C if one or more of the rule antecedents are *true* for *x*. Therefore we can say that $x \in \mathcal{U}$ is a member of the concept *C;* that is, *C(x)* is true if and only if

$$\tau\left(\bigvee_{j=1}^{m} \bigwedge_{i=1}^{nj} Q_i^j(p_{Q_i^j}(x))\right) = 1$$

where τ is the the truth function. Since we are allowing some predicates in $\mathcal{P}$ to be fuzzy, whereas *C* is not, we make the following assumptions:

- A security parameter $0 < \theta < 1$ is given;

- *C(x)* is θ-true if and only if

$$\tau\left(\bigvee_{j=1}^{m} \bigwedge_{i=1}^{nj} = 1 \, Q_i^j(p_{Q_i^j}(x))\right) > \theta$$

  and where the truth value above is computed according to the min-max semantic; that is,

$$\tau\left(\bigvee_{j=1}^{m} \bigwedge_{i=1}^{nj} Q_i^j(p_{Q_i^j}(x))\right) = \max_{j=1,\ldots,m} \left(\min_{i=1,\ldots,nj} (Q_i^j(p_{Q_i^j}(x)))\right).$$

Moreover, it is possible that some of the predicates in $\mathcal{P}$ are either unknown or analytically given, and at the same time they can be either unconstrained or constrained to have values higher than a threshold α only within a given subset of $\mathcal{U}$.

Given a set $F = \{\mu_1, \cdots, \mu_n\}$ of membership functions associated to the predicates in $\mathcal{P}$, the fuzzy classification system (FCS for short) (1) will be denoted by S_m^F. The notation S_m will then denote the collection of all possible FCS's S_m^F, which in turn can be characterized as the collection of all sets *F* of membership functions. Such FCSs will be called *convex* fuzzy classification systems.

By definition, S_m is connected to a nonfuzzy predicate, that is, a nonfuzzy concept *C*. Our goal is to learn the membership functions from positive and negative examples of the concept *C*, in the hypothesis that a classification system S_m^F will be used with respect to the fixed threshold value θ. The obtained truth value will be denoted by $S_m^F(x)$. In the end, *x* is classified as a θ-positive example of *C* if $S_m^F(x) > \theta$.

10.4. Some Comments on the Learning Model

At this point, some comments are needed in order to have a better grasp of the learning model we are describing. As we mentioned, our starting point is that an "expert" provides a system of fuzzy rules that define a crisp concept. We also ask the expert to provide the linguistic orders. For instance, "high" follows "medium" that follows "low." However, we do not ask the expert to justify the rules; that is to say, to provide a "minimal" system of rules. Some rules may be redundant and fire always when others are firing. Some others may be useless and never fire. Moreover, we do not ask for the expert to give a "complete" system. Therefore, there may be some factors that are not taken into account. This way, we think we stay close to reality, expecially when dealing with complex decisional systems such as the one about the emergency room in a hospital, where it is certainly not feasible to expect any one to be able to explicit a complete and minimal set of rules to be followed for the admission of patients.

Once the system of fuzzy rules is given, the "learner" starts observing examples. These examples are drawn from a fixed but unknown distribution. Intuitively, these assumptions try to formalize the fact that the learner lives in a certain environment and that he/she learns according to what happens in this specific environment. At the end, his/her ability will be measured according to the same environment. Thus, if at the end of the training period we change environment, we cannot expect the learner to "function" well. Once again, common sense and common life events help us in understanding how much this assumption is natural. Going back to the hospital examples, we can certainly say that in different parts of the world, we find different diseases (or at least the statistical presence of many diseases and their symptoms change). At the end of this chapter, we will discuss a problem of understanding words spoken in Italian. Here again, things may change if the learning process happens in different parts of the country where strong differences in the accent may occur.

10.5. PAC-Learnability of Convex FCS

As we saw in our brief introductory section to Valiant's model of learning, it is extremely important to show that the concept class has a "good" Vapnik-Chervonenkis dimension. In our case, the following holds

Theorem 1: Let S_m be a class of convex FCS's of type (3.1). Let $C \subseteq \mathcal{R}^k$. We then have:

$$vc(S_m) < 2m + 1.$$

From this theorem and the result in [5] we have that a polynomial number of examples suffices to guarantee that with probability at least $1 - \delta$ we are able to produce a ϵ-approximation of a given convex FCS.

In order to obtain PAC-learnability we need to show that we are able to output a convex FCS consistent with the observed examples in polynomial time as well. Assuming that the correct fuzzy classification system S_m^F lies within the hypothesis space S_m, the preceding implies that we want to learn a class of concepts *by* the same class [8,10], which in our case means that we want to learn S_m by S_m. The problem of PAC-learning the class of convex FCS can then be approached as follows:

- given ϵ and δ draw at least

$$\max\left(\frac{4}{\epsilon} \ln \frac{2}{\delta}, \frac{16m}{\epsilon} \ln \frac{13}{\epsilon}\right),$$

examples from the distribution D;

- determine the hypercubes of $\mathcal{R}^k$ where there are θ-positive examples only (the *positive hypercubes*); suppose the hypercubes are $m' \leq m$;
- use one rule of S_m to cover each θ-positive hypercube.
- project the m' positive hypercubes on the k-th component, obtaining $m'_k \leq m_k$ positive intervals $\{[a_1, b_1], \ldots, [a_{m_k}, b_{m_k}]\}$
- define Q^i_j as a trapezoidal fuzzy set *using* the above defined intervals.

The problem of producing an FCS consistent with the given examples is then reduced to the problem of defining *good* trapezoidal fuzzy set using the obtained intervals in each component. However, this general problem is $\mathcal{NP}$-hard (see [3]). As a consequence, though a relatively small number of examples is sufficient to obtain a good training set, the process of elaborating such information may take quite a long time. We need then to turn our attention to some specific cases or we need to empower the learner with some specific features.

It is well known that the satisfiability problem for conjunctions of clauses with at least three literals is $\mathcal{NP}$-hard, whereas the case with at most two literals can be solved polynomially. Analogously, if we consider linguistic orders where only two elements are allowed—for each component (linguistic term) of the FCS only two linguistic values are allowed—we obtain PAC-learnability. In this case, we are dealing with systems where for instance for the linguistic term "pain" we can only have two values such as "strong" and "weak"; for "fever" only two values "high" and "low." Therefore, we have systems that are still useful.

Formally, the system $S_m{}^2$ of classification rules is given by:

$$Q^1_1(p_{Q^1_1}(x)) \wedge \cdots \wedge Q^1_{n_1}(p_{Q^1_{n_1}}(x)) \to C(x)$$

$$\cdots \qquad \cdots \qquad\qquad \cdots \qquad\qquad (2)$$

$$Q^m_1(p_{Q^m_1}(x)) \wedge \cdots \wedge Q^m_{n_m}(p_{Q^m_{n_m}}(x)) \to C(x)$$

where

- the predicates Q^j_i are taken from a set $\mathcal{P} = \{Q_1, \cdots, Q_n\}$ of given unary predicates;
- for all Q_j, p_{Q_j} is a projection function that returns the parameter that is of significance for Q_j.
- for every component k, there are at most two predicates Q_1, Q_2 corresponding to k (i.e., such that p_{Q_i} returns the value of the k-th component) and they define a linguistic order.

In the case of FCS S_m^2 the following is a PAC-learning algorithm.

Algorithm 1: Learning algorithm for S_m^2
  Input: θ, ϵ, δ and $N = \max(4/\epsilon \ln 2/\delta, 16m/\epsilon \ln 13/\epsilon)$ examples in $\mathcal{R}^k$;

Output: with probability at least $(1 - \delta)$, membership functions for predicates in S_m^2 which are ϵ-approximations of the unknown ones.

for every component k do

    compute the $m' \leq m$ positive hypercubes using the given examples

    project the m positive hypercubes on the k-th component,

        obtaining at most 2 positive intervals $\{[a_1^k, b_1^k], [a_2^k, b_2^k]\}$ for each component

    if two positive intervals are obtained

    define Q_1^k, Q_2^k as the trapezoidal fuzzy sets

    $Q_1{}^k = (a_1^k, a_1^k, b_1^k, a_2^k),$

    $Q_2{}^k = (b_1^k, a_2^k, b_2^k, b_2^k),$

        where $a_0 = a_1$ and $b_{m_k+1} = b_{m_k}$.

    if only one positive $[a^k, b^k]$ interval is obtained

    define Q_1^k, Q_2^k as the trapezoidal fuzzy sets

    $Q_1{}^k = (a^k, a^k, b^k, b^k + z^k),$

    $Q_2{}^k = (a^k - z^k, a^k, b^k, b^k),$

        where z^k is a positive constant.

    define θ so that no negative examples are covered.

For the general case, notice that if every rule of the correct system S_m^F is represented by some positive example, and separated from the other rules by some negative example, then if we draw the preceding number of examples, there are exactly m positive hypercubes, and, in turn, for each component there are exactly m_k positive intervals, where the number of predicates in the linguistic order for the k-th component that occur in S_m is also m_k. This follows from the hypotheses that every rule is represented by some positive example and the correct classification system belongs to the hypothesis space S_m. If we assume that the distribution is such that every rule *fires* at least once, then we can bypass the $\mathcal{NP}$-hardness problem. In particular, this assumption implies that in the classification system there are no useless rules relative to the *world* (i.e., the probability distribution of events) the expert lives in. A learning algorithm for convex FCS that will work if the previous assumption can be obtained quite easily from the one shown (see [3] for more details).

As we mentioned, we can try to empower the learner to speed up the learning process. In the model we have discussed so far, the learner is quite passive. He/she receives the system as input and then the examples according to the underlying distribution. No questions or doubts are allowed. Let us suppose then to make the process interactive; that is to say, at some instant the learner can make guesses and ask the teacher to confirm whether the guess is good or to give counter-examples. A particular type of guess, called "equivalence query" has been introduced in [2]. This guessing mechanism is able to enrich the collection of examples, so that important missing examples have to be provided by the teacher. In the end, the learner is able to quickly provide a good guess.

10.6. Speech Recognition

As a more complex case, we consider the classification problem for speech recognition described in [4]. The goal of the authors was to distinguish the 10 digits, uttered in Italian by several speakers, and acquired through a microphone. The signals are then sampled and turned into two time-dependent features: zero crossing and total energy. Each of these features is segmented into time intervals by means of syntactic pattern recognition techniques, and each interval is labeled with four attributes: shape, length, maximum value, and total area under the curve in that interval. The shape can either be bell-like (C1), flat (C2), ascending (C3), or descending (C4). Coming to what is more interesting for our discussion here, the length, maximum value and total area attributes, being numeric, had to be turned into symbolic predicates with a fuzzy semantics:

- $hs(x), hm(x), hl(x)$ stand, respectively, for the linguistic values *small, medium, large,* of the term "height";
- analogously, $as(x), am(x), al(x)$ stand, respectively, for the linguistic values *small, medium, large,* of the term "area"; and,
- $as(x), am(x), al(x)$ are, respectively, the linguistic values *small, medium, large,* of the term "length."

In [4], the fuzzy truth values of the previous predicates were fixed and given by a domain expert, based on appropriately chosen trapezoidal fuzzy sets. The logical structure of the classification rules was instead learned from a set of 220 examples, 22 for each class. A system of 33 rules was obtained. For instance:

$$zerocrossing(x) \wedge C1(x) \wedge$$
$$n205: \quad hl(x) \wedge al(x) \wedge \qquad\qquad \rightarrow \text{class 7}$$
$$energy(y) \wedge C1(y) \wedge wl(y)$$
$$zerocrossing(x) \wedge C1(x) \wedge$$
$$n208: \quad hl(x) \wedge al(x) \wedge \qquad\qquad \rightarrow \text{class 7}$$
$$energy(y) \wedge C1(y) \wedge al(y)$$

contain literals that are fuzzy—$hl(x), al(x), wl(x), al(y)$—each corresponds to a different dimension, and literals that are not fuzzy, such as $zerocrossing(x), C1(x), energy(y), C1(y)$, which are not significant for our purposes. We then need to consider two hypercubes (one for each rule) in a four-dimensional space, where the four dimensions are: height(x), area(x), length(y), area(y).

Examples are sampled for class 7 (positive examples) and for the other classes (negative examples); and for each example, the following four numeric values are computed: height of x, area of x, length of y, area of y. This turns one example into a point in our four-dimensional space. Our assumptions on the distributions will guarantee that the points corresponding to the positive examples can be included in exactly two hypercubes, so that the points corresponding to the negative examples are not included.

For our particular rules, as more examples are seen, the hypercubes, and therefore the semantics of "large height of x," "large area of x," "large length of y," "large area of y," are tuned to more appropriate values that enhance the classification rate for class 7. This solves the problems that are due to a bad expert's choice for the corresponding fuzzy sets.

10.7. Conclusion and Open Problems

In this chapter we have presented a new model for efficient learning of membership functions for linguistic orders in classification systems. The proposed theoretical framework combines Valiant's probabilistic approach to learning and linguistic orders for characterizing semantic terms. Though the general learning problem is computationally hard, under meaningful restrictions either on the underlying probability distribution or on the syntactic structure of the classification systems, fuzzy membership functions can be quickly learned by observing positive and negative examples. Analogous results may be obtained by allowing the learner to make guesses and ask for counter-examples (if any). The obtained membership functions are probably approximately correct within a particular classification problem. Therefore, with respect to such a classification problem, future examples will be correctly classified with high probability. Summing up, we can claim that the learning framework we have presented provides the mathematical means for validating fuzzy rules (i.e., the membership functions within fuzzy rules) within a probabilistic context. This way, there is no longer any need to rely completely on a domain expert for providing the membership functions.

Many problems are yet to be solved, among which we can highlight:

- Minimizing and completing the set of rules: The set of rules may be redundant or semantically incomplete. In particular, incompleteness will reflect heavily upon the final output for the membership functions, in order to account for all those examples that would be more naturally explained by adding extra rules and therefore extra (linguistic) parameters.

- Dealing with errors: Some examples may be (either maliciously or not) misclassified. Can our learner deal with this problem?

10.8. References

[1] Bergadano, F., and V. Cutello. "Learning Membership Functions." *Proceedings, ECSQARU '93, 2nd European Conference on Symbolic and Quantitative Approaches to Reasoning and Uncertainty,* Vol. 747, pp. 25–32. Granada, Spain: 1993.

[2] ———. "Learning Fuzzy Sets." *Proceedings, EUFIT '95,* ed. G.J. Zimmermann. Aachen, Germany: 1995.

[3] ———. "Probably Approximate Correct (PAC) Leaning in Fuzzy Classification Systems." To appear, *IEEE Transactions on Fuzzy Systems,* 1995.

[4] Bergadano, F., et al. "Automated Concept Acquisition in Noisy Environments" *IEEE Transactions on PAMI,* Vol. 10, No. 4. (1988).

[5] Blumer, A., et al. "Learnability and the Vapnik-Chervonenkis Dimension." *Journal of ACM,* Vol. 36, No. 4 (1989), pp. 929–965.

[6] Chang, A.M., and L.O. Hall. "The Validation of Fuzzy Knowledge-based Systems." *Fuzzy Logic for the Management of Uncertainty,* eds. L.A. Zadeh and J. Kacprzyk. pp. 589–604. New York: John Wiley and Sons Inc., 1992.

[7] Hudson, D.L., and M.E. Cohen. "The Role of Approximate Reasoning in a Medical Expert System." *Fuzzy Expert Systems,* ed. A. Kandel. Boca Raton: CRC Press, 1991.

[8] Kearns, M.J. *The Computational Complexity of Machine Learning.* MIT Press, 1990.

[9] Klir, G.J., and T.A. Folger. *Fuzzy Sets Uncertainty and Information.* Englewood Cliffs: Prentice Hall, 1988.

[10] Natarajan, B.K. *Machine Learning, A Theoretical Approach.* Morgan Kaufmann, 1991.

[11] Pitt, L., and L. G. Valiant. "Computational Limitations on Learning from Examples." *Journal of ACM,* Vol. 35, No. 4 (1988), pp. 965–984.

[12] Valiant, L. "A Theory of the Learnable." *Communications of the ACM,* Vol. 27, No. 11 (1984), pp. 1134–1142.

[13] Vapnik, V., and A. Y. Charvonenkis. "On the Uniform Convergence of Relative Frequencies of Events to their Probabilities." *Theory of Probability and its Applications,* Vol. 16, No. 2 (1971), pp. 264–280.

11 Nonlinear Channel Equalization by Adaptive Fuzzy Filter

Li-Xin Wang
Department of Electrical and Electronic Engineering
The Hong Kong University of Science and Technology
Clear Water Bay, Kowloon, Hong Kong

Jerry M. Mendel
Signal and Image Processing Institute
Department of Electrical Engineering-Systems
University of Southern California
Los Angeles, California

ABSTRACT: This chapter develops an adaptive fuzzy filter and applies it to the equalization of nonlinear communication channels. The adaptive fuzzy filter is constructed from a set of fuzzy If-Then rules whose parameters are adjusted by a recursive least squares (RLS) algorithm based on input-output data. The initial rules can be specified by human experts, therefore the approach provides a mechanism to combine linguistic information (in the form of fuzzy If-Then rules) and numerical information (in the form of input-output data) in a uniform fashion. The simulation results show that: 1) without using any linguistic information, the RLS adaptive fuzzy filter is a well-performing nonlinear adaptive filter (similar to polynomial and neural-net adaptive filters); 2) by incorporating some linguistic description (in fuzzy terms) about the channel into the adaptive fuzzy filter, the adaptation speed is greatly improved; and, 3) the bit error rates of the fuzzy equalizer are close to that of the optimal equalizer.

11.1. Introduction

Nonlinear distortion over a communication channel is now a significant factor hindering further increase in the attainable data rate in high-speed data transmission [1,6]. Because the received signal over a nonlinear channel is a nonlinear function of the past values of the transmitted symbols, and the nonlinear distortion varies with time and from place to place, effective equalizers for nonlinear channels should be nonlinear and adaptive.

In [1,6], ploynomial adaptive filters were developed for nonlinear channel equalization. In [2,3], multilayer perceptrons and radial basis function expansions were used as adaptive equalizers for nonlinear channels. Because nonlinear channels include a very broad spectrum of nonlinear distortion, it is very difficult to say which nonlinear adaptive filter is dominantly better than the others. Therefore, it is worth trying other new nonlinear structures as prototypes of nonlinear adaptive filters in addition to the existing Volterra series, multilayer perceptron, radial basis function expansions, and so on. In this chapter, we develop a recursive least squares (RLS) adaptive fuzzy filter and use it for nonlinear channel equalization.

11.2. RLS Adaptive Fuzzy Filter

Our RLS adaptive fuzzy filter solves the following problem. Consider a real-valued vector sequence $[\mathbf{x}(k)]$ and a real-valued scalar sequence $[d(k)]$, where $k = 0, 1, 2, \ldots$ is the time index, and $\mathbf{x}(k) \in U \equiv [C_1^-, C_1^+] \times [C_2^-, C_2^+] \times \cdots \times [C_n^-, C_n^+] \subset R^n$ (we call U and R the input and output spaces of the filter, respectively). At each time point k, we are given the values of $\mathbf{x}(k)$ and $d(k)$. The problem is: at each time point $k = 0, 1, 2, \ldots$, determine an adaptive filter $f_k : U \subset R^n \to R$ such that:

$$J(k) = \sum_{i=0}^{k} \lambda^{k-i} [d(i) - f_k(\mathbf{x}(i))]^2 \tag{1}$$

is minimized, where $\lambda \in (0, 1]$ is a forgetting factor.

This problem is quite general. If we constrain the f_k's to be linear functions, the problem becomes an FIR adaptive filter design problem [4]. If the f_k's are Volterra series expansions, we have an adaptive polynomial filter design problem [6]. If the f_k's are multilayer perceptrons or radial basis function expansions, the problem becomes the neural nets adaptive filter design problem [2,3].

11.2.1. Design of the RLS Adaptive Fuzzy Filter

Step 1: Define m_i fuzzy sets in each interval $[C_i^-, C_i^+]$ of the input space U, which are labeled as F_i^{ji} ($i = 1, 2, \ldots, n, ji = 1, 2, \ldots, m_i$; note that ji is a single index) in the following way: the m_i membership functions $\mu_{F_i^{ji}}$ cover the interval $[C_i^-, C_i^+]$ in the sense that for each $x_i \in [C_i^-, C_i^+]$ there exists at least one $\mu_{F_i^{ji}}(x_i) \neq 0$. These membership functions are fixed and will not change during the adaptation procedure in Step 4.

Step 2: Construct a set of $\prod_{i=1}^{n} m_i$ fuzzy If-Then rules in the following form:

$$R^{(j1,\ldots,jn)} : IF\ x_1\ is\ F_1^{j1}\ and\cdots and\ x_n\ is\ F_n^{jn},$$
$$THEN\ d\ is\ G^{(j1,\ldots,jn)}, \tag{2}$$

where $\mathbf{x} = (x_1, \ldots, x_n)^T \in U$ (the filter input), $d \in R$ (the filter output), $ji = 1, 2, \ldots, m_i$ with $i = 1, 2, \ldots, n$, F_i^{ji}'s are the same labels of the fuzzy sets defined in Step 1, and the $G^{(j1,\ldots,jn)}$'s are labels of fuzzy sets defined in the output space, which are determined in the following way: if there are linguistic rules from human experts in the form of (2), set $G^{(j1,\ldots,jn)}$ to be the corresponding linguistic terms of these rules; otherwise, set $\mu_{G^{(j1,\ldots,jn)}}$ to be an arbitrary membership function over the output space R. *It is in this way that we incorporate linguistic rules into the adaptive fuzzy filter; that is, we use linguistic rules to construct the initial filter.*

Step 3: Construct the filter f_k based on the $\prod_{i=1}^{n} m_i$ rules in Step 2 as follows:

$$f_k(\mathbf{x}) = \frac{\sum_{j1=1}^{m_1} \cdots \sum_{jn=1}^{m_n} \theta^{(j1,\ldots,jn)} (\mu_{F_1^{j1}}(x_1)\cdots\mu_{F_n^{jn}}(x_n))}{\sum_{j1=1}^{m_1} \cdots \sum_{jn=1}^{m_n} (\mu_{F_1^{j1}}(x_1)\cdots\mu_{F_n^{jn}}(x_n))}, \tag{3}$$

where $\mathbf{x} = (x_1, \ldots, x_n)^T \in U$, $\mu_{F_i^{ji}}$'s are membership functions defined in Step 1, and $\theta^{(j1,\ldots,jn)} \in R$ is the point at which $\mu_{G^{(j1,\ldots,jn)}}$ achieves its maximum value. Due to the way in which we defined the $\mu_{F_i^{ji}}$'s in Step 1, the denominator of 3 is nonzero for all the points of U; therefore, the filter f_k of 3 is well-defined. The fuzzy system 3 is obtained by combining the $\prod_{i=1}^{n} m_i$ rules of Step 2 using product inference and center-average defuzzification [8,9].

In 3, the weights $\mu_{F_i^{ji}}(x_1)\cdots\mu_{F_n^{jn}}(x_n)$ are fixed functions of $\mathbf{x}$; therefore, the free design parameters of the adaptive fuzzy filter are the $\theta^{(j1,\ldots,jn)}$'s which are now collected as a $\prod_{i=1}^{n} m_i$-dimensional vector:

$$\theta = (\theta^{(1,1,\ldots,1)}, \ldots, \theta^{(m_1,1,\ldots,1)}; \theta^{(1,2,1,\ldots,1)}, \ldots, \theta^{(m_1,2,1,\ldots,1)};$$
$$\ldots; \theta^{(1,m_2,1,\ldots,1)}, \ldots, \theta^{(m_1,m_2,1,\ldots,1)}; \ldots; \theta^{(1,m_2,\ldots,m_n)}, \tag{4}$$
$$\ldots, \theta^{(m_1,m_2,\ldots,m_n)})^T.$$

Define the *fuzzy basis functions* [9]

$$p^{(j1,\ldots,jn)}(\mathbf{x}) = \frac{\mu_{F_1^{j1}}(x_1)\cdots\mu_{F_n^{jn}}(x_n)}{\sum_{j1=1}^{m_1} \cdots \sum_{jn=1}^{m_n} (\mu_{F_1^{j1}}(x_1)\cdots\mu_{F_n^{jn}}(x_n))}, \tag{5}$$

and collect them as a $\prod_{i=1}^{n} m_i$-dimensional vector $\mathbf{p}(\mathbf{x})$ in the same ordering as the θ of (4); that is,

$$\mathbf{p}(\mathbf{x}) = (p^{(1,1,\ldots,1)}(\mathbf{x}), \ldots, p^{(m_1,1,\ldots,1)}(\mathbf{x}); p^{(1,2,1,\ldots,1)}(\mathbf{x}),$$

$$\ldots, p^{(m_1,2,1,\ldots,1)}(\mathbf{x}); \ldots; p^{(1,m_2,1,\ldots,1)}(\mathbf{x}), \ldots,$$

$$p^{(m_1,m_2,1,\ldots,1)}(\mathbf{x}); \ldots; p^{(1,m_2,\ldots,m_n)}(\mathbf{x}), \ldots,$$

$$p^{(m_1,m_2,\ldots,m_n)}(\mathbf{x}))^T. \tag{6}$$

Based on 4 and 6 we can now rewrite 3 as:

$$f_k(\mathbf{x}) = \mathbf{p}^T(\mathbf{x})\,\theta. \tag{7}$$

Step 4: Use the following RLS algorithm [4] to update θ: let the initial estimate of θ, $\theta(0)$, be determined as in Step 2, and $P(0) = \sigma I$, where σ is a small positive constant, and I is the $\prod_{i=1}^{n} m_i - by - \prod_{i=1}^{n} m_i$ identity matrix; at each time point $k = 1, 2, \ldots$, do the following:

$$\phi(k) = \mathbf{p}(\mathbf{x}(k)), \tag{8}$$

$$P(k) = \frac{1}{\lambda}[P(k-1) \tag{9}$$
$$- P(k-1)\phi(k)(\lambda + \phi^T(k)P(k-1)\phi(k))^{-1}\phi^T(k)P(k-1)],$$

$$K(k) = P(k-1)\phi(k)[\lambda + \phi^T(k)\,P(k-1)\phi(k)]^{-1}, \tag{10}$$

$$\theta(k) = \theta(k-1) + K(k)(d(k) - \phi^T(k\theta(k-1)), \tag{11}$$

where $[\mathbf{x}(k)]$ and $[d(k)]$ are the sequences defined above in the Problem, $\mathbf{p}(*)$ is defined in 6, and λ is the forgetting factor in 1.

Remark 1: The RLS algorithm 9-11 is obtained by minimizing $J(k)$ of 1 with f_k constrained to be the form of 7. Because f_k of 7 is linear in the parameters, the derivation of 9-11 is the same as that for the FIR linear adaptive filter [4]; therefore, we omit the details.

Remark 2: It was proven in [8,9] that functions in the form of 3 are universal approximators; that is, for any real continuous function g on the compact set U, there exists a function in the form of 3 such that it can uniformly approximate g over U to arbitrary accuracy. Consequently, our adaptive fuzzy filter is a powerful nonlinear adaptive filter in the sense that it has the capability of performing any nonlinear filtering operation.

Remark 3: Linguistic information (in the form of the fuzzy If-Then rules of 2) and numerical information (in the form of desired input-output pairs $(\mathbf{x}(k), d(k))$) are combined into the filter in the following way: due to Steps 2–4, linguistic If-Then rules are directly incorporated into the filter 3 by constructing the initial filter based on the linguistic rules; and, due to the adaptation Step 4, numerical pairs $(\mathbf{x}(k), d(k))$ are incorporated into the filter by updating the filter parameters such that the filter output "matches" the pairs in the sense of minimizing 1. It is natural and reasonable to assume that linguistic information from human experts is provided in the form of 2 because the rules of 2 state what the filter outputs should be in some input situations, where "what should be" and "some situations" are represented by linguistic terms that are characterized by fuzzy membership functions. On the other hand, it is obvious that the most natural form of numerical information is provided in the form of input-output pairs $(\mathbf{x}(k), d(k))$.

11.3. Application to Nonlinear Channel Equalization

The digital communication system considered in this chapter is shown in Figure 11.1, where the "channel" includes the effects of the transmitter filter, the transmission medium, the receiver matched filter, and other components. The transmitted data sequence $s(k)$ is assumed to be an independent sequence taking values from $\{-1, 1\}$ with equal probability. The inputs to the equalizer, $x(k), x(k-1), \cdots, x(k-n+1)$, are the channel outputs corrupted by an additive noise $e(k)$. The task of the equalizer at the sampling instant k is to produce an estimate of the transmitted symbol $s(k-d)$ using the information contained in $x(k), x(k-1), \cdots, x(k-n+1)$, where the integers n and d are known as the order and the lag of the equalizer, respectively.

We use the geometric formulation of the equalization problem due to [2,3]. Using similar notation to that in [2,3], define:

$$P_{n,d}(1) = \{\hat{\mathbf{x}}(k) \in R^n | s(k-d) = 1\}, \tag{12}$$

$$P_{n,d}(-1) = \{\hat{\mathbf{x}}(k) \in R^n | s(k-d) = -1\}, \tag{13}$$

where

$$\hat{\mathbf{x}}(k) = [\hat{x}(k), \hat{x}(k-1), \cdots, \hat{x}(k-n+1)]^T, \tag{14}$$

$\hat{x}(k)$ is the noise-free output of the channel (see Figure 11.1), and $P_{n,d}(1)$ and $P_{n,d}(-1)$ represent the two sets of possible channel noise-free output vectors $\hat{\mathbf{x}}(k)$ that can be produced from sequences of the channel inputs

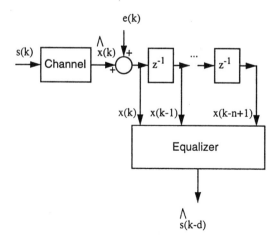

Figure 11.1   Schematic of data transmission system.

containing $s(k - d) = 1$ and $s(k - d) = -1$, respectively. The equalizer can be characterized by the function:

$$g_k : R^n \rightarrow \{-1, 1\} \tag{15}$$

with

$$\hat{s}(k - d) = g_k(\mathbf{x}(k)), \tag{16}$$

where

$$\mathbf{x}(k) = [x(k), x(k - 1), \cdots, x(k - n + 1)]^T \tag{17}$$

is the observed channel output vector. Let $p_1[\mathbf{x}(k)|\hat{\mathbf{x}}(k) \in P_{n,d}(1)]$ and $p_{-1}[\mathbf{x}(k)|\hat{\mathbf{x}}(k) \in P_{n,d}(-1)]$ be the conditional probability density functions of $\mathbf{x}(k)$ given $\hat{\mathbf{x}}(k) \in P_{n,d}(1)$ and $\hat{\mathbf{x}}(k) \in P_{n,d}(-1)$, respectively. It was shown in [2,3] that the equalizer, which is defined by:

$$f_{opt}(\mathbf{x}(k)) = sgn[p_1(\mathbf{x}(k)|\hat{\mathbf{x}}(k) \in P_{n,d}(1))$$
$$-p_{-1}(\mathbf{x}(k)|\hat{\mathbf{x}}(k) \in P_{n,d}(-1))] \tag{18}$$

achieves the minimum bit error rate for the given order n and lag d, where $sgn(y) = 1(-1)$ if $y \geq 0$ $(y < 0)$. If the noise $e(k)$ is zero-mean and Gaussian with covariance matrix:

$$Q = E[(e(k), \ldots, e(k - n + 1))(e(k), \ldots, e(k - n + 1))^T], \tag{19}$$

then from $x(k) = \hat{x}(k) + e(k)$ we have that:

$$p_1[\mathbf{x}(k)|\hat{\mathbf{x}}(k) \in P_{n,d}(1)] - p_{-1}[\mathbf{x}(k)|\hat{\mathbf{x}}(k) \in P_{n,d}(-1)]$$

$$= \sum exp\left[-\frac{1}{2}(\mathbf{x}(k) - \hat{\mathbf{x}}_+)^T Q^{-1} (\mathbf{x}(k) - \hat{\mathbf{x}}_+)\right] \tag{20}$$

$$-\sum exp\left[-\frac{1}{2}(\mathbf{x}(k) - \hat{\mathbf{x}}_-)^T Q^{-1}(\mathbf{x}(k) - \hat{\mathbf{x}}_-)\right],$$

where the first (second) sum is over all the points $\hat{\mathbf{x}}_+ \in P_{n,d}(1)$ $(\hat{\mathbf{x}}_- \in P_{n,d}(-1))$.

Now consider the nonlinear channel:

$$\hat{x}(k) = s(k) + 0.5s(k - 1) - 0.9[s(k) + 0.5s(k - 1)]^3, \tag{21}$$

and white Gaussian noise $e(k)$ with $E[e^2(k)] = 0.2$. For this case, the optimal decision region for $n = 2$ and $d = 0$:

$$[\mathbf{x}(k) \in R^2|p_1[\mathbf{x}(k)|\hat{\mathbf{x}}(k) \in P_{2,0}(1)]$$
$$-p_{-1}[\mathbf{x}(k)|\hat{\mathbf{x}}(k) \in P_{2,0}(-1)] \geq 0], \tag{22}$$

is shown in Figure 11.2 as the shaded area. The elements of the sets $P_{2,0}(1)$ and $P_{2,0}(-1)$ are illustrated in Figure 11.2 by the o and *, respectively. From Figure 11.2, we see that the optimal decision boundary for this case is severely nonlinear. We now use the RLS adaptive fuzzy filter to solve

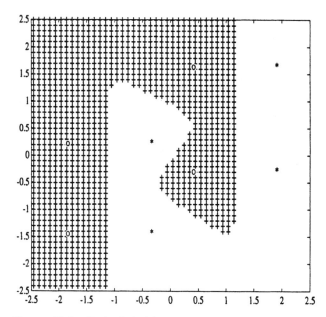

Figure 11.2 Optimal decision region for the channel (21), Gaussian white noise with variance $\sigma_e^2 = 0.2$, and equalizer order $n = 2$ and lag $d = 0$, where the horizontal-axis denotes $x(k)$ and the vertical-axis denotes $x(k - 1)$.

this specific equalization problem (channel (21), $e(k)$ white Gaussian with variance 0.2, equalizer order $n = 2$ and lag $d = 0$).

Example 1: Here we used the RLS adaptive fuzzy filter without any linguistic information. We chose $\lambda = 0.999$, $\sigma = 0.1$, $m_1 = m_2 = 9$, and $\mu_{F_i^j}(x_i)$ $= exp[-1/2(x_i - \bar{x}_i^j/0.3)^2]$ with $\bar{x}_i^j = -2, -1.5, -1, -0.5, 0, 0.5, 1, 1.5, 2$ for $j = 1, 2, \ldots, 9$, respectively, where $i = 1, 2$, $x_1 = x(k)$ and $x_2 = x(k - 1)$. For the same realization of the sequence $s(k)$ and the same randomly chosen initial parameters $\theta(0)$ (within $[-0.5, 0.5]$), we simulated the cases when the adaptation algorithm (9)-(11) stopped at: (i) $k = 30$, and (ii) $k = 100$. The final decision regions, $[\mathbf{x}(k) \in R^2 | f_k(\mathbf{x}(k)) \geq 0]$, for the two cases are shown in Figures 11.3 and 11.4, respectively. From Figures 11.3 and 11.4 we see that the decision regions obtained from the RLS adaptive fuzzy filter tended to converge toward the optimal decision region.

Example 2: Next we used the RLS adaptive fuzzy filter and incorporated the following linguistic information about the decision region. From the geometric formulation we see that the equalization problem is equivalent to determining a decision boundary in the input space of the equalizer. Suppose that there are human experts who are very familiar with the specific situation, such that although they cannot draw the specific decision boundary in the input space of the equalizer, they can assign degrees to different regions in the input space that reflect their belief that the regions should belong to 1-catalog

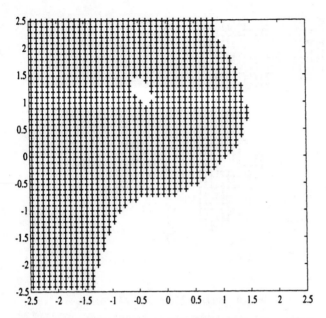

Figure 11.3 Decision region of the RLS adaptive fuzzy filter without using any linguistic information and when the adaptation stopped at $k = 30$, where the horizontal-axis denotes $x(k)$ and the vertical-axis denotes $x(k-1)$.

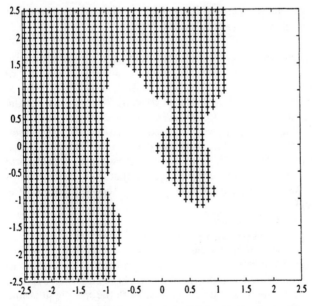

Figure 11.4 Decision region of the RLS adaptive fuzzy filter without using any linguistic information and when the adaptation stopped at $k = 100$, where the horizontal-axis denotes $x(k)$ and the vertical-axis denotes $x(k-1)$.

or -1-catalog. Take Figure 11.2 as an example. We see from that figure that the difficulty is to determine which catalog the middle portion should belong to; in other words, as we move away from the middle portion, we have less and less uncertainty about which catalog the region should belong to. For example, for the leftmost region in Figure 11.2, we have more confidence that it should belong to the 1-catalog rather than the -1-catalog. Similarly, for the rightmost region in Figure 11.2, we have more confidence that it should belong to the -1-catalog rather than the 1-catalog. So, we assume that the human experts know that a portion of the boundary is somewhere around $x(k) = -1.2$ for $x(k-1)$ less than 1 and around $x(k) = 1.2$ for $x(k-1)$ greater than 1. To make these observations more specific, we have the fuzzy rules shown in Figure 11.5 where the membership functions N3, N2, etc. are the $\mu_{F_i^j}$'s defined in Example 1. We have 48 rules in Figure 11.5, corresponding to the boxes with numbers; for example, the bottom left box corresponds to the rule: "If $x(k)$ is N4 and $x(k-1)$ is N4, then f_k is G," where f_k is the filter output, and the center of μ_{F^j} is 0.6. Because the filter output f_k is a weighted average of these centers (see 3), the numbers 0.6, 0.4, -0.4, -0.6 in Figure 11.5 reflect our belief that the regions should correspond to the 1-catalog in the -1-catalog. For example, if the input point $[x(k), x(k-1)]$ falls in the leftmost region of Figure 11.5, then we have more confidence that the transmitted $s(k)$ should be 1 rather than -1, and we present this confidence by assigning the center of the fuzzy term in the corresponding Then **px** to be 0.6.

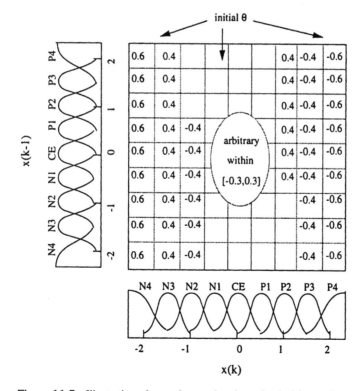

Figure 11.5   Illustration of some fuzzy rules about the decision region.

It should be emphasized that the rules in Figure 11.5 provide very fuzzy information about the decision region, because: 1) the regions are fuzzy; that is, there are no clear boundaries between the regions, and 2) the numbers 0.6, 0.4, −0.4, −0.6 are conservative; that is, they are away from the real transmitted values 1 or −1. We now show that although these rules are fuzzy, the speed of adaptation is greatly improved by incorporating them into the RLS adaptive fuzzy equalizer (filter). Figure 11.6 shows the final decision region determined by the RLS fuzzy adaptive filter, $[\mathbf{x}(k) \in R^2 | f_k(\mathbf{x}(k)) \geq 0]$ (shaded area), when the adaptation stopped at $k = 30$ after the rules in Figure 11.5 were incorporated, where the $\mu_{F_i^l}$'s and the sequence $s(k)$ were the same as those in Example 1. Comparing Figures 11.6 and 11.3, we see that the adaptation speed was greatly improved by incorporating these fuzzy rules.

Example 3: In this final example, we compared the bit error rates achieved by the optimal equalizer (18) and the adaptive fuzzy equalizer for different signal-to-noise ratios, for the channel (21) with equalizer order $n = 2$ and lag $d = 1$. The optimal bit error rate was computed by applying the optimal equalizer (18) to a realization of 10^6 points of the sequences $s(k)$ and $e(k)$. We chose the filter parameters to be the same as in Example 1. We ran the RLS adaptive fuzzy filters for the first 1000 points in the same 10^6 point realization of $s(k)$ and $e(k)$ as for the optimal equalizer, and then used the trained fuzzy equalizers to compute the bit error rate for the same 10^6 point realization. Figure 11.7 shows the bit error rates of the optimal equalizer and the RLS fuzzy equalizer for different signal-to-noise ratios. We see from Figure 11.7 that the bit error rate of the fuzzy equalizer is very close to the optimal one.

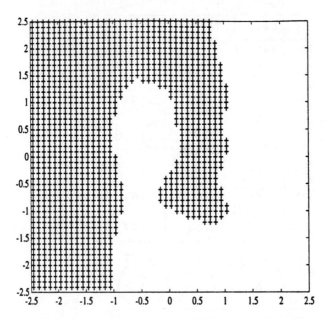

Figure 11.6 Decision region of the RLS adaptive fuzzy filter after incorporating the fuzzy rules illustrated in Figure 11.5 and when the adaptation stopped at $k = 30$, where the horizontal-axis denotes $x(k)$ and the vertical-axis denotes $x(k-1)$.

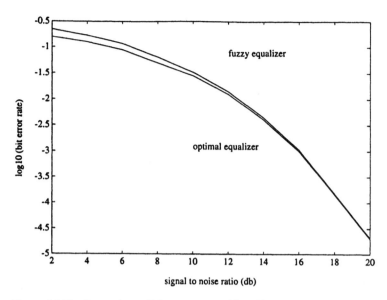

Figure 11.7   Comparison of bit error rates achieved by the optimal and fuzzy equalizer.

11.4. References

[1] Bigleieri, E., et al. "Adaptive Cancellation of Nonlinear Intersymbol Interference for Voiceband Data Transmission." *IEEE Journal on Selected Areas in Communications,* Vol. SAC-2, No. 5 (1984), pp. 765–777.

[2] Chen, S., et al. "Adaptive Equalization of Finite Nonlinear Channels using Multilayer Perceptions." *Signal Processing,* Vol. 20, (1990), pp. 107–119.

[3] ———. "Reconstruction of Binary Signals using an Adaptive Radial-basis Function Equalizer." *Signal Processing,* Vol. 22 (1991), pp. 77–93.

[4] Cowan, C.F.N., and P.M. Grant. *Adaptive Filters.* Englewood Cliffs: Prentice Hall, 1985.

[5] Falconer, D.D. "Adaptive Equalization of Channel Nonlinearities in QAM Data Transmission Systems." *The Bell System Technical Journal,* Vol. 57, No. 7 (1978), pp. 2589–2611.

[6] Mathews, V.J. "Adaptive Polynomial Filters." *IEEE Signal Processing Magazine,* July, 1991. pp. 10–26.

[7] Mulgrew, B., and C.F.N. Cowan. *Adaptive Filters and Equalisers.* Boston: Kluwer Academic Publishers, 1988.

[8] Wang, L.X. *Adaptive Fuzzy Systems and Control: Design and Stability Analysis.* Englewood Cliffs: Prentice Hall, 1994.

[9] Wang, L.X., and J.M. Mendel. "Fuzzy-basis Functions, Universal Approximation, and Orthogonal Least Squares Learning." *IEEE Transactions on Neural Networks,* Vol. 3, No. 5 (1992), pp. 807–814.

12 Possibilistic Time-Series Model and Analysis of Consumption

Junzo Watada
Osaka Institute of Technology
Omiya, Asahi, Osaka 535 Japan

ABSTRACT: A multivariant analysis, methods of which have been developed from the statistical point of view, is one of most important techniques that analyze data in various fields. From the fuzzy-set theoretical and possibilistic viewpoint, E. Ruspini and J.C. Bezdek proposed a clustering method [7]. Hitherto, many methods including fuzzy regression, principal component analysis, quantification methods, and time-series analysis are proposed and employed in analyzing data obtained from the real world.

Time-series data can be analyzed in terms of possibility by the model illustrated here. The possibilistic time-series model is proposed based on a possibilistic regression model. A fuzzy smoothing method is proposed in order to remove the irregular changes from the trend. Using the trend, the seasonal circle can be abstracted from time-series data.

This time-series model is applied to analyze data of consumptions of alcoholic beverage and gas energy at Osaka, and illustrates the latent structure of the consumptions at Osaka, Japan.

12.1. Introduction

A multivariant analysis, methods of which have been developed from the statistical point of view, is one of most important techniques that analyze data in various fields. From the fuzzy-set theoretical and possibilistic viewpoint, E. Ruspini and J.C. Bezdek proposed a clustering method [7]. Hitherto, many methods including fuzzy regression [4, 5, 9], principal component analysis [8], quantification methods [11] and time-series analysis [10, 12] are proposed and employed in analyzing data obtained from the real world.

Time-series analysis based on the concept of statistics is widely applied to many economic, social, managerial, and engineering problems for explaining the change of a variable depending on time as explained by Box & Jenkins [1] and Pindyck & Rubinfeld [3].

In this chapter, vague or possibilistic observation data are defined as fuzzy numbers that are fuzzy sets in a real line, and a possibilistic time-series model is formulated by using a fuzzy function of time whose parameters are fuzzy numbers. A fuzzy function based on fuzzy set theory can be effectively employed to cope with the vagueness of phenomena in various systems. This fuzzy function of time enables us to forecast the future of systems or events in terms of possibilities that Zadeh first defined on the basis of fuzzy sets [13].

The possibilistic time-series model obtained from fuzzy data in time series explains their trend and seasonal cycles in time series. As an example, this method is applied to the consumptions of alcoholic beverage and gas energy at Osaka City, Japan, to compare the trends and seasonal cycles between both of their consumptions.

12.2. Problem Formulation

To describe the problem considered here, in Table 12.1, let us show fuzzy data in time series and time variables that are used in the possibilistic time-series analysis. These time variables are explanatory variables. An observed value Y is a fuzzy number characterized by its membership function μ_Y. It is assumed through this chapter that fuzzy numbers Y are normal and convex.

The possibilistic time-series model is described by a fuzzy function with fuzzy parameters as:

$$Y = A_1 \cdot t_1 + A_2 \cdot t_2 + \cdots + A_K \cdot t_K = \mathbf{A} \cdot \mathbf{t'} \tag{1}$$

where $\mathbf{t'}$ is a transpose vector of a column vector $\mathbf{t'} = (t_1, t_2, \ldots, t_K)$ whose i^{th} element t_i denotes t^{i-1}, and $\mathbf{A}$ is a parameter vector whose i^{th} element is a fuzzy number A_i. $\mathbf{A}$ is defined by a direct product set on the direct product space R^K as:

Table 12.1   Data in Time Series

Sample number	Time series	Observed value	Time variables				Estimated value
1	$-n$	Y_{-n}	t_{-n}^0,	t_{-n}^1,	$\cdots$	t_{-n}^{k-1},	Y_{-n}^*
2	$-(n-1)$	$Y_{-(n-1)}$	$t_{-(n-1)}^0$,	$t_{-(n-1)}^1$,	$\cdots$	$t_{-(n-1)}^{k-1}$,	$Y_{-(n-1)}^*$
$\vdots$	$\vdots$	$\vdots$	$\vdots$	$\vdots$	$\vdots$	$\vdots$	$\vdots$
n	-1	Y_{-1}	t_{-1}^0,	t_{-1}^1,	$\cdots$	t_{-1}^{k-1},	Y_{-1}^*

$$\mathbf{A} = A_1 \times A_2 \times \cdots \times A_K \tag{2}$$

whose membership function is denoted by:

$$\mu_{\mathbf{A}}(\mathbf{a}) = \bigvee_{i=1}^{k} \{\mu_{A_i}(a_i)\} \tag{3}$$

where $\mathbf{a} = (a_1, a_2, \ldots, a_K)$.

Through the extension principle, the membership function of a fuzzy number $Y = \mathbf{At'}$ can be defined by its membership functions as follows:

$$\mu_Y(y) = \begin{cases} \displaystyle\bigvee_{\{\mathbf{a}|\mathbf{at'}=y\}} \mu_{\mathbf{A}}(\mathbf{a}); \{\mathbf{a}|\mathbf{at'}=y\} \neq 0 \\ 0 \qquad\qquad ; \text{otherwise} \end{cases} \tag{4}$$

In this chapter, $\mu_{A_i}(a_i); (i = 1, 2, \ldots, K)$ is assumed to be a triangular membership function:

$$\mu_{A_i}(a_i) = \begin{cases} 1 - \dfrac{|\alpha_i - a_i|}{c_i}; \alpha_i - c_i \leq a_i \leq \alpha_i + c_i \\ 0 \qquad\qquad ; \text{otherwise} \end{cases} \tag{5}$$

where α_i is a center of a fuzzy number A_i and c_i denotes the fuzziness of a fuzzy number A_i. Figure 12.1 illustrates a pyramidal membership function. The center and the fuzziness of a fuzzy vector $\mathbf{A}$ are denoted by α and $\mathbf{c}$, respectively. Then this fuzzy vector $\mathbf{A}$ means "about α." Let us employ a simple notation $\mathbf{A} = \{\alpha, \mathbf{c}\}$ for convenience.

The membership function (4) can be rewritten by using pyramidal fuzzy parameters $\mathbf{A}$ as:

$$\mu_{Y_r}(y_r) = \begin{cases} 1 - \dfrac{|y_r - \alpha \mathbf{t}'_r|}{\displaystyle\sum_{i=1}^{K} c_i|t_{ri}|}; \{\alpha \mathbf{t}'_r - \sum_{i=1}^{K} c_i|t_{ri}| \leq y_r \leq \alpha t'_r + \sum_{i=1}^{K} c_i|t_{ri}| \\ 0 \qquad\qquad ; \text{otherwise} \end{cases} \tag{6}$$

where it is assumed that $0/0 = 0$.

When normal convex fuzzy numbers $Y_{-1}, Y_{-2}, \ldots, Y_{-n}$ as shown in Table 12.1 are given in time series, our aim is to decide the fuzzy function of

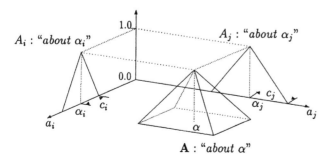

A_i : "about α_i" A_j : "about α_j"

$\mathbf{A}$: "about α"

Figure 12.1 Fuzzy set A or parameters in possibilistic time-series model.

time that best expresses the change of observed values Y_{-r}. Two indices will be introduced to measure the appropriateness of the possibilistic time-series model. One is fitness of fuzzy function to the given data and the other is fuzziness included in the fuzzy function.

The following definition shows the degree of the fitting of the possibilistic linear model Y_r^* to the fuzzy observation data Y_r, which means a possibility:

$$h_r = \bigvee_{y \in R} \{\mu_{Y_r}(y) \wedge \mu_{Y_r^*}(y)\} \tag{7}$$

This fitness means the index of closeness of the estimated value Y_r^* to the observed value Y_r as shown in shown in Figure 12.2.

On the other hand, the fuzziness S included in the model is defined by:

$$S = \sum_{i-1}^{k} w_i c_i = \mathbf{w}\mathbf{c}' \tag{8}$$

where w_i is the weight of each parameter a_i. These two indices are incompatible with each other. The better the model becomes in terms of fitness, the more extensive the fuzziness of the model is. Therefore, the trade-off between the two indices of fuzziness and fitness must be maintained.

The possibilistic time-series analysis decides α and $\mathbf{c}$ of a fuzzy function (1) with the minimum fuzziness S under the conditions that:

$$h_r \geq h_0; r = -1, -2, \ldots, -n \tag{9}$$

The condition (9) says that each fitness h_r of an estimated value Y_r^* to an observed value Y_r should not be smaller than given fitness standard h_0.

12.3. Determination of the Model

The α-level sets of observed value Y_r and estimated value Y_r^* at the fitness standard h_0 are respectively denoted by:

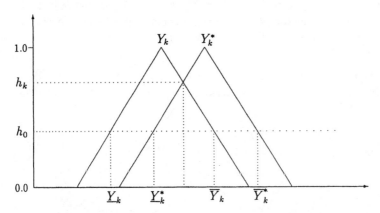

Figure 12.2 Fitness h_k between observed value A_k and estimated value A_k^* and fitness standard h_0.

$$Y_r^{h_0} = [\underline{Y}_r, \overline{Y}_r] \tag{10}$$

$$Y_r^{*h_0} = [\underline{Y}_r^*, \overline{Y}_r] \tag{11}$$

As Figure 12.2 illustrates, the conditions (9) are rewritten in the following inequalities:

$$\underline{Y}_r^* \leq \overline{Y}_r; r = -1, -2, \ldots, -n \tag{12}$$

$$\underline{Y}_r \leq \overline{Y}_r^*; r = -1, -2, \ldots, -n \tag{13}$$

By these inequalities, an α-level set $Y_r^{*h_0}$ at h_0 can be easily rewritten as:

$$Y_r^{*h_0} = \left\{ y \mid h_0 \leq 1 - \frac{|y - \alpha \cdot \mathbf{t}_r'|}{\sum\limits_{i-1}^{k} c_i |t_{ri}|} \right\} \tag{14}$$

Equivalently, we have:

$$Y_r^{*h_0} = \left[-(1 - h_0) \sum_{i=1}^{k} c_i |t_{ri}| + \alpha \mathbf{t}_r', (1 - h_0) \sum_{i=1}^{k} c_i |t_{ri}| + \alpha \mathbf{t}_r' \right] \tag{15}$$

These equalities (15) reduce our problem to the following linear programming problem as described in Tanaka et al. [4, 5, 9].

12.3.1. Linear Programming Problem

The problem is to decide α and $\mathbf{c}$ which minimize the criterion function:

$$S = w_1 c_1 + w_2 c_2 + \cdots + w_k c_k \tag{16}$$

under the constraints that:

$$\alpha \mathbf{t}_r' - (1 - h_0) \sum_{i=1}^{k} c_i |t_{ri}| \leq \overline{Y}_r$$

$$\alpha \mathbf{t}_r' + (1 - h_0) \sum_{i=1}^{k} c_i |t_{ri}| \geq -\underline{Y}_r ; r = -1, -2, \ldots, -n \tag{17}$$

$$\mathbf{c} \geq 0 \tag{18}$$

This linear programming problem can be easily solved by a conventional technique.

12.4. Trend and Seasonal Cycle

A linear trend model is simply expressed by $\mathbf{Y}_{rm}^* = \mathbf{A}\mathbf{t}'$. The α-level set $[\underline{Y}^*, \overline{Y}^*]$ of estimated value Y^* at the fitness standard h_0 is written as:

$$\underline{Y}^* = \alpha \mathbf{t}' - \mathbf{c}\mathbf{t}' \tag{19}$$

$$\overline{Y}^* = \alpha \mathbf{t}' + \mathbf{c}\mathbf{t}' \tag{20}$$

The trend of fuzzy data in time series expresses "approximate $\alpha \mathbf{t}'$." In other words, the trend is described in terms of the center $\alpha \mathbf{t}'$ and the fuzziness **ct'**. the fuzziness represents the possibility area in the trend of the original series as Figure 12.3 shows.

Seasonal cycles are defined as the deviation from the trend at each month. It is assumed that original series and its estimation of the trend are given as Y_{rm} and Y_{rm}^* where r (r = 1, 2, . . . , L) and m (m = 1, 2, . . . , 12) denote the year and the month, respectively. The mean deviation from the trend at each month $Y_{.m}^*$ can be written in the form:

$$Y_{.m}^* = \frac{1}{L} \sum_{r=1}^{L} (Y_{rm} - Y_{rm}^*); m = 1, 2, \ldots, 12 \qquad (21)$$

This seasonal cycle $Y_{.m}^*$ is a fuzzy number derived from the fuzziness of Y_{rm} and Y_{rm}^* (r = 1, 2, . . . , L). This fuzzy number expresses possibilities included in the seasonal cycle.

The following lemma is necessary for the proof of Proposition 1. It is assumed that membership functions are continuously nondecreasing in $(-\infty, m]$ and continuously nonincreasing in $[m, +\infty)$. Moreover, the function f, which carries a fuzzy set from its domain to its region, is an increasing function. We have the following lemma.

12.4.1. Lemma 1

Given an increasing function $f(\cdot)$, the fuzzy set:

$$Y = f(A_1, A_2, \ldots, A_n) \qquad (22)$$

can be calculated in such a manner that the increasing part and the decreasing part of the membership function of Y can be separately determined by the increasing part and decreasing part of each membership function μ_{A^i}, respectively as in Dubois and Prade [2].

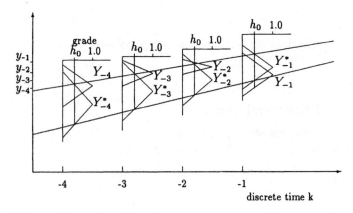

Figure 12.3   Estimated trend.

12.4.2. Proposition 1

Given fuzzy numbers X_i $(i = 1, 2, \ldots, n)$ with their membership functions:

$$\mu_{X_i}(x) = 1 - \frac{|x - \alpha_i|}{c_i}; i = 1, 2, \ldots, n \tag{23}$$

the membership function of their mean:

$$\overline{X} = \frac{1}{n} \sum_{i=1}^{n} X_i \tag{24}$$

results in the form:

$$\mu_{\overline{x}}(x) = 1 - \frac{|x - \overline{\alpha}|}{\overline{c}}; i = 1, 2, \ldots, n \tag{25}$$

where

$$\overline{c} = \frac{1}{n} \sum_{i=1}^{n} c_i \tag{26}$$

and

$$\overline{\alpha} = \frac{1}{n} \sum_{i=1}^{n} \alpha_i \tag{27}$$

12.4.3. Proof

Lemma 1 says that the increasing part and the decreasing part of a membership function can be separately and independently calculated. Let us show the proof in the case where:

$$X \geq \frac{1}{n} \sum_{i=1}^{n} \alpha_i \tag{28}$$

if we define v by:

$$v = \frac{x_i - \alpha_i}{c_i} \tag{29}$$

then:

$$x_i = c_i v + \alpha_i \tag{30}$$

The summation of x_i in equation 30 is reduced to:

$$x = \frac{1}{n} \sum_{i=1}^{n} x_i$$

$$= \frac{1}{n} \left(\sum_{i=1}^{n} c_i \right) v + \frac{1}{n} \sum_{i=1}^{n} \alpha_i \tag{31}$$

Therefore, using the notation $\overline{c}$ in equation 26 and $\overline{\alpha}$ in equation 27, equation 31 leads to:

$$v = \frac{x - \overline{\alpha}}{\overline{c}} \tag{32}$$

Then we have:

$$\mu_{\overline{X}}(x) = 1 - \frac{|x - \overline{\alpha}_i|}{\overline{c}_i} \tag{33}$$

The proof in the other case where:

$$X \leq \frac{1}{n} \sum_{i=1}^{n} \alpha_i \tag{34}$$

is omitted, because the procedure is the same as in the above proof.
Employing this proposition, seasonal cycles can be described by:

$$Y^*_{\cdot m} = \frac{1}{L} \sum_{r=1}^{L} (Y_{rm} - Y^*_{rm}) \tag{35}$$

$$\mu_{Y_m}(y) = 1 - \frac{|y - \overline{\alpha}_{\cdot m}|}{\overline{c}_{\cdot m}} \tag{36}$$

where:

$$\overline{\alpha}^*_{\cdot m} = \frac{1}{L} \sum_{r=1}^{L} (\alpha_{rm} - \alpha^*_{rm}) \tag{37}$$

$$\overline{c}^*_{\cdot m} = \frac{1}{L} \sum_{r=1}^{L} (c_{rm} - c^*_{rm}) \tag{38}$$

12.5. Analysis of Consumption

In this section we are focusing on the application of the possibilistic time-series model to the consumptions of alcoholic beverage and gas energy per household per month at Osaka City, Japan [6]. The possibilistic time-series model can forecast their consumptions in the future.

12.5.1. Fuzzy Observation

Original data are given as real values in time series. Employing these data, let us regard data at $r-1, r$ and $r+1$ as the possibilistic output of the system at r in the following way.

A fuzzy number Y_r at time r is constructed from actual values y_{r-1}, y_r and y_{r+1} at times $r-1, r$ and $r+1$, respectively. As illustrated in Figure 12.4, Y_r is a fuzzy number with the least fuzziness whose support Y^{+0} includes those three actual values y_{r-1}, y_r and y_{r+1}. In other words, these values y_{r-1}, y_r and y_{r+1} are considered as realization from among the possibilities that the fuzzy number Y_r is defined by:

$$\mu_{Y_r}(y) = 1 - \frac{|y - \alpha_r|}{c_r} \tag{39}$$

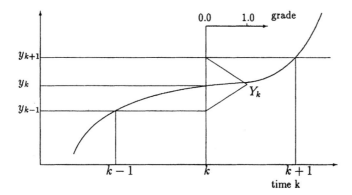

Figure 12.4 Construction of possibility distribution at time k.

where:

$$c_r = \frac{1}{2}(\overline{Y}_r - \underline{Y}_r) \tag{40}$$

$$\alpha_r = \overline{Y}_r - c_r = \underline{Y}_r + c_r \tag{41}$$

$$\overline{Y}_r = max\{y_{r-1}, y_r, y_{r+1}\} \tag{42}$$

$$\underline{Y}_r = min\{y_{r-1}, y_r, y_{r+1}\} \tag{43}$$

In this section we will analyze time-series data as possibilistic observation data in the sense of Equation 39.

12.5.2. Results

The linear trend model of the consumptions of alcoholic beverage and gas energy is written by:

$$Y = A_0 + A_1 t \tag{44}$$

the measurement S of fuzziness is defined as:

$$S = 0.5 \, c_0 + c_1 \tag{45}$$

And ratio of fuzziness, c/α, is defined by:

$$\frac{c}{\alpha} = \frac{(fuzziness)}{(central\ value)} \tag{46}$$

this ratio of fuzziness is employed to make a comparison between different fuzzy numbers.

In this analysis, original series come from the reference [6]. Table 12.2 shows the results of possibilistic time-series analysis, telling the following facts. Concerning the term of time, fuzziness ratio 1.63 of the consumption of alcoholic beverage was larger than −0.375 of the consumption of gas energy. The inclination of alcoholic consumption is large, but that of

Table 12.2   Results of Analysis (Fuzziness Standard = 0.5)

	Parameters (α, c)	Ratio of Fuzziness	Fuzziness S
Alcoholic Beverage	$A_0, (5.091, 0.000)$	0.000	0.018
	$A_1, (0.011, 0.018)$	1.636	
Gas Energy	$A_0, (5.535, 0.000)$	0.000	0.012
	$A_1, (-0.032, 0.012)$	−0.375	

gas consumption is a little bit declined. These values mean that the growth of the alcoholic consumption was faster and more, but that of gas energy is shrinking, because of the economical decession in the term. Furthermore, the model of alcoholic beverage had more fuzziness of a time term than that of gas energy as Table 12.2 illustrates. This fact indicates the following. The increasing ratio of consumption of gas energy was rather constant and its increasing curve was approximately declined. On the contrary, the increasing ratio of the consumption of alcoholic beverage was not constant.

Figures 12.5 and 12.6 illustrate the trends in the consumptions of alcoholic beverage and gas energy, respectively. The possibilistic time-series model can express the possibility area of the trend by using the width of the trend as these figures show.

Figures 12.7 and 12.8 illustrate their seasonal cycles, which are derived from the estimated trend and original series.

It is possible to forecast the consumption per household per month of the following year by means of adding the seasonal cycle to the trend value of the following year. Figures 12.9 and 12.10 illustrate estimated consumptions of alcoholic beverage and gas energy in each month for the following year, respectively.

The width of fuzziness in the estimated consumption in the figures declares that the consumption will be realized within the width of their

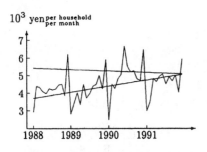

$$Y = (5.091, 0.000) + (0.011, 0.018)X$$

Figure 12.5   Trend with possibility area (Alcoholic Beverage).

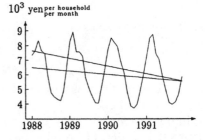

$$Y = (5.535, 0.000) + (-0.032, 0.012)X$$

Figure 12.6   Trend with possibility area (Gas Energy).

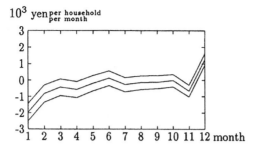

Figure 12.7   Seasonal cycle (alcoholic beverage).

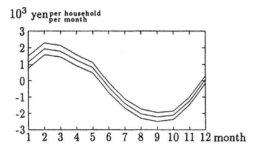

Figure 12.8   Seasonal cycle (gas energy).

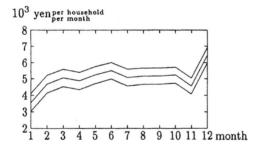

Figure 12.9   Forecast of sales volume in 1993 (alcoholic beverage).

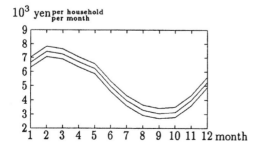

Figure 12.10   Forecast of sales volume in 1993 (gas energy).

possibility. Our possibilistic time-series model can forecast the consumption by the possibility area.

12.6. Conclusion

The possibilistic time-series model interprets the fuzziness included in data as the possibility of a system. The possibilistic model obtained from fuzzy data can be employed to forecast the possible output for the future. Since the system can be allowed to behave in many ways because of the possibility that the system has, the obtained expression should be necessarily interpreted possibilistically. The application of the possibilistic time-series model in analyzing and forecasting consumptions has proved that it is of great use for coping with possibilistic phenomena in time series.

The following can be concluded concerning the characteristics of the possibilistic time-series model according to the results of analysis and forecasting of the consumptions at Osaka City, Japan.

1. This model can represent trend and seasonal cycles in terms of possibility. The time-series model with the possibility area can successfully handle and interpret the vagueness of forecasting.

2. Fitness standard h_0 and measurement of fuzziness S are incompatible with each other. The more strictly the fitness standard h_0 is set, the fuzzier the model is. If all data can be discussed only at the high possibility, it would be better to assign the fitness standard h_0 to a large value in (0, 1], although the high fitness standard makes the model fuzzier. Otherwise, the low fitness standard might be taken.

3. If it is assumed that the latent structure has possibility distribution or fuzziness at a cross-section, it is possible to construct the possibility distribution at time k from original series y_k in the manner that its support y_k^{+0} of a fuzzy number Y_k includes actual values at times $k - 1, k$ and $k + 1$. This treatment is of great use for analyzing a system by the possibilistic time-series model even when original series are given clear-cut values.

12.7. References

[1] Box, G.P., and G.M. Jenkins. *Time Series Analysis: Forecasting and Control.* San Francisco: Holden-day, 1970.
[2] Dubois, D., and H. Prade. "Operations on Fuzzy Numbers." *International Journal of Systems Sciences,* Vol. 9 (1978), pp. 613–626.
[3] Pindyck, R.S., and D.C. Rubinfeld. *Econometric Models and Economic Forecast.* New York: McGraw-Hill, 1976.
[4] Tanaka, H., et al. "Linear Regression Analysis with Fuzzy Model." *IEEE Transactions on Systems, Man, and Cybernetics,* Vol. SMC-12, No. 6 (1982), pp. 903–907.

[5] ———. "Possibilistic Linear Regression for Fuzzy Data." *European Journal of Operational Research,* Vol. 39 (1989), pp. 1–8.

[6] Census of Osaka City, Japan in 1988–1992. (In Japanese). Research and Statistics Department, Printing Bureau of Osaka City.

[7] Watada, J. "Fuzzy Classification Method." (In Japanese). *Fuzzy OR, Journal of Japan Society for Fuzzy Theory and Systems,* Vol. 4, No. 1 (1992), pp. 61–73.

[8] Watada, J., and Y. Yabuuchi. "Fuzzy Principal Component Analysis." *Proceeding of Brazil-Japan Joint Symposium on Fuzzy Systems,* 1994.

[9] ———. "Fuzzy Robust Regression Analysis." *Proceedings, 3rd International Conference on Fuzzy Systems.* pp. 1370–1376. Florida: June, 1994.

[10] Watada, J., et al. "Analysis of Time-Series Data by Possibilistic Model." *Proceeding of International Workshop on Fuzzy System Applications.* pp. 228–229. Fukuoka, Japan: 1988.

[11] Watada, J., and H. Tanaka. "Fuzzy Quantification Methods." *Proceedings, 2nd IFSA Congress.* pp. 66–69. Tokyo, Japan: 1987.

[12] Watada, J. "Fuzzy Time-Series Analysis and Forecasting of Sales Volume." *Fuzzy Regression Analysis,* eds. J. Kacprzyk and M. Fedrizzi. pp. 211–227. 1992.

[13] Zadeh, L.A. "Fuzzy Sets as a Basis for a Theory of Possibility." *International Journal of Fuzzy Sets and Systems,* Vol. 1 (1978), pp. 3–28.

13 Virtual Worlds in Feedback Fuzzy Systems

Julie A. Dickerson
Department of Electrical and Computer Engineering,
Iowa State University,
Ames, Iowa

Bart Kosko
Department of Electrical Engineering—Systems, Signal and
Image Processing Institute,
University of Southern California,
Los Angeles, California

ABSTRACT: Feedback fuzzy systems can model complex dynamical systems. Virtual worlds are dynamical systems in which the user interacts with the dynamical process. Math models may prove too fine-grained and too brittle to model these virtual worlds. Feedback fuzzy systems can approximate the dynamics of such virtual worlds with a fixed number of sets (nodes) and rules (edges). The fuzzy sets or nodes in the rules control the granularity of the dynamical model.

A fuzzy cognitive map is a fully interconnected feedback fuzzy system that models a dynamic causal web. The map's sets or nodes can change with neural-like functions or with more complex nonlinear functions. Its rules or edges change with unsupervised causal learning laws that differ from the correlation learning laws of synapses. A user can model each virtual world with its own cognitive map and then combine the maps to combine the virtual worlds. More complex systems can replace each node with its own cognitive map or with its own feedforward fuzzy system. This allows cognitive maps to act as multiresolution approximators of dynamical systems.

This chapter uses adaptive fuzzy cognitive maps to model a nonlinear undersea world of predators and prey. The causal-map technique can apply to other dynamical systems where the user interacts with the dynamical process and where the user wants to model or partially control the process with a multiresolution rule-based framework.

13.1. Fuzzy Virtual Worlds

What is a virtual world? It is what changes in a "virtual reality" [9] or "cyberspace" [2]. A virtual world links humans and computers in a causal medium that can trick the mind or senses. At the broadest level, a virtual world is a dynamical system

$$\frac{d\mathbf{V}}{dt} = f(\mathbf{V}).$$

How the virtual world changes depends on its past state and many other variables. It changes with time as the user or an actor moves through it. In the simplest case, only the user moves in the virtual world. In general, both the user and the virtual world change and they change each other.

Change in a virtual world is causal. Actors cause events to happen as they move in a virtual world. They add new patterns of cause and effect and respond to old ones. In turn, the virtual world acts on the actors or on their physical or social environments. The virtual world changes their behavior and can change its own web of cause and effect. This feedback causality between actors and their virtual world makes up a complex dynamical system that can model events, actors, actions, and data as they unfold in time.

Virtual worlds are fuzzy as well as fedback. Events occur and concepts hold only to some degree. Events cause one another to some degree. In this sense, virtual worlds are fuzzy causal worlds. They are fuzzy dynamical systems.

How do we model the fuzzy feedback causality? One way is to write down the differential equations that show how the virtual "flux" or "fluid" changes in time. This gives an exact model. The Navier-Stokes equations [1] used in weather models give a fluid model of how actors move in a type of virtual world. They can show how clouds or tornadoes form and dissolve in a changing atmosphere or how an airplane flies through pockets of turbulence. Such math models are hard to find, hard to solve, and hard to run in real time. They paint too fine a picture of the virtual world.

Fuzzy cognitive maps (FCMs) can model the virtual world in large fuzzy chunks. They model the causal web as a fuzzy directed graph [5, 7]. The nodes and edges show how causal concepts affect one another to some degree in the fuzzy dynamical system. The "size" of the nodes gives the chunk size. In a virtual world, the concept nodes can stand for events, actions, values, moods, goals, or trends. The causal edges state fuzzy rules or causal flows between concepts. The fuzzy rule states how much one node grows or falls as some other node grows or falls.

Experts draw the FCMs as causal pictures. They do not state equations. They state concept nodes and link them to other nodes. The FCM system turns each picture into a matrix of fuzzy rule weights. The system weights and adds the FCM matrices to combine any number of causal pictures. More FCMs tend to sum to a better picture of the causal web with rich tangles of feedback and fuzzy edges even if each expert gives binary (present or absent) edges. This makes it easy to add or delete actors or to change the background of a virtual world or to combine virtual worlds that are disjoint or overlap. We can also let an FCM node control its own FCM to give a nested FCM in a hierarchy of virtual worlds. The node FCM can model the complex nonlinearities between the node's input and output. It can drive the motions, sounds, actions, or goals of a virtual actor.

The FCM itself acts as a nonlinear dynamical system. Like a neural net it maps inputs to output equilibrium states. Each input digs a path through the virtual state space. In simple FCMs, the path ends in a fixed point or limit cycle. In more complex FCMs, the path may end in an aperiodic or "chaotic" attractor. We illustrate the FCM technique with a simple FCM that learns and converges to a binary limit cycle.

In contrast, an AI expert system [16] models a system as a binary rule tree with graph search. Each input fires one rule or a few rules, and the search spreads down the tree branch to a leaf or leaves. Reactive systems [3] choose from a set of precompiled actions in the tree. This means that the virtual world designer must anticipate what action to select under all possible conditions. Situated agents with goals can also help choose actions in diverse situations [10]. Each of these systems keeps the feedforward tree structure. The lack of feedback loops allows the tree search. But each serial inference uses only a small part of the stored knowledge. Each FCM input fires all the rules to some degree. The causal "juice" swirls through the tangles of fuzzy feedback and equilibrates in a global system response. In this way, FCMs model the "circular causality" [12] of real and virtual worlds.

13.2. Fuzzy Cognitive Maps

Fuzzy cognitive maps are fuzzy signed digraphs with feedback [5, 7]. Nodes stand for fuzzy sets or events that occur to some degree. The nodes are causal concepts. They can model events, actions, values, goals, or lumped-parameter processes.

Directed edges stand for fuzzy rules or the partial causal flow between the concepts. The sign (+ or −) of an edge stands for causal increase or decrease. The positive edge rule:

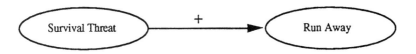

states that a survival threat increases runaway. It is a positive causal connection. The runaway response grows or falls as the threat grows or falls. The negative edge rule:

states that running away from a predator decreases the survival threat. It is a negative causal connection. The survival threat grows the less the prey runs away and falls the more the prey runs away. The two rules define a minimal feedback loop in the FCM causal web:

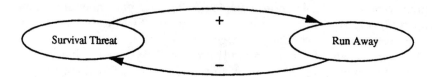

An FCM with n nodes has n^2 edges. The nodes $C_i(t)$ are fuzzy sets and so take values in $[0, 1]$. So an FCM state is the *fit* (fuzzy unit) vector $\mathbf{C}(t) = (C_1(t), \ldots, C_n(t))$ and thus a point in the fuzzy hypercube $I^n = [0, 1]^n$. An FCM inference is a path or point sequence in I^n. It is a fuzzy process or indexed family of fuzzy sets $\mathbf{C}(t)$. The FCM can only "forward chain" [16] to answer what-if questions. Nonlinearities do not permit reverse causality. FCMs cannot "backward chain" to answer why questions.

The FCM nonlinear dynamical system acts as a neural network. For each input state $\mathbf{C}(0)$, it digs a trajectory in I^n that ends in an equilibrium attractor $\mathbf{A}$. The FCM quickly converges or "settles down" to a fixed point, limit cycle, limit torus, or chaotic attractor in the fuzzy cube.

The output equilibrium is the answer to a causal what-if question: What if $\mathbf{C}(0)$ happens? In this sense, each FCM stores a set of global rules of the form "If $\mathbf{C}(0)$, then equilibrium attractor $\mathbf{A}$."

The size of the attractor regions in the fuzzy cube governs the number of these global rules or "hidden patterns" [7]. All points in the attractor region map to the attractor. An FCM with a global fixed point has only one global rule. All input balls "roll" down its "well." FCMs can have large and small attractor regions in the fuzzy cube. The attractor types can vary in complex FCMs with highly nonlinear concepts and edges. Then one input state may lead to chaos and a more distant input state may end in a fixed point or limit cycle.

13.2.1. Simple FCMs

Simple FCMs have bivalent nodes and trivalent edges. Concept values C_i take values in $\{0,1\}$. Causal edges take values in $\{-1,0,1\}$. So, for a concept, each simple FCM state vector is one of the 2^n vertices of the fuzzy cube I^n. The FCM trajectory hops from vertex to vertex. I^n ends in a fixed point or limit cycle at the first repeated vector.

We can draw simple FCMs from articles, editorials, or surveys. A delphi process can also produce the FCMs [11]. Most persons can state the sign of causal flow between nodes. The hard part is to state its degree or magnitude. We can average expert responses [7, 15] as in equation (3) or use neural systems to learn fuzzy edge weights from data. The expert responses can initialize the causal learning or modify it as a type of forcing function.

Figure 13.1 shows a simple FCM for a virtual dolphin. It lists a causal web of goals and actions in the life of a dolphin [13]. The connection matrix $\mathbf{E}_D$ states these causal relations in numbers:

	D_1	D_2	D_3	D_4	D_5	D_6	D_7	D_8	D_9	D_{10}
D_1	0	−1	−1	0	0	1	0	0	0	0
D_2	0	0	0	0	1	0	0	0	0	0
D_3	0	0	0	1	1	−1	−1	0	0	−1
D_4	1	0	−1	0	0	−1	−1	0	0	−1
D_5	0	0	1	0	0	0	0	0	−1	0
D_6	0	0	0	0	−1	0	1	0	0	0
D_7	0	0	0	0	0	0	0	1	0	0
D_8	−1	1	−1	0	1	0	−1	0	0	0
D_9	0	0	0	0	1	−1	−1	−1	0	1
D_{10}	−1	−1	1	0	−1	−1	−1	−1	−1	0

$\mathbf{E}_D = $ (label at left of matrix)

The ith row lists the connection strength of the edges e_{ik} directed out from causal concept D_i and the ith column lists the edges e_{ki} directed into D_i. Row 9 shows how the concept SURVIVAL THREAT changes the other concepts. Column 9 shows the concepts that change SURVIVAL THREAT.

13.2.2. FCM Recall

FCMs recall as the FCM dynamical system equilibrates. Simple FCM inference thresholds a matrix-vector multiplication [6, 7]. State vectors $\mathbf{C}_n$ cycle through the FCM adjacency matrix $\mathbf{E}$: $\mathbf{C}_1 \rightarrow \mathbf{E} \rightarrow \mathbf{C}_2 \rightarrow \mathbf{E} \rightarrow \mathbf{C}_3 \rightarrow$ .... The system nonlinearly transforms the weighted input to each node C_i:

$$C_i(t_n + 1) = S\left[\sum_{k=1}^{N} e_{ki}(t_n)C_k(t_n) \right] \quad (1)$$

Here, $S(y)$ is a bounded signal function. For simple FCMs, the sigmoid function:

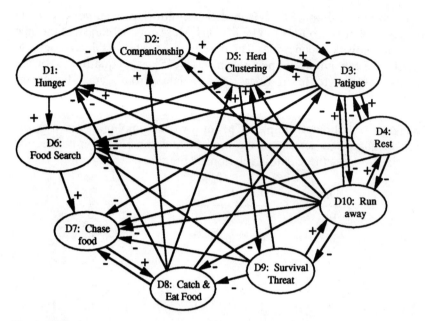

Figure 13.1 Trivalent fuzzy cognitive map for the control of a dolphin actor in a fuzzy virtual world. The rules or edges connect causal concepts in a signed connection matrix.

$$S(y) = \frac{1}{1 + e^{-c(y - T)}} \tag{2}$$

with large $c > 0$ approximates a binary threshold function.

Simple threshold FCMs quickly converge to stable limit cycles or fixed points [6, 7]. These limit cycles show "hidden patterns" in the causal web of the FCM.

We can model the effect of a survival threat on the dolphin FCM as a sustained input to D_9. This means $D_9 = 1$ for all time t_k. C_0 is the initial input state of the dolphin FCM:

$$C_0 = [0\,0\,0\,0\,0\,0\,0\,0\,1\,0].$$

Then:

$$C_0\,E_D = [0\,0\,0\,0\,1\,-1\,-1\,-1\,0\,1] \rightarrow C_1 = [0\,0\,0\,0\,1\,0\,0\,0\,1\,1].$$

The arrow stands for a threshold operation with 1/2 as the threshold value. C_1 keeps D_9 on since we want to study the effect of a sustained threat. C_1 shows that when threatened, the dolphins cluster in a herd D_5 and flee the threat. The negative rules in the ninth row of E_D show that a threat to survival turns off other actions. The FCM converges to the limit cycle $C_1 \rightarrow C_2 \rightarrow C_3 \rightarrow C_4 \rightarrow C_5 \rightarrow C_1 \ldots$ if the threat lasts:

$$C_1\ E_D = [-1\ -1\ 2\ 0\ 0\ -2\ -2\ -2\ -2\ 1] \rightarrow C_2 = [0\ 0\ 1\ 0\ 0\ 0\ 0\ 0\ 1\ 1],$$
$$C_2\ E_D = [-1\ -1\ 1\ 1\ 1\ -3\ -3\ -2\ -1\ 0] \rightarrow C_3 = [0\ 0\ 1\ 1\ 1\ 0\ 0\ 0\ 1\ 0],$$
$$C_3\ E_D = [1\ 0\ 0\ 1\ 2\ -3\ -3\ -1\ -1\ -1] \rightarrow C_4 = [1\ 0\ 0\ 1\ 1\ 0\ 0\ 0\ 1\ 0],$$
$$C_4\ E_D = [1\ -1\ -1\ 0\ 1\ -1\ -2\ -1\ -1\ 0] \rightarrow C_5 = [1\ 0\ 0\ 0\ 1\ 0\ 0\ 0\ 1\ 0],$$
$$C_5\ E_D = [0\ -1\ 0\ 0\ 1\ 0\ -1\ -1\ -1\ 1] \rightarrow C_1 = [0\ 0\ 0\ 0\ 1\ 0\ 0\ 0\ 1\ 1],$$

Flight causes fatigue (C_2). The dolphin herd stops and rests, staying close together (C_3). All the activity causes hunger (C_4, C_5). If the threat persists, they again try to flee (C_1). A threat surpresses hunger. This limit cycle shows a "hidden" global pattern in the causal virtual world.

The FCM converges to the new limit cycle $C_6 \rightarrow C_7 \rightarrow C_8 \rightarrow C_9 \rightarrow C_{10} \rightarrow C_{11} \rightarrow C_{12} \rightarrow C_{13} \rightarrow C_6 \dots$ when the shark gives up the chase or eats a dolphin and the threat ends $(D_9 = 0)$:

$$C_6\ \ \ = [0\ 0\ 1\ 1\ 1\ 0\ 0\ 0\ 0\ 0],$$
$$C_6\ E_D = [1\ 0\ 0\ 1\ 1\ -2\ -2\ 0\ -1\ -2] \rightarrow C_7 = [1\ 0\ 0\ 1\ 1\ 0\ 0\ 0\ 0\ 0],$$
$$C_7\ E_D = [1\ -1\ -1\ 0\ 0\ 0\ -1\ 0\ -1\ -1] \rightarrow C_8 = [1\ 0\ 0\ 0\ 0\ 0\ 0\ 0\ 0\ 0],$$
$$C_8\ E_D = [0\ -1\ -1\ 0\ 0\ 1\ 0\ 0\ 0\ 0] \rightarrow C_9 = [0\ 0\ 0\ 0\ 0\ 1\ 0\ 0\ 0\ 0],$$
$$C_9\ E_D = [0\ 0\ 0\ 0\ -1\ 0\ 1\ 0\ 0\ 0] \rightarrow C_{10} = [0\ 0\ 0\ 0\ 0\ 0\ 1\ 0\ 0\ 0],$$
$$C_{10}\ E_D = [0\ 0\ 0\ 0\ 0\ 0\ 0\ 1\ 0\ 0] \rightarrow C_{11} = [0\ 0\ 0\ 0\ 0\ 0\ 0\ 1\ 0\ 0],$$
$$C_{11}\ E_D = [-1\ 1\ -1\ 0\ 1\ 0\ -1\ 0\ 0\ 0] \rightarrow C_{12} = [0\ 1\ 0\ 0\ 1\ 0\ 0\ 0\ 0\ 0],$$
$$C_{12}\ E_D = [0\ 0\ 1\ 0\ 1\ 0\ 0\ 0\ -1\ 0] \rightarrow C_{13} = [0\ 0\ 1\ 0\ 1\ 0\ 0\ 0\ 0\ 0],$$
$$C_{13}\ E_D = [0\ 0\ 1\ 1\ 1\ -1\ -1\ 0\ -1\ -1] \rightarrow C_6\ = [0\ 0\ 1\ 1\ 1\ 0\ 0\ 0\ 0\ 0],$$

The dolphin herd rests from the previous chase (C_6, C_7). Then they begin a hunt of their own (C_9, C_{10}). They eat (C_{11}) and then they socialize and rest (C_{12}, C_{13}, C_6). This makes them hungry and the feeding cycle repeats.

Each node in a simple FCM turns actions or goals on and off. Each node can control its own FCM, fuzzy control system, goal-directed animation system, force feedback, or other input-output map. The FCM can control the temporal associations or timing cycles that structure virtual worlds. These patterns establish the rhythm of the world.

13.2.3. Augmented FCMs

FCM matrices additively combine to form new FCMs [5]. This allows combination of FCMs for different actors or environments in the virtual world. The new (augmented) FCM includes the union of the causal concepts for all the actors and the environment in the virtual world. If an FCM does not include a concept, then those rows and columns are all zero. The sum of the augmented (zero-padded) FCM matrices for each actor forms the virtual world:

$$F = \sum_{i=1}^{n} w_i F_i \qquad (3)$$

The w_i are positive weights for the ith FCM F_i. The weights state the relative value of each FCM in the virtual world and can weight any subgraph of the FCM. Figure 13.2a shows two simple FCMs that might come from

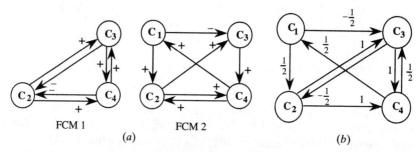

Figure 13.2 FCMs combine additively. (a) Two bivalent FCMs. (b) Augmented FCM. The augmented FCM takes the union of the causal concepts of the smaller FCMs and sums the augmented connection matrices: $\mathbf{F} = \frac{1}{2}(\mathbf{F}_1 + \mathbf{F}_2)$.

a simple delphi process [11]. Equation 3 combines these FCMs to give the new simple FCM in Figure 13.2b that has fuzzy or multivalued edges:

$$\mathbf{F} = \frac{1}{2}(\mathbf{F}_1 + \mathbf{F}_2) = \frac{1}{2} \cdot \begin{bmatrix} 0 & 1 & -1 & 0 \\ 0 & 0 & 2 & 2 \\ 0 & -1 & 0 & 2 \\ 1 & 0 & 1 & 0 \end{bmatrix} \qquad (4)$$

The FCM sum (3) helps knowledge acquisition. Any number of experts can describe their FCM virtual world views and (3) will weight and combine them. In contrast, an AI expert system [16] is a binary tree with graph search. Two or more trees need not combine to a tree. Combined FCMs tend to have feedback or closed loops that precludes graph search with forward or backward "chaining."

13.3. Virtual Undersea World

Figure 13.1 shows a simple FCM for a virtual dolphin. It lists a causal web of goals and actions in the life of a dolphin [13]. The connection matrix $\mathbf{E}_D$ states these causal relations in numbers. Figure 13.3 shows an augmented FCM for an undersea virtual world. It combines fish school, shark, and dolphin herd FCMs with (1): $\mathbf{F} = \mathbf{F}_{\text{fish}} + \mathbf{F}_{\text{shark}} + \mathbf{F}_{\text{dolphin}}$. The new links among these FCMs are those of predator and prey where the larger eats the smaller. The actors chase, flee, and eat one another. A hungry shark chases the dolphins and that leads to the limit cycle $(\mathbf{C}_1, \mathbf{C}_2, \mathbf{C}_3, \mathbf{C}_4)$ above. Augmenting the FCM matrices gives a large but sparse FCM since the actors respond to each other in few ways.

The augmented FCM moves the actors in the virtual world. The binary output states of this FCM move the actors. Each FCM state maps to equations or function approximations for movement.

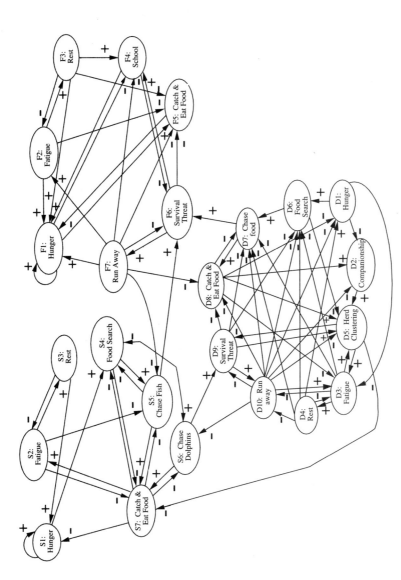

Figure 13.3 Augmented FCM for different actors in a virtual world. The actors interact through linked common causal concepts such as chasing food S_5 or D_7 and avoiding a threat F_7 or D_7.

We used a simple update equation for position:

$$\mathbf{p}(t_{n+1}) = \mathbf{p}(t_n) + \Delta t \cdot \mathbf{v}(t_n) \qquad (5)$$

where $\mathbf{p}$ is the position of an actor at time t, and $\mathbf{v}(t)$ is the velocity of the actor at time t. The velocity depends on which nodes are active. For example, the velocity increases when a predator chases prey. The velocity $\mathbf{v}(t)$ does not change at time step Δt. The FCM finds the direction and magnitude of movement. The magnitude of the velocity depends on the FCM state. If the FCM state is "run away," then the velocity is FAST. If the FCM state is "rest," then the velocity is SLOW. The prey choose the direction that maximizes the distance from the predator. The predator chases the prey. When a predator searches for food, it swims at random [4]. Each state moves the actors through the sea.

The FCM in Figure 13.3 encodes limit cycles between the actors. For example, if we start with a hungry shark and set the causal link between concept S4: FOOD SEARCH and S6: CHASE DOLPHINS equal to zero we can look at shark interactions with the fish school. Then the first state $\mathbf{C}_1$ is:

$$\mathbf{C}_1 = [0\ 0\ 0\ 0\ 0\ 0\ 0\ 0\ 0\ 0\ 1\ 0\ 0\ 0\ 0\ 0\ 0\ 0\ 0\ 0\ 0\ 0]$$

This vector gives a seven-step limit cycle with four transition steps:

$$\mathbf{C}_1\mathbf{E}_A = [0\ 0\ 0\ 0\ 0\ 0\ 0\ 0\ 0\ 0\ 1\ 0\ 0\ 1\ 0\ 0\ 0\ 0\ 0\ 0\ 0\ 0] \rightarrow$$
$$\mathbf{C}_2 = [0\ 0\ 0\ 0\ 0\ 0\ 0\ 0\ 0\ 0\ 1\ 0\ 0\ 1\ 0\ 0\ 0\ 0\ 0\ 0\ 0\ 0],$$
$$\mathbf{C}_2\mathbf{E}_A = [0\ 0\ 0\ 0\ 0\ 0\ 0\ 0\ 0\ 1\ 0\ 0\ 1\ 1\ 0\ -1\ 0\ 0\ 0\ 0\ 0\ 0] \rightarrow$$
$$\mathbf{C}_3 = [0\ 0\ 0\ 0\ 0\ 0\ 0\ 0\ 0\ 1\ 0\ 0\ 1\ 1\ 0\ 0\ 0\ 0\ 0\ 0\ 0\ 0],$$
$$\mathbf{C}_3\mathbf{E}_A = [0\ 0\ 0\ 0\ 0\ 0\ 0\ 0\ 0\ 1\ 0\ 0\ 0\ 1\ 0\ 0\ 0\ 0\ 0\ 0\ 1\ 0] \rightarrow$$
$$\mathbf{C}_4 = [0\ 0\ 0\ 0\ 0\ 0\ 0\ 0\ 0\ 1\ 0\ 0\ 0\ 1\ 0\ 0\ 0\ 0\ 0\ 0\ 1\ 0],$$
$$\mathbf{C}_4\mathbf{E}_A = [0\ 0\ 0\ 0\ 0\ 0\ 0\ 0\ 0\ 1\ 0\ 0\ 0\ 0\ 1\ 0\ 0\ 0\ 1\ -1\ 1\ 1] \rightarrow$$
$$\mathbf{C}_5 = [0\ 0\ 0\ 0\ 0\ 0\ 0\ 0\ 0\ 1\ 0\ 0\ 0\ 0\ 1\ 0\ 0\ 0\ 1\ 0\ 1\ 1],$$
$$\mathbf{C}_5\mathbf{E}_A = [0\ 0\ 0\ 0\ 0\ 0\ 0\ -1\ 0\ 0\ 0\ 1\ 0\ 0\ -2\ -1\ 0\ 2\ 1\ 0\ 0\ -2\ -2\ 1] \rightarrow$$
$$\mathbf{C}_6 = [0\ 0\ 0\ 0\ 0\ 0\ 0\ 0\ 0\ 0\ 0\ 1\ 0\ 0\ 0\ 0\ 1\ 1\ 0\ 0\ 0\ 1],$$
$$\mathbf{C}_6\mathbf{E}_A = [0\ 0\ 0\ 0\ 0\ 0\ 0\ -1\ 0\ 0\ 0\ 1\ 0\ -2\ 0\ -1\ 3\ 1\ 1\ -2\ -1\ -1\ 0] \rightarrow$$
$$\mathbf{C}_7 = [0\ 0\ 0\ 0\ 0\ 0\ 0\ 0\ 0\ 0\ 0\ 0\ 1\ 0\ 0\ 0\ 1\ 1\ 1\ 0\ 0\ 0\ 0],$$
$$\mathbf{C}_7\mathbf{E}_A = [0\ 0\ 0\ 0\ 0\ 0\ 0\ 0\ 0\ 1\ -1\ 0\ 0\ 0\ 0\ 3\ -1\ 1\ 0\ -1\ 0\ 0] \rightarrow$$
$$\mathbf{C}_8 = [0\ 0\ 0\ 0\ 0\ 0\ 0\ 0\ 0\ 1\ 0\ 0\ 0\ 0\ 0\ 1\ 0\ 1\ 0\ 0\ 0\ 0],$$
$$\mathbf{C}_8\mathbf{E}_A = [0\ 0\ 0\ 0\ 0\ 0\ 0\ 0\ 0\ 1\ 0\ 0\ 1\ 0\ 0\ 0\ 2\ -1\ 0\ 0\ 0\ 0] \rightarrow$$
$$\mathbf{C}_9 = [0\ 0\ 0\ 0\ 0\ 0\ 0\ 0\ 0\ 1\ 0\ 0\ 1\ 0\ 0\ 0\ 1\ 0\ 0\ 0\ 0\ 0],$$
$$\mathbf{C}_9\mathbf{E}_A = [0\ 0\ 0\ 0\ 0\ 0\ 0\ 0\ 0\ 1\ 0\ 0\ 1\ 1\ 0\ -1\ 1\ 0\ 0\ -1\ 1\ 0\ 0] \rightarrow$$
$$\mathbf{C}_{10} = [0\ 0\ 0\ 0\ 0\ 0\ 0\ 0\ 0\ 1\ 0\ 0\ 1\ 1\ 0\ 0\ 1\ 0\ 0\ 0\ 1\ 0\ 0],$$
$$\mathbf{C}_{10}\mathbf{E}_A = [0\ 0\ 0\ 0\ 0\ 0\ 0\ 0\ 0\ 1\ 0\ 0\ 0\ 1\ 0\ 0\ 0\ 0\ 0\ -1\ 1\ 1\ 0] \rightarrow$$
$$\mathbf{C}_{11} = [0\ 0\ 0\ 0\ 0\ 0\ 0\ 0\ 0\ 1\ 0\ 0\ 0\ 1\ 0\ 0\ 0\ 0\ 0\ 0\ 1\ 1\ 0],$$
$$\mathbf{C}_{11}\mathbf{E}_A = [0\ 0\ 0\ 0\ 0\ 0\ 0\ 0\ 0\ 1\ 0\ 0\ 0\ 0\ 0\ 1\ -1\ 0\ 0\ 1\ -1\ 1\ 1] \rightarrow$$
$$\mathbf{C}_5 = [0\ 0\ 0\ 0\ 0\ 0\ 0\ 0\ 0\ 1\ 0\ 0\ 0\ 0\ 0\ 1\ 0\ 0\ 0\ 1\ 0\ 1\ 1].$$

In this limit cycle, a shark searches for food (C_1,C_2,C_3). The shark finds some fish (C_4), chases the fish (C_5), and then eats some of the fish (C_6). To avoid the shark, most fish run away and then regroup as a school (C_5,C_6,C_7). Then the fish rest and eat while the shark rests (C_8,C_9). In time, the shark gets hungry again and searches for fish (C_{10},C_{11}).

The result is a complex dance among the actors as they move in a 2D ocean. Figure 13.4 shows these movements. The forcing function is a hungry shark $(S_1 = 1)$. The shark encounters the dolphins, which cluster and then flee the shark. The shark chases but cannot keep up. The shark still searches for food and finds the fish. It catches a fish and then rests with its hunger sated. Meanwhile, the hungry dolphins search for food and eat more fish. Each actor responds to the actions of the other.

13.4. Adaptive Fuzzy Cognitive Maps

An adaptive FCM changes its causal web in time. The causal web learns from data. The causal edges or rules change in sign and magnitude. The

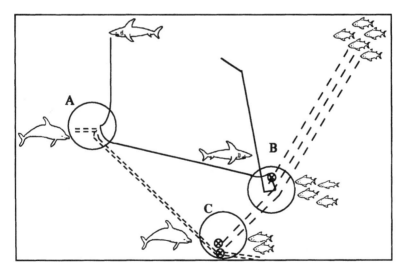

Figure 13.4 FCMs control the virtual world. The augmented FCM controls the actions of the actors. In event A, the hungry shark forces the dolphin herd to run away. Each dashed line stands for a dolphin swim path. In event B, the shark finds the fish and eats some. Each dashed line stands for the path of a fish in the school. The cross shows the shark eating a fish. In event C, the fish run into the dolphins and suffer more losses. The solid lines are the dolphin paths. The dashes are the fish swim paths. The cross shows a dolphin eating a fish.

additive scheme (3) is a type of causal learning since it changes the FCM edge strengths. In general, an edge e_{ij} changes with some first-order learning law:

$$\dot{e}_{ij} = f_{ij}(\mathbf{E}, \mathbf{C}) + g_{ij}(t) \tag{6}$$

Here, g_{ij} is a forcing function. Data fires the concept nodes and in time this leaves a causal pattern in the edge. Causal learning is local in f_{ij}. It depends on just its own value and on the node signals that it connects [7, 8]:

$$\dot{e}_{ij} = f_{ij}(e_{ij}, C_i, C_j, \dot{C}_i, \dot{C}_j) + g_{ij}(t) \tag{7}$$

Correlation or Hebbian learning can encode some limit cycles in the FCMs. It adds pairwise correlation matrices to encode patterns [7,8]. This method can only store a few patterns. Differential Hebbian learning encodes changes in a concept in equation 7. Both types of learning are local and light in computation.

The differential Hebbian learning law [7,8] correlates concept changes or velocities:

$$\dot{e}_{ij} = -e_{ij} + \dot{C}_i(x_i)\dot{C}_j(x_j) \tag{8}$$

So, $\dot{C}_i(x_i)\dot{C}_j(x_j) > 0$ iff concepts C_i and C_j move in the same direction. $\dot{C}_i(x_i)\dot{C}_j(x_j) < 0$ iff concepts C_i and C_j move in opposite directions. In this sense, 8 learns patterns of causal change. The first-order structure of (8) implies that $e_{ij}(t)$ is an exponentially weighted average of paired (or lagged) changes. The most recent changes have the most weight. The *discrete* change $\Delta C_i(t) = C_i(t) - C_i(t-1)$ lies in $\{-1,0,1\}$. The discrete differential Hebbian learning can take the form:

$$e_{ij}(t+1) = \begin{cases} e_{ij}(t) + c_t[\Delta C_i(x_i)\Delta C_j(x_j) - e_{ij}(t)] & \text{if } \Delta C_i(x_i) \neq 0 \\ e_{ij}(t) & \text{if } \Delta C_i(x_i) = 0 \end{cases} \tag{9}$$

Here, c_t is a learning coefficient that decreases in time [7]. $\Delta C_i \Delta C_j > 0$ iff concepts C_i and C_j move in the same direction. $\Delta C_i \Delta C_j < 0$ iff concepts C_i and C_j move in opposite directions. $\mathbf{E}$ changes only if a concept changes.

The changed edge slowly "forgets" the old causal changes in favor of the new ones. This causal law can learn higher-order causal relations if it correlates multiple cause changes with effect changes.

We used differential Hebbian learning to encode a feeding sequence and a chase sequence in a FCM. We correlated changes between adjacent time steps at i and $i + 1$. The concepts in the ith row learn only when $\Delta C_i(x_i)$ equals 1 or -1. The update equation took the form of (9) with $j =$

$i + 1$. We used $c_i(t_k) = 0.1[1 - t_k/1.1N]$. Figure 13.5 lists the two training sequences. This gave the $\mathbf{E_D}$:

	D_1	D_2	D_3	D_4	D_5	D_6	D_7	D_8	D_9	D_{10}
D_1	−0.25	0.00	0.00	−0.24	−0.24	0.76	−0.51	0.00	0.00	0.00
D_2	0.00	−0.49	0.49	−0.51	0.00	0.00	0.00	0.00	0.00	0.00
D_3	−0.26	0.00	−0.25	1.00	0.75	0.00	0.00	0.00	0.00	0.00
D_4	1.00	0.00	−0.25	−0.25	−0.25	−0.50	0.00	0.00	0.00	0.00
D_5	0.51	−0.16	0.49	−0.34	−0.51	−0.33	0.00	0.00	0.00	−0.16
D_6	0.00	0.00	0.00	0.00	0.00	−0.49	1.00	−0.51	0.00	0.00
D_7	0.00	−0.51	0.00	0.00	−0.51	0.00	−0.49	1.00	0.00	0.00
D_8	0.00	1.00	−0.33	0.00	0.67	0.00	0.00	−0.67	0.00	0.00
D_9	0.00	0.00	−1.00	0.00	1.00	0.00	0.00	0.00	0.00	1.00
D_{10}	0.00	0.00	1.00	−0.51	−1.00	0.00	0.00	0.00	0.00	−0.49

$\mathbf{E_D} =$ (applied to the rows D_5 region of the matrix above)

This learned edge matrix $\mathbf{E_D}$ resembles the FCM matrix in Figure 13.1. The causal links it lacks between $\mathbf{D_{10}}$ and $\{\mathbf{D_6, D_7, D_8}\}$ were not in the training set. The diagonal links terms for self-inhibition of each concept. This occurs since each concept is on for one cycle before the matrix tran-

Time Step	Hunting Sequence									
	C_1	C_2	C_3	C_4	C_5	C_6	C_7	C_8	C_9	C_{10}
1	0	0	1	1	1	0	0	0	0	0
2	1	0	0	1	1	0	0	0	0	0
3	1	0	0	0	0	0	0	0	0	0
4	0	0	0	0	0	1	0	0	0	0
5	0	0	0	0	0	0	1	0	0	0
6	0	0	0	0	0	0	0	1	0	0
7	0	1	0	0	1	0	0	0	0	0
8	0	0	1	0	1	0	0	0	0	0
9	0	0	1	1	1	0	0	0	0	0
10	1	0	0	1	1	0	0	0	0	0

Time Step	Chase Sequence									
	C_1	C_2	C_3	C_4	C_5	C_6	C_7	C_8	C_9	C_{10}
1	0	0	0	0	0	0	0	0	1	0
2	0	0	0	0	1	0	0	0	0	1
3	0	0	1	0	0	0	0	0	0	0
4	0	0	0	1	1	0	0	0	0	0
5	1	0	0	0	0	0	0	0	0	0
6	0	0	0	0	0	1	0	0	0	0
7	0	0	0	0	0	0	1	0	0	0
8	0	0	0	0	0	0	0	1	0	0
9	0	1	0	0	1	0	0	0	0	0

Figure 13.5 The two training sequences used for the differential competitive learning. The FCM in Figure 13.1 generated these sequences.

sitions to the next state. The hunger input $\mathbf{CL}_0 = [1\ 0\ 0\ 0\ 0\ 0\ 0\ 0\ 0\ 0]$ with a threshold of 0.51 now leads to the limit cycle:

$\mathbf{CL}_0\ \mathbf{E}_D = [-0.25\ 0.00\ 0.00\ -0.24\ -0.24\ 0.76\ -0.51\ 0.00\ 0.00\ 0.00] \rightarrow$
$\qquad \mathbf{CL}_1 = [0\ 0\ 0\ 0\ 0\ 1\ 0\ 0\ 0\ 0],$
$\mathbf{CL}_1\ \mathbf{E}_D = [0.00\ 0.00\ 0.00\ 0.00\ 0.00\ -0.49\ 1.00\ -0.51\ 0.00\ 0.00] \rightarrow$
$\qquad \mathbf{CL}_2 = [0\ 0\ 0\ 0\ 0\ 0\ 1\ 0\ 0\ 0],$
$\mathbf{CL}_2\ \mathbf{E}_D = [0.00\ -0.51\ 0.00\ 0.00\ -0.51\ 0.00\ -0.49\ 1.00\ 0.00\ 0.00] \rightarrow$
$\qquad \mathbf{CL}_3 = [0\ 0\ 0\ 0\ 0\ 0\ 0\ 1\ 0\ 0],$
$\mathbf{CL}_3\ \mathbf{E}_D = [0.00\ 1.00\ -0.33\ 0.00\ 0.67\ 0.00\ 0.00\ -0.67\ 0.00\ 0.00] \rightarrow$
$\qquad \mathbf{CL}_4 = [0\ 1\ 0\ 0\ 1\ 0\ 0\ 0\ 0\ 0],$
$\mathbf{CL}_4\ \mathbf{E}_D = [0.51\ -0.65\ 0.98\ -0.85\ -0.51\ -0.33\ 0.00\ 0.00\ 0.00\ -0.16] \rightarrow$
$\qquad \mathbf{CL}_5 = [0\ 0\ 1\ 0\ 0\ 0\ 0\ 0\ 0\ 0],$
$\mathbf{CL}_5\ \mathbf{E}_D = [-0.26\ 0.00\ -0.25\ 1.00\ 0.75\ 0.00\ 0.00\ 0.00\ 0.00\ 0.00] \rightarrow$
$\qquad \mathbf{CL}_6 = [0\ 0\ 0\ 1\ 1\ 0\ 0\ 0\ 0\ 0],$
$\mathbf{CL}_6\ \mathbf{E}_D = [1.51\ -0.16\ 0.25\ -0.59\ -0.76\ -0.83\ 0.00\ 0.00\ 0.00\ -0.16] \rightarrow$
$\qquad \mathbf{CL}_1 = [1\ 0\ 0\ 0\ 0\ 0\ 0\ 0\ 0\ 0],$

This resembles the sequence of rest, eat, play, and rest from section 13.3. Figure 13.6a shows the hand-designed limit cycle from section 13.3. Figure 13.6b shows the limit cycle from FCM found with differential Hebbian learning. The learned limit cycle is one step shorter since the value of $\mathbf{E}_{D5}$ does not change over two intervals in the original FCM. The learning law in (9) learns only if there is a change in the node.

13.5. Conclusion

Fuzzy cognitive maps can model the causal web of a virtual world. The FCM can control its local and global nonlinear behavior. The local fuzzy rules or edges and the fuzzy concepts they connect model the causal links within and between events. The global FCM nonlinear dynamics give the virtual world an "arrow of time." A user can change these dynamics at will and thus change the causal processes in the virtual world. FCMs let experts and users choose a causal web by drawing causal pictures instead of by stating equations.

FCMs can also help visualize data. They show how variables relate to one another in the causal web. The FCM output states can guide a cartoon of the virtual world. The cartoon animates the FCM dynamics as the system trajectory moves through the FCM state space, as Figure 13.7 shows. This can apply to models in economics, medicine, history, and politics [14] where the social and causal web can change in complex ways that may arise from changing the sign or magnitude of a single FCM causal rule or edge.

The additive structure of combined FCMs permits a Delphi [11] or questionnaire approach to knowledge acquisition. These new causal webs can change an adaptive FCM that learns its causal web as neural-like learning laws process time-series data. Experts can add their FCM matri-

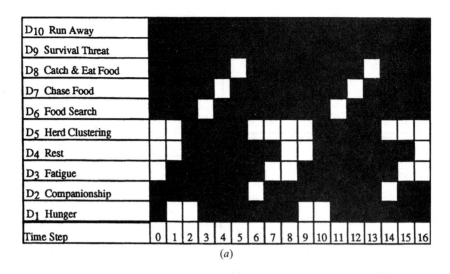

(a)

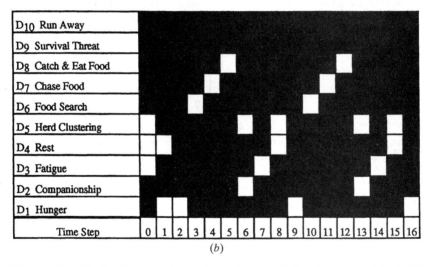

(b)

Figure 13.6 Limit cycle comparison between the hand-designed system and the FCM found with differential Hebbian learning. Each column is a binary state vector. (a) Rest, feed, play, rest limit cycle for the FCM in Figure 13.1. (b) Limit cycle for the FCM found with (9).

ces to the adaptive FCM to initialize or guide the learning. Such a causal web can learn the user's values and action habits and perhaps can test them or train them.

More complex FCMs have more complex dynamics and can model more complex virtual worlds. Each concept node can fire on its own time scale and fire in its own nonlinear way. The causal edge flows or rules can have their own time scales too and may increase or decrease the causal

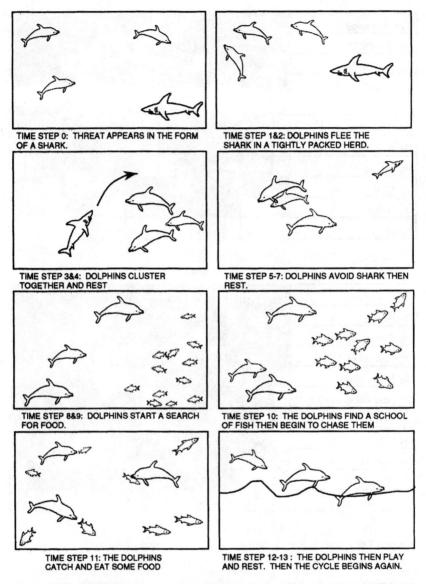

Figure 13.7 The FCM output states can guide a cartoon of the virtual world. This cartoon shows the dolphin chase, rest, eat sequence described in section 13.3. The cartoon animates the FCM dynamics as the system trajectory moves through the FCM state space.

flow through them in nonlinear ways. This behavior does not fit in a simple FCM with threshold concepts and constant edge weights.

An FCM can model these complex virtual worlds if it uses more nonlinear math to change its nodes and edges. The price paid may be a chaotic virtual world with unknown equilibrium behavior. Some users may want this to add novelty to their virtual world or to make it more exciting. A user might choose a virtual world that is mildly nonlinear and has periodic equilibria. At the other extreme, the user might choose a virtual world that is so wildly nonlinear it has only aperiodic equilibria.

Fuzziness and nonlinearity are design parameters for a virtual world. They may give a better model of a real process. Or they may be just more fun to play with.

13.6. References

[1] Brown, R.A. *Fluid Mechanics of the Atmosphere.* New York: Academic Press, 1991.

[2] Gibson, W. *Neuromancer.* New York: Ace Books, 1984.

[3] Kaelbling, L.P. "An Architecture for Intelligent Reactive Systems," in *Reasoning About Actions and Plans,* eds. M.P. Georgeff and A.L. Lansky. pp. 395–410. San Mateo: Morgan Kaufmann, 1987.

[4] Koopman, B.O. *Search and Screening.* New York: Pergamon Press, 1980.

[5] Kosko, B. "Fuzzy Cognitive Maps." *International Journal Man-Machine Studies,* Vol. 24 (1986), pp. 65–75.

[6] ———. "Bidirectional Associative Memories." *IEEE Transactions on Systems, Man, and Cybernetics,* Vol. 18 (1988), pp. 49–60.

[7] ———. "Hidden Patterns in Combined and Adaptive Knowledge Networks." *International Journal of Approximate Reasoning,* Vol. 2 (1988), pp. 337–393.

[8] ———. *Neural Networks and Fuzzy Systems.* Englewood Cliffs: Prentice Hall, 1992.

[9] Krueger, M. *Artificial Reality II,* Second ed. Reading: Addison-Wesley, 1991.

[10] Maes, P. "Situated Agents can have Goals." *Robotics and Autonomous Systems,* Vol. 6 (1990), pp. 49–70.

[11] Martino, J.P. *Technological Forecasting for Decision Making.* American Elsevier, 1972.

[12] Minsky, M.L. *The Society of Mind.* New York: Simon & Schuster, 1985.

[13] Shane, S.H. "Comparison of Bottlenose Dolphin Behavior in Texas and Florida, with a Critique of Methods for Studying Dolphin Behavior," in *The Bottlenose Dolphin,* eds. S. Leatherwood and R.R. Reeves, pp. 541–558. New York: Academic Press, 1990.

[14] Taber, W.R. "Knowledge Processing with Fuzzy Cognitive Maps." *Expert Systems with Applications,* Vol. 2 (1991), pp. 83–87.

[15] Taber, W.R., and M. Siegel. "Estimation of Expert Weights with Fuzzy Cognitive Maps." *IEEE, 1st International Conference on Neural Networks* (ICNN-87). San Diego: 1987.

[16] Winston, P.H. *Artificial Intelligence,* Second ed. Reading: Addison-Wesley, 1984.

Retrieving Information

PART 1
Querying

GUIDING NOTE

This section includes chapters devoted to flexible database querying and information retrieval. Fuzzy set methods can be used in these problems for dealing with at least three different tasks:

i) Representing the flexibility of the query expressing the preferences of the user: using fuzzy methods the extent to which an object, whose description is stored in the base, satisfies the request becomes a matter of degree,

ii) Manipulating information, stored in a database, pervaded with imprecision and uncertainty. Using this approach, ill-known attribute values are represented by means of possibility distributions.

iii) Modeling similarity between close values. If an attribute value v satisfies an elementary requirement, a value "close" to v should still somewhat satisfy the requirement.

Queries are usually compound, and this raises the issue of finding the appropriate aggregation operations for combining the elementary degrees of matching. An important benefit of dealing with flexible queries is then to provide a basis for rank-ordering the retrieved items according to user's preferences. It also avoids too strict requirements leading to empty sets of answers and too permissive requirements resulting in too large sets of answers where no help is provided to the user for choosing between them.

The issue of allowing for flexible queries is discussed in the first six chapters with emphasis on various aspects of the idea. Kacprzyk and Zadrozny show how fuzzy querying system can be incorporated in existing database systems. They put a particular stress on the use of OWA operations for performing aggregations in queries where it is required that "most" of the conditions be satisfied rather than all. Bosc and Pivert investigate in detail how to extend the classical SQL language in order to process fuzzy queries. Rasmussen and Yager discuss how linguistic summaries of the form "few people in the database are tall" can be evaluated and validated. They show how these types of statements can be incorporated as predicates within the SQL framework and thus be easily included as extensions of existing systems. While the three first chapters were database-oriented, Bordogna and Pasi deal with information retrieval. The relevance of an index term of a document is now a matter of degree and somewhat reflects the frequency of the term in the document. However, this occurrence has to be appreciated on the basis of specific criteria according to the considered document sections and the relevance also depends on user's interests. The evaluation of the relevance of a document with respect to a compound query requires the use of OWA operations. Isomoto, Yoshine, and Ishii suggest an application in the multicriteria area where scenic images are retrieved from fuzzy descriptions of what they represent. Larsen and Yager show the interest of softening queries and how evaluations of stored items can be modified when the importance given to the elementary requirements varies.

Vanderberghe and De Caluwe deal with a fuzzy information database where fuzzy information is represented by possibility distributions. Then the evaluation of a (fuzzy) query is pervaded by the uncertainty and the imprecision coming from the stored data. One is then led to distinguish between items that more or less *possibly* match the query and those that *certainly* match it to some degree (because the available information for those items is sufficiently precise with respect to the query). George, Srikanth, Buckles, and Petry use fuzzy similarity relations in an object-oriented data model. Consequences on database operations of the introduction of similarity relations modelling approximate equalities are fully discussed.

14 Fuzzy Queries in Microsoft Access V.2

Janusz Kacprzyk, Sławomir Zadrożny
Systems Research Institute, Polish Academy of Sciences

ABSTRACT: A fuzzy querying "add-on" to Microsoft Access v.2 is presented. Fuzzy descriptions and linguistic quantifiers are accommodated to allow for queries as "find (all) records such that *most* of the (*important*) clauses (possibly containing vague notions) are satisfied (to a degree from [0,1]." Calculi of linguistically quantified propositions and OWA operators are employed.

14.1. Introduction

Relational DBMSs based on a graphical user interface (GUI), Microsoft Windows 3.1 in our case, are increasingly popular due to their ease of use and intuitiveness, even for an inexperienced user. These are exemplified by Microsoft's FoxPro for Windows, Access, Borland's Paradox for Windows, SPC's Superbase, Lotus' Approach, and others.

One often faces an inherent vagueness in the description of what is to be really retrieved, and then it may be cumbersome to formulate a proper query using standard database capabilities.

This chapter is a continuation of our previous works (Kacprzyk and Ziółkowski, 1986; Kacprzyk, Zadrożny, and Ziółkowski, 1989) and later Kacprzyk and Zadrożny (1994a–1995d). Their essence is the use of a commercial DBMS, and then the implementation of fuzzy querying as an add-on. So, the family of FQUERY (. . . , III+) fuzzy querying systems, for the dBase type DBMSs, and then FQUERY for Access, for Microsoft Access v.1, have been proposed.

We present here the implementation of that fuzzy querying system for Access v.2. The system supports the queries of the type "find (all) records such that *most* (almost all, much more than a half . . . or any other suitable linguistic quantifier) of the *important* attributes are as specified (e.g., equal to 5, greater than 10, much less than 100, etc.)" as proposed in Kacprzyk and Ziółkowski (1986a, 1986b), and Kacprzyk, Zadrożny, and Ziółkowski (1989). In this work, we (re)develop and implement that basic fuzzy querying system for Access v.2. Its open architecture, as well as some new features ("add-in") makes it an ideal candidate for our purposes. Its enhanced speed plays some role, too.

14.2. Fuzzy Elements in a Query

The FQUERY family supports various fuzzy elements in queries, and the problem is how to include in a classical query language such terms as "low," "much greater than," "most," and so on. That is: (1) how to extend the syntax and semantics of the query, and (2) how to provide an easy way of eliciting and manipulating those terms by the user; these aspects will now be discussed.

Access represents a query in the SQL formalism exemplifed by:

```
SELECT <list of fields>
WHERE
cond₁₁ AND cond₁₂ AND...AND cond₁ₖ
OR...OR
condₙ₁ AND condₙ₂ AND...AND condₙₘ
```

where each of $cond_{ij}$, an atomic condition, involves fields of tables and relational symbols, such as PRICE > 1000 or AMOUNT_IN_STOCK > AMOUNT_ON_ORDERS; the ANDed sequence of atomic conditions is referred to as a subcondition.

FQUERY for Access extends this scheme allowing for the use of fuzzy terms. Hence, we obtain the following general form of the query accepted by the FQUERY for Access in BNF-like notation:

```
<query> ::=
        SELECT <list of fields>*
        FROM <list of tables>*
        WHERE <fuzzy quantifier>
        <sequence of subconditions> ;
<sequence of subconditions> ::=
        <subcondition> |
        <subcondition> OR <sequence of subconditions>
<subcondition> ::=
        <fuzzy quantifier> <importance coefficient>
        <sequence of atomic conditions>
<sequence of atomic conditions> ::=
```

```
        <atomic condition> |
        <atomic condition> AND
        <sequence of atomic conditions>
<atomic condition> ::=
        <attribute> = <fuzzy value> |
        <attribute> <fuzzy relation> <attribute> |
        <attribute> <fuzzy relation> <number>*|
        <other forms obeying Microsoft Access's syntax>*
<attribute> ::= <numeric field>
<fuzzy quantifier> ::= <OWA-tag><quantifier name>|
<OWA-tag> ::= OWA |
```

The meaning of the main entities may be summarized as:

- **<attribute>**   A (numerical!) field to be used in a query and sub-jected to a fuzzy term has to be declared as an attribute. For each attribute, the user should give: the lower limit (LL) and upper limit (UL). They determine the interval of possible values, and are used for scaling the values while calculating the (degree of) compatibility (matching) with a fuzzy value used, or the degree of membership in a fuzzy relation. They need not describe the real value interval.

- **<fuzzy value>**   These are equivalents of imprecise linguistic terms, such as, "large" in "salary is large," and are defined by trapezoidal membership functions on $[-10, +10]$ (to avoid, e.g., context dependency).

   For an attribute with a fuzzy value, its actual value, V, for a given record is first linearly mapped into $[-10, +10]$ preserving the mapping of its range of values, that is, $[LL, UL]$ onto $[-10, 10]$. Then, as the matching degree, the membership degree of the transformed value V in the fuzzy value is assumed.

- **<fuzzy relation>**   An imprecise relation as "not much greater than" is represented by a binary fuzzy relation with a trapezoidal membership function. The two operands may be both attributes' names and numbers. For two attributes, the *difference* of their actual values, D, for a given record is first linearly mapped into $[-10, 10]$ preserving the range of variability; that is $[LL1 - UL2, UL1 - LL2]$ onto $[-10, 10]$, where LL1, LL2, UL1 and UL2 are the lower and upper bounds of variability ranges. Then, as the matching degree, the membership degree of D in the fuzzy relation is assumed. If the second operand is a number, the matching degree is calculated analogously, assuming as the variability range of the number the one of the first operand.

   For example, if we have an attribute PRICE with the range of values "PRICE:(0, 1000000)," a fuzzy relation AROUND with the trapezoidal membership function "AROUND:$(-2, -1, 1, 2)$," a query

"PRICE IS AROUND 250,000," and a record with "PRICE = 260,000," then the query is referred to two attributes with the same range $[0, 1000000]$. The value $10000 (= 260000 - 250000)$ is mapped into $[-10, 10]$, thus we obtain 0.1. Then we take its membership degree in the fuzzy relation, equal 1.0, which is the matching degree sought; for "PRICE = 400000," the matching degree is equal 0.5.

- **<fuzzy quantifier> <importance coefficient> <OWA-tag>** The fuzzy quantifiers are used in statements as "*most* clauses of the query are to be satisfied." Initially, in FQUERY for Access v.1 (Kacprzyk and Zadrożny, 1994) the fuzzy linguistic quantifiers were defined as fuzzy sets in $[0.0, 10.0]$ (cf. Zadeh, 1983) with piecewise linear membership functions. To calculate the truth value of "$QP(x)$," for example, "*most* (Q) subconditions *of the query are fulfilled*," we map the nonfuzzy cardinality of the fuzzy set of the subconditions fulfilled, S, into the $[0, 10]$. Then, we take the membership degree of the transformed value of S in the set representing fuzzy quantifier, as the degree of the satisfaction of the whole query.

  In FQUERY for Access v.2 (Kacprzyk and Zadrożny, 1995a–d), first, importance is added allowing for the following queries "*most of the important subconditions of the query are fulfilled.*" The use of importance makes it possible to differentiate between primary subconditions whose fulfillment is essential for the concept represented by the query, and secondary ones, being less important for the meaning of this concept. Second, the OWA operators (Yager, 1988) are supported. The user can use either a predefined fuzzy quantifier, or can add to the name the prefix "OWA" to employ its OWA interpretation.

  The use of OWA operators instead of plain Zadeh's (1983) quantifiers may sometimes be convenient. It also may alleviate some rigidness of the proposed extended SQL syntax as, for example, it may be easier to have a subcondition being an ORed sequence of atomic conditions instead of an ANDed sequence as it is originally. That is, instead of:

  atomic_condition$_1$ AND ... AND ... atomic_condition$_n$

  one can put

  OWAFuzzy_MAX atomic_condition$_1$ AND ... AND ... atomic_condition$_n$

  where the OWAFuzzy_MAX is defined by the OWA weights $[1, 0, 0, \ldots, 0]$.

14.3. Remarks on Implementation

FQUERY for Access v.2 system is embedded in the native Access environment as an add-on (or add-in). Due to the lack of specific tools in

Access v.1.x, the use of, and especially the installation of the former FQUERY for Access 1.x was more difficult (Kacprzyk and Zadrożny, 1994a, b).

To embed fuzzy elements into the Access environment, two representation problems should be solved. First, the definitions of attributes, fuzzy values, and so on should be stored in proper locations. Second, a possibility to express the query involving fuzzy elements should be provided; this requires a mechanism for putting such a fuzzy element into the Query By Example (QBE) sheet (grid).

The former problem is solved using the Access library feature. More specifically, all the code and data necessary for the representation and processing of fuzzy elements are located in a specific database file, a library. It can be installed by the user and then made available during any session with the DBMS. This feature was already present in Access v. 1.x, but in v. 2.0 it becomes more operational securing an easy installation/deinstallation. For each category of fuzzy elements, there is a table in the library database storing all information needed. Those tables store descriptions of the predefined elements (e.g., fuzzy quantifier "most" or fuzzy value "low") and the elements defined by the users during the subsequent sessions.

The latter problem, how to include fuzzy elements in the queries, is solved through the use of parameters. Access allows for parameters in the queries of any name. By a special parameter naming convention, we make it possible to refer to previously defined fuzzy elements. For example, to use the fuzzy value "low," one has to put into an appropriate cell of the QBE sheet a parameter named [FfA_FV Low]; that is, one has to precede the name of the selected fuzzy element with an appropriate prefix (brackets are the part of the standard Access notation for parameters in queries).

The correspondence between fuzzy elements and prefixes is:

<fuzzy quantifier>:	FfA_FQ
<importance coefficient>:	FfA_FI
<fuzzy value>:	FfA_FV
<fuzzy relation>:	FfA_FR

For further details on naming parameters, see, for example, Kacprzyk and Zadrożny (1995a, b).

14.3.1. The Toolbar

The proposed parameters naming convention is easy and intuitively appealing. Nevertheless, a manual composition of the required parameters' names may be inconvenient. FQUERY for Access v. 2.0 provides its own toolbar. It is not a regular toolbar in the sense of Access due to some implementational difficulties in a library database but the solution adopted yields virtually all the features of a regular toolbar. There is one button for every category of fuzzy elements—fuzzy values, fuzzy relations, fuzzy quantifiers, and fuzzy importances. These buttons are supplemented by one for declaring attributes, one for starting the querying process, and two standard buttons for closing the toolbar and for help.

14.3.2. Basic Rules of Interaction

Generally, the user interacts with the FQUERY for Access v.2.0 in order to:

- declare attributes,
- define fuzzy elements and put them automatically into the QBE sheet, and
- start the querying process.

All these activities are initiated by pressing a button on the toolbar. The toolbar is displayed after selecting a special menu item which is added to the standard Access's menu File|Add-in during the installation process.

The user inserts fuzzy elements into the QBE sheet selecting them from a menu that appears on the screen. These menus are accompanied by other buttons for defining fuzzy elements. Such a definition, or an attribute declaration, consists in filling a special form displayed on the screen.

After the query definition, the user initiates the search by pressing the GO button. FQUERY for Access v.2.0 is designed to use the standard Access querying procedure. If the query contains fuzzy elements, they are still legitimate; that is, parameters (the user is asked to provide actual values for them). If the query has no fuzzy elements, the pressing of either the standard Access button or that of FQUERY for Access v.2.0 gives the same result.

14.3.3. Query Transformation

The composition of a query with fuzzy elements is done through the standard Access interface. FQUERY for Access provides, moreover, some specific tools enabling a seamless introduction of fuzzy elements into the query; except for that, the user interacts with a familiar interface. The same applies to the running of a fuzzy query. Again, the native Access engine is employed to run such a query, which, obviously, has to be transformed before.

The query is transformed into a legitimate Access query, and at the same time an intended interpretation of fuzzy elements is provided. The idea of that transformation may be briefly described as follows, in the terms of SQL syntax. All conditions are removed from the WHERE clause of the query, and are replaced by a call to the FQUERY for the Access internal function, which computes the matching degrees of subsequent records. An artificial (calculated) field is added to the SELECT clause to display this matching degree for each query (preserving all fields originally present in the SELECT clause). The function responsible for the computation of the matching degree is called with a number of arguments equal to the number of fuzzy elements in the query. Each of these arguments (actually, function calls) puts fields' values necessary for the matching degree computation into the FQUERY for Access internal data structure. Being called during the querying process for each record, this function gathers all information needed.

Thus, by pressing the GO button, the original SQL type query is translated according to the preceding rules and replaced by the modified one. The structure of the original fuzzy query is mirrored in the FQUERY for Access internal data structures, and the modified query contains calls to functions filling this data structure with all information required for computing the matching degree for the subsequent records of the database. Then, the query is run by Access as usual and the results are displayed. The original SQL form of the query is restored. It is done "on the fly," so that the user cannot even see its modified form on which the currently displayed information is based.

Finally, since the output of our querying add-on is a modified Access SQL query, the efficiency depends on the efficiency of Access's own query optimization techniques.

14.4. Example

Consider a databases of houses for sale. The record for each house contains, for example, the price and the number of bedrooms and bathrooms. We seek a house with four bedrooms, three bathrooms, and not much more expensive than $250,000 which can be expressed using FQUERY's for Access syntax as:

```
SELECT ADDRESS, PRICE, BEDROOMS, BATHROOMS
FROM HOUSES
WHERE ((PRICE=[FfA_FR Not much'greater than|250000]) AND
(BEDROOMS=[FfA_FR Around|4]) AND (BATHROOMS=[FfA_FR
    Around|3]));
```

and the composition of such a query is shown in Figure 14.1.

We obtain the following (best) records in response:

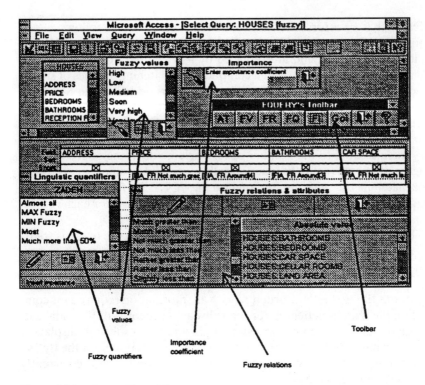

Figure 14.1 Composition of the query.

Address	Price	Bedrooms	Bathrooms	Md
4 Church St.	260,000	4	3	0.964912280701754
76 Cambridge Rd	147,000	3	2	0.888888888888889
12 Upper St.	271,700	4	4	0.888888888888889
249 Regent St.	270,800	3	2	0.888888888888889
179 Bayswater Rd	249,800	4	2	0.888888888888889

Without fuzzy elements in the query, we may have first:

```
SELECT ADDRESS, PRICE, BEDROOMS, BATHROOMS
FROM HOUSES
WHERE ((PRICE<=250000) AND (BEDROOMS=4) AND
(BATHROOMS=3));
```

which yields no record; that is, an empty response. Further, we may have:

```
SELECT ADDRESS, PRICE, BEDROOMS, BATHROOMS
FROM HOUSES
```

```
WHERE ((PRICE <=250000) AND (BEDROOMS<=5 And
BEDROOMS>=3) AND (BATHROOMS<=4 And BATHROOMS>=2))
```

and obtain:

Address	Price	Bedrooms	Bathrooms
76 Cambridge Rd	147,000	3	2
77 Hollywood Rd	174,600	3	3
34 Matlock St.Lane	176,000	5	2
302 Regent St.	183,900	3	2
12 Glengall St.	191,600	3	2

Notice that the record with a highest matching degree is absent because the price slightly exceeds $250,000; however, to most people, $260,000 is not much greater than this. Still, it is not so simple to overcome this difficulty in a nonfuzzy approach. If we just use another, slightly higher limit for the price in our nonfuzzy query, it may still happen that we will miss some houses slightly more expensive. Hence, the problem is in a fuzziness of requirements, and FQUERY for Access provides us with a quick and elegant tool to handle this.

14.5. Conclusion

We have presented the essence of FQUERY for Access v.2, an add-on to Microsoft's popular Windows-based DBMS, which allows for the use of fuzzy elements in querying, making querying more flexible and human-consistent.

14.6. References

[1] Bosc, P., et al. "Fuzzy Querying with SQL: Extensions and Implementation Aspects." *Fuzzy Sets and Systems*, Vol. 28 (1988), pp. 333–349.

[2] ———. *Fuzziness in Database Management Systems.* Physica-Verlag, Heidelberg: 1995.

[3] Bosc, P., and O. Pivert. "Fuzzy Querying in Conventional Databases," in *Fuzzy Logic for the Management of Uncertainty,* eds. L.A. Zadeh and J. Kacprzyk. pp. 645–671. New York: John Wiley & Sons Inc., 1992.

[4] Chang, S.K., and J.S. Ke. "Database Skeleton and its Application to Fuzzy Query Translation." *IEEE Transactions on Software Engineering,* SE-4. pp. 31–43. 1978.

[5] Kacprzyk, J., and S. Zadrozny. "Fuzzy Querying for Microsoft Access." *Proceedings, 3rd International Conference on Fuzzy Systems,* Vol. 1, pp. 167–171. Orlando, Fla.: 1994.

[6] ———. "Fuzzy Queries in Microsoft Access: Toward a More Intelligent Use of Microsoft Windows-based DBMS's." *Proceedings, ANZIIS '94.* pp. 492–496. Brisbane, Australia: 1994.

[7] ———. "Fuzzy Queries in Microsoft Access." *Proceedings, FUZZ-IEEE/IFES '95 Workshop on Fuzzy Database Systems and Information Retrieval.* pp. 61–66. Yokohama, Japan: 1995.

[8] ———. "Fuzzy Queries in Microsoft Access." *Proceedings, 6th IFSA Congress,* Vol. 2. pp. 341–344. Sao Paolo, Brazil: 1995.

[9] ———. "FQUERY for Access: Fuzzy Querying for a Windows-based DBMS," in *Fuzziness in Database Management Systems,* eds. P. Bosc and J. Kacprzyk. pp. 415–433. Physica-Verlag, Heidelberg: 1995.

[10] Zadrozny, S., and J. Kacprzyk. "Fuzzy Querying using the Query-by-Example Option in a Windows-based DBMS." *Proceedings, 3rd European Congress on Intelligent Techniques and Soft Computing,* Vol. 2. pp. 733–736. Aachen, Germany: 1995.

[11] Kacprzyk, J., et al. "FQUERY III+: A Human Consistent Database Querying System based on Fuzzy Logic with Linguistic Quantifiers." *Information Systems,* Vol. 6 (1989), pp. 443–453.

[12] Kacprzyk, J., and A. Ziolkowski. "Retrieval from Bases using Queries with Fuzzy Linguistic Quantifiers," in *Fuzzy Logics in Knowledge Engineering,* eds. H. Prade and C.V. Negoita. Verlag TUV Rheinland, Cologne: 1986.

[13] ———. "Database Queries with Fuzzy Linguistic Quantifiers." *IEEE Transactions on Systems, Man, and Cybernetics.* SMC-16. (1986), pp. 474–479.

[14] Yager, R.R. "Aggregating Evidence using Quantified Statements." *Information Science,* Vol. 36 (1985), pp. 179–206.

[15] ———. "On Ordered, Weighted Averaging Operators in Multicriteria Decision Making." *IEEE Transactions on Systems, Man, and Cybernetics.* SMC-18 (1988), pp. 183–190.

[16] Zadeh, L.A. "A Computational Approach to Fuzzy Quantifiers in Natural Languages." *Computers and Maths with Applications,* Vol. 9 (1983), pp. 149–184.

[17] Zemankova-Leech, M., and A. Kandel. "Fuzzy Relational Databases—A Key to Expert Systems." Verlag TUV Rheinland, Cologne: 284.

15 Extending SQL Retrieval Features for the Handling of Flexible Queries

Patrick Bosc
Olivier Pivert
IRISA/ENSSAT

ABSTRACT: An important issue in extending database management systems (DBMS) functionalities is to allow the expression of imprecise queries in order to make these systems able to satisfy some user needs more closely. This paper deals with flexible querying of regular relational databases in order to incorporate preferences inside user queries. The basic idea is to enrich the SQL language, which is currently used as a standard interface to current DBMSs, by introducing flexible predicates interpreted in the context of fuzzy sets. The syntax and semantics of the extended components as well as the relationships between SQL and the extended language are discussed. Some aspects related to feasibility and implementation of such a language are also addressed.

15.1. Introduction

In the field of databases, numerous efforts have been made to meet new needs and requirements. In particular, a stream of research has focused on the introduction of imprecision and/or uncertainty in database management systems (DBMSs). This issue covers several different aspects, among which two are striking: the storage and handling of imperfect information on the one hand and the expression of imprecise queries on the other hand. These two aspects are somewhat independent and we are only concerned with the latter whose objective is to propose alternatives to the use of Boolean logic, which, in most database management systems, remains the only way for the selection of information. Sometimes,

Boolean expressions are too rigid in the specification of the authorized values and limited in the choice of the connectors (conjunction and disjunction). For instance, if one is looking for a hotel room, a query like "price between $40 and $55 and distance to conference site < 1 km" involves the conjunction of two crisp predicates and will reject a hotel with an excellent location whose price is $57. This fact may be particularly unconvenient if no hotel satisfies both conditions, in which case the answer is empty.

The approach advocated here is situated in the context of usual relational databases (where data are precisely known). It is based on the use of fuzzy set theory to define imprecise conditions. The overall objective is the design of a language allowing for queries where (flexible) predicates are more or less satisfied rather than true or false. In this context, a grade (of membership or satisfaction) is attached to any element of the answer, which provides a natural ordering. Beyond some syntactic appeal, such as the possible use of linguistic terms (young, about 15, much greater than, etc), the interest of fuzzy querying is to allow for the expression of preferences in the selection conditions and consequently to provide users with discriminated answers (since some elements are better than others according to these preferences).

In [1], the fuzzy set framework is shown to be a sound scientific choice. In particular, it is a natural basis to express the graduality involved in the notion of preference. Moreover, it offers a means to express some other approaches based on more particular techniques such as distances or numeric combination of Boolean predicates. It is also able to deal with some kinds of needs that are not permitted (or supported) by these specific approaches (for instance, it allows for various types of combination of predicates).

The choice of SQL as a basis for the design of a flexible query language SQLf, has been done for the sake of continuity with respect to tools widely used in the database community. SQLf has the same general philosophy as SQL (as to querying features and syntax in particular), which is enlarged with new possibilities regarding flexible querying. The objective is to enrich the original language with capabilities related to flexibility wherever it makes sense, for example, not only for the selection of individual tuples but also for the qualification of sets of tuples. Furthermore, SQLf is in the continuity of the language described in [2], and it has been made as similar to SQL as possible, particularly regarding query equivalences [3].

The chapter is organized as follows. Section 15.2 is dedicated to a brief presentation of the basic elements of the SQL language (regarding querying functionalities). In section 15.3, various kinds of fuzzy predicates applying to individual tuples are reviewed, whereas fuzzy quantified statements applying to sets of tuples are presented in section 15.4. The basic component of SQLf, the base block, is described in section 15.5. Its syntactic and semantic specificities with respect to SQL on the one hand and its expressive power in terms of algebraic operations on the other hand are pointed out. Section 15.6 is devoted to conditions based on the use of nested blocks. Equivalences between various formulations as well as the connection between the use of nested predicates and set operations (intersection and difference) are discussed. The extension of the partitioning mechanism of SQL, which is the basis for queries applying to sets of tuples, is presented in section 15.7. Beyond the syntactic and semantic definition of the language, one important point concerns the evaluation of fuzzy queries with the further objective of an efficient implementation of a DBMS supporting such queries. Fuzzy (as well as regular) query processing is a very complex topic, and an exhaustive coverage can only be a long-term objective. Nevertheless, some initial directions are suggested in section 15.8 as a starting point for deeper investigations. Finally, the conclusion summarizes the principal ideas of the chapter and suggests some trends for future work.

15.2. SQL—A Survey

The objective of this section is to recall the principles and the basic features of SQL regarding querying capabilities. SQL was designed in the '70s, and it aims at the provision of a powerful, easy-to-use language for relational databases. It offers the capabilities of the relational algebra and some additional features to cope with practical needs such as arithmetic operations, aggregate functions, or variables. From a syntactic point of view, SQL is a block-structured language, and the basic structure of an SQL query is the base block whose general format is: **select** <attributes> **from** <relations> **where** <condition>.

The "from" clause specifies the relations of the database that are concerned by the block. The "select" clause describes the resulting relation made of attributes taken from the input relations (* is used when all attributes are desired). The "where" clause contains some condition (expressed as a logical expression where attribute values are compared to literals or to other attribute values) to be satisfied and the interpretation of such a sentence is the following:

Step 1: Perform the Cartesian product of the input relations.

Step 2: Restrict the Cartesian product to those elements that satisfy the condition.

Step 3: Remove unnecessary attributes (those that are not mentioned in the "select" part).

During this last phase, duplicates may appear (so the result is not a pure relation) and they can be eliminated using the keyword "distinct." With respect to the relational algebra, one may observe that this construct covers the projection, the Cartesian product, and the selection (and consequently joins that are nothing but the composition of Cartesian products and selections).

> **Example:** Throughout this chapter, the database made of the relations: EMP(#emp, e-name, salary, job, age, city, #dep) and DEP(#dep, d-name, manager, budget, location) describing employees and departments of a company are used for illustration. The query: "find the triples <employee number, employee name, department name> such that the employee lives in Chicago, earns more than $2500 and works in a department with a budget less than $2.5M" may be expressed:
>
> > **select** #emp, e-name, d-name **from** EMP, DEP
> > **where** city = "Chicago" **and** salary > 2500 **and** budget <2.5 **and** EMP.#dep = DEP.#dep.
>
> In this case, the condition in the "where" clause involves four elementary components, and the predicate EMP.#dep = DEP.#dep is a joining condition between the relations EMP and DEP.

An interesting feature of SQL lies in the ability for the combination of blocks. One possibility is to build elementary predicates using one (or several) nested blocks instead of predicates of the form: <attribute> <comp.operator> <literal>. Two blocks can be connected by means of several operators: i) set membership ([not] in); ii) set existence ([not] exists); iii) existential or universal quantification (any, all); iv) scalar comparison if the inner block returns a single value by means of an aggregate (min, sum, ...). The inner block (also called subquery) is seen as a set (possibly a singleton), and it has to be evaluated for each tuple of the outer block (except if it does not depend on the outer block).

> **Example:** Consider the query: "find the number and name of any employee who works in a department located in Phoenix." If it is expressed:
>
> > **select** #emp, e-name **from** EMP **where** #dep **in**
> > (**select** #dep **from** DEP **where** location = "Phoenix")
>
> the inner block does not depend on the outer one. However, another possible expression uses the "exists" operator:
>
> > **select** #emp, e-name **from** EMP **where exists** (**select** * **from** DEP
> > **where** #dep = EMP.#dep **and** location = "Phoenix")
>
> and in this case, the inner block depends on the outer block due to the reference to EMP in the predicate: #dep = EMP.#dep. From a semantic point of view, these two formulations are equivalent, but they may slightly differ in terms of performances.

The other possibility is to combine several selection blocks using set operators since the result of a block is a relation (which is also a set). However, it may be remarked that the intersection and difference of two relations R and S result in a subset of the first one. As a consequence, these two operations do not require a specific syntactic feature and they may be formulated using a block nesting whose expression is given in section 15.6 for SQLf. On the contrary, the union does not match this restriction-based scenario since it enlarges the participating relations. That is the reason why the union requires a specific construct that operates on two base blocks at the same level (no nesting takes place):

select $A_1, \ldots, A_p$ **from R where** cond-1 **union**
select $A_1, \ldots, A_p$ **from S where** cond-2.

Finally, it appears that the relational algebra is completely covered thanks to the base block and some appropriate combinations.

SQL also offers the possibility to operate at the level of sets of tuples. The principle is to define partitions of a relation based on a common value of one or several attributes (keyword "group by"). It then becomes possible to select those subsets of the partition that satisfy a (set-oriented) condition involving aggregates (keyword "having").

Example: The query: "find the departments (number) where the average salary of the clerks is over \$1500 and none earns more than \$2000" is formulated:

select #dep **from** EMP **where** job = "clerk"
group by #dep
having avg(salary) > 1500 and max(salary) ≤ 2000.

From a logical point of view, the evaluation of such a query leads to the two steps described in Figure 15.1: i) employees who are clerks are split into subsets according to the department number; and ii) the condition on the salaries of the clerks of each subset is checked and in case of success the department number associated to the subset is put into the answer.

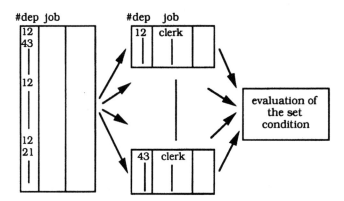

Figure 15.1 The grouping mechanism in SQL.

15.3. Fuzzy Predicates Used in SQLf

There are different kinds of fuzzy predicates applied to individual elements. First are base (or atomic) predicates, each represented by a membership function over a subset of the underlying domains (P: $D_1 \times \ldots \times D_n \to [0, 1]$). As suggested by V. Tahani [4], one may use simple fuzzy conditions like age = "young," salary $\approx$ 40, and so on.

Moreover, fuzzy predicates may call on linguistic modifiers to define modified predicates using unary operators [5]. Modifiers are represented by functions from [0, 1] to [0, 1] and are applied to fuzzy set membership functions in order to model the effect of linguistic hedges such as "very," "more or less," "rather," and so on. The most usual modifier functions are of the form: $\mu_{mod\,P}(x) = (\mu_p(x))^n$ ($n > 1$ for a concentrator and $n < 1$ for a dilator), or $\mu_{mod\,P}(x) = o^n(\mu_P(x))$ where o is a nonidempotent norm (resp. co-norm) for a concentrator (resp. dilator) or $\mu_{mod\,P}(x) = \mu_P(x \pm a)$ (translations [6]).

Lastly, it is possible to build compound predicates based on n-ary operators. Fuzzy set theory offers a panoply of aggregation attitudes [7, 8] richer than the Boolean framework, in particular a variety of conjunctions and disjunctions and trade-off operations. Conjunctive (resp. disjunctive) aggregations of elementary degrees of matching are performed usually by applying min (resp. max) operation to the degrees. Using min for evaluating a conjunction of required properties means that the grading of the least satisfied property will reflect the global level of satisfaction. This type of logical conjunction may be felt as too requiring in some situations. In some applications, one may like to express that some elementary conditions are less important than others. Conjunctive and disjunctive aggregations have been generalized into weighted conjunction and disjunction [9]. Operators called "means" (arithmetic, geometric, harmonic, weighted, generalized [10]) as well as the OWA aggregator [11] allow for compromises between the predicates used as parameters.

15.4 Fuzzy Quantified Statements

Fuzzy conditions based on the use of fuzzy quantifiers have also been proposed. Fuzzy quantifiers represent linguistic expressions such as "many of," "at least 3" (Figure 15.2) and they are used in fuzzy quantified statements. Two main families of fuzzy quantified statements may be distinguished: "Q elements of set X are satisfying the fuzzy predicate A" ("Q X's are A") and "Q elements of set X that satisfy the fuzzy predicate B also satisfy the fuzzy predicate A" ("Q X's B are A"). From a practical point of view, statements of the form "Q X's are A" are more common and the focus is put on them in the rest of this chapter. "At least half of the employees are well-paid" illustrates this kind of statement.

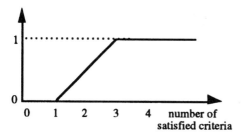

Figure 15.2 The fuzzy quantifier "at least 3."

Fuzzy quantifiers were first introduced by L.A. Zadeh [12], and it is possible to distinguish between absolute quantifiers and relative ones. Absolute quantifiers are expressed with a number (or a counter) while relative quantifiers refer to a proportion. A typical example of an absolute (resp. relative) quantifier could be "at least 3" (resp. "at least half"). Thus, an absolute quantifier is represented by a function Q from an integer (or real) range to [0, 1], whereas a relative quantifier is represented by a function Q from [0, 1] to [0, 1]. In both cases, the value Q(j) defines the truth value of the statement "Q X's are A" when exactly j elements from X fully satisfy A (whereas it is assumed that A is fully unsatisfied for the other elements).

Several methods to determine the truth value of quantified statements of the type "Q X are A" have been proposed. For homogeneity purposes with respect to fuzzy predicates (previous section), we restrict ourselves to approaches whose result is a degree. R. Yager [13] considers only increasing quantifiers, and he defines the truth value of "Q X's are A" as the value of an ordered weighted average (OWA operator). The use of this operator has been extended to the case of decreasing quantifiers in [14] and [15]. L.A. Zadeh [12] proposes to use the Σcount operation to define the cardinality of a fuzzy set. Thus, the degree of truth of "Q X's are A" is Q(ΣCount(A)) in the case of an absolute quantifier, and Q(ΣCount(A)/n) in the case of a relative one (n being the cardinality of the set X). A last solution relies on fuzzy integrals (in particular Sugeno and Choquet integrals [16]). In that case, a fuzzy quantifier is defined by a nonadditive measure whose arguments are regular sets. When the predicate A is regular, the truth value of "Q X's are A" is the measure of the regular set made of the elements from X that satisfy A. When A is fuzzy, to evaluate "Q X's are A" is then to measure a fuzzy set, according to a measure (Q) defined on regular sets. It has been shown [17] that both Sugeno and Choquet fuzzy integrals are tools enabling such a computation, and then it is possible to utilize these two fuzzy integrals to compute the truth value of "Q X's are A." This last method seems the more general for increasing, decreasing, and unimodal fuzzy quantifiers. Any of these approaches may be chosen as a basis for interpreting quantified statements in SQLf depending on the semantics desired by the user.

15.5. The Base Block in SQLf

In SQLf, the select block remains fundamentally the same as in SQL. It returns a fuzzy relation (whose tuples are weighted) instead of a usual relation. The differences concern essentially two points: i) a parameter intended for the calibration of the final result (either a number of desired responses denoted n, or a qualitative threshold denoted t, or both) is introduced for the outermost block; and ii) selection conditions are no longer solely Boolean. In SQLf, the formulation of a simple select block is:

> **select** [n | t | n, t] <attributes> **from** <relations>
> **where** <fuzzy-condition>

where <relations> corresponds to a list of usual (crisp) relations defined in the database schema, and <fuzzy condition> can involve fuzzy and Boolean basic conditions. This statement is a generalization of the usual SQL base block, and its interpretation is basically the same (cf. section 15.2) except that in step 2, the restriction is a fuzzy one, which will attach a degree to each tuple. According to the query: **select** t A, B **from** R **where** fc, where R denotes a base (crisp) relation and fc is a fuzzy condition, a tuple $x = <a, b, \ldots >$ of R will lead to a tuple $<a, b>$ in the resulting relation whose degree is $\mu_{fc}(x)$. This tuple will be kept in the result if $\mu_{fc}(x)$ is over t. It is possible to have several tuples with the same value and different degrees in the result. To avoid this situation, the keyword "distinct" is used to ensure that the result is a "pure" fuzzy relation (the highest degree is kept). A query like:

> **select distinct** R.A, S.B **from** R, S
> **where** $fc_1(R)$ **and** $fc_2(S)$ **and** R.C θ S.D

involves a join of the relations R and S, which may be a fuzzy one if the predicate R.C θ S.D is itself fuzzy. A pair (a, b) belonging to the result Rf (before calibration) receives the degree:

$$\mu_{Rf}(a, b) = \sup_{(x,y) | x \in R \wedge x.A = a \wedge y \in S \wedge y.B = b} \min(\mu_{fc1}(x), \mu_{fc2}(y), \mu_{\theta}(x.C, y.D)).$$

The consideration of fuzzy quantified statements has led to extend the base block with a specific feature initially suggested by Kacprzyk and Ziolkowski [18]. This construct allows queries of the form: "find the employees such that almost all out of {salary = "very large," age = "young," budget much greater than 30, . . . } match." Let us consider an extension of a relation R made of a set of tuples $\{t_1, \ldots, t_m\}$. The idea is to consider that the determination of the extent to which a tuple t satisfies : "<quantifier> **out of** $\{fc_1, \ldots, fc_n>\}$ match" relies on a calculus similar to that of a quantified statement of the type Q X's are A. In this case, the quantifier applies to a set of values $(fc_1(t), \ldots, fc_n(t))$ resulting from a same tuple t by several fuzzy predicates). Consequently, this kind of statement can be a component of a **where** clause according to the syntax:

select ... from ... where ... Q **out-of** $(fc_1, \ldots, fc_n)$.

The user chooses the desired interpretation of the quantified statement with the help of different names for a same quantifier ($Q_{o\,w\,a}$ for Yager's OWA-based interpretation, Q_{I-C} for an interpretation based on a Choquet integral and so on).

15.6. Subqueries and Combination of Blocks

Similar to SQL, several nesting operators are available in SQLf, for instance to evaluate the extent to which an element belongs to a fuzzy set or the degree of emptiness of a fuzzy set.

15.6.1. Set Membership

In SQLf, the operator "in" allows for testing if the value of an attribute in the current tuple belongs to the (fuzzy) set of values returned by a subquery. The predicate "a **in** (**select** b **from** S **where** fc)" is then defined by: $\mu_{in}(a, SQ) = sup_{b \in SQ \wedge b = a}\mu_{SQ}(b)$ where SQ denotes the fuzzy subset of b-values returned by the inner block applied to relation S.

> **Example:** The query: "find the young employees who work in a high-budget department" can be expressed:
>   **select** #emp **from** EMP **where** age = "young" **and** #dep **in**
>   (**select** #dep **from** DEP **where** budget = "high").

A situation somewhat similar to the previous one occurs when one wants to know if a given value is close (no longer equal) to one of those returned by a nested block. The syntax of this sort of predicate is: a **in$_f$** (**select** b **from** S **where** fc). Its definition is based on the composition of the set membership ("in") and an approximate equality ($\approx$): $\mu_{in_f}(a, SQ) = sup_{b \in SQ}min(\mu_{\approx}(a, b), \mu_{SQ}(b))$.

> **Example:** The query: "find the young employees whose salary is close to the salary of at least one employee having a large commission" can be expressed:
>   **select** #emp **from** EMP **where** age = "young" **and** sal **in$_f$**
>   (**select** sal **from** EMP **where** commission = "large").

15.6.2. Set (Non)emptiness

SQL allows for the use of the connector "exists" which checks whether a set is empty. The extension of this operator to fuzzy sets raises the question of the measure of emptiness of a fuzzy set. One possible interpretation is founded on a quantitative view (cardinality or "surface"), and it requires a measurement tool. The other has been chosen since it preserves some equivalences. It is merely qualitative and it relies upon the height of the fuzzy set. The predicate: "**exists** (**select** * **from** S **where** fc)" is defined as: $\mu_{exists}(SQ) = \sup_{b \in SQ}\mu_{SQ}(b)$.

This operator, as well as "in" and "in$_f$" may be negated, in which case, the formulas are derived from the previous ones using the complement.

15.6.3. Comparison Involving Quantifiers

The predicates of the form: <attribute> θ Q <SQ> (where θ is a comparison operator, Q is a quantifier, "any" for the existential one or "all" for the universal one, and <SQ> denotes a subquery) available in SQL are extended in three ways: i) the subquery may return a fuzzy relation; ii) θ may be any fuzzy relational operator ($\approx$, slightly greater, etc); and iii) Q may represent a fuzzy quantifier. When the subquery returns a fuzzy set and/or θ is any (fuzzy) comparison operator, the meaning of the predicate "a θ **any** (**select** b **from** S **where** fc)" becomes:

$$\mu_{\theta\ any}(a, SQ) = \sup_{b \in SQ}\min(\mu_{\theta}(a, b), \mu_{SQ}(b)).$$

In SQL, the predicate "a θ **all** (**select** b **from** S **where** bc)" is interpreted: "$\forall s \in S, bc(s) \Rightarrow (a\ \theta\ s.b)$." Its meaning in SQLf:

$$\mu_{\theta\ all}(a, SQ) = \inf_{b \in SQ}\max(1 - \mu_{SQ}(b), \mu_{\theta}(a, b))$$

relies on Dienes implication $(a \Rightarrow b = \max(1 - a, b))$, and it preserves the equivalence: $[a\ \theta\ \textbf{all} <SQ>] \Leftrightarrow [\textbf{not}(a\ \bar{\theta}\ \textbf{any} <SQ>)]$.

The introduction of fuzzy quantifiers instead of "any" and "all" is worthy of a fairly long development and cannot be detailed here (see [19]). The general form of these statements is just given:

select <atts> **from** R **where** A θ Q(**select** B **from** S **where** fc)

and an illustration with the query: "find the employees whose salary is much greater than that of **almost all** the young employees working in the same department" which would be stated:

select #emp, e-name **from** EMP E **where** salary >> almost-all
(**select** salary **from** EMP **where** #dep= E.#dep **and** age = "young").

15.6.4. Scalar Comparison

SQLf queries can involve fuzzy comparisons between values. This kind of mechanism can be used to extend predicates involving a comparison between an attribute value and the result of an aggregate function returned by a **usual** nested block (since only aggregates defined on crisp sets are considered) according to:

select X **from** R **where** A θ (**select** agg(B) **from** S **where** bc)

where A and B are attributes defined on the same domain, θ is a comparison operator, bc is a Boolean condition, and agg denotes an aggregate function. The semantics of such a query are given by: $\mu_{Res}(x) = \sup_{r \in R \wedge r.X = x} \mu_\theta(r.A, v)$ where Res denotes the result of the query, and v is the value returned by the nested block.

Example: The query: "find the employees whose salary is much greater than the average of the salaries of the employees in the same department" can be expressed as:

    select #emp **from** EMP E **where** sal >>
        (**select** avg(sal) **from** EMP **where** #dep = E.#dep).

15.6.5. Set Operations

As in SQL, the only necessary set operation in SQLf is the union. The expression:

    select $A_1, \ldots, A_p$ **from** R **where** fc_R **union**
    select $A_1, \ldots, A_p$ **from** S **where** fc_S

performs the union of the fuzzy relations R' and S' issued from the projection onto $(A_1, \ldots, A_p)$ of the restriction of $R(A_1, \ldots, A_m)$ by fc_R (resp. $S(A_1, \ldots, A_n)$ by fc_S) according to:

$$\mu_{R' \cup S'}(x) = \max(\mu_{R'}(x), \mu_{S'}(x)).$$

The intersection and difference may be achieved by restrictions (using the "exists" nesting operator). The expressions:

    select $A_1, \ldots, A_p$ **from** R **where** fc_R **and exists**
        (**select** * **from** S **where** fc_S **and** $A_1 = R.A_1$ **and** ... **and** $A_p = R.A_p$)

    select $A_1, \ldots, A_p$ **from** R **where** fc_R **and not exists**
        (**select** * **from** S **where** fc_S **and** $A_1 = R.A_1$ **and** ... **and** $A_p = R.A_p$)

perform, respectively, the intersection and the difference of the (fuzzy) relations R' and S' previously defined according to:

$$\mu_{R' \cap S'}(x) = \min(\mu_{R'}(x), \mu_{S'}(x)) \text{ and } \mu_{R' - S'}(x) = \min(\mu_{R'}(x), 1 - \mu_{S'}(x)).$$

Example: The query: "find the cities with at least a department with a high budget and an employee who is young and well-paid" is basically the intersection of two fuzzy relations (departments with a high budget projected onto the attribute location on the one hand and young and well-paid employees projected onto the attribute city on the other hand). It may be expressed:

select location **from** DEP **where** budget = "high" **and exists**
(**select** * **from** EMP **where** salary = "well-paid" **and**
age = "young" **and** city = DEP.location").

15.6.6. Nestings and Query Equivalences

To provide users with some degree of freedom, high-level languages allow a given need (natural language sentence) to be expressed in slightly different ways (although the result is the same). Some equivalences in SQLf, which generalize those valid in SQL, are now pointed out.

If fc_1 and fc_2 are fuzzy predicates, the following equivalences between SQLf expressions hold:

- a) **select** R-attributes **from** R **where** fc_1 **and** A **in**
   (**select** B **from** S **where** fc_2)
- a') **select** R-attributes **from** R **where** fc_1 **and exists**
   (**select** * from S **where** fc_2 **and** R.A = B)

- b) **select** R-attributes **from** R **where** fc_1 **and** A **in**$_f$
   (**select** B **from** S **where** fc_2)
- b') **select** R-attributes **from** R **where** fc_1 **and exists**
   (**select** * from S **where** fc_2 **and** R.A. $\approx$ B)

- c) **select** R-attributes **from** R **where** fc_1 **and** A θ **any**
   (**select** B **from** S **where** fc_2)
- c') **select** R-attributes **from** R **where** fc_1 **and exists**
   (**select** * **from** S **where** fc_2 **and** R.A θ B)

- d) **select distinct** R-attributes **from** R, S
   where fc_1 **and** fc_2 **and** R.A. θ S.B
- d') **select distinct** R-attributes **from** R **where** fc_1 **and exists**
   (**select** * **from** S **where** fc_2 **and** R.A θ B)

- e) **select** R-attributes **from** R **where** fc_1 **and** A **not in**
   (**select** B **from** S **where** fc_2)
- e') **select** R-attributes **from** R **where** fc_1 **and not exists**
   (**select** * **from** S **where** fc_2 **and** R.A = B)

- f) **select** R-attributes **from** R **where** fc_1 **and** A **not in**$_f$
   (**select** B **from** S **where** fc_2)
- f') **select** R-attributes **from** R **where** fc_1 **and not exists**
   (**select** * **from** S **where** fc_2 **and** R.A $\approx$ B)

- g) **select** R-attributes **from** R **where** fc_1 **and** A θ **all**
  (**select** B **from** S **where** fc_2)
- g') **select** R-attributes **from** R **where** fc_1 **and not exists**
  (**select** * **from** S **where** fc_2 **and** (R.A $\bar{\theta}$ B)).

This list is not exhaustive (especially due to some "transitivity"), and it is mainly intended to show the genericity of "exists," since the other nestings may be expressed with this operator (or its negation).

Example: It is possible to express the query "find the best 5 departments (number) that have a medium budget and no very young employee":

> **select** 5 #dep **from** DEP **where** budget = "medium" **and** #dep $\neq$
> **all** (**select** #dep **from** EMP **where** age = "very young")

or:

> **select** 5 #dep **from** DEP **where** budget = "medium" **and** #dep
> **not in** (**select** #dep **from** EMP **where** age = "very young")

or:

> **select** 5 #dep **from** DEP **where** budget = "medium" **and not**
> **exists** (**select** * **from** EMP **where** age = "very young" **and** #dep =
> Emp.#dep).

15.7. Partitioning

The grouping functionality is retained in SQLf, and in this context, the "having" clause can be used along with a (fuzzy) set-oriented condition aimed at the selection of subsets. In this section, the various possible conditions, from conditions involving aggregate functions (min, etc) to more complex ones involving fuzzy quantifiers or fuzzy sets comparisons, are discussed.

15.7.1. Use of Aggregate Functions

In SQLf, it is possible to use the result of an aggregate function (min, max, sum, average, or count) as an argument of a fuzzy criterion. The general form of these statements is described below:

> **select** <atts-1> **from** R **where** bc **group by** <atts-2>
> **having** $fc_1(agg_1)$ **connector** ... **connector** $fc_p(agg_p)$

where <atts-1> is a subset of the attributes present in <atts-2>, bc is a Boolean condition, and fc_i is a fuzzy condition applying to the result of the aggregate agg_i.

Example: The query: "find the departments where the average salary of the engineers is about $3500" is expressed in SQLf by:

> **select** #dep **from** EMP **where** job = "Engineer"
> **group by** #dep **having** avg (salary) $\approx$ 3500.

It should be noticed that the "where" clause must involve a Boolean condition. A fuzzy condition would lead to partitions made of fuzzy (weighted) tuples for which aggregate functions do not deliver a grade. Thus, such an extension would not be semantically compatible with the homogeneity of the language. Consequently, queries such as: "find the average salary of the young employees of each department" is not permitted in SQLf.

An equivalence holds between the queries:

select A **from** R **where** bc **group by** A
having $fc_1(agg_1)$ **connector ... connector** $fc_p(agg_p)$

and:

select A **from** R R_1 **where** bc **and**
    $(fc_1($**select** agg_1 **from** R **where** $A = R_1.A$ **and** bc$)$
    connector ... connector
    $fc_p($**select** agg_p **from** R **where** $A = R_p.A$ **and** bc$))$.

15.7.2. Use of Quantified Statements

Hereafter, the case where conditions applying to partitions do not only involve vague predicates but also vague quantifiers is considered. An example of such a query is: "find the departments where most of the employees are young." The interpretation of this query is the following:

1. The relation EMP is split into subsets of employees working in a same department.

2. For each subset, the quantified proposition "most of the employees are young" is calculated. Due to the multiple interpretations of quantified statements (cf. section 15.4), this proposition may have different meanings, and the user's choice is made through an appropriate name of the quantifier ("Q_i").

In SQLf, the previous query is expressed:

select #dep **from** EMP
group by #dep **having** $most_i$ **are** age = "young".

15.7.3. Comparisons of Fuzzy Sets

In an earlier version of SQL, it was possible to select a subset depending on a condition based on the comparison of sets. This feature has not been kept in the present versions of SQL. However, it turns out that such a possibility is mandatory to express the various semantics of a generalized division. The regular division of $R(A, X)$ by $S(A, Y)$ denoted by $R[A \div A]S$, where A is a set of attributes common to R and S, aims at determining the X-values in R connected with all the A-values appearing in S. Formally, this operation can be defined in the following way:

$$x \in R[A \div A]S \Leftrightarrow S[A] \subseteq \Gamma^{-1}(x) \qquad \text{where } \Gamma^{-1}(x) = \{a \mid (x, a) \in R\}.$$

In this expression, the relation R is viewed as inducing a multiple-valued mapping Γ which associates to a value x the set $\Gamma(x) = \{a \mid (x, a) \in R\}$; in other words, the division $R[A \div A]S$ is nothing but the lower image of $S[A]$ by Γ. Considering the relations PRODUCT(p#, price) and ORDERS(store, p#, quantity), the query: "find the stores that have ordered at least 10 pieces of all products over \$15" is the division: $O[p\# \div p\#]P$ where O is the restriction of ORDERS with quantity > 10 projected onto (store, p#), and P is the restriction of PRODUCT such that price ≥ 15. If this question is turned into: "find the stores that have ordered a **moderate** number of pieces of all **medium-priced** products," it corresponds to the division of two fuzzy relations (moderate orders divided by medium-priced products). It has been shown in [20, 21, 22] that such a division may be seen in terms of an inclusion:

$$\mu_{R[A \div A]S}(x) = \deg(S[A] \subseteq \Gamma^{-1}(x))$$

which generalizes the view just given. But the major difference with the regular case is that such an expression may convey different semantics depending on: i) the type of inclusion retained (degree based on an implication or a cardinality); and ii) the interaction between the degrees (the degree of an S-tuple may be seen either as a threshold to attain or as the importance of the related A-value). To reach these semantics in SQLf, it is convenient to allow for a new type of construct, namely the set containment, for which appropriate names ("contains$_i$") will cover the various semantics depending on the user's choice. The SQL expression corresponding to the previous query is:

> **select** store **from** ORDERS **where** qty = "moderate"
> **group by** store **having** set(p#) **contains**$_i$
>   (**select** p# **from** PRODUCTS **where** price = "medium").

15.8. On the Evaluation of SQLf Queries

The evaluation of queries in the context of declarative languages (such as SQL) remains an open problem due to its combinatorial nature. Indeed, given a query, the optimal plan (algorithm) to process it cannot be found in a "reasonable" time (in general). This applies to imprecise queries too, especially because they are more complex than ordinary ones. The increase in complexity is mainly due to the fact that the operations to be carried out depend on a larger volume of data since selections, joins, and so on require more tuples to be examined than in the Boolean context. One might think of two principal ways (and architectures) to process fuzzy queries: i) to use a regular DBMS and to develop an additional layer playing the role of an interface; or ii) to build a completely new system including fuzzy query processing techniques (algorithms) in its kernel. These two lines are under consideration and the objective here is just to illustrate them.

The first strategy, called derivation, assumes that a threshold (λ) is associated with an SQLf query in order to retrieve its λ-level cut. The principle is to express the λ-cut in terms of a query involving only regular (Boolean) expressions, which requires to distribute the λ-cut operation onto the constitutive elements of a complex predicate [23]. It is then possible to use an existing relational database management system to process the (derived) regular SQL query. Depending on the connectors used in the initial SQLf query, the Boolean query obtained may deliver the exact λ-cut or a superset (in which case, extra elements must be removed by means of a complementary processing). The ratio of extra tuples (which may be seen as an indice of efficiency) is examined in [24]. In so doing, one can expect to take advantage of the implementation mechanisms handled by the DBMS to reach acceptable performances. In addition, fuzzy query processing reduces mainly to a transformation procedure located on top of an existing DBMS according to the architecture depicted in Figure 15.3, which should keep the development effort limited. This strategy applies only to SQLf queries that do not contain partitioning, nor fuzzy quantified statements.

The other strategy is completely different (Figure 15.4) and it relies on: i) the decomposition of an SQLf query into elementary operations; and ii) the evaluation of these basic operations by means of "efficient algorithms" (to implement fuzzy selections, joins, semi-joins and anti-joins for instance). Some works have been undertaken along this line [25] and their principle is given for the case of an SQLf query involving a (fuzzy) semi-join:

select λ * **from** R **where** fc_1 **and exists**
   (**select** * **from** S **where** fc_2 **and** R.A θ S.B).

The evaluation of this query is devised assuming that relations of the database can be accessed and (re)organized appropriately if necessary. A first idea is to design a naïve algorithm based on a Cartesian product of R and S (i.e., the entire S relation is accessed for each R-tuple). Then, refinements are suggested in order to improve the efficiency of this algorithm by preventing the exhaustive scan of relation S in the inner loop. Such conditions play the role of success or failure heuristics which reduce the complexity of the procedure. It may be noticed that it is also possible to design "improved" algorithms (with respect to algorithms performing exhaustive scans of relations) for the evaluation of quantified statements when a degree of satisfaction to attain is given [26].

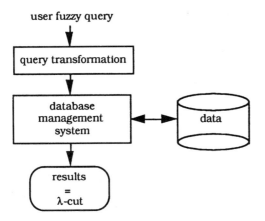

Figure 15.3 Architecture for the "derivation" strategy.

15.9. Conclusion

A language supporting the expression of imprecise queries addressed to a relational database is considered. The interpretation of the queries is founded on the fuzzy set theory and the language, named SQLf, extends the SQL language.

First, the main characteristics of SQL are recalled. Then, the two main types of fuzzy conditions useful for SQLf (tuple and set-oriented fuzzy predicates) are reviewed. The extension of the various constructs of SQLf are then presented. The multirelation block aims at the extension of the capabilities of (fuzzy) selection, join, and projection. Nesting operators ("in," "exists," and quantifiers especially) allow for the use of subqueries (or predicates involving one or several base blocks). Two types of extension are considered: i) the operator is applied to fuzzy relations; and ii) the operator is "fuzzyfied." It has been shown that the usual equiva-

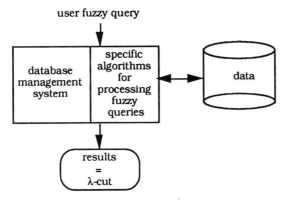

Figure 15.4 Architecture for the "direct evaluation" strategy.

lences in SQL remain valid in SQLf provided that appropriate definitions are chosen for the nesting operators. The next point deals with the partitioning capability. In this framework, set-oriented (fuzzy) conditions may be used by means of aggregate functions (min, average . . .), fuzzy quantified statements or set comparisons (in particular to express different semantics of an extended division). The last section is dedicated to the processing of fuzzy queries. This aspect is of prime importance since a database management system should be efficient. Two possible approaches are briefly discussed: i) the transformation of SQLf queries into regular SQL queries; and ii) the decomposition of a query into elementary operations for which appropriate algorithms are available.

One of the aims of this chapter is to show that it seems realistic to define a query language supporting imprecise conditions as an extension of a regular relational query language. SQLf offers an open framework for future extensions if needed and a wide range of equivalences are preserved (this fact is essential for users who are familiar with SQL). The aspects related to query processing need to be further investigated in order to refine and compare the strategies devised here.

15.10 References

[1] Bosc, P., and O. Pivert. "Some Approaches for Relational Databases Flexible Querying." *Journal of Intelligent Information Systems,* Vol. 1 (1992), pp. 323–354.

[2] Bosc, P., et al. "Fuzzy Querying with SQL: Extensions and Implementation Aspects." *Fuzzy Sets and Systems,* Vol. 28 (1988), pp. 333–349.

[3] Bosc, P., and O. Pivert. "About Equivalences in SQLf, A Relational Language Suporting Imprecise Querying." *Proceedings, 1st International Fuzzy Engineering Symposium (IFES '91).* pp. 309–320. Yokohama, Japan: 1991.

[4] Tahani, V. "A Conceptual Framework for Fuzzy Query Processing: A Step Toward Very Intelligent Database Systems." *Information Processing and Management,* Vol. 13 (1977), pp. 289–303.

[5] Zadeh, L.A. "A Fuzzy Set Theoretic Interpretation of Linguistic Hedges." *Journal of Cybernetics,* Vol. 2 (1972), pp. 4–34.

[6] Bouchon-Meunier, B., and J. Yao. "Linguistic Modifiers and Imprecise Categories." *Journal of Intelligent Systems,* Vol. 7 (1992). pp. 25–36.

[7] Dubois, D., and H. Prade. "A Review of Fuzzy Set Aggregation Connectives." *Information Sciences,* Vol. 36 (1985), pp. 85–121.

[8] Yager, R.R. "Connectives and Quantifiers in Fuzzy Sets." *Fuzzy Sets and Systems,* Vol. 40 (1991), pp. 39–75.

[9] Dubois, D., and H. Prade. "Weighted Minimum and Maximum Operations in Fuzzy Set Theory." *Information Sciences,* Vol. 39 (1986), pp. 205–210.

[10] Dyckhoff, H., and W. Pedrycz. "Generalized Means as a Model of Compensative Connectives." *Information Sciences,* Vol. 14 (1984), pp. 143–154.

[11] Yager, R.R. "On Ordered Weighted Averaging Aggregation Operators in Multicriteria Decision Making." *IEEE Transactions on Systems, Man, and Cybernetics,* Vol. 18 (1988), pp. 183–190.

[12] Zadeh, L.A. "A Computational Approach to Fuzzy Quantifiers in Natural Languages." *Computer Mathematics with Applications,* Vol. 9 (1983), pp. 149–183.

[13] Yager, R.R. "Applications and Extensions of OWA Aggregations." *International Journal of Man-Machine Studies,* Vol. 37 (1991), pp. 103–132.

[14] Bosc, P., and L. Lietard. "On the Extension of the Use of the OWA Operator to Evaluate some Quantifications." *Proceedings, 1st European Congress on Fuzzy and Intelligent Technologies.* pp. 332–338. Aachen, Germany: 1993.

[15] Yager, R.R. "Families of OWA Operators." *Fuzzy Sets and Systems,* Vol. 59 (1993), pp. 125–148.

[16] Bosc, P., and L. Lietard. "Monotonic Quantified Statements and Fuzzy Integrals." *Proceedings of the NAFIPS/IFIS/NASA '94 Joint Conference.* pp. 8–12. San Antonio, Tex.: 1994.

[17] Grabisch, M., et al. "Fuzzy Measure of Fuzzy Events Defined by Fuzzy Integrals." *Fuzzy Sets and Systems,* Vol. 50 (1992), pp. 293–313.

[18] Kacprzyk, J., and A. Ziolkowski. "Database Queries with Fuzzy Linguistic Quantifiers." *IEEE Transactions on Systems, Man, and Cybernetics,* Vol. 16 (1986), pp. 474–478.

[19] Bosc, P., et al. "Quantified Statements in a Flexible Relational Query Language." *Proceedings, ACM-SAC '95 Conference.* pp. 488–492. Nashville, Tenn.: 1995.

[20] Bosc, P., et al. "Fuzzy Division for Regular Relational Databases." *Proceedings, 4th International IEEE Conference on Fuzzy Systems.* pp. 729–734. Yokohama, Japan: 1995.

[21] Bosc, P., et al. "Flexible Queries in Relational Databases—The Example of the Division Operator." *Proceedings of the Workshop Uncertainty in Databases and Deductive Systems.* pp. 83–94. Ithaca, New York: 1994.

[22] Bosc, P. "Some Views of the Division of Fuzzy Relations." *Proceedings, 5th International Workshop on Current Issues on Fuzzy Technologies.* pp. 14–22. Trento, Italy: 1995.

[23] Bosc, P., and O. Pivert. "On the Evaluation of Simple Fuzzy Relational Queries: Principles and Measures," in *Fuzzy Logic: State of the Art.* eds. R. Lowen and M. Roubens. pp. 355–364. Boston: Kluwer Academic Publishers: 1993.

[24] ———. "On the Efficiency of the Alpha-Cut Distribution Method to Evaluate Simple Fuzzy Relational Queries." *Proceedings, 5th Information Processing and Management of Uncertainty Conference.* pp. 11–16. Paris: 1994.

[25] Bosc, P. "Some Approaches for Processing SQLf-nested Queries." To appear, *Journal of Intelligent Systems.*

[26] Bosc, P., et al. "Quantified Statements and Database Fuzzy Querying," in *Fuzziness in Database Management Systems.* eds. P. Bosc and J. Kacprzyk. pp. 275–308. Physica Verlag, Heidelberg: 1995.

16 A Fuzzy SQL Summary Language for Data Discovery

Dan Rasmussen
Computer Science Department, Roskilde University

Ronald R. Yager
Machine Intelligence Institute, Iona College

ABSTRACT: The increasing use of computers for transactions and communication have created mountains of data that contain potentially valuable knowledge. To search for this knowledge, we have to develop a new generation of tools, which have the ability of flexible querying and intelligent searching. In this chapter we will introduce an extension of a fuzzy query language called Summary SQL which can be used for knowledge discovery and data mining. We show how it can be used to search for typical values and fuzzy rules.

16.1. Introduction

The increasing use of computers in businesses and governmental agencies has created mountains of data that contain potentially valuable knowledge. To uncover this knowledge, we have to develop a new generation of sophisticated tools with the ability to do flexible querying and intelligent searching. This rapidly growing field is known as Data Mining (DM) or Knowledge Discovery in Databases (KDD), and was introduced by Piatetsky-Shapiro and others. [1–5] Basically, we require two categories of Data Mining tools; the first one is able to perform an automatic search for knowledge (a bottom-up dredging of raw facts to discover connections), and the other one is an interactive tool that needs an analyst to ask questions (a top-down search to test hypotheses).

In this chapter we introduce an SQL-like query language for top-down mining. In this language, we combine the idea of a fuzzy query language [6–7] and linguistic summaries [8–13] to make a more powerful language. In the new language we can define queries that make it possible to find typical values and fuzzy rules.

A crisp rule is a relation between values associated with a data object, which have to be satisfied by all or most of the data objects in the database. An example of a rule could be "if x has a salary > $80,000, then x is an executive," but a rule does not always describe the data 100 percent. Sometimes there can exist exceptions among the data. For this reason, rules are often shown in percents like "if x has a salary > $80,000, then x is an executive—90%," where 90 percent of the data satisfy the rule.

Fuzzy rules are different from crisp rules in several ways. First, a fuzzy rule has a degree of truth, which is a value in [0,1], where 1 is true and 0 not true. Second, we can use fuzzy terms like *small, high,* and *close to* in the predicates to write fuzzy rules like: "If x has a *high* salary then x is an executive," or "If x has a salary *close to* or *above* $80,000 then x is an executive."

In this work, considerable use is made of the concept of a linguistic summary [8–13]. A linguistic summary is a quantified fuzzy expression, and like a fuzzy expression, it has a degree of truth in the unit interval. *Many, most,* and *few* are all examples of fuzzy quantifiers and combined with a fuzzy rule we can use them to describe patterns in data like "*most* x with a salary *close to* $80,000 are executives" or "*few* x with a *small* salary are executives." The fuzzy quantifiers can in some way be compared to the percentage satisfaction used in a crisp rule.

The rest of this chapter is organized as follow. First we briefly describe the concept of a fuzzy query and linguistic summary, then we show how a linguistic summary can be a part of a fuzzy query, and how it can be used to find fuzzy rules and typical values. We then present a new query language called Summary SQL and some practical examples.

16.2. Fuzzy Queries and Linguistic Summaries

In this section we provide a brief introduction to fuzzy queries and linguistic summaries. We first consider fuzzy queries.

A common way to select objects from a database system is to formulate a query where the selection part is a logical expression. In classic databases we use crisp Boolean concepts to describe the objects we are looking for. A legal crisp query could be "select all persons where the height is greater then 1.8 m." This is different from a fuzzy query where the selection part is a fuzzy expression. In a fuzzy query we are able to use fuzzy terms like *tall, small,* and *close to* to define linguistic concepts. If we want to select all the *tall* persons we can make the query "*select all persons where the height is tall,*" in this case we use the fuzzy concept *tall* to select the tall people.

To illustrate how fuzzy queries can be used to select objects we will give some examples. Let **DB** be a database of objects and let o_i be an object in the database, $o_i \in$ **DB**. Associated with the database we have a set of attributes $\mathbf{A} = \{a_1, \ldots, a_n\}$ where each attribute has a corresponding domain. For example, the objects in the database **DB** could be people and the attributes Name, Height and Weight. The notation $o_i.a_j$ or $a_j(o_i)$ is used to refer to the value of attribute a_j for the object o_i. Furthermore, we can associate with each attribute a collection of fuzzy concepts. These concepts can be defined via membership functions as fuzzy subsets over the domain of the attribute. For example, the membership function $\mu_{tall}(\textbf{Height})$ defines the concept *tall* over domain(Height) and is shown in Figure 16.1a. Then $\mu_{tall}(1.8) = 0.5$ would indicate the degree to which 1.8 m. is compatible with the idea of the concept *tall*. Figure 16.1b would define the concept *heavy* over the domain of weights.

The result of a fuzzy query Q on the **DB** is a fuzzy subset over the elements in the **DB**, the persons o_i, and their membership grades are their degree of satisfaction to the query Q. A useful way to present the answer is a ranked list, where the persons with the highest degree of membership are the first elements.

Let our database consist of three objects:

$$\mathbf{DB} = \{(Hans,1.8,100), (Peter,1.7,90), (Ben,1.9,85)\}$$

where the first value is the Name, the second the Height, and the third the Weight. If we want to retrieve the *tall* persons from **DB** we have to make the query:

$$Q_{\text{Height} = tall}(\mathbf{DB}) = \{o_i \in \mathbf{DB} \mid \mu_{tall}(o_i.\text{Height})\}.$$

The answer to this query is the fuzzy set $\{1/(ben,1.9,85), 0.5/(hans,1.8,100), 0/(peter,1.7,90)\}$.

As in the case of crisp queries we can make multicriteria searching where we use the functions *AND* ($\wedge$) and *OR* ($\vee$) to aggregate the predicates or use of negation *NOT* ($\neg$). Normally, the minimum will be used as the *AND* aggregation and the maximum for the *OR* aggrega-

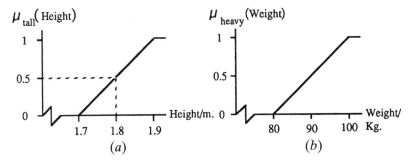

Figure 16.1   The membership functions for tall (*a*) and heavy (*b*).

tion. For example if $\mu_{heavy}(o_i.\text{Weight})$ is defined as in Figure 16.1b we can make the query:

$$Q_{\text{Height} = tall \text{ and Weight} = heavy}(\textbf{DB})$$

$$= \{o_i \in \textbf{DB} \mid \mu_{tall}(o_i.\text{Height}) \wedge \mu_{heavy}(o_i.\text{Weight})\}$$

$$= \{o_i \in \textbf{DB} \mid \min(\mu_{tall}(o_i.\text{Height}), \mu_{heavy}(o_i.\text{Weight}))\}$$

In this case, the answer to our query will be the fuzzy subset:

$$\{0.5/(\text{hans},1.8,100,0.25/(\text{ben},1.9,85), 0/(\text{peter},1.7,90)\}.$$

For the query:

$$Q_{\text{Height} = tall \text{ or Weight} = heavy}(\text{DB})$$

$$= \{o_i \in \textbf{DB} \mid \mu_{tall}(o_i.\text{Height}) \vee \mu_{heavy}(o_i.\text{Weight}))\}$$

$$= \{oi \in \textbf{DB} \mid \max(\mu_{tall}(o_i.\text{Height}), \mu heavy(o_i.\text{Weight}))\}$$

we get the fuzzy subset:

$$\{1/(\text{hans},1.8,100), 1/(\text{ben},1.9,85), 0.5/(\text{peter},1.7,90)\}.$$

Normally, negation is defined as 1, minus the membership degree of the negated expression. For example if $\mu_{tall}(o_i.\text{Height}) = 0.25$, then $\mu_{nottall}(o_i.\text{Height}) = 1 - \mu_{tall}(o_i.\text{Height}) = 1 - 0.25 = 0.75$. For the query:

$$Q_{\text{Height} = tall \text{ and Weight} = not\ heavy}(\textbf{DB})$$

$$= \{o_i \in \textbf{DB} \mid \min(\mu_{tall}(o_i.\text{Height}), 1 - \mu_{heavy}(o_i.\text{Weight}))\}$$

In this case, we get the fuzzy set:

$$\{0.75/(\text{ben},1.9,85), 0/(\text{hans},1.8,100), 0/(\text{peter},1.7,90)\}.$$

As we have seen, a fuzzy querying language is a very flexible tool. In this framework, the selected objects do not have to match the search criteria exactly, which gives the system a more human-like behavior.

We now turn to a brief introduction of linguistic summaries. A linguistic summary is a meta description of the information in the database, and can be used to express relational knowledge about the data. Examples of linguistic summaries are:

Most people in **DB** are **about 1.8 meters**

Few people in **DB** are **tall**

Formally, a linguistic summary is a statement of the form:

Q *objects in* **DB** *are* **S,**

where **S** is called the **summarizer, Q** is called the **quantity in agreement**, and **DB** is a data collection. Also associated with a linguistic summary is a truth value $\mathcal{T} \in [0,1]$, called **the measure of validity** of the summary [9]. The summarizer **S** is a fuzzy expression, linguistic concept, defined over the domain of some attribute associated with the database. The second component in a linguistic summary, the quantity in agreement, belongs to a class concept that Zadeh [14] called linguistic quantifiers. Examples of these objects are terms such as *most, few,* or *about half.* Essentially, linguistic quantifiers are fuzzy proportions or fuzzy probabilities. In [14], Zadeh suggested we can represent any of these linguistic terms as a fuzzy subset **Q** of the unit interval. In this representation, the membership grade of any $r \in [0,1]$ is a measure of the compatibility of the proportion r with the linguistic quantifier we are representing by the fuzzy subset **Q**.

The measure of validity $\mathcal{T}$ provides an indication of how compatible the linguistic summary is with the database. We now describe the methodology used to calculate the validity $\mathcal{T}$ of a linguistic summary. Assume $\mathbf{DB} = \{o_1, \ldots, o_n\}$ is our collection of data objects and the summarizer **S** is a fuzzy expression on the attributes **A** of $o_i \in \mathbf{DB}$, and **Q** is the fuzzy quantifier. The procedure for obtaining the validity of a linguistic summary in the face of the data **DB** is as follows:

1. For each $o_i \in \mathbf{DB}$, calculate $\mathbf{S}(o_i)$, the degree to which o_i satisfies the summarizer **S**.

2. Let $r = \dfrac{1}{n}\sum_{i=1}^{n} \mathbf{S}(o_i)$, the proportion of objects in the **DB** that satisfy **S**.

3. Then $\mathcal{T} = \mathbf{Q}(r)$, the grade of membership of r in the proposed quantity in agreement.

Another type linguistic summary is of the form:

Most tall *objects in* **DB** *are* **young**

In this case, we only say something about a subpopulation of the data (*the tall objects*). As we shall see, this type of summary will be useful for obtaining fuzzy rules from a database. The generic form of this class of linguistic summaries is:

Q R *objects in* **DB** *are* **S**

The procedure for calculating $\mathcal{T}$ is the same as the previous, except in step 2. In this case, we calculate r as the proposition of the **R** objects in **DB** that satisfy **S**:

$$r = \frac{\sum_{i=1}^{n} T(\mathbf{S}(o_i), \mathbf{R}(o_i))}{\sum_{i=1}^{n} \mathbf{R}(o_i)}$$

where **R** and **S** are fuzzy subsets representing the concepts used in the summary, and T is a t-norm. A t-norm is a class of binary operators used for implementing an AND operation to which minimum and product belong [15].

Closely related and semantically equivalent to the preceding type of linguistic summary is the situation in which we have a fuzzy database and desire to make a summary over some attribute of this fuzzy database. We recall that a fuzzy database [6], $\mathcal{DB}$, is of the same form as a crisp database except that each of the objects has a degree of membership in $\mathcal{DB}$, which may be different from 1. In this framework, if we desire to validate the linguistic summary "**Q** *objects in* $\mathcal{DB}$ are **S**," we proceed in a manner similar to the previous. We calculate for each $o_i \in \mathcal{DB}$, $\mathbf{S}(o_i)$, the degree to which o_i satisfies the summarizer **S**. We then calculate:

$$r = \frac{\sum_{i=1}^{n} T(\mathbf{S}(o_i), \mathcal{DB}(o_i))}{\sum_{i=1}^{n} \mathcal{DB}(o_i)}$$

where $\mathcal{DB}(o_i)$ is the membership grade of an object in the fuzzy database. Finally, we calculate $\mathcal{T} = \mathbf{Q}(r)$.

16.3. Summary as a Predicate

A linguistic summary, like a fuzzy predicate, has a truth value in the unit interval, the truth value being the measure of validity of the summary. Based on this observation, we can use linguistic summaries in the same way that we use predicates in formation of fuzzy queries to a database. This fact will enable us to develop an SQL-like summary language for use in data mining. We will now show how linguistic summaries can be adopted into a fuzzy query language and how they can be used to find typical values and fuzzy rules of the form "**Q R** *objects in* **DB** *are* **S**."

We first look at the issue of finding typical values in a database. We can define a typical value for an attribute in a **DB** as a value which is *close to* most of the values found in the **DB** for that attribute. Yager [16] discusses how we can use fuzzy subsets to represent typical values.

Consider a database having as one of its attributes salary. Consider a salary S and the linguistic summary "**Most** *objects in* **DB** *have a* Salary **close to** S." The validity of this summary is a measure of the typicality of the salary S. We can denote this as a predicate Σ_{Most} ($o_j \in$ **DB** | Salary(o_j) $\approx$ S). As noted, the predicate Σ_{Most} ($o_j \in$ **DB** | Salary(o_j) $\approx$ S) is semantically identical to the linguistic summary "**Most** *objects in* **DB** *have a* Salary **close to** S," where Σ_Q represents a summary with a linguistic quantifier **Q**, $o_j \in$ **DB** are the data objects we want to summarize, and Salary(o_j) $\approx$ S is the summarizer **S**. The term $\approx$ is used to indicate the predicate **close to**. The predicate x **close to** y can be represented as a fuzzy relation on the domain of salaries whose truth value indicates the nearness between x and y.

In our approach we shall let the objects in the database themselves provide the values that are considered as potential typical values. Thus, if o_i is an object in the database and Salary(o_i) is the salary of this object, then Σ_{Most} ($o_j \in$ **DB** | Salary(o_j) $\approx$ Salary(o_i)) is the measure of typicality of the object o_i in the context of salary, as well as the measure of typicality of the value salary(o_i).

If we want to find the set of people in the database who have a typical income, we can pose the following question: *"Select all persons with a salary close to most of the other salaries."* We can formulate this as a query to the database over the attribute salary:

$$Q_{\text{Salary} = S \wedge \Sigma_{Most}(o_j \in \text{DB} \mid \text{Salary}(o_j) \approx S)}(\textbf{DB})$$

$$= \{o_i \in \textbf{DB} \mid \Sigma_{Most}(o_j \in \textbf{DB} \mid \mu_{close\ to}(\text{Salary}(o_j), \text{Salary}(o_i))\}$$

The result of the query will be a ranked list where the people with the highest membership degree (degree of typicality) have the most typical salary. Of course, the degree of typicality could be so small for the highest ranked persons that we do not want to call their salary typical. In the next section, we will give some examples.

We now investigate how we can use these ideas to help in the discovery from a database of fuzzy rules of the form exemplified by "**tall** *objects in* **DB** *are* **heavy**." The justification of such a rule can be based upon the validity of the linguistic summary "**Most tall** *objects in* **DB** *are* **heavy**." Thus we see that the discovery of rules from a database is closely related to the validation of linguistic summaries.

Assume we conjecture a rule *"tall persons are heavy"* and would like to have it confirmed. This can be done by validating the summary: "**Most tall** *objects in* **DB** *are* **heavy**."

As we have indicated in the previous section an equivalent formulation of this summary is the summary: "**Most** *objects in* **tall persons** *are* **heavy**," in which **tall persons** is a fuzzy database having the same structure as the original database **DB**, except that each object has a membership in **tall persons** where **tall persons**$(o_i) = \mu_{tall}(\text{Height}(o_i))$. Thus the membership grade of an object in the fuzzy database **tall persons** is the same as the membership grade of the object in the fuzzy predicate *tall*. Using this equivalence, we formulate the preceding as a two-part query to our original database.

First, select from the database the fuzzy database **tall persons** where:

$$\textbf{Tall\_Persons} = Q_{\text{Height} = tall}(\textbf{DB})$$

and then pose the linguistic summary to this new database:

$$\sum_{Most} (o_i \in \textbf{Tall\_Persons} \mid o_i.\text{Weight}=heavy)(\textbf{Tall\_Persons})$$

$$= \sum_{Most} (o_i \in \{o_j \in \textbf{DB} \mid \mu_{tall}(o_j.\text{Height})\} \mid \mu_{heavy}(o_i.\text{Weight}))$$

Implicit in this approach to rule generation is the conjecture of a potential rule for validation, *tall persons are heavy*. Generally, the process of conjecturing rules requires some kind of expert knowledge to help in this process. In Explora [17, 18] and the approach introduced by Yager [13, 19], they suggest the use of templates to help in this conjecturing process. As suggested by Yager [13, 19], a template associated with an attribute is a collection of linguistic concepts, fuzzy subsets, used to talk about that attribute. For example, associated with the attribute height could be the template {*tall, medium, short*}, and associated with the attribute weight could be the template {*heavy, average, skinny*}. Using these templates, we can then conjecture all rules of the form most **E** type objects in the database are **F**, where **E** is a linguistic value from the template set associated with height and **F** is a linguistic value from the template set associated with the attribute weight. Our testing for validation would then be performed on all these possible rules. As noted in [13, 19], the template sets can be seen as a kind of expert knowledge about the domains, which helps in the conjecture of potential rules. In Explora [17, 18], a conceptual hierarchy is used to guide the search and to prevent redundant discoverings. More generally our tool for validation can be used in any situation in which some kind of expert knowledge is used to conjecture rules. In this spirit, the summary tool can be part of a human-machine interactive system for rule discovery.

In the following, we describe a naive, but more automated, approach to rule generation from databases which, rather than requiring expert knowledge to conjecture the potential rules, uses the values of the objects in the database themselves to generate the rules, and then uses our validation procedure to confirm the rules. In this approach, as we shall subsequently see, the objects in the database form the prototypes for the potential rules.

Consider a database with the attributes Age and Salary. The spirit of this approach is as follows. For each object o_i in the database **DB**, we form a fuzzy database $\mathcal{DB}_i$ where the membership grade of any o_j is equal to the degree of closeness of the age of the object o_j to the age of the focus element o_i. Then for each of these databases, we test the validity of the summary "**Most** objects in $\mathcal{DB}_i$ have Salary **close to** salary(o_i)." The validity of such a summary can be seen as the confirmation of a rule from the original database of the form if Age is *close to* Age(o_i) then Salary is *close to* Salary(o_i). We shall denote this kind of rule as Rule-Object$_i$. A significant feature of this method is that the whole procedure just described can be expressed as a query to the database **DB** in form:

$$Q_{\text{Age} = A \land \text{Salary} = S \land \Sigma_{\text{Most}}(o_j \in Q_{\text{Age} = A}(\textbf{DB})| o_j.\text{Salary} = S)}(\textbf{DB})$$

$$= \{o_i \in \textbf{DB} \mid \Sigma_{\text{Most}} (\{o_j \in \textbf{DB} \mid \mu_{\text{close to}}(o_j.\text{Age}, o_i.\text{Age})\} \mid \mu_{\text{close to}}(o_j.\text{Salary}, o_i.\text{Salary}))\}$$

The result of this query is a fuzzy relation over the objects in the database in which the membership grade indicates the degree of validity of Rule-Object$_i$. We note in the worst cases the complexity of this algorithm will be $O(x^2)$ where x is the number of objects in **DB**.

In the preceding we have suggested two approaches, both based on the use of linguistic quantifiers, to the construction of fuzzy rules from a database. In the first approach, an interactive one, external expert knowledge is used to generate potential rules, which are then tested for validity. In the second approach, an automated one, the objects in the database are used as prototypes for potential rules.

16.4. Summary SQL

Summary SQL is the name of a prototype and a summary query language we have developed. The syntax of the query language is nearly similar to SQL, and a normal fuzzy query has the syntax:

select *attributes*

from *tables*

where *conditions*

The result of this query is a sort table where the membership degree of the objects indicate how much they belong to the table. The syntax of a summary query is:

summary *quantifier*

from *tables*

where *conditions*

The *conditions* in the **where** clause are a fuzzy expression where we can conjunct (AND), disjunct (OR) and negate (NOT) the predicates. The predicates can be summaries or have the form *attribute* **IS** *fuzzyterm.* The result of a summary query is the truth value of that summary.

In the following, we shall provide some examples of the application of this language. In our examples we will use the concept *tall* defined in Figure 16.1a and the concepts *most* and *close to* defined in Figure 16.2a,b. The concept *close to* x is defined as a fuzzy relation where the membership grade of the two arguments x and *Weight* is 1 for x = *Weight* and 0 when the distance between x and *Weight* is greater than 10 Kg. We assume a triangular form.

Persons is a datatable where each person has the attributes Name, Height and Weight. In Figure 16.3 we show the result of the query "*select all tall persons.*" In this case, Table_0 is an alias for the tall persons. At right, we can see the persons membership degree (μ) to the query.

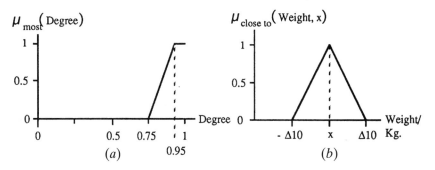

Figure 16.2   Definitions of the fuzzy concepts *most* (a) and *close to* (b).

```
from Persons
where height is tall;

table name:   Table_0

              name      height      weight          μ

              John       195          96            1
               Ben       193         101            1
              Jake       191          97            1
             Harry       190          99            1
             Jerry       187          96          0.85
               Sam       185          97          0.75
              Burt       185          96          0.75
               Dan       180          93          0.5
            Dustin       177          87          0.35
              Adam       173          83          0.15
           Michael       170          78            0
              Eric       168          75            0
              Paul       166          70            0
```

Figure 16.3   The table of the tall persons.

We next consider a simple summary query. The summary "*most tall persons are heavy*" is evaluated in Figure 16.4, where Table_0 is the *tall* persons. The summary has the true value $T \approx 0.94$.

We now consider the problem of finding typical values. To find the typical weight among *tall* persons, we have to rename the tall persons (Table_0) because we have to refer to two different objects from the same table; this is done in the **from** clause by (<table> <new name>). See Figure 16.5. The query in Figure 16.5 is implemented by iterating over each object in *tall* persons (Table A) and summarizes the weight with respect to all the *tall* persons (Table B). The result Table_1 is a fuzzy subset where the values μ indicate the degree of typically for the weight among the *tall* persons (Figure 16.6).

16.5. Conclusion

In this chapter, we have shown how a fuzzy query language and linguistic summaries can be combined to make a more powerful query language. This new query language makes it possible to search for typical values and fuzzy rules without losing the ability to make fuzzy queries. We suggest

```
summary most
from Table_0
where weight is heavy;

result: 0.943878
```

Figure 16.4   Result of the summary "most tall persons are heavy."

```
from Table_0 A
where summary most
      from Table_0 B
      where weight:A is close_to weight:B;

table name:  Table_1

              name      height     weight           μ

              Jake       191        97       0.433673
               Sam       185        97       0.433673
              John       195        96       0.365646
             Jerry       187        96       0.365646
              Burt       185        96       0.365646
             Harry       190        99       0.229592
               Ben       193       101              0
               Dan       180        93              0
            Dustin       177        87              0
              Adam       173        83              0
           Michael       170        78              0
              Eric       168        75              0
              Paul       166        70              0
```

Figure 16.5   Typical weight among *tall* persons.

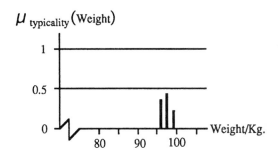

Figure 16.6   Membership function for typical weight among tall persons.

how a summary query language could look, and we call it Summary SQL. A simple implementation of a prototype of Summary SQL has been developed. Use was made of this prototype for the examples in the chapter. In the future, we expect to make a more complete implementation of Summary SQL, which will take advantage of the full fuzzy query language.

16.6. References

[1] Piatetsky-Shapiro, G., and B. Frawley. *Knowledge Discovery in Databases.* Cambridge: MIT Press, 1991.

[2] ———. *Knowledge Discovery in Databases: Papers from the 1993 AAAI Workshop.* Menlo Park: AAAI Press, 1993.

[3] Matheus, C.J., et al. "Systems for Knowledge Discovery in Databases." *IEEE Transactions on Knowledge and Data Engineering,* Vol. 5 (1993), pp. 903–913.

[4] Fayyad, U.M., and R. Uthurusamy. *Knowledge Discovery in Databases.* Menlo Park: AAAI Press, 1994.

[5] ———. *Proceedings, 1st International Conference on Knowledge Discovery and Data Mining.* Menlo Park: AAAI Press, 1995.

[6] Zemankova, M., and A. Kandel. "Fuzzy Relational Databases—A Key to Expert Systems." Verlag TUV Rheinland, Cologne: 1984.

[7] Larsen, H.L., and T. Andreasen. "Flexible Query-Answering Systems." Roskilde, Denmark: Roskilde University, 1994.

[8] Yager, R.R., and T.C. Rubinson. "Linguistic Summaries of Databases." *Proceedings, IEEE Conference on Decision and Control.* pp. 1094–1097. San Diego, C.A.: 1981.

[9] Yager, R.R. "A New Approach to the Summarization of Data." *Information Sciences,* Vol. 28 (1982), pp. 69–86.

[10] Zadeh, L.A. "Test Score Semantics as a Basis for a Computational Approach to the Representation of Meaning." *Literary and Linguistic Computing,* Vol. 1 (1986), pp. 24–35.

[11] Yager, R.R. "On Linguistic Summaries of Data," in *Knowledge Discovery in Databases.* eds. G. Piatetsky-Shapiro and B. Frawley. pp. 347–363. Cambridge: MIT Press, 1991.

[12] ———. "Linguistic Summaries as a Tool for Database Discovery." *Workshop on Fuzzy Database Systems and Information Retrieval at FUZZ-IEEE/IFES.* pp. 79–82. Yokohama, Japan: 1995.

[13] ———. "Fuzzy Summaries in Database Mining." *Proceedings, 11th Conference on Artificial Intelligence for Applications.* pp. 265–269. Los Angeles, Calif.: 1995.

[14] Zadeh, L.A. "A Computational Approach to Fuzzy Quantifiers in Natural Languages." *Computing and Mathematics with Applications,* Vol. 9 (1983), pp. 149–184.

[15] Dubois, D., and H. Prade. "A Review of Fuzzy Sets Aggregation Connectives." *Information Sciences,* Vol. 36 (1985), pp. 85–121.

[16] Yager, R.R. "A Fuzzy Measure of Typicality." Technical Report # MII-1513. Machine Intelligence Institute, Iona College. New Rochelle, N.Y., 1995.

[17] Hoschka, P., and W. Klosgen. "A Support System for Interpreting Statistical Data," in *Knowledge Discovery in Databases,* ed. G. Piatetsky-Shapiro and B. Frawley. pp. 325–345. Cambridge: MIT Press, 1991.

[18] Klosgen, W. "Problems for Knowledge Discovery in Databases and their Treatment in the Statistics Interpreter Explora." *International Journal of Intelligent Systems,* Vol. 7 (1992), pp. 649–673.

[19] Yager, R.R. "Database Discovery using Fuzzy Sets." Technical Report # MII-1601. Machine Intelligence Institute, Iona College. New Rochelle, N.Y., 1996.

17 A Fuzzy Information Retrieval System Handling Users' Preferences on Document Sections

Gloria Bordogna, Gabriella Pasi
Istituto per le Tecnologie Informatiche Multimediali—CNR

ABSTRACT: The synthesis of a document's information content is a crucial preliminary activity of information retrieval. Common indexing models adopt the simplifying assumption that information is homogeneously distributed in documents and that it cannot be interpreted on the basis of users' needs. In this chapter, an approach to represent documents as structured entities composed of sections is proposed. Further, by considering that the documents' information content can be regarded differently according to the users' needs, a mechanism is defined, which allows users to express preferences on the document sections bearing more interesting information. In this way, the significance of the index terms is dynamically computed during a retrieval session based on the users' specifications. Finally, a compared evaluation of the retrieval results produced by a system using this fuzzy representation of structured documents and the same system with a traditional fuzzy representation is discussed.

17.1. Introduction

One of the main objectives of current research in information retrieval is the improvement of the system's effectiveness; the aim is to retrieve all the documents in the archive as far as possible concerned with the topics of interest expressed in a user query. The production of effective results is dependent both on subjective factors, such as users' ability to express their information needs in a query, and on the characteristics of the Information Retrieval System (IRS). The main components of an IRS are:

- the representation of documents, in which the documents' information content is synthesized and organized in a data structure suitable for direct access;
- the query language; and
- the retrieval mechanism, which evaluates a query and retrieves the documents that satisfy it.

In an attempt to improve the effectiveness of Information Retrieval Systems, some authors have defined new retrieval models, based on more expressive query languages and more accurate representations of documents. Others authors have defined relevance feedback mechanisms that enhance the interaction with users in order to grasp more useful information on their needs [1,2,3,4,5,6,7,8].

In this chapter an approach is proposed that is based on a twofold consideration:

- the representation of documents plays a key role in determining the effectiveness of the retrieval. In fact, providing information retrieval systems with powerful query languages or sophisticated retrieval mechanisms is not sufficient to achieve effective results if the representation of documents strongly simplifies their information content;
- the interaction with the user is fundamental not only at the level of query formulation or analysis of the retrieved documents, but also to specify the criteria to be used to interpret the documents' content.

Many works have been done to improve the representation of documents in a static manner, which does not provide for the possibility of an interaction with users for the interpretation of the documents' content [9,10,11]. In this chapter a fuzzy representation of structured documents is presented that is subjected to a user interpretation [12]. In this model, documents are described as structured entities composed of sections. Different degrees of significance are computed for a given term in a document, one for each document section, based on the section's semantics; these values are then aggregated to obtain the overall significance of a term in a document. The aggregation function is defined on the basis of a two-level interaction between the system and the user. At the first level, the user can express preferences on the document sections, outlining those that the system should more heavily take into account in evaluating the relevance of a document to a user query. At the second level, the user can decide which aggregation function has to be applied for producing the overall significance degree. This is done by the specification of a linguistic quantifier such as *at least one, at least k,* or *all.* By adopting this document representation, the same query can select documents in different relevance order depending on the user indications. In section 17.2, the indexing problem is introduced; in section 17.3, the representation of structured documents is defined; its implementation to extend the functionalities of a fuzzy information retrieval system is described in section 17.4. Finally, in section 17.5, it is evaluated in comparison with the same system using a traditional fuzzy representation. The results show an improvement of the effectiveness of the system and suggest further evolutions.

17.2. Document Indexing

To automatically evaluate a user query, a system must be provided with a representation of the document's content: the basic problem is to capture and synthesize the meaning of a document written in natural language. Currently, general tools for interpreting natural language texts are far from being generally applicable [13]. The major impediment to their application is that the interpretation of the document's meaning needs a too-large number of decision rules even in narrow domains. The semantic analysis of texts yields acceptable performances only when it is applied to index documents about specific and narrow subject areas [13,14,15].

Other approaches renounce to explicitly define the indexing function and adopt neural retrieval models; they are based on the conviction that document indexing is a too-complex activity, subject to various factors difficult to be explicitly described [16,17,18,19]. These models need a training phase in order to generate the associations between the documents and the index terms, and their application is still experimental.

More feasible approaches are those based either on manual indexing or on a statistical analysis of the texts. Manual indexing procedures are generally carried out by a group of experts in the archive application field; the experts are involved to select some terms, single words, or phrases, named indexes, which they judge meaningful to synthesize the information contained in each document. The manual procedure is characterized by inefficient performances when applied to index a large amount of information. Moreover, this process is based on heuristic considerations producing a subjective representation [4].

Automatic indexing procedures have been advocated and designed in order to cope with the drawbacks of manual indexing. At present, the most common automatic indexing procedure is based on the assumption that the presence of a term in a document is an indication of the topics dealt with in the document: in full-text indexing, all terms, named index terms, are automatically extracted from the documents [4] and organized in a data structure, the so-called inverted-file. Full-text indexing is often associated with low-level linguistic analysis, that is, morphological and lexical analysis. In order to expand index terms, some authors have designed associative mechanisms based on statistical co-occurrences of terms in documents [6,20].

The most adopted information retrieval model is the Boolean one, which is generally associated with full-text indexing; in this model, a document d is formally represented by the mathematical set of its index terms, $R(d) = \{t\}$ in which $t \in T$, and the membership function correlating terms and documents ($F: D \times T \to \{0,1\}$) is defined on the set of documents D, and on the set of terms T. A value $F(d,t) = 1$ ($F(d,t) = 0$) indicates the presence (absence) of term $t \in T$ in document $d \in D$.

Queries are defined as Boolean expressions on terms. The retrieval function then applies an exact matching; it selects the documents that are pointed in the inverted-file by the terms in the query, and evaluates the AND, OR, and NOT operators as the set operations of intersection, union, and complement respectively. As in the Boolean document representation, there is no means to express the varying degree of concern of a term to a document; a partial matching mechanism cannot be applied in order to rank documents in decreasing order of their relevance to the query [4]. Such a ranking is very useful, since what generally happens in real situations is that users can have preferences on the retrieved documents.

To improve the retrieval activity with a ranking ability, the Boolean representation has been extended by the introduction of index term weights [4,10]. Within fuzzy set theory, the F correlation function is allowed to take values in the unit interval, $F: D \times T \to [0,1]$. Here the index term weight $F(d,t) \in [0,1]$ represents the degree of significance of t in d; this value can be specified between no significance, $F(d,t) = 0$, and full significance $F(d,t) = 1$. Consequently, in the fuzzy document representation, a document is represented as a fuzzy set of terms, $R(d) = \{\langle t, \mu_d(t)\rangle | t \in T\}$ in which $\mu_d(t) = F(d,t)$.

Through this extension, the retrieval mechanism can compute the relevance of each document to the query expressed by a numeric score, called Retrieval Status Value (RSV), which denotes how well a document satisfies the query [21].

The definition of the criteria for an automatic computation of $F(d,t)$ is a crucial aspect; generally this value is defined on the basis of statistical measurements with the aim of balancing the values of recall and precision, which are parameters commonly used to measure the effectiveness of the retrieval activity. Recall is the ratio of the number of relevant documents retrieved to the total number of documents relevant; it is an indicator of the exhaustivity of the indexing; precision is the ratio of the number of relevant documents retrieved to the total number of documents retrieved; it is thus an indicator of the specificity of the indexing [4].

When the indexing vocabulary is narrow and specific (terms occur frequently in a few documents), the retrieval precision is favored at the expense of recall; the reverse is obtained when the indexing vocabulary is broad and nonspecific (terms occur frequently in almost all documents of the archive).

On the basis of these considerations, the significance F(d,t) of a term in a document has been defined so as to increase with the frequency of term t in the document d, and to decrease with the frequency of the term in all the documents of the archive [4,10,11]:

$$F(d,t) = tf_{dt} * IDF_t \tag{1}$$

in which:

- tf_{dt} is a normalized term frequency, which can be defined as: $tf_{dt} = OCC_{dt}/MAXOCC_d$; OCC_{dt} is the number of occurrences of t in d, and $MAXOCC_d$ is the number of occurrences of the most frequent term in d;
- IDF_t is a normalized inverse document frequency, which can be defined as a function of $Log\ (N/NDOC_t)$; where N is the total number of documents in the archive and $NDOC_t$ is the number of documents indexed by t. The computation of IDF_t is particularly costly in the case of large collections that are updated online.

Notice that the F function defined in (1), does not take into account that a term within a document text can play a different role according to the location of its occurrences. To define a significance degree that considers this dependency, we have proposed a new representation of documents, which can be interpreted by users according to their information needs [12].

17.3. A User Adaptive Fuzzy Representation of Structured Documents

Definition (1) is based on the assumption that the information is homogeneously distributed in documents. However, this assumption does not hold for a variety of applications, such as the management of bibliographic archives, medical reports, proposals for scientific and technical projects, in which documents are naturally structured in logic subparts and sections, containing information semantically self-consistent and self-contained. For example, in an archive of scientific project proposals, the documents are structured in sections such as title, project leader, funding organization, keywords, objectives, descriptions, and so on, in these documents, a single occurrence of a term in the title suggests that the project is deeply concerned with the concept expressed by the term, while a single occurrence in the reference may suggest that the project refers to other publications dealing with that concept. The information role of each term occurrence depends then on the semantics of the sub-part where it is located; the single occurrences of a term may then contribute differently to the significance of the term in the whole document.

Besides this semantic dependency, the subparts of a document may have a different importance determined by users' needs. For example, when looking for project proposals that have been funded by a certain organization, the most important subpart is the funding organization, while when looking for projects on a certain topic, the title, keywords, objectives, and description subparts are those preferred.

These considerations outline two distinct aspects that should be considered to compute the significance of a term in a structured document:

- the occurrences of a term in different document sections have to be taken into account according to specific criteria;
- users' interests may influence the computation of the F function by either enhancing or reducing the contribution of the term's occurrences, depending on the subpart to which they belong. For example, a user might specify the different importances of the sections and even decide that a term must be present in all the sections of the document or in at least a certain number of them in order to consider the term fully significant.

Some commercial widespread systems provide the ability of searching terms in specific document sections [4]. Nevertheless, they do not provide for the ability of associating different importances with the sections.

The need for a user adaptive representation of documents led us to define a fuzzy representation of structured documents in which documents are managed as structured entities, partitioned into sections. A section is a logical subpart identified by s_i, where $i \in 1, \ldots, n$ and n is the total number of sections in the documents. We assume here that an archive contains documents sharing a common structure. In the proposed representation, each term-document pair is not associated with a single index term weight, $F(d,t)$, but with a set of values, $F_1(d,t), \ldots, F_n(d,t)$, denoting the significance degree of term t in section i of document d. A function $F_i : DxT \rightarrow [0,1]$ is then defined for each section i. The overall significance degree $F(d,t)$ is computed by combining the single significance degrees of the sections, the $F_i(d,t)$s, through a decision function specified by the user. This function is identified by a fuzzy linguistic quantifier such as *all, at least k, at least 1,* and it aggregates the significance degrees of the sections according to their importance values, also specified by the user.

The fuzzy binary relation $R(d) = \{\langle (t,s), \mu_d(t,s) \rangle \mid (t,s) \in T \times S\}$ is defined to represent a document d; the value $\mu_d(t,s) = F_s(d,t)$ expresses the significance of term t in section s of document d. A section s is then represented by the fuzzy binary relation $R(s) = \{\langle (t,d), \mu_s(t,d) \rangle \mid (t,d) \in T \times D\}$, in which $\mu_s(t,d) = F_s(d,t)$.

The criteria for the definition of μ_s are based on the semantics of section s. For example, for sections containing short texts or formatted texts, such as the project leader and the keywords, a single occurrence of a term makes it fully significant in that section; in this case, it can be assumed that $\mu_s(t,d) = 1$, if t is present in s, $\mu_s(t,d) = 0$ otherwise. On the other side, for sections containing textual descriptions of variable length, such as the abstract and project description sections, $\mu_s(t,d)$ can be computed as a function of the normalized term frequency in the section.

The single $\mu_s(t,d)$s are aggregated according to a twofold specification of the user:

- users can express preferences on sections by associating a numeric score $\alpha_i \in [0,1]$ to each section s_i so that the most important sections have an importance weight close to 1, the less important ones a weight close to 0;

- users can specify through a linguistic quantifier how many sections of the documents must be taken into account; the quantifier can be *all* (the most restrictive one), *at least one* (the weakest one), or *at least k* which is associated with an intermediate aggregation criterion.

Within fuzzy set theory, there are several approaches to formalize linguistic quantifiers [22,23,24,25,26]. As Yager pointed out, the formalization based upon Ordered Weighted Average operators is suited to model a linguistic quantifier as a connective lying between the AND and the OR [23]. For this reason, we have adopted OWA operators on criteria of different importances to model the quantifier-guided aggregation function F. As pointed out previously, the criteria to be aggregated are the n significance degrees of the sections, $\mu_1(d,t), \ldots, \mu_n(d,t)$ of a document d. When setting a retrieval session, the user can specify an importance weight $\alpha_i \in [0,1]$ to each section *i*, and a linguistic quantifier lq which identifies the aggregation function. When processing a query, the first step accomplished by the system for evaluating F(d,t) is the selection of the OWA operator associated with the linguistic quantifier lq, OWA_{lq}.

When the user does not specify any preferences on the document sections, the overall significance degree F(d,t) is obtained by applying directly the OWA_{lq} operator to the values $\mu_1(d,t), \ldots, \mu_n(d,t)$:

$$F(d,t) = OWA_{lq} (\mu_1(d,t), \ldots, \mu_n(d,t))$$

When different importances $\alpha_1, \ldots, \alpha_n$ are associated with the sections, it is first necessary to modify the values $\mu_1(d,t), \ldots, \mu_n(d,t)$ in order to increase the "contrast" between the contributions due to important sections with respect to those of less important ones. The modified degrees $a_1, \ldots, a_n$ of significance of the sections are obtained as follows:

$$a_i = (\alpha_i \vee (1 - orness(W))) \mu_i^{\alpha_i \vee orness(W)}$$

The second step is the evaluation of the overall significance degree $F(d,t)$ by applying the operator OWA_{lq} to the modified degrees $a_1, \ldots, a_n$:

$$F(d,t) = OWA_{lq}(a_1, \ldots, a_n)$$

The user can select a linguistic quantifier among a set of possible ones: *all, at least k,* with k varying between 1 and n. The *at least k* quantifier is usually defined by a weighting vector $W_{at\ least\ k}$ in which $w_k = 1$. This quantifier acts as the specification of an exact threshold of value k on the number of the sections. As this definition is too crisp, we have provided another definition of *at least k* in which the k value is interpreted as a fuzzy threshold. When users specify *at least k,* they mean that a term has a full overall significance if it is present in k or more sections, but they want to get a certain significance degree even if the term is present in k − 1, k − 2, . . . , 1 sections. $W_{at\ least\ k}$ is thus defined in which $w_i = 1/k$ for $i \leq k$, and $w_i = 0$, for $i > k$.

When the user does not make any specification about the aggregation operator, the system should provide at least the same performance as it does with the traditional fuzzy representation of documents. For dealing with this case, another quantifier, named *at least a few* has been defined; its desired behavior is that when a term is present in *m* or more sections of a document, the overall significance degree should be maximum (i.e., 1); the increase of satisfaction in having the term present in *i + 1* sections with respect to having it in *i* sections should be greater as *i* approaches the threshold *m*. The weighting vector $W_{at\ least\ a\ few}$ is then defined as: $w_i = i/n + r/m$ in which r/m is a constant value depending solely on n; *m* is defined as the maximum value j for which:

$$\sum_{j=1}^{m} j \leq n \quad \text{and} \quad r = 1 - \sum_{j=1}^{m} \frac{j}{n} \ \forall i \leq m; w_i = 0 \ \forall i > m.$$

17.4. Implementation of the Fuzzy Representation of Structured Documents

The fuzzy representation of structured documents has been implemented on the Information Retrieval System DOMINO, and has been evaluated on an archive containing 2500 textual documents that describe research projects of the "Consiglio Nazionale delle Ricerche" (CNR). DOMINO is a prototypal information retrieval system developed in C programming language at the CNR; the most recent version runs on PC 486 under Windows. DOMINO was originally conceived and implemented as a Boolean system based on a full-text indexing with a stoplist for eliminating useless words, and a traditional inverted file data structure [7].

A first evolution of the system was the implementation of the traditional fuzzy representation of documents based on the computation of the index term weight $F(d,t)$ through definition (1). Further extensions have concerned the Boolean query language to allow users to specify the "importance" that the search terms must have in the desired documents [7,27]. Two query languages have been implemented in which each query term can be associated with either a numeric weight or a linguistic descriptor of the desired importance of the term, respectively. The semantics of the numeric query term weight is that of ideal index term weight, and has been defined as the fuzzy restriction *close to w;* linguistic descriptors have been defined as values of the linguistic variable *importance*. Examples of queries in the two languages are:

$$q_1 = \langle t_1, w_1 \rangle \text{ OR } \langle t_2, w_2 \rangle \text{ AND NOT } \langle t_3, w_3 \rangle$$

and

$$q_2 = \langle t_1, important \rangle \text{OR} \langle t_2, fairly\ important \rangle \text{AND} \langle t_3, not\ very\ important \rangle$$

respectively, in which t_1, t_2, t_3, are search terms, w_1, w_2, $w_3, \in [0,1]$ are numeric weights and *important, fairly important, not very important* are linguistic weights.

The scheme of the retrieval activity in this prototypal version of DOMINO is represented in Figure 17.1. The input to the retrieval activity is a user's query, which is either a Boolean expression on pairs term-numeric weight or a Boolean expression on pairs term-linguistic weight.

The query is interpreted by the query interpreter module, which builds an evaluation binary tree: the leaves contain the terms with the compatibility functions defining the semantics of either the numeric weights or linguistic descriptors; the intermediate nodes contain the Boolean operators. The partial matching mechanism evaluates this binary tree in post-order against the fuzzy document representation. This bottom-up procedure yields consistent results since the retrieval mechanism satisfies the separability property of the wish-list [2,5,7]. The retrieval status values produced by this phase can be used either to rank directly the documents retrieved or to classify the documents into relevance classes.

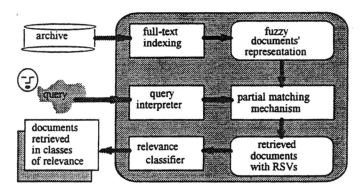

Figure 17.1   Scheme of the DOMINO system with the traditional fuzzy representation of documents.

In Figure 17.2, the extension of DOMINO obtained by implementing the fuzzy representation of structured documents is sketched. Here the retrieval activity is fired by a query; the user may also specify the importance weights $(\alpha_1, \ldots, \alpha_n)$ associated with the sections of a document, and may choose a linguistic quantifier lq as aggregation criterion of the degrees of significance of the sections. This information is used by the control mechanism to interpret the document's content.

The control mechanism module aggregates the degrees of significance modified by the importance weights $\alpha_1, \ldots, \alpha_n$ of the sections by applying the OWA_{lq} operator.

The results of this module are the overall degrees of significance, F(d,t)s, which are passed to the partial matching mechanism for the computation of the Retrieval Status Value (RSV). This last module and the query interpreter module are the same of the previous version of the system. The type and the number of document sections depend on the semantics of the archive; their definition is made by an expert before starting the archive generation phase. During this phase, it is necessary to specify the criteria by which to compute the significance degrees of the terms in each section. In the archive of CNR research projects, two kinds of sections have been identified based on heuristics: the "structured" sections, containing short texts, such as the *research code, title, research leader,* and so on, and the "narrative" sections, containing unstructured textual descriptions, such as the *description* and the *objective.* For the *structured sections,* the μ_s function has been defined as follows:

$$\mu_s(d,t) = \begin{cases} 1 & \text{if t is present in the structured section s of d} \\ 0 & \text{otherwise} \end{cases} \tag{2}$$

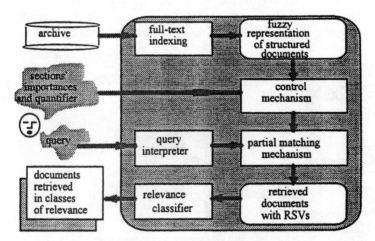

Figure 17.2 Scheme of the DOMINO system with the fuzzy representation of structured documents.

For the *narrative sections,* the μ_s function should be defined based on the normalized term frequency:

$$\mu_s(d,t) = \begin{cases} 1 & \text{if } tf_{dst} * IDF_t \geq 1 \\ tf_{dst} * IDF_t & \text{otherwise} \end{cases} \qquad (3)$$

in which IDF_t is the inverse document frequency of term t (see definition (1)), tf_{dst} is the normalized term frequency defined as:

$$tf_{dst} = \frac{OCC_{dst}}{MAXOCC_{sd}}$$

in which OCC_{dst} is the number of occurrences of term t in section *s* of document d, and $MAXOCC_{sd}$ is a normalization parameter depending on the section's length so as not to underestimate the significance of short sections with respect to long ones. For example, it can be computed as the frequency of the term with the highest number of occurrences in the section. As the computation of this value would be very time-consuming, it is convenient to heuristically approximate it: during the archive generation phase, the expert indicates the estimated percentage of the average length of each section with respect to the average length of documents ($PERL_s$). Given the number of occurrences of the most frequent term in each document d, $MAXOCC_d$, the heuristic approximation of the number of occurrences of the most frequent term in section *s* of document d is:

$$MAXOCC_{sd} = PERL_s * MAXOCC_d$$

17.5. Evaluation of the Fuzzy Representation of Structured Documents

In this section, some results produced by DOMINO extended with the fuzzy representation of structured documents are illustrated. First, the different rankings obtained for two documents by adopting the traditional fuzzy document representation and the fuzzy representation of structured documents are outlined by an example.

The two documents considered in the archive of CNR research projects contain the term "genoma." With traditional fuzzy document representation, the degree of significance of "genoma" in representing the content of the documents, $F(d_i, genoma)$, is computed by applying definition (1); it depends on the number of occurrences of "genoma" in the document and in the whole archive, and not on its location in the various sections.

Table 17.1 shows the normalized frequency of "genoma" in the sections of the two documents; notice the term "genoma" has the same total number of occurrences in both the documents. Since the normalization factors are the same, by applying function (1), the significance of "genoma" in both documents gets the same value $F(d_1, genoma) = F(d_2, genoma) = 0.8$.

Table 17.2 shows the significance degrees for each section in which the term "genoma" occurs. These degrees are obtained using the fuzzy representation of structured documents; since the *title* and *keywords* sections are short texts, $\mu_{title}(d, genoma)$ and $\mu_{keywords}(d, genoma)$ are computed through definition (2). After estimating that the *objective* section takes up averagely 30 percent of the document's length, and the *description* section is around 40 percent, $\mu_{objective}(d, genoma)$ and $\mu_{description}(d, genoma)$ are computed on the basis of definition (3).

When the user does not specify any criterion to aggregate the single degrees of the sections, the default quantifier, *at least a few* is used; given 13 sections, the weighting vector of the $OWA_{at\ least\ a\ few}$ operator is defined as:

$$W_{at\ least\ a\ few} = [0.13, 0.21, 0.29, 0.37, 0, 0, 0, 0, 0, 0, 0, 0, 0];$$

since no importance is specified to differentiate the contributions of the sections, all of them are assumed with the maximum importance weight: $(\alpha_i = 1, \forall i \mid 1 \le i \le 13)$. Notice that the document d_1, which contains "genoma" in the *keywords* and *title,* is now considered more significant with respect to the document d_2 containing the term just in the *objective* and *description.*

These results can be reversed; for example, when the user specifies that the presence of the term "genoma" in the *objective* is fundamental. Table 17.3 illustrates this situation: it shows the modified degrees of significances of the sections when the user sets the aggregation criterion equal to *at least 1* and $\alpha_{objective} = 1$, $\alpha_{title} = \alpha_{keywords} = \alpha_{description} = 0.5$, and $\alpha_i = 0$ otherwise. In order to evaluate the improvement in the retrieval effectiveness of DOMINO, a compared evaluation of the system results produced by using the traditional fuzzy representation of documents and the fuzzy representation of structured documents has been carried out on the archive of the CNR research projects. Recall and precision have been computed for a set of 11 sample queries consisting of a single pair ⟨term,*important*⟩. When using the fuzzy representation of structured doc-

Table 17.1 The Normalized Frequency of "Genoma" in the Sections of the Two Documents

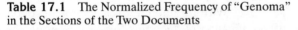

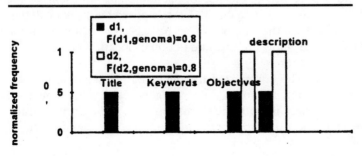

Table 17.2   The Significance Degrees of the Term "Genoma" in Each Section oɪ the Two Documents

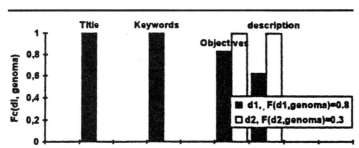

uments, the user specifies for each query the importance weights of the sections (α_i for $i = 1, \ldots, 13$) and the quantifier to aggregate the contributions of the sections.

A crucial aspect in the evaluation of the recall parameter is the estimation of the set of documents relevant to the user, N_{rel}, when the archive contains large collections. To reduce this burdensome operation, a sample subset of the archive is generally selected [4]. Due to the reduced cardinality of the sample set, the feasibility and reliability of users' estimation of relevant documents increase. In our experiment, instead of using a subset of the archive randomly selected, we have identified a meaningful subset, consisting of all documents pertaining to the subject area of the test queries.

This has been achieved by considering that each CNR research project is uniquely classified into one of the subject areas, through the value assumed by the section *Research Number,* labeled *RN.*

For each test query, the following procedure has been adopted: first, a sample collection of the archive has been obtained by selecting the documents in which the value of *RN* corresponds to the subject area of the query; then this sample collection has been browsed by the user to determine all documents worth retrieving, that is, the set N_{rel}. In a second step,

Table 17.3   The Modified Significance Degrees of the Term "Genoma" in Each Section of the Two Documents

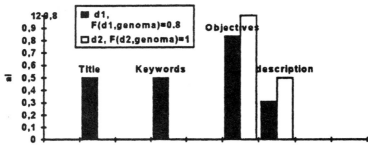

the query has been evaluated by the system that has classified the documents retrieved into four classes: *Very Relevant (VR), Relevant (R), Fairly Relevant (FR)*, and *Not Very Relevant (NR)*. Finally, to compare the results produced by the system with the user classification of the document retrieved, the user has been asked to specify his/her classifications in the relevance classes. Due to both the synthetic description of the projects (they have an average length of 40 lines) and to the full-text indexing procedure, the precision is high, and the set of documents judged worth retrieving by the users, N_{rel}, is a subset of the documents retrieved by the system. In their classification process, the users have placed the documents they judged worth retrieving in the first three classes of relevance (*Very Relevant (VR), Relevant (R)*, and *Fairly Relevant (FR)*). For each query, two matrices such as those in Table 17.4 have been filled. They report the comparisons of the human and system classifications in relevance classes by applying the traditional fuzzy representation in Table 17.4a and the representation of structured documents in Table 17.4b respectively. In each row (column), the user's (system's) classification of documents into relevance classes is reported. The last row (column) reports the total number of documents classified in the same class by the system (user). The values in bold cases on the main diagonal correspond to the documents on which the human and system classifications agree. Notice that the system with the fuzzy representation of structured documents (agreement degree of 58 percent; in fact there is agreement on 7 out of 12 documents) performs better than the system with the traditional fuzzy representation (agreement degree of 42 percent; in fact there is agreement on 5 out of 12 documents).

Table 17.5 summarizes the retrieval results of 11 queries produced by DOMINO when applying the traditional fuzzy representations of documents and the fuzzy representations of structured documents respectively. Salton's increasing output methodology has been applied to analyze the distribution of documents judged worth retrieving by the

Table 17.4 Comparison of the Results of the Query q: ⟨**grafica**; *important*⟩ **in** *at least 1* **section with** ($\alpha_{title} = 1$; $\alpha_{objective} = 0.5$; $\alpha_{keywords} = 0.6$)

		s y s t e m						s y s t e m				
		VR	R	FR	NR	Tot			VR	R	FR	NR	Tot
u'	VR	-	-	2	1	3	u	VR	3	-	-	-	3
s	R	-	1	-	2	3	s	R	-	-	2	1	3
e	FR	-	-	2	2	4	e	FR	-	-	4	-	4
r	NR	-	-	-	2	2	r	NR	-	-	2	-	2
	Tot	-	1	4	7	12		Tot	3	-	8	1	12

| (a) | (b) |

(a) user and system with fuzzy representation;
(b) user and system with the fuzzy representation of structured documents

Table 17.5 Average Values of Recall and Precision Obtained for a Sample Set of Queries by Applying the Two Representations of Documents

CLASSES	N_{retr}	$VR \cup R \cup FR$		$VR \cup R$		VR		
Average values	Prec.	Rec.	Prec.	Rec.	Prec.	Rec.	Prec.	Agreement
Traditional fuzzy representation	87%	58%	98%	31%	100%	20%	100%	36%
Fuzzy representation of structured documents	87%	87%	97%	55%	100%	40%	100%	61%

user, N_{rel}, in the various relevance classes by applying the definitions of recall and precision in Figure 17.3.

Each column lists the average values of Recall (Rec.) and Precision (Prec.) on the 11 test queries for documents classified by the system in different groups of relevance classes, except the second column which reports only the precision values for all the documents retrieved ($N_{retr} = VR \cup R \cup FR \cup NR$). The third column refers to the documents classified by the system in one of the most relevant classes, that is, in one of the classes *Very Relevant (VR), Relevant (R), Fairly Relevant (FR)*. The fourth column refers to the documents classified as *Very Relevant (VR)* or *Relevant (R)*. The fifth column refers to the documents classified by the system as *Very Relevant (VR)*. It can be observed that while the values of precision remain unchanged in the two versions of the system, the values of recall are higher by using the new representation than those obtained by using the traditional fuzzy representation. The last column reports the degrees of agreement between the system and the user classifications; also, for this parameter, the system with the fuzzy representation of structured documents classifies documents more closely to the user than the same system with the traditional fuzzy document representation.

17.6. Conclusion

In this chapter, a fuzzy representation of structured documents has been proposed that makes an IRS capable to suit the interpretation of the doc-

$$\text{Recall} = \frac{N_{\text{retr class}} \cap N_{\text{rel}}}{N_{\text{rel}}} \qquad \text{Precision} = \frac{N_{\text{retr class}} \cap N_{\text{rel}}}{N_{\text{retr\_class}}}$$

$N_{\text{retr\_class}}$ = number of documents retrieved in the specified class

N_{rel} = total number of documents relevant to the user query

Figure 17.3 Definitions of recall and precision.

ument's content to the users' needs; the documents are represented as composed of sections on which users can express preferences. A control mechanism has been defined that evaluates the significance of query terms in the archived documents based on the user's specification. A system implementing the representation of structured documents has been described and some evaluations presented. It has been shown that a system using this representation is characterized by a higher effectiveness with respect to the same system with the traditional fuzzy representation. In particular, the possibility of specifying different importance weights of the sections has been considered a very useful feature, which can be applied in many situations; it makes it possible to represent more accurately the document content based on criteria which are closer to user interpretation.

17.7. References

[1] Van Rijsbergen, C.J. *Information Retrieval.* Butterworths & Co. Ltd. 1979.
[2] Waller, W.G., and D.H. Kraft. "A Mathematical Model of a Weighted Boolean Retrieval System." *Information Processing & Management,* Vol. 15 (1979), pp. 235–245.
[3] Buell, D.A., and D.H. Kraft. "A Model for a Weighted Retrieval System." *Journal of the American Society for Information Science,* Vol. 32, No. 3 (1981), pp. 211–216.
[4] Salton, G., and M.J. McGill. *Introduction to Modern Information Retrieval.* New York: International Book Company, McGraw-Hill, 1984.
[5] Cater, S.C., and D.H. Kraft. "A Generalization and Clarification of the Waller-Kraft Wish-List." *Information Processing & Management,* Vol. 25, No. 1 (1989), pp. 15–25.
[6] Miyamoto, S. *Fuzzy Sets in Information Retrieval and Cluster Analysis.* Boston: Kluwer Academic Publishers, 1990.
[7] Bordogna, G., and G. Pasi. "A Fuzzy Linguistic Approach Generalizing Boolean Information Retrieval: A Model and Its Evaluation." *Journal of the American Society for Information Science,* Vol. 44, No. 2 (1993), pp. 70–82.
[8] ———. "Linguistic Aggregation Operators of Selection Criteria in Fuzzy Information Retrieval." *International Journal of Intelligent Systems,* Vol. 10 (1995), pp. 233–248.
[9] Sparck-Jones, K.A. "A Statistical Interpretation of Term Specificity and its Application in Retrieval." *Journal of Documentation,* Vol. 28, No. 1 (1972), pp. 11–20.
[10] Radecki, T. "Fuzzy Set Theoretical Approach to Document Retrieval." *Information Processing & Management,* Vol. 15 (1979), pp. 247–260.
[11] Salton, G., and C. Buckley. "Term Weighting Approaches in Automatic Text Retrieval." *Information Processing & Management,* Vol. 24, No. 5 (1988), pp. 513–523.
[12] Bordogna, G., et al. "A Fuzzy Document Representation Supporting User Adaptation in Information Retrieval." *Proceedings, 2nd IEEE International Conference on Fuzzy Systems.* pp. 974–979. San Francisco, Calif.: 1993.
[13] Doszkocs, T. "Natural Language Processing in Information Retrieval." *Journal of the American Society for Information Science,* Vol. 13, No. 4 (1986), pp. 191–196.
[14] Bolc, L., et al. "A Natural Language Information Retrieval System with Extensions towards Fuzzy Reasoning (Medical Diagnostic Computing)." *International Journal of Man-Machine Studies,* Vol. 23, No. 4 (1985).
[15] Frappaolo, C. "Artificial Intelligence and Text Retrieval: A Current Perspective on the State-of-the-Art." *Proceedings, 13th National Online Meeting.* pp. 113–114. New York, N.Y.: 1992.
[16] Mori, H., et al. "An Adaptive Document Retrieval System using a Neural Network." *International Journal of Human-Computer Interaction,* Vol. 2, No. 3 (1990), pp. 267–280.

[17] Wong, S.K.M., et al. "Computation of Term Associations by a Neural Network." *Proceedings, ACM SIGIR '93*. pp. 107–114. Pittsburgh, Penn.: June, 1993.

[18] Chen, H. "Machine Learning for Information Retrieval: Neural Networks, Symbolic Learning, and Genetic Algorithms." *Journal of the American Society for Information Science*, Vol. 46, No. 3 (1995), pp. 194–216.

[19] Crestani, F. "Learning Strategies for an Adaptive Information Retrieval System Using Neural Networks." *Proceedings, 2nd IEEE International Conference on Neural Networks*. San Francisco, Calif.: 1995.

[20] Bezdek, J. C., et al. "Transitive Closures of Fuzzy Thesauri for Information Retrieval Systems." *International Journal of Man-Machine Studies*, Vol. 25, No. 3 (1986).

[21] Buell, D.A. "An Analysis of Some Fuzzy Subset Applications to Information Retrieval Systems." *Fuzzy Sets and Systems*, Vol. 7 (1982), pp. 35–42.

[22] Zadeh, L.A. "A Computational Approach to Fuzzy Quantifiers in Natural Languages." *Computing Math Applications*, Vol. 9 (1983), pp. 149–184.

[23] Yager, R.R. "On Ordered Weighted Averaging Aggregation Operators in Multicriteria Decision Making." *IEEE Transactions on Systems, Man, and Cybernetics*, Vol. 18, No. 1 (1988), pp. 183–190.

[24] Prade, H. "A Two-Layer Fuzzy Pattern Matching Procedure for the Evaluation of Conditions Involving Vague Quantifiers." *Journal of Intelligent and Robotic Systems*, Vol. 9 (1994), pp. 541–569.

[25] Yager, R.R. "Interpreting Linguistically Quantified Propositions." *International Journal of Intelligent Systems*, Vol. 9 (1994), pp. 541–569.

[26] Bosc, P., and L. Lietard. "Monotonic Quantified Statements and Fuzzy Integrals." *NAFIPS/IFIS/NASA '94 Joint Conference*. pp. 8–12. San Antonio, Tex.: 1994.

[27] Bordogna, G., et al. "Query Term Weights as Constraints in Fuzzy Information Retrieval." *Information Processing & Management*, Vol. 27, No. 1 (1991), pp. 15–26.

18 Data Model and Fuzzy Information Retrieval for Scenic Image Database: Theoretical Extension of a Traditional Crisp Model to Fuzzy Model

Yukuo Isomoto
Computation Center,
Nagoya City University

Katsumi Yoshine
Faculty of Economics,
Nanzan University

Naohiro Ishii and Hiroto Nakatani
Department of Intelligence and Computer Science,
Nagoya Institute of Technology

ABSTRACT: This chapter deals with a scenic image database, which consists of three kinds of data: composition, documents, and scenic atmosphere. Owing to much fuzziness of their numerical or linguistic data, it needs to improve the database model and the information retrieval in terms of the fuzzy set theory. In this chapter, the authors formulate an extended information retrieval from the viewpoint of a satisfaction grade of the stored data, which are estimated by two logical products: a stored data and a retrieval condition, and a stored data and the complement of a retrieval condition. The information retrieval method discussed in this chapter is suitable to the database whose stored data and a retrieval condition are very fuzzy.

18.1. Introduction

Recent multimedia technologies encourage us to develop a scenic image database in which paintings, photographs, or sketches are stored (see Figure 18.1). In the last few years, image databases have been discussed regarding their information retrieval [1][2][3][4][5], which searches stored data as similar to a retrieval condition as possible. Generally speaking, the more complicated the stored data are, the more vague its data model and retrieval condition become relatively. Especially, the data of scenic images are so fuzzy that the data model and its information retrieval method should be improved to implement the scenic image database. For instance, in order to describe allocation data of the object in a scenic image, we propose a description method with a "fuzzy rectangle." The object is nearly allocated inside the rectangular (see Figure 18.2). In this chapter, the authors design the data model with many fuzzy data items, and formulate the information retrieval with a fuzzy condition described in a fuzzy set [6].

An attribute of the stored data and a retrieval condition are described in a fuzzy set and its membership function. In order to estimate how much the stored data satisfy a retrieval condition, a satisfaction grade is formulated by taking account of both of the retrieval condition and its complement. In section 18.2, the information retrieval is formulated in the fuzzy set theory. In section 18.3, its method is applied to the scenic image database.

18.2. Extended Model of Fuzzy Information Retrieval

In the information retrieval, retrieved data are loosely searched within a fuzzy retrieval condition. Let a_D be an attribute value of the stored data,

Figure 18.1   A sample scenic image.

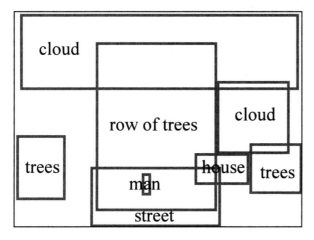

Figure 18.2 Allocation data of a scenic image.

and a_C be the one of a retrieval condition. In a conventional crisp model, they satisfy the following rules:

$$\begin{cases} \text{if } a_D \subseteq a_C \text{ then } \pi_{DC} = 1, \\ \text{if } a_D \subseteq c_C \text{ then } \pi_{DC} = 0 \end{cases} \tag{1}$$

where c_C is a complement of a_C. Let π_{DC} be a satisfaction grade. π_{DC} is 1 (true) when an attribute of stored data is a subset of a retrieval condition. On the contrary, π_{DC} is 0 (false) when an attribute of stored data is a subset of complement of a retrieval condition. Owing to much fuzziness of the scenic image data, (1) should be extended to the fuzzy set theory.

For the extension of (1) to the fuzzy set theory, let A_D be a fuzzy attribute of the stored data with a membership function $\mu_D(u)$, and A_C be a fuzzy attribute of a retrieval condition with a membership function $\mu_C(u)$. In order to estimate how much the A_D is included within a subset of the A_C, calculate a satisfaction possibility $\mu_{SDC}(u)$ and an unsatisfaction one $\mu_{UDC}(u)$, which are defined as follows (see Figure 18.3):

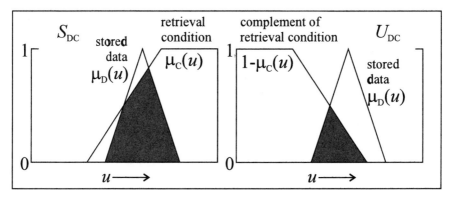

Figure 18.3 A satisfaction factor S_{DC} and an unsatisfaction one U_{DC}.

$$\mu_{SDC}(u) = \min \{\mu_D(u), \mu_C(u)\},$$

$$\mu_{UDC}(u) = \min \{\mu_D(u), (1 - \mu_C(u))\}. \tag{2}$$

The $\mu_{SDC}(u)$ and $\mu_{UDC}(u)$ are in the interval $[0,1]$:

$$0 \le \mu_{SDC}(u) \le 1 \text{ and } 0 \le \mu_{UDC}(u) \le 1.$$

According to a pair of $\mu_{SDC}(u)$ and $\mu_{UDC}(u)$, we can estimate how much an attribute of the stored data is a subset of a retrieval condition at u (see Figure 18.3). "$\mu_{SDC}(u) = 1$" means that the stored data is absolutely a subset of the retrieval condition at u, but "$\mu_{UDC}(u) = 1$" means that an attribute of the stored one is absolutely not a subset of a retrieval condition at u.

By integrating the functions $\mu_{SDC}(u)$ and $\mu_{UDC}(u)$ over u, define the fuzzy satisfaction grade Π_{DC} as follows:

$$\Pi_{DC} = S_{DC}/(S_{DC} + U_{DC}) \tag{3}$$

where

$$S_{DC} = \int \mu_{SDC}(u) \, du, \ U_{DC} = \int \mu_{UDC}(u) \, du.$$

The u is defined in the interval $[u_{\min}, u_{\max}]$. The Π_{DC} in (3) is normalized to be 1 at the maximum, and has the same value as π_{DC} of (1) at the limit to a crisp model. Both $\mu_C(u)$ and $(1 - \mu_C(u))$ contribute to estimate the fuzziness of the information retrieval (see Figure 18.3). If an attribute of the stored data is absolutely within the constraint of a retrieval condition, Π_{DC} is 1. On the contrary, when the 1 is absolutely without the retrieval condition, Π_{DC} is 0. When stored data is partially within the retrieval condition, Π_{DC} is between 0 and 1. The larger the satisfaction grade gets, the more the stored data satisfy the retrieval condition.

18.3. Fuzzy Retrieval for an Image Database

The image database consists of four kinds of data items:

P_n: Raw data of a scenic image,

A_n: Allocation data of a scenic image,

D_n: Document data of a scenic image,

L_n: Lyrical atmosphere of a scenic image.

Here, we define the fuzzy sets of these data items with membership functions. Let $f_{nk}(x,y)$ be an occupation possibility of a k-th object at a point (x,y) in the n-th image:

"$f_{nk}(x,y) = 1$" means an absolute occupation,

"$f_{nk}(x,y) = 0$" does an absolute unoccupation,

"$0 < f_{nk}(x,y) < 1$" does a fuzzy occupation.

Moreover, define a fuzzy set δ of the depth of an object in a painting with associated membership functions:

$\delta \in$ {absolutely near, very near, near, far, very far, absolutely far}.

D_n consists of a painter, a painted date, painting method, and so on. L_n consists of linguistic fuzzy data about a lyrical atmosphere such as "bright," "happy," or "lovely" about the raw images like paintings.

In our data model, for simplicity, we apply the following form to the membership functions (see Figure 18.4):

$$F(u; U_1, U_2, U_3, U_4) = \begin{cases} 0 & \text{for } u \leq U_1, \\ (u - U_1)/(U_2 - U_1) & \text{for } U_1 < u < U_2, \\ 1 & \text{for } U_2 \leq u \leq U_3, \\ (U_4 - u)/(U_4 - U_3) & \text{for } U_3 < u < U_4, \\ 0 & \text{for } U_4 \leq u \end{cases} \quad (4)$$

where u is a real number. Hereafter, membership functions are defined by the F. The occupation possibility $f_{nk}(x, y)$, the depth $d_{nk}(z)$, and any other fuzzy numbers $v_{nki}(r)$ are defined by the F as follows:

$$f_{nk}(x, y) = F(x; X_1, X_2, X_3, X_4)$$
$$\times F(y; Y_1, Y_2, Y_3, Y_4), \text{ for } 0 < x < x_{max}, 0 < y < y_{max}, \quad (5)$$

$$d_{nk}(z) = F(z; Z_1, Z_2, Z_3, Z_4), \text{ for } 0 < z < z_{max}, \quad (6)$$

$$v_{nki}(r) = F(r; R_1, R_2, R_3, R_4), \text{ for } r_{min} < r < r_{max} \quad (7)$$

where x, y, z and r are real numbers. Also, a membership function $l_{nkj}(u)$ on a truth value u of linguistic fuzzy data is expressed by the function F as follows:

$$l_{nkj}(u) = F(u; U_1, U_2, U_3, U_4), \text{ for } 0 \leq u \leq 1 \quad (8)$$

where u is a truth value of a linguistic fuzzy set L_{nkj} and the $l_{nkj}(u)$ denotes the membership function of the L_{nkj}. Lyrical atmosphere data is expressed as the linguistic fuzzy set τ with membership functions $a_\tau(u)$ (see Figure 18.5):

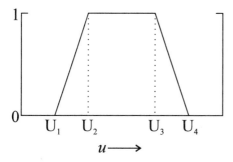

Figure 18.4 Membership functions for numeric fuzzy sets.

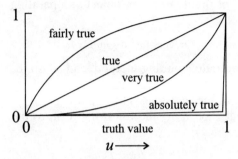

Figure 18.5 Membership functions for linguistic fuzzy sets.

$\tau \in \{\text{absolutely true, very true, true, fairly true}\}.$

$$a_{\text{absolutely true}}(u) = \begin{cases} 0 & \text{for } 0 \leq u < 1, \\ 1 & \text{for } u = 1, \end{cases}$$

$$a_{\text{very true}}(u) = u^2, \tag{9}$$

$$a_{\text{true}}(u) = u,$$

$$a_{\text{fairly true}}(u) = u^{1/2}$$

where $0 \leq u \leq 1$. The function $a_{\tau}(u)$ is arranged in the same series as the fuzzy set τ.

The process of our information retrieval consistes of two steps. In the first step, the stored data are searched in a traditional crisp retrieval. In the second step, the retrieved data are sorted in the fuzzy satisfaction grades (3):

Π_{An}: satisfaction grade for the A_n,

Π_{Dn}: satisfaction grade for the D_n,

Π_{Ln}: satisfaction grade for the L_n,

w_A: weight factor for the Allocation data,

w_D: weight factor for the Document data,

w_L: weight factor for the Lyrical atmosphere

where $0 \leq w_A \leq 1, 0 \leq w_D \leq 1$, and $0 \leq w_L \leq 1$. The total satisfaction grade T_n is defined in the following equation:

$$T_n = w_A\Pi_{An} + w_D\Pi_{Dn} + w_L\Pi_{Ln}. \tag{10}$$

The retrieved data set is sorted in order of the values of their satisfaction grades: T_n is the primary sort key. The other sort keys are the weights w_A, w_D, and w_L. For example, the second key is w_A, the third one is w_D, and fourth one is w_L when $w_A > w_D > w_L$.

18.4. Conclusion

The extended fuzzy information retrieval formulated in this chapter is suitable for the image database whose stored data are very fuzzy. Taking account of a retrieval condition and its complement, the authors defined a satisfaction grade in order to estimate how much the attributes of the stored data are included within a retrieval condition. This estimation method is suitable to very fuzzy data such as paintings, pictures, drawings, and so on.

In this chapter, the authors did not discuss how to determine fuzzy sets and their membership functions of the stored data. This theme is connected with human factors, on which the shapes of membership functions depend. The production of the allocation data is the other open problem. At present, it is very difficult to determine mechanically the data of object names, allocation, atmosphere, and so on, even if we apply the advanced technologies of "image understanding." Therefore, for the implementation of the image database, the database administrators have to produce the fuzzy data such as allocations, documents, and lyrical atmosphere by themselves. For efficient database administration, they need to develop a supporting system that assists an administrator to edit the fuzzy sets with membership functions.

18.5. References

[1] Kato, T., and T. Kurita. "Visual Interaction with Image Database Systems—Electronic Art Gallery, Art Museum." *Transactions of Information Processing Society of Japan,* Vol. 33 (1992), pp. 466–477.

[2] Tanabe, K., et al. "A Similarity Retrieval Method using Shape Similarity Measure based on Mean Opinion Scores." *NTT R&D,* Vol., 39 (1990), pp 697–707.

[3] Kawafuchi, A. "An Image Grouping System for Use in the Administration of Visual Material Databases." *Japan Journal of Education Technology II.* (1991), pp. 159–167.

[4] Miyamoto, S., et al. "Document Retrieval and Large Retrieval-based on Fuzzy Prepositional Index." *Journal of Japan Society for Fuzzy Theory and Systems,* Vol. 3 (1991), pp. 98–107.

[5] Matsuyama, T., et al. "SIGMA—A Framework for Image Understanding Integration of Bottom-Up and Top-Down Analysis." *Transactions of Information Processing Society of Japan,* Vol. 26 (1985), pp. 877–889.

[6] Zadeh, L.A. "Fuzzy Sets." *Information and Control,* Vol. 8 (1965), pp. 338–353.

19 Query Fuzzification for Internet Information Retrieval

Henrik Legind Larsen
Computer Science Dept.,
Roskilde University,
P.O. Box 260, DK-4000 Roskilde

Ronald R. Yager
Machine Intelligence Institute,
Iona College,
New Rochelle, New York

ABSTRACT: After outlining the basic structure of an information retrieval system, we discuss the process of softening user queries based on the use of fuzzy subsets, and introduce the concept of importance modification. We then describe the construction of a crisp query, a so-called envelope, applied to retrieve the potentially relevant items, as characterized by the softened query, using a traditional information base management system. The process of criteria aggregation based on MOM and MAM operators is investigated. We discuss the use of a MAM operator to provide a ranking of the relevant items in the information base. Finally, we present for illustration snapshots from the user interface of a test application based on the approach.

19.1. Introduction

The ascendancy of the Internet, and in particular the World Wide Web, is making the development of intelligent information retrieval an extremely important issue. An information retrieval system [1] is a system to retrieve relevant information objects from an *information base.*

The information base stores a collection of objects some of which are of potential interest to the users. Each object is represented by an item that can be seen to be made up of two components. The first component is the index and the second component is the body. The index usually consists of highly organized pieces of information that can be used to help identify and select the objects that may be relevant to a user. The body consists of information that may not be organized but it contains the material that is of interest to the user. The fundamental problem in information retrieval is to find the subset of objects in the information base that is relevant to a given user. In a fuzzy information retrieval system, one can supply the list of relevant items with an ordering as to their potential interest to the user. Figure 19.1 shows a top-level view of the information retrieval system processes.

In the first step, the user enters a request in terms of features of interest employing the keywords in the indexing system used to describe the objects. The information in this query is then used by the information retrieval system to select items that may be potentially relevant to the user. The final step is a process where the user looks at the items suggested by the system and decides the ultimate relevance of the items. This final step greatly reduces the burden of the information retrieval process, for it allows the *user* to look at the items selected and decide the ultimate relevance. This means that not all the knowledge about the decision has to be formalized in a manner that can be manipulated by the computer. The user must only supply the information that is used to search through the index.

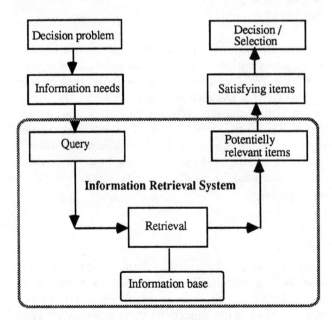

Figure 19.1   Information retrieval framework.

As an example, we will consider the problem of selecting a house for purchase and assume that the user has access to an information base consisting of a collection of houses for sale. Here the user would express desired properties about the kind of house desired (price, size, location, etc.) in the query. The system would then search the information base and produce a listing of houses that closely match the user's request. This information could include text, more detailed information about the house, as well as perhaps a picture of the house. The user then looks at this information and decides which houses he or she wants to visit. In making this decision, the user may use all kinds of subjective criteria, which may be hard to quantify and not necessarily specified in his or her query.

In this chapter we describe an information retrieval system that uses fuzzy sets to help in the selection process; this kind of system can be viewed as an intelligent inquiry system. Figure 19.2, which is an expansion of the information retrieval system box of Figure 19.1, illustrates the steps involved in the information retrieval process.

In the first step, the crisp information provided by the user is softened with the aid of fuzzy sets. Using the index and a modified version of the requirements ("crisp envelope," step 2), we search through the information base (step 3), to find a subset of objects in the information base that can be considered as potentially relevant to the user. Step 3 can be based on an ordinary crisp querying language. The set of objects found in this step is called the "crisp envelope" answer. The final step in the process is a ranking of the elements in this crisp envelope, which is then presented to the user.

This chapter is organized as follows. In section 19.2, we introduce the idea of fuzzifying a crisp constraint, expressed as a criterion in the user

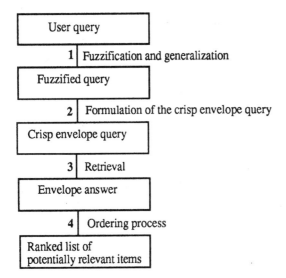

Figure 19.2   The process of the information retrieval system.

query, and show how information on importance of satisfying the constraint can be utilized in the fuzzification. Although here we consider constraints on numerical attributes, the approach can be transformed to non-numerical domains through introducing a similarity relation on the domain. In section 19.3, we outline the construction of a crisp query, a so-called envelope, for retrieving the answer to a fuzzified query using an information base management system that only supports a crisp query language. Here we build on the ideas introduced by Bosc and Pivert [2]. In section 19.4, we focus on the aggregation of the criterion scores to the query score, which is a measure of the overall satisfaction of the query, given some object. After recalling the basics of t-norms and t-conorms for *and* and *or* aggregation, we present the MAM and MOM operators, which generalize the first mentioned norms, and introduce the (importance) weighted form of these operators, including the additive weighted form. In section 19.5, we propose the application of an additive weighted MAM operator for aggregation of criterion scores. For an illustration of the application of our approach we finally (in section 19.6) present and comment on some snapshots from the user interface of a test application implemented.

19.2. Fuzzification of Requirements

An important characteristic of many of the criteria supplied in a user query is that the needs they intend to represent are not crisp. If persons looking for a house indicate their desire to spend between $100,000 and $140,000 for the house, it is not the case that they will be totally uninterested in a house costing $145,000. They may be less satisfied but not completely unsatisfied. The central observation here is that the boundary between a criterion being completely satisfied and not being satisfied is fuzzy rather than crisp. In building intelligent information retrieval systems, we must take advantage of this fuzziness in the criteria. As we shall subsequently see, we use this fuzziness in two ways. First, we use it to soften the user query to allow potential interesting items to be retrieved, even if they do not directly satisfy the original user query. In particular, we use it in providing a query envelope, that is, a crisp query applied to retrieve the potentially most interesting items from the information base. The second way we use this fuzzy characteristic is to provide an ordering (ranking) of the items according to the degree to which they satisfy the softened user query.

The first step in the process of taking advantage of the lack of crispness in the user's requirements is to provide an appropriate representation of the requirements taking into account their noncrisp boundaries. The most appropriate tool for representing this imprecise information is the fuzzy subset structure introduced by Zadeh [3]. As originally discussed by Zadeh, one application of the fuzzy subset is to represent concepts that have noncrisp boundaries. We recall that if X is a set, then a fuzzy subset A of X is characterized by a membership function $A(x) \in [0,1]$, such that for any element x in X, $A(x)$ indicates the degree to which the concept represented by A is satisfied by the element x. Considerable experience with fuzzy logic controllers [4] has indicated that trapezoidal type functions are a very effective class of of functions for the representation of fuzzy concepts that have typical values.

Let $[a,b]$ be the range of values specified in the user query as being acceptable for some attribute, such as the price of a house. One can then *fuzzify* the range $[a,b]$ to be considered as "approximately $[a,b]$." Figure 19.3 shows the fuzzy subset A representing the fuzzified range.

Formally, we can represent the fuzzy subset A by the following membership function:

$$A(x) = \begin{cases} 0 & x \leq c \text{ or } x \geq d \\ 1 & a \leq x \leq b \\ \dfrac{x-c}{a-c} & c \leq x \leq a \\ \dfrac{d-x}{d-b} & b \leq x \leq d \end{cases}$$

In some situations, the extension of the original interval doesn't necessarily imply a decrease in satisfaction. For example, if $[a,b]$ is the range for the price one is willing to pay for a house, then paying anything less than a is completely satisfying. In this case, our fuzzy subset becomes as shown in Figure 19.4. We see that in one direction—costs less then those in the range $[a,b]$—the extension of the specifications provided by the user results in no loss of satisfaction, while in the other direction there exists a satisfaction decay, a fuzzy boundary manifested by a sloping line from b to d. The specifications provided by the user results in no loss of satisfaction, while in the other direction there exists a decay of satisfaction, a fuzzy boundary manifested by a sloping line from b to d.

While many of the criteria in a user query can be softened (fuzzified) with the aid of fuzzy subsets, some criteria are not amenable to this kind of softening. For example, the desire to have a fireplace or two bathrooms is not easily fuzzified.

The preceding technique is most useful for numeric variables; however, it can be extended to non-numeric domains by introducing a simi-

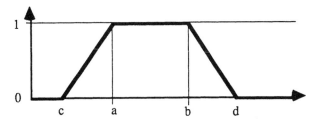

Figure 19.3 Representation of "approximately."

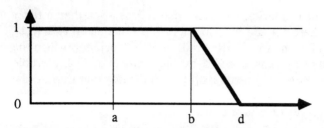

Figure 19.4 Unbalanced Extension of $[a,b]$.

larity relation [5]. Larsen and Yager [6] described a solution for information retrieval in the case of non-numeric domains characterized by a set of terms with a similarity relation. They proposed an oriented similarity relation, in the form of a fuzzy implication (or, preorder) relation, for broadening (softening) the user query, allowing, for instance, the request for a carport to be broadened to carport *or* garage.

In addition to providing information about the values of the variables describing the objects, users can provide information about the importance of the various characteristics. Yager [7, 8, 9] investigated the effect of importance on criteria (concepts describing desired items) used in decision processes. In [10], it is suggested that if $\alpha \in [0, 1]$ is a measure of importance, 0 being the lowest and 1 the highest, associated with a criterion represented by a fuzzy subset A on X, then we can transform this into another fuzzy subset B, $B(x) = (A(x))^{\alpha}$.

Yager [11] describes the effect of the inclusion of importance as being closely related to modification of the original concept by a linguistic hedge, such as "sort of." Figure 19.5 illustrates, for an exponential type fuzzy subset, the effect of the modification of a concept by importance. The principle effect of this operation is to cause, in the transformed fuzzy subset B, an increase in membership grade, a widening of bandwidth, as we decrease the importance of the original set A. Thus, if $\alpha_1 > \alpha_2$, then for all x, $B_1(x) \le B_2(x)$.

Recently, Yager [12] has provided a general formal characterization of the association of importance with criteria. Assume A is a fuzzy subset and $\alpha \in [0,1]$ is a measure of importance; then we can transform A into a

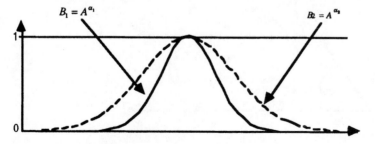

Figure 19.5 Effect of different importance weights ($a_1 > a_2$).

fuzzy subset B such that $B(x) = g(\alpha, A(x))$ where $g(\alpha, A(x))$ is a function having the following properties:

1. $g(\alpha, A_1(x)) \geq g(\alpha, A_2(x))$ if $A_1(x) > A_2(x)$
2. $g(\alpha_1, A(x)) \leq g(\alpha_2, A(x))$ if $\alpha_1 > \alpha_2$
3. $g(1, A(x)) = A(x)$
4. $g(0, A(x)) = 1$

We see from property 2 that the effect of decreasing importance is to increase the width of the transformed fuzzy subset B. It does this by increasing the membership grade. Thus, the less important a characteristic, the less restrictive the effective requirement expressed by the criterion. At the extreme (property 4), if something has zero importance, any object in the information base satisfies it.

Because of their inherent piecewise linearity, we earlier suggested the use of trapezoidal type membership functions, as shown in Figure 19.3, to soften (fuzzify) the crisp ranges, $[a,b]$, given by a user. Figure 19.6 illustrates a new proposed method for including importances associated with trapezoidal type membership functions. In this figure, it is assumed that $\alpha_1 > \alpha_2$, α_2 is less important. We see that if we denote $S_i = [c_i, d_i]$ as the support of the fuzzy subset, the less important a criterion, the wider the support. Using this approach for the inclusion of importance, we may obtain an alternative representation of the fuzzy subset membership grade.

We recall that for the left fuzzy part, $c_i \leq x \leq a$, we get $A_i(x) = (x - c_i)/(a - c_i)$. Let $u_i = (a - c_i)/a$. Thus u_i is the proportion of a the user is willing to give up, consider as dispensable, if the importance is α_i. The proportion u_i can be reviewed as a measure of the *flexibility*, how much a can be relaxed, as a function of the importance. We see that $c_i = a - u_i a$, and thus for $x \in [a - u_i a, a]$:

$$A_i(x) = \frac{x - a + u_i a}{u_i a} = 1 - \frac{1}{u_i}\left(1 - \frac{x}{a}\right).$$

Since $a - c_i$ decreases as the importance increases, we see that the larger the importance, the smaller the u_i. In particular, we need some function

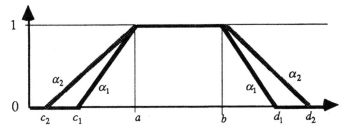

Figure 19.6 Including importance weights with trapezoidal membership functions.

$f_L, f_L(\alpha) = u$, such that as α increases, u decreases to help us get u directly from the importance value. Subsequently, we say more about the construction of f_L.

In an analogous manner, we get for the right fuzzy part, $b < x < d_i$, that:

$$A_i(x) = 1 - \frac{1}{v_i}\left(\frac{x}{b} - 1\right)$$

We note that the two fuzzy parts do not have to be symmetric. Again, we must obtain some function f_R that transforms importance values α_i into corresponding values of v_i. Both functions, f_L and f_R, must depend on the context.

While we have implicitly assumed the importance to be provided in terms of numeric values in the unit interval, this is neither necessary nor desirable. A preferred means of getting importance information from the user is in terms of a linguistic scale. A typical example of such a scale is: (1) very high, (2) high, (3) moderate, (4) low, and (5) very low. Using such a scale, we again need functions to transform the importance value into a pair (u_i, v_i). This transformation, while dependent on the domain, must be such that as the importance decreases, the width of the support increases.

An issue that must be considered in the construction of the approximate fuzzy ranges from the crisp ranges is how we get the c_i and d_i that are used for the extensions. A number of observations must be made regarding this issue. Experience with human-machine systems tells us that we do not want to overburden the user with requests for to much information.

A second observation that bears on the process of selection of the extended ranges results from the way in which the fuzzy information retrieval system is used. In using such a system, the user inputs, through the query, his or her requirements and importances. This information is then transformed into a fuzzy subset which is used to *extend* the boundaries of the request by providing a crisp *envelope* query for objects (items) that satisfy the user, as illustrated by Figure 19.7. This step allows us to rely on an ordinary (crisp) database management system for the searching. We call this the extended crisp condition (see Figure 19.7). The objects in the database falling in the crisp envelope are ranked with the aid of the fuzzy subset. A given number of the highest ranked objects are presented to the user for taking the appropriate action.

Figure 19.7   Crisp envelope of query.

From this discussion we see that all that the fuzzification process does is help in providing the crisp extension of the user query and the final ranking of the objects. The issue of determining the values of c_i and d_i then becomes one of appropriately relaxing the original requirements, as given in the user query, and to obtain an appropriate ordering for the objects presented to the user as the answer to the query.

Based upon the preceding observations, we feel that the values of c_i and d_i can be obtained via *default values.* A default value of course depends on the application domain and attribute range. These default values are obtained from the importance values through functions f_L and f_R previously introduced.

We should emphasize a very important distinction between the problem of multicriteria-based information retrieval (MCIR) and multicriteria decision making (MCDM). The important thing to highlight is that in MCIR it is the user who makes the final decision as to what action to take (which houses to visit or buy), whereas in MCDM it is the computer that makes the final decision. The implication of this distinction is that the representational requirements in MCIR are less demanding then in MCDM. Since the final decision in MCIR is made by the user, this final decision can be based upon additional knowledge and criteria that the user has but that he or she need not represent in the query presented to the system (see Figure 19.1). This characteristic type of human-machine interaction inherent in information retrieval systems greatly simplifies the burden on the system and the requirements that the user must formally express. Thus, once having the highest ranked objects he or she can bring to bear some very sophisticated reasoning and preference information in actually making the final decision. On the other hand, in MCDM systems, the user must present to the computer all the criteria he or she desires to be considered, which may be beyond both the representational ability of the system and the cognitive ability of the user.

19.3. Computation of Envelopes

A fuzzy query to an information base may be seen as a multicriteria, or multidimensional, characterization of the user needs with respect to the information base domain; that is, the objects in the search space, represented by items in the information base. From this point of view, the response to a query is the set of those objects that provide the best instances of the (fuzzy) *concept* represented by the characterization of the user needs. From another point of view, fuzzy querying is a decision problem. In this view, the query describes a multicriteria *decision problem,* and the answer to the query is the set of the objects with the best overall satisfaction of the decision problem.

In general, a query criterion induces a linear ordering of the objects in the search space. Thus, a multicriteria query determines a partial ordering of the objects. The global (linear) ordering needed for the answer is obtained by an aggregation of the satisfaction of the criteria. In this aggregation, each criterion is weighted with the importance of satisfying the criterion in recognizing the concept or in the decision problem. Thus, to answer a query, we must, in principle, compute the aggregated value for each item in the information base. To do this in an efficient way, we should provide fuzzy indexes organized as inverted files. However, in fuzzy querying in traditional information base management systems, only access through the crisp querying language of the systems is possible. There are two de facto standards to consider in crisp querying languages, namely SQL (Structured Query Language) [13] for the relational database model, and CCL (Common Command Language) [14] for document bases. Both languages support a crisp Boolean formulation of query criteria. We will address the problem of fuzzy querying through such a crisp language as SQL.

The basic idea of our approach is to compute a so-called envelope for the fuzzy query. An envelope is a *crisp query* such that the answer to the fuzzy query is a subset of the answer to the envelope; the envelope defines the query used for accessing the database.

Assume our information base comprises a set of objects X. Let $A_1, \ldots,$ A_n be a set of criteria, fuzzy subsets, representing the user's needs. Our procedure is to transform these fuzzy criteria into crisp criteria, $D_1, \ldots,$ D_n, and then use an SQL language to search the information base to find the subset Y of X of objects that satisfy this crisp query. We call the subset Y the *envelope answer*. Once having the subset Y we can use the original fuzzy criteria to rank the objects. The advantage of using this envelope is to reduce the search burden as well as allow the use of available, efficient SQL search techniques. In this section, concentrate on the issue of formulating the envelope.

Consider a fuzzy criteria A represented by a trapezoidal fuzzy subset of the type shown in Figure 19.8. We obtain from the fuzzy criteria A a related crisp criteria D, as shown in Figure 19.9. The membership grade $D(x)$ of this crisp criteria is 1 for $l \leq x \leq r$ and otherwise 0.

We obtain the bounds, l and r, of the criteria D from A in the following manner. Let δ, called the threshold for satisfaction of a query, be a num-

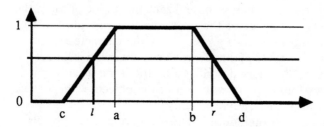

Figure 19.8 Fuzzy criteria *A*.

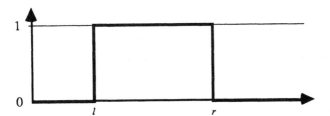

Figure 19.9   Crisp criteria *D*.

ber in the unit interval; for example, we can select $\delta = 0.5$. From the membership function of *A* we obtain *l* and *r* as the δ level points, thus *D* is the δ-level set of *A*. In particular, in Figure 19.8, $A(l) = \delta = (l - c)/(a - c)$, from which we obtain the lower (left) bound $l = \delta(a - c) + c$. Similarly, we have $A(r) = \delta = (d - r)/(d - b)$, and the upper (right) bound $r = d - \delta(d - b)$.

In this way, we transform each of the fuzzy criteria, $A_i, i = 1, \ldots n$, into crisp criteria D_i. We then determine the envelope answer as the subset *Y* of *X* of objects *y* such that, for all *i*, $D_i(y) = 1$. That is, the envelope is the subset of elements that satisfy *all* the transformed criteria.

Figure 19.10 illustrates the construction of the envelope for a two-dimensional query. The area contained within the bold lines constitutes set *X* of objects represented in the information base. The black rectangle indicates the subset of objects that satisfy the user query. The black rectangle plus the gray area indicates the envelope answer *Y* obtained by the fuzzification of the user query followed by the crispization to *D*. It is on the elements in *Y* that we shall subsequently provide a ranking as to their potential usefulness to the user. Thus, via the process of fuzzification followed by crispization, we have essentially reduced the domain of objects to be considered from the global search space *X* to the smaller space *Y*.

It should be pointed out that using our approach, the importances of the criteria have been factored into the process of obtaining the envelope.

Figure 19.11 illustrates the effect of importance inclusion on the construction of the envelope. Retrieved set (b) shows that if we *decrease* the importance of the criteria represented along the abscissa coordinate, we effectively *increase* the size of the envelope in that direction. This effect results because in decreasing the importance we have increased the val-

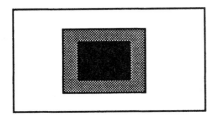

Figure 19.10   Construction of the envelope.

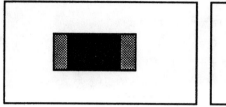 

Figure 19.11   Effect of decreasing the importance in one dimension.

ues of the membership grade (see Figure 19.6) and essentially relaxed the criterion and thus allowed more objects in the information base to pass through our filter.

As a result of this step, we have a collection of objects, the envelope answer, which contains the subset of potentially relevant objects to the user. The next step is to rank these objects. To do this, we use an aggregation type process and use the original fuzzy criteria, the A_i, to provide the scores used in this aggregation process.

19.4. MOM and MAM Aggregation of Criteria

19.4.1 Basic Properties of t-norms and t-conorm Operators

In fuzzy logic systems, the basic aggregation operations are performed by the logical connectives *and* and *or*, which provide pointwise implementations of the intersection and union operations. It has been well established in the literature [15] that the appropriate characterization of these operators in the multivalued logic environment are the triangular norm operators. The t-norm operator provides the characterization of the *and* operator. It is a mapping $T: \mathbf{I} \times \mathbf{I} \to \mathbf{I}$, where $\mathbf{I} = [0, 1]$, having the following properties:

T_1: $T(a,b) = T(b,a)$ commutativity

T_2: $T(a,b) \geq T(c,d)$ for $a \geq c$ and $b \geq d$ monotonicity

T_3: $T(a,T(b,c)) = T(T(a,b),c)$ associativity

T_4: $T(a,1) = a$ *one* identity element

Its dual, the t-conorm, characterizes the *or* operator. It is a mapping $S: \mathbf{I} \times \mathbf{I} \to \mathbf{I}$ having properties:

S_1: $S(a,b) = S(b,a)$ commutativity

S_2: $S(a,b) \geq S(c,d)$ for $a \geq c$ and $b \geq d$ monotonicity

S_3: $S(a,S(b,c)) = S(S(a,b),c)$ associativity

S_4: $S(a,0) = a$ *zero* identity element

Examples of t-norms are: $T(a,b) = 1 - \min(1,((1-a)^\beta + (1-b)^\beta)^{1/\beta})$, $\beta \in \mathbf{R}^+$; $T(a,b) = \min(a,b)$; and $T(a,b) = a \cdot b$. The corresponding t-conorms are: $S(a,b) = \min(1,(a^\beta + b^\beta)^{1/\beta})$, $\beta \in \mathbf{R}^+$; $S(a,b) = \max(a,b)$; $S(a,b) = a + b - a \cdot b$.

A fundamental property of t-norms is $T(a_1, \ldots, a_n) \geq T(a_1, \ldots, a_n, a_{n+1})$; Yager [16, 17, 18] called this property the *anti-monotonicity in cardinality* property. This property says that as more conditions are *required* to be satisfied by an *and* aggregation, the overall satisfaction can't increase. The related property associated with the t-conorms is $S(a_1, \ldots, a_n) \leq S(a_1, \ldots, a_n, a_{n+1})$; Yager [16] called this the *monotonicity in cardinality* property: as more conditions are *allowed* to contribute to an *or* aggregation, the overall satisfaction can't decrease.

It can be shown that 1 acts as an identity element in the t-norm aggregation while 0 acts as an identity element in the t-conorm aggregation.

19.4.2. MOM and MAM Operators

We now introduce a more generalized class of operators that provide for generalized formulations of the *and* and *or* aggregations. A *bag* (or multiset) drawn from a set X is any collection of elements, each of which is contained in X. A bag allows multiple copies of the same element. In the following, we restrict ourselves by constraining X to be the unit interval, **I**. We let U^I be the subset of all bags drawn from **I**. Assume $B = \langle b_1, \ldots, b_n \rangle$ is a bag of cardinality n. We say that B is in its *fundamental form* if the elements are indexed such that $b_i \geq b_j$ if $i > j$. If A and B are two bags of the same cardinality, and, when expressed in fundamental form, we have the property that $a_i \geq b_i$ for all i, we denote this as $A \geq B$. If A and B are two bags, we denote the *sum* of the bags (or the *bag union*) by $D = A \oplus B$ where D is the bag consisting of the members from A and B.

Example: Assume $A = \langle 0.2, 0.4, 0.8, 1, 1 \rangle$ and $B = \langle 0, 0.4, 0.6, 1 \rangle$
then $D = A \oplus B = \langle 0, 0.2, 0.4, 0.4, 0.6, 0.8, 1, 1, 1 \rangle$

Definition: A bag mapping $H: U^I \to \mathbf{I}$ is called a MAM (Monotonic Anti-Monotonic) [16] operator if it has the following properties:

MA.1 $H(A) \geq H(B)$ for $A \geq B$ (monotonicity in values)

MA.2 $H(A \oplus \langle 1 \rangle) = H(A)$ (*one* identity element)

As in the case of all bag mappings, the MAM operator is commutative with respect to its arguments. We call this a *generalized symmetry condition*. It is easily seen that the following property holds for MAM operators:

PA.1 $H(A \oplus B) \leq H(A)$ (antimonotonicity in cardinality)

We see that the MAM operator is a generalization of the t-norm operator and can be viewed as a generalized *and* aggregation. In particular, the boundary condition of the t-norm, T_4, has been weakened and included as MA.2. The associativity property of the t-norm, T_3, has been eliminated. The condition MA.1 is essentially the monotonicity condition, T_2, and the commutativity condition, T_1, is implicitly satisfied by all bag mappings. Yager [16] has shown that the t-norm is a special class of MAM operators.

For any bag A, since $A = \Phi \oplus A$ (Φ being the empty bag $\langle\rangle$), from condition PA.1, it follows that $H(\Phi) \geq H(A)$. Based upon this condition, we say that H is *normal* if $H(\Phi) = 1$. Further, we say that the MAM operator is *regular* if $H(\langle 0\rangle) = 0$. It can be seen that if H is regular, then for any bag E having zero as one of its arguments, it is the case that $H(E) = 0$: We can express $E = \langle 0\rangle \oplus B$ where B is the bag E less the element 0. From PA.1, we have $H(\langle 0\rangle \oplus B) \leq H(\langle 0\rangle) \leq 0$, hence $H(E) = 0$.

Yager [16] introduced a family of operators that generalized the t-conorm operator and thus induced generalized *or*-like aggregations. This class of bag mappings are called MOM (Monotonic on Monotonic) operators.

Definition: A bag mapping $G:U^I \to \mathbf{I}$ is called a MOM (Monotonic on Monotonic) operator [16] if it has the following properties:

MO.1 $G(A) \geq G(B)$ for A $\geq$ B   (monotonicity in values)

MO.2 $G(A \oplus \langle 0\rangle) = G(A)$ (*zero* identity element)

It can be shown that the following property holds for MOM operators:

PO.1 $G(A \oplus B) \geq G(A)$ (monotonicity in cardinality)

It can further be shown that the MOM operator is a generalization of the t-conorm operators [17]. We say that a MOM operator G is *normal* if $G(\Phi) = 0$. We shall call G *regular* if $G(\langle 1\rangle) = 1$. It can be shown that if G is regular and E is any bag containing 1 as an element, then $G(E) = 1$.

There exists a De Morgan-like duality between MOM and MAM operators.

Definition: Assume $F:U^I \to \mathbf{I}$ is any bag mapping that takes bags from the unit interval into the unit interval. We define the *dual* of F, $\hat{F}$, as $\hat{F}(A) = 1 - F(A^C)$, where A^C is the complement of A defined to be the bag consisting of the elements b_i, where $b_i = \bar{a}_i = 1 - a_i$.

The following theorems proven in [16] show that MAM and MOM operators are duals of each other.

Theorem: Assume G is a MOM operator, then $\hat{G}$ is a MAM operator.

Theorem: Assume H is a MAM operator, then $\hat{H}$ is a MOM operator.

As we have already indicated, the t-norm and t-conorm are MAM and MOM operators. In the following we introduce another important class of MAM and MOM operators. Assume $g:\mathbf{R} \rightarrow \mathbf{I}$ is a monotonic nondecreasing function from the real line into the unit interval; that is, $g(x) \geq g(y)$ if $x > y$.

Let A be a bag drawn from the unit interval and let us define $\text{Sum}(A) = \sum_{i=1}^{n} a_i$, where n is the cardinality of A. We call this the *bag sum*. It can be shown that the bag mapping $G(A) = g(\text{Sum}(A))$ is a MOM operator.

Using our duality theorem, we can show that if $h:\mathbf{R} \rightarrow \mathbf{I}$ is a monotonic nonincreasing function, $h(x) \leq h(y)$ if $x > y$, then $H(A) = h(\text{Sum}(A^C))$ is a MAM operator.

19.4.3. Weighted MOM and MAM Operators

We now introduce the concept of weighted bags and the related ideas of weighted MOM and MAM operators. These operators will generalize the concept of weighted aggregations, which can be used to associate importances with the aggregates.

Definition: A *weighted bag* is a bag A whose elements are tuples (w_i, a_i) where both w_i and a_i are drawn from the unit interval. For each tuple in A, we call a_i *the value of the tuple*, and w_i the *weight of the tuple*.

Let A and B be two weighted bags of the same cardinality. Assume to each tuple (w_i, a_i) in A there exists a corresponding tuple (w'_i, b_i) in B where $w'_i = w_i$. If it is the case that $a_i \geq b_i$ for all i, we say that $A \geq_V B$. Assume that for each tuple (w_i, a_i) in A there exists a corresponding tuple (w'_i, b_i) in B where $a_i = b_i$. If it is the case that $w_i \geq w'_i$, we say that $A \geq_W B$. We now extend the MOM operator to act on weighted bags.

Definition: A bag mapping $G_W:U^{I \times I} \rightarrow \mathbf{I}$ is called a *weighted MOM operator* if it has the properties:

    WO.1 $G_W(A) \geq G_W(B)$ if $A \geq_V B$
    WO.2 $G_W(A \oplus B) \geq G_W(A)$
    WO.3 $G_W(A \oplus \langle(1,0)\rangle) = G_W(A)$
    WO.4 $G_W(A) \geq G_W(B)$ if $A \geq_W B$

We now turn to the corresponding definition for weighted MAM operators.

Definition: A bag mapping $H_W:U^{I \times I} \rightarrow \mathbf{I}$ is called a *weighted MAM operator* if it has the properties:

    WA.1 $H_W(A) \geq H_W(B)$ if $A \geq_V B$
    WA.2 $H_W(A \oplus B) \leq H_W(A)$
    WA.3 $H_W(A \oplus \langle(1,1)\rangle) = H_W(A)$
    WA.4 $H_W(A) \leq H_W(B)$ if $A \geq_W B$

The introduction of these weighted bags along with the weighted mappings will provide a framework for generalizing the idea of weighted aggregations. The weighted operators allow us to consider aggregations where the elements differ in importance.

Assume A is a weighted bag. We define the *right-pointed complement* of this bag as A^{RC} where every element (w_i, a_i) in A is replaced by $(w_i, \bar{a}_i)$, with $\bar{a}_i = 1 - a_i$. We now define the concept of the dual of a weighted bag mapping in a similar way to which we defined it in the earlier section. Let $F_W : U^{I \times I} \to I$ be a weighted bag mapping; the dual of $F_W, \hat{F}_W$, is $\hat{F}_W(A) = 1 - F(A^{RC})$.

Weighted MOM and MAM operators are related by duality:

Theorem: Assume G_W is a weighted MOM operator, then $\hat{G}_W$ is a weighted MAM operator.

Theorem: Assume H_W is a weighted MAM operator, then $\hat{H}_W$ is a weighted MOM operator.

We now look at some classes of weighted bag operators; the proofs of all the results in this section are found in [16]. We first define a class of weighted MOM operators based on the logical connectives.

Theorem: If S is a t-conorm and T a t-norm, then $G_W(A) = S_{i=1}^n(T(w_i,a_i))$ is a weighted MOM operator.

The following are examples of this class of operators: (1) $\max_i(\min(w_i,a_i))$; (2) $\max_i(w_i \cdot a_i)$; (3) $\min(1,\sum_{i=1}^n \min(w_i,a_i))$; (4) $\min(1,\sum_{i=1}^n(w_i \cdot a_i))$; and (5) $1 - \prod_{i=1}^n(1 - w_i \cdot a_i)$.

Using the duality relationship we obtain the following theorem:

Theorem: If S is a t-conorm and T a t-norm, then $H_W(A) = T_{i=1}^n(S(\bar{w}_i,a_i))$ is a weighted MAM operator.

Among this class are: (1') $\min_i(\max(\bar{w}_i,a_i))$; and (2') $\prod_{i=1}^n(\bar{w}_i + w_i \cdot a_i)$

The following theorem introduces another class of weighted MOM operators.

Theorem: Assume $g : \mathbf{R} \to \mathbf{I}$ is a monotonic nondecreasing function, then $G_W(A) = g(\sum_{i=1}^n(w_i \cdot a_i))$ is a weighted MOM operator. We shall call this class *additive weighted MOM* operators.

Using our duality theorem, we can obtain a class of dual *additive weighted MAM* operators, generalized weighted *and* aggregators.

Theorem: Assume $h : \mathbf{R} \to \mathbf{I}$ is a monotonic nonincreasing function, then $H_W(A) = h(\sum_{i=1}^n(w_i \cdot \bar{a}_i))$ is a weighted MAM operator.

We see that G_W essentially increases as $\sum_{i=1}^{n}(w_i \cdot a_i)$ increases; that is, as more important elements are satisfied, we increase our satisfaction. On the other hand, H_W works by considering the unsatisfaction, $\bar{a}_i$, and as more important aggregates are not satisfied, we decrease the total aggregate score.

19.5. Ranking Objects in the Retrieval System

In the preceding, we discussed the issue of criteria aggregation. We now specialize this to the ranking of objects for an information retrieval system. We discussed two classes of aggregation, MOM and MAM operators. We recall that the MOM operator is a generalized *or*-like aggregation while the MAM operator is a generalized *and*-like operator. In information retrieval systems we see the criteria specified by the user as being connected by an *and*-like operator, assuming the user generally wants all the criteria satisfied. That is, a person desires to obtain further information about houses in a certain price range *and* in a particular location *and* having certain amenities. Thus, the appropriate family of operators are the MAM operators. We have described two classes of MAM operators, the t-norm and the additive. We shall consider here the additive class. Thus, in the weighted additive formulation the score in the query of an object y is the importance weighted aggregation of the n criterion scores:

$$\text{score}(y) = H_W(A(y)) = h\left(\sum_{i=1}^{n}\left(w_i \cdot \overline{A_i(y)}\right)\right)$$

However, in constructing the criteria function, as discussed in section 19.2, we can implicitly include the importance weights; thus, we can use an alternative version:

$$\text{score}(y) = h\left(\sum_{i=1}^{n} \overline{B_i(y)}\right)$$

where B_i are the importance modified criteria.

In addition, since all we need is a ranking of the objects, we can use any monotonically nonincreasing function for h. We shall use the exponential function; that is:

$$\text{score}(y) = e^{-\sum_{i=1}^{n}\overline{B_i(y)}}$$

Since $e^{-\sum_{i=1}^{n}\overline{B_i(y)}} = e^{-\sum_{i=1}^{n}(1-B_i(y))} = e^{-\sum_{i=1}^{n}1} \cdot e^{\sum_{i=1}^{n}B_i(y)}$, and $e^{-\sum_{i=1}^{n}1} = e^{-n} > 0$, we obtain the same ranking by using $\text{score}(y) = e^{\sum_{i=1}^{n}B_i(y)}$, and, further, by using $\text{score}(y) = \ln(e^{\sum_{i=1}^{n}B_i(y)}) = \sum_{i=1}^{n}B_i(y)$. Thus, the ranking of the objects can be obtained simply by ordering them according to the sum of their scores of the importance modified criteria.

19.6. An Example System

Figure 19.12 shows cuts of screen snapshots from a test application of the approach outlined. The objects represented in the informations base are apartments in Paris advertised for sale through a newspaper using a public videotex service (like the French Minitel) as an alternative media for advertising.

Users are assumed to be persons that want to purchase an apartment in Paris, and want to find those offers that best satisfy their needs. An apartment item contains three kinds of information: the location area, numerical attributes, and a free text field from which the non-numeric information is extracted. The snapshots are from the English version of the user interface to the system. Figure 19.12(a) and (b) show numeric and non-numeric (term) criteria in a user query example; the desired locations are selected in a Paris map (not shown) and fuzzified to "similar" locations. Each criterion is associated an importance level indicated by a symbol with the semantics given by the following list:

⩓   very high importance

∧   high importance

•   medium importance

∨   low importance

⩔   very low importance

The user may change the importance by clicking on the symbol causing the list to pop up, and allowing the user to select any of the five levels.

Figure 19.13 is copied from the answer presented to the query example in Figure 19.12. Figure 19.13(a) lists the three most interesting offers, ranked by decreasing score. Figure 19.13 further shows for the first offer in the list, (b) the free text (French) as supplied from the newspaper, and (c) the terms (English) identified in this text.

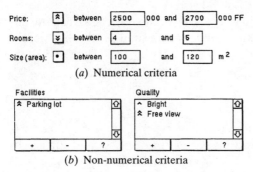

(a) Numerical criteria

(b) Non-numerical criteria

Figure 19.12   Numerical and non-numerical (term) criteria example.

No.	Category	Location	Price	Rooms	Area (m²)
✓ 5	App	3 EME ARRONDI	2800000	5	110
308	App	16 EME ARROND	2500000	4	100
20	App	12 EME ARROND	2500000	4	94

(a) List over the three most satisfying apartments

4/5 PIECES:IMMEUBLE RECENT-8EME ETAGE ET DERNIER AVEC ASCENSEUR-SOLEIL- SEJOUR ENVIRON 60 M2-3 CHAMBRES- 2 BAINS-VUE PANORAMIQUE-CHARME ET CARACTERE- POSSIBLE PARKING

(b) Free text (French) information on the first in the list above

●Recent ●Parking lot ●Elevator ●Sun ●Panoramic view ●Charming

(c) Identified terms (English) in the free text

Figure 19.13   Answer to the query example in Figure 19.12.

We notice that the price is a higher than specified by the user, while the number of rooms and the size of the apartment actually are in the intervals specified. Considering the non-numeric (term) criteria, we see that "parking lot" is directly satisfied. Through the similarity relation, we have further satisfied "bright" to some degree (through "sun"), and "free view" (through "panoramic view"). Though the second choice in the last satisfied completely on all the numerical criteria, it must fail on at least one of the important non-numeric criteria (actually it fails to satisfy "free view"). Thus, a (relatively) minor increase of the price above the interval specified has been considered worthwhile to satisfy the strong desire for "free view."

19.7. Conclusion

We presented an approach to a weighted multicriteria information retrieval system that uses fuzzy subsets as mechanism to allow for the flexible evaluation of user requirements. Although we focused on numerical criteria, the approach is also applicable for non-numerical criteria (concepts, terms)—in the first case, the semantic similarity utilized relies on the numerical scale; in the second case, it relies on a similarity relation. We discussed the potential use of MAM and MOM operators as a tool for the aggregation of user requirements. Finally, we illustrated the application of the mechanism and tools in an application for a real estate agency. Our an approach is in particular interesting for retrieval through the Internet WWW. In this situation, the semantic elasticity supported by our approach allows the user to retrieve the most interesting objects, even when the description applied in the information base does not directly match the query formulation chosen by the user.

19.8. References

[1] Miyamoto, S., and T. Miyake. "On Fuzzy Information Retrieval." *Japanese Journal of Fuzzy Theory and Systems,* Vol. 3 (1991), pp. 93–105.

[2] Bosc, P., and O. Pivert. "Fuzzy Querying in Conventional Databases," in *Fuzzy Logic for the Management of Uncertainty,* eds. J. Kacprzyk and L.A. Zadeh. pp. 645–671. New York: John Wiley and Sons, 1992.

[3] Zadeh, L.A. "Fuzzy Sets." *Information and Control,* Vol. 8 (1965), pp. 338–353.

[4] Lee, C.C. "Fuzzy Logic in Control Systems: Fuzzy Logic Controller, Part I." *IEEE Transactions on Systems, Man, and Cybernetics,* Vol. 20 (1990), pp. 404–418.

[5] Zadeh, L.A. "Similarity Relations and Fuzzy Orderings." *Information Sciences,* Vol. 3 (1971), pp. 177–200.

[6] Larsen, H.L., and R.R. Yager. "The Use of Fuzzy Relational Thesauri for Classificatory Problem Solving in Information Retrieval and Expert Systems." *IEEE Transactions on Systems, Man, and Cybernetics,* Vol. 23 (1993), pp. 31–41.

[7] Yager, R.R. "A New Methodology for Ordinal Multiple Aspect Decisions based on Fuzzy Sets." *Decision Sciences,* Vol. 12 (1981), pp. 589–600.

[8] ———. "Forms of Multicriteria Decision Functions and Preference Information Types," in *Approximate Reasoning in Expert Systems,* eds. M.M. Gupta, A. Kandel, W. Bandler, and J.B. Kiska. pp. 167–177. North Holland, Amsterdam: 1985.

[9] ———. "A Note on Weighted Queries in Informational Retrieval Systems." *Journal of the American Society of Informational Sciences,* Vol. 38 (1987), pp. 23–24.

[10] ———. "Fuzzy Decision Making using Unequal Objectives." *Fuzzy Sets and Systems,* Vol. 1 (1978), pp. 87–95.

[11] ———. "Multiple Objective Decision Making using Fuzzy Sets." *International Journal of Man-Machine Studies,* Vol. 9 (1977), pp. 375–382.

[12] ———. "On Weighted Median Aggregation." Technical Report #MII-1317. Machine Intelligence Institute, Iona College. New Rochelle, N.Y.: 1993.

[13] Date, C.J. *An Introduction to Database Systems.* Reading: Addison-Wesley, 1986.

[14] Salton, G. *Automatic Text Processing.* Reading: Addison-Wesley, 1989.

[15] Dubois, D., and H. Prade. "A Review of Fuzzy Sets Aggregation Connectives." *Information Sciences,* Vol. 36 (1985), pp. 85–121.

[16] Yager, R.R. "A Unified Approach to Aggregation based upon MOM and MAM Operators." *Technical Report #MII-1316.* Machine Intelligence Institute, Iona College. New Rochelle, N.Y.: 1993.

[17] ———. "MAM and MOM Operators for Aggregation." *Information Sciences,* Vol. 69 (1993), pp. 259–273.

[18] ———. "Toward a Unified Approach to Aggregation in Fuzzy and Neural Systems." *Proceedings, World Conference on Neural Networks.* Vol. II, pp. 619–622. Portland, Ore.: 1993.

20 Fuzzy Database Techniques: An Application to Criminal Investigation

R. Vandenberghe, R. De Caluwe
Computer Science Laboratory
(Department of Telecommunication and Information Processing)
University of Gent, Belgium

ABSTRACT: There are essentially two approaches for dealing with incomplete and imprecise information in the framework of (relational) databases. On the one hand, fuzzy similarity relations, as introduced by Buckles and Petry, are used to express the degree of interchangeability of the different values from the same attribute domain. On the other hand, in the approach of Dubois, Prade, and Testemale, possibility distributions are used to represent all possible kinds of incompletely or fuzzily known attribute values.

In this chapter, a combination of both techniques is studied and applied to the very specific domain of criminal investigation, in particular to criminal identification by means of a personal description. The proposed method can however be applied to any other domain where one has to deal with a similar kind of fuzziness and uncertainty.

The method consists of a fuzzy pattern matching process, in which the description of the pattern (the wanted profile in our case), is matched against the available data, both of which can be cursed with imprecision and uncertainty. Hereby, a Prade-Testemale-like technique is used, based on possibility distributions, but also involving likeness relations, defined on the attribute domains, resulting in the fuzzy matching aimed at.

20.1. Introduction

In solving crimes, personal description is an important tool. Known criminals are listed by our judicial institutions. In case a new crime occurs, this list is often consulted because, according to a well-founded hypothesis, the greater number of crimes is perpetrated by recidivists or suspected people who have already been listed for other delicts. Basically, such consultation can be considered as a pattern matching process. Due to witnesses and external circumstances, a profile of the criminal(s) is made up. This profile is matched against the available data.

According to the forms used by the police department, the physical description of a criminal consists of about 40 attributes, 25 single-valued and 15 multivalued. Single-valued attributes are for instance Build, Face.Shape, Hair.Style, and so on. The domain of Build for example consists of the values: thin, slim, average, sturdy, and corpulent. On the contrary, the attributes Face.Details, Hair.Particularities, are multivalued. For Face.Details, for example, each value must selected from the domain: asymmetric, wrinkled, freckles, birthmarks, and pimples. Notice that we make use of multivalued and of composite attributes, since this allows the most natural and best suited way of modelling the information, for what we have in view.

Obviously, personal descriptions are pervaded with imprecision and uncertainty. This must be taken into account in the matching process. With a few exceptions, all attributes acting in a personal description have a discrete domain, consisting of inherently fuzzy values. Hence, we will focus our approach on this kind of attribute. The chapter reconsiders the same problem as [1], [2].

The rest of the chapter is organized as follows. In section 20.2, a model is outlined—using Boolean-like expressions—for the representation of "fuzzy" values of single-valued and multivalued attributes, used for the description of the data in the database as well as of the wanted profile. Section 20.3 shows how, with these attribute values, possibility distributions are associated on the power class of the attribute domain. For the representation of the profile, the likeness relations are involved. The pattern matching process is described in section 20.4. It uses a Prade-Testemale-like technique based on possibility distributions. In section 20.5, the method is illustrated on criminal identification.

20.2. Expressions for Describing Attribute Values

Looking for an appropriate model for the representation of our data and profiles, the following issues arise. In the first place, the meaning of inherently fuzzy attribute values, such as "square" (attribute Face.Shape) cannot be expressed in terms of a measurable quantity. This implies that no fuzzy sets can be associated with these attribute values in a natural way, and consequently a model as in [3], is not suitable here.

Secondly, it is possible that, in the case of a single-valued attribute, none of the selectable attribute values (a limited number, for simplicity) really suits. Yet a choice must be made (the most suitable one).

Moreover, it is not always easy to distinguish between different attribute values (e.g., Eyes.Color: blue, gray; Face.Details: freckles, birthmarks, and so on), so that one can easily be mistaken. To be able to take into account this kind of mistake, and the subjectiveness of a witness, we define a likeness-relation (sup-W-transitive) on each attribute domain. Due to this likeness relation, possible mistakes are flattened. As an example we present the likeness-relation for the attribute Build in Table 20.1.

Due to the similarity of certain values, one can also doubt between values; for instance, "freckles or birthmarks" (multivalued attribute Face.Details), "possibly foreheadbaldness" (multivalued attribute Hair. Baldness), and so on.

Furthermore, sometimes a witness can only state with certainty which values are not applicable, but cannot make any further statements; for example, "not corpulent" (single-valued attribute Build), "no glasses" (multivalued attribute Eyes.Particularities).

Summarizing, we can represent the description of an attribute value as a kind of Boolean expression, composed of (sets of) domain values, the operators & (AND), OR, NOT (or NO) and CERTAINLY, adopting one of the forms given here.

1. *A is a single-valued attribute with domain D_A:*

   $u, \qquad u \in D_A$
   $OR(U), \quad U \subseteq D_A$
   $NOT(U), U \subseteq D_A$

   We introduce the following abbreviation: unknown $\equiv OR(D_A)$
   A few examples:

   Hair.Style (Chris) is OR({curly, wavy})
   Face.Shape (John) is NOT({square})

Table 20.1 Likeness-Relation for Build

	Thin	Slim	Average	Sturdy	Corpulent
Thin	1.0	0.9	0.5	0.3	0.0
Slim	0.9	1.0	0.6	0.4	0.1
Average	0.5	0.6	1.0	0.8	0.4
Sturdy	0.3	0.4	0.8	1.0	0.6
Corpulent	0.0	0.1	0.4	0.6	1.0

2. *A is a multivalued attribute with domain D_A:*

$$\text{CERTAINLY}(D_1) \ \& \ \text{OR}(D_2) \ \& \ \text{NOT}(D_3)$$

with $\{D_i | \ i = 1,2,3\}$ a set of three disjoint (possibly empty) subsets of D_A, where D_2 is not a singleton.

The subset $D_A \backslash (D_1 \cup D_2 \cup D_3)$ denotes the set of attribute values that can be neither included nor excluded with certainty. We use the notation unknown, when $D_1 = D_2 = D_3 = \emptyset$, and introduce the abbreviation none $\equiv$ NOT(D_A).

Furthermore, we introduce the keyword "REST," for conciseness of the representation:

$$\text{Operator}(\text{REST}) \Leftrightarrow \text{Operator}(D_A \backslash \bigcup_{j \neq i} D_j)$$

where $i = 1$ if Operator = CERTAINLY, $i = 2$ if Operator = OR and $i = 3$ if Operator = NOT.

A few examples:

Eyes.Particularities (Nancy) is NOT({glasses, tics})

Face.Details (John) is CERTAINLY({pimples})
                                      & OR({freckles, birthmarks})
                                      & NOT(REST)

Notice that, in the approach of Buckles & Petry [4], [5] attribute-values can be subsets of the concerning domain, indicating the possible values for the attribute; this is equivalent to the use of an expression of the form "OR(D) & NOT(REST)" in our representation.

20.3. Representation of the Data and Pattern Attributes

Each of the expressions for an attribute value $A(X)$ of A, proposed previously, is in fact an indication for the various possible values that A can take for X. Hence a possibility distribution can be associated with each of these expressions. Since we have to deal with multivalued attributes, we have to consider possibility distributions on $\mathcal{P}(D_A)$, the power class of the domain D_A of the attribute A. For uniformity, we use such distributions in the case of single-valued attributes too. The possibility distributions are deduced in the way suggested by Prade & Testemale [6].

20.3.1. Representation of Data Attributes

1. *A is a single-valued attribute with domain D_A:*

"$A(X)$ is u", with $u \in D_A$: $\pi_{A(X)}(\{u\}) = 1$
"$A(X)$ is OR(U)", with $U \subseteq D_A$: $\pi_{A(X)}(\{u\}) = 1, \forall u \in U$
"$A(X)$ is NOT(U)", with $U \subseteq D_A$: $\pi_{A(X)}(\{u\}) = 1, \forall u \in D_A \backslash U$

In each case, $\pi_{A(X)}(D) = 0$ if $D \subseteq D_A$ is not a singleton.

2. *A is a multivalued attribute with domain* D_A:

"A(X) is $A^{(1)}(X)$ & $A^{(2)}(X)$ & $A^{(3)}(X)$,"

where $A^{(1)}(X) \equiv$ CERTAINLY(D_1), $A^{(2)}(X) \equiv$ OR(D_2), $A^{(3)}(X) \equiv$ NOT(D_3), and $\{D_i | i = 1,2,3\}$ a set of disjoint subsets of D_A, where D_2 is not a singleton. We omit $A^{(i)}(X)$ from the expression if $D_i = \varnothing$.

First we write down the possibility distribution for each of the subexpressions $A^{(i)}(X)$:

$$\pi_{A^{(1)}(X)}(D) = 1, \quad \text{if } D \subseteq D_A \text{ and } D \supseteq D_1,$$
$$= 0, \quad \text{otherwise.}$$

$$\pi_{A^{(2)}(X)}(D) = 1, \quad \text{if } D \subseteq D_A \text{ and } D \cap D_2 \neq \varnothing;$$
$$= 0, \quad \text{otherwise.}$$

$$\pi_{A^{(3)}(X)}(D) = 1, \quad \text{if } D \subseteq D_A \text{ and } D \cap D_3 = \varnothing,$$
$$= 0, \quad \text{otherwise.}$$

The distribution for the complete expression $A(X)$ is then obtained as:

$$\pi_{A(X)}(D) = \min_{i=1}^{3} \pi_{A^{(i)}(X)}(D),$$

$$\pi_{A(X)}(D) = 1, \quad \text{if } \pi_{A^{(i)}(X)}(D) = 1 \; \forall i \in \{1,2,3\},$$
$$= 0, \quad \text{otherwise.}$$

This means that the only possible subsets of values from D_A for $A(X)$ are those that contain all the elements of D_1, at least one of D_2 and none of D_3.

In particular, the attribute values unknown and none, are represented as follows:

A(X) is unknown: $\pi_{A(X)}(D) = 1, \forall D \subseteq D_A.$

A(X) is none: $\pi_{A(X)}(\varnothing) = 1, \pi_{A(X)}(D) = 0,$ elsewhere in $D_A.$

Consider for example the multivalued attribute $A \equiv$ Chin.Particularities, with domain {spherical, wry, protruding, dimple}. A possible value A(X) for this attribute can be expressed as "CERTAINLY({spherical,protruding}) & NO({dimple})." The associated possibility distribution $\pi_{A(X)}$ is then given by:

$$\pi_{A(X)}(\{\text{spherical,protruding}\}) = \pi_{A(X)}(\{\text{spherical,protruding,wry}\}) = 1;$$

$$\pi_{A(X)}(D) = 0, \text{ for all other combinations } D \text{ of particularities.}$$

20.3.2. Representation of Pattern Attributes

Since we are only interested in obtaining all the criminals who, to some extent, conform to a description (given by witnesses), we only need to consider queries of the following form, involving only "atomic" conditions:

"SELECT ALL X WHERE $A_1(X)$ IS P_1 ... AND $A_m(X)$ IS P_m"

where $A_1(X), A_2(X), \ldots, A_m(X)$ indicate the values (expressions !) of the attributes $A_1, \ldots A_m$ for criminal X, and $P_1, \ldots P_m$ are expressions describing the desired profile with respect to these attributes, all of the form proposed in section 20.2.

For instance, a possible condition could be: "Eyes.Color(X) IS gray." It is clear that a person X with Eyes.Color(X) = blue, still matches the description "gray" to some extent, due to the existing similarity between "blue" and "gray." To obtain this kind of fuzzy matching, each crisp value v appearing in the profile description will be translated implicitly into a fuzzy value like(v), where:

$$\mu_{LIKE(v)}(d) = s(d,v), \forall d \in D_A,$$

That is, v will be replaced by the fuzzy set of all values that are similar to v, according to the likeness relation defined on the attribute domain D_A.

Now the simplest form of an atomic condition, is "A(X) IS P," where P is v, $v \in D_A$. In the case of a single-valued attribute A, we can associate the following possibility distribution (on $\mathcal{P}(D_A)$) with P:

$$\pi_P(\{d\}) = s(d,v), \forall d \in D_A.$$

For a multivalued attribute A, we obtain (by applying the common technique for extending a fuzzy set toward the powerclass of its domain):

$$\pi_P(D) = \max_{d \in D} s(d,v), \forall D \subseteq D_A.$$

Using Zadeh's classical operations, we obtain distributions for a general expression for the profile P: applying the operators OR, NOT, and AND (&), is translated into, taking the maximum, complement with respect to 1, and minimum of the corresponding possibility distributions respectively. The results are presented next.

1. *A is a single-valued attribute with domain D_A:*

   "P is v", with $v \in D_A$: $\pi_P(\{u\}) = s(u,v),$ $\forall u \in D_A$

   "P is OR(V)", with $V \subseteq D_A$: $\pi_P(\{u\}) = \max_{v \in V} s(u,v),$ $\forall u \in D_A$

   "P is NOT(V)", with $V \subseteq D_A$: $\pi_P(\{u\}) = \min_{v \in V} (1 - s(u,v)),$ $\forall u \in D_A$

In each case, $\pi_P(D) = 0$ if $D \subseteq D_A$ is not a singleton. In particular: "P is unknown": $\pi_P(\{u\}) = 1, \forall u \in D_A$

2. *A is a multivalued attribute with domain D_A:*

   "P is $P^{(1)}$ & $P^{(2)}$ & $P^{(3)}$"

where $P^{(1)} \equiv CERTAINLY(P_1)$, $P^{(2)} \equiv OR(P_2)$, $P^{(3)} \equiv NOT(P_3)$ and $\{P_i | i = 1,2,3\}$ a set of disjoint subsets of D_A, where P_2 is not a singleton. Again, we omit $P^{(i)}$ if $P_i = \varnothing$.

The possibility distributions for each of the subexpressions $P^{(i)}$ are given as:

$$\pi_{P^{(1)}}(\varnothing) = \pi_{P^{(2)}}(\varnothing) = \pi_{P^{(3)}}(\varnothing) = 0$$

$$\pi_{P^{(1)}}(D) = \min_{v \in P_1} \max_{d \in D} s(d,v), \qquad \forall D \subseteq D_A, D \neq \varnothing$$

$$\pi_{P^{(2)}}(D) = \max_{v \in P_2} \max_{d \in D} s(d,v), \qquad \forall D \subseteq D_A, D \neq \varnothing$$

$$\pi_{P^{(3)}}(D) = \min_{v \in P_3} (1 - \max_{d \in D} s(d,v)), \qquad \forall D \subseteq D_A, D \neq \varnothing$$

$$\forall i \in \{1,2,3\}: \text{if } P_i = \varnothing \text{ then } \pi_{P^{(i)}}(D) = 1 \; \forall D \subseteq D_A.$$

The following properties can be deduced:

$$\text{if } D \supseteq P_1 \qquad \text{then } \pi_{P^{(1)}}(D) = 1,$$

$$\text{if } D \cap P_2 \neq \varnothing \qquad \text{then } \pi_{P^{(2)}}(D) = 1,$$

$$\text{if } D \cap P_3 \neq \varnothing \qquad \text{then } \pi_{P^{(3)}}(D) = 0.$$

For the complete expression P, the possibility distribution is then obtained as:

$$\pi_P(D) = \min_{i=1}^{3} \pi_{P^{(i)}}(D), \forall D \subseteq D_A.$$

As an example, consider the multivalued attribute Face.Details with domain {asymmetric, wrinkled, freckles, birthmarks, pimples}, and the following expression for the pattern P with respect to this attribute: "CERTAINLY({asymmetric,pimples}) & OR({freckles,birthmarks}) & NOT({wrinkled}))." The following possibility distribution π_P is then associated with P:

$$\pi_P(D) = \min (\min (\max_{d \in D} s(d,\text{asymmetric}), \max_{d \in D} s(d,\text{pimples})),$$

$$\max (\max_{d \in D} s(d,\text{freckles}), \max_{d \in D} s(d,\text{birthmarks})),$$

$$1 - \max_{d \in D} s(d,\text{wrinkled})) \qquad \forall D \subseteq D_A.$$

For example: $\pi_P(\{\text{asymmetric,freckles,pimples}\}) = 1 - \max \{s(\text{asymmetric,wrinkled}),$
$s(\text{freckles,wrinkled}), s(\text{pimples,wrinkled})\} = 1,$
since $s(d,\text{wrinkled}) = 0 \; \forall d \in D_A \backslash \{\text{wrinkled}\}$.

In the case of a crisp matching process (i.e. $s(x,x) = 1, s(x,y) = 0 \; \forall x \neq y$), the possibility distribution π_P can be described by means of the following rules:

$$\pi_P(D) = 1, \text{if } D \supseteq P_1 \text{ and } (P_2 = \varnothing \text{ or } D \cap P_2 \neq \varnothing) \text{ and } D \cap P_3 = \varnothing$$

$$= 0, \text{otherwise.}$$

20.4. The Matching Process

The matching process consists of the calculation of a fuzzy truth value, being the average of a possibility- and a necessity-measure, for each criminal. This is done in a way similar to that of the possibility-based approach. Here, the likeness relations, defined on the domains, are involved. The list of all the registrated criminals is then ordered by descending truth-values.

For each individual attribute A, appearing in the description of the wanted profile, the desired possibility- and necessity-measure can be calculated using the generalized formulae for distributions defined on the powerclass $\mathcal{P}(D_A)$ of the domain D_A of the attribute A; that is:

$$\pi(P|A(X)) = \sup \{\min (\pi_{A(X)}(D), \pi_P(D)) \mid D \in \mathcal{P}(D_A)\}$$

$$N(P|A(X)) = \inf \{\max (1 - \pi_{A(X)}(D), \pi_P(D)) \mid D \in \mathcal{P}(D_A)\}$$

Notice that these formulae can be simplified to:

$$\pi(P|A(X)) = \sup \{\pi_P(D) \mid D \subseteq D_A \wedge \pi_{A(X)}(D) = 1\}$$

$$N(P|A(X)) = \inf \{\pi_P(D) \mid D \subseteq D_A \wedge \pi_{A(X)}(D) = 1\}$$

Taking into account the formulae deduced in section 20.3 for expressing the distributions $\pi_P(D)$ and $\pi_{A(X)}(D)$, for $D \subseteq D_A$, in terms of those for the subexpressions ($\pi_{P^{(i)}}(D)$ resp. $\pi_{A^{(i)}(X)}(D)$, i = 1,2,3), we obtain:

$$\pi(P|A(X)) = \sup \{ \min_{i \in \{1,2,3\}} \pi_{P^{(i)}}(D) \mid D \subseteq D_A \wedge D \supseteq D_1 \wedge D \cap D_2 \neq \varnothing \wedge D \cap D_3 = \varnothing\}$$

$$\pi(P|A(X)) = \inf \{ \min_{i \in \{1,2,3\}} \pi_{P^{(i)}}(D) \mid D \subseteq D_A \wedge D \supseteq D_1 \wedge D \cap D_2 \neq \varnothing \wedge D \cap D_3 = \varnothing\}$$

Following, a few rules are presented to obtain $\pi(P|A(X))$ and $N(P|A(X))$ without making any calculations, under certain conditions.

1. $\pi(P|A(X)) = N(P|A(X))$ when the expression for A(X) doesn't contain a subexpression $OR(D_2)$ (i.e. $D_2 = \varnothing$) and $D_1 \cup D_3 = D_A$.

   Interpretation: For a crisp description (one expressing no doubts), it is equally possible as necessary that it matches a given profile.

2. If $P_3 = \varnothing$ then $N(P|A(X))$ remains unchanged when in the expression for A(X), $NOT(D_3)$ is replaced by $NOT(D_3')$, with $D_3' = Co(D_1 \cup D_2)$.

   Interpretation: The necessity is the worst case possibility, so values about which there is no certainty may be excluded from this calculation.

3. If $P_3 = \varnothing$, $P_1 \subseteq Co(D_3)$, and ($P_2 \not\subseteq D_3$ or $P_2 = \varnothing$), then $\pi(P|A(X)) = 1$.

   Interpretation: If the profile does not exclude any attribute values, and the given description does not exclude any of the "certain" profile values *and* admits at least one of the profile values between which doubt exists, then matching is completely possible. As a corollary of this rule, we obtain:

If $P_3 = \varnothing$ and $D_3 = \varnothing$, then $\pi(P|A(X)) = 1$.

Interpretation: If neither the given description nor the profile explicitly excludes certain values for the attribute, then matching is completely possible.

4. If $P_3 \cap D_1 \neq \varnothing$, then $\pi(P|A(X)) = N(P|A(X)) = 0$.

   Interpretation: A description stating certainty about a value can impossibly satisfy a profile that excludes that value explicitly.

5. If $P_3 \nsubseteq D_3$, then $N(P|A(X)) = 0$.

   Interpretation: A description cannot completely satisfy a profile excluding a value that is not explicitly excluded in the description.

6. If $P_3 = \varnothing$, $P_1 \subseteq D_1$, and ($P_2 \subseteq D_2$ or $P_2 \cap D_1 \neq \varnothing$), then $\pi(P|A(X)) = N(P|A(X)) = 1$.

   Interpretation: When the profile does not exclude any values, then a given description completely matches the profile, if it confirms all the values about which certainty exists, and at least one of the values between which doubt exists. As a corollary of the previous rule, we find:

   If $P_3 = \varnothing$, $P_1 = D_1$, and $P_2 = D_2$, then $\pi(P|A(X)) = N(P|A(X)) = 1$.

As an example, consider again the attribute $A \equiv$ Face.Details, and the following profile: "P is CERTAINLY({asymmetric}) & OR({birthmarks, pimples})."

1. A(X) is CERTAINLY({asymmetric,wrinkled}) & OR({freckles, birthmarks}) & NO({pimples}).

   $P_1 = \{\text{asymmetric}\} \subseteq D_A \backslash \{\text{pimples}\}$, and
   $P_2 = \{\text{birthmarks,pimples}\} \cap D_A \backslash \{\text{pimples}\} = \{\text{birthmarks}\} \neq \varnothing$,
   so according to rule 3, $\pi(P|A(X)) = 1$.

2. A(X) is CERTAINLY({asymmetric,pimples}) & OR({freckles, birthmarks}) & NOT({wrinkled}).

   $P_1 = \{\text{asymmetric}\} \subseteq D_1$ and $P_2 \cap D_1 = \{\text{pimples}\} \neq \varnothing$.
   Hence, according to rule 6, $\pi(P|A(X)) = N(P|A(X)) = 1$.

Particular cases:

* "P is unknown": $\pi(P|A(X)) = N(P|A(X)) = 1$, for each expression A(X).

* "P is none": $\pi(P|A(X)) = N(P|A(X)) = 0$, if A(X) contains a CERTAINLY-and/or OR-part;

   $\pi(P|A(X)) = N(P|A(X)) = 1$, otherwise.

In the case of *crisp matching*, $\pi(P|A(X))$ and $N(P|A(X))$ are solely determined by the relative position of the subsets D_1, D_2, D_3, and P_1, P_2, P_3, and can be calculated by means of the following rules:

(a) $\pi(P|A(X)) = 1$, if $P_1 \subseteq Co(D_3) \wedge (P_2 = \varnothing \vee P_2 \not\subseteq D_3) \wedge P_3 \cap D_1 = \varnothing \wedge P_3 \not\supseteq D_2$,

$\quad = 0$, otherwise.

(b) $N(P|A(X)) = 1$, if $P_1 \subseteq D_1 \wedge (P_2 = \varnothing \vee P_2 \supseteq D_2 \vee P_2 \cap D_1 \neq \varnothing) \wedge P_3 \subseteq D_3$

$\quad = 0$, otherwise.

As a corollary of rule (b) we obtain:

If $P_1 = D_1, P_2 = D_2$ and $P_3 = D_3$, then $\pi(P|A(X)) = N(P|A(X)) = 1$

This is the expected result for a perfect matching between query and data in the crisp case. Notice, however, that in the general case, no such rule can be formulated.

When an arbitrary likeness-relation s is used to obtain a fuzzy matching, $\pi(P|A(X))$ and $N(P|A(X))$ can be calculated in terms of the sets $\{D_i|i = 1, \ldots, 3\}$ and $\{P_j|j = 1, \ldots, 3\}$ and the similarities existing between their elements. General formulae can be derived for each type of profile P. Next we illustrate this for a profile of the form "P is $CERT(P_1)$" and an arbitrary expression for $A(X)$.

$$\pi_P(D) = \pi_{P^{(1)}}(D) = \min_{v \in P_1} \max_{d \in D} s(d,v),$$

$$\pi(P|A(X)) = \sup \{\pi_P(D) \mid D \subseteq D_A \backslash D_3 \wedge D \supseteq D_1 \wedge D \cap D_2 \neq \varnothing\}$$

$$= \pi_P(D^*) \quad \text{with } D^* = Co(D_3),$$

$$= \min_{v \in P_1} \max_{d \in D_A \backslash D_3} s(d,v).$$

$$N(P|A(X)) = \inf \{\pi_P(D) \mid D \subseteq D_A \wedge \pi_{A(X)}(D) = 1\}$$

$$= \min_{D = D_1 \cup \{d_2\}} \min_{v \in P_1} \max_{d \in D} s(d,v)$$

$$= \min_{v \in P_1} \min_{d_2 \in D_2} \max \left(\max_{d_1 \in D_1} s(d,v), s(d_2,v) \right)$$

$$= \min_{v \in P_1} \max \left(\max_{d_1 \in D_1} s(d_1,v), \min_{d_2 \in D_2} s(d_2,v) \right).$$

Having obtained the possibility- and necessity-measure $\pi(A_i(X)$ is $P_i | A_i(X))$ resp. $N(A_i(X)$ is $P_i | A_i(X))$ for each individual attribute A_i ($i = 1 \ldots m$), the possibility $\pi(X)$ and necessity $N(X)$ that criminal X matches the complete profile "$A_1(X)$ is P_1 and $\ldots A_m(X)$ is P_m," and finally the truth-value, are calculated as follows:

$$\pi(X) = \min_{i \in \{1,\ldots,m\}} \pi(P_i|A_i(X)),$$

$$N(X) = \min_{i \in \{1,\ldots,m\}} N(P_i|A_i(X)),$$

$$T(X) = (\pi(X) + N(X))/2.$$

20.5. Application of the Method to Criminal Identification

Here, the matching process is illustrated on a realistic example of a wanted profile (limited here to the description of the face) and a fictitious criminal X.

Wanted profile

Face: Thickness is filled

   Shape is NOT ({square})

   Details is CERTAINLY({pimples}) & OR({freckles, birthmarks})

   Color is red

   Hair is NO({beard})

Personal description of criminal X

Face: Thickness is chubby

   Shape is round

   Details is CERTAINLY({freckles}) &

                  NOT({birthmarks, asymmetric, wrinkled})

   Color is fresh

   Hair is CERTAINLY({moustache}) & NO({beard})

For the individual attributes $A_1 \equiv$ Face.Thickness, $A_2 \equiv$ Face.Shape, $A_3 \equiv$ Face.Details, $A_4 \equiv$ Face.Color and $A_5 \equiv$ Face.Hair, we obtain respectively:

$$* \pi(P_1|A_1(X)) = N(P_1|A_1(X)) = s(\text{filled, chubby}) = 0.6$$

$$* \pi(P_2|A_2(X)) = N(P_2|A_2(X)) = 1 - s(\text{round,square}) = 0.8$$

$$* \pi(P_3|A_3(X)) = \min (\pi_1,\pi_2)$$

$$N(P_3|A_3(X)) = \min (N_1,N_2)$$

with

   $\pi_1 = \max (s(\text{freckles,pimples}), s(\text{pimples,pimples})) = 1,$

   $\pi_2 = \max (\max (s(\text{freckles,freckles}), s(\text{pimples,freckles})), \ldots) = 1,$

   $N_1 = s(\text{freckles, pimples}) = 0.2,$

   $N_2 = \max (\max (s(\text{freckles,freckles}), \ldots), \max (\ldots , \ldots)) = 1.$

Hence:

$$\pi(P_3|A_3(X)) = 1; N(P_3|A_3(X)) = 0.2.$$

Notice that $\pi(P_3|A_3(X)) = 1$ follows from rule (3), with D = {freckles, pimples}.

$*\pi(P_4|A_4(X)) = N(P_4|A_4(X)) = s(red,fresh) = 0.7$

$*\pi(P_5|A_5(X)) = 1 - s(moustache,beard) = 1 - 0 = 1,$

$N(P_5|A_5(X)) = min (1 - s(moustache,beard), 1 - s(whiskers,beard)) = min (1, 0.8)$

$= 0.8.$

Finally we obtain: $\pi(X) = 0.6$, $N(X) = 0.2$, and hence $T(X) = 0.4$. This means that our fictious criminal X matches the wanted profile to a degree 0.4.

Notice that, when multiple descriptions are available (from several witnesses), the matching process should be carried out for each of these descriptions, and the maxima of the resulting truth-values should be used to obtain the final ordered list of suspects.

20.6. Conclusion

The approach presented here is focused on attributes with a discrete domain, where the domain values are inherently fuzzy. Each of these domains is provided with a likeness relation. Furthermore, attributes are allowed to be composite and multivalued. General expressions are proposed for representing "fuzzy" values of single-valued and multivalued attributes, for the description of the data as well as the wanted profile. With these attribute values, possibility distributions are associated on the power class of the domain. The likeness relations are involved in the representation of the profile. In this way, a combination of the possibility-based technique on the one hand, and the similarity-based approach on the other hand, is used to make possible the desired fuzzy pattern matching.

The issue of fuzzy pattern matching has also been treated by R. De Caluwe et al. in the context of a more general, fuzzy relational database model [7]. Recent related work has been done by Melton and Shenoi [8], by Rundensteiner et al. [9] and by J.M. Medina et al. [10], among others. The models proposed by these authors can also be considered as generalizations of the model of Buckles and Petry.

20.7. References

[1] Vandenberghe, R., et al. "A Practical Application of Fuzzy Database Techniques to Criminal Investigation." *Preprints of the Proceedings of the 2nd IFSA Congress.* pp. 661–665. Tokyo, Japan: 1987.

[2] ———. "Some Practical Aspects of Fuzzy Database Techniques: An Example." *Information Systems,* Vol. 14, No. 6 (1989), pp. 465–472.

[3] Dubois, D., and H. Prade. *Théorie des Possibilities.* Paris: 1985.

[4] Buckles, B.P., et al. "Design of Similarity-based Relational Databases," in *Fuzzy Logic in Knowledge Engineering,* eds. H. Prade and C. Negoita. pp. 3–7. TUV, Rheinland. 1986.

[5] Yazici, A., et al. "A Survey of Conceptual and Logical Data Models for Uncertainty Management," in *Fuzzy Logic for the Management of Uncertainty,* eds. L.A. Zadeh and J. Kacprzyk. pp. 607–644. New York: John Wiley and Sons Inc., 1992.

[6] Prade, H., and C. Testemale. "Representation of Soft Constraints and Fuzzy Attribute Values by Means of Possibility Distributions in Databases," in *The Analysis of Fuzzy Information,* Vol. II, ed. J.C. Bezdek. Boca Raton: CRC Press, 1987.

[7] De Caluwe, R., et al. "Integrating Fuzziness in Database Models," in *Fuzziness in Database Management Systems,* ed. P. Bosc and J. Kacprzyk. pp. 71–113. Physica-Verlag, Heidelberg: 1995.

[8] Melton, A., and S. Shenoi. "Fuzzy Relations and Fuzzy Relational Databases." *Computers Mathematical Applications,* Vol. 21, No. 11–12. (1991), pp. 129–138.

[9] Rundensteiner, E.A., et al. "On Nearness Measures in Fuzzy Relational Data Models." *International Journal of Approximate Reasoning,* Vol. 3 (1989), pp. 267–298.

[10] Medina, J.M., et al. "GEFRED: A Generalized Model of Fuzzy Relational Databases." *Information Sciences,* Vol. 76 (1994), pp. 87–109.

21 An Approach to Modelling Impreciseness and Uncertainty in the Object-Oriented Data Model*

R. George, R. Srikanth
Department of Computer Science
Clark Atlanta University
Atlanta, Georgia

B. P. Buckles, F. E. Petry
Department of Computer Science
Tulane University
New Orleans, Louisiana

ABSTRACT: An Object-Oriented Data Model (OODM) capable of representing uncertainty is described in this chapter. The modelling capability is derived by utilizing fuzzy logic to generalize equality to similarity. Similarity permits the impreciseness in data to be represented explicitly. Imprecision in data results in uncertainty in classification. Both these mechanisms are facilitated in the model. A primitive operator, the merge, that preserves nonredundancy in the data model is defined.

21.1. Introduction

Object-Oriented Database Management Systems (OODBMS) have been developed to meet the challenge of complex data modeling require-

* This work is supported in part by the Army Center of Excellence in Information Sciences, Clark Atlanta University under ARO Grant DAAL03-G-0377.

ments of large-scale, data-intensive applications. They are suitable for a variety of applications, including VLSI design, CAD/CAM, CASE, Geographic Information Systems, and so on [2, 7, 16]. This range of applicability can be attributed to the natural representation of the real world facilitated by the object-oriented paradigm. Despite this representational power, OODBMS are ill equipped in dealing with inherently vague, uncertain, or imprecise data. Traditionally, the solution has been to conform these types of data to precise values.

This approach detracts from the representational capability of the object-oriented paradigm and semantically overloads application programs. In this chapter we present a fuzzy logic-based extension to the data model, permitting imprecise and uncertain data to be explicitly represented. Consequently, the ability to manipulate such data via semantically richer query languages is facilitated. The similarity relation, which replaces equality, is the basis of the extended data model. Any two values, **x** and **y** in a fuzzy attribute domain **D** obey the properties of symmetry, reflexivity, and transitivity.

$$s(x, x) = 1 \textbf{ reflexivity}$$

$$s(x, y) = s(y, x) \textbf{ symmetry}$$

$$s(x, y) \leq max_{z \in D}[min(s(x, z), s(z, y))] \textbf{ transitivity}$$

This generalization of equality to similarity has important bearing on class structure as well as database operations. Traditionally, the view in databases (and artificial intelligence) has been that specialization (or, alternately, generalization) and instantiation produce classes and objects that are subsumed by their classes and superclasses respectively (in other words, with a crisp membership) [2, 6]. It has been shown that in an object-class and class-superclass hierarchical relationship, it is the prototypical object that is modelled [13]. Also, certain set operations, such as symmetric difference, can result in subclasses that inherit only some attributes and methods of their superclass [18]. We generalize subsumption of objects/classes in classes/superclasses so that the conventional view is a special case. The motivation for this extension is twofold. First, it permits more accurate knowledge representation of the Universe of Discourse. This has its advantages; for example, in coupled Artificial Intelligence-Database System, where an outstanding bottleneck has been the mismatch between the two knowledge representation paradigms [11]. Another possible application area is in Object-Oriented Geographical Information Systems, where querying is not always on precise objects (i.e., those whose attributes are precisely known, a priori [12]). Secondly, a more powerful retrieval mechanism is facilitated by this extension. It becomes possible to retrieve fuzzy data, as well as typical and atypical members of a class via the query language. It should be noted that the retrieval of precise attributes and crisp members of a class is a special case of imprecise retrieval.

Previously, Rudensteiner and Bandler [17] studied the problem of fuzzy semantic networks, proving equivalence with the binary relational representation models. Torrasso et al. [20], defined a frame-based representation with three kinds of weighted attributes: necessary, sufficient, and supplementary. For object-oriented databases, Zicari [21] has considered issues of incompleteness, albeit without use of fuzzy concepts. In particular, incomplete data in an object is handled by the introduction of explicit null values similar to the relational and nested relational models. Dubois et al. [8], have utilized possibility theory to represent vagueness and uncertainty in class hierarchies. For single-valued attributes they define the inclusion between classes to be the inclusion between the fuzzy ranges (which are possibility distributions). The emphasis in our approach is to define a data model that preserves the underlying features of its logical paradigm, while accommodating uncertainties in hierarchies. So, we account for nonsingular object attribute values that may be connected through logical operators such as the AND [19], the OR [3], and so on. This is a reflection of the fact that in semantically expressive data models (for instance, the object-oriented and semantic data models), there exist data with a variety of semantics, resulting from different database operations. Furthermore, we distinguish between uncertainty and impreciseness. Impreciseness is a property of data, which the similarity relationship tries to capture. Uncertainty arises out of the "aggregation" of the imprecision in object attribute values, and occurs at the class level. The "aggregation" is application-dependent and so this model accounts for the relevance of the attributes to the fuzzy class and the conceptual (semantic) distance between the class and the objects (or subclasses).

In section 21.2, we define the basic terminology, and section 21.3 discusses how impreciseness in object (or subclasses) attribute values result in membership values in classes. Fuzzy Class Schemas and a consistency preserving operation—the **Merge**—are defined in section 21.4. An example query in the system is described in section 21.5, and section 21.6 concludes the paper.

21.2. Objects and Classes

The object-oriented data model represents the universe of discourse as a collection of interacting objects. Identity and state characterize objects. Identity distinguishes one object from another. The state of an object consists of the values of its attributes. Similar objects are grouped together to form a class. The structure and the permitted behavior define the class. The attributes of a given object may be basic or composite, and a composite attribute may itself be composed of simple or composite attributes. This results in a directed, possibly cyclical graph, called the class-composition hierarchy [14]. A class may be derived from another resulting in class-subclass relationships (inheritance). The inheritance graph is a directed acyclic graph. Thus the object-oriented paradigm models real-world situations through a class hierarchy and a class composition hierarchy (aggregation).

The domain of an attribute, *dom*, is the set of values the attribute may take, irrespective of the class it falls into. The range of an attribute, *rng*, is the set of allowed values that a member of a class, an object, may take for the attribute; and, in general, $rng \subseteq dom$. For instance, assume that age is an attribute and the domain of age is between 0 and 150. If there exists a class Employee, the range of age for the class may be 20 to 70. The range is clearly a subset of the domain of age, but is the subset that is most pertinent to the class definition of Employee.

A feature that distinguishes the fuzzy hierarchy from the classical one (crisp) is that the concepts that form the classes have "imprecise" boundaries. This uncertainty is a result of the imprecision in the values of the object attributes that form the class. For example, if we consider the class of Young-Students, the uncertainty in the class is directly a result of the fuzziness of the meaning of "young." Fuzzy logic, which explicitly premits the representation of "soft" thresholds, is utilized to solve this problem. The presence of a soft threshold for the data suggests that, unlike the classical case (1,0 type approaches), it is possible to have objects that are members of a class with a degree of membership. There is another interesting aspect to this issue. A formal range is associated with each attribute value in a class. But it is possible the actual attribute values within the class might be different from the formal value(s). Since the similarity relation links the attribute values in a domain (through transistivity), an object may be a member of a class though its attribute values might be different from the elements of the formal range. The extent to which these values differ affects the membership of the object in the class and will be a part of the formulation of membership values. The relevance of the attribute to the concept modelled and the conceptual (or semantic) distance between a superclass and a class, or between a class and an object, have to be accounted in deriving membership values of the class/object in the superclass/class. In fuzzy hierarchies it is important to consider the conceptual (or semantic) distance between links. A class may not necessarily be contained in a superclass but may be only an approximate subclass. Thus, there can exist situations in which the membership of a class in its superclasses increases as the inheritance hierarchy is ascended (strong ISA). Conversely, the membership could also decrease as the inheritance hierarchy is ascended (weak ISA).

21.2.1. Application: Oceanographic Modelling

The principal features of our modelling approach will be illustrated next through a running example based on a database schema (Figure 21.1) founded on the representations of oceanographic features. Associated sim-

```
CLASS: Seasonal_North_Atlantic_Features
PROPERTIES:
        Location
        Radius
        Season
END;

CLASS: Cold_Core_Ring
INHERIT:
        Seasonal_North_Atlantic_Features
PROPERTIES:
        Curvature
        Radius
        Temperature
END;
```

Figure 21.1   Schema of an oceanographic database.

ilarity matrices for fuzzy attributes are shown in Tables 21.1–21.5. Oceanographic or geographical databases are ideal for illustration since classification of the various features can be very difficult and subjective due to cloud cover, lighting, seasonal variables, and so on. The sample we give here is only a simplified part of a more complex database for such features. We will use it to illustrate the uncertain information in a similarity-based object-oriented model and to provide examples of the calculations of object-class and class-subclass relationships.

Satellite remote sensing is producing huge volumes of data that will require new approaches to data modelling and databases to effectively utilize the data. We have been involved in the design of approaches using fuzzy object-oriented databases for geographical information systems [12], and the development of a knowledge-based system to assist in interpretation of satellite imagery of the North Atlantic region [5].

Table 21.1   Curvature = {Very High, High, Medium}

	Curvature		
Very High	1.0	0.85	0.55
High	0.85	1.0	0.55
Medium	0.55	0.55	1.0

Table 21.2   Season = {Fall, Winter, Spring}

	Season		
Fall	1.0	0.8	0.6
Winter	0.8	1.0	0.6
Spring	0.6	0.6	1.0

Table 21.3   Location = {W, WSW, WNW, SW, SSW, S, SSE}

			Location			
W	1.0	0.8	0.4	0	0	0	0
WSW	0.8	1.0	0.4	0	0	0	0
WNW	0.4	0.4	1.0	0	0	0	0
SW	0	0	0	1.0	0.5	0.5	0.5
SSW	0	0	0	0.5	1.0	1.0	0.9
S	0	0	0	0.5	1.0	1.0	0.9
SSE	0	0	0	0.5	0.9	0.9	1.0

Table 21.4   Rain Fall = {Torrential, Very Heavy, Heavy, Moderate, Normal, Medium, Low, Very Low}

			Rainfall			
Torrential	1.0	0.9	0.9	0.85	0.75	0.75	0.75	0
Very Heavy	0.9	1.0	0.95	0.85	0.75	0.75	0.75	0
Heavy	0.9	0.95	1.0	0.85	0.75	0.75	0.75	0
Moderate	0.85	0.85	0.85	1.0	0.75	0.75	0.75	0
Normal	0.75	0.75	0.75	0.75	1.0	0.8	0.8	0
Medium	0.75	0.75	0.75	0.75	0.8	1.0	0.85	0
Low	0.75	0.75	0.75	0.75	0.8	0.85	1.0	0
Very Low	0	0	0	0	0	0	0	1.0

Table 21.5   Temperature = {Arctic, Frigid, Very Low, Low, Moderate, Normal, Mild}

			Temperature			
Arctic	1.0	0.81	0.81	0.75	0.75	0.75	0.25
Frigid	0.81	1.0	0.9	0.75	0.75	0.75	0.25
Very Low	0.81	1.0	1.0	0.75	0.75	0.75	0.25
Low	0.75	0.75	0.75	1.0	0.75	0.75	0.25
Moderate	0.75	0.75	0.75	0.75	1.0	0.75	0.25
Normal	0.75	0.75	0.75	0.75	0.75	1.0	0.25
Mild	0.25	0.25	0.25	0.25	0.25	0.25	1.0

The North Atlantic region has very dynamic oceanographic features, such as the Gulf Stream, which is a rapidly varying warm water current flow from the Gulf of Mexico. It flows north and north-eastward across the North Atlantic, and in the area of interest it can be over 100 km. in width. Its boundaries may be detected as edges in remote-sensed infrared images due to temperature gradients as the stream is much warmer than surrounding waters. The Gulf Stream has large meanders from its mean position. In a large southward meander, a loop may pinch off and surround a mass of cold water, which then separates as a large eddy called a cold core ring. Similar northward meanders surround warm water and form warm core rings. These features range from 50–300 km. in diameter and persist for several weeks. Their motion and characteristics can impact fishing, ocean acoustics and many other diverse interests.

21.3. Modelling Uncertainty in Class Hierarchies

We assume the following notation:

$Attr(C) = \{a_1, a_2, \ldots, a_n\}$, are the attributes of class C, and

$SClass(C) = \{C_1, C_2, \ldots, C_n\}$, are the superclasses of class C.

21.3.1. Object-Class Relationships

We first formulate the membership of an object o_j in class C with attributes $Attr(C)$. Based on the considerations of relevance and ranges of attribute values outlined in the previous section, the membership of object o_j in C is defined as:

$$\mu_C(o_j) = \mathbf{g}[\mathbf{f}(RLV(a_i, C), INC(rng_C(a_i)/o_j(a_i)))] \tag{1}$$

where $RLV(a_i, C)$ indicates the relevance of the attribute a_i to the concept C, and $INC(rng_C(a_i)/o_j(a_i))$ denotes the degree of inclusion of the attribute values of o_j in the formal range of a_i in the class C.

The degree of inclusion determines the extent of similarity between a value (or a set of values) in the denominator with the value in the numerator (or a set of values). The function $\mathbf{f}$ represents the aggregation over the $\mathbf{n}$ attributes in the class and $\mathbf{g}$ reflects the nature of the semantic link existing between an instance(object) and a class/superclass. The value of $RLV(a_i, C)$ may be supplied by the user or computed in a manner similar to that in [9]. We consider several cases for the evaluation of $INC(rng(a_i)/o_j(a_i))$.

Example: For the class Cold_Core_Ring (abbreviated CCR) discussed previously, assume the following attribute ranges:

$rng_{CCR}(curvature) = \{very\_high\}$

$rng_{CCR}(temperature) = \{frigid, very\_low, low\}$

$rng_{CCR}(radius) = 10\text{–}50$ miles

$rng_CCR(season) = \{winter\}$

$rng_CCR(rainfall) = \{heavy, very\_heavy\}$

$rng_CCR(location) = \{S\}$

CASE I:

1. $o_j(a_i) \subseteq rng(a_i) : INC = 1$

   If $o(temperature) = \{frigid, very\_low\}$. Since $o(temperature) \subseteq rng_{CCR}(temperature)$

   $INC(rng_{CCR}(temperature)/o(temperature)) = 1$

2. trivial case where $o_j(a_i) = \phi : INC = 0$

   If $o(temperature) = \{\}$, i.e., a null value, (perhaps indicating unknown)

   $INC(rng_{CCR}(temperature)/o(temperature)) = 0$

CASE II:

If the cardinality of the attribute value, $card(o_j(a_i)) = 1$ and $o_j(a_i) \notin rng_C(a_i))$, then we base the value on the most similar element in the range of a_i for this class:

$$INC = Max(s(x, y)) \text{ where } x \in o_j(a_i) \text{ and } y \in rng_C(a_i)$$

If $o(temperature) = \{arctic\}$, that is, a singleton value:

$$INC(rng_{CCR}(temperature)/o(temperature)) = Max[s(x', arctic')] = 0.81$$

$$\text{where } x \in rng_C CR(temperature)$$

CASE III:

If $card(o_j(a_i)) > 1$ and $o_j(a_i) \nsubseteq rng_C(a_i)$, then three different interpretations are possible on $o_j(a_i)$. This is consonant with the different semantics that arise in databases when an object attribute takes more than one value. The attribute values may be connected through AND, XOR or inclusive OR semantics [3, 19]. The value for inclusion, INC, is now dependent on the attribute semantics.

TYPE I (AND semantics): Under AND semantics, an attribute takes more than one value, and all values exist simultaneously (are true). The Nest operation results in data with AND semantics.

Cohesion (**Coh**) indicates the minimum level of similarity between the elements of the object attribute value, $INC(rng_C(a_i)/o_j(a_i)) = Min[Max(s(x,y)), Coh(o_j(a_i))]$, where $x, z \in o_j(a_i)$, and $y \in rng_C(a_i)$.

Coh$(o_j(a_i))$, that is, $Min(s(x,z))$, puts an upper bound on the inclusion of $o_j(a_i)$ in $rng_C(a_i)$. In other words, whatever the similarity between the elements of the attribute value and the range, the degree of inclusion cannot exceed the degree of cohesion or similarity existing between the elements of the object attribute value itself.

TYPE II (OR semantics): With OR semantics an attribute takes more than one value, all or some of which may exist simultaneously (are true). When attribute values are linked through OR semantics, there is less certainty about the data values in comparison with AND semantics. OR semantics may be exclusive OR inclusive OR, with different interpretations.

1. Type IIa (Exclusive OR semantics): Exclusive OR semantics dictate that exactly one of the object attribute values is true.

   $$INC(rng_C(a_i)/o_j(a_i)) = Max(s(x,z)) \text{ where } x \in o_j(a_i), z \in rng_C(a_i)$$

   In this case, we take an optimistic view of the inclusion of the individual attribute values in the range and assign the value to be the maximum of the similarities that exist between the elements of the range.

2. Type IIb (Inclusive OR Semantics): Assume an object attribute has two values say, a and b. Under inclusive OR interpretation, the possible situations for this attribute's value may be $\{a\}$, $\{b\}$, or $\{a, b\}$. So here we find the value of INC to be:

$INC(rng_C(a_i)/o_j(a_i)) = Max[Max(s(x, y)), Min[Max(s(x, y)), Thresh(o_j(a_i))]],$

where $x \in o_j(a_i)$ and $y \in rng_C(a_i)$.

Note, however that the inclusion of object value attributes with XOR or inclusive OR are nonetheless identical when evaluated in this approach.

Assume $o(temperature) = \{moderate, low\}, x \in o(temperature)$ and $y \in rng_{CCR}(temperature)$:

1. OR Semantics(XOR or Inclusive OR):

   $INC(rng_{CCR}(temperature)/o(temperature)) = Max[s(x, y)] =$
   $Max[0.75, 0.75, 1.0, 0.75, 0.75, 0.75] = 1.0$

2. AND Semantics:

   Threshold$(o(temperature)) = 0.75$. Therefore $INC(rng_{CCR}(temperature)/o(temperature)) = Min[0.75, Max[0.75, 0.75, 1.0, 0.75, 0.75, 0.75]] = 0.75$

We can now compute the membership of an object in the class Cold_Core_Ring. Assume the following object attribute instantiations:

o(curvature) = {high}

o(temperature) = {moderate, low}

o(radius) = {25}

o(season) = {winter}

o(rainfall) = {heavy}

o(location) = {SSW, SSE}

and the following relevance rules hold:

RLV(curvature,CCR) = 2.5

RLV(temperature,CCR) = 0.25

RLV(radius,CCR) = 0

RLV(season,CCR) = 0.5

RLV(rainfall,CCR) = 0.5

RLV(location,CCR) = 2.0

RLV_{Max} in this case is 2.5. Note that we follow the convention that if X very much determines Y, then RLV(X,Y) = 2.0 and if X more-or-less determines Y, RLV(X,Y) = 0.5 and so on. We use the max function for g and assume $f(a,b) = b * (a/RLV_{Max})$ i.e., normalizing the relevances [9]. Hence computing the membership of o in the class Cold_Core_Ring,

$$\mu_{CCR}(o) = Max(0.85 * 1, 0.75 * .1, 1 * 0, 1 * .2, 1 * .2, .9 * .8) = 0.85$$

As previously, the membership of a class in its superclass has to account for the semantics of the attributes contributing to the class concept, the degree of inclusion of the attribute ranges of the class in the superclass and the conceptual distance between a class and its superclass. A similar approach can be taken with class-superclass relations [10].

21.4. A Fuzzy Class Schema

The generalization of equality to similarity has important consequences for the data model and its permitted operations. In this section we formally define the data model and describe the effects of this generalization on database operations. A primitive operation of the model, the merge is defined, and it is shown that merge preserves the desired database property of non-redundancy. The results from Section 4 will be utilized in describing Fuzzy Class Schema, and the assumption made is that all membership values are thus derived.

We assume the following notation

$D_1, D_2, \ldots, D_n$ are a finite set of domains.

$dom(a_i)$ is the domain of attribute a_i.

$val(a_i)$ is the value of attribute a_i.

Definition [Domains]:

1. a_i is a simple (atomic) attribute if $dom(a_i) = D_i$, $val(a_i) \in D_i$, and $card(val(a_i)) = 1$.

2. a_i is a simple set attribute if $dom(a_i) = 2^{D_i}$ where 2^{D_i} represents the power set of D_i excluding the null set, and $val(a_i) \in 2^{D_i}$.

3. a_i is a composite tuple attribute if $a_i = \{a_{i+1}, a_{i+2}, \ldots, a_j, \ldots, a_n\}$, where a_j is a composite tuple or a simple attribute and $dom(a_i) = dom(a_{i+1}) \times dom(a_{i+2}) \times \ldots \times dom(a_j) \times \ldots \times dom(a_n)$

4. a_i is a composite set attribute if $dom(a_i) = 2^{dom(a_j)}$ where a_j is a composite tuple attribute.

Definition [Class]: A class, C_i, is defined as a set of attributes, $\{a_1, a_2, \ldots, a_j, \ldots, a_n\}$ where a_j may be a simple atomic, simple set, composite tuple or composite set attribute. A composite tuple attribute is identical with the root of a class-composition hierarchy. The extension of C_i, $ext(C_i)$ is the set of objects that populate the class, that is, the data, and $o(a_i)$ represents the value of attribute a_i of object, o, where $o \in ext(C)$.

Definition [Range Similar]: If $o(a_i) \not\subseteq rng_{C_i}(a_i)$, where a_i is an attribute of C_i (or o). $o(a_i)$ can be said to be range similar to $rng(a_i)$, denoted by $o(a_i) \sim_s rng_{C_i}(a_i)$. At the limit, when $INC(rng_{C_i}(a_i)/o(a_i)) = 1$, range similarity is the subset relation. For composite tuple and composite set valued objects range similarity is a vector.

Definition [Imprecise Object]: o is a fuzzy object in C_i if $(\forall j)o(a_j) \sim_s rng_{C_i}(a_j)$ and $\mu_{C_i}(o)$ takes values in the range $[0,1]$. By this definition, only objects that have the same structure as its class may be imprecise objects; in other words, an object in the hierarchical tree is permitted to be an imprecise object only in its classes and superclasses (thus disallowing arbitrary objects from being imprecise members of arbitrary classes). Structure thus is the defining character of the imprecise object.

Definition [Similarity Threshold]: Assume a_j is a noncomposite attribute of the class, C_i. By definition of the fuzzy object $o(a_j) \sim_s rng_{C_i}(a_j)$. The threshold of a_j is defined to be $Thresh(a_j) = min_{(\forall o)}(Coh(o(a_j)))$. The threshold denotes the minimum similarity between the values of a class attribute. If the attribute domain is crisp, or values are atomic, then threshold = 1. As the threshold value approaches zero, larger chunks of information group together and the information conveyed about that attribute of the class decreases.

The threshold value of a composite attribute is undefined. A composite domain is constituted (at some level) by simple domains each of which has a threshold; that is, the threshold for a composite object is a vector composed of the thresholds of simple domains.

We now define the merge, which is a primitive operator. A level value, for an attribute given a priori, L_j, determines which objects may be combined through the set union of the respective values. Note that the level value may be specified via the query language with the constraint that it never exceed the threshold value.

Definition [Merge]: Assume objects, o, and o', belonging to a class, C_i with degrees of membership, $\mu_{C_i}(o)$ and $\mu_{C_i}(o')$ respectively (since the discussion is at object level, identities are used for object attribute values). The objects may be represented most generally as:

$$o = (i, \langle\, a_k : i_k, a_{k+1} : i_{k+1}, \ldots, a_j : i_j, \ldots, a_m : i_m \,\rangle, \mu_{C_i}(o)), \text{ and}$$

$$o' = (i', \langle\, a_k : i'_k, a_{k+1} : i'_{k+1}, \ldots, a_j : i'_j, \ldots, a_m : i'_m \,\rangle, \mu_{C_i}(o'))$$

where i and i' are the identities of o and o', i_j and i'_j, the identity of o_j and o'_j, etc. (i.e., each attribute value is an object itself). If $\forall j : j = 1, 2, \ldots, m$; a_j is noncomposite, L_j is the level value for the attribute a_j and $x \in o(a_j)$ and $y \in o'(a_j)$ so that $min_{\forall x, \forall y}[s(x, y)] \geq L_j$ and $L_j \leq Thresh(a_j)$, then

$$\textbf{Merge}(o, o') = o'' = (i'', \langle\, a_k : i''_k, a_{k+1} : i''_{k+1}, \ldots, a_j : i''_j, \ldots, a_m : i''_m \,\rangle, \mu_{C_i}(o'')),$$

where $o''_j = (i''_j, \{i_j, i'_j\})$ (i.e., two existing objects are used to create a new object, with a new identity) $\mu_{C_i}(o'')$ is the membership of o'' in class, C_i.

Note that the membership of the new object o'' in class, C_i is computed as described in the previous section. The semantics of this operation is OR. Merge combines two objects provided the similarity between every attribute value in each of the objects is greater than some arbitrary level value set by the user. As in the case for threshold, the definition can be extended to composite objects.

A sample query would be of the form:

Query: Retrieve the coordinates of "Cold_Core_Rings" in the "North_Atlantic_Basic" characterized by "frigid" temperatures and "moderate" rainfall.

Translated to SQL-like code:

SELECT	CCR_Latitude, CCR_Longitude
FROM	CCR: $\mu_{CCR} \geq 0.8$
WHERE	CCR.Temperature = "Frigid" and CCR.Rainfall = "Moderate":
LEVEL	CCR.Temperature ≥ 0.9 and CCR.Rainfall ≥ 0.85

Note that the retrieval involves membership values of the objects in the class and the fuzzy attribute values. This query would ensure for instance that all the objects retrieved are members of the class Cold_Core_Ring and have temperatures that were "frigid" to the level of 0.9; that is, they could be any temperature in the set {arctic, frigid, very_low} and with rainfall in the set {torrential, very_heavy, heavy, moderate}.

21.5. Conclusion

Uncertainty arises in a variety of ways—from the data values themselves, the semantics of the data, and the type of hierarchy being modelled. At the data level, fuzziness arises from multivalued attributes, which may be connected through Boolean functions such as AND, OR, and XOR. Attribute semantics and fuzzy data combine to produce uncertainty at object levels. All these aspects were accommodated in the data model defined. Fuzziness in data values has an effect on redundancy in databases, and it was shown that no two objects in the data model have the same interpretation. We are currently investigating a query algebra for the data model. The effect of set operation on fuzzy classes and the consequences of multiple inheritance on the data model also needs to be studied.

A powerful knowledge representation methodology is facilitated in databases through this approach. Using classic knowledge representation considerations such normality, typicality, atypicality, and so on, it is possible to constrain the attribute value ranges between the two classes, with correspondingly different class-subclass memberships. A point also needs to be made about implementation issues. Changes in similarity or relevance values can be considered to be schema changes, to be executed with care. Insertion and modification can be constrained to invoke methods that compute object membership. Since only queries that query fuzzy attributes or objects need utilize these values, the average cost of evaluation would then be only slightly higher than a nonfuzzy database.

21.6. References

[1] Ankebrandt, C., et al. "Scene Recognition using Genetic Algorithms with Semantic Nets." *Pattern Recognition Letters,* Vol. 11 (1990), pp. 285–293.

[2] Bertino, E., and L. Martino. "Object-Oriented Database Management Systems: Concepts and Issues." *IEEE Computer* (1991), pp. 65–81.

[3] Buckles, B.P., and F.E. Petry. "A Fuzzy Representation of Data for Relational Databases." *Fuzzy Sets and Systems,* Vol. 7 (1982), pp. 213–226.

[4] ———. "Uncertainty Models in Information and Database Systems." *Journal of Information Science: Principles and Practice,* Vol. 11 (1985), pp. 77–87.

[5] Buckles, B.P., et al. "Ocean Feature Recognition using Genetic Algorithms with Fuzzy Fitness Functions (GA/F3)." *Proceedings, NAFIPS '90* (1990), pp. 394–397.

[6] Brachman, R.J. "What IS-A Is and Isn't: An Analysis of Taxonomic Links in Semantic Networks." *IEEE Computer,* Vol. 16 (1983), pp. 30–37.

[7] Cattell, R.G.G. *Object Data Management.* Reading, MA Addison-Wesley, 1991.

[8] Dubois, D., et al. "Vagueness, Typicality and Uncertainty in Class Hierarchies." *International Journal of Intelligent Systems,* Vol. 6 (1991), pp. 167–183.

[9] Dutta, S. "Approximate Reasoning by Analogy to Answer Null Queries." *International Journal of Approximate Reasoning,* Vol. 5 (1991), pp. 373–398.

[10] George, R., et al. "Modeling Class Hierarchies in the Fuzzy Object-Oriented Data Model." *International Journal of Fuzzy Sets and Systems,* Vol. 60 (1993), pp. 259–272.

[11] ———. "Integrating Artificial Intelligence and Database Systems." *Proceedings, IJCAI '91 Workshop on Integrating Artificial Intelligence and Database Systems.* pp. 77–84. 1991.

[12] George, R., et al. "Uncertainty Modeling in Object-Oriented Geographical Information Systems." *Proceedings, Conference on Database and Expert System Applications (DEXA).* 1992.

[13] Lakoff, G. *Women, Fire, and Dangerous Things.* Chicago: University of Chicago Press, 1987.

[14] Kim, W. "A Model of Queries for Object-Oriented Database Systems." *Proceedings, International Conference on Very Large Databases (VLDB).* 1989.

[15] Motoro, A. "Accommodating Imprecision in Database Systems: Issues and Solutions (SIGMOD RECORD 19)." pp. 15–23. 1990.

[16] Orenstein, J., and F.A. Manola. "PROBE Spatial Data Modeling and Query Processing in Image Database Applications." *IEEE Transactions on Software Engineering,* Vol. 4, No. 5 (1988).

[17] Rundensteiner, E., and W. Bandler. "The Equivalence of Knowledge Representation Schemata: Semantic Networks and Fuzzy Relational Products." *Proceedings, NAFIPS Conference.* pp. 477–501. 1986.

[18] Rundensteiner, E., and B. Lubomir. "Set Operations in Object-based Data Models." *IEEE Transactions on Knowledge and Data Engineering. 1992.*

[19] Schek, H.J, and M.H. Scholl. "The Relational Model with Relation-valued Attributes." *Information Systems,* Vol. 11 (1986), pp. 103–115.

[20] Torasso, P., and L. Console. "Approximate Reasoning and Prototypical Knowledge." *International Journal of Approximate Reasoning,* Vol. 3 (1989), pp. 157–177.

[21] Zicari, R. "Incomplete Information in Object-Oriented Databases." *SIGMOD RECORD,* Vol. 19 (1990), pp. 33–40.

[22] Zemenkova, M., and A. Kandel. "Implementing Imprecision in Information Systems." *Information Sciences,* Vol. 37 (1985), pp. 107–141.

Retrieving Information

PART 2
Reasoning

GUIDING NOTE

Automated reasoning allows implicit information contained in a knowledge base to be retrieved via inference. As distinct from the previous part, the retrieval process here is not simply a matter of matching a query against stored items, but information is produced by combining several pieces of information, so as to uncover conclusions that were only implicitly present. Fuzzy sets have been used in most kinds of knowledge representation structures: rules, frames, belief networks, classical logic, sequent systems, as shown by the contributions in this part.

The most popular representation tool for fuzzy knowledge is the fuzzy rule, which originally was devised to represent the way human operators control complex processes. The first application was to partially automatize the control of cement kilns, done in the late seventies by Danish researchers. Fuzzy rules have the merit of both being linguistically expressible and lending themselves to numerical calculations for interpolation purposes. The paper by Holmblad and Østergaard testifies that fuzzy rules have been useful for implementing human knowledge in an industrial setting. Since then, many other applications of fuzzy rule-based systems have been devised, and there are books specifically dedicated to this subfield. What the FLS experience suggests, though, is that the overall architecture of the fuzzy expert system is much more complex than just a bunch of fuzzy rules, since often several objectives must be satisfied, requiring some priority management; furthermore, the dynamic aspects of these systems turns out to be very important, hence requiring a timing calculation for appropriately triggering control actions.

At the same time as the emergence of fuzzy rule-based control, another artificial intelligence tool started being successful—the expert systems. Pioneering expert systems were the MYCIN system in medicine and PROSPECTOR in geology. These systems did not use fuzzy rules but crisp rules with certainty factors attached to them. There has been a lot of debate as to the meaning of certainty factors, some claiming that they were degrees of probability, others strongly disagreeing with this interpretation. It also became very natural to try to use fuzzy set operations to combine certainty factors. MILORD is one of the most comprehensive expert systems based on putting together ideas from the MYCIN tradition and fuzzy sets. It not only uses fuzzy set operations for uncertainty propagation, but considers the fact that certainty factors are more qualitative than quantitative. The MILORD proposal is to model certainty factors as fuzzy numbers, and use fuzzy arithmetic plus linguistic approximation to devise symbolic uncertainty combination tables. MILORD thus computes with words.

The early generation of expert systems suffered from a systematic truth-functionality assumption, which is not valid in general, and limits the type of knowledge to be processed (no cycles, tree structures, etc.). The new generation has seen a blossoming of other type of systems. First, when knowledge is hierarchical, it is natural to implement it in a semantic network form using classes, subclasses, and instances. The use of fuzzy sets in inheritance networks is discussed by Yager who tries to handle the presence of exceptional subclasses or instances by means of nonmonotonic fuzzy set operations. These fuzzy set operations combine the information specific to a class with information stemming from its father-class, the former having priority over the latter if they contradict each other.

As Bayesian nets have repaired the theoretical flaws of early probabilistic expert systems, possibilistic graphical models may become the rigorous approach to fuzzy expert systems. Since the main difficulty is to properly combine local pieces of knowledge, a natural idea is to start with a rigorous representation of a knowledge base as a joint possibility distribution on a space of attributes. Then conditions are defined under which this joint possibility distribution can be split into smaller components without losing information. These conditions represent conditional independence assumptions. The paper by Gebhardt and Kruse describe the theoretical foundation of possibilistic networks whose origin is basically Zadeh's calculus of fuzzy restrictions presented 25 years ago. These results have been exploited in the software POSSINFER that has been used for data fusion by the German aerospace industry.

Possibility theory is a very flexible uncertainty framework because it lends itself to representation in many frameworks such as belief nets as well as logical settings. It is far easier to develop possibilistic extensions of logic than probabilistic logic. On this basis, a logic-based tool such as the ATMS (Assumption-Based Truth-Maintenance System) devoted to the management of hypotheses has been generalized to uncertain pieces of knowledge. It enables groups of hypotheses that form explanations, diagnoses, or that lead to extracting maximal consistent subbases, to be ranked in terms of plausibility. Benferhat, Chehire, and Monai propose an application of the possibilistic ATMS to a problem of determination of the most plausible scenario that fits a set of observations in the military setting.

Possibility theory has also been used in causal diagnosis problems when it is relevant to distinguish between symptoms that are certainly produced by a disease from symptoms that are only possibly produced by it. It gives rise to a rather simple relational model, which differs from the other fuzzy relational models of diagnosis, because it copes with incomplete knowledge and handles uncertainty in a very qualitative way. On the contrary, older fuzzy relational methods model intensity of presence of symptoms rather than uncertainty. The possibilistic relational diagnosis method has been successfully applied to a problem of satellite fault analysis, both through the exploitation of incomplete fault trees, and for networks of components. In the latter case reported by Cayrac, Dubois, and Prade each component is described via a relational model pervaded with uncertainty. This component model is simple enough to be used in practice, and realistic enough to be useful.

Fuzzy sets are flexible enough to be associated to many automated reasoning tools in order to enhance their expressive power for the qualitative handling of uncertainty and preference. This is due to the various existing semantics of fuzzy sets. An example of preference handling in a formal sequent-based deductive system described by Corrêa da Silva and Kon. It is a very original application to music analysis, based on Lambek calculus. In fact, this chapter belongs to an old tradition of fuzzy logic that has not been so active in the last 15 years, dealing with fuzzy grammars. The chapter on musical analysis may be the forerunner of a revival of this trend.

22 The Progression of the First Fuzzy Logic Control Application

L.P. Holmblad, J.J. Østergaard
FLS Automation A/S, 2500 Valby Copenhagen, Denmark.

ABSTRACT: This chapter will survey the application of the first industrial application of fuzzy logic control. The application was developed by F.L. Smidth & Co. A/S (FLS) for control of rotary cement kilns. The presentation is given in retrospect, starting in 1974 when FLS heard about fuzzy logic for the first time. The most important milestones in our work with high-level process control are presented, with special emphasis on the role of fuzzy logic. The present status of the FLS FuzzyExpert system is outlined, and the development trend for high-level process control systems as expected by FLS Automation is discussed.

22.1. Introduction

FLS is a major supplier of cement plants and has been developing applications of fuzzy logic for controlling cement plants since 1974. Before the 1960s, the operator controlled the cement kiln by looking into its hot end, the burning zone, and by watching the smoke leaving the chimney. As shown in Figure 22.1, the operator was on a platform just behind the kiln, with a blue glass to protect his or her eyes. At that time, the blue glass was the most important aid for controlling the formation of cement clinker. The operation was 100 percent manual and very few measurements were available. In addition to the blue glass for inspection of the burning zone and the darkness of the smoke, a temperature measurement was normally available at the cold end of the kiln. Later, an oxygen analyzer was installed, thereby permitting more accurate control of the fuel/air ratio than was possible simply by observing the smoke.

Figure 22.1   Cement kiln burner platform with local control panel from the 1960s.

Central control was introduced in the cement industry in the 1960s. Temperature measurements, pressure measurements, voltage and amps indications, pen recorders, alarms, and other indicators were gathered in a central control room. PID controllers were also installed, mainly for uniform feeding of the raw material and the fuel. The operator no longer sat next to the hot, noisy, and dusty kiln, but controlled the process by looking at instruments. However, if there was uncertainty about the readings, he or she would still go to the platform and pick up the blue glass to make a visual inspection of the burning zone.

Computers for process supervision and control were introduced in the cement industry in the late 1960s. FLS, as one of the world's leading manufacturers of cement plants, accepted the challenge of computerized control of cement kiln operation from the very beginning. The cement kiln is the main machine at a cement plant, and the overall economy of cement production very much depends on the operation of the kiln. A medium-size cement kiln producing 5000 tons of cement clinker per day consumes about 20 tons of coal per hour. Economically, it is thus very attractive if even a few percent of coal can be saved and production increased a little through proper control of the kiln.

After experimental work in the 1970s, FLS in 1980 launched the first commercial computer system for automatic kiln control based on fuzzy logic. Today, nearly 200 kilns have been equipped with high-level fuzzy control by FLS. Modern control systems include comprehensive instrumentation, PLC sequence control, extensive alarm treatment, reporting functions, operator color screens, and high-level control strategies.

A modern control room is shown in Figure 22.2. But the blue glass has not disappeared. The operator may still want to look inside the kiln to check that everything is in order. However, modern control systems, including high-level fuzzy control, are of invaluable help to the operator in the safe and profitable production of cement.

This chapter presents how FLS has been working with the technology of fuzzy logic from the start in 1974 to the present version of our Fuzzy-Expert system, which is based on the FUZZY II structure.

22.2. The Start

Before we had even heard of fuzzy logic, some experiments with automatic kiln control were carried out in 1972 at a cement plant in Denmark. The most interesting aspect of these experiments is the approach that was chosen for the implementation of the kiln controller. The fuel control strategy, as shown in Figure 22.3, was programmed as a two-dimensional decision table with an error signal and the change in error as inputs. The error and the change in error were both divided into three levels, resulting in nine actions on the fuel. Today, many fuzzy controllers are implemented along exactly the same lines, except that control actions and input conditions are expressed in terms of fuzzy membership functions, as illustrated in Figure 22.4.

The idea of implementing a control strategy as a decision table, which basically is a rough description of the manual control scheme, was thus born before we learned of the theory of fuzzy logic.

Figure 22.2   Central control room at a modern cement plant.

E	–	+1	+2	+3
	0	-1	0	+1
	+	-3	-2	-1

▲	+	0	–
OIL		T	

▲   = Oil feed rate change
E   = Error on kiln drive load
T   = Trend in kiln drive load
-3/+3 = ▲ Oil units

Figure 22.3 Fuel control decision table.

The rule-based approach that underlies the decision tables was also inspired by the instructions we found in a textbook for kiln operators, which contained the control rules for manual operation of a cement kiln shown in Figure 22.5.

The first time we heard about fuzzy logic was at the The IFAC/IFIP International Conference on Digital Computer Applications to Process Control, held in Zürich, Switzerland, in 1974. As a postscript to a paper on learning controllers [1], fuzzy logic was proposed as an alternative approach to human-like controllers. The last remark of the concluding section says:

> "Greater dividends can be expected however if information is processed in a higher-level framework of conceptional representation. The potentiality of this approach has been demonstrated by successful implementation of the fuzzy logic controller and further research in this area is strongly recommended."

It was immediately clear to us that we had come upon a theoretical basis for our early attempts to achieve automatic kiln control. The recommendation was accepted and FLS started to investigate the feasibility of fuzzy logic control in cooperation with The Technical University of Denmark.

22.3. The First Experiments

Before applying the theory of fuzzy logic to control of a cement kiln, we wanted to investigate the theory under circumstances where experiments

Position deviation \ Velocity deviation	Negative	Zero	Positive
Negative	Negative Big	Negative Small	Zero
Zero	Negative Small	Zero	Positive Small
Positive	Zero	Positive Small	Positive Big

Figure 22.4 A fuzzy logic decision table.

Case	Condition	Action to be taken	Reason
10	BZ OK	a. Increase I.D. fan speed	To raise back-end temperature and increase oxygen percentage for action 'b'
	OX low		
	BE low	b. Increase fuel rate	To maintain burning zone temperature
11	BZ OK	a. Decrease fuel rate slightly	To raise percentage of oxygen
	OX low		
	BE OK		
12	BZ OK	a. Reduce fuel rate	To increase percentage of oxygen for action 'b'
	OX low	b. Reduce I.D. fan speed	To lower back-end temperature and maintain burning zone temperature
	BE high		
13	BZ OK	a. Increase I.D. fan speed	To raise back-end temperature
	OX OK	b. Increase fuel rate	To maintain burning zone temperature
	BE low		
14	BZ OK	NONE. However, do not get overconfident, and keep all conditions under close observation.	
	OX OK		
	BE OK		
15	BZ OK	When oxygen is in upper part of range	
	OX OK	a. Reduce I.D. fan speed	To reduce back-end temperature
	BE high	When oxygen is in lower part of range	
		b. Reduce fuel rate	To raise oxygen percentage for action 'c'
		c. Reduce I.D. fan speed	To lower back-end temperature and maintain burning zone temperature
16	BZ OK	a. Increase I.D. fan speed	To raise back-end temperature
	OX high	b. Increase fuel rate	To maintain burning zone temperature and reduce percentage of oxygen
	BE low		
17	BZ OK	a. Reduce I.D. fan speed slightly	To lower percentage of oxygen
	OX high		
	BE OK		

Figure 22.5 Extract from Peray's textbook for kiln operators.

were possible. The experiments allowed in a working cement kiln are very limited. Experimental work was therefore carried out at The Technical University of Denmark. The theoretical understanding and inspiration in relation to process control were gained mainly from papers written by Zadeh and Mamdani [6, 2], and control experiments were performed in laboratory-scale processes such as a small heat exchanger [4].

The first experiments using a real cement kiln were carried out at the beginning of 1978 at a Danish cement plant, using the control rules for manual operation shown in [5]. The ambition of the original control strategy was relatively low. We wanted to start with a strategy that was clear, easy to discuss, and likely to work—at least when the kiln was in stable operation near the desired operating point. The idea was to develop a control system that could keep the kiln cruising at a given production level, like the autopilot for an airplane.

During the experiments, which lasted for about three months, it was possible to change the strategy by modifying the existing rules or by adding new control rules. Modifications had to be made by the computer expert on the basis of advice and criticism from the burner specialist.

At this stage of the development work, the attitude of the management in FLS toward the new kiln control attempts was sceptical, both because of the earlier failures of others who had attempted computerized kiln control, but perhaps also to some extent because of the strange name "fuzzy." Other names were suggested like "verbal controllers," "pragmatic controllers," and "rule-based controllers," but eventually, with an increasing understanding by the management of the concept, it was decided to stay with the word fuzzy, a decision that has never been regretted since.

22.4. Fuzzy Control Language

The first two industrial installations of fuzzy controllers occurred toward the end of 1979. One system was installed at the Danish cement plant where the first experiments had been carried out; the second system was supplied to a Swedish paper mill for control of a rotary kiln for reburning of lime.

The programming technique was based on a block-oriented approach. Control rules were programmed by interrelating calculation blocks evaluating the terms LOW, OK, HIGH, AND, OR, and so on, as shown in the example in Figure 22.6. But the possibilities were very limited for adding conventional logic schemes and normal calculations to supplement the fuzzy control rules. It soon became obvious that the block representation of the strategy was inflexible and lost its comprehensibility as more rules and parameters were added.

To address these problems, we developed the programming language FCL (an abbreviation of fuzzy control language). The first version of an FCL-based fuzzy controller was installed at the cement plant in Denmark in 1981. To some extent, FCL is similar to Fortran and Basic, but it is also different as it includes evaluation of fuzzy control rules of the form:

IF ⟨condition⟩ THEN ⟨control actions⟩

where the ⟨condition⟩ and the ⟨control actions⟩ are expressed as fuzzy membership functions.

Using FCL for programming of the control rules in Figure 22.6 results in the following two program lines, which are easier and more direct to understand than the block diagram:

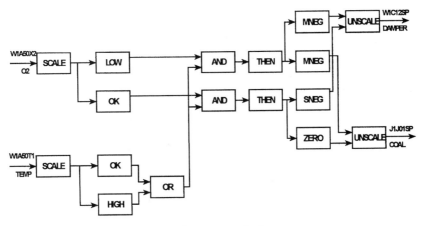

Figure 22.6 Block representation of fuzzy control rules.

IF LOW(O2) AND (OK(TEMP) or HIGH(TEMP)) THEN
                                                MNEG(DAMPER),MNEG(COAL)

IF OK(O2) AND (OK(TEMP) OR HIGH(TEMP)) THEN
                                                SNEG(DAMPER),ZERO(COAL)

where MNEG and SNEG are abbreviations for medium negative and small negative, respectively.

In general, a cement kiln is a process involving rather long time constants. From the point of view of automatic control, this is normally a complication; on the other hand, you do not face the demand for very fast execution of control programs. On this basis, the first version of FCL was based on an interpreter translation of the program lines at each execution. Typically, a control strategy consisted of 200–500 program lines, and the minimum time interval between execution of programs was one minute.

However, as applications developed, the execution time did become a problem. The control strategy increased in complexity through the inclusion of additional process parameters to obtain better and more accurate control performance, more than one kiln was controlled by one computer, and faster-responding processes were also being controlled by the fuzzy. It was therefore found necessary to modify FCL to include a compiler, so that programs to be executed appear in a directly executable form. This second, much faster version of FCL was launched in 1984, and today the minimum time interval between execution of thousands of program lines is one second.

This, of course, still puts a limit on the extent to which fast-responding processes can be controlled by our fuzzy system. We are, however, not considering that issue because our main application remains implementation of control strategies on the human operator level, rather than underlying basic controllers.

350   FUZZY INFORMATION ENGINEERING

22.5. The Second Generation

The mid-1980s were very busy, with production and installation of fuzzy systems at cement kilns all over the world. It was a very exciting period, too, with growth and a lot of encouraging and successful projects, resulting in increasingly advanced and complicated control strategies. Problems, however, started to emerge like small clouds coming over the horizon, as it turned out that some of our fuzzy systems were not performing satisfactorily after a period of time. Although they were claimed to be easy to comprehend and adapt because of their inherent pragmatic and human modelling approach, it was found in practice that the control strategies became rather complex and not always easy for plant engineers to maintain.

Against this background, development work for the second generation of our fuzzy system was initiated in 1988, with the main design objectives focusing on user maintainability. The new fuzzy system was launched in early 1990 under the name of FUZZY II. The objectives relating to comprehensibility and maintainability have been met through a simple and well-defined structure for implementation of high-level control strategies. For an operator, control of the process consists in achieving various goals, which are more or less precisely defined: maximum output, minimum consumption of raw materials and energy, high product quality, safe process operation, and so on.

Different processes have different control objectives but, in general, good process control may be defined through a list of control objectives that should be fulfilled as much as possible. The concept of control objectives is a key element in the structure of a FUZZY II control strategy. For a cement kiln, typical control objectives are:

- stable operation,
- good cement clinker quality,
- complete combustion,
- low fuel consumption.

As control objectives are frequently in conflict, coordination means approaching optimal conditions in succession of importance. Priorities, in other words, have to be assigned to the various control objectives, specifying which objectives are considered the most important to fulfill.

Control objectives with different priorities are thus among the basic elements of a FUZZY II high-level control strategy.

22.6. The FUZZY II Structure

The elements of a FUZZY II process control strategy are the following:

State indices   Calculations concerning the actual
                         process condition.

Control groups	Arrangements of the overall control strategy into groups of control objectives.
Priority management	Determines the extent to which the control actions to fulfill the individual objectives should be executed.
Control objectives	Specifications of the goals of the fuzzy control strategy.

Normally, a state index combines various measurements into a single figure. The degree of process stability, the product quality, the production level, and so on, are all typical examples of state indices for a kiln control strategy. The state indices are important to the structure of a FUZZY II control strategy, as they form the basis for dividing the overall strategy into control groups which can be treated independently. The state indices are used to coordinate control actions from the various control groups. Figure 22.7 shows a diagram of the control strategy structure for which the FUZZY II system has been prepared.

Design of a control strategy consists in filling in the structure with specific state index calculations, control groups, and control objectives, whereas the priority management system is a fixed module in the system. For a new process, it is perhaps not so clear which are the most appropriate indices and control groups. This is not a major problem, however, as the structure facilitates a stepwise implementation of control objectives and index calculations concurrent with more and more process control knowledge being available.

Every control objective is implemented as what is known as an objective module, made up of the following four basic elements:

- deviation calculation
- rule block
- output program
- timing calculation

Figure 22.8 shows the objective module diagram, which is used for implementation of all types of control objectives.

22.6.1. Deviation Calculation

The deviation calculation evaluates the degree to which the objective is fulfilled. Normally, the calculation results in a "fuzzy value" between −1 and +1, which expresses how far the actual process situation is from fulfilment of the objective.

22.6.2. Rule Block

The rule block holds the set of control rules for fulfillment of the specific objective. Normally, the rule block is formulated as a set of fuzzy control

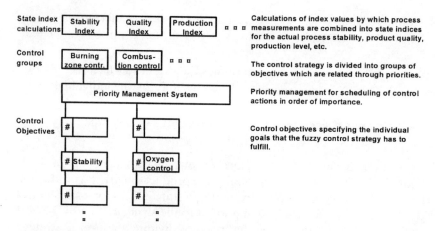

Figure 22.7   FUZZY II control strategy structure.

rules using FCL, but other techniques may also be used, like PID, neural nets, mathematical models, and so on.

22.6.3. Priority Management

The rule block for each control objective results in control actions that are multiplied by a weight factor between 0 and 1. The smaller the weight factor, the more the control actions are suppressed. The weight factor for a given objective is a function of the deviation values for the higher priority objectives, which ensures that control actions to fulfill a given objective are reduced if higher-priority objectives are not fulfilled.

22.6.4. Output Program

The output program evaluates process constraints and selects among alternative control actions based upon the actual index values. The logic for selecting alternative adjustments may be fuzzy or nonfuzzy depending on whether a gradual or an either/or switch is the most appropriate.

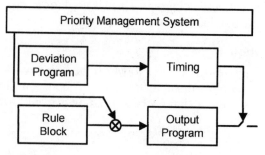

Figure 22.8   Control objective module diagram.

In most cases, the fuzzy logic approach gives the best control performance, simply because no process operates with sudden changes between alternative control actions.

22.6.5. Timing Calculation

The timing calculation determines when control actions are to be executed. It is just as important as the rule block for determining the proper function of the control strategy. Also, the timing calculation is normally fuzzy in the sense that the time interval between control actions changes gradually as a function of the deviation value. The larger the deviation, the more frequent the control actions.

The priority management system reflects our "fuzzy way of thinking," as it is designed to give a smooth and gradual transition between the objectives, as opposed to the nonfuzzy approach, in which only one objective at a time would be active.

Years ago, oxygen control was used to illustrate the way FLS has applied the theory of fuzzy logic to process control [5]. At that time, the purpose was to explain membership functions, the combination of rules, and the fuzzy control language. Now oxygen control will be used to illustrate the structure of a control objective module.

The *deviation calculation,* shown in Figure 22.9, consists of a transformation of the actual oxygen percentage into a deviation value (DEVI) between −1 and +1, applying the user-specified low limit, set point and high limit.

The *rule block,* shown in Figure 22.10, specifies more or less draught (DRAF) as a function of the deviation value. For instance, a negative DEVI value indicates that oxygen is too low, and the control rules specify an increase in the draught.

The weight factor W, calculated by the priority management, determines the actual degree of influence of the oxygen control objective. W is a function of the deviation values for the higher-priority objectives. The larger these higher-priority deviation values, the more the oxygen control actions will be suppressed, whereas low values of the higher-priority deviations will allow oxygen control actions to be executed.

As shown in Figure 22.11, the *timing* program calculates the time interval between control actions, applying a linear function of the absolute value of DEVI. The closer the oxygen is to either the low limit or the high limit, the more frequent the control actions.

The *output program,* shown in Figure 22.12, implements the evaluated increase or decrease of the draught by adjustment of the I.D. fan speed or the damper position, or by another action if the I.D. fan speed or damper position has reached high or low limit. The alternative actions will be decided on the basis of the actual values of the state indices.

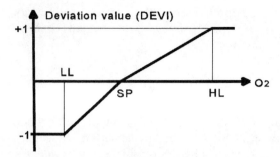

Figure 22.9   Deviation calculation.

22.7. The Next Generation

Even though an increasing trend has been registered for beneficial application of more advanced control schemes to solve SI/SO problems, our main application of the fuzzy system is still high-level MI/MO process control, which may be defined as coordination of interrelated process controllers set points, normally done by a human operator.

To a certain extent, the FuzzyExpert system acts as a human operator by taking over most of the job of controlling the process, including coordination of set points and decisions on production level. A FuzzyExpert system may thus be used to reduce the number of operators in the control room. However, an unmanned control room at a cement plant is not yet possible, nor is it a goal that one should aim for.

If the operator does not agree with the way the fuzzy system controls the process, he or she can switch off the fuzzy controller and control the process manually. If the operator judges rightly that the fuzzy controller is not producing optimal operation, then the need is simply to adjust the control strategy.

If, however, the operator does not judge the situation correctly, a conflict situation may arise between the operator and the FuzzyExpert system. The fuzzy controller is generally well accepted by the operators, but there is no doubt that the system will be even better if conflicts can be

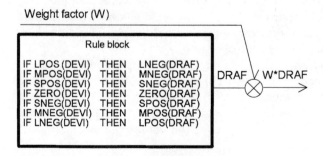

Figure 22.10   Rule block for oxygen control.

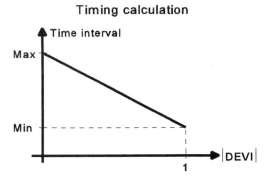

Figure 22.11   Timing calculation.

avoided and real cooperation between the system and the operator can be established.

It is even possible that the conflict is of a psychological nature. The operator may feel that the computer has been appointed to do the job better than he or she can do it. Perhaps the operator is of the opinion that the fuzzy controller has taken away the most interesting part of his or her daily work. The operator, in other words, does not always consider the fuzzy *his or her* tool for producing optimal process control but a competitor that he or she is very much inclined to switch off at the first opportunity.

The fuzzy logic development work within FLS Automation is thus focusing on: "How to get the operator back into the driver's seat."

The goal is still to approach optimal operation through automatic control of the process. But the high-level control system should be placed in the hands of the operator to enable him or her to use the system as a tool instead of the either/or operator control situation. The fuzzy control system should be able to accept and process inputs from the operator, who very often possesses useful information for the achievement of optimal operation. A control system that works with inputs from a human operator who expresses him- or herself in everyday terms is another step in the direction of applying the basic ideas of fuzzy logic control.

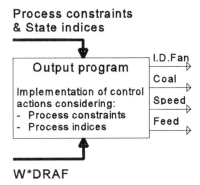

Figure 22.12   Output coordination.

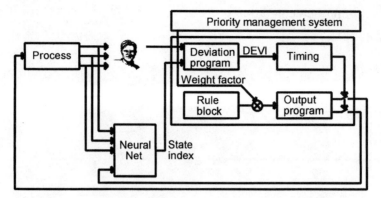

Figure 22.13   FuzzyExpert system applying operators' information.

For future high-level control systems, FLS Automation is working with integration of various control and prediction techniques. In our opinion, the optimal overall control system is most likely to be a combination of the rule-based fuzzy logic approach, neural network techniques, and model-based systems, with the possibility of operator interference. In particular, neural nets seem to be a promising technique for integrating the operator in a structured way as an active part of the automatic control system.

Figure 22.13 shows a diagram of an operator-activated control objective. The neural net has been trained to reveal key information about the actual process state, the so-called state indices in FUZZY II terminology. The operator may judge the same index variables, and a FUZZY II control objective has been defined to cope with the situation in which the neural net and the operator do not agree.

In this way, the operator has the possibility of interfering with the automatic control strategy. Operator interference is not necessary, but when he or she interferes, it is done in a well-defined way that has been decided through the definition of the special operator-activated control objective.

22.8. References

[1] Assilian, S., and E.H. Mamdani. "Learning Control Algorithms in Real Dynamic Systems." *Proceedings, IFAC/IFIP International Conference on Digital Computer Applications to Process Control.* Springer: Zurich, Berlin: 1974.

[2] Eshragh, F., and E.H. Mamdani. "A General Approach to Linguistic Approximation." *International Journal of Man-Machine Studies,* Vol. 11 (1979), pp. 501–519.

[3] Holmblad, L.P., and J.J. Ostergaard. "Control of a Cement Kiln by Fuzzy Logic." FLS Review No. 67, FLS Automation A/S, Hoffdingsvej 77, DK-2500. Valby, Copenhagen, Denmark.

[4] Ostergaard, J.J. "Fuzzy Logic Control of a Heat Exchanger Process," in *Fuzzy Automata and Decision Processes.* eds. M.M. Gupta, et al. North Holland: 1977.

[5] Peray, K.E., and J.J. Wadell. *The Rotary Cement Kiln.* New York: Chemical, 1972.

[6] Zadeh, L.A. "Outline of a New Approach to the Analysis of Complex Systems and Decision Processes." *IEEE Transactions on Systems, Man, and Cybernetics,* Vol. 1 (1973), pp. 28–44.

23 MILORD: The Architecture and the Management of Linguistically Expressed Uncertainty*

L. Godo, R. López de Mántaras, and C. Sierra
Centre d'Estudis Avançats, Consell Superior d'investigacions Científiques, 17300 Blanes, Girona, Spain

A. Verdaguer
Institut Municipal d'Investigacio Mèdica, Barcelona, Spain

ABSTRACT: The objective of this chapter is to describe the MILORD Shell and particularly its architecture and its management of uncertainty. MILORD is an expert systems building tool consisting of two inference engines and an explanation module. The system allows one to perform different calculi of uncertainty on an expert-defined set of linguistic terms expressing uncertainty. Each calculus corresponds to specific conjunction, disjunction, and implication operators. The internal representation of each linguistic uncertainty value is a fuzzy subset of the interval [0,1]. The different calculi of uncertainty applied to the set of linguistic terms give, as a result, a fuzzy subset that is approximated, by means of a linguistic approximation process, to a linguistic certainty value belonging to the set of linguistic terms. This linguistic approximation keeps the calculus of uncertainty closed. This has the advantage that, once the linguistic certainty values have been defined, the system computes, off-line, the conjunction, disjunction, and implication operations for all the pairs of linguistic uncertainty values in the term set and stores the results in matrices. Therefore, when MILORD is run, the propagation and combination of uncertainty is performed simply by accessing these precom-

* Reprinted from INTERNATIONAL JOURNAL OF INTELLIGENT SYSTEMS, VOL. 4, 471-501 (1989), John Wiley & Sons, Inc.

puted matrices. MILORD also deals with nonmonotonic reasoning in the same framework of uncertainty management. Finally, an application to the diagnosis and treatment of pneumoniae is presented.

23.1. Knowledge Representation in MILORD

23.1.1. Basic Entities: Facts, Rules, Modules, Strategies, and Contexts

MILORD consists of four types of objects: facts, rules, modules, strategies, and contexts. There are two types of rules, depending on its conclusions: rules and metarules.

Contexts. The Knowledge Base (KB) is partitioned into a set of contexts. Each context is specialized in a particular task, for example diagnosis, treatment, and so on. Each context is composed of several modules, one of them containing the metarules that control the search strategy over the other modules.

Modules. A module is a set of rules grouped by several criteria: same conclusions, similar conditions, and so on. For example, in our application to medical diagnosis, each module has a set of diagnoses and treatments to which the rules are related. The diagnoses and treatments may be shared by different module structures, allowing them to perform different steps toward the same objectives. Each module has a set of metarules that supervise the applicability of the rules in that module. These metarules apply only to the rules of the module to which they belong. The result, in each module, is a certainty value associated to each one of the diagnoses or treatments to which the module is related.

Strategies. A strategy is a set of modules to be evaluated and a set of modules rejected. Strategies are built by metarules, and are dynamically generated at run time depending on the metarules that can be fired. When more than one strategy is generated in a given point of execution, some metarules combine them into one that will be used by the system as the current one. When evaluating a strategy, the system follows one after another of those modules contained in it to be visited.

Rules and Metarules. The rules are the basic components of a module. They are composed of a set of conditions: facts, predicates on facts or computations on numerical values of facts. Each condition will have a certainty value as a result of its evaluation. The rules have a conclusion that is a predicate over a given object: a fact (in the case of the conclusion of a rule) or a rule or module (in the case of a conclusion of a metarule). Each rule has a certainty value associated that is used in the propagation of the certainty from the conditions to the conclusion. Obviously, it only makes sense when the conclusion refers to the certainty value of a fact, but not when the conclusion is a binary decision. The examples of rules given in this article are those of PNEUMON-IA, (an application in medical diagnosis using MILORD).

The metarules are of three different types:

Rule-oriented metarules. These metarules, as has mentioned, are related to the applicability of the rules within a module. Depending on contextual facts, some rules are removed from the active rule set; for example, the rules that deduce some kind of virus disease depending on a blood analysis cannot be applied unless the results of the analysis are available.

Module-oriented metarules. These metarules refer to the global strategy of selecting subgoals. After the application of each module, the set of metarules modifies the strategy, adding or deleting modules from the list of objectives; for example, a very high certainty value about the conclusion of a bacterial disease will probably discard the modules concerning nonbacterial diseases.

Strategy-oriented metarules. When more than one strategy is generated, they are responsible for combining them into only one. They use domain knowledge and control knowledge (knowledge referring the conflicting strategies) in their premises.

Facts. Facts are the most elementary objects of the system. They are of four different types:

- Boolean
- Fuzzy—The value is a certainty degree, represented by a linguistic fuzzy number or a linguistic fuzzy label. [1,2]
- Numerical—The value of the fact is a number.
- Subsets—The value of a fact is a subset of a given set of possible values.

In rule definition it is necessary to perform type checking of the facts, as well as of the predicates. MILORD keeps track of the rules that deduce each fact and the rules they belong to, as part of the premise. This is necessary to perform forward and backward chaining in an efficient way.

23.1.2. KB Edition and Verification

This system has a rule-oriented editor that provides the functions necessary to develop the knowledge base (KB). The main features are:

- Basic commands to add, modify, or delete every object in the KB.
- Automatic prompting of the attributes of the objects, with syntactic control.
- Type checking for the typified attributes.
- Advanced commands to search, rename (with automatic changes of all pointers within the system), and copy objects.

The editor can insert new objects in the KB, automatically updating it. To provide flexibility, it is possible to use objects before defining them. The editor maintains all previous commands in an agenda. At the session closure, every object in which an operation has been made is connected with the original KB. If any connection fails, the editor asks the user for a solution. If he or she cannot resolve the question, the editor restores the last correct situation for this object.

Logical verification requires detection of any KB situations that could cause improper behavior of the inference engine. These situations can be logical errors (contradictory rules or circular rules), missing knowledge (unreachable conclusions) or knowledge duplication (redundant rules, subsumed rules or unnecessary IF-conditions). In Boolean logic, all these situations are detected with a static rule analysis. [3] In fuzzy systems, further extensions are required. These are discussed next.

Redundant rules. Two rules are redundant if they are identical, ignoring the certainty values. For example, these rules are redundant (the values between parentheses represent the certainty values):

$$(a)$$
$$p \rightarrow q$$

$$(b)$$
$$p \rightarrow q$$

These rules are not a logic problem in a Boolean system, but they are in a fuzzy system. The same information may be counted twice, with an erroneous certainty value in the conclusion.

Subsumed rules. A rule is subsumed by another if: (1) both have the same conclusion, and (2) both share a set of IF-conditions but one of them has additional IF-conditions. If the following example $R1$ is subsumed by $R2$:

$$(a)$$
$$R1: p,q \rightarrow r$$

$$(b)$$
$$R2: p \rightarrow r$$

This is a legal construction. To avoid an erroneous combination of the certainty values, care must be taken not to fire $R2$ if $R1$ has been fired.

Unnecessary IF-conditions. An unnecessary IF-condition is contained in two rules if: (1) the conclusions are identical, (2) both rules have the same IF-conditions except one, and (3) that IF-condition is the same in both rules, but is affirmed in one and negated in the other. For example:

$$(a)$$
$$R1: p,q \rightarrow r$$

$$(b)$$
$$R2: p, \neg q \rightarrow r$$

It is possible to eliminate this IF-condition in Boolean logic and collapse the two rules in one. In general, this is not possible in fuzzy logic. This situation must be detected to warn the user.

Circular rules. A set of rules is circular if they create an infinite loop in the backward engine. For example, the following set of rules is circular:

$$R1\!: p \to q \quad {}^{(a)}$$

$$R2\!: q \to r \quad {}^{(b)}$$

$$R3\!: r \to p \quad {}^{(c)}$$

If the goal is p, the backward engine tries to validate r (rule $R3$). Next it tries to validate q (rule $R2$) and then p (rule $R1$), which returns it to the original goal. The problem is the same in fuzzy and Boolean logic.

Contradictory rules. In Boolean logic, two rules are contradictory if they have the same IF-conditions and opposite conclusions. For example:

$$R1\!: p \to q \quad {}^{(a)}$$

$$R2\!: p \to \neg q \quad {}^{(b)}$$

In fuzzy logic, this is a legal construction. It is possible to have some degree of belief in some fact q and also a degree of belief in the opposite fact $\neg q$. A contradiction may be considered when for an expert-defined threshold π, we have:

$$\textbf{certainty(q)} + \textbf{certainty(}\neg\textbf{q)} > \pi$$

To detect such contradictions it is necessary to keep for every fact q the opposite fact $\neg q$, and compute the certainty values of q and $\neg q$, in every step of every deduction chain. In any case, the rules that are contradictory in a Boolean sense (without considering the certainty values) are displayed.

Unreachable conditions. If the conclusion of a rule is not a goal and it does not match any IF-condition of another rule, this conclusion is unreachable and this rule will not be fired. In fuzzy logic, a conclusion may match an IF-condition of another rule. However, the rule will not be fired if the rules chaining always propagates a certainty value lower than a given validity threshold (in MYCIN is 0.2, in MILORD is SLIGHTLY POSSIBLE). Therefore, this is also a situation of unreachable conclusion.

Dead-end IF-conclusions and dead-end goals. If a goal or an IF-condition does not match a conclusion of any rule, this is a dead-end goal or IF-condition. They will not be validated and there is a gap in the KB. In fuzzy logic another type of dead-end IF-condition is possible: it occurs when the rules chaining always stops because the certainty value is below the validity threshold.

Redundant rules, subsumed rules, unnecessary IF-conditions, circular rules, unreachable conclusions, and dead-end IF-conditions and goals (the two last in the Boolean case only), can be detected by a static rule analysis. Problems associated with the propagation of the certainty values below the validity threshold (unreachable conclusions and dead-end IF-conditions) can be detected traversing the AND/OR deduction tree. Given a goal, an upper bound of the certainty value reachable for each possible deduction chain can be computed. This is done by applying the implication function to the certainty values of the rules in the deduction chain. If some deduction chain is cut because the upper bound falls below the mentioned validity threshold, the cutting point is a dead-end IF-condition, and the remainder of the chain becomes a set of unreachable conclusions (for this goal). If none of these rules is used in another deduction chain, it can never be fired.

23.1.3. Semantic Network Organization

There is an obvious hierarchical structure, (inclusion relationship), among the objects defined in MILORD. Each element has, in this sense, some inherited properties. A fact inherits the names of the rules it is related to. The rules and the facts inherit the name of the module they appear in, and so on.

This structure can be seen as a three-level semantic network. In each level objects have interrelations that express priority, subsumption, inclusion by property chains, specificity, and so on. These relations are obtained from a syntactic analysis of the Knowledge Base (KB) that is performed by the editor described previously. Together with this explicit structure, there are explicit relations among these objects given by the metarules. Let us see a set of examples of these relations.

In the following examples, a semantic network is established in such a way that it allows the system to fulfill the restrictions imposed by the knowledge base. In Figures 23.1 to 23.3 bold lines represent the relationships inferred from the information given in the definition of the KB.

The next example shows an inclusion via property chains. In this case the property type is "is a kind of":

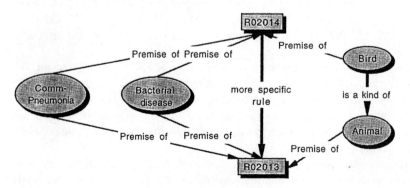

Figure 23.1 Schematic representation of the relation between $R02013$ and $R02014$.

MILORD: The Architecture of Linguistically Expressed Uncertainty   363

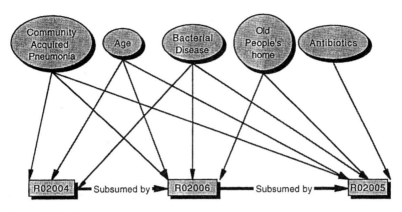

Figure 23.2 Subsumption of rules (all links are POs).

```
R02013        IF    1) Community-acquired pneumonia
                    2) Frequent contacts with animals
                    3) Bacterial disease
              THEN  [Quite possible]
                    Pneumococcus

R02014        IF    1) Community-acquired pneumonia
                    2) Frequent contacts with birds
                    3) Bacterial disease
              THEN  [Very possible]
                    Pneumococcus
```

There is a relation "bird is a kind of animal" that makes the rule R02014 more specific than the rule *R*02013.

What follows is an example of *subsumption* among three rules:

```
R02006        IF    1) Community-acquired pneumonia
                    2) (> age 70)
                    3) Lives in an old people's home.
                    4) Bacterial disease
              THEN  [Moderately possible]
                    Pneumococcus
```

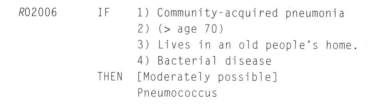

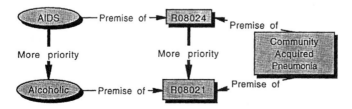

Figure 23.3 Priority relationship.

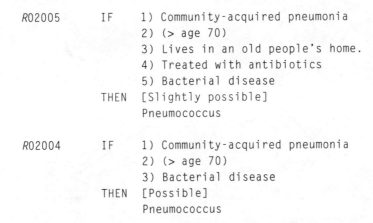

```
RO2005      IF     1) Community-acquired pneumonia
                   2) (> age 70)
                   3) Lives in an old people's home.
                   4) Treated with antibiotics
                   5) Bacterial disease
            THEN   [Slightly possible]
                   Pneumococcus


RO2004      IF     1) Community-acquired pneumonia
                   2) (> age 70)
                   3) Bacterial disease
            THEN   [Possible]
                   Pneumococcus
```

Figure 23.3 shows a priority relationship between conditions of different rules.

23.1.4. Knowledge Translation from External to Internal Representation

In order to improve the system's performance, a translation of the external representation is made. The internal object representation is based on a framelike structure. Each object, fact, rule, or module, is represented by a structure that holds the properties, relations, and general information of each object. This representation makes explicit the implicit relations of the external representation. Moreover, some computation may be done; for example, the maximum reachable value of a fact, also some misspellings, as well as syntactic and sematic errors can be detected. Type checking is applied here in order to test the KB. Next, we can see a partial result of the compilation process over a rule and a fact:

The external aspect of a rule is:

```
RO10014     IF     1) Community-acquired pneumonia
                   2) No expectoration
                   3) Not dehydrated
            THEN   [Moderately possible]
                   Atypical disease
```

The internal representation of a rule contains information that is not explicit in the external one, such as contextual and control information to perform a more efficient explanation of the reasoning strategies. The control slots EX-P-CUT and EX-O-CUT (see III-B), which are nil by default, retain information about the evaluation process.

The internal representation is implemented using the "defstruct" primitive of Common-Lisp. For example:

```
#S(RULE) :   :KB              PNEUMON-IA
             :NAME            R01014
             :MODULE          BACT-ATIP
             :IF              (C-A-PNEU
                              (NO EX)
                              (NO DEHYDRATED)

             THEN             (CONCLUDE ATIIP)
             :VALUE           MODERATELY POSSIBLE
             :APPLIED         NIL
             :SUBSUMED          (R01023 R03045)
             :METARULES         (M01003 M01015)
             :EX-P-CUT        NIL
             :EX-O-CUT        NIL)
```

The internal representation contains information about context, cross-reference, control, value, and type of value. The contextual information is given by the location of the fact in the KB, its name, the KB to which it belongs, and the modules where it appears. Each fact has two lists that contain the names of the rules where it appears as part of the premise, and the rules where it appears as conclusion. This is a very useful way to perform cross-reference tables that are mainly used in the development stage. Each fact has a type and a set of legal values that are included in the representation of the facts, assuming by default that a fact is of a fuzzy type. Control information is related to the cuts the system may perform in the evaluation of a fact (see IV-B).

The internal representation of the fact **LOBAR PATTERN** is:

```
#S(FACT :    BC               PNEUMON-IA
             :NAME            LOBAR PATTERN
             :MODULE          (PNEUMON MENU)
             :QUESTION "Has the pneumonia a lobar pattern in
               the x-ray?"
             :LONG-NAME       "LOBAR PATTERN"
             :RULES           NIL
             :PREMISE-OF        (R10058 R02022)
             :VALUE-TYPE      FUZZY
             :VALUE           NIL
             :ANSWERS
                 (IMPOSSIBLE, ALMOST-IMPOSSIBLE
                  SLIGHTLY-POSSIBLE MODERATELY-POSSIBLE
                  POSSIBLE QUITE-POSSIBLE VERY-POSSIBLE
                  ALMOST-SURE SURE)
             :DEDUCTIBLE      NIL
             :CUT             NO
             :USED-RULES      NIL
```

```
:EXP-C-CUT          NIL
:EXP-I-CUT          NIL)
```

The knowledge translation, performed off-line, must of course be recomputed when modifications are introduced into the KB. This recomputation could be done incrementally.

23.2. MILORD Multilevel Architecture

When defining an application (a KB), two main aspects of the problem must be solved by a given shell: The representation of Domain Knowledge and of Control Knowledge. The second aspect is the main one in most AI applications. In this section the relations between them will be pointed out.

The architecture of MILORD presents a multilevel structure in both the domain representation and the control representation. There is a relation between these two representations as can be seen in Figure 23.4.

The Semantic Network acts over the facts, structuring their interdependencies and controlling mechanisms such as semantic subsumption between concepts (for example, if the fact *AIDS* is present in the context of a bacterial disease then the fact *Alcoholic* is not relevant and should not be considered).

The metarules hierarchy controls the application of their corresponding domain knowledge. Before moving down in the domain level hierarchy (from strategies to rules and facts), the corresponding control level is consulted.

This separation between different levels of control and of domain representation matches quite well various design processes in KB definition:

1. Allows a top-down design of the KB, because the decisions about domain knowledge and the corresponding control items are independent of later refinements. For example, in the case of strategy definitions and resolution of conflicts between strategies, you can first define strategies based only on domain knowledge, and later you can define how to solve the possible conflicts between them.

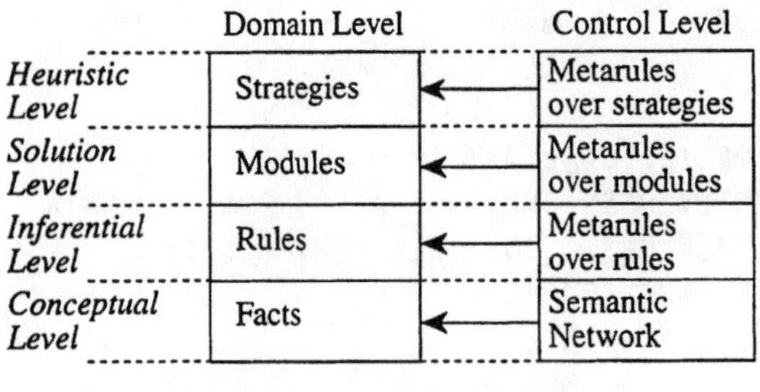

	Domain Level	Control Level
Heuristic Level	Strategies	←	Metarules over strategies
Solution Level	Modules	←	Metarules over modules
Inferential Level	Rules	←	Metarules over rules
Conceptual Level	Facts	←	Semantic Network

Figure 23.4   Multilevel architecture of MILORD.

2. Allows defining different problem solving methods, due to the flexibility at the operational level. For example, you can define simple classification or heuristic classification processes. [4]

3. Allows defining different hierarchical structures: mixed hierarchies or pure hierarchies in the domain knowledge, and the corresponding control level that supervises the use of the different strategies.

However, this architecture is not suitable to define generative systems, that is, systems that can generate or build the solutions to the problem. MILORD presumes that all the solutions are known *a priori*.

This multilevel definition has also some interesting issues from the point of view of the knowledge engineer:

Extensibility: adding new domain knowledge and new control knowledge is easy and safe.

Debugability: to correct mistakes and validate the KB is easier.

Explainability: to explain the behavior of the system is easier because upper levels in the hierarchy provide the correct justifications.

23.3. Uncertain Reasoning

The numerical approaches to the representation of uncertainty imply hypothesis of independence, mutual exclusiveness, and so on about the information they deal with. On the other hand, they oblige the expert and the user to be unrealistically precise and consistent in the assignment of such numerical values to rules and facts. Furthermore, these approaches are computationally expensive.

Two approaches, based on a linguistic characterization of uncertainty, have been developed in MILORD. The certainty values are linguistic terms defined by the expert. In the first approach, the internal representation of each term is a fuzzy number on the interval [0,1], following the work of Bonissone, [5] and allows to deal with uncertain facts and with rules whose uncertainty concerns the strength of the implication. The second approach is an extension of the first one that allows one to deal with rules containing linguistically expressed uncertainty that modifies the conditions and conclusions. Such type of uncertainty is internally represented by fuzzy labels. [6] For computational reasons, both representations are parametrized at the very beginning of each application design. In our application to pneumonia diagnosis, we have first been using the first approach, and later, we have switched to the second approach according to the preference of our medical expert.

MILORD has also been parametrized in order to perform different calculi of uncertainty operating on the expert defined term set of linguistic certainty values.

23.3.1. The Calculus of Uncertainty

It can be shown [7] that Triangular norms (*T*-norms) and Triangular conorms (*T*-conorms) are the most general families of two-place functions from **[0,1]** × **[0,1]** onto **[0,1]** that respectively satisfy the requirements of conjunction and disjunction operators.

A *T*-norm $T(p,q)$ performs a conjunction operator, on the degrees of certainty of two or more conditions in the same premise, satisfying the following properties:

$$T(0,0) = 0$$

$$T(p, 1) = T(1, p) = p$$

$$T(p, q) = T(q, p)$$

$$T(p, q) \leq T(r, s) \text{ if } p \leq r \text{ and } q \leq s$$

$$T(p, T(q, r)) = T(T(p, q), r)$$

A *T*-conorm $S(p,q)$ computes the degree of certainty of a conclusion derived from two or more rules. It is a disjunction operator satisfying the following properties:

$$S(1, 1) = 1$$

$$S(0, p) = S(p, 0) = p$$

$$S(p, q) = S(q, p)$$

$$S(p, q) \leq S(r, s) \text{ if } p \leq r \text{ and } q \leq s$$

$$S(p, S(q, r)) = S(S(p, q), r)$$

For suitable negation operators $N(x)$, *T*-norms and *T*-conorms are dual in the sense of De Morgan laws.[8]

An implication function $I(p,q)$ gives the certainty degree of a rule as a function of the certainty degree of the premise and the certainty degree of the conclusion. The more usual types of implication functions are:

1. S-Implications, defined by $I_S(p,q) = S(N(p),q)$. *S* being a *T*-conorm and *N* a negation operator.

2. *R*-Implications, defined by $I_R(p,q) = \text{SUP}\{c \in [0,1] \mid T(p,c) \leq q\}$. Being *T* a *T*-norm.

A "Modus Ponens-generating function" (m.p.g.f.),[9] for an implication function *I*, propagates a certainty value to the conclusion from the certainty values of the premise and the rule:

1. For an *S*-Implication generated by a *T*-conorm *S*, a m.p.g.f. can be defined by $m_I(p,r) = \text{INF}\{c \in [0,1] \mid S(N(p),c) \geq r\}$.

2. For an *R*-Implication generated by a *T*-norm *T*, *T* itself is a m.p.g.f.

Some usual pairs of dual T-norms and T-conorms are:

$$T_0(x,y) = \begin{cases} \min(x,y), \text{ if } \max(x,y) = 1 \\ 0, \text{ otherwise} \end{cases} \qquad S_0(x,y) = \begin{cases} \min(x,y), \text{ if } \max(x,y) = 1 \\ 0, \text{ otherwise} \end{cases}$$

$$T_1(x,y) = \max(0, x + y - 1) \qquad S_1(x,y) = \min(1, x + y)$$

$$T_{1.5}(x,y) = \frac{xy}{2 - (x + y - xy)} \qquad S_1(x,y) = \frac{x + y}{1 + xy}$$

$$T_2(x,y) = xy \qquad S_1(x,y) = x + y - xy$$

$$T_{2.5}(x,y) = \frac{xy}{x + y - xy} \qquad S_{2.5}(x,y) = \frac{x + y - 2xy}{1 - xy}$$

$$T_3(x,y) = \min(x,y) \qquad S_3(x,y) = \max(x,y)$$

It can be shown that they are ordered as follows:

$$T_0 \le T_1 \le T_{1.5} \le T_2 \le T_{2.5} \le T_3$$

$$S_3 \le S_{2.5} \le S_2 \le S_{1.5} \le S_1 \le S_0$$

Some usual Implication functions and its m.p.g.f. are:

$$I_R^1(x,y) = I_S^1(x,y) = \min(1 - x + y, 1) \quad m_I = T_1$$

$$I_S^2(x,y) = 1 - x + xy \qquad m_I(x,y) = \begin{cases} \dfrac{\max(x + y - 1, 0)}{x}, \text{ if } x \ne 0 \\ 0, \text{ otherwise} \end{cases}$$

$$I_R^2(x,y) = \begin{cases} 1, \text{ if } x \le y \\ \dfrac{x}{y}, \text{ otherwise} \end{cases} \qquad m_I = T_2$$

$$I_S^3(x,y) = \max(1 - x, y) \qquad m_I(x,y) = \begin{cases} 0, \text{ if } y \le 1 - x \\ y, \text{ otherwise} \end{cases}$$

$$I_R^3(x,y) = \begin{cases} 1, \text{ if } x \le y \\ y, \text{ otherwise} \end{cases} \qquad m_I = T_3$$

In MILORD we have specially considered the pairs (T_1, S_1), (T_2, S_2), and (T_3, S_3) following the experimental results obtained by Bonissone [10] which consisted in applying nine T-norms to three different term sets. Bonissone analyzed the sensitivity of each operator with respect to the granularity (number of elements) in the term sets and concluded that only the T-norms T_1, T_2, and T_3 generated sufficiently different results for term sets that do not have more than nine elements. On the other hand, according to the results of Miller [11] concerning the span of absolute judgment, it is unlikely that any expert or user would consistently qualify uncertainty using more than nine different terms.

23.3.2. The Linguistic Certainty Values

MILORD allows the expert to define the term set of linguistic certainty values which constitutes the verbal scale that he or she and the users will use to express their degree of confidence in the rules and facts respectively. Recent psychological studies have shown the feasibility of such verbal scales: ". . . A verbal scale of probability expressions is a compromise between people's resistance to the use of numbers and the necessity to have a common numerical scale" [12]; ". . . people asked to give numerical estimations on a common-day situation err most of the time and in a nonconsistent way. Furthermore, they are unable to appreciate their judgments imprecision (errors are by far bigger than the maximum error accepted as possible by the subjects themselves). Nevertheless, judgments embodied in linguistic descriptors appear consistent in this same situation . . ." [13].

23.3.3. The Management of Uncertainty with Fuzzy Numbers

Each linguistic value is represented internally by a fuzzy interval (fuzzy number) that is, the membership function of a fuzzy set on the real line, or, more precisely, on the truth space represented by the interval [0,1]. These membership functions can be interpreted as the meanings of the terms in the term set. The conjunction and disjunction operators applied to these functions will produce another membership function as a result that will have to be matched to a term in the term set, in order to keep the term set closed. This can be done by a linguistic approximation process that will be described later (see Bonissone [5] for an extensive study of the linguistic approximation process).

23.3.3.1. The Term Set for PNEUMON-IA and Its Representation. Although the expert can define its own term set together with its internal representation, MILORD provides a default term set obtained by means of a survey conducted among several hundred medical professionals in the Barcelona area. A similar study was also performed [15] although the goal there was not to use the term set in an expert system. The default term set is:

{IMPOSSIBLE, ALMOST-IMPOSSIBLE, SLIGHTLY-POSSIBLE, MODERATELY-POSSIBLE, POSSIBLE, QUITE-POSSIBLE, VERY-POSSIBLE, ALMOST-SURE, SURE}

Each term T_i is represented by a membership function $\mu_i(x)$, for x in the interval [0,1].

Each membership function is represented by four parameters $T_i = (a_i, b_i, c_i, d_i)$, corresponding to the weighted interval in Figure 23.5.

The nine-element term set has the following representation resulted from the conducted survey:

IMPOSSIBLE	$= (0,0,0,0)$
ALMOST IMPOSSIBLE	$= (0,0,0.05,0.08)$
SLIGHTLY POSSIBLE	$= (0.05,0.07,0.14,0.17)$
MODERATELY POSSIBLE	$= (0.10,0.15,0.35,0.45)$
POSSIBLE	$= (0.25,0.35,0.55,0.65)$
QUITE POSSIBLE	$= (0.45,0.55,0.75,0.85)$
VERY POSSIBLE	$= (0.65,0.75,1,1)$
ALMOST SURE	$= (0.95,0.98,1,1)$
SURE	$= (1,1,1,1)$

corresponding to following functions in Figure 23.6.

In order to be able to evaluate the T-norms T_1, T_2, T_3 and the T-conorms S_1, S_2, S_3 on the elements of the term set, we apply the following formulæ according to the arithmetic rules on fuzzy numbers: [1]

Given two fuzzy intervals $\iota = (a, b, c, d)$ and $\iota' = (a', b', c', d')$, we have:

$$\iota + \iota' = (a + a', b + b', c + c', d + d')$$

$$\iota - \iota' = (a - d', b - c', c - b', d - a')$$

$$\iota * \iota' = (aa', bb', cc', dd')$$

$$min(\iota, \iota') = (min(a, a'), min(b, b'), min(c, c'), min(d, d'))$$

$$max(\iota, \iota') = (max(a, a'), max(b, b'), max(c, c'), max(d, d'))$$

23.3.3.2. The Linguistic Approximation.   A linguistic approximation process is performed in order to find a term (linguistic value) in the term set whose "meaning" (membership function) is the closest (according to a given metric) to the "meaning" (membership function) of the result of the conjunction or disjunction operation performed on any two linguistic values of the term set. This allows maintenance of closed operations for

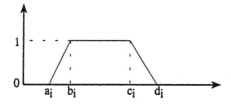

Figure 23.5   Parametric representation of membership functions.

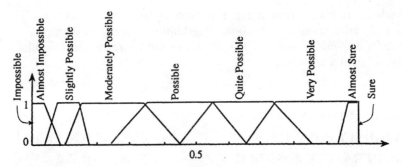

Figure 23.6   Term set for PNEUMON-IA.

any T-norm and T-conorm. The problem is, therefore, that of computing a distance between two trapezoidal membership functions. In order to do so, we have adopted for the sake of simplicity a solution consisting in the computation of a weighted Euclidean distance of two relevant features of the functions: the first moment and the area under the function. Figure 23.7 shows the results obtained with the selected T-norm T_2 on the term set of Figure 23.6.

23.3.4. The Management of Uncertainty Using Fuzzy Linguistic Labels

As it has been mentioned, this is the approach that has been finally preferred by our expert.

23.3.4.1. Introduction.   This is an alternative approach that allows to combine imprecision and uncertainty. Let us consider a proposition such as 'X is A' where X is a variable that takes its values from a fuzzy subset A of a Universe of Discourse U. Then X induces a possibility distribution [2] on A:

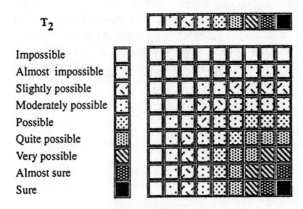

Figure 23.7   AND matrix computed using T_2.

$$\Pi(x) = \mu_A(x), \text{for all } x \in U$$

where μ_A stands for the membership function of the fuzzy subset A.

From now on, we will identify A with the possibility distribution Π_x on A. We can define a fuzzy label [6] by means of a function $t: [0,1] \to [0,1]$ such that the proposition '$(X$ is $A)$ is t' would be equivalent to 'X is A'' ' where $A'' = t \circ A$, in the sense of the usual functions composition. See, for example, Figure 23.8.

From this point of view, a fuzzy label can be understood as a linguistic modifier of the fuzzy subset A. But on the other hand, given A and A'', we can interpret t as the compatibility of A with A'', that is, the fuzzy label we have to apply to A to get A''. The compatibility is defined as follows:

$$t(x) = \begin{cases} \sup\{A''(u) \mid u \in A^{-1}(x)\}, \text{if } A^{-1}(x) \neq \varnothing \\ 0, \text{otherwise} \end{cases}$$

23.3.4.2. Connective Operators between Fuzzy Labels.
In order to propagate and combine uncertainty, it is necessary to define the following operators.

In what follows, A will stand for a fuzzy subset of a universe U, and B a fuzzy subset of a universe V.

1. **Composition.** If we apply a linguistic modifier t_2 to a fact that is already labeled by t_1 what we are doing is to apply consecutively two functions to a possibility distribution; in other words, we are modifying the fact by the composition of two labels:

   $$((X \text{ is } A) \text{ is } t_1) \text{ is } t_2 = (X \text{ is } A) \text{ is } t, \text{ being } t = t_2 \circ t_1$$

2. **Compatibility.** The compatibility of '$(X$ is $A)$ is t_1' with respect to '$(X$ is $A)$ is t_2' is $t_{1,2}$ if $t_{1,2}$ is the least fuzzy label (w.r.t. the pointwise order) such that:

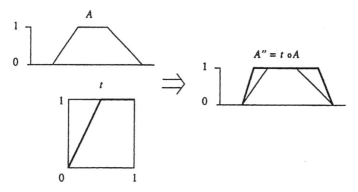

Figure 23.8   Modification of a fuzzy set by a fuzzy label.

$$((X \text{ is } A) \text{ is } t_1) \text{ is } t_{1,2} \cong (X \text{ is } A) \text{ is } t_2$$

in the sense that $t_{1,2} \circ t_1 \geq t_2$, where $t_{1,2}$ is defined as:

$$t_{1,2}(x) = \text{Sup}\{ t_2(y) \mid t_1(y) = x \}, \text{for all } x \in [0,1]$$

3. **Conjunction.** A composed proposition of the kind "$[(X \text{ is } A) \text{ AND } (Y \text{ is } B)]$" has an associated two-dimensional possibility distribution, $\Pi_1(u,v) = T(A(u), B(u))$, T being the T-norm conjunction operator. In the same way, if the proposition is "$[(X \text{ is } A) \text{ is } t_1] \text{ AND } [(Y \text{ is } B) \text{ is } t_2]$" the possibility distribution will be $\Pi_2(u,v) = T(A'(u), B'(v))$, being $A' = t_1 \circ A$ and $B' = t_2 \circ B$. Then, for a given T-norm T, we define $t_1 \wedge_T t_2$ as a label that transforms Π_1 into Π_2, as follows:

$$[(X \text{ is } A) \text{ is } t_1] \text{ AND } [(Y \text{ is } B) \text{ is } t_2] \cong [(X \text{ is } A) \text{ AND } (Y \text{ is } B)] \text{ is } t_1 \wedge_T t_2$$

where $(t_1 \wedge_T t_2)(z) = \text{Inf}\{ T(t_1(x), t_2(y)) \mid z = T(x,y) \}$, for all $z \in [0,1]$.

4. **Disjunction.** A composed proposition of the kind "$[(X \text{ is } A) \text{ OR } (Y \text{ is } B)]$" has an associated two-dimensional possibility distribution $\Pi_1(u,v) = S(A(u), B(v))$, S being the T-conorm disjunction operator. In the same way, if the proposition is "$[(X \text{ is } A) \text{ is } t_1] \text{ OR } [(Y \text{ is } B) \text{ is } t_2]$" the possibility distribution will be $\Pi_2(u,v) = S(A'(u), B'(u))$, being $A' = t_1 \circ A$ and $B' = t_2 \circ B$. Then, for a given T-conorm S, we define $t_1 \vee_S t_2$ as a label that transforms Π_1 into Π_2, as follows:

$$[(X \text{ is } A) \text{ is } t_1] \text{ OR } [(Y \text{ is } B) \text{ is } t_2] \cong [(X \text{ is } A) \text{ OR } (Y \text{ is } B)] \text{ is } t_1 \vee_S t_2$$

where $(t_1 \vee_S t_2)(z) = \text{Inf}\{ S(t_1(x), t_2(y)) \mid z = S(x,y) \}$, for all $z \in [0,1]$.

5. **Negation.** Given a proposition "$(X \text{ is } A) \text{ is } t$", we define the negation of t as a label $\neg t$ that transforms the possibility distribution $\neg A$ into $\neg(t \circ A)$, that is:

$$\neg((X \text{ is } A) \text{ is } t) = (X \text{ is } \neg A) \text{ is } \neg t$$

where $\neg A$ stands for the standard complement of A that is:

$$\mu_{\neg A}(u) = 1 - \mu_A(u)),$$

and $\neg t = n \circ t \circ n$, with $n(x) = 1 - x$.

With these definitions, notice that, if T and S are dual, the following De Morgan's equality can be easily verified:

$$t_1 \vee_S t_2 = \neg((\neg t_1) \wedge_T (\neg t_2))$$

6. **Inference (Modus Ponens).** Following the "modified" Compositional Rule of Inference, [16] the basic scheme of inference is:

$$\frac{[\text{IF } (X \text{ is } A) \text{ THEN } (Y \text{ is } B)] \text{ is } t_1 \quad (X \text{ is } A) \text{ is } t_2}{(Y \text{ is } B) \text{ is } t_3 = \text{INFER}(t_1, t_2)}$$

where $t_3(y) = \text{Sup}\{ m_I(t_2(x), t_1(I(x,y))) \mid x \in [0,1] \}$, for all $y \in [0,1]$.

Here $I(x,y)$ is the Implication function chosen to represent the conditional statement, and m_1 is its corresponding "modus ponens generating function."

This formulation can be generalized if the conditions and the conclusions contain linguistically expressed uncertainty modifiers. In such a case, the inference process needs three steps:

$$[IF ((X \text{ is } A) \text{ is } t_1) \text{ THEN } ((Y \text{ is } B) \text{ is } t_2] \text{ is } t_3$$
$$\frac{(X \text{ is } A) \text{ is } t_4}{(Y \text{ is } B) \text{ is } t_5 = (INFER(t_3, t_{1,4})) \circ t_2}$$

that is:

1. computing the compatibility of t_1 with t_4, we get $t_{1,4}$
2. applying the Compositional Rule of Inference $t \circ t_{1,4}$ and t_3, we get $INFER(t_3, t_{1,4})$
3. and, finally, the composition of $INFER(t_{1,4}, t_3)$ with t_2 gives t_5

23.3.4.3. Selection of a Family of Labels. Because of the arbitrary ways to modify a possibility distribution, it is necessary to work on a restricted family of fuzzy labels. The labels we have considered have a two-parameter representation $t = (a,b)$, where $a = 0$ or $b = 1$, leading to the two following types of labels:

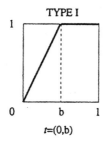
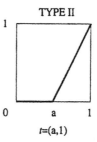

These labels perform two kinds of transformations (see Figure 23.9).

A' is a less restrictive fuzzy subset than A, while A'' is a more restrictive one. Therefore, modifications of Type I can be viewed as a linguistic way to emphasize the fact of having less confidence on the premise 'X is A', whereas modifications of Type II emphasize more confidence.

Furthermore, a set of certainty degrees can be established according to the different modifications of A (see Figure 23.10). Thus, an implicit order relation "$\leq_L$" is defined: if $t_1 = (a_1, b_1)$ and $t_2 = (a_2, b_2)$ then: $t_1 \leq_L t_2$ if $a_1 + b_1 \leq a_2 + b_2$ (i.e., $t_1 \leq_L t_2$ if $t_1(x) \geq t_2(x)$, for all $x \in [0,1]$.

Finally, notice that this set of labels actually applies over values with a possibility degree between 0 and 1 (increasing it or decreasing it), and has no effect on values that are totally possible.

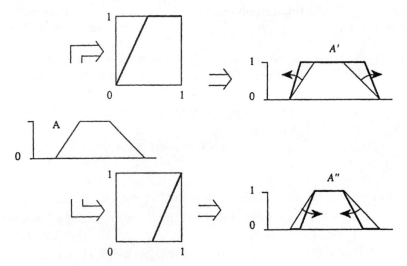

Figure 23.9 Types of modifications.

23.3.4.4. The Connective Operations over the Family of Labels and Its Approximation. The results of the connective operations defined in section 23.4.2 are shown in Table 23.1 for the family of labels mentioned in the last section with the two-parameter representation. In some cases the result of such operations will be a label not belonging to our family. Therefore, a first approximation process is performed in order to keep the family closed under the connective operations.

23.3.4.5. Selection of the Term Set and Its Linguistic Approximation. MILORD works with two term sets of linguistic certainty values. One, given by the expert, is used externally, and the other one is automatically generated from the first and used transparently by the user. The reason of this is explained later in this section.

Each linguistic certainty value, as it has been explained in section 23.4.3 is internally represented by a fuzzy label, which can be understood as the meaning of the terms in the term sets.

The connective operators applied to these linguistic certainty values will produce another certainty value, that will be matched to a term in

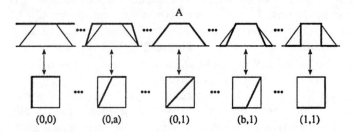

Figure 23.10 Ordered set of certainty labels.

Table 23.1 Connective Operations Over the Family of Labels

	Composition $t_1 \circ t_2$	Compatibility of t_1 with t_2	Conjunction* $t_1 \wedge_T t_2$	Disjunction $t_1 \vee_S t_2$	Inference t_1 (rule) t_2 (premise) with S-Implication Generated bu S_2	S-Implication Generated by S_3
$t_1 = (0,a)$ $t_2 = (b,1)$	$(0,ab)$	$(0,b/a),\ a>b$ $((b-a)/b,1),\ a\le b,\ b\neq 0$ $(0,1),\ a=b=0$	$(0,T(a,b))$	$(0,\max(a,b))$	$(0,0),\ a<1$ $(0,b),\ a=1$	$(0,0),\ a\neq 1\ \text{or}\ b\neq 1$ $(0,1),\ a=b=1$
$t_1 = (0,a)$ $t_2 = (b,1)$	$(0,a(1-b)),\ a+b\le 1\ b\neq 1$ $(a,1),\ a+b>1$	$(1-a+ab,1)$	$(0,a)$	$(b,1)$	$(0,0),\ a+b<1$ $(0,2d-d^2/b),\ a+b>1$ $d=(a+b-1)/b$	$(0,0),\ a+b<1$ $(0,a),\ a+b\ge 1$
$t_1 = (a,1)$ $t_2 = (0,b)$	$(0,b(1-a)),\ a+b\le 1\ a\neq 1$ $((a+b-1)/b,1),\ a+b>1$	$(0,b(1-a))$	$(0,b)$	$(a,1)$	$(0,b/(1-a)),\ a+b\le 1, a\neq 1$ $((a+b-1)/b,1),\ a+b>1$	$(0,0),\ a+b<1$ $(a,1),\ a+b\ge 1$
$t_1 + (a,1)$ $t_2 = (b,1)$	$(a+b-ab,1)$	$((b-a)/(1-a),1),\ b\ge a\ a\neq 1$ $(0,(1-a)/(1-b)),\ b<a$ $(0,1),\ a=b=1$	$(\min(a,b),1)$	$(S(a,b),1)$	$(a,1)$	

*Also valid for inference using R-implication generated by T.
$(0,0) \circ (1,1) = (1,1)$
$(1,1) \circ (0,0) = (0,0)$

one of the two term sets, depending on the operator used as it will be described later.

In the expert term set E of PNEUMON-IA (see section 23.4) there are nine linguistic values with the following parametric representation:

t_1: UNKNOWN	(0,0)
t_2: VERY-LITTLE-POSSIBLE	(0,0.05)
t_3: SLIGHTLY-POSSIBLE	(0,0.1)
t_4: MODERATELY-POSSIBLE	(0,0.65)
t_5: POSSIBLE	(0,1)
t_6: QUITE-POSSIBLE	(0.35,1)
t_7: VERY-POSSIBLE	(0.9,1)
t_8: ALMOST-SURE	(0.95,1)
t_9: SURE	(1,1)

These labels are applicable to facts and rules. If no label is specified, MILORD assumes the default value ALMOST-SURE (t_8), instead of SURE (t_9) because t_9 has a behavior different from the others: it *cannot be modified* by composition (e.g. $t \circ t_9 = t_9$, for any t), and it is *totally incompatible* with anything else (e.g., compatibility of t_9 with t is t_0 for every $t \neq t_9$). Therefore, t_9 and, by duality, t_0 are reserved for nonfuzzy reasoning.

As mentioned, after every logical operation, an approximation process is performed to keep the expert term set closed. In this process, the extreme labels (t_0 and t_9) are not considered. For example, the following conjunction operation for three different T-norms:

$$\text{(slightly possible } [(0, 0.1)]) \wedge_T \text{ (moderately possible } [(0, 0.65)]) \rightarrow$$

$$\text{gives} \rightarrow \begin{cases} (0,0), & \text{if } T = T_1 \\ (0,0.65), & \text{if } T = T_2 \\ (0,0.1), & \text{if } T = T_3 \end{cases}$$

Then, the linguistic approximation process gives:

very-little-possible (for (0,0))

very-little-possible (for (0,0.65)), and

slightly-possible (for 0,0.1))

The linguistic certainty label used by the expert to qualify a rule is internally substituted by its compatibility with the default value (ALMOST SURE). The reason is that the basic inference process:

$$\frac{[\text{IF } ((X \text{ is } A) \text{ is } t_1) \text{ THEN } ((Y \text{ is } B) \text{ is } t_2] \text{ is } t_3}{(X \text{ is } A) \text{ is } t_4}$$
$$(Y \text{ is } B) \text{ is } t_5 = (\text{INFER}(t_3, t_{1,4})) \circ t_2$$

actually works only with compatibility labels: the first one is the matching degree of the premise $(t_{1,4})$; the second one, the certainty value of the rule (t_3), is in fact a satisfaction degree; and the last one $(\text{INFER}(t_3,t_{1,4}))$, is the result of combining the first two, and has to be interpreted as the matching degree propagated to the conclusion. This degree will be composed with t_2 in order to obtain the final certainty degree of the conclusion.

Thus, the labels produced by a compatibility or inference process do not really have the same linguistic interpretation as the labels of the expert term set E. Hence, it is meaningless to match them. Moreover, the term set is not large enough to avoid approximation errors. For example, the compatibilities of t_8 with t_5, t_4, t_3, and t_2 would all be linguistically approximated to t_2; in the same way, the compatibilities of t_2 with t_5, t_6, t_7, and t_8 would all be approximated to t_8. Because of this, MILORD generates an extended term set E^* that is only internally used and transparent to the user.

In MILORD the default extended term set contains the following 15 terms:

$$t_1{}^* = t_1 \qquad t_2{}^* = t_{8,2} \qquad t_3{}^* = t_{8,3} \qquad t_4{}^* = t_{8,4}$$

$$t_5{}^* = t_2 \qquad t_6{}^* = t_3 \qquad t_7{}^* = t_4 \qquad t_8{}^* = t_5$$

$$t_9{}^* = t_6 \qquad t_{10}{}^* = t_7 \qquad t_{11}{}^* = t_8 \qquad t_{12}{}^* = t_{4,8}$$

$$t_{13}{}^* = t_{3,8} \qquad t_{14}{}^* = t_{2,8} \qquad t_{15}{}^* = t_9$$

And the domain and image of each operator is:

OR	$:E \times E$	$\rightarrow E$
COMPATIBILITY	$:E \times E$	$\rightarrow E^*$
AND	$:E^* \times E^*$	$\rightarrow E^*$
INFERENCE	$:E^* \times E^*$	$\rightarrow E^*$
COMPOSITION	$:E^* \times E$	$\rightarrow E$
NEGATION	$: \quad E^*$	$\rightarrow E^*$

Let us see an example of the inference process:

```
R08004    IF   1. Community acquired pneumonia is almost sure
               2. Bacterial disease is possible
               3. (No aspiration) is very possible
          THEN [Possible]
               Enterobacteria is quite possible
```

Observed facts:

1. Community acquired pneumonia is *very possible*
2. Bacterial disease is *almost sure*
3. Aspiration is *slightly possible*

Inference steps:

(a) Compatibility between (1) and (1') gives: *moderately possible*

(b) Compatibility between (2) and (2') gives: *almost sure*

(c) Negation of (3'): (no aspiration) is (not *slightly possible*) i.e., *very possible*

(d) compatibility between (3) and (c) gives: *possible*

(e) [(a) and (b) and (d)] gives: *moderately possible*

(f) Inference: (e) and the rule value (possible) gives: *moderately possible*

(g) Composition between (f) and the conclusion label (*quite possible*) gives: **possible**

23.3.5. Nonmonotonic Reasoning

Let us suppose that at a given moment, the inference engine has deduced a fact 'Y is B' with a certainty fuzzy label t_B, and later a new fact 'X is C' provides evidence against 'Y is B'. Then, a mechanism to modify (decrease) the certainty of 'Y is B' is needed. This can be performed introducing a new rule, whose conclusion is not a fact but its certainty expressed by a fuzzy label, that is:

$$\text{If } (X \text{ is } C) \text{ Then } ((\text{certainty-of } Y \text{ is } B) \text{ is } t^*)$$

being t^* a fuzzy label of Type I (e.g., $t^*(x) \geq x$).

After applying this rule, the new fuzzy label associated to 'Y is B' will be $t_B^* = t^* \circ t_B$. Where t_B^* is smaller than t_B because t^* is of type I. But, what is the expected behavior of this type of nonmonotonic rule? It is expected that the less certain is 'X is C', the less the certainty of 'Y is B' will decrease. Taking into account the behavior of the Modus Ponens Inference Rule (23.4), the only way to achieve this is increasing the certainty of 'Y is ¬B' instead of decreasing the certainty of 'Y is B'. Then, the internal formulation of these rules is the following:

$$[\text{If } ((X \text{ is } C) \text{ is } t_1) \text{ Then } ((\text{certainty-of } Y \text{ is } \neg B) \text{ is } \neg t^*)] \text{ is } t_2$$

So, if we have the fact 'X is C' with a fuzzy label t_3, then the inference mechanism will infer:

$$(\text{certainty-of } Y \text{ is } \neg B) \text{ is } t^{**}$$

$$\text{where, } t^{**} = (\text{INFER}(t_{1,3}, t_2)) \circ (\neg t^*)$$

and, finally we obtain:

$$(Y \text{ is } B) \text{ is } t_B^{**} = (\neg t^{**}) \circ t_B$$

Remark. t^* is a term of the expert defined term set, but, again, it is internally substituted by its compatibility with the default value (almost-sure) and matched against a term of the extended term set. In section 23.4 we give an example of nonmonotonicity.

23.4. Inference Engines

23.4.1. Tabular Representation of Logical Operations

We have pointed out in the preceding sections some advantages of representing the uncertainty by a set of linguistic values. In particular we have seen that this allows precomputing of all the logical operations off-line and storing of the results in matrices. Then, at execution time, the computation of an operation is reduced to accessing a matrix. For example, to apply a rule that contains n conditions would require, in the worst case, $3n + 2$ additive operations, $n + 1$ division operations, and $2n + 1$ comparisons to compute the certainty of the conclusion from the certainty of the conditions and of the rule itself, if the computation is performed on-line, whereas with our approach only $n + 1$ matrix accesses are necessary.

This method has another interesting advantage from the implementation point of view: to perform an access to a matrix there is no need for extra memory space, whereas a function call and the use of local variables needed in other approaches do need extra memory space. This point is very important, in terms of computing time, in languages like LISP that have a dynamic management of memory and produce extra calls to the garbage collector.

The tabulation of the logical operations gives an enormous flexibility to the system. A change in the logical connectives is performed just by changing the matrices. Hence, it is easy for the expert to experiment with different reasoning schemes during the development of an application. The only problem with this approach is that the linguistic approximation introduces an error in the propagation of uncertainty through the rules. This error can be important in a long reasoning chain and a compensation mechanism has to be found. In the application to pneumoniæ diagnosis, the longest chain so far encountered contains only six rules and the accumulated error was small. Figure 23.11 shows an example of such matrices, in the case of the OR connective, and with the linguistic term set of the pneumonia application.

23.4.2. The Lookahead Technique in the Backward Engine Based on a Generalized Alpha-Beta Pruning Technique

To be accepted, any hypothesis has to be verified with a linguistic certainty value greater than a threshold defined by the expert. This allows application of a lookahead technique in the backward reasoning process, whose advantage is to guide the selection of questions and to minimize the search.

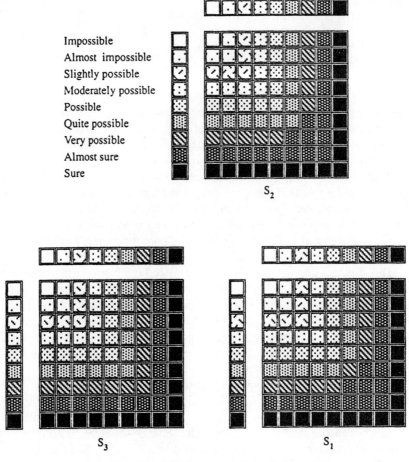

Figure 23.11   OR matrices computed from the PNEUMON-IA term set.

Traversing the AND/OR search tree from the hypotheses to the non-deducible facts depends on the heuristic selection of rules and conditions in the rules. At each selection step, MILORD checks whether the linguistic values obtained until that moment are sufficiently high to allow the hypothesis to reach the acceptance value.

To do that, the lookahead process starts computing the maximum reachable value (MRV) of the hypothesis, assuming that all the unknown nondeducible conditions have the highest linguistic certainty value in the ordered set of linguistic values defined by the expert. The known nondeducible facts assume their real values. The MRV is a function of the premises that are known at each moment. Given an MRV the system selects a rule R_i and calculates the minimum quantum of certainty that this rule must propagate in order to reach the threshold. Then, this quantum is passed back to its premises and constitutes the threshold they must reach. In the evaluation of the premises, the system calculates again the minimum value that each one of them must reach in order to get over the threshold. Then this value is passed back as the threshold for the conclusions of the rules above R_i. This is a recursive procedure. When the process arrives to a nondeducible fact and asks the user for a value, it already knows the minimal value that this fact should have. If the value given by the user is smaller, the process stops (the search tree is cut) and the system backtracks to another rule concluding the hypothesis under evaluation. If there are no more rules, it backtracks to another hypothesis.

In the procedure explained previously, all the computations are, again, performed off-line just once, and the results stored in matrices that represent a kind of inverse operator of the AND, OR, and INFER operators. Figure 23.12 is the inverse operator matrix of the T-norm T_2.

The cuts produced by this method are recorded as slot values in the internal representation of facts and rules. This is very useful for explanation purposes. There are four possible cuts in MILORD:

1. The system is evaluating a deducible fact and detects that it will not reach the threshold. A report is recorded as the value of the slot EX-C-CUT in the frame representation of that fact. This report states which rule was the cause of the cut and which rules were not yet applied. This cut is propagated forward.

2. The system is evaluating a rule and the conditions do not reach the threshold. The report is recorded as the value of the slot EX-P-CUT in the rule representation frame. This cut is propagated forward.

3. The system is evaluating a rule whose conditions have reached the lowest linguistic certainty value (that cannot be increased, due to the characteristics of the T-norms). A report is recorded as the value of the slot EX-O-CUT in the rule representation frame. This cut is not always propagated.

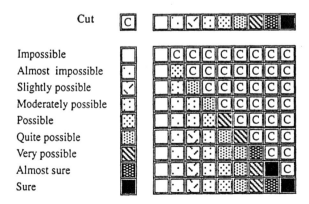

Figure 23.12 AND inverse operator for T_2.

4. The system detects that a fact will never reach the threshold because it is greater than the MRV. This cut is recorded as the value of the slot EX-I-CUT in the fact representation frame, and it is propagated forward. This information is very useful during the design of the knowledge base.

23.4.3. Cooperation between Engines

In MILORD, the two engines, forward and backward, can cooperate during the reasoning process. The forward engine is applied to the rule sets that are driven by the conditions, such as metarules or treatment modules. The backward engine is applied to the rule sets that are driven by the goals, such as diagnostic modules. However, in some cases, the two engines may cooperate to perform concrete tasks. When the forward engine reaches a conclusion with a certainty value near the acceptance threshold value, it calls the backward engine in order to try to increase this certainty value over the threshold, by considering other rule paths that conclude the same hypothesis. Furthermore, when the amount of information furnished by the user in the evaluation of a concrete case is large, the backward engine can call the forward engine in order to perform a first inference step that could clarify the possible diagnoses. Also, when new information is voluntarily introduced by the user, a call to the forward engine is performed in order to immediately take into account this new information.

This cooperation is not presently specified in the KB definition. It is internal to MILORD, although it will be soon possible to specify it at definition time using metarules.

23.5. PNEUMON-IA: An Application in Medicine

This application concerns the diagnosis and treatment of pneumonia diseases. This application, as many others in medicine, has a lot of complex and interesting characteristics that serve as a benchmark for expert systems environments. Among them nonmonotonic reasoning, uncertain, and incomplete information can be pointed out.

These problems have several solutions in MILORD. Uncertain reasoning may be accomplished by the methods described in 23.2.3 and 22.2.4. Nonmonotonic reasoning is performed by the inheritance mechanism of the frame oriented representation and by the mechanism described in 23.2.5. The present implementation includes the methodology described in 23.2.3.

Let us see an example of nonmonotonic reasoning. We focus our attention on a smoker, bronchitic, 62-year-old patient with a community-acquired pneumonia, and with grampositive coccus in pairs. First of all, let us assume that the system deduces that it is *very possible* that the disease has a bacterial origin and only *slightly possible* that it has an atypical origin. Afterwards, a control metarule deduces that, for a patient with these characteristics, the system should first try to validate the hypothesis: *Streptococcus pneumoniæ* (a kind of bacteria). Now, suppose that there are only two applicable rules in this case:

```
R02003 IF    1. Community-acquired pneumonia
             2. Respiratory chronic disease
             3. Bacterial disease
         THEN [Possible]
             Streptococcus pneumoniæ


R02026 IF    1. Community-acquired pneumonia
             2. Pleuresy
             3. Grampositive coccus in pairs or strings
         THEN [very possible]
             Streptococcus pneumoniæ
```

After applying these two rules, it deduces that it is *very possible* that the bacteria is *Streptococcus pneumoniæ*. Two days later, we obtain an X-ray and observe that cavitations are present, which is evidence against streptococcus. This implies that our certainty of *Streptococcus pneumoniae* was too high and, therefore, it must be decreased. In this case, the following nonmonotonic rule is applied:

```
R02034 IF    1) Streptococcus Pneumoniæ is quite possible
             2) X-ray-cavitations
         THEN [Sure]
                 The certainty of Streptococcus pneumoniæ is
                 moderately possible
```

This rule forces the certainty of *Streptococcus pneumoniæ* to go down according to the certainty degree propagated by the rule as described in 23.2.5. The final result is that the certainty value of *Streptococcus pneumoniæ* is *slightly possible*.

When a diagnosis or a treatment fails it has to be modified. The modification has to take into account the new information related to the failure and the previous diagnosis and treatment. The modification is monitored by metarules whose conditions are relevant to the wrong diagnosis or treatment.

At any time, the user may input new relevant information that, depending on a set of metarules, may trigger a change in the search process, which consists in adding modules to or deleting modules from the list of objectives.

The use of control metarules for rules and modules has led us to design a hierarchical structure of the knowledge base. The Knowledge Base of

PNEUMON-IA has three different contexts: DIAGNOSIS, TREAT-MENT, and COMPLICATIONS, supervised by a module containing module oriented metarules (see Figure 23.13). The supervising module allows different interactions, depending on what the user is interested in. For example, a user who already knows the diagnosis will only be interested in the treatment. At present, the diagnosis context, almost completed for community acquired pneumonia, contains ten modules: a metarule module and nine rule modules that cluster rules concluding the same germ or family of germs. The treatment context is also in progress, while the complications context will be soon started.

23.6. Conclusion

We have described some aspects of the MILORD system and in particular its architecture and its management of uncertainty. The most relevant features of our approach is the representation of uncertainty by means of expert-defined linguistic statements.

The main advantage of this approach is that once the linguistic values have been defined by the expert, the system computes and stores the matrices corresponding to the different conjunction, disjunction, and implication operations on all the pairs of terms in the term set. When MILORD is run on a particular application, *the propagation and combination of uncertainty is performed by simply accessing these precomputed matrices.*

This approach also allows management of nonmonotonic reasoning using the uncertain reasoning framework. Furthermore, the frame-based representation allows one to deal with incomplete information through inheritance mechanisms.

The hierarchical knowledge base structure allows expression of the knowledge with rules containing a small number of conditions, increasing in this way the efficiency of the system.

The application to the diagnosis and treatment of pneumoniæ presently contains around 1000 rules and 350 facts covering more than 95 percent of the community-acquired pneumoniæ. In the near future, we

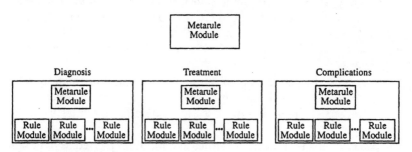

Figure 23.13   PNEUMON-IA KB structure.

are planning to cover also hospital-acquired pneumoniæ as well as post-treatment complications.

Other applications using MILORD include VLSI design [17] and Automatic Control [18]. Future extensions of MILORD will concern the management of imprecise information and an interface with a knowledge acquisition system, based on personal construct psychology, under development in our group. MILORD is implemented in VaxLisp DEC VAX machines.

23.7. References

[1] Dubois, D., and H. Prade. *Theories des Possibilities.* Masson, Paris: 1985.

[2] Zadeh, L.A. "The Role of Fuzzy Logic in the Management of Uncertainty in Expert Systems." *International Journal of Fuzzy Sets and Systems,* Vol. 11 (1983), pp. 119–227.

[3] Nguyen, T.A., et al. "Knowledge Base Verification," *AI Magazine* (summer, 1987), pp. 67–75.

[4] Clancey, W.J. "Heuristic Classification." *Artificial Intelligence,* Vol. 27 (1985), pp. 289–350.

[5] Bonissone, P.P. "The Problem of Linguistic Approximation in System Analysis." *Ph.D. Dissertation, EECS Department,* University of California at Berkeley, 1979.

[6] Baldwin, J.F. "A New Approach to Approximate Reasoning using Fuzzy Logic." *International Journal on Fuzzy Sets and Systems,* Vol. 2 (1979), pp. 309–325.

[7] Alsina, C., et al. "On Some Logical Connective for Fuzzy Set Theory." *Journal of Mathematical Analysis and Applications,* Vol. 93, No. 1 (1983), pp. 15–26.

[8] Trillas, E. "Sobre Funciones de Negacion en la Teoria de Conjuntos Difusos." *Stochastica,* Vol. 3, No. 1 (1979), pp. 47–60.

[9] Trillas, E., and L. Valverde. "On Mode and Implication in Approximate Reasoning," in *Approximate Reasoning and Expert Systems.* eds. M.M. Gupta. North Holland: 1985.

[10] Bonissone, P.P., and K.S. Decker. "Selecting Uncertainty and Granularity: An Experiment in Trading Off Precision and Complexity." General Electric Corporate Research and Development Center, *KBS Working Paper.* Schenectady, New York.

[11] Miller, G.A. "The Magical Number Seven, Plus or Minus Two: Some Limits on Our Capacity for Processing Information." *Psychological Review,* Vol. 63 (1956), pp. 81–97.

[12] Beyth-Marom, R. "How Probable is Probable? A Numerical Taxonomy Translation of Verbal Probability Expressions." *Journal of Forecasting,* Vol. 1 (1982), pp. 257–269.

[13] Freksa, C., and R.L. de Mantaras. "A Learning System for Linguistic Categorization of Soft Observations." *Actes Collogue de la Association pour la Recherche Cognitive.* Orsay: Universite de Paris-Sud: 1984.

[14] de Mantaras, R.L., et al. "MILORD: An Expert Systems Building Tool with Approximate Reasoning," in *Fuzzy Logic in Knowledge Engineering.* eds. C.V. Negoita and H. Prade. TUV Verlag: 1986.

[15] Augustine, A.M., et al. "How Medical Professionals Evaluate Expressions of Probability." *The New England Journal of Medicine* (1986), pp. 740–744.

[16] Valverde, L., and E. Trillas. "On Modus Ponens in Fuzzy Logic." 15th International Symposium Multi. Logics. Kingston, Canada: 1985.

[17] Felix, R., et al. A Rule-based System using Reasoning with Uncertainty for VLSI Chip Architecture Selection. CEAB Research Report 88/5. 1988.

[18] Sanz, R., et al. "Adaptative Control with a Supervisor Level using a Rule-based Inference System with Approximate Reasoning. IMACS 88. Paris: 1988.

24 Fuzzy Set Methods in Inheritance Networks

Ronald R. Yager
Machine Intelligence Institute, Iona College

ABSTRACT: Frame-based reasoning systems in which the slot values are expressed as fuzzy sets are described. It is noted that inheritance networks are generated from frame-based systems as a result of *is a kind of* links connecting the frames. We introduce a prioritized aggregation operator for making inferences in these types of inheritance networks with fuzzy set slot values. We look at a number of typical inheritance network structures and provide machinery for making inferences. We also look at inheritance networks with partial links.

24.1. Introduction

A fundamental contribution of artificial intelligence has been the development of useful structures for the representation of knowledge. One such structure is the frame-based reasoning system [1–3]. In these systems we have a collection of objects called frames, each of which corresponds to a type or class of object in our system. A frame is defined by a collection of slots (variables), particular to that object, denoting meaningful properties that can be associated with that object. For example, with human beings, it is meaningful to associate a slot corresponding to the number of eyes, whereas such a slot would be meaningless with a rock. Furthermore, these slots are filled with typical values associated with that slot. For example, the slot number of eyes would have the value 2. In most cases, these frame-based systems involve hierarchical schemes connecting the different frames via **is a kind of** and **is an element of** links. These links allow us to infer the inheritance of properties from one frame type to another. For example, because human beings are a kind of mammal, we are able to associate with human beings the characteristics associated with mammals. In these frame-based inheritance networks, we follow the convention of calling the more general object a parent of a less general object, which is called its child; thus, the mammal frame is a parent of the human being frame.

The use of fuzzy sets via the theory of approximate reasoning allows for an extension of the representational capabilities of frame-based systems by providing, with the use of linguistic values, the ability to represent imprecise linguistic values as the slot values associated with objects. As an example, we can associate with the slot height in the frame corresponding to basketball player the linguistic value *tall*. In [4, 5], Yager discussed the use of fuzzy logic in frame-based inference systems.

In many situations, the properties inherited rather than being immutable are typical and are considered as default. For example, exceptional people can be found having only one eye. Formal difficulties arise when the values inherited are typical (defeasible) and allow themselves to be overrode. Many of the issues and problems that are pervasive in nonmonotonic logics [6] also arise in these systems. The problems and properties of these inheritance networks have been investigated by a number of researchers. Touretzky [7–9] has been particularly active in this area. Sanderwall [10] and Brewka [11] have also concerned themselves with complex inheritance systems. Etherington and Reiter [12] and Etherington [13] have looked at inheritance networks with exceptions using the framework of Reiter's default logic [14].

In this chapter we consider inheritance networks in which the knowledge representation scheme uses the fuzzy set-based theory of approximate reasoning. We suggest some procedures for making inferences in inheritance networks that have both default (defeasible) and absolute knowledge (nondefeasible) information. The motivation for our suggestions is based upon the use of possibility qualification for representing typical or default values. The concept of possibility qualification was first applied to defeasible reasoning in [15].

24.2. Knowledge Representation in Approximate Reasoning

In this section, we introduce some of the basic ideas of the theory of approximate reasoning needed for our discussion of inheritance networks. More detailed and comprehensive information about the theory of approximate reasoning can be found in [16–19].

Assume V is a variable that can take its value in the set X, called the base set. For illustrative purposes we let V be the variable corresponding to age of John. In this case, X would be the set [0, 100]. If John's age is known to be *young* we can represent the concept *young* as a fuzzy subset A over the set X. In this fuzzy subset, the membership grade A(x) is the compatibility of the age x with the concept young. Alternatively, A(x) can be viewed as the truth of using the imprecise predicate young to describe someone whose age is x.

The theory of approximate reasoning uses this fuzzy subset to provide a representation of our knowledge in terms of a canonical proposition **V is A**. This statement is meant to indicate that the value of V lies in the set A. It does this by associating with V a possibility distribution Π_v, a mapping from X into the unit interval, such that $\Pi_v(x) = A(x)$, where $\Pi_v(x)$ indicates the possibility that V assumes the value x. At the core of the use of the theory of approximate reasoning is the ability to provide a semantics associated with the linguistic term *young*. While the theory of approximate finds its most profound usefulness in environments with linguistic information, it can be used to represent very precise information. For example, if we know that John is 15 years old, we can represent this in a canonical statement V is B where B = {15}. Here we see the only possible age is 15.

The ability to represent knowledge in terms of fuzzy sets allows us to be able to answer questions regarding the validity of some statement about a variable given our knowledge of that variable. For example, we may be interested in determining the validity of the statement John is 15 years old given that we know he is young. As discussed in the literature, when our knowledge is imprecise, one can't uniquely answer such questions. Assume we have the knowledge that V is A and we are interested in determining the validity of V is B. Two measures have been introduced to help us address this issue [20]. The first measure, called the measure of **possibility**, is defined as $Poss(B/A) = Max_x[A \cap B]$. The second measure, called the measure of **certainty**, is defined as $Cert(B/A) = 1 - Poss[\overline{B}/A]$. Taken together, these measures provide a bound on the truth of B given A:

$$Truth(B/A) \in [Cert(B/A), Poss(B/A)]$$

Essentially, Poss[B/A] measures the degree of intersection or compatibility of B with A, and can be seen as an optimistic value of the truth. The measure of certainty measures the degree to which A is contained in B and can be seen as a pessimistic value of the truth.

The theory of approximate reasoning provides a number of tools for translating natural language statements into canonical propositions. We briefly describe some of these. In the following, we again let V stand for the attribute John's age and A indicate the fuzzy subset *young*. The statement *John is not young* gets translated into the proposition V is B where B(x) = 1 − A(x). The proposition *John is very young* gets translated into the proposition V is C where $C(x) = (A(x))^2$. The proposition *John is sort of young* gets translated into the proposition V is D where $D(x) = (A(x))^{1/2}$. Another translation rule pertains to certainty qualified propositions [21]. The statement *John is young is α-certain* gets translated into the proposition V is E where $E(x) = A(x) \vee (1 - \alpha)$.

An important class of operations in theory of approximate reasoning are those that allow us to combine information contained in separate statements. Consider the two pieces of information V is A and V is B. The conjunction of these two pieces of information results in the proposition V is A **and** B. We can represent this as the single statement V is E. Using the intersection operation to model the **anding** of A and B, we get $E = A \cap B$ where $E(x) = A(x) \wedge B(x), \wedge$ is the Min operator. (Alternative definitions for the intersection of fuzzy sets using t-norms are widely discussed in the literature [22,23]).

Let us first look at the formal properties associated with this operation. We first note that this operation is pointwise; $E(x)$ solely depends on $A(x)$ and $B(x)$ and no other elements in X. Among the significant properties associated with the intersection operations are: **1.** Commutativity-$A \cap B = B \cup A$; **2.** Associativity-$A \cap (B \cup C) = (A \cap B) \cap C$; **3.** Monotonicity-If $A_1 \subset A_2$ and $B_1 \subset B_2$ then $A_1 \cap B_1 \subset A_2 \cap B_2$; **4.** $A \cap X = A = X \cap A$; **5.** $\varnothing \cap A = \varnothing = A \cap \varnothing$; **6. a.** $A \cap B \subset A$ **b.** $A \cap B \subset B$; **7. a.** If $A \subset B$ then $A \cap B = A$ **b.** If $B \subset A$ then $A \cap B = B$; **8.** Idempotency: $A \cap A = A$.

In the preceding we recall that $A \subset B$ if $A(x) \leq B(x)$ for all $x \in X$. We also recall [24] that a fuzzy subset A is called **normal** if there exists at least one x such that $A(x) = 1$. Fuzzy subsets that are not normal are called **subnormal**. Subnormality provides a generalization of the concept of the null set from ordinary set theory. Subnormality is seen as some indication of conflict between the information being aggregated.

Let us now look at some of the implications of these formal properties with respect to the combination of knowledge. Commutativity tells us that both pieces of information are treated in the same way. Idempotency implies that if both pieces of knowledge are the same, then we have gained nothing by combining them. Since a statement V is X essentially corresponds to having no information about V, property 4 tells us that combining this information with this any other information provides no additional information.

In some situations, rather than treating both pieces of information on an equal footing, we may want to give some preference to one piece of information over another. This may occur for example if one piece of information is more strongly believed than another. In [25], Yager introduced another type of conjunction of fuzzy sets that we call a **prioritized conjunction**.

Definition: Assume A and B are two fuzzy subsets of X. We denote the prioritized conjunction of A and B by $\eta(A, B) = D$ where D is also a fuzzy subset of X defined such:

$$D(x) = ((1 - \text{Poss}[A/B]) \wedge A(x)) \vee (A(x) \wedge B(X)),$$

where $\vee$ = max and $\wedge$ = min. We note that we can also express η as:

$$\eta(A, B)(x) = (A(x) \wedge (B(X) \vee (1 - \text{Poss}[A/B]))$$

Let us look at the functioning of this operator to see why we call it a priority operator. First we see that if there exists complete compatibility between A and B, Poss[A/B] = 1, then D = A ∩ B, the usual intersection of the two sets. If A and B are completely conflicting, $A(x) \wedge B(x) = 0$ for all x, then Poss[A/B] = 0 then D = A. Thus we see that a kind of priority exists with respect to the information being aggregated; conflict is always resolved in favor of A. Thus, using this operator allows B to refine A, in the case where D = A ∩ B, but never allows B to contradict A. Thus the information contained in A is seen to have a priority over that contained in B.

We note that this priority implies that this operation is not commutative, $\eta(A, B) \neq \eta(B, A)$. In addition, we note that this operator is not pointwise; the value of D(x) depends on the membership grades of elements other than x via the Poss [A/B] term.

In addition to not being commutative and associative, as the following example illustrates, the prioritized intersection is not monotonic.

Example: Assume $A = \{x_1, x_2, x_3\}$ and $B = \{x_5\}$. Since Poss[A/B] = 0 we get $\eta(A,B) = A = \{x_1, x_2, x_3\}$. Next consider the sets $G = \{x_1, x_2, x_3, x_4\}$ and $H = \{x_1, x_5\}$ noting that $A \subset G$ and $B \subset H$. Since Poss[G/H] = 1, then $\eta(G, H) = G \cap H = \{x_1\}$ and thus $\eta(A, B) \not\subset \eta(G, H)$.

A significant implication of this observation to common sense reasoning systems is that the gaining of knowledge doesn't necessitate a better answer.

In [25], Yager shows that the fourth property associated with the usual intersection is essentially satisfied by the prioritized intersection; $\eta(A, X) = A$ and $\eta(X, A) = A$ if A is normal; however, $\eta(X, A)(x) = (1 - Max_x[A(x)]) \vee A(x)$ if A is subnormal.

Because of the prioritized nature of η, the fifth property is not completely shared by these two forms of intersection; $\eta(\emptyset, A) = \emptyset$ whereas $\eta(A, \emptyset) = A$. It is interesting to note, as shown in [25], that $\eta(A, B) = \emptyset$ iff $A = \emptyset$.

Let us now investigate property 6. In [25], it is shown that 6a is always satisfied while 6b is semi-satisfied; a. $\eta(A, B) \subset A$ and b. $\eta(A, B)(x) \leq B(x)$ for all x where $B(x) \geq 1 - Poss [A/B]$.

Property 7 is also only partially shared; if $A \subset B$, then $\eta(A, B) = A$, whereas if $B \subset A$, then $\eta(A, B)(x) = ((1 - \beta) \wedge A(x)) \vee B(x)$, where $Max_x[B(x)] = \beta$; however, if B is normal, then $\eta(A, B) = B$. We note that when $B \subset A$, the closer B is to being normal, the closer $\eta(A, B)$ is to B, while the further B is from normal, the closer $\eta(A, B)$ is to A. Finally, we note that η is idempotent $\eta(A, A) = A$.

We note one further important distinction between the standard intersection operation and the η operation. We recall that ∩ is a pointwise operator; if F = A ∩ B, then $F(x) = A(x) \wedge B(x)$ and F(x) just depends upon A(x) and B(x). On the other hand, η is *not* a pointwise operator. If

$E = \eta(A, B)$, then $E(x) = ((1 - \text{Poss } [A/B]) \wedge A(x)) \vee A(x) \wedge B(x))$, $E(x)$ depends upon the membership grades of A and B via the Poss [A/B] term.

Let us look at the distributivity of this operation. Consider $D = \eta(A, B_1 \cup B_2)$. In this case, $D(x) = A(x) \wedge (B_1(x) \vee B_2(x) \vee (1 - \text{Poss}[A/B_1 \cup B_2)]))$. We note that $\text{Poss}[A/B_1 \cup B_2)] = \text{Poss}[A/B_1] \vee \text{Poss } [A/B_1]$, and from De Morgan's law see that:

$$1 - \text{Poss } [A/(B_1 \cup B_2)] = (1 - \text{Poss } [A/B_1]) \wedge (1 - \text{Poss } [A/B_2]).$$

Using these equivalences we get that:

$$D(x) = A(x) \wedge (B_1(x) \vee B_2(x) \vee ((1 - \text{Poss } [A/B_1]) \wedge (1 - \text{Poss } [A/B_2]))).$$

From this we see that if both $P(A/B_1) = P(A/B_2) = 0$, then we get $D = A$. If any of the $P(A/B_i) = 1$, then we get $D(x) = A(x) \wedge (B_1(x) \vee B_2(x))$.

If we consider $E = \eta(A_1 \cup A_2, B)$ we get:

$$E(x) = (A_1(x) \vee A_2(x)) \wedge (B(x) \vee ((1 - \text{Poss}[A_1/B]) \wedge (1 - \text{Poss}[A_1/B]))).$$

Let us return to our basic definition of η, $\eta(A, B) = A(x) \wedge [B(x) \vee \overline{P}]$, we have used $\overline{P} = 1 - \text{Poss } [A/B])$. We recall that $\vee$ (Max) is an example of a t-conorm. Actually, it is the weakest t-conorm. We can consider using other t-conorms in place of Max. We consider three other t-conorms:

Algebraic Sum: $S_1(a, b) = a + b - ab$

Bounded Sum: $S_2(a, b) = 1 \wedge (a + b)$

Drastic Sum: $S_3(a, b) = a$ when $b = 0$

$\qquad\qquad\qquad\qquad = b$ when $a = 0$

$\qquad\qquad\qquad\qquad = 1$ otherwise

In this context, we denote $S_0(a, b) = a \vee b$. Using these different operations we get the following formulations for η:

t-conorm(S_i)	η_i	
S_0	$\eta_0 = A(x) \wedge [B(x) \vee \overline{P}]$	
S_1	$\eta_1 = A(x) \wedge [\overline{P} + PB(x)]$	
S_2	$\eta_2 = A(x) \wedge [\overline{P} + B(x)]$	
S_3	$\eta_3 = A(x) \wedge B(x)$	if $\overline{P} = 0$
	$\eta_3 = A(x) \wedge \overline{P}$	if $B(x) = 0$
	$\eta_3 = A(x)$	otherwise

We note that cases 1 and 2 can be expressed in alternative forms:

$$\eta_1(A, B)(x) = A(x) \wedge [1 - \overline{B}(x) P]$$

$$\eta_2(A, B)(x) = A(x) \wedge [1 + B(x) - P]$$

24.3. Frame-Based Structures

The concept of a frame was originally introduced by Minsky [1] and has been developed by a number of other researchers [2, 3]. A frame provides a data structure that can be used to model typical elements of a class. The structure of a frame consists of a name identifying the frame. Affiliated with a frame is a collection of slots corresponding to attributes possessed by the type of object the frame is representing. In addition, assigned to each slot of the frame is a typical value associated with that slot. Figure 24.1 shows an example of a frame.

In [4] we suggested the use of fuzzy subsets for the representation of the values associated with the slots in a frame. The use of fuzzy subsets allows us to provide a representational language that allows for a semantics for the values associated with the slots in a frame. Essentially, in this representation, the information about the slot values are of the form of canonical statements of the type used in the theory of approximate reasoning. As we will see, this representation allows for a formal method for the combination of information contained in different frames.

A special class of frame objects are *instance* frames. These frames rather than being associated with classes of objects correspond to particular objects. For example, we may have a frame corresponding to Bill Clinton. The structures of these instance frames are the same as class frames; they have slots and slot values. One difference is that the information contained in these instance frames can be considered as definitive rather than typical as in the case of frames corresponding to classes of objects.

Frame objects, both instance and class types, in addition to having slots with associated frame variables, can have one other component. This component is called **kind of links**. Essentially, these links point to other frames of which the current frame is a subclass. With the aid of these links we can construct networks of interconnected frames. Using these connections a frame can inherit the properties, slot values, of frames it is connected to by kind of links. More generally, a frame can inherit properties from any of its ancestor frames through paths of these types of links. In this spirit, frame networks can be seen as inheritance networks. A central problem in the use of frame systems is the determination of properties associated with an instance frame based upon its connection with other frames. A problem that arises in pursuing this endeavor occurs when a conflict exists between the information contained in a frame and one of its ancestors. For example, an instance frame corresponding to John

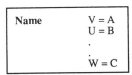

Figure 24.1   Frame structure.

Smith may inherit the property of having two eyes from an ancestor frame mammals via the intermediary frame of human being. However, if the instance frame corresponding to John Smith says that he only has one eye, we must adjudicate between these two conflicting facts.

The general imperative for inheriting information from different frames is based upon associating a priority with the pieces of information. This priority is based upon the proximity of the frame to the instance of which we are interested. Thus a piece of information in a frame closer to the instance is given more priority than one further away. Implicit in this imperative is that information contained in the instance frame itself is given the highest priority. The association of a priority with the information being combined requires us to use a prioritized conjunction.

In the following we look at some inheritance network structures and see the procedure for aggregating the information.

24.4. Inference in Inheritance Structures

In this section we look at the inheritance mechanism in frame-based inheritance systems for some standard arrangement of frames. In Figure 24.2 we consider a purely hierarchical arrangements of the frame structures.

In the following we let D_j indicate the inferred value of V resulting from combining the knowledge about V contained in the first j frames closest to our object. All fuzzy subsets will be assumed normal. In addition, any frame that has no knowledge about the value V will be assumed to have a value $V = X$, "unknown."

We initiate our structure by assigning $D_0 = A_0$, the value found in the instance frame. To calculate the inferred value after combining this with

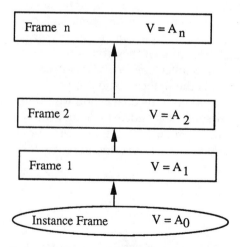

Figure 24.2 Pure hierarchical structure.

the information contained in first ancestor we get, using our prioritized conjunction, $D_1 = \eta(D_0, A_1)$, thus:

$$D_1(x) = D_0(x) \wedge (A_1(x) \vee (1 - \text{Poss } (A_1/D_0))).$$

In order to find the inferred value of V after including the information in the second ancestor, we get $D_2 = \eta(D_1, A_2)$, and hence $D_2(x) = D_1(x) \wedge (A_2(x) \vee (1 - \text{Poss } (A_2/D_1)))$. More generally, after the inclusion of the jth ancestor, we get $D_j = \eta (D_{j-1}, A_j)$, and hence:

$$D_j(x) = D_{j-1}(x) \wedge (A_j(x) \vee (1 - \text{Poss } (A_j/D_{j-1}))).$$

From this we see that this structure leads to a recursive formulation for the calculation of the inferred slot value.

We note that in this inheritance network we can use any of the other formulations for the prioritized aggregation discussed in the previous section.

A number of observations can be made regarding the information aggregation procedure. Consider the case in which a frame provides no information. For example, assume the jth ancestor has $A_j = X$, thus $D_j = \eta(D_{j-1}, X)$, hence $D_j(x) = D_{j-1}(x) \wedge [X(x) \vee (1 - \text{Max}_x(D_{j-1}(x))] = D_{j-1}(x)$. Thus the resulting information is unaffected by this frame.

Consider next the case in which $\text{Poss}(A_j/D_{j-1}) = 1$; that is, there exists a value in A_j that is completely compatible with a value in D_{j-1}. In this case, we get $D_j = D_{j-1} \cap A_j$. In this situation we get a refinement of the knowledge contained in D_{j-1} by the knowledge contained in A_j.

In the case where $\text{Poss}(A_j/D_{j-1}) = 0$, no compatibility values, then $D_j = D_{j-1}$. Here we see that the information in A_j is completely disregarded.

The following example illustrates the application of the inference mechanism just described. In this example, we use $\eta_2(A, B) = A(x) \wedge [(1 - \text{Poss}[B/A]) + B(x)]$.

Example: We assume we have an inheritance network of the type shown in Figure 24.2 having two ancestor levels above the instance frame, $n = 2$. Assume V is defined on the space $X = \{a, b, c, d\}$. Let the slot values associated with this problem be $A_0 = \{0/a, 1/b, 1/c, 1/d\}$, $A_1 = \{1/a, 0.7/b, 0.3/c, 1/d\}$ and $A_2 = \{1/a, 0.8/b, 1/c, 0.8/d\}$. In this case, $D_0 = A_0$ and $D_1 = \eta_2(D_0, A_1)$. Since $\text{Poss}[D_0/A_1] = 0.7$ we get $(1 - \text{Poss}[D_0/A_1]) = 0.3$ and thus $D_1(x) = D_0(x) \wedge [A_1(x) + 0.3]$. In this case, we get $D_1(a) = 0$, $D(b) = 1$, $D(c) = 0.6$ and $D(d) = 0$. Next we calculate:

$$D_2(x) = D_1(x) \wedge [A_2(x) + (1 - \text{Poss}(D_1/A_2))].$$

Since $\text{Poss } (D_1/A_2) = 0.8$, we get $1 - \text{Poss}(D_1/A_2) = 0.2$ and $D_2(x) = D_1(x) \wedge [A_2(x) + 0.2]$. From this we see $D_2(a) = 0$, $D_2(b) = 1$, $D_2(c) = 0.6$ and $D_2(d) = 0$; therefore $D = \{0/a, 1/b, 0.6/c, 0/d\}$.

We now consider a second typical inheritance network generated from a frame-based reasoning system (see Figure 24.3). In this situation, the ancestors of the instance object rather than forming a pure hierarchy diverge into different paths.

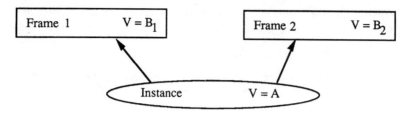

Figure 24.3   Inheritance network with diverging ancestors.

In this figure it is assumed that the instance object has two *kind of links,* which lead to unrelated ancestors. Each of the ancestors provide independent information.

In this situation we use as our formulation for obtaining the information, D, and infer from all the frames of this network the formulation $D = \eta(A, B_1 \cap B_2) \cap \eta(A, B_1 \cup B_2)$. In the following, we denote $E = \eta(A, B_1 \cap B_2)$ and $F = \eta(A, B_1 \cup B_2)$.

Let us look at the functioning of this formulation for aggregating the frame information. In order to get a more intuitive understanding of how this structure works, we assume that all sets are crisp. We also use the following notation $\alpha_1 = Poss[A/B_1]$, $\alpha_2 = Poss[A/B_2]$, $\alpha_3 = Poss[A/B_1 \cap B_2)]$ and $\alpha_4 = Poss[A/B_1 \cup B_2)] = \alpha_1 \vee \alpha_2$.

Case 1: In this case, we assume there is a value common to all frames, $A \cap B_1 \cap B_2 \neq \Phi$ Because of our assumption of crispiness in the case we get $\alpha_1 = \alpha_2 = \alpha_3 = \alpha_4 = 1$. From this we obtain $E = A_1 \cap B_1 \cap B_2, F = A \cap (B_1 \cup B_2)$, and finally $D = E \cap F = A_1 \cap B_1 \cap B_2$. Thus we see that the inferred value is the conjunction of the information contained in each of the frames.

Case 2: In this case, we assume A is individually compatible with each of the ancestor frames but all three are conflicting, $A \cap B_1 \neq \varnothing, A \cap B_2 \neq \varnothing$ and $A \cap B_1 \cap B_2 = \varnothing$. Therefore, in this case, we have $\alpha_1 = \alpha_2 = \alpha_4 = 1$ and $\alpha_3 = 0$; this gives us $E = A, F = (A \cap B_1) \cup (A \cap B_2)$, and finally $D = E \cap F = (A \cap B_1) \cup (A \cap B_2)$. Thus, in this case, we see our inferred value is the union of the solutions that A has individually in common with each of its ancestors.

Case 3: In this case, we assume that A is compatible with only one of the ancestors and conflicting with the other, $A \cap B_1 \neq \varnothing, A \cap B_2 = \varnothing$ and $A \cap B_1 \cap B_2 = \varnothing$. From this we get $\alpha_1 = 1, \alpha_2 = 0, \alpha_3 = 0$, and $\alpha_4 = 1$, which gives us $E = A$, $F = A \cap B_1$ and $D = E \cap F = A \cap B_1$. Thus, in this case, our inferred value is the intersection of A with the ancestor with which it is compatible.

Case 4: Here we consider the situation where A is conflicting with both its ancestors, $A \cap B_1 = \varnothing, A \cap B_2 = \varnothing$ and $A \cap B_1 \cap B_2 = \varnothing$. From this we get $\alpha_1 = \alpha_2 = \alpha_3 = \alpha_4 = 0$. Using these values we calculate $E = A, F = A$ and finally $D = A$. Thus, in this case, the information in the ancestor frames is disregarded.

The following provides an illustrative example of the inference process in this type of inheritance network. We again use η_2 as our prioritized aggregation operator.

Example: Again we assume V is defined on the base set X = {a, b, c, d}. We let the frame values be A = {0/a, 1/b, 1/c, 0/d}, B_1 = {1/a, 0.8/b, 0.2/c, 0/d} and B_2 = {0/a, 0.6/b, 0.8/c, 1/d}. We denote G = $B_1 \cap B_2$ = {0/a, 0.6/b, 0.2/c, 0/d} and H = $B_1 \cup B_2$ = {1/a, 0.8/b, 0.8/c, 1/d}. Since E = η_2(A, G) and Poss[A/G] = 0.6 we get E(x) = A(x) $\wedge$ [G(x) $\vee$ 0.4] and hence E(a) = 0, E(b) = 1, E(c) = 0.6 and E(d) = 0. Since F = η_2(A, H) and Poss[A/H] = 0.8 we get F(x) = A(x) $\wedge$ [H(x) + 0.2] and hence F(a) = 0, F(b) = 1, F(c) = 1 and F(d) = 1. From this we get D = F $\cap$ E = {0/a, 1/b, 0.6/c, 0/d}.

In Figure 24.4 we show an extension of the previous situation with n diverging immediate ancestors.

To express the formulation used to calculate the inferred value in this structure, we make use of the following notational convention. Let **B** = {$B_1, B_2, \ldots, B_n$} and let $\mathcal{B} = 2^B$, the power set of **B**. Let F be any element in $\mathcal{B}$, a subset of B_j's. We denote Conj(F) as the intersection of the subsets in F. Finally, we let E_j be the subset of $\mathcal{B}$ consisting of all subsets of **B** that have j components. Using this notation we express the combined information as:

$$D = \bigcap_{j=1}^{n} \eta(A, \bigcup_{F \in E_j} Conj(F))$$

For example, in the case when n = 3, we get:

$$D = \eta(A, B_1 \cup B_2 \cup B_3) \cap \eta(A, (B_1 \cap B_2) \cup (B_1 \cap B_3) \cup (B_2 \cap B_3)) \cap$$
$$\eta(A, B_1 \cap B_2 \cap B_3)$$

In Figure 24.5 we consider a third structure that can arise in hierarchical frame networks. In this structure, rather than the independent paths diverging from a frame, we have n paths *converging* into an ancestor frame.

To express the aggregation operator used in this situation we use the notation introduced in the preceding. In the following, D is the inferred value obtained from all the information. Our method is an iterative procedure described as follows. We calculate $D_1 = \eta(X, \bigcup_{F \in E_1} Conj(F))$. From this we then calculate $D_2 = \eta(D_1, \bigcup_{F \in E_2} Conj(F))$ and continue calculating in this manner using $D_i = \eta(D_{i-1}, \bigcup_{F \in E_i} Conj(F))$. After calculating D_n, we obtain final inferred value as $D = \eta(D_n, A)$. In the case when n = 3, we have $D_1 = \eta(X, B_1 \cup B_2 \cup B_3)$, $D_2 = \eta(D_1, ((B_1 \cap B_2) \cup (B_1 \cap B_3) \cup (B_2 \cap B_3)))$, $D_3 = \eta(D_2, B_1 \cap B_2 \cap B_3)$ and then $D = \eta(D_3, A)$.

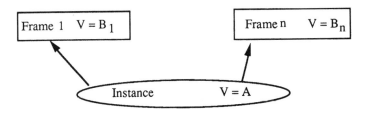

Figure 24.4   Instance with n diverging ancestors.

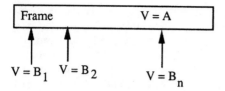

Figure 24.5 Network with links converging into a frame.

In this section we have described the inference mechanism for various typical formulations of inheritance networks. In calculating the inherited values in more complex networks, these standard structures can be used to obtain the inferences of subparts of the network.

24.5. Partially Connected Links

In the preceding we have assumed that all links were fully connected links. Here we consider the possibility that links are partial. In particular, we provide a framework in which a child is a partial descendent of its immediate ancestor. For example, if we have a frame corresponding to writers and John is a part-time writer, then the *is a kind of* link connecting the instance frame John to the writers frame is partial. More generally, we allow that the subset of ancestors is fuzzy rather than crisp. Specifically, we are allowing for degrees of *is a kind of* connection. Figure 24.6 shows a simple case of the situation we are now considering.

In Figure 24.6, by α, we are indicating that the object is only partially, to degree α, a kind of the ancestor frame. In this case, the inferred value, D, obtained by combining information in both these frames is obtained using $D = \eta(A, B; \alpha)$ where:

$$D(x) = A(x) \wedge [B(x) \vee (1 - \alpha) \vee (1 - \text{Poss}(A/B))]$$

In the above we note the addition of the term $(1 - \alpha)$ in the aggregation process. We note that if the connection is full, $\alpha = 1$, then this formulation reduces to the original case. If no connection exists, $\alpha = 0$, then $D = A$. If the connection is a partial one, $0 < \alpha < 1$, the effect of B is reduced even if it is fully compatible with A.

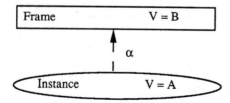

Figure 24.6 Partially connected is a kind of link.

Alternative forms can be considered in the formulation of η. Essentially, we have formulated $\eta(A, B; \alpha)$ by $D(x) = A(x) \wedge S(B(x), (1 - \alpha), (1 - \text{Poss} (A/B)))$ where S is a t-conorm and have used the Max for S. If we use the bounded sum instead of the max in the preceding, we get:

$$D(x) = A(x) \wedge [B(x) + (1 - \alpha) + (1 - \text{Poss} (A/B))]$$

We now consider a more general hierarchical network (see Figure 24.7) in which each link has a partial connection, α_i, to its parent node.

In the following we let $\omega_i = \text{Min}_{j=1 \text{ to } i}[\alpha_j]$, which is the value of the weakest link in the chain from instance frame to the ith frame. The process of calculating the overall inferred value D in this partially connected network uses an iterative process similar to the one used in the network in Figure 24.2. At each level we calculate $D_i = \eta(D_{i-1}, B_i; \omega_i)$ where we initialize the process with $D_0 = A$. The final inferred value D is obtained as $D = D_n$.

It is interesting to consider an alternative view of the basic aggregation process in the case of partial linkage, Figure 24.6. This view is based upon the use of certainty transformation introduced earlier. We can consider the effect of a partial link to reduce the certainty of our belief in B. Thus we can look at a partial link as effectively saying *V is B is α-certain*. From our translation rules this gives us V is F where $F(x) = B(x) \vee (1 - \alpha)$. We then form $D = \eta(A, F)$, and hence we get:

$$D(x) = A(x) \wedge [F(x) \vee (1 - \text{Poss}(A/F))]$$

$$D(x) = A(x) \wedge [B(x) \vee (1 - \alpha) \vee (1 - \text{Poss}(A/F))]$$

Since $\text{Poss}(A/F) = \text{Max}_x[A(x) \wedge (B(x) \vee (1 - \alpha))] = \text{Max}_x[A(x) \wedge B(x)] \vee [(1 - \alpha) \wedge \text{Max}_x A(x)]$. With $a = \text{Max}_x A(x)$ and $P = \text{Poss}(A/B)$ we get $D(x) =$

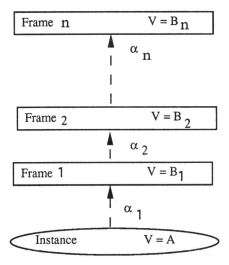

Figure 24.7 Pure hierarchy with partial links.

$A(x) \wedge [B(x) \vee \overline{\alpha} \vee (1 - (P \vee (\overline{\alpha} \wedge a)))]$. We can also express this as $D(x) = A(x) \wedge [B(x) \vee \overline{\alpha} \vee (\overline{P} \wedge (\alpha \vee \overline{a}))]$ after the use of DeMorgan's laws. A further simplification can be had. Since $\overline{P} \wedge (\alpha \vee \overline{a}) = \overline{P} \wedge \alpha \vee \overline{P} \wedge \overline{a}$ and noting that $a = \text{Max}_x A(x) \geq \text{Poss}(A/B)$, and hence $\overline{a} \leq \overline{P}$, we get $\overline{P} \wedge (\alpha \vee \overline{a}) = \overline{P} \wedge \alpha \vee \overline{a}$. This gives us a the form $D(x) = A(x) \wedge (B(x) \vee \overline{\alpha} \vee (\overline{P} \wedge \alpha) \vee \overline{a})$. If we use the bounded sum instead of the max, we get $D(x) = A(x) \wedge (B(x) + \overline{\alpha} + \overline{P} \wedge \alpha + \overline{a})$.

24.6. Conclusion

The use of fuzzy subsets in frame-based reasoning systems provides an ability to represent and manipulate linguistic information in this class of structures. We have studied inheritance networks generated from frame-based models. Our specific interest was in the case where the slot values are fuzzy subsets. We introduced and studied a prioritized conjunction operator for combining information from different frames. We showed how this operator works in different typical inheritance network structures. Finally we considered inheritance networks with partial links.

24.7. References

[1] Minsky, M. "A Framework for Representing Knowledge," in *The Psychology of Computer Vision.* ed. P. Winston. pp. 211–277. New York: McGraw-Hill, 1975.

[2] Brachman, R. "I Lied about Trees, or Defaults and Definitions in Knowledge Representation." *AI Magazine,* Vol. 6, No. 3 (1985), pp. 80–93.

[3] Brachman, R., and J.G. Schmolze. "An Overview of the KL-ONE Knowledge Representation System." *Cognitive Science,* Vol. 9 (1985), pp. 171–216.

[4] Yager, R.R. "Linguistic Representation of Default Values in Frames." *IEEE Transactions on Systems, Man, and Cybernetics,* Vol. 18 (1984), pp. 630–633.

[5] ———. "Nonmonotonic Inheritance Systems." *IEEE Transactions on Systems, Man, and Cybernetics,* Vol. 18 (1988), pp. 1028–1034.

[6] Ginsberg, M.L. *Readings in Nonmonotonic Reasoning.* Los Altos: Morgan Kaufmann, 1987.

[7] Touretzky, D.S. "Implicit Ordering of Defaults in Inheritance Systems." *Proceedings, 5th National Conference on Artificial Intelligence.* pp. 322–325. Austin, Tex.: 1984.

[8] ———. *The Mathematics of Inheritance Systems.* Los Altos: Morgan Kaufmann, 1986.

[9] Touretzky, D.S., et al. "A Clash of Intuitions: The Current State of Nonmonotonic Inheritance Systems." *Proceedings, 10th IJCAI Conference.* Milan: 1987.

[10] Sandewall, E. "Nonmonotonic Inference Rules for Multiple Inheritance with Exceptions." *Proceedings, IEEE 74.* pp. 1345–1353. 1986.

[11] Brewka, G. "The Logic of Inheritance in Frame Systems." *Proceedings, 10th IJCAI.* pp. 483–488. Milan: 1987.

[12] Etherington, D.W., and R. Reiter. "On Inheritance Hierarchies with Exceptions." *Proceedings, 3rd National Conference on Artificial Intelligence.* pp. 104–108. Washington, D.C.: 1983.

[13] Etherington, D.W. "Formalizing Nonmonotonic Reasoning Systems." *Artificial Intelligence,* Vol. 31 (1987), pp. 41–85.

[14] Reiter, R. "A Logic for Default Reasoning." *Artificial Intelligence,* Vol. 13 (1980), pp. 81–132.

[15] Yager, R.R. "Using Approximate Reasoning to Represent Default Knowledge." *Artificial Intelligence,* Vol. 31 (1987), pp. 99–112.

[16] Zadeh, L.A. "A Theory of Approximate Reasoning," in *Machine Intelligence.* eds. J. Hayes, et al. New York: Halstead Press, 1979.

[17] Yager, R.R., et al. *Fuzzy Sets and Applications: Selected Papers by L.A. Zadeh.* New York: John J. Wiley and Sons, 1987.

[18] Yager, R.R. "Deductive Approximate Reasonings Systems." *IEEE Transactions on Knowledge and Data Engineering,* Vol. 3 (1991), pp. 399–414.

[19] Dubois, D., and H. Prade. "Fuzzy Sets in Approximate Reasoning Part I: Inference with Possibility Distributions." *Fuzzy Sets and Systems,* Vol. 40 (1991), pp. 143–202.

[20] Zadeh, L.A. "Fuzzy Sets and Information Granularity," in *Advances in Fuzzy Set Theory and Applications.* eds. M.M. Gupta, et al. pp. 3–18. North Holland: 1979.

[21] Yager, R.R. "Approximate Reasoning as a Basis for Rule-based Expert Systems." *IEEE Transactions on Systems, Man, and Cybernetics,* Vol. 14 (1984), pp. 636–643.

[22] Yager, R.R., and D.P. Filev. *Essentials of Fuzzy Modeling and Control.* New York: John J. Wiley and Sons, 1984.

[23] Klir, G.J., and Y. Bo. *Fuzzy Sets and Fuzzy Logic: Theory and Applications.* Upper Saddle River: Prentice Hall, 1995.

[24] Zadeh, L.A. "Fuzzy Sets." *Information and Control,* Vol. 8 (1965), pp. 338–353.

[25] Yager, R.R. "Nonmonotonic Set Theoretic Operations." *Fuzzy Sets and Systems,* Vol. 42 (1991), pp. 173–190.

25 POSSINFER: A Software Tool for Possibilistic Inference*

Jörg Gebhardt and Rudolf Kruse
Department of Mathematics and Computer Science
University of Braunschweig
D-38106 Braunschweig, Germany

ABSTRACT: Probabilistic graphical models such as Bayesian networks and Markov networks have proved to be powerful normative tools for uncertain reasoning in the presence of crisp data. On the other hand, many applications show that the explicit modelling of *imprecise* (multivalued) data is desirable to fit the needs of industrial practice, so that graphical models based on nonstandard numerical settings should be studied in more detail. Possibility theory has turned out to be a very promising framework for this purpose. It provides a justified form of information compression and efficient approximate reasoning techniques without affecting the expressive power of decision making in systems that are nonsensitive to slight changes in the knowledge base.

Following this line we present the theoretical background and application features of the software tool POSSINFER (POSSibilistic INFERence) which we have developed in cooperation with Deutsche Aerospace in order to support graphical modelling and inference mechanisms with respect to the possibilistic setting, similar to HUGIN in the probabilistic setting.

25.1. Introduction

One of the major aims of graphical modelling in knowledge-based systems is to provide a framework for the efficient decision making-

* This work has partially been funded by CEC-ESPRIT III Basic Research Project 6156 (DRUMS II)

oriented conditioning of *imperfect generic knowledge* about a current object state of interest (e.g., rules, uncertain relations), given any application-dependent *pieces of evidence* (e.g. facts, instantiations of variables) [17].

More particularly, let V denote a set of variables taking their values on attached finite domains $\Omega^{(v)}$, $v \in V$. Furthermore, let Ω denote their joint domain and Ω^A the marginal domain of all variables in $A \subseteq V$.

The variables in V are assumed to characterize an object type under consideration, so that the current state of a certain object of this type can be specified with the aid of an element ω_0, taken from the chosen set Ω of alternatives.

Imperfect generic knowledge concerns the prior uncertainty about the truth of the proposition "$\omega_0 = \omega$," quantified for all possible alternatives $\omega \in \Omega$. Such knowledge can often be represented in terms of a distribution function on Ω, which is, for instance, a probability distribution, a mass distribution, or a possibility distribution, referred to the respective numerical setting.

The consideration of evidential knowledge consists in conditioning this distribution based on additional available information about ω_0, and to calculate the resulting marginal distributions for each of the single variables in V.

Due to the high cardinality of multidimensional sets of alternatives, it is reasonable to search for appropriate *decomposition techniques* that allow to confine to calculations in lower-dimensional joint domains.

The *qualitative part* of a graphical model therefore consists of a graphical structure; for example, a directed acyclic graph (DAG), an undirected graph (UG), or a chain graph (CG), each of which specifies existing dependencies and independencies between the variables.

The *quantitative part* of a graphical model is a family of distribution functions on joint domains that are determined by means of the graphical structure. In the case of a DAG representation, conditional distribution functions are used to quantify the uncertainty about the value of a variable, given any instantiation of its parent nodes in the DAG; whereas, for example, in a hypertree representation, for each hyperedge, one has to deal with unconditioned distribution functions, defined on the joint domains of the variables that are contained in the respective hyperedge.

In both cases, the stated decomposability allows to establish efficient reasoning processes that enjoy *local propagation algorithms* rather than global conditioning procedures.

The most advanced graphical models for uncertain reasoning in knowledge-based systems are *Bayesian networks* and *Markov networks* [20, 18], for which successful software tools such as HUGIN [1, 14], PATHFINDER [12], and BAIES [3] are available.

A more general approach to graphical modelling in various uncertainty calculi that covers the probabilistic setting and the belief function setting as well as the possibilistic setting in the framework of *valuation-*

based systems (*VBS*) [25] has been proposed in [26, 24] and implemented in PULCINELLA [22].

In this chapter, we outline the formal underpinnings and the features of the interactive software tool POSSINFER that supports graphical modelling in terms of possibilistic networks. Section 25.2 deals with the notion of a possibilistic network, its semantical background, and how to use it for reasoning tasks. In this context it is important to clarify in which way a possibilistic network reflects possibilistic independence. It turns out that *possibilistic noninteractivity* is a proper alternative type of possibilistic independence, when directly compared with the standard independence concept used in valuation-based systems, which is strongly related to Dempster's rule of conditioning, specialized to possibility measures. Based on the presented concepts and methods, Section 25.3 gives a brief illustration of the functionality of POSSINFER. Section 25.4 is for some concluding remarks, and Section 25.5 for the list of references.

25.2. Possibilistic Networks

A *possibilistic network* is a graphical model $N = (H, \Pi)$ that consists of a hypertree $H = (V, \varepsilon)$ and a family $\Pi = (\Pi_E)_{E \in \varepsilon}$ of possibility distributions. The set ε of hyperedges specifies, from a qualitative point of view, all relevant dependencies between the variables V under consideration. Additionally, for each hyperedge $E \in \varepsilon$, the attached possibility distribution π_E : $\Omega^E \to [0, 1]$ quantifies the uncertainty about the occurrence of particular relationships $\omega_E \in \Omega^E$.

25.2.1. Interpretation of a Possibilistic Network

The idea of a possibilistic network is to represent a *lossless join decomposition* of a possibility distribution $\pi : \Omega \to [0, 1]$ that specifies our imperfect general knowledge about the current object state $\omega_0 \in \Omega$ of interest, so that for any $\omega \in \Omega$, the quantity $\pi(\omega)$ is the degree of possibility for the truth of the proposition "$\omega_0 = \omega$". Lossless join decomposability means that π can be recovered from the family $(\pi_E)_{E \in \varepsilon}$ of possibility distributions.

Formally spoken, for any nonempty subsets U and W of variables, let Π_W^U denote the *projection* from Ω^U onto Ω^W, and $\hat{\Pi}_W^U$ the *cylindrical extension* from Ω^W to Ω^U. Furthermore, for any $\alpha \in [0, 1]$, let:

$$[\pi]_\alpha \overset{\text{Df}}{=} \{\omega \in \Omega \mid \pi(\omega) \geq \alpha\} \tag{1}$$

denote the α-*cut* of π.

Using this notion, the possibility distributions π_E occur as projections of π onto Ω^E:

$$[\pi_E]_\alpha \overset{\text{Df}}{=} \Pi_E^V([\pi]_\alpha). \tag{2}$$

The possibilistic network $N = (H, \Pi)$ constitutes a *lossless join decomposition* of π, iff:

$$[\pi]_\alpha = \bigcap_{E \in \varepsilon} \hat{\Pi}_E^V([\pi_E]_\alpha) \qquad (3)$$

holds for all $\alpha \in [0, 1]$.

Note that for each possibility degree α, condition (3) corresponds to lossless join decomposability of the relation $[\pi]_\alpha$, which is a property well known from database theory (e.g. [28]). In this sense, we deal with a generalization from the relational approach of handling imprecise data to the uncertainty calculus of possibility theory, simply introducing an ordering of *possibilistic confidence levels* $\alpha \in [0, 1]$.

25.2.2. Independence in Possibilistic Networks

Condition (3) reflects *independence assumptions* for each of the relations $[\pi]_\alpha$ that we want to study in some more detail:

Let X, Y, and Z be disjoint subsets of variables, and $X \neq \varnothing$. X is called *independent of Y given Z* with respect to a nonempty relation $R \subseteq \Omega$, iff for any instantiations $Y = y$ and $Z = z$ (i.e.: $y = \Pi_Y^V(\omega_0)$ and $z = \Pi_Z^V(\omega_0)$) it is:

$$R(X \mid z) = R(X \mid yz), \qquad (4)$$

where

$$R(X \mid z) \overset{\text{Df}}{=} \Pi_X^V(R \cap \hat{\Pi}_Z^V(z)),$$
$$R(X \mid yz) \overset{\text{Df}}{=} \Pi_X^V(R \cap \hat{\Pi}_Y^V(y) \cap \hat{\Pi}_Z^V(z)). \qquad (5)$$

The background of this definition is as follows. A relation $R \subseteq \Omega$ that is chosen as a set-valued specification of ω_0 is called *correct* w.r.t. ω_0, iff $\omega_0 \in R$. For any $R' \subseteq \Omega$, the relation R' is *at least as specific as R*, iff $R' \subseteq R$.

A correct relation R is therefore most specific w.r.t. ω_0, iff for all proper subsets R' of R, considering our actual knowledge about ω_0, specified by R, it is not guaranteed that R' is correct w.r.t. ω_0.

If R is correct and of maximum specificity w.r.t. ω_0, then $R(X \mid z)$ is the most specific correct set-valued specification of $\Pi_X^V(\omega_0)$, given the information that $\Pi_X^V(\omega_0) = z$. The independence condition (4) simply says that any additional information about Y does not further specify our knowledge about X, which perfectly fits the intuitive meaning of independence.

Using the concept of relational independence as formalized in equality (4), we are now in the position to analyze which kind of possibilistic independence is represented in a possibilistic network:

Let $\varepsilon = \{E_1, \ldots, E_m\}$, so that $(E_1, \ldots, E_m)$ is a *construction sequence* [19] for the hypertree H. For $j = 1, \ldots, m$, define $V_j \overset{\text{Df}}{=} V_1 \cup \ldots \cup V_{j-1}$, $Z_j \overset{\text{Df}}{=} V_{j-1} \cap E_j$, and $Y_j \overset{\text{Df}}{=} E_j \setminus Z_j$, where $V_0 \overset{\text{Df}}{=} \varnothing$.

Let $X_j \in \varepsilon$ such that $Z_j \subseteq X_j$. It is easy to prove that lossless join decomposability (3) is satisfied, iff $I_{[\pi]_\alpha}(X_j \setminus Z_j, Y_j \mid Z_j)$ holds for all $j = 1, \ldots, m$ and all $\alpha \in [0, 1]$. This is the case, iff the possibility distributions π_E are pairwise *noninteractive*, which means that for any pair $(E, E') \in \varepsilon \times \varepsilon$ of hyperedges such that $X = E \setminus E'$, $Y = E' \setminus E$, and $Z = E \cap E'$, we obtain:

$$\pi(X \cup Y \mid z) \equiv \min(\pi(X \mid z), \pi(Y \mid z)), \tag{6}$$

where the conditioned projection of π onto Ω^W, $\varnothing \neq W \subseteq V$, is defined as:

$$[\pi(W \mid z)]_\alpha \overset{\text{Df}}{=} \Pi_W^V([\pi]_\alpha \cap \hat{\Pi}_Z^V(z)). \tag{7}$$

This result establishes possibilistic noninteractivity [13] as a reasonable approach to the definition of independence in possibilistic networks. Subsection 25.2.4. will provide further arguments why possibilistic noninteractivity seems to be the best choice among the various existing proposals for a concept of possibilistic independence.

25.2.3. Reasoning in Possibilistic Networks

The reasoning task in a possibilistic network is to calculate possibility distributions $\pi_\upsilon : \Omega^{(\upsilon)} \to [0, 1]$, $\upsilon \in V$, as the most specific correct specifications of the values $\omega_0^{(\upsilon)} = \Pi_{\{\upsilon\}}^V(\omega_0)$ of the current object state ω_0 of interest, given the generic knowledge π and additional application-dependent pieces of evidence in form of an instantiation $Z = z$ of a subset $Z \subseteq V$ of variables. Since π is supposed to be the most specific correct specification of ω_0 in terms of a possibility distribution, which means that $[\pi]_\alpha$ is correct and of maximum specificity w.r.t. ω_0, given any possibilistic confidence level α, it is easy to verify that:

$$[\pi_\upsilon]_\alpha = [\pi(\{\upsilon\} \mid z)]_\alpha. \tag{8}$$

A propagation algorithm for possibilistic networks can take advantage of the lossless join decomposability property of π, by calculating:

$$[\pi_\upsilon]_\alpha = \Pi_{\{\upsilon\}}^E([\pi(E \mid z)]_\alpha) \tag{9}$$

for an arbitrary hyperedge such that $\upsilon \in E$. For more details on this topic, we refer to [16].

25.2.4. Some Additional Notes on Possibilistic Independence

Although the necessity of justifying an appropriate concept of possibilistic independence has been well known for a couple of years [13], a unique approach has not been successful yet. Some recent discussions can be found in [6, 7, 4]. In our opinion, the main cause for the existence of competing proposals arises from the fact that concerning the treatment of imperfect information, there are two different levels of reasoning, which are the *credal level*, where *knowledge representation* and all operations on the given knowledge take place (e.g., conditioning in the light of new pieces of evidence), and the *pignistic level*, where the final step of *decision making* follows [27]. In probabilistic reasoning, we do not find a real distinction between these two levels, since all imperfect information is represented with the aid of probability distributions.

On the other hand, the distinction becomes obvious in the nonstandard calculi that deal with uncertainty in the presence of imprecise (multivalued) data. For example, in the belief function setting [23], knowledge representation and any belief change operation on the credal level is realized in terms of belief functions or mass distributions, whereas the so-called *pignistic transformation,* using a *generalized insufficient reason principle,* ends in a probability distribution for decision making [27]. In possibility theory [5], the basis for knowledge representation on the credal level is the concept of a (not necessarily normalized) possibility distribution and Zadeh's *extension principle* [29] for operating on possibility distributions. On the pignistic level, a possibility distribution may be normalized and transformed into its induced possibility measure, which is the starting point for the decision-making task. Due to the existence of the mentioned levels of reasoning, we find at least two different approaches to the definition of a concept of independence in possibility theory, namely *imprecision-driven* possibilistic independence on the credal level (without normalization) and *uncertainty-driven* possibilistic independence (with normalization) on the pignistic-level. The generalization of (4) to the possibilistic setting reads as follows:

X is *independent of Y given Z* w.r.t. a possibility distribution π, iff for any instantiations $Y = y$ and $Z = z$:

$$(a) \quad \pi(X \mid z) \equiv \pi(X \mid yz), \text{ or}$$
$$(b) \quad \pi^*(X \mid z) \equiv \pi^*(X \mid yz), \tag{10}$$

where

$$\pi^*(X \mid \cdot) \overset{Df}{=} \frac{\pi(X \mid \cdot)}{\pi(V \mid \cdot)} \tag{11}$$

denotes the normalization of the respective possibility distribution, and $\pi(V \mid yz) > 0$ is assumed to be satisfied; (a) is called *imprecision-driven* possibilistic independence (in symbols: $I_\pi(X, Y \mid Z)$) and (b) is *uncertainty-driven* possibilistic independence (in symbols: $I_\pi^*(X, Y \mid Z)$).

$I_\pi(X, Y \mid Z)$ is equivalent to (conditional) *possibilistic noninteractivity,* while $I_\pi^*(X, Y \mid Z)$ corresponds to independence with respect to *Dempster's rule of conditioning,* specialized to possibility measures. Furthermore, it turns out that $I_\pi(X, Y \mid Z)$ is a *semi-graphoid* and $I_\pi^*(X, Y \mid Z)$ even a *graphoid,* so that the two independence models are in agreement with the main axioms for graphical models that were proposed by J. Pearl [21]. The fact that $I_\pi(X, Y \mid Z)$ does not satisfy the intersection axiom of graphoids is not surprising, because imprecision-driven possibilistic independence can be viewed as a generalization of the relational independence model, which itself is only a semi-graphoid. An extensive discussion of this topic is given in [4].

Conditions (6) and (10) provide good reasons to apply possibilistic noninteractivity as the fundamental concept of independence in the software tool POSSINFER.

An additional important argument arises from the fact that possibilistic noninteractivity conforms with the *extension principle*, which can be envisaged as the essential concept for operating on possibility distributions and thus for possibilistic reasoning on the credal level within a possibilistic network.

In this context it should also be pointed out that a strict formal and semantical approach to possibility theory confirms the extension principle not just as a principle, but as the only way of operating on possibility distributions; that is, correctness- and maximum specificity-preserving [8, 9].

Note that uncertainty-driven possibilistic independence is *not* consistent with applying the extension principle, but it can be justified in Shenoy's valuation-based systems, by treating possibility theory in its restricted view as a special case of Dempster-Shafer theory when confined to consonant mass distributions.

25.3. POSSINFER: An Implementation

The presented concept of a possibilistic network has been applied successfully in cooperation with the Mathematics and Computer Science Department of the University of Braunschweig and Deutsche Aerospace in a project for uncertainty modelling and data fusion [2]. A part of the cooperation is the conception and implementation of a prototype version of the software tool POSSINFER (POSSibilistic INFERence) in order to support reasoning with the aid of possibilistic networks, using the programming language C on SUN Workstations under SUN-UNIX, X-Windows, and OSF/Motif.

POSSINFER distinguishes between two basic application modes, which are modelling of generic knowledge and evidential reasoning, respectively.

25.3.1. Modelling of Generic Knowledge

In this mode, an expert is supported in providing a possibilistic network for the representation of the available generic knowledge about a certain application domain of interest.

25.3.1.1. Qualitative Part of the Possibilistic Network. The first step of building the knowledge base is to fix the set V of variables, to define their attached domains, and to construct the dependency hypertree $H = (V, \varepsilon)$ of the network on the screen.

The domains $\Omega^{(\upsilon)}$ of the variables $\upsilon \in V$ correspond to self-defined enumerations types or the standard datatypes *real* and *integer*, which are well known from imperative programming languages. In the case of *real* or *integer,* POSSINFER needs a partitioning of the respective domain into a finite number of intervals, so that $\Omega^{(v)}$ can be viewed as a set of selected representative values.

The restriction to finite domains (at least for internal calculations) allows an efficient execution of the main operations that are necessary for the propagation algorithm. Using the vertical representation of possibility distributions as mappings from domains into the unit interval, rather than the horizontal representation with the aid of a finite number of α-cuts, the calculation of cylindrical extension, intersection, and projection is simply based on the operators *min* and *max,* and arrays may be employed instead of linked dynamic data structures, by which a costly heap management is rendered dispensible.

25.3.1.2. Quantitative Part of the Possibilistic Network. The second step of building the knowledge base is to introduce the quantitative part of the network, namely the family $\Pi = (\pi_E)_{E\epsilon\epsilon}$ of possibility distributions. The definition of π_E is either pointwise by input of the possibility degrees $\pi_E(\omega_E)$ for all $\omega_E \in \Omega^E$, or by formulation of a finite number of inference rules of the type:

$$R_i^E : if\ A_i\ is\ \pi_{A_i}\ then\ B_i\ is\ \pi_{B_i}, \tag{12}$$

where $A_i \cup B_i = E, A_i \cap B_i = \varnothing, i = 1, \ldots, k_E$, and π_{A_i}, π_{B_i} are possibility distributions on Ω^{Ai} and Ω^{Bi}, respectively.

The meaning of such a rule is as follows: If π_{A_i} is the most specific correct imperfect specification of $\Pi_{A_i}^V(\omega_0)$, then π_{B_i} is the most specific correct imperfect specification of $\Pi_{B_i}^V(\omega_0)$.

It can be shown that π_E, when interpreted as the conjunction of the rules R_i^E, equals the minimum of the Gödel relations that are induced by pairs (π_{A_i}, π_{B_i}). For more details, see [9].

In order to make the specification of the generic knowledge in form of a possibilistic rule base more expressive, POSSINFER supports the declaration of a finite set of names for user-defined (parametrized) possibility distributions, taken from various available classes of functions with standard shapes such as rectangles, triangles, and trapezoids, respectively.

25.3.2. Evidential Reasoning

In this mode, the specified possibilistic network can be used for the reasoning process, given any piece of evidence for the single variables $\upsilon \in V$, be it precise, imprecise, or possibilistic. Based on local propagation techniques described in [16], POSSINFER calculates the conditioned possibility distributions π_υ that we mentioned in Section 2.3. An illustrative example of a POSSINFER session is presented in Figure 25.1.

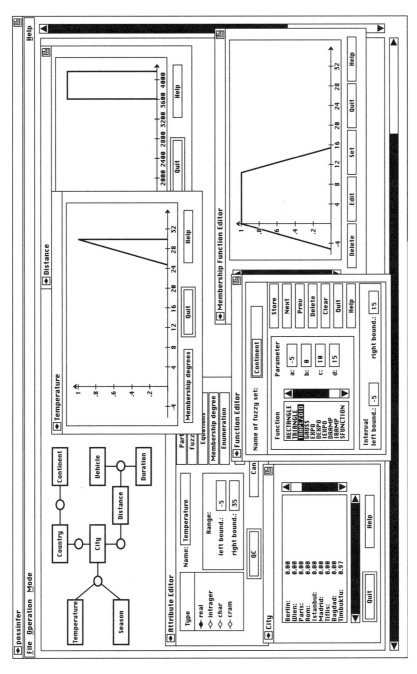

Figure 25.1 An example of a POSSINFER session.

25.4. Conclusion

POSSINFER is a theoretically well-founded software tool for possibilistic graphical modelling based on hypertree structures and noninteractivity as the fundamental concept of possibilistic independence. Contrary to probabilistic approaches, the possibilistic setting supports the treatment of uncertainty in the presence of imprecise (multivalued) data, but in order to reach efficiency, a certain kind of information compression, considered in the interpretation of possibility distributions and approximate instead of crisp reasoning has to be accepted [11]. Practical experience shows that such a restriction or simplification is tolerable in many systems. As a consequence, it is near at hand that possibilistic graphical modelling may grow up to play a similar role in the field of uncertain reasoning in knowledge-based systems as current fuzzy control as a tool for (information-compressed) interpolation between crisp points in vague environments in the field of control engineering [15].

Concerning the design of possibilistic networks, the effort to specify the qualitative part as well as the quantitative part is considerable, so that an automated induction by using underlying background knowledge could alleviate such specification difficulties. In our current research, we therefore investigate methods of learning possibilistic networks (with DAG or hypertree structure) from databases of sample cases. Preliminary results on the successful induction of a nontrivial network can be found in [10] and will be implemented in POSSINFER.

25.5. References

[1] Andersen, S.K., et al. "HUGIN—A Shell for Building Bayesian Belief Universes for Expert Systems." *Proceedings, 11th International Joint Conference on Artificial Intelligence.* pp. 1080–1085. 1989.

[2] Beckmann, J., et al. "Possibilistic Inference and Data Fusion." *Proceedings, 2nd EUFIT Conference.* pp. 46–47. 1994.

[3] Cowell, R. "BAIES—A Probabilistic Expert System Shell with Qualitative and Quantitative Learning," in *Bayesian Statistics 4.* eds. J. Bernardo, et al. pp. 595–600. Oxford: Oxford University Press, 1992.

[4] de Campos, L.M., et al. "Syntactic and Semantic Approaches to Possibilistic Independence," in *Symbolic and Quantitative Approaches to Reasoning and Uncertainty, Lecture Notes in Artificial Intelligence 946.* eds. C. Froidevaux and J. Kohlas. pp. 77–88. Springer, Berlin: 1995.

[5] Dubois, D., and H. Prade. *Possibility Theory.* New York: Plenum Press, 1988.

[6] del Cerro, L.F., and A. Herzig. "Possibility Theory and Independence." *Proceedings, 5th IPMU Conference.* pp. 820–825. 1994.

[7] Fonck, P. "Conditional Independence in Possibility Theory," in *Uncertainty in Artificial Intelligence, Proceedings of the 10th Conference.* eds. R.L. de Mantaras and D. Poole. pp. 221–226. Los Altos: Morgan and Kaufmann, 1994.

[8] Gebhardt, J., and R. Kruse. "A Possibilistic Interpretation of Fuzzy Sets by the Context Model." *Proceedings, FUZZ-IEEE 1992.* pp. 1089–1096. San Diego, Calif.: 1992.

[9] ———. "A New Approach to Semantic Aspects of Possibilistic Reasoning," in *Symbolic and Quantitative Approaches to Reasoning and Uncertainty, Lecture Notes in Computer Science 747.* eds. M. Clarke, et al. pp. 151–160. Springer, Berlin: 1993.

[10] Gebhardt, J., and R. Kruse. "Learning Possibilistic Networks from Data." *Proceedings, 5th International Workshop on Artificial Intelligence and Statistics.* pp. 233–244. Fort Lauderdale, Fla.: 1995.

[11] Gebhardt, J., and R. Kruse. "Reasoning and Learning in Probabilistic and Possibilistic Networks: An Overview," in *Machine Learning: ECML '95, Lecture Notes in Artificial Intelligence,* 912. pp. 3–16. 1995.

[12] Heckerman, D. *Probabilistic Similarity Networks.* Cambridge: MIT Press, 1991.

[13] Hisdal, E. "Conditional Possibilities, Independence, and Noninteraction." *Fuzzy Sets and Systems,* Vol. 1 (1978), pp. 283–297.

[14] Jensen, F.V., and J. Liang. "drHUGIN—A System for Value of Information in Bayesian Networks." *Proceedings, 5th Conference on Information Processing and Management of Uncertainty in Knowledge-based Systems (IPMU '94).* pp. 178–183. Paris: 1994.

[15] Klawonn, F., et al. "Fuzzy Control on the Basis of Equality Relations with an Example from Idle Speed Control." *IEEE Transactions on Fuzzy Systems,* Vol. 3 (1995), pp. 336–350.

[16] Kruse, R., et al. *Foundations of Fuzzy Systems.* Chichester: Wiley, 1994.

[17] Kruse, R., et al. *Uncertainty and Vagueness in Knowledge-based Systems: Numerical Methods.* Springer, Berlin: 1991.

[18] Lauritzen, S.L., and D.J. Spiegelhalter. "Local Computations with Probabilities on Graphical Structures and their Application to Expert Systems." *Journal of the Royal Statistics Society Series B,* Vol. 2, No. 50 (1988), pp. 157–224.

[19] Maier, D. *The Theory of Relational Databases.* Rockville: Computer Science Press, 1983.

[20] Pearl, J. *Probabilistic Reasoning in Intelligent Systems: Networks of Plausible Inference.* New York: Morgan Kaufmann, 1992.

[21] Pearl, J., and A. Paz. "Graphoids: A Graph-based Logic for Reasoning about Relevance Relations," in *Advances in Artificial Intelligence 2.* eds. B.D. Boulay, et al. pp. 357–363. North Holland: 1987.

[22] Saffiotti, A. and E. Umkehrer. "PULCINELLA: A General Tool for Propagating Uncertainty in Valuation Networks," in *Proceedings 7th Conference on Uncertainty in Artificial Intelligence.* eds. B. D'Ambrosio, et al. San Mateo: Morgan Kaufmann, 1991.

[23] Shafer, G. *A Mathematical Theory of Evidence.* Princeton: Princeton University Press, 1976.

[24] Shafer, G., and P.P. Shenoy. "Local Computation in Hypertrees." School of Business, University of Kansas at Lawrence, 1988.

[25] Shenoy, P.P. "A Valuation-based Language for Expert Systems." *International Journal of Approximate Reasoning,* Vol. 3 (1989), pp. 383–411.

[26] Shenoy, P.P., and G.R. Shafer. "Axioms for Probability and Belief-Function Propagation," in *Uncertainty in Artificial Intelligence (4).* eds. R.D. Shachter, et al. pp. 169–198. North-Holland: 1990.

[27] Smets, P., and R. Kennes. "The Transferable Belief Model." *Artificial Intelligence,* Vol. 66 (1994), pp. 191–234.

[28] Ullman, J.D. *Principles of Database and Knowledge-base Systems.* Rockville: Computer Science Press Inc., 1988.

[29] Zadeh, L.A. "The Concept of a Linguistic Variable and its Application to Approximate Reasoning." *Information Sciences,* Vol. 9 (1975), pp. 43–80.

26 Possibilistic ATMS in a Data Fusion Problem

Salem Benferhat
I.R.I.T., University of Toulouse III, France

Thomas Chehire, Francesco Fulvio Monai
Thomson-CSF/RCC, Colombes, France

ABSTRACT: Possibilistic ATMS are truth maintenance systems oriented toward hypothetical reasoning where both assumptions and justifications can bear an uncertainty weight. Uncertainty is represented in the framework of possibility theory. In possibilistic logic, uncertain clauses are handled as such, and then in possibilistic ATMS, the management of uncertainty is not separated from the other classical capabilities of the ATMS. The main interest of a possibilistic ATMS is to take advantage of the uncertainty pervading the available knowledge so as to rank-order environments in which a given statement is true. Basic algorithms associated with possibilistic ATMS are given. Finally, we detail the suitability and the advantages of using a possibilistic ATMS to a data fusion application.

26.1. Introduction

Assumption-based truth-maintenance systems (ATMS) [3, 4] are automated reasoning systems oriented toward hypothetical reasoning since they are able to determine under which set of assumption(s) a given proposition is true. This set is called the "label" of the proposition. In this chapter we present an extension of the ATMS, called "possibilistic ATMS" (or Π-ATMS for short), where the management of uncertainty is integrated inside the basic capabilities of the ATMS. Uncertainty pervading justifications or grading assumptions is represented in the framework of possibility and necessity measures ([18], [9]); these measures agree with the ordinal nature of what we wish to represent (it enables us to distinguish between what is plausible and what is less plausible). The certainty of each granule in the knowledge base (represented by a clause in possibilistic logic [8]) is evaluated under the form of a lower bound of a necessity measure. This uncertainty in the deduction process is propagated by means of an extended resolution principle. Uncertainty degrees are then naturally attached to the configurations of assumptions in which a given proposition is true; one can also evaluate to what degree a given configuration of assumptions is inconsistent or compute the more or less certain consequences of a configuration of assumptions. This approach enables us to handle disjunctions and negations of assumptions without particular problem. Moreover, by rank-ordering configurations according to the degrees attached to them, Π-ATMS provides a way of limiting combinatorial explosion when using ATMS in practice.

We present the basic definitions and results of possibilistic logic first. In section 26.3 we give the basic definitions and functionalities of the Π-ATMS. Section 26.4 presents an algorithm for the computation of labels and contradictory environments ("nogoods") based on an extension of the so-called CAT-correct resolution, initially developed by Cayrol and Tayrac [1, 16]. An application to a data fusion problem will be widely described in section 26.5.

26.2. Possibilistic Logic

26.2.1 Modeling Uncertainty with Possibility and Necessity Measures

Possibilistic logic [11, 13] is an extension of classical logic where one manipulates propositional or first-order calculus closed formulas weighted by lower bounds of possibility or necessity degrees that belong to [0,1]. In this chapter we restrict ourselves to a fragment of possibilistic logic, the "clausal possibilistic propositional logic," where the considered formulas are exclusively conjunctions of possibilistic propositional clauses weighted by necessity degrees [8, 10].

A possibility measure Π satisfies the following axioms [18, 9]:

(i) $\Pi(\perp) = 0; \Pi(\top) = 1$

(ii) $\forall p, \forall q, \Pi(p \vee q) = \max(\Pi(p), \Pi(q))$

where $\perp$ and $\top$ denote respectively contradiction and tautology. We emphasize that we only have $\Pi(p \wedge q) \leq \min(\Pi(p), \Pi(q))$ in the general case. A necessity measure is associated by duality with a possibility measure by $\forall p, N(p) = 1 - \Pi(\neg p)$. Axiom (ii) is then equivalent to $\forall p, \forall q, N(p \wedge q) = \min(N(p), N(q))$ and, as a consequence, $N(p) > 0$ implies that $\Pi(p) = 1$. We adopt the following conventions:

- $N(p) = 1$ means that, given the available knowledge, p is certainly true.

- $1 > N(p) > 0$ means that p is somewhat certain and ¬p not certain at all (since the axioms imply that $\forall p$, min $(N(p),N(\neg p)) = 0$).

- $N(p) = N(\neg p) = 0$ (equivalent to $\Pi(p) = \Pi(\neg p) = 1$) corresponds to the case of total ignorance; namely, from the available knowledge, nothing enables us to say if p is rather true or rather false.

Possibilistic logic is well-adapted to the representation of states of incomplete knowledge, since we can distinguish between the complete lack of certainty in the falsity of a proposition p $(N(\neg p) = 0)$ and the total certainty that p is true $(N(p) = 1)$.

26.2.2. Possibilistic Clauses and Possibilistic Resolution

An uncertain clause will be a classical logic clause c to which a valuation is attached, taken as a lower bound of its necessity measure. Thus, in the following, we write (c α) as soon as the inequality $N(c) \geq \alpha$ is taken for granted. Resolution has been extended to possibilistic logic [8, 11] as follows:

$$\frac{(c\ \alpha)}{(c'\ \beta)}$$
$$\overline{(c''\ \min(\alpha,\beta))}$$

where c″ is a classical resolvent of the classical clauses c and c′. The refutation method is generalized to possibilistic logic [7, 8]. If we are interested in proving that a formula f is true, we add to the knowledge base Σ the assumption $N(\neg f) = 1$, that is, that f is certainly false. Let Σ′ be the resultant knowledge base. Then we can show that any valuation attached to the empty clause produced by the extended resolution pattern from Σ′ is a lower bound α of the necessity measure of the conclusion f. It entails the existence of "optimal refutations," that is, derivations of an empty clause with a maximal valuation. We take the notation $\Sigma \vdash (c\ \beta)$ if and only if there exists a β′-refutation with $\beta' \geq \beta$, that is, a deduction of $(\perp \beta')$, from $\Sigma' = \Sigma \cup \{(\neg c\ 1)\}$.

26.2.3. Semantics and Partial Inconsistencies

A semantics has been defined for clausal possibilistic logic [10, 13]. Let c be a clause and M(c) the set of the models of c, then the models of (c α) are defined by a fuzzy set M (c α) with a membership function:

$$\mu_{M(c\ \alpha)}^{(\omega)} = 1 \quad \text{if } \omega \in M(c)$$

$$= 1 - \alpha \text{ if } \omega \in M(\neg c),$$

where ω is a (classical) interpretation. Then the fuzzy set of models of a set of weighted clauses $\Sigma = \{C_1, C_2, \ldots, C_n\}$, where C_i stands for $(c_i\ \alpha_i)$, is the intersection of the fuzzy sets $M(C_i)$; thus:

$$\mu_{M(\Sigma)}(\omega) = \min_{i=1,\ldots,n} \mu_{M(C_i)}(\omega).$$

The consistency degree of Σ is defined by $\mathrm{cons}(\Sigma) = \max_\omega\{\mu M(\Sigma)^{(\omega)}\}$; it estimates the degree to which the set of models of Σ is not empty. The quantity $\mathrm{Inc}(\Sigma) = 1 - \mathrm{cons}(\Sigma)$ is called degree of inconsistency of Σ. We say that F is a logical consequence of Σ if $\forall \omega$, $\mu_{M(F)}(\omega) \geq \mu_{M(\Sigma)}(\omega)$, which will be written $\Sigma \vDash F$. Finally, we have the completeness theorem ([10, 13]): $\Sigma \vdash (c\ \beta)$ iff $\Sigma \vDash (c\ \beta)$.

26.2.4. Hypothetical Reasoning

As it was pointed out in [12], the weighted clause $(\neg p \vee q\ \alpha)$ is semantically equivalent to the weighted clause $(q\ \min(\alpha, v(p)))$ where $v(p)$ is the truth value of p; therefore, $v(p) = 1$ if p is true and $v(p) = 0$ if p is false. Indeed, for any uncertain proposition $(p\ \alpha)$ we can write $\mu_{M(p\,\alpha)}(\omega)$ under the form $v(p\ \alpha) = \max(v(p), 1 - \alpha)$, where $v(p)$ is assigned by interpretation ω. Then obviously:

$$v(\neg p \vee q\ \alpha) = \max(v(\neg p \vee q), 1 - \alpha) = \max(1 - v(p), v(q), 1 - \alpha)$$

$$= \max(v(q), 1 - \min(v(p), \alpha)) = v(q\ \min(v(p), \alpha))$$

The equivalence between the weighted clauses $(\neg p \vee \neg s \vee q\ \alpha)$ and $(\neg p \vee q\ \min(\alpha, v(s)))$ expresses that the rule "if p and s are true then q is certain to the degree α" means that "in an environment where s is true, if p is true then q is certain to the degree α," when we decide to consider s as an assumption. This enables us to express that if the clause $\neg p \vee q$ is certain to the degree α in an environment where s is true, and if the clause $p \vee r$ is certain to the degree β in an environment where t is true, then the resolvent clause $q \vee r$ is certain to the degree $\min (\alpha, \beta)$ in an environment where s *and* t are true. It turns out that when $\alpha = \beta = 1$, the previous resolution rule is very close to the CAT-correct resolution rule [1, 16], which separates the assumptions from the other literals by sorting them, and where resolution is restricted so as to get rid of the nonassumption literals. Hence, possibilistic logic can capture not only the propagation of uncertainty, but at the same time the propagation of the reasons for uncertainty.

26.3. Basic Definitions of a Possibilistic ATMS

Classical ATMS require that the clauses contained inside the knowledge base are certain; we may wish to handle more or less uncertain information without losing the capacities of the ATMS. ATMSs make the distinction between *assumptions* (or *hypotheses*) and other data (or *facts*). In the following, assumptions and facts are considered as Π-ATMS nodes.

The basic principle of the Π-ATMS introduced in [12] is to associate to each clause a weight α that is a lower bound of its necessity degree. Assumptions may also be weighted; that is, the user or the inference engine may decide at any time to believe an assumption with a given certainty degree. A Π-ATMS is able to answer the following questions:

1. Under what configuration of the assumptions is a fact d certain to some degree (i.e., what assumptions shall we consider as true in order to have d certain to degree α)?

2. What is the inconsistency degree of a given configuration of assumptions?

3. In a given configuration of assumptions, to what degree is each observed fact certain?

The kind of classical ATMS extended here is Cayrol and Tayrac's [1, 16] generalized ATMS, where each piece of information is represented by a (general) propositional clause. It make it possible to have:

- A uniform representation for all pieces of knowledge (no differentiated storage and treatment between justifications and disjunctions of assumptions).

- The capability of handling negated assumptions as assumptions; thus environments and nogoods may contain negations of assumptions; this approach differs from DeKleer "NATMS" [5] where negated assumptions do not appear inside the environments.

- A simple and uniform algorithm for the computation of labels, based on a restricted form of resolution (see section 26.4).

26.3.1. Environments and Labels

First, the basic notions attached to the classical ATMS can be generalized. Let Σ be a set of necessity-valued clauses. Let E be a set of assumptions; we only consider nonweighted assumptions (i.e., they will have the implicit weight 1). The following definitions are useful:

- $[E\ \alpha]$ is an *environment* of the fact d if $N(d) \geq \alpha$ is a logical consequence of $E \cup \Sigma$;

- $[E\ \alpha]$ is an α-*environment* of d if $[E\ \alpha]$ is an environment of d and if $\forall \alpha' > \alpha, [E\ \alpha']$ is not an environment of d (α is maximal);

- $[E\ \alpha]$ is an α-contradictory environment, or α-*nogood*, if $E \cup \Sigma$ is α-inconsistent with α maximal. The α-nogood $[E\ \alpha]$ is said to be minimal if there is no β-nogood $[E'\ \beta]$ such that $E \supset E'$ and $\alpha \leq \beta$.

The label of the fact d, $L(d) = \{[E_i\ \alpha_i], i \in I\}$ is the unique fuzzy subset of the set of environments for which the four following properties hold:

- *(weak) consistency:* $\forall [E_i\ \alpha_i] \in L(d)$, $E_i \cup \Sigma$ *is* β*-inconsistent, with* $\beta <$ α_i (i.e., $Inc(E_i \cup \Sigma) < \alpha_i$); it guarantees that either E_i is consistent (i.e., $\beta = 0$), or its inconsistency degree is anyway strictly less than the certainty with which d can be deduced from $E_i \cup \Sigma$ (i.e., we are sure to use a consistent subbase of $E_i \cup \Sigma$ to deduce d, see [13]).

- *soundness:* $L(d)$ is sound if $\forall [E_i\ \alpha_i] \in L(d)$ we have $E_i \cup \Sigma \vDash (d\ \alpha_i)$; that is, $L(d)$ contains only environments of d.

- *completeness:* $L(d)$ is complete if for every environment E' such that $E' \cup \Sigma \vDash (d\ \alpha')$ then $\exists i \in I$ such that $E_i \subset E'$ and $\alpha_i \geq \alpha'$. That is, all minimal α-environments of d are present in $L(d)$.

- *minimality:* $L(d)$ is minimal if it does not contain two environments $(E_1\ \alpha_1)$ and $(E_2\ \alpha_2)$ such that $E_1 \subset E_2$ and $\alpha_1 \geq \alpha_2$. It means that $L(d)$ only contains the most specific α-environments of d (i.e., all their assumptions are useful).

Ranking environments according to their weight in the label of each fact provides a way for limiting the consequences of combinatorial explosion: indeed when a label contains too many environments, the $\prod$-ATMS can help the user by giving the environments with the greatest weight(s) only. We will illustrate this advantage in section 26.5 (See also [6]).

26.3.2. Contexts

To extend the ATMS notion of context, we now consider *weighted assumptions.* A weighted assumption is a couple $(H\ \alpha)$ where H is an assumption and $\alpha \in [0,1]$ is the *a priori* certainty degree assigned to H. The *context* associated with the set of weighted assumptions $\mathscr{E}$ is the set of all couples $(d, val\mathscr{E}(d))$, where d is a fact or an assumption, and $val\mathscr{E}(d)$ $= \sup\{\alpha, \mathscr{E} \cup \Sigma \vDash (d\ \alpha)\}$. Let us now give the following theorem: Let $\mathscr{E}$ be a set of valued assumptions. Let d be a fact; it can be shown that $\mathscr{E} \cup \Sigma \vDash$ $(d\ \alpha)$ in possibilistic logic if and only if $\exists [E_i\ \alpha_i] \in Label(d)$, $E_i =$ $\{H_{i,1}, H_{i,2}, \ldots, H_{i,n}\}$ such that:

1. $\mathscr{E}^* \supset E_i$ where $\mathscr{E}^*$ is the classical set of assumptions obtained from $\mathscr{E}$ by ignoring the weights.
2. $\alpha \leq \min(\alpha_i, \beta_1, \beta_2, \ldots, \beta_n)$ where $\beta_1, \beta_2, \ldots, \beta_n$ are the weights attached to $H_{i,1}, H_{i,2}, \ldots, H_{i,n}$ in $\mathscr{E}$.
3. $\alpha > Inc(\mathscr{E} \cup \Sigma)$.

26.3.3. Interpretations

In the classical ATMS, an environment E is said to be an *interpretation* if it is consistent and if adding any assumption to it make it inconsistent.

Interpretations are complete descriptions of a given situation in terms of assumptions. In possibilistic logic, an interpretation E may be partially inconsistent, namely it may contain a nogood that does not however violate weak consistency. We say that an interpretation E is totally consistent if it satisfies the two following requirements:

1. $\text{Incons}(\sum \cup E) = 0$
2. $\forall\, H \notin E$ (H is an assumption), $\text{Incons}(\sum \cup E \cup \{H\}) > 0$.

where $\text{Incons}(X)$ is the degree of the inconsistency of X.

Totally consistent interpretations can be defined using the notion of *candidates* that are environment C such that for each nogood N we have $N \cap C = \varnothing$. A candidate C is said to be *minimal* if it does not exist a candidate C such that $C' \subset C$. We can show that the complement of a minimal candidate is a totally consistent interpretation, that is:

$$I = \{T - C\,/T \text{ is the set of all assumptions, and C is a minimal candidate}\}.$$

In general, the number of totally consistent interpretations is very important and in practice it is not possible to take into account all the totally consistent interpretations. The certainty weights can then be used to rank the interpretations. Let T be the set of all assumptions and N the set of all nogoods. The following algorithm gives the best interpretations:
While N is nonempty:

- Select the most certain nogood and remove it from N.
- Remove from T the least certain assumption involved in the selected nogood.
- Remove from N all nogoods involving the selected assumption. The resulting T is the best maximal set of assumptions.

26.4. Basic Algorithms of a Possibilistic ATMS

The type of ATMS that we extend to possibilistic logic is the one proposed by Cayrol and Tayrac [1, 16]. Contrary to De Kleer's [3, 4] classical ATMS, this system, called π-RCO (Oriented CAT-correct Possibilistic Resolution) (CAT: Clause whose Antecedent is Typed) uses possibilistic resolution in order to deduce a specific type of clauses of interest for the ATMS, called π-CATI (Possibilistic Clause whose Antecedent is Typed and Interesting). As in the classical ATMS, the set of data is divided into two groups: T and NT containing respectively the assumption data and the nonassumption ones. The computation of labels and nogoods requires some further definitions.

26.4.1. Definition of a π-CATI and a π-RCO Possibilistic Resolution

A clause is of the form A → B where A is a conjunction of positive literals and B is a disjunction of positive literals. A is called antecedent and B consequent. A weighted clause (C α) is a π-CATI, if and only if:

1. every literal in the antecedent side of C is an assumption, and,

2. it contains at most one nonassumption literal in the consequent side of C.

If (C α) satisfies only the first condition, we call it a π-CAT (Possibilistic Clause with Typed Antecedent).

The basic idea of the π-RCO is to use the possibilistic resolution rule in order to deduce every π-CATI that is logically entailed from the initial set of clauses. In order to minimize the number of applications of possibilistic resolution, an arbitrary but complete ordering O is introduced on the set of nonassumption data NT. The π-RCO consists in applying possibilistic resolution between two weighted clauses C_1 and C_2 of the form:

C_1:	A_1	→{x} ∪ B_1	α_1
C2:	$A_2 \cup \{x\}$	→B_2	α_2

$\mathcal{R}(C_1,C_2)$:	$A_1 \cup A_2$	→ $B_1 \cup B_2$	$\min(\alpha_1,\alpha_2)$

under one of the two following conditions:

1. C_1 and C_2 are π-CATI such that the consequent side of $\mathcal{R}(C_1,C_2)$ contains at most one nonassumption literal.

2. The three following conditions are satisfied:

2.1. C_1 is a π-CAT,

2.2. x is the smallest (relatively to O) nonassumption datum in the antecedent side of C_2.

2.3. x is one of the two smallest nonassumption data in the consequent side of C_1.

26.4.2. The Algorithm

As in the classical ATMS, π-RCO is incremental, provided that the set of clauses $\sum$ is saturated, which means that before the introduction or the deduction of a new clause, all possible possibilistic resolutions π-RCO are executed, thus only the possibilistic resolutions that are enabled by the newly introduced clause are processed. On the other hand, after the introduction or the inference of the new clause, the set of clauses $\sum$ must be minimized by removing every tautology and every subsumed clause.

We recall that a clause (A→B α_1) is a tautology iff A ∩ B = ∅. The clause (A_1→B_1 α_1) subsumes the clause (A_2→B_2 α2) iff $A_2 \supseteq A_1$, $B_2 \supseteq B_1$ and $\alpha_1 \geq \alpha_2$.

Each time a new clause is introduced in the system, it is checked if it is a tautology or a subsumed clause; then, if none of these holds, all clauses that are subsumed by the newly introduced clause are removed, and lastly all possible π-RCO resolutions are triggered with this new clause. This cycle is repeated for every deduced clause, and the following is an algorithm summarizing these operations:

```
Procedure introduce (cl)
Begin
   ; cl is the newly introduced clause, Σ represents the
   knowledge base.
   J:={cl}; J contains all deduced or introduced clauses.
   while (J≠∅) do
       .choose a weighted clause c of J.
       .remove c from J.
       .if c is not subsumed· and c is not a tautology then
           .remove all clauses from Σ which are subsumed by c.
           .add c to Σ.
           .K:=all-π-RCO(c) ; K contains all possible clauses
           which allow us to
                           ; apply π-RCO resolution with c.
           .while (K≠∅) do
               .remove a weighted clause cl from K
               .add to J the π-RCO resolvent ℛ(cl,c)
End introduce
```

26.4.2. Using π-RCO in a Possibilistic ATMS

We show in this section how possibilistic resolution π-RCO can be used to compute every minimal nogood and the label of each datum. By definition, [E α] is an environment of a literal d, wrt the set of clauses Σ iff E $\cup \Sigma \vDash (d\ \alpha)$; this is equivalent to $\Sigma \vDash (E \rightarrow d\ \alpha)$ [13]. Thus an environment of a literal d is characterized by a clause containing exactly the literal d in his consequent side, and only assumptions or negated assumptions in his antecedent side. Obviously, this clause is a π-CATI. Thus, the label of a nonassumption literal d is:

$$L(d) = \{(P \cup \{\neg x\ /\ x \in Q\}\ \alpha]\ /\ (P \rightarrow \{d\} \cup Q\ \alpha) \in \Sigma \text{ is a } \pi\text{-CATI}\}.$$

An environment [E α] is a nogood if and only if ($\bot$ α) is a logical consequence of E$\cup\Sigma$, i.e $\Sigma \vDash (E \rightarrow \bot\ \alpha)$. Thus a nogood is denoted by a clause containing only assumptions in their antecedent part; these clauses are also π-CATI. Hence, the nogoods are computed as here:

$$Nogood = \{[P \cup \{\neg x\ /\ x \in Q\}\ \alpha]\ /\ (P \rightarrow Q\ \alpha) \in \Sigma \text{ is a } \pi\text{-CATI and } T \supseteq Q\}.$$

26.5. A Data Fusion Application

Data fusion allows the elaboration and the evaluation of a situation synthesized from low-level information provided by different kinds of sensors. The fusion of the collected data will result in fewer and higher-level information more easily assessed by a human operator and that will assist him or her effectively in the decision process.

SEFIR (Système Expert de Fusion Interactive du Renseignement) is a prototype of a data fusion expert system that receives messages about observations provided by intelligence officers describing the nature, the number and the disposition of enemy units on the battle field, and tries to derive the enemy formation [15]. Units can be of several types (tank, motorized rifle, etc.) and are organized in hierarchical levels ranging from the higher division level down to the regiment, battalion, company, and section levels. A data fusion process consists normally of three phases [17]:

- the *correlation* phase, that is the association and combination of different information concerning the same unit, obtained from different sources;

- the *aggregation* phase, that is the identification of a unit of a certain hierarchical level given partial evidence of its component units of the lower hierarchical level;

- the *fusion* phase, that is the elaboration of a(some) consistent situation(s) given partial information provided by several sources.

The correlation phase is not implemented in SEFIR since we assume that each intelligence officer sends the informations concerning the units moving on the axis that has been allocated to him solely. Each unit is thus observed only once. The messages received by SEFIR contain symbolic and numeric informations such as: (i) the type and level of the observed unit; (ii) the time of the observation; (iii) the axis of enemy progress on which the observer is located.

SEFIR aggregates the observations described in the messages into higher hierarchical level units relying on its (incomplete) knowledge of the enemy's organization and doctrine. This knowledge is encoded in rules of the form: "if three tank sections are observed on the same axis within an interval of time of one hour, then they may belong to the same tank company."

The uncertainty resulting from such incomplete knowledge induces the generation of a relevant number of somewhat contradictory hypotheses (nogoods) of possible aggregations of units for a given situation. For example, if four tank sections are observed on the same axis within one hour, it is possible to create two hypotheses of aggregation at the superior hierarchical level of companies, as shown in Figure 26.1.

These two hypotheses are contradictory since they contain two common sections and thus they can't be both considered for a further aggre-

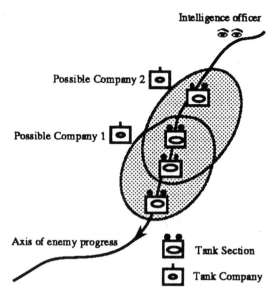

Figure 26.1   Creation of two contradictory hypotheses
of companies, given evidence of four sections.

gation at the battalion higher hierarchical level. Moreover, an expert
would prefer the *Possible Company 1* hypothesis because it is more compact than the other one. Possibility theory is well adapted to represent
such preferences.

When dealing with such uncertain knowledge, one should be able to
distinguish in the set of hypotheses the ones that are too uncertain to be
considered as true, the ones that are almost certain and the ones that
have an intermediary degree of certainty. An additional requirement
comes from the fact that a data fusion system has to free the operator
from low-level details and to draw his or her attention on the higher
level (fused) informations for a timely decision-making process. This
can be achieved only if the possible contradictory choices provided by
the system are limited enough. It is thus necessary to take advantage of
all the available knowledge and induced constraints to limit the potential hypotheses to the most realistic (i.e., certain) ones. In the case of
SEFIR, the knowledge that guides the discrimination among hypotheses is given by:

- the hierarchical structure of the observed enemy disposition;
- the movement strategies of units depending on their level.

Three main features are thus requested for developing such a data
fusion application: i) handling both numeric and symbolic data; ii) handling multiple uncertain hypotheses somewhat contradictory; and iii)
reducing these multiple hypotheses.

The first SEFIR prototype relied completely on the knowledge engineer for all the stated functionalities. This resulted in ad hoc algorithms that are neither proven to be correct nor easily reusable in similar applications by another knowledge engineer. This section describes a new prototype of the SEFIR expert system, using a Π-ATMS, that can ease the development of data fusion applications.

26.5.1. Coupling a Π-ATMS and an Inference Engine

In the Π-ATMS, justifications are clauses without variables (Propositional Logic). However, most applications require more expressiveness power and rely on an OPS-like forward chaining inference engine with first order rules. These engines encode usually a *match-select-act* cycle. The propositions contained in the fact base may match some rules condition parts, and thus instantiate one or more rules. Instantiated rules are queued in a so-called conflict set for future selection and eventual firing. When a rule is fired, it may create new facts that will in turn instantiate new rules. In this framework, justifications are dynamically generated and link facts created by a rule's right-hand side to the facts that instantiated the rule. We thus implemented a toolkit integrating an inference engine and a Π-ATMS, as shown in Figure 26.2. A similar architecture in the case of a standard ATMS is presented in [14].

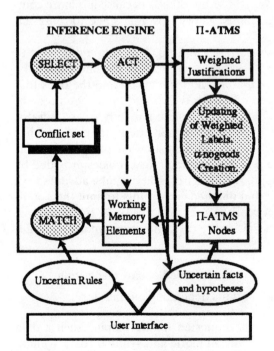

Figure 26.2 Coupling a Π-ATMS and an OPS-like inference engine.

The user can create uncertain hypotheses, facts, and rules. Facts and hypotheses are stored as Π-ATMS nodes, and corresponding working memory elements are created in the inference engine and can eventually match rules conditions. When a rule is selected and then fired, its action part does not modify directly the working memory of the inference engine (as it normally does in the standard match-select-act cycle). Instead, new uncertain facts and hypotheses can be created and associated to new working elements, or new justifications can be installed on existing facts and hypotheses.

The role of the inference engine is thus to produce the weighted justifications, while the role of the Π-ATMS is to manage the uncertainty by updating weighted environments in labels and handling weighted contradictions, as it was described in section 26.4.

26.5.2. The Aggregation Phase in SEFIR

We are now going to describe how the proposed toolkit architecture supports the new SEFIR expert system. Units are represented as uncertain facts with the following informations:

- *id:* internal reference of the unit;
- *level:* section, company, battalion, regiment, or division;
- *type:* tank, motorized rifle, and so on;
- *time:* interval of time during which the unit has been observed;
- *axis:* axis on which the unit has been observed to move;
- *subunits:* units of the lower level composing the unit itself.

The uncertainty degree of each unit is computed from its type, its level, its completeness (number and type of subunits), and the covered spatiotemporal surface.

In SEFIR, the generation of weighted hypotheses is limited by applying domain knowledge. However, a significant number of hypotheses is produced at each level in the enemy organization hierarchy, entailing intractable Π-ATMS computations. It is thus crucial to select only the "best" aggregation hypotheses, for an efficient assistance in the enemy threat assessment by the operator. The algorithm given in the end of section 26.3 shows how to select the "best" aggregation hypotheses.

We started by breaking down the global problem in smaller, more tractable ones. This was eased by the use of the Thomson-CSF proprietary XIA inference engine. XIA allows to structure the knowledge base in many independent rule-bases (or Knowledge Sources), each of which can infer on many independent private working memories (pwm). A similar functionality is provided by the GBB-OPS5 integrated problem-solving architecture [2].

The reasoning process has been structured in order to handle the different levels of units in different private working memories. Each level is treated separately by a specialized knowledge source with rules that formalize:

- the available knowledge on the enemy organization at that level;
- the constraints that restrict the aggregation of units of that level into units of the higher hierarchical level.

The possible aggregations done at each level have been segmented in different phases: (i) aggregation of sections into companies; (ii) aggregation of companies into battalions; (iii) aggregation of battalions into regiments; (iv) aggregation of regiments into divisions.

At the end of each of these phases, the Π-ATMS allows to identify just the most certain among the possible combinations and to eliminate the ones that would have been most probably discarded by an expert. We detail in the following the aggregation mechanism of units of level n in units of level n + 1. The best possible aggregations of units of level n ordered by certainty are treated separately in different private working memories to produce the best possible aggregations of units of level n + 1:

- For each private working memory of level n:

  The inference engine computes, starting from the units of this private working memory and using the rules of the level n, all the hypotheses of possible *complete* units for level n + 1 that are compatible with the aggregation and spatio-temporal constraints.

  The Π-ATMS computes the best k maximal consistent combinations of these hypotheses (i.e., k best interpretations, see section 26.3.), using the fact that two hypotheses are contradictory if they correspond to two units which have at least one common subunit.

- For each of these best consistent combinations:

  The inference engine computes, starting from the units of the private working memory and using the rules of the level n, all the hypotheses of possible *incomplete* units for level n + 1 that are compatible with the aggregation and spatio-temporal constraints and that are not in the current consistent combination.

  The Π-ATMS completes the current consistent combination with the best newly created hypotheses to obtain the final consistent combination.

- Finally, all the best combinations produced by the different private working memories are sorted by certainty. The best k generate private working memories for level n + 1: each hypothesis of the selected combination is asserted as a fact in the new working memory.

This cycle is repeated for each phase until the best m solutions for the division level are obtained. Then the operator can evaluate the enemy threat by analyzing the proposed division hypotheses.

26.5.3. A Test Scenario

We detail in the following the solutions given by the first SEFIR prototype and the ones given by the possibilistic version for a test scenario in which three intelligence officers provided information on the enemy units they observed during six hours. The symbols used to represent the observed and aggregated units in the figures are:

🔲	Tanks Section	....	Company
🔲	Motorized rifles Company	,,,,,,,,,	Battalion
🔲	Motorized rifles Battalion		
🔲	Tanks Company	∞∞⌃⌃⌃⌃	Regiment
🔲	Tanks Battalion	▬▬	Division

The criteria used for the evaluation of the certainty of an aggregated unit take into account:

- the unit level and type;
- the covered spatio-temporal surface;
- the unit completeness.

We can note that this criteria doesn't take into account the completeness of the subunits composing the aggregated unit, thus it is not optimal. However, since the first SEFIR prototype used this criteria, we retained

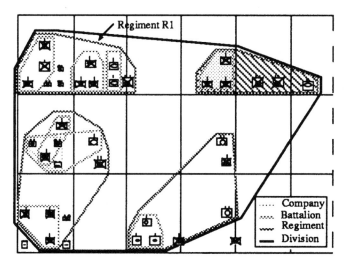

Figure 26.3 First solution given by the first SEFIR prototype.

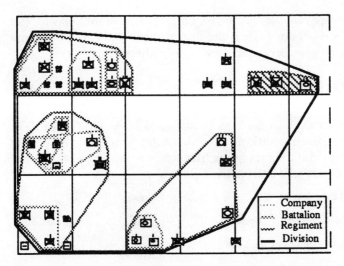

Figure 26.4 Second solution given by the first SEFIR prototype.

it to better compare the solutions provided by the two prototypes. The best (with respect to the criteria) three solutions given by the first SEFIR prototype are represented, respectively, in Figures 26.3, 26.4, and 26.5.

First, we remark that the second solution is a subset of the first one since the grayed regiment of the Figure 26.4 is included in the grayed regiment of the Figure 26.3. Thus, this second solution should not appear in the solutions proposed to the operator. Moreover, the third solution (see Figure 26.5) is not optimal since the aggregation of the companies noted C1, C2, and C3 in a battalion, and its insertion in the grayed regiment represents a better alternative. The presence of these solutions is due to the

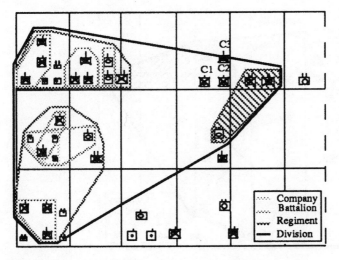

Figure 26.5 Third solution given by the first SEFIR prototype.

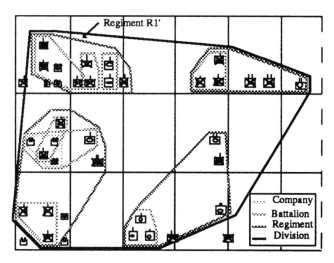

Figure 26.6   First solution given by the possibilistic SEFIR prototype.

fact that the reduction of the generated uncertain hypotheses was done heuristically in this first prototype.

The best three solutions given by the possibilistic SEFIR prototype for the same scenario are represented, respectively, in Figures 26.6, 26.7 and 26.8. The first solution is better than the corresponding one proposed by the first prototype since the regiment noted R1' in Figure 26.6 is more compact than the regiment noted R1 in Figure 26.3. Thus the certainty of R1' is greater than the certainty of R1 (with respect to the criteria). The second solution represents an effective alternative to the first one since

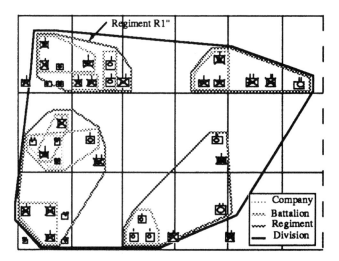

Figure 26.7   Second solution given by the possibilistic SEFIR prototype.

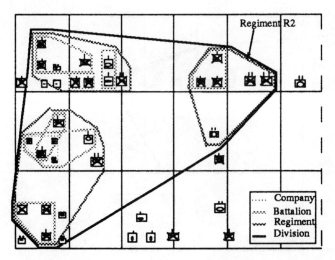

Figure 26.8 Third solution given by the possibilistic SEFIR prototype.

the battalions composing the regiment noted R1″ (see Figure 26.7) are not the same composing the regiment noted R1′ (see Figure 26.6). Finally, the third solution is correct since the regiment noted R2 (see Figure 26.8) is complete. In fact, R2 includes the companies noted C1, C2, and C3 in the Figure 26.5.

As a final remark we can say that the solutions given by the possibilistic SEFIR prototype are really compatible with the selected criteria.

26.6 CONCLUSION

Possibilistic ATMS enable a joint handling of assumptions and uncertainty relative to a knowledge base, in the framework of possibilistic logic. The fact that possibilistic logic remains on many points close to classical logic facilitates the extension of efficient procedures, such as those based on Oriented CAT-correct resolution for the computation of labels, nogoods and contexts, by ordering the environments of a datum according to the certainty with which it can be deduced from each of them.

The truth maintenance system based on the π-RCO resolution seems to have a number of advantages over the classical ATMS. Firstly, it allows the use of general clauses without requiring the creation of new data, justifications and disjunctions of assumptions as in [4]. The second advantage is that all justifications of the knowledge base are stored under the form of general weighted clauses, while in the classical ATMS, the justifications are stored in four different areas depending on the clause type: Horn clauses, disjunctions of assumptions, nogoods and environments. Finally, we have seen that negated assumptions are naturally taken in account, which is not possible in the classical ATMS, and they may appear in environments, nogoods and labels.

From the application point of view, the use of an architecture coupling a Π-ATMS and a first order inference engine enables a quicker development of more readable, efficient, maintainable and reusable solutions to the problems of uncertain data management and multiple hypotheses handling in data fusion applications. The approach presented in this paper is well adapted to the aggregation phase of a data fusion process.

26.7 REFERENCES

[1] Cayrol, M. and Tayrac, P. Les résolutions CAT-correcte et CCT-correcte, la résolution CAT-correcte dans l'ATMS. *Colloque International sur l'Informatique Cognitive des Organisations (ICO'89),* Québec, Canada, 1989.

[2] Corkill, D.D. Embedable problem-solving architectures: A study of integrating OPS5 with GBB. *Proceedings of CAIA,* 1990, 176-182

[3] De Kleer, J. An assumption-based TMS. *Artificial Intelligence 28,* 127-162, 1986.

[4] De Kleer, J. Extending the ATMS. *Artificial Intelligence 28,* 163-196, 1986.

[5] De Kleer, J. A general labeling algorithm for assumption-based truth maintenance. *Proceedings of the National Conference on Artificial Intelligence (AAAI'88),* Saint Paul, Minnesota, Aug. 21-26, 1988, 188-192.

[6] Bos-Plachez C., Apport d'un ATMS possibiliste pour les diagnostic des circuits electroniques analogiques. In Proc. of Rencontres Francophones sur la Logique floue et ses Applications, Cépadues edition, pp 111-118.

[7] Dubois, D., Lang, J. and Prade, H. Theorem proving under uncertainty—A possibility theory-based approach, *Proceedings of the 10th Intern. Joint Conf. on Artificial Intelligence (IJCAI'87),* Milano, Italy, August, 1987, 984-986.

[8] Dubois, D. and Prade, H. Necessity measures and the resolution principle. *IEEE Trans. Systems, Man and Cybernetics 17,* 474-478, 1987.

[9] Dubois, D. and Prade, H. (with the collaboration of Farreny, H., Martin-Clouaire, R. and Testemale, C.) *Possibility Theory—An Approach to Computerized Processing of Uncertainty,* Plenum Press, New York, 1988.

[10] Dubois, D., Lang, J. and Prade, H. Advances in automated reasoning using possibilistic logic. In: A. Kandel (Ed.), *Fuzzy Expert Systems,* CRC Press, Boca Raton, FL, 1992, 125-134.

[11] Dubois, D. and Prade, H. Resolution principles in possibilistic logic. *Int. J. of Approximate Reasoning 4(1),* 1-21, 1990.

[12] Dubois, D., Lang, J. and Prade, H. A possibilistic assumption-based truth maintenance system with uncertain justifications and its application to belief revision. In: J.P. Martins and M. Reinfrank (Eds.), *Truth Maintenance Systems,* Springer Verlag, Berlin, 1991, 87-106.

[13] Dubois, D., Lang, J. and Prade, H. Possibilistic logic. In: D.M. Gabbay (Ed.), *Handbook of Logic in Artificial Intelligence and Logic Programming, Vol. 2,* Oxford University Press, 1994, 439-513.

[14] Morgue, G. and Chehire, T. Efficiency of production systems when coupled with an assumption based truth maintenance system. *Proceedings of AAAI'91,* 1991, 268-274.

[15] Lastic Saint-Jal, T.de. SEFIR: Interactive intelligence data fusion. Proceedings MILCOMP, Wembley Conference Centre, London, England 1989.

[16] Tayrac, P. ARC: An extended ATMS based on directed CAT-correct resolution. In: J.P. Martins and M. Reinfrank (Eds.), *Truth Maintenance Systems,* Springer Verlag, Berlin, 1991, 107-124.

[17] Waltz, E. and Llinas, J. *Multi-Sensor Data Fusion,* Artech House Inc., Boston, London, 1990.

[18] Zadeh, L.A. Fuzzy sets as a basis for a theory of possibility. *Fuzzy Sets and Systems 1,* 3-28, 1978.

27 Possibilistic Handling of Uncertainty in Practical Fault Isolation*

Didier Cayrac[†]
Matra Marconi Space, Toulouse, France

Didier Dubois
Henri Prade
I.R.I.T., University of Toulouse III, France

ABSTRACT: An approach to fault isolation that exploits vastly incomplete models is presented. It relies on separate descriptions of each component behavior, together with the links between them, which enables a focusing of the reasoning to the relevant part of the system. As normal observations do not need explanation, the behavior of the components is limited to anomaly propagation. Diagnostic solutions are disorders (fault modes or abnormal signatures) that are consistent with the observations, as well as abductive explanations.

An ordinal representation of uncertainty based on possibility theory provides a simple exception-tolerant description of the component behaviors. We can for instance distinguish effects that are more or less certainly present (or absent) and effects that are more or less possibly present (or absent) when a given anomaly is present. A realistic example illustrates the benefits of this approach.

27.1. Introduction and Rationale

Developing models of systems that are both expressive enough to support effective diagnosis and cheap enough to keep knowledge acquisition cost-

* This is a fully revised and expanded version of a paper collected in the Proceedings of the 11th Conference on Uncertainty in Artificial Intelligence, Montréal, 1995, pp. 68–76.
† Current affiliation: Hewlett-Packard France, 5 avenue Raymond Chanas - Eybens, 38053 Grenoble Cedex 9, France.

FUZZY INFORMATION ENGINEERING

affordable in real-world contexts remains an open problem. This seems to prevent a wide acceptance of model-based diagnosis [11] in industry. Models of the system to be diagnosed traditionally consist of a description of its structure, in terms of components linked together, and of a description of the behavior of the individual components. On the one hand, acquisition of the structure is "cheap," as it can often be derived directly from design information (the detection of faults altering the structure of the system cannot be handled in this framework). On the other hand, the behavior of the individual components of the system is much more difficult to model in an appropriate way. Two approaches are usually followed: the correct behavior and/or the fault modes of each component are represented. The representation choice is conditioned to a large extent by the diagnostic approach chosen: consistency-based or abductive.

Consistency-based diagnosis [6], [7] exploit a nominal behavior model to derive explanations that allow the restoration of the consistency of the predicted behavior with the observations. This approach requires an expensive model because it must allow an effective detection of the discrepancies between predicted and observed behaviors (i.e., real anomalies are indeed detected, and there are few spurious ones). We believe that the cost of a model capable of such a high-quality simulation (and expressed in first order logic) would be prohibitive for most real-world applications (except maybe digital circuitry), if it were even feasible.

Abductive diagnosis [13] relies on a causal model between faults and manifestations, and looks for explanations (faults) that cause, or "cover" the symptoms observed. Explanation as consistency is a weaker notion than explanation as covering: the consistent explanations form a superset of the abductive explanations. Abductive diagnosis requires completeness of the identified fault modes [5]. Proposals for handling incompleteness [4] still require the identification of all possible sources of incompleteness, at the level of each rule, which makes their application unfit to vastly incomplete models.

If all observations were to be explained abductively, a model of the nominal *and* fault behavior of the system that is just as fine as for the consistency-based approach would be required. However, Console and Torasso also show that if only part of the observations (for instance, the abnormal ones) need to be abductively explained, a model describing how anomalies are propagated is sufficient.

Section 27.2 distinguishes between fault detection and fault isolation, which require different kinds of knowledge. The approach to fault isolation we outline exploits vastly incomplete models, and allows the identification of fault modes that are not explicitly described. An ordinal representation of uncertainty based on possibility theory allows a qualitative and incomplete description of the component behaviors, at an appropriate level of abstraction. Section 27.3 presents the possibilistic logic treatment. The proposed approach is formalized in section 27.4, and illustrated by a realistic example in section 27.5.

27.2. Overview of the Approach

The diagnostic problem at large (which may be summarized by "what is wrong with my system?") includes two goals: determining what is wrong from the "outside" point of view, that is, identifying the symptoms; and determining what is wrong from the "inside" point of view, that is, identifying the part of the system that is originally responsible for the symptoms. These two tasks (which often are not distinguished) actually make best use of different kinds of knowledge, and thus would benefit from being treated separately, with distinct models of the system. Indeed, sets of simple nominal behavior models of restricted scope are often sufficient for monitoring; besides, simple influence models describing anomaly propagation are sufficient for fault isolation if a well-focused inference is used.

27.2.1. Fault Detection

In order to detect a fault (i.e., at first, to detect that something is wrong with the system), a model of the nominal, that is, correct, behavior of the system is necessary. To put it plainly, *"you can't know that something is wrong if you don't know what the system is supposed to do when it is okay."* This task is often performed by some dedicated monitoring facilities. In the case of satellites, the telemetry flow is monitored in real time. Typically, the value of some observable parameter is compared to some thresholds, or its evolution is matched to a standard pattern. This model of the nominal behavior is thus a lot simpler than a simulator (either qualitative or numerical), and therefore preferred, as it is sufficient to fulfill the monitoring task.

The output from the monitoring phase is a first set of symptoms (typically abnormal states of variables, or abnormal evolutions). Further analysis performed off-line (for instance through additional probing or finer analysis of collected data) allows the discovery of additional symptoms. As this additional analysis is expensive, it should be focused, and driven by the fault isolation task.

This simple approach has only one drawback: using model-based terms, it generates discrepancies, but not conflicts (minimal sets of components of which at least one is faulty): fault hypotheses have to be generated in the fault isolation phase.

27.2.2. Fault Isolation

At this stage, given abnormal observations, we are looking for explanations in terms of anomalies inside the system, that is, fault(s) of some parts of the system. The absence of a full-fledged nominal behavior model rules out the application of the conventional consistency-based approach. An abductive approach only requires a model describing how anomalies are propagated, but, as pointed out, it still demands exhaustive identification of:

- fault modes of components; and
- influences within components (i.e., how an anomaly in input of a component affects its outputs).

These two constraints are relaxed, allowing more incompleteness in the model, while recovering all relevant explanations through focused consistency-based and/or abductive reasoning on the subset of the model relevant to the symptoms.

27.2.2.1. Identification of "New" Fault Modes. In addition to conventional "abducibles" formed by identified fault modes of each component (e.g., relay "stuck at 1" or "stuck at 0"), we also accept as diagnostic solutions abnormal states of the outputs of a given component. For instance, "noisy output" of a filter may be accepted as a fault hypothesis, even if no identified fault mode specifically predicts this abnormal output. This allows the characterization of fault modes that were not identified. The "new" fault modes are characterized by an abnormal signature on the component outputs. This information may be sufficient for repair, or an expert may decide whether they correspond to possible fault modes.

Preidentified fault modes may be preferred, and thus get a higher priority in the discrimination. Among fault hypotheses formed by abnormal output of components, those associated to components for which the anomaly cannot be explained by anomalies located further upstream may be preferred. This heuristic preference order allows a better exploitation of the results (e.g., "conventional" abducibles come first). The possibility of accepting as candidates the characterization of possible abnormal behavior improves the exploitation of incomplete models, while the preference heuristics allow a sorting of the potentially numerous hypotheses generated.

27.2.2.2. Incomplete Model Exploitation. To relax the completeness assumption on influences (anomaly propagation) within components, we propose to use a form of consistency-based reasoning on a *relevant* subset of the model, in complement to abductive reasoning. This relevant subset corresponds to a restriction of the model to the parts that are somehow related to observed symptoms (a formal definition of this approach is given in section 27.4). A *relevant consistent explanation* is then a fault mode or an abnormal signature that belongs to this subset, and is consistent with all the observations.

Introducing uncertainty in the behavior representation avoids the need for complete elicitation of exceptional cases. It is also in agreement with incompleteness of the description of the diagnosed situation. In the following, we propose an ordinal representation of uncertainty of the behavior of individual components [10], [2], [3]. It allows the expression of:

- (more or less) certain influences between inputs and outputs (possibly taking into account the configuration of the component, e.g., "on" or "off" for a relay);
- (more or less) impossible influences (e.g., a given input cannot lead to a given output).

It thus leaves room for influences that are (more or less) possible.

The basic principle of the reasoning used at the local (component) level is as follows: all abnormal inputs that *may* cause the abnormal output (i.e., the influence is not impossible) are gathered; they are relevant consistent explanations. Among these, the ones that (more or less) certainly cause the anomaly (i.e., the influence is certain) are preferred; they are abductive explanations.

27.2.2.3. The Fault Isolation Process.

- *Hypotheses generation:* As no hypotheses are provided by the monitoring phase, it is necessary to generate them as a first step of fault isolation. We want to find disorders that are directly or indirectly "related" to the observed manifestations, that is, components that may be responsible for the symptoms. The fact that a disorder is "related" to a manifestation can have two meanings: a strong (abductive) meaning, in which the hypotheses entail the manifestation, or a weaker (consistency-based) meaning, in which the hypotheses are just consistent with the symptom and there is a possible influence path between them (this notion will be formalized in the next section). We thus have to follow upstream "influence paths," and collect as candidates the acceptable disorders found on the way.

- *Additional manifestations prediction:* The monitoring phase only provides an incomplete set of symptoms. It is therefore useful to generate additional expected manifestations for the fault hypotheses, in order to allow discrimination.

- *Probing and hypotheses discrimination:* The expected manifestations are tested, and whether these new observations are entailed by or are consistent with the disorders is verified. This allows the update of the plausibility of the disorders: an inconsistent hypothesis will be rejected, a covering hypothesis (abductive solution) will be preferred over hypotheses that are just consistent with the symptoms.

This discussion suggests that a simple fault influence propagation model may be sufficient for the fault isolation task, given proper focusing. The ideas introduced are formalized in the next section.

27.3. Possibilistic Logic Approach

In possibilistic logic [8], [9], classical logic formulas are weighted by lower bounds of the necessity degree with which the formula is held for true. A weighted formula (φ, α) is thus interpreted as the semantic constraint $N(\varphi) \geq \alpha$ where N is a necessity measure. A necessity measure is associated with a plausibility ordering of the possible interpretations of the world encoded by a so-called $[0,1]$-valued possibility distribution π. $\pi(\omega) > \pi(\omega')$ means that interpretation ω is more plausible than interpretation ω'. It is assumed that $\exists \omega, \pi(\omega) = 1$. Then N is defined from π by:

$$N(\varphi) = \min\{1 - \pi(\omega) | \omega \models \neg\varphi\} = 1 - \max\{\pi(\omega) | \omega \models \neg\varphi)\} = 1 - \Pi(\neg\varphi)$$

where Π is the possibility measure [14] associated with π and the necessity of φ corresponds to the impossibility of $\neg\varphi$. It follows that:

$$N(\varphi \wedge \psi) = \min(N(\varphi), N(\psi)).$$

$N(\varphi) = 1$ indicates that it is certain that φ is true $N(\varphi) = 0$ indicates that φ is unknown. Automated reasoning in possibilistic logic is a generalization of the situation in classical logic, and is based on the axioms of propositional calculus (with a necessity degree equal to 1) and on a many-valued extension of modus ponens:

$$N(\varphi) \geq \alpha, N(\neg\varphi \vee \psi) \geq \beta \vdash N(\psi) \geq \min(\alpha, \beta),$$

also written as $\{(\varphi, \alpha), (\neg\varphi \vee \psi, \beta)\} \vdash (\psi, \min(\alpha, \beta))$.

A model-based diagnosis problem can be characterized by a logical theory SD describing the behavior of the system, a set of atoms CXT describing contextual data expressing the configurations of the components, and a set of literals OBS representing the observations to be explained. Two kinds of solutions are then defined, with $T = SD \cup CXT$:

- consistency-based approach: an explanation H (i.e., a set of literals representing disorders) is a solution iff:

$$T \cup OBS \cup H \text{ is consistent}$$

- abductive approach: an explanation H is a solution iff:

$$T \cup H \vdash OBS$$

The extension of these two approaches to the handling of uncertainty using possibilistic logic is now briefly outlined.

Let us consider a knowledge base T made of uncertain implication relations between possible disorders (explanations) $d_i, i = 1, n$ and effects, that is, present or absent, manifestations $m_j, j = 1, u$. This is encoded by weighted clauses of the form:

$$N(\neg d_i \vee m_j) \geq \alpha_{ij} > 0 \text{ and } N(\neg d_k \vee \neg m_r) \geq \lambda_{kr} > 0.$$

A constraint of the form $N(\neg d_i \vee m_j) \geq \alpha_{ij}$ means that the presence of disorder d_i causes the presence of manifestation m_j almost certainly, independently of the context and of the presence of other disorders. Besides, we have a set OBS of uncertain observations represented by weighted formulas of the form:

$$N(m_s) \geq \beta_s > 0 \qquad \text{(present manifestations)}$$

$$N(\neg m_t) \geq \rho_t > 0 \qquad \text{(absent manifestations)}$$

It is assumed that $\forall i, \forall j, \forall r, N(\neg d_i \vee m_j) > 0$ and $N(\neg d_i \vee \neg m_r) > 0$ entail $j \neq r$, thus, the behavioral knowledge is coherent. In the approach presented in this chapter, $\mathcal{T}$ can be interpreted as the behavior of a given component, the disorders d_i being fault modes and abnormal inputs, and the manifestations m_j or $\neg m_r$ corresponding to what is observed. Applying the possibilistic modus ponens rule, we obtain:

$$\forall j, N(\neg d_i) \geq \min(\alpha_{ij}, \rho_j) \text{ and } \forall r, N(\neg d_i) \geq \min(\lambda_{ir}, \beta_r)$$

and thus

$$N(\neg d_i) \geq \max[\max_j \min(\alpha_{ij}, \rho_j), \max_r \min(\lambda_{ir}, \beta_r)] \tag{1}$$

Thus, from (1) we compute an upper bound of possibility degree of the explanation d_i, $\Pi(d_i) = 1 - N(\neg d_i)$ which is the *level of consistency* $\text{cons}\mathcal{T}(d_i; \text{OBS}) \geq 1 - N(\neg d_i)$ of $\mathcal{T} \cup \text{OBS} \cup \{d_i\}$ in the possibilistic setting. Indeed, in possibilistic logic, the level of inconsistency (the complement to 1 of the level of consistency) of a knowledge base $\mathcal{K} \cup \{\varphi\}$ is nothing but the greatest lower bound α such that $N(\neg \varphi) \geq \alpha$ is compatible with the constraints on the necessity measure N encoding the pieces of knowledge in $\mathcal{K}$.

Let M^+ be the set of present manifestations m_j, such that $\exists \, \beta_j > 0$, $N(m_j) \geq \beta_j$. Abductive solutions of the diagnosis problems are computed by looking for the disorders d_i that alone cover, explain all the manifestations in M^+. Thus, we are interested in disorders d_i such that $\forall \, m_j \in M^+$, $d_i \cup \mathcal{T} \vdash m_j$ in the classical case. In case of a possibilistic theory $\mathcal{T}$, if $(\neg d_i \vee m_j, \alpha_{ij}) \in \mathcal{T}$, then $(d_i, 1) \cup \mathcal{T} \vdash (m_j, \alpha_{ij})$. If the observation is uncertain $(N(m_j) \geq \beta_j)$, then $(d_i, 1) \cup \mathcal{T} \vdash (m_j, \beta_j)$ only if $\beta_j \leq \alpha_{ij}$ (by weakening of the conclusion). Then d_i can be considered as a totally acceptable abductive explanation of (m_j, β_j). If $\alpha_{ij} < \beta_j$, the plausibility of d_i as an abductive explanation would be only considered as equal to α_{ij}. Thus d_i is excluded as an abductive explanation as soon as $\nexists \, \alpha_{ij} > 0$ $(\neg d_i \vee m_j, \alpha_{ij}) \in \mathcal{T}$. An explanation d_i, which certainly causes the observations that are somewhat certain (in particular, $\forall j$, if $\beta_j = 1$ then we should have $\alpha_{ij} = 1$), will be preferred to an explanation d_k which does not cause with a total certainty the certainly present manifestations $(\exists j, \beta_j = 1$ and $\alpha_{kj} < 1)$. It amounts to computing the degree of plausibility $\Delta^*(d_i)$ of an abductive explanation d_i of an uncertain observation (m_j, β_j) as:

$$\Delta^*(d_i) = \beta_j \rightarrow \alpha_{ij} \tag{2}$$

where $a \to b = 1$ if $a \leq b$ and $a \to b = 0$ if $a > b$ (Gödel implication). This holds for any m_j in M^+, and d_i is an abductive explanation of M^+ if and only if:

$$\Delta^*(d_i) = \min_j (\beta_j \to \alpha_{ij}). \tag{3}$$

Then (3) expresses a coverage of the fuzzy set of manifestations more or less certainly observed by the fuzzy set of manifestations more or less certainly caused by d_i. Note that Δ^* is not a necessity degree strictly speaking since $\Delta^*(d_i) = 1$ means only that d_i is highly plausible.

In the computation of abductive solutions, only observed manifestations are accounted for. Indeed, we do not wish to explain the nominal behavior. Moreover, negative causal knowledge is often scarce (i.e., many λ_{ir} will be 0 in practice). It is easy to see that when $\lambda_{ir} = 0$, accounting for an absent manifestation ($N(\neg m_r) \geq \rho_r > 0$) will destroy the abductive information in (3) since then $\rho_r \to \lambda_{ir}$ is equal to 0.

A consequence of this logical modelling is the hypothesis that the effects of simultaneously present disorders accumulate without interfering with each other. Indeed, $N(\neg d_i \vee m_j) \geq \alpha_{ij}$ and $N(\neg d_k \vee m_l) \geq \alpha_{kl}$ entail $N(\neg d_i \vee \neg d_k \vee m_j) \geq \alpha_{ij}$, $N(\neg d_k \vee \neg d_j \vee m_l) \geq \alpha_{kl}$ and then $N(\neg d_i \vee \neg d_k \vee m_j) \geq \max(\alpha_{ij}, \alpha_{kj})$. Thus:

$$\Delta^*(\{d_i, d_k\}) = \min_j (\beta_j \to \max(\alpha_{ij}, \alpha_{kj}))$$
$$= \min_j \max(\beta_j \to \alpha_{ij}, \beta_j \to \alpha_{kj})$$
$$\geq \max(\Delta^*(d_i), \Delta^*(d_k)).$$

This expresses that $\{d_i, d_k\}$ covers M^+ at least as well as d_i or d_k alone, and shows that Δ^* is not a necessity measure. This does not prevent the simplest explanations from being preferred; that is, the unique disorder solutions when they are as plausible as the multiple disorder solutions.

27.4. Formal Description

The model of the system consists of a description of its individual components and their behavior, and of the links defining the relation between them.

27.4.1. Component Description

The components have identified inputs, outputs, configuration modes (i.e., states), and possibly identified fault modes. All these can be viewed as the parameters of the model. They will be represented as predicates defined on discrete domains.

Definition 1: A **component** C_i is characterized by:

- A set of predicates describing:

  its input $\{c_i\_in_1, \ldots, c_i\_in_m\}$,

  its output $\{c_i\_out_1, \ldots, c_i\_out_p\}$,

its configuration mode c_i_state (if applicable),

its fault mode c_i_fault.

- A theory CD_i concerning these predicates, expressed in possibilistic logic and describing its behavior:

  how an abnormal input signature affects its outputs, given its configuration mode,

  the impact of each identified fault mode on its outputs

Component is used here as a generic term: a component may be an actual electric component, or a whole equipment, or a function, and so on.

Inputs and outputs are defined on a set of abnormal states such as "absent," "noisy," "at_zero," and so on. Nominal states need not be represented, as they are not propagated. We consider that the system is static, that the configuration mode of the component does not change during the diagnostic session.

As we only require the explanation of abnormal observations, the behavior representation proposed (anomaly propagation) is sufficient. The information regarding the behavior of each component is kept separate, as this "partitioning" is exploited by the diagnostic task.

It should be noted that even if no gradual representation of uncertainty was used, we could distinguish between influences that are certain and those that are only possible. For example, in Figure 27.1, the behavior of C_1, "i_1 cannot cause an anomaly on o_1, but may impact o_2, and will impact o_3" would be expressed as $CD_1 = \{i_1(abnormal) \rightarrow \neg o_1(abnormal),$ $i_1(abnormal) \rightarrow o_3(abnormal)\}$. At the component level, $i_1(abnormal)$ is an abductive explanation of $o_3(abnormal)$, a consistent explanation of $o_2(abnormal)$, and there is no explanation for $o_1(abnormal)$ above component C_1 (then $o_1(abnormal)$ will be considered as a disorder in itself). Note that in this simple example, the component has only one input; in the general case, an abnormal input signature should be considered.

By default, it is assumed here that consequences of abnormal inputs can be added without interference (otherwise interferences should be explicitly described). In case of impossible effects, the logical formalism obliges us to specify when several inputs are available, that the effect is impossible if the other inputs are not abnormal (e.g., $i_1(abnormal) \wedge \neg i_2(abnormal) \rightarrow \neg o_1(abnormal)$. Moreover, in this model it is not allowed to write both $i_1(abnormal) \rightarrow o_1(abnormal)$ and $i_1(abnormal) \wedge \neg i_2(abnormal) \rightarrow \neg o_1(abnormal)$ without contradiction. Thus the model is somewhat simplistic.

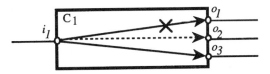

Figure 27.1   Certain versus possible influences.

The use of both consistency-based and abductive approaches at the component level captures of a form of incompleteness. However, as mentioned previously, a greater expressivity of uncertainty is desirable. We may for instance want to express that a fault mode is more likely to impact one output of the component than another, or distinguish unlikely impacts from those that are plainly impossible. The goal of this refinement is to allow a ranking of the diagnostic solutions, for instance through the identifications of fault hypotheses that are more or less consistent with the observations, or that more or less cover them.

The behavior CD_i of the component C_i can thus be equivalently defined by:

- a set of uncertain clauses encoded in possibilistic logic,
- a global relation on the Cartesian product of the set of variables formed by the input, output, configuration mode, and fault mode of the component, weighted in terms of necessity degrees [2].

A subset of the outputs of the components is assumed to be observable. However, some observations may be pervaded with uncertainty.

27.4.2. Links between Components

The links describe the way in which the components are connected, and characterize their possible interactions. As components have distinct inputs and outputs, the links are directed. They just carry the value of the output of a component to some inputs of other components, without modification.

Definition 2: A **link** is a proposition of the form:

$$c_i\_out_j(x) \rightarrow c_k\_in_1(x) \wedge \ldots \wedge c_p\_in_q(x)$$

expressing that the output state $c_i\_out_j(x)$ of the component C_i is propagated to the inputs $c_k\_in_1(x), \ldots, c_p\_in_q(x)$ of components $C_k, \ldots, C_p$.

Definition 3: The set **LINKS** contains all the links between the components of the system.

Although this is usually not done in most model-based diagnostic approaches, we choose to identify the links as individual entities. Indeed, in case several components are related through more that one possible interaction path (e.g., two links exist between them), this allows to focus the reasoning to the relevant links.

As defined, the links only allow distribution of information (fan-out), but no fusion (fan-in). This limitation allows a clear separation between components, which encapsulate all the behavior and the "wiring" represented by links. In a fan-in situation, when the effects can be superposed (they do not interfere), the relation can be represented by several links; when they do interfere, an additional component must be created.

27.4.3. The Diagnostic Problem

Definition 4: The **model of the system, SD,** is formed by the component behaviors and the links between them:

$$SD = \{CD_1, \ldots, CD_n, LINKS\}$$

Definition 5: We call **context, CXT,** the set of configuration modes of the components at the time of diagnosis. This is assumed to be known *a priori*: $CXT = \{c_i\_state(state_k), \ldots\}$.

Definition 6: We call **set of observations, OBS,** the set of the output states that have been observed. OBS is partitioned into two subsets M^+ (manifestations whose presence is confirmed) and M^- (those whose absence is confirmed).

$$OBS = \{c_i\_out_h(state_q), \ldots, \neg c_j\_out_k(state_t), \ldots\}$$

$$= M^+ \cup M^- = \{m_1, \ldots, \neg m_n, \ldots\}$$

$c_5\_out_1(noisy)$ is an example of a present manifestation. It should be noted that an observation is here equivalent to an abnormal state of a link, as a link is tied to exactly one component output. The observations may also be more or less certain. M^+ and M^- are in fact fuzzy sets whose membership degrees are interpreted as certainty levels: $N(m_1) \geq \mu_{M+}(m_1), \ldots, N(\neg m_n) \geq \mu_{M-}(m_n), \ldots$

Definition 7: A **diagnostic problem** is the tuple **DP**, formed by the model of the system, its configuration at the time of diagnosis, and the set of observations:

$$DP = \{SD, CXT, OBS\}.$$

In addition to a possibilistic version of "conventional" abductive reasoning, we propose a form of possibilistic consistency-based reasoning. It exploits a theory formed by the behaviors of components that are on an upstream influence path and the relevant links between them. The following two definitions characterize its elements.

The **set of possible influence paths leading to a manifestation m** (given output state $c_p\_out_q(state_r)$ of a component C_p) is the subset **REL_LINKS**(m) of LINKS containing links that may propagate the cause of m. REL_LINKS(m) is defined recursively as follows: a link $c_i\_out_j(x) \rightarrow c_k\_in_v(x) \wedge \ldots \wedge c_s\_in_t(x)$ of LINKS belongs to REL_LINKS if and only if:

- It is tied to an input $c_p\_in_\tau(x)$ of C_p, and there is at least one state of this input that is (at least partially) consistent with m; that is, with $c_p\_out_q(state_r)$: $p \in \{k, \ldots, s\}$, and $\exists \tau, \exists state_\gamma, CD_p \cup \{c_p\_in_\tau(state_\gamma)\}$ is consistent to a strictly positive degree.

- It is tied to the input $c_\omega\_in_\tau(x)$ of a component C_ω of which an output $c_\omega\_out_\lambda$ matches the premise of one of the links of REL_LINKS, and there is at least one state s of $c_\omega\_in_\tau$ that is at least partially consistent with m and the model of the system (i.e., there is a possible influence path between $c_\omega\_in_\tau$ and $c_p\_out_q(state_r))$: $\exists\,\omega \in \{k, \dots, s\}, \exists\lambda, \exists state_\gamma,$ $c_\omega\_out_\lambda(x) \to \dots \in$ REL_LINKS(m) and SD $\cup\ \{c_\omega\_in_\tau(state_\gamma)\}\ \cup$ $\{c_p\_out_q(state_r)\}$ is consistent to a strictly positive degree.

REL_LINKS (relevant links) forms a restriction of the theory LINKS to the links that are relevant to a given symptom. This restriction is performed on the basis of possible influence paths *between* components (links), and *inside* them.

The **set REL_COMPS(m) of components relevant to a manifestation m** (given output state $c_p\_out_q(state_r)$ of C_p), contains C_p and all the components of which an output is tied to a possible influence path to m:

$$\text{REL\_COMPS(m)} = \{C_i, i = p \text{ or } \exists\lambda, c_i\_out_\lambda(x) \to \dots \in \text{REL\_LINKS(m)}\}$$

REL_COMPS(m) contains all the components that may be responsible for the state observed on the output of a given component (manifestation m).

27.4.4. Single Fault Solutions

An **elementary solution d of the diagnostic problem** DP is either:

- a fault mode $d = c_i\_fault(fault\_mode_j)$ of component C_i, or
- a set of abnormal states $d = \{c_i\_out_j(state_k), \dots\}$ on the outputs of C_i, (and $d \cap OBS = \emptyset$: d is not a trivial solution),

such that:

- d causes more or less certainly all present manifestations:

    SD $\cup$ CXT $\cup$ {d} $\vdash M^+$ with a strictly positive necessity degree α, and SD $\cup$ CXT $\cup$ {d} $\cup M^-$ is completely consistent with the observations d is then an **abductive explanation to the degree α** of the abnormal observations.

- there is a possible influence path between d and each present manifestation, and d is not completely inconsistent with the observations:

    $d = c_i\_fault(fault\_mode_j); \forall\ m \in M^+, C_i \in$ REL_COMPS(m) and SD $\cup$ CXT $\cup$ {d} $\cup$ OBS is consistent to a srictly positive degree β

    or:

    $\forall\lambda, \forall s$ such that $c_i\_out_\lambda(s) \in d, \forall\ m \in M^+, c_i\_out_\lambda(s) \to \dots \in$ REL_LINKS(m), and SD $\cup$ CXT $\cup$ {d} $\cup$ OBS is consistent to a strictly positive degree β.

d is then a **relevant explanation consistent to the degree** β with the observations.

Clearly, in the preceding expressions, SD can be replaced by its relevant (useful) parts:

$$\cup_{m \in M+}[\text{REL\_LINKS(m)} \cup \text{REL\_COMPS(m)}]$$

The single fault solutions are thus fault modes or abnormal output signatures which:

- (*more or less*) entail all the manifestations (abductive explanations),
- are (*more or less*) consistent with the observations, and there exists an influence path between the hypothesis and each manifestation.

Thus, a ranking of more or less plausible solutions to the diagnosis problem is obtained.

27.4.5. Probing Points

An **expected manifestation** m with respect to a solution d of a diagnostic problem DP, is any abnormal observable output state of a component, $m = c_i\_out_j(state_k)$, such that:

SD $\cup$ CXT $\cup$ {d} $\vdash$ m with a strictly positive necessity degree.

m is then expected to be present when d is present.

or:

SD $\cup$ CXT $\cup$ {d} $\vdash$ ¬m with a strictly positive necessity degree.

m is then expected to be absent when d is present.

The observation of whether an expected manifestation m is present or not allows the diagnostic system to check whether d is still a consistent and/or an abductive explanation: m is added to OBS.

27.5. A Realistic Example

27.5.1 A Satellite Solar Array Equipment

The goal of the power regulation subsystem is to meet the power requirements of the equipments connected on the bus. A ladder of comparators connects as many solar arrays (SA) as necessary (Figure 27.2). When the voltage is too high on the power bus, SAs are progressively disconnected. If, due to an anomaly, this is not enough, a protection resistor is connected to create an extra load. On the contrary, if all SAs are connected and the power demand still cannot be met, the control system assumes that the sun is no longer visible (it is behind the Earth), and sends an eclipse signal to an on-board computer, so that batteries can be used to

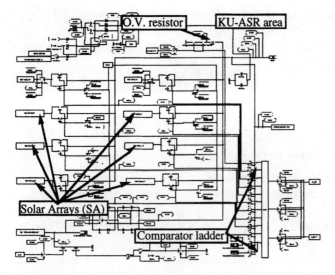

Figure 27.2   Comparator ladder connection to Solar Arrays.

supply extra power. A simplified view of the control system is given in Figure 27.3.

27.5.2. Main Components

In this example, we distinguish between analog and digital input/output. Analog i/o identified states are *DEG* and *ABS* (respectively for degraded and absent; only abnormal states are used). Digital i/o identified states are *ZERO, ONE*. Similar extremely simple sets of qualification turned out to be a good trade-off between knowledge acquisition cost and solutions quality for the modeling of complex systems.

We choose to represent explicitly (more or less) certain and (more or less) impossible influences between inputs and outputs of components. The uncertainty is limited to the following qualitative levels: "certain,"

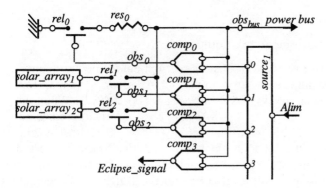

Figure 27.3   The control system.

"almost certain," "likely," "possible" (i.e., unknown); "unlikely," "almost impossible," "impossible." In other words, we use a discrete linearly ordered scale. In practice, levels of certainty of presence of, for instance, a manifestation m ($\mu_{M_+}(m)$), can be represented by a number: 1.0 for "certain," 0.8 for "almost certain," and so on, 0.0 for "possible"; the levels of certainty of absence of m can be similarly encoded: 1.0 for "impossible," 0.8 for "almost impossible," and so on, 0.0 for "possible." Note that only the ordering between these numbers is meaningful, and not their exact value. Since only purely ordinal operations such as min, max, order-reversing and Gödel implication are used, the formulas used can be straightforwardly transposed from the [0,1] scale to a discrete scale.

Behavior of the components used in the simplified example:

Comparator: $comp_i$

input: ref (analog), in; (analog) *output:* out. (digital)
behavior:
$comp_i\_ref(ABS) \rightarrow comp_i\_out(ONE)$, certain
$comp_i\_ref(ABS) \rightarrow comp_i\_out(ZERO)$, impossible
$comp_i\_ref(DEG) \rightarrow comp_i\_out(ONE)$, likely
$comp_i\_in(ABS) \rightarrow comp_i\_out(ZERO)$, certain
$comp_i\_in(ABS) \rightarrow comp_i\_out(ONE)$, impossible
Note that the behavior of the comparator is fully described when its "ref" or "in" input is ABS. However, when it "ref" input is DEG, the output may be ONE (likely) or, implicitly, ZERO (possible); when its "in" input is DEG, any output state is possible. Note also that we explicitly state that when something is certain, its contrary is impossible (since nothing is stated about the mutual exclusiveness of values ZERO and ONE here).

Solar array section: $solar\_array_i$

output: out (analog)

Relay: rel_i

input: command (digital), in (analog); *output:* out (digital)
behavior:
$rel_i\_state(ON) \land rel_i\_in(ABS) \rightarrow rel_i\_out(ABS)$, certain
$rel_i\_state(ON) \land rel_i\_in(DEG) \rightarrow rel_i\_out(DEG)$, certain
$rel_i\_state(OFF) \land rel_i\_in(ABS) \rightarrow rel_i\_out(ABS)$, impossible
$rel_i\_state(OFF) \land rel_i\_in(DEG) \rightarrow rel_i\_out(DEG)$, impossible

Note that nothing is said about the response of the relay to an ON or OFF command input since we do not represent the dynamic behavior of the components.

Voltage source: source$_i$

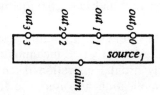

The voltage source gives in output a scale of voltages used as references for comparators. Its input is its alimentation.
input: alim (analog); *output:* out$_1$, out$_2$, out$_3$, out$_4$ (analog)
behavior:
for all j, source$_i$_alim(ABS) $\rightarrow$ source$_i$_out$_j$(ABS), certain
source$_i$_alim(DEG) $\rightarrow$ source$_i$_out$_0$(DEG), unlikely
source$_i$_alim(DEG) $\rightarrow$ source$_i$_out$_2$(DEG), likely
source$_i$_alim(DEG) $\rightarrow$ source$_i$_out$_3$(DEG), likely

Ground: ground$_i$

output: out (analog)

Resistor: res$_i$

res

input: in (analog); *output:* out (analog)
behavior:
res$_i$_in(ABS) $\rightarrow$ res$_i$_out(ABS), almost certain
res$_i$_in(DEG) $\rightarrow$ res$_i$_out(DEG), likely

27.5.3. Diagnostic Session

Initial symptom: OBS = M$^+$ = {(*Eclipse_signal*(*ONE*), certain)}: observation of an eclipse signal, which is abnormal because at this time the satellite is still facing the sun. CXT = {*rel$_0$*(*OFF*), *rel$_1$*(*ON*), *rel$_2$*(*OFF*)}

Hypotheses generation phase
    Figure 27.4 shows the theory relevant to the original symptom. Hypotheses (which in this example consist only in abnormal output of some components) are denoted in boldface.
    Abductive explanations, computed using the Formula (3):

D^* = {(*source_out$_3$*(*ABS*), 1.0), (*alim*(*ABS*), 1.0),

                                  (*source_out$_3$*(*DEG*), 0.3), (*alim*(*DEG*), 0.3)}

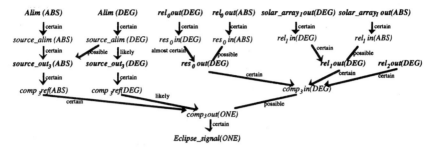

Figure 27.4   Subset of the theory relevant to the symptom Eclipse_signal(ONE).

Eclipse_signal(ONE) is a certain consequence of *source_out₃(ABS)* and *alim(ABS)*, but only a likely consequence of *source_out₃(DEG)* and *alim(DEG)*. The former explanations, which are abductive explanations in the conventional sense, are thus preferred at this point.

Consistent explanations, computed using the Formula (1) (all of them are fully consistent with the eclipse signal symptom):

$$\hat{D} = \{(source\_out_3(ABS), possible), (source\_out_3(DEG), possible),$$

$$(res_0\_out(DEG), possible), (rel_1\_out(DEG), possible),$$

$$(rel_2\_out(DEG), possible), (rel_0\_out(DEG), possible),$$

$$(rel_0\_out(ABS), possible), (solar\_array_1\_out(DEG), possible),$$

$$(solar\_array_1\_out(ABS), possible), (alim(ABS), possible),$$

$$(alim(DEG), possible)\}$$

Additional manifestation prediction phase

A prediction phase allows the elicitation of additional manifestations that may further discriminate among pending hypotheses. Figure 27.5 summarizes this phase of the reasoning.

The additional manifestations predicted by the various fault hypotheses are therefore: *obs_bus(DEG)*, *obs_bus(ABS)*, *obs₀(ONE)*, *obs₁(ONE)*, *obs₂(ONE)*.

Additional manifestation probing phase

We observe: {(*obs_bus(DEG)*, almost certain), (*obs_bus(ABS)*, impossible), (*obs₀(ONE)*, impossible), (*obs₁(ONE)*, certain), (*obs₂(ZERO)*, certain)}.

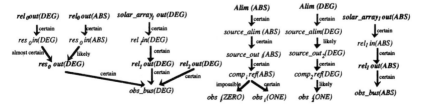

Figure 27.5   Additional manifestation prediction phase.

$(obs_0(ZERO)$, certain), which is equivalent to $(obs_0(ONE)$, impossible) is completely inconsistent with $alim(ABS)$, which predicts $(obs_0(ONE)$, certain) and $(obs_0(ZERO)$, impossible), and partially inconsistent with $alim(DEG)$, which predicts $(obs_2(ONE)$, likely). The hypothesis $alim(ABS)$ is therefore discarded and $alim(DEG)$ is unlikely. Similarly, $(obs\_bus(ABS)$, impossible) is inconsistent with $solar\_array_1\_out(ABS)$, which predicts $(obs\_bus(ABS)$, certain), and is therefore completely rejected.

The other hypotheses remain completely possible, i.e., they are located on a possible influence path leading to some of the symptoms, and they are completely consistent with all the observed symptoms. However, no abductive hypothesis remains: $source_1\_out_3(ABS)$ and $source\_out_3(DEG)$ do not abductively explain the symptom $(obs\_bus(DEG)$, almost certain), $obs_1(ONE)$, certain) and $(obs_2(ZERO)$, certain).

Conclusion of the diagnosis session – exploitation of the results

Abductive explanations: $D^* = \emptyset$

Consistent relevant explanations:

$\hat{D} = \{(source\_out_3(ABS)$, possible), $(source\_out_3(DEG)$, possible),

$(rel_0\_out(ABS)$, possible), $(rel_0\_out(DEG)$, possible),

$(res_0\_out(DEG)$, possible), $(solar\_array_1\_out(DEG)$, possible),

$(rel_1\_out(DEG)$, possible), $(rel_2\_out(DEG)$, possible),

$(alim(DEG)$, unlikely)$\}$

$source\_out_3(ABS)$, $source\_out_3(DEG)$ are rejected by the user because they cannot explain the abnormal bus voltage. $solar\_array_1\_out(DEG)$ is relevant: if the array is damaged, it will produce less power, and this may trigger the eclipse signal. It is preferred over $rel_1\_out(DEG)$, which can be one of its manifestations. $rel_2\_out(DEG)$ is quickly discarded by the user: an extra solar array connected cannot produce the symptoms observed. $rel_1\_out(DEG)$ is actually irrelevant, since the relay is off.

$rel_0\_out(ABS)$ and $rel_0\_out(DEG)$ are preferred over $(res_0\_out(DEG)$, possible), which may be their manifestations. $rel_0\_out(ABS)$ is in fact the explanation that is the closest to the real fault. Indeed, rel_0 is actually faulty: it connected unduly res_0 to the power bus, causing the voltage to go down, and, as the bus was heavily loaded, triggering the eclipse signal.

27.6. Conclusion

Preliminary ideas that led to the proposed approach were introduced in [12], and experimented through the DIAMS project led by Matra Marconi Space since 1987. Its goal is the delivery of operational diagnostic support systems for satellites. Early experiments of model-based approaches were judged not fully satisfactory, especially with respect to the knowledge acquisition costs. During the last nine years, several systems were developed, based on the joint use of various diagnostic knowledge: fault trees, causal knowledge, and functional (model-based) knowledge. They include one preoperational version installed in the Telecom-2 satellite control center early 1994 [1].

In this chapter, we proposed a route that may improve the feasibility of operational applications of model-based reasoning. It allows the exploitation of a vastly incomplete model through well-focused diagnostic strategies. However, it clearly falls in the scope of diagnostic *support* systems, as the number of possible hypotheses generated is clearly larger than if a complete model were available. However, we recover part of the lost discrimination power through the introduction of an ordinal treatment of uncertainty, which enables to rank-order the remaining candidates. Possibilistic logic seems to be well-adapted to contexts in which information is scarce or expensive to gather (significant incompleteness, absence of priors).

27.7. References

[1] Brenot, J.M., et al. "On the Design and Development Choices to Bring to Operation a Diagnostic Expert System for the Telcom 2 Satellite." *Proceedings, Tooldiag International Conference on Fault Diagnosis.* pp. 368–377. Toulouse, France: 1993.

[2] Cayrac, D., et al. "Possibility Theory in Fault Mode Effect Analyses—A Satellite Fault Diagnosis Application." *Proceedings, 3rd International Conference on Fuzzy Systems 1994.* pp. 1176–1181. 1994.

[3] Cayrac, D., et al. "Qualitative and Logical Handling of Uncertainty in a Relational Model for Operational Fault Diagnosis." *Proceedings of the DX-94 5th International Workshop on Principles of Diagnosis.* pp. 47–55. New York: 1994.

[4] Console, L., et al. "A Theory of Diagnosis for Incomplete Causal Models." *Proceedings, 11th International Joint Conference on Artificial Intelligence (IJCAI 1989).* pp. 1311–1317. Detroit, Mich.: 1989.

[5] Console, L., and P. Torasso. "Integrating Models of the Correct Behavior into Abductive Diagnosis." *Proceedings, 9th European Conference on Artificial Intelligence (ECAI 1990).* pp. 160–166. Stockholm, Sweden: 1990.

[6] Davis, R., and W. Hamscher. "Model-based Reasoning—Troubleshooting," in *Exploring Artificial Intelligence.* ed. H.E. Shrobe. pp. 297–346. Los Altos: Morgan Kaufmann, 1988.

[7] De Kleer, J., and B.C. Williams. "Diagnosing Multiple Faults." *Artificial Intelligence,* Vol. 32 (1987), pp. 97–130.

[8] Dubois, D., et al. "Automated Reasoning using Possibilistic Logic: Semantics, Belief Revision and Variable Certainty Weights." *IEEE Transactions on Knowledge and Data Engineering,* Vol. 6 (1994), pp. 64–69.

[9] ———. "Possibilistic Logic," in Handbook of Logic in Artificial Intelligence and Logic Programming—Vol. 3: *Nonmonotonic Reasoning and Uncertainty Reasoning.* eds. D.M. Gabbay, et al. pp. 439–513. Oxford: Clarendon Press, 1994.

[10] Dubois, D., and H. Prade. "A Fuzzy Relation-based Extension of Reggia's Relational Model for Diagnosis," in *Proceedings, 9th Conference on Uncertainty in Artificial Intelligence.* eds. D. Heckerman and E.H. Mamdani. pp. 106–113. Washington: 1993.

[11] Hamscher, W., et al. *Readings in Model-based Diagnosis.* San Mateo: Morgan Kaufmann, 1992.

[12] Haziza, M. "An Expert System Shell for Satellite Fault Isolation based on Structure and Behaviour." *Proceedings, ESTEC Workshop on Artificial Intelligence and Knowledge-based Systems for Space.* Noodwijk, The Netherlands: 1988.

[13] Poole, D. "Normality and Faults in Logic-based Diagnosis." *Proceedings, 11th International Joint Conference on Artificial Intelligence (IJCAI 1989).* pp. 1304–1310. Detroit, Mich.: 1989.

[14] Zadeh, L.A. "Fuzzy Sets as a Basis for a Theory of Possibility." *Fuzzy Sets and Systems,* Vol. 1 (1978), pp. 3–28.

28 A Fuzzy Categorial Grammar for the Harmonization of Melodies

Flávio S. Corrêa da Silva, Fábio Kon
Instituto de Matemática e Estatística da Universidade de São Paulo—Cid. Universitária "ASO"—CP 66281—05389-970—São Paulo (SP)—Brazil

ABSTRACT: In [5] we have stretched the analogy of "Music as Language" and employed techniques from Categorial Grammar for functional harmonic analysis. In the present chapter we extend those techniques to characterize local stylistic preferences in terms of pertinence relations to a fuzzy set of "highly appraised" harmonic structures. The formal structures employed to represent these stylistic preferences are triples [fuzzy preference value: sequence of chords: harmonic function], herewith coined Fuzzy-Syntactic Categories. We illustrate the potential applicability of Fuzzy-Syntactic Categories by the harmonization of a well-known popular song and present the results of an experiment in which we tested the characterization of personal aesthetic preferences in terms of these structures*.

28.1. Introduction

It is commonplace in everyday conversation to refer to the "*Language of Music,*" and the study of musical phenomena as linguistic objects has been developed by many authors (see [1, 4, 8, 13]). In [5], we used some techniques from linguistics—namely, *Categorial Grammar*—to represent a rather specific and simple problem of music theory, which we believe nevertheless to be of widespread interest: functional harmonic analysis [3].

---

* This chapter is a revised and extended version of [6].

The aim of Categorial Grammar [2, 10] is the analysis of syntactic well-foundedness of sentences. The fundamental concept underlying Categorial Grammar is that of *syntactic categories,* which are classes to which words in a sentence must belong. Syntactic categories can be organized as formulae of some substructural logic—for example, the so-called *Lambek Calculus* [10]—in such way that syntactic well-foundedness can be checked via an appropriate *proof theory* related to the logic.

In [5] we presented an encoding of the harmonic functions of chords as syntactic categories and showed how the generation of proofs of "harmonic well-foundedness" could be implemented and used as a tool to verify and to display the harmonic functional structuring of cadences.

We can apply the same ideas to automatically *generate* accompaniments for a melody, by superimposing chords on selected notes of a melodic line. In this case, the melody acts as a series of *constraints* for the resulting sequence of chords, which can be requested for instance to contain the notes of the melody upon which they are placed, as well as to be "well-founded" cadences.

Clearly, for most melodies the sequence of accompanying chords generated this way is not unique (indeed, this set is most of time very large). From the standpoint of the theory of functional harmony encoded as a grammar, all different variations are "correct," in the sense that they obey the harmonic rules encoded in the syntactic categories. Stylistic (and personal) judgment, however, give preference to some sequences of chords over others. For example, the melodic sequence { C,F,D,C } can have as accompaniments the chords { **C, F, G, C** } or { **C, d, G7-, C** } (among many others). (Capital letters stand for notes from a melodic line, and boldfaced letters stand for chords: a boldfaced capital letter denotes a major triad, a boldfaced small letter denotes a minor triad, a boldfaced capital letter followed by a "7-" indicates a dominant seventh chord, and so on.) One sequence of chords may be considered preferable over the others, depending on individual taste or on what musical style is being considered.

It is this type of preference that we intend to characterize. We represent these preferences as Fuzzy-Syntactic Categories, which are pairs [sequences of chords: harmonic functions], accompanied by *fuzzy membership values* to a set of "highly-appraised" sequences. These values are attached to chords and sequences of chords as labels in a propositional doubly labelled deductive system [7, 11] (see also [12] for a general discussion on labelled deductive systems). The system is doubly labelled because the fuzzy values are attached to pairs [chords: harmonic function], which are themselves formulae of a propositional labelled deductive system. The values are then propagated to cadences and fragments of cadences according to Zadeh norms and conorms [9, 14, 15]. Our aim is to provide an automatic assessment of generated accompaniments of melodies based on the fuzzy preference relations in use.

The rest of this chapter is organized as follows: in section 28.2 we briefly review the concepts of Lambek Calculus that we need to use in the rest of this paper; in section 28.3 we formally introduce the Fuzzy-Syntactic Categories, and show how they can be applied to encode aesthetic preferences among different harmonizations of a single melody; in section 28.4 we present the empirical results we have obtained; finally, in section 28.5 we present some conclusions and proposed future work.

28.2. The Lambek Calculus

J. Lambek introduced the Syntactic Calculus—most often called Lambek Cálculus—in [10], as a tool to encode the English grammar, such that grammaticality of sentences could be tested deductively.

Essentially, the Lambek Calculus corresponds to classical propositional logic devoid of any structural rule, in which implication is broken in two connectives, heretofore referred to as left-implication and right-implication. In this work, we have used only the implicative fragment of that Calculus.

A Gentzen-style presentation of implicative Lambek Calculus can be given by the following rules, in which x, y, z are syntactic categories generated by the members of a set S of basic syntactic categories, and $\Gamma, \overline{\Gamma}, \Delta$ are sequences of syntactic categories. The sequences $\overline{\Gamma}$ are assumed to be nonempty.

axiom: $x \vdash x$.

right-inclusion: left-inclusion:

right-implication
$$\frac{\overline{\Gamma},y\vdash x}{\overline{\Gamma}\vdash x/y} \qquad \frac{\overline{\Gamma}\vdash y;\Gamma,x,\Delta\vdash z}{\Gamma,x/y,\overline{\Gamma},\Delta\vdash z}$$

left-implication
$$\frac{y,\overline{\Gamma}\vdash x}{\overline{\Gamma}\vdash y\backslash x} \qquad \frac{\overline{\Gamma}\vdash y;\Gamma,x,\Delta\vdash z}{\Gamma,\overline{\Gamma},y\backslash x,\Delta\vdash z}$$

For example, Lambek assumes that $S = \{n, s\}$, in which n stands for "noun" and s stands for "sentence." The words of the English language are attached as labels to formulae, in such way that they can only occur in specific sequences from which the category "s(entence)" can be derived.

Giving a more specific example, if we assume the words **John** and **milk** to be of category "n(oun)," the word **fresh** to be of category "n/n" (a qualifier—must precede the noun it is qualifying to produce a qualified noun) and the word **likes** to be of category $n\backslash s/n$ (a transitive verb—forms a sentence if preceded by a noun—the subject—and followed by another noun—the object of the sentence), we can prove the grammaticality of **John likes fresh milk** with the deduction tree presented in Figure 28.1 (we abbreviate **John, likes, fresh,** and **milk** with their initials **J, l, f,** and **m**). This proves that from the sequence **J:** n, **l:** $n\backslash s/n$, **f:** n/n, **m:** n we can derive the sentence **Jlfm:** s.

In [5] we showed how this Calculus could be used for harmonic analysis. We have employed a set of three basic syntactic categories $S = \{a, b, c\}$, a and c loosely corresponding to the functions of *tonic* and *cadence,* related

$$\frac{\text{fm: } n \vdash \text{fm: } n \qquad \text{Jlfm: } s \vdash \text{Jlfm: } s}{\cfrac{\text{m: } n \vdash \text{m: } n \qquad \text{Jl: } s/n, \text{ fm: } n \vdash \text{Jlfm: } s}{\cfrac{\text{Jl: } s/n, \text{ f: } n/n, \text{ m: } n \vdash \text{Jlfm: } s \qquad \text{J: } n \vdash \text{J: } n}{\text{J: } n, \text{ l: } n\backslash s/n, \text{ f: } n/n, \text{ m: } n \vdash \text{Jlfm: } s}}}$$

Figure 28.1 Deduction for **John likes fresh milk**.

to Lambek's *noun* and *sentence* functions (see [4] for a similar analogy), and *b* corresponding to an intermediate function of *subdominant*.

In order to present an example, we encode in Table 28.1 a fragment of Functional Harmony [3], sufficient to generate complete, perfect and plagal cadences in major and minor modes of any key. The table indicates, for each chord considered in this work, what function it performs, in what mode, and in which key. Keys are given in terms of relative degrees to the root of the chords. For example, the major triad C-E-G has function "*a*" in the major first degree of C (Imaj), that is, the key of C major.

With this in hand, we can prove the "grammaticality" of the complete cadence { **C,F,G,C** }. We omit the keys and modes in our deduction trees to make our presentation more concise. Following Table 28.1, if we attach the triads *C, F, G* as labels to the categories *a, a\b* and *b\c/a*, we can obtain the deduction tree presented in Figure 28.2.

Now assume we have a melody for which we want to build an accompaniment. Based on the rhythmic structure of the melody, we select the points in the melody upon which we want to superimpose chords. We require that the harmonic cadences thus obtained have to be "grammatically well-founded," and that each chord must contain the notes in the melody lying at the point upon which it is placed. (The actual set of rules we find in manuals for building accompaniments to melodies is larger and quite more convoluted than this. Nevertheless, these overtly simplified rules are sufficient for the presentation of our proposed techniques: they are correct (in the sense that any accompaniment built this way shall be considered acceptable, from a music-theoretical point of view), rich

Table 28.1 Dictionary of Syntactic Categories of Chords

chord	function					
	a	$a\backslash a$	a/a	$a\backslash b$	$a\backslash c/a$	$b\backslash c/a$
major triad	Imaj	Imaj	Imaj	Vmaj	Vmaj IVmaj IVmin	IVmaj IVmin
minor triad	Imin	Imin	Imin	Vmin VIImaj	Vmin VIImaj	
dominant seventh					IVmaj IVmin	IVmaj IVmin
major seventh added ninth	Imaj	Imaj	Imaj	Vmaj	Vmaj	

$$\frac{\frac{\text{CF: } b \vdash \text{CF: } b \quad \text{CFGC: } c \vdash \text{CFGC: } c}{\text{C: } a \vdash \text{C: } a \quad \text{CF: } b, \text{GC: } b\backslash c \vdash \text{CFGC: } c}}{\frac{\text{C: } a, \text{F: } a\backslash b, \text{GC: } b\backslash c \vdash \text{CFGC: } c \quad \text{C: } a \vdash \text{C: } a}{\text{C: } a, \text{F: } a\backslash b, \text{G: } b\backslash c/a, \text{C: } a \vdash \text{CFGC } c}}$$

Figure 28.2 A deduction for the complete cadence.

enough to generate musically interesting examples, and small enough to fit into this chapter.)

For example, we could similarly deduce that the cadence { **C,d,G7-,C** } is grammatically well-founded (Figure 28.3), and both { **C,F,G,C** } and **C,d,G7-,C** } (among other alternatives) can be taken as accompaniments for the simple melody {C,F,D,C}.

The choice upon which accompaniment to choose is based on stylistic and personal preferences. Nonetheless, it seems reasonable to request from a composer/arranger (or listener) that his or her style and personal preferences be somehow consistent. A rather unrestraining framework for this consistency requirement can be based on the supposition that cadences and segments of cadences can be ordered in such way that one would not accept a segment of cadence to entail a second segment they did not like.

One interesting way of envisaging this framework is therefore to admit that segments of cadences have different fuzzy membership degrees to a set of "highly appraised" cadences such that, if $\alpha \vdash \beta$, then the fuzzy membership degree of β cannot be smaller than that of α. It should be remarked that what we regard as segments of cadences are pairs [chords: harmonic function], like the ones presented in Figure 28.2. Our framework is detailed next.

28.3. Fuzzy-Syntactic Categories

We introduce here the concept of *Fuzzy-Syntactic Categories*. Fuzzy-Syntactic Categories are triples of the form $\mu:\mathbf{C}:c$, where $\mu \in [0,1]$ is a *fuzzy degree of appraisal,* **C** is a *sequence of chords* and c is a *syntactic category*. Assuming that a segment of cadence cannot entail a second segment less-appraised than itself, we formulate the following propagation rule for degrees of appraisal, which is in accordance with Zadeh's triangular norms and conorms for fuzzy sets: if we can have in a proof the sequent $\mu_1:\mathbf{C}_1:c_1, \mu_2:\mathbf{C}_2:c_2 \vdash \mu:\mathbf{C}_1\mathbf{C}_2:c$, then we have that $\mu \geq min\{\mu_1,\mu_2\}$.

Our computational implementation is based on constraint propagation for maintaining consistency among degrees of appraisal. At the ini-

$$\frac{\frac{\text{Cd: } b \vdash \text{Cd: } b \quad \text{CdG7-C: } c \vdash \text{CdG7-C: } c}{\text{C: } a \vdash \text{C: } a \quad \text{Cd: } b, \text{G7-C: } b\backslash c \vdash \text{CdG7-C: } c}}{\frac{\text{C: } a, \text{d: } a\backslash b, \text{G7-C: } b\backslash c \vdash \text{CdG7-C: } c \quad \text{C: } a \vdash \text{C: } a}{\text{C: } a, \text{d: } a\backslash b, \text{G7-: } b\backslash c/a, \text{C: } a \vdash \text{CdG7-C } c}}$$

Figure 28.3 Another deduction for the complete cadence.

$$\frac{\dfrac{0:\mathbf{CF}:b\vdash 0:\mathbf{CF}:b\qquad 0:\mathbf{CFGC}:c\vdash 0:\mathbf{CFGC}:c}{\dfrac{0:\mathbf{CF}:b,0:\mathbf{GC}:b\backslash c\vdash 0:\mathbf{CFGC}:c\qquad 0:\mathbf{C}:a\vdash 0:\mathbf{C}:a}{0:\mathbf{C}:a,0:\mathbf{F}:a\backslash b,0:\mathbf{GC}:b\backslash c\vdash 0:\mathbf{CFGC}:c\qquad 0:\mathbf{C}:a\vdash 0:\mathbf{C}:a}}}{0:\mathbf{C}:a,0:\mathbf{F}:a\backslash b,0:\mathbf{G}:b\backslash c/a,0:\mathbf{C}:a\vdash 0:\mathbf{CFGC}:c}$$

Figure 28.4   Initial values for the complete cadence.

tial configuration, the set of appraised segments of cadences is empty, and the user builds his or her own set of degrees of appraisal incrementally, that is initially, $\mu = 0$ for all triples $\mu{:}\mathbf{C}\ c$. Each time the user updates the values of μ, all values that have already occurred in any deduction are updated in order to preserve consistency, and from that point on each newly used segment of cadence is constrained by the actual values. The input points for the user to update values are individual chords, and compound segments of cadences must obey the propagation rule above.

We have proposed the utilization of Fuzzy-Syntactic Categories, implemented as previously, as a tool to encode individual preferences among complete harmonic cadences by encoding preferences among functions that individual chords may have, and thus obtaining an induced ordering for more complex combinations of chords.

As an example, let us consider again the complete cadence { $\mathbf{C},\mathbf{F},\mathbf{G},\mathbf{C}$ }. The initial Fuzzy-Syntactic Categories corresponding to our previous deduction are as in Figure 28.4.

Now, if the user updates the degrees of appraisal to, for example, 0.5 : $\mathbf{C}$: a, 0.1 : $\mathbf{F}$: $a\backslash b$ and 0.6 : $\mathbf{G}$: $b\backslash c/a$, the remaining values are changed as in Figure 28.5.

As the process is iterated, the database of values for degrees of appraisal is enriched. If then the user wants to evaluate the cadence {$\mathbf{C},\mathbf{d},$ $\mathbf{G},\mathbf{C}$}, the starting point is as in Figure 28.6.

If the user adds for example the value 0.3 : $\mathbf{d}$: $a\backslash b$ to the collection of degrees of appraisal, the resulting values become as in Figure 28.7.

We have developed an initial experiment on generating a database of values for degrees of appraisal. The results are presented in the following section.

28.4. Empirical Results

Our experiment consisted of encoding a fragment of tonal harmony [3] in terms of Fuzzy-Syntactic Categories, and then of providing all grammatically well-founded harmonizations for a given melody that we could

$$\frac{\dfrac{0.1:\mathbf{CF}:b\vdash 0.1:\mathbf{CF}:b\qquad 0.1:\mathbf{CFGC}:c\vdash 0.1:\mathbf{CFGC}:c}{\dfrac{0.1:\mathbf{CF}:b,0.5:\mathbf{GC}:b\backslash c\vdash 0.1:\mathbf{CFGC}:c\qquad 0.5:\mathbf{C}:a\vdash 0.5:\mathbf{C}:a}{0.5:\mathbf{C}:a,0.1:\mathbf{F}:a\backslash b,0.5:\mathbf{GC}:b\backslash c\vdash 0.1:\mathbf{CFGC}:c\qquad 0.5:\mathbf{C}:a\vdash 0.5:\mathbf{C}:a}}}{0.5{:}\mathbf{C}{:}a,0.1{:}\mathbf{F}{:}a\backslash b,0.6{:}\mathbf{G}{:}b\backslash c/a,0.5{:}\mathbf{C}{:}a\vdash 0.1:\mathbf{CFGC}:c}$$

Figure 28.5   Updated values for the complete cadence.

$$\frac{\dfrac{0:\mathbf{Cd}:b \vdash 0:\mathbf{Cd}:b \qquad 0:\mathbf{CdGC}:c \vdash 0:\mathbf{CdGC}:c}{0:\mathbf{Cd}:b,0.5:\mathbf{GC}:b\backslash c \vdash 0:\mathbf{CdGC}:c \qquad 0.5:\mathbf{C}:a \vdash 0.5:\mathbf{C}:a}}{\dfrac{0.5:\mathbf{C}:a,0:\mathbf{d}:a\backslash b,0.5:\mathbf{GC}:b\backslash c \vdash 0:\mathbf{CdGC}:c \qquad 0.5:\mathbf{C}:a \vdash 0.5:\mathbf{C}:a}{0.5:\mathbf{C}:a,0:\mathbf{d}:a\backslash b,0.6:\mathbf{G}:b\backslash c/a,0.5:\mathbf{C}:a \vdash 0:\mathbf{CdGC}:c}}$$

Figure 28.6   Initial values for the altered cadence.

derive from the encoded fragment of tonal harmony. With this in hand, we ordered the set of harmonizations according to an informal perception of "closeness" to the original arrangement for that melody. Then we looked for a fuzzy labelling of pairs [individual chord: harmonic function] that reflected this ordering, to check whether this methodology was capable of expressing stylistic harmonic preferences, as we had suggested.

The melody we used is an excerpt from the well-known "Girl from Ipanema" (Jobim and Moraes) (Figure 28.8).

Based on table 1, the collection of 46 well-founded cadences to harmonise this melody is the set $\mathcal{H}$ presented below:

$\mathcal{H} = \{$

C7 + 9C7 + 9GC,	C7 + 9C7 + 9GC7 + 9,	C7 + 9C7 + 9G7 – C
C7 + 9C7 + 9G7 – C7 + 9,	C7 + 9DGC,	C7 + 9DGC7 + 9,
C7 + 9DG7 – C,	C7 + 9DG7 – C7 + 9,	C7 + 9DC7 + 9C,
C7 + 9DC7 + 9C7 + 9,	C7 + 9GC7 + 9C,	C7 + 9GC7 + 9C7 + 9,
C7 + 9G7 – C7 + 9C,	C7 + 9G7 – C7 + 9C7 + 9,	G7 + 9G7 + 9C7 + 9G7 + 9,
G7 + 9G7 + 9C7 + 9G,	G7 + 9GC7 + 9G7 + 9,	G7 + 9GC7 + 9G,
GG7 + 9C7 + 9G7 + 9,	GG7 + 9C7 + 9G,	GGC7 + 9G7 + 9,
GGC7 + 9G,	G7 + 9C7 + 9G7 + 9G7 + 9,	G7 + 9C7 + 9G7 + 9G,
G7 + 9C7 + 9GG7 + 9,	G7 + 9C7 + 9GG,	GC7 + 9G7 + 9G7 + 9,
GC7 + 9G7 + 9G,	GC7 + 9GG7 + 9,	GC7 + 9GG,
G7 + 9D7 – G7 + 9G7 + 9,	G7 + 9D7 – G7 + 9G,	G7 + 9D7 – GG7 + 9,
G7 + 9D7 – GG,	GD7 – G7 + 9G7 + 9,	GD7 – G7 + 9G,
GD7 – GG7 + 9,	GD7 – GG,	G7 + 9DG7 + 9G7 + 9,
G7 + 9DG7 + 9G,	G7 + 9DGG7 + 9,	G7 + 9DGG,
GDG7 + 9G7 + 9,	GDG7 + 9G,	GDGG7 + 9,
GDGG	}.	

$$\frac{\dfrac{0.3:\mathbf{Cd}:b \vdash 0.3:\mathbf{Cd}:b \qquad 0.3:\mathbf{CdGC}:c \vdash 0.3:\mathbf{CdGC}:c}{0.3:\mathbf{Cd}:b,0.5:\mathbf{GC}:b\backslash c \vdash 0.3:\mathbf{CdGC}:c \qquad 0.5:\mathbf{C}:a \vdash 0.5:\mathbf{C}:a}}{\dfrac{0.5:\mathbf{C}:a,0.3:\mathbf{d}:a\backslash b,0.5:\mathbf{GC}:b\backslash c \vdash 0.3:\mathbf{CdGC}:c \qquad 0.5:\mathbf{C}:a \vdash 0.5:\mathbf{C}:a}{0.5:\mathbf{C}{:}a,0.3{:}\mathbf{d}{:}a\backslash b,0.6{:}\mathbf{G}{:}b\backslash c/a,0.5{:}\mathbf{C}{:}a \vdash 0.3:\mathbf{CdGC}:c}}$$

Figure 28.7   Updated values for the altered cadence.

Figure 28.8 Excerpt from "Girl from Ipanema."

The first 14 cadences are in the key of C major, whereas the remaining 32 cadences are in the key of G major. From all these cadences, the "closest" one to the original harmonization by A. C. Jobim is { **C7 + 9dG7 – C**}. Moreover, every harmonization in C major must be considered "closer" to the original harmonization than harmonizations in other keys.

We added the following fuzzy degrees of appraisal to the pairs [individual chord: harmonic function] occurring in the cadences preceding:

1:**C7 + 9**:*a*	1:**C**:*a*	1:**d**:*a\b*
1:**G7-**:*b\c/a*	0.9:**G**:*b\c/a*	0.6:**C7 + 9**:*a\a*
0.6:**C**:*a\a*	0.3:**G**:*a\c/a*	0.3:**G7-**:*a\c/a*
0.4:**C7 + 9**:*a/a*	0.5:**C**:*a/a*	0.3:**G**:*a*
0.3:**G7 + 9**:*a*	0.4:**G**:*a\a*	0.4:**G7 + 9**:*a\a*
0.3:**C7 + 9**:*a\c/a*	0.3:**D**:*b\c/a*	0.4:**D7-**:*b\c/a*
0.1:**G**:*a/a*	0.1:**G7 + 9**:*a/a*	

These values induce the following values for the harmonizations in

{ **1:C7 + 9dG7 – C,**	**1:C7 + 9dG7 – C7 + 9,**
0.9:C7 + 9dGC,	**0.9:C7 + 9dGC7 + 9,**
0.5:C7 + 9dC7 + 9C,	**0.4:C7 + 9dC7 + 9C7 + 9,**
0.3:C7 + 9C7 + 9GC,	**0.3:C7 + 9C7 + 9GC7 + 9,**
0.3:C7 + 9C7 + 9G7 – C,	**0.3:C7 + 9C7 + 9G7 – C7 + 9,**
0.3:C7 + 9GC7 + 9C,	**0.3:C7 + 9GC7 + 9C7 + 9,**
0.3:C7 + 9G7 – C7 + 9C,	**0.3:C7 + 9G7 – C7 + 9C7 + 9,**
0.3:G7 + 9G7 + 9C7 + 9G7 + 9,	**0.3:G7 + 9G7 + 9C7 + 9G,**
0.3:G7 + 9GC7 + 9G7 + 9,	**0.3:G7 + 9GC7 + 9G,**
0.3:GG7 + 9C7 + 9G7 + 9,	**0.3:GG7 + 9C7 + 9G,**
0.3:GGC7 + 9G7 + 9,	**0.3:GGC7 + 9G,**
0.1:G7 + 9C7 + 9G7 + 9G7 + 9,	**0.1:G7 + 9C7 + 9G7 + 9G,**
0.1:G7 + 9C7 + 9GG7 + 9,	**0.1:G7 + 9C7 + 9GG,**

0.1:GC7 + 9G7 + 9G7 + 9,	**0.1:GC7 + 9G7 + 9G,**
0.1:GC7 + 9GG7 + 9,	**0.1:GC7 + 9GG,**
0.1:G7 + 9D7 − G7 + 9G7 + 9,	**0.1:G7 + 9D7 − G7 + 9G,**
0.1:G7 + 9D7 − GG7 + 9,	**0.1:G7 + 9D7 − GG,**
0.1:GD7 − G7 + 9G7 + 9,	**0.1:GD7 − G7 + 9G,**
0.1:GD7 − GG7 + 9,	**0.1:GD7 − GG,**
0.1:G7 + 9DG7 + 9G7 + 9,	**0.1:G7 + 9DG7 + 9G,**
0.1:G7 + 9DGG7 + 9,	**0.1:G7 + 9DGG,**
0.1:GDG7 + 9G7 + 9,	**0.1:GDG7 + 9G,**
0.1:GDGG7 + 9,	**0.1:GDGG }.**

As can be observed, the desired ordering is thus obtained. However, the framework is not sensitive enough to permit the characterization of *all possible orderings* by means of updates on degrees of appraisal to individual chords.

28.5. Conclusion

Clearly, there is still much to be done to turn Fuzzy-Syntactic Categories into a more user-friendly tool for musicians. Nonetheless, our initial experimental results indicate that the representation of stylistic preferences in terms of fuzzy sets can be interesting.

Immediate future work on Fuzzy-Syntactic Categories will include optimizing their implementation as a computational tool, and developing more thorough experiments to assess the applicability of these structures in more complex harmonizations. It will also be interesting to study the possibilities of automating the generation of the values for fuzzy values, perhaps by training an appropriate neural network for this task.

The major restriction that we have imposed onto the framework at implementation level is that update values are allowed only for individual chords. As a consequence, some harmonizations must be deemed indistinguishable, and an evaluation can only be lowered by inserting chords that have not yet occurred in the harmonization. It will be interesting to search for more flexible ways to update values that preserve appropriate computational complexity degrees for the corresponding implementations.

28.6. References

[1] Baroni, M., and L. Callegari. *Musical Grammars and Computer Analysis.* University degli Studi di Bologna e Modena: 1984.

[2] Benthem, J. "Categorial Grammar and Type Theory." *Journal of Philosophical Logic,* Vol. 19 (1990), pp. 115–168.

[3] Brisolla, C.M. *Principios de Harmonia Funcional.* Novas Metas: 1979.

[4] Cope, D. *Computers and Musical Style.* A-R Editions: 1991.

[5] Correa da Silva, F.S., and F. Kon. *Categorial Grammar and Harmonic Analysis.* In II Brazilian Symposium on Computer Music. Brazil: 1995.

[6] ———. "Stylistic Musical Choices via Fuzzy Preference Rules." *6th International Fuzzy Sets Association World Congress.* Brazil: 1995.

[7] Gabbay, D.M. "Abduction in Labelled Deductive Systems—A Conceptual Abstract," in *European Conference on Symbolic and Quantitative Aspects of Uncertainty, LNCS 548.* 1991.

[8] Holtzman, S.R. "A Generative Grammar Definition Language for Music." *Interface,* Vol. 9 (1980), pp. 1–48.

[9] Klement, E.P. "Construction of Fuzzy O-Algebras using Triangular Norms." *Journal of Mathematical Analysis and Applications,* Vol. 85 (1982), pp. 543–565.

[10] Lambek, J. "The Mathematics of Sentence Structure." *American Mathematics Monthly,* Vol. 65 (1958), pp. 154–169.

[11] Oliveira, A.J., and R.J.G.B. Queiroz. "Term Rewriting Systems with LDS." In *SBIA 1994.* Brazil: 1994.

[12] Queiroz, R.J.G.B., and D. Gabbay. "An Introduction to Labelled Natural Deduction." In *3rd Advanced Summer School in Artificial Intelligence.* 1992.

[13] Schurmann, E.F. *A Musica como Linguagem.* Brasiliense/CNPq. 1989.

[14] Zadeh, L.A. "Fuzzy Sets." *Information and Control,* Vol. 8 (1965), pp. 338–353.

[15] ———. "Probability Measures of Fuzzy Events." *Journal of Mathematical Analysis and Applications,* Vol. 23 (1968), pp. 421–427.

Exploiting Information

PART 1
Decision Making

GUIDING NOTE

Fuzzy sets offer a very extensive framework for multiaspect evaluation due to the existence of a very rich and axiomatically well-understood body of fuzzy set-theoretic operations. In traditional numerical approaches such as multiattribute decision making, the central idea was that of a trade-off between objectives, underlying a compensatory aggregation scheme. Namely a bad rating according to one criterion can be counterbalanced by a good rating according to another one. The fuzzy set approach encompasses compensatory and noncompensatory modes of aggregation, and is actually best known for the minimum based noncompensatory proposal of Bellman and Zadeh. The chapter by Zimmermann examines the behavioral relevance of fuzzy set connectives, and develops the methodology for devising hierarchical models of complex linguistic categories that embody high-level objectives. The next chapter by Maeda and Murakami is an application of this methodology to a practical problem of choice of a computer system. These chapters are typical of a wide class of application of fuzzy set theory, namely subjective evaluation.

As a dual notion to fuzzy sets, the concept of a fuzzy measure was proposed by Sugeno in 1974, along with an integral that is closely related to the min-max calculus of Zadeh. The Sugeno integral plays the same role for possibility theory as does the Lebesgue integral for probability theory. While the usual interpretation of set-functions, like probability measures, is in terms of uncertainty modelling, the fuzzy measure and the fuzzy integrals were also used as a natural and very general approach to the notion of criteria importance. The chapter of Grabisch gives a very informed overview of fuzzy integrals, and their applications to subjective multiple-criteria evaluation, multisource data fusion, pattern-recognition and image processing. The theory of fuzzy measures is also a point of tangency between fuzzy set theory and upper/lower probabilities because part of the fuzzy set connectives can be described as a Choquet integral. These generalized integrals (Choquet or Sugeno) are appealing because they account for the notion of interaction between criteria, contrary to the case of a weighted sum that presupposes their independence. This field of investigation is rather new and is potentially very attractive both from theoretical points of views and fruitful for applications in decision making and related areas. An example of aggregation operation that is closely related to Choquet integral is the Ordered Weighted Average operation of Yager. In his chapter with Engemann and Miller, they show how the OWA operation can account for a decision-maker's attitude toward risk. This chapter shows how ideas borrowed from expected utility theory, fuzzy set theory, and Shafer's belief function theory can lead to a realistic choice method under uncertainty. This method is illustrated on the problem of purchasing an electricity generator for a bank in order to cope with power outages.

The representation of attitude toward risk is also at the heart of the contribution by Kikuchi in the field of transportation research. It deals with the behavior of a driver approaching a crossroad when the traffic lights become yellow. It is shown how possibility theory can account for extreme attitudes of aggressive drivers or very cautious ones. This study is validated on real data.

The last contribution to this section illustrates another kind of application of fuzzy sets to decision making: reaching consensus in a group that must agree on a course of action. It is shown how to build graded evaluations of consensus, which incorporate fuzzy quantifiers so as to model consensus criteria of the form "most people agree." The interaction between fuzzy sets and social choice or group-decision making are again a fruitful field of investigation.

29 Operators in Models of Decision Making

Prof. Dr. H.-J. Zimmermann
*Lehrstuhl für Unternehmensforschung (Operations Research),
RWTH Aachen, D-52062 Aachen, Federal Republic of Germany*

ABSTRACT: Models of human decision making—especially in multicriteria decision making—generally include the aggregation of criteria or criteria and constraints. For the case that criteria and/or constraints cannot be modelled crisply but as fuzzy sets, L.A. Zadeh suggested in his seminal paper in 1970, that this aggregation can be modelled by either the minimum or the product operator. Subsequently, it was shown empirically that this model might have to be modified in order to model human decision making adequately. This paper presents some empirical evidence and suggests other models to describe aggregation in models of human decision making.

29.1. Introduction

A decision in a "fuzzy environment" has been defined by Bellman and Zadeh [1] as the intersection of fuzzy sets representing either objectives or constraints. The grade of membership of an object in the intersection of two fuzzy sets, that is, the fuzzy set "decision," was determined by use of either the min-operator or the product operator. The following example is an illustration of this [29]:

Example 1: The board of directors is trying to find the "optimal" dividend to be paid to the shareholders. For financial reasons it ought to be attractive and for reasons of wage negotiations it should be modest. The fuzzy set of the objective function "attractive dividends" could, for instance, be defined by:

$$\mu_o(x) = \begin{cases} 1, & x \geq 5,8, \\ \dfrac{1}{2100}[-29x^3 - 366x^2 - 877x + 540] \\ 0, & x \leq 1. \end{cases}$$

The fuzzy set (constraint) "modest dividend" could be represented by:

$$\mu_c(x) = \begin{cases} 1, & x \leq 1,2, \\ \dfrac{1}{2100}[-29x^3 - 243x^2 + 16x + 2388], \\ 0, & x \geq 6. \end{cases}$$

The fuzzy set "decision" is then:

$$\mu_D = \mathrm{Min}\ (\mu_o(x), \mu_c(x)).$$

The optimal dividend to be paid to the shareholders would be 3.5 percent, considering the dividend with the highest degree of membership in the fuzzy set "decision" as the "most desirable." Rather than viewing a decision as the intersection of several fuzzy sets, as we did in [30], one could describe it also as the union of all relevant fuzzy sets, using the maximum operator for aggregation (see Figure 29.1).

Example 2: An instructor at a university has to decide how to grade written test papers. Let us assume that the problem to be solved in the test was a linear programming problem and that the student was free to solve it either graphically or using the simplex method. The student has done both. The student's performance is expressed—for graphical solution as well as for the algebraic solution—as the achieved degree of membership in the fuzzy sets "good graphical solution" (G) and "good simplex solution" (S), respectively. Let us assume that he or she reaches:

$$\mu_G = 0.9 \text{ and } \mu_S = 0.7.$$

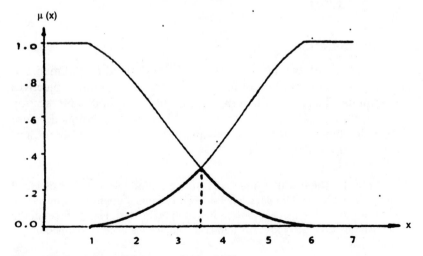

Figure 29.1 A fuzzy decision; x = dividend (%).

If the grade to be awarded by the instructor corresponds to the degree of membership of the fuzzy set "good solutions of linear programming problems" it would be quite conceivable that this grade μ_{LP} could be determined by:

$$\mu_{LP} = Max(\mu_G, \mu_S) = Max(0.9, 0.7) = 0.9.$$

The two definitions of decisions—as the intersection or the union of fuzzy sets—imply essentially the following: The interpretation of a decision as the intersection of fuzzy sets implies no positive compensation (trade-off) between the degrees of membership of the fuzzy sets in question, if either the minimum or the product is used as an operator. Each of them yields degrees of membership of the resulting fuzzy set (decision), which are on or below the lowest degree of membership of all intersecting fuzzy sets (see Example 1). This is also true if any other t-norm [30] is used to model the intersection, or operators, which are no t-norms but map below the min-operator. It should be noted that, in fact, there are decision situations in which such a "negative compensation" (i.e., mapping below the minimum) is appropriate. This case will be discussed later.

The interpretation of a decision as the union of fuzzy sets, using the max-operator, leads to the maximum degree of membership achieved by any of the fuzzy sets representing objectives or constraints. This amounts to a full compensation of lower degrees of membership by the maximum degree of membership (see Example 2). No membership will result, however, that is larger than the largest degree of membership of any of the fuzzy sets involved. Observing managerial decisions, one finds that there are hardly any decisions with no compensation between either different degrees of goal achievement or the degrees to which restrictions are limiting the scope of decisions. It may be argued that compensatory tendencies in human aggregation are responsible for the failure of some classical operators (min, product, max) in empirical investigations [7, 19].

The following conclusions can probably be drawn: Neither t-norms that map below the minimum nor t-conorms that map above the maximum operator can alone cover the scope of human decision making. It is very unlikely that a single nonparametric operator can model appropriately the meaning of "and" or "or" context-independently, that is for all persons, at any time and in each context. There seem to be three ways to remedy this weakness of t-norms and t-conorms: one can either define parameter-dependent t-norms or t-conorms [Dubois, Frank, Hamacher, Sugeno, Yager], which cover with their parameters the scope of some of the nonparametric t-norms or t-conorms and can, therefore, be adapted to a context [3]. The advantage of these operators is that most of them keep the good property of t-norms. Their disadvantage is that they do not go beyond the t-norms, that is, they all map below the minimum.

A second way is to combine t-norms and their respective t-conorms and so cover also the range between t-norms and t-conorms (which could be called the space of "partial positive compensation"). The disadvantage of this approach is that generally some of the useful properties of t-norms or t-conorms, such as transitivity, get lost.

The third way is, eventually, to design operators that are neither t-norms nor t-conorms, but that are efficient and model one particular context well enough. In this chapter we concentrate on the second approach and present some empirical evidence for the suitability of these operators.

Zadeh already pointed out that the type of operator for the aggregation of fuzzy sets in the sense of an intersection might depend on whether the sets are "interactive" or "noninteractive" [26], which sometimes was interpreted as "dependent" or "independent." We feel, however, that "interaction" in this sense is not a feature of the fuzzy sets aggregated but of the type of aggregation that does not necessarily depend on the sets in question. Before developing more promising models for aggregation we felt it necessary to obtain some more empirical knowledge on the presumption that people do not avoid the area between the minimum and maximum when merging subjective categories. It is possible that human beings use many nonverbal connectives in their thinking and reasoning.

These connectives may be located between the intersection operators (t-norms) and union operators (t-conorms). Being forced to verbalize them may possibly map the set of "intermediate connectives" into the set of the corresponding language connectives ("and" "or"). Hence, when talking, they use the verbal connective that they feel closest to their "real" nonverbal connective. In analogy to the verbal connectives, the logicians defined the connectives "$\wedge$" and "$\vee$," assigning certain properties to each of them. By this, compound sentences can be examined for their truth values. In contrary to this constructive process, the empirical researcher has to analyze a given structure. Therefore, in order to induce subjects to use their "own connectives," we avoided the verbal connectives "and" and "or" in our experiment, but tried to ask for combined membership values implicitly presenting a suitable experimental design and instruction, respectively.

29.2. Experiment [28]

As a simple example of a decision or evaluation using such a "connective" consider the following situation in which the quality of dovetailing of tiles and their solidity determine together the quality of a tile.

29.2.1. A "Realistic" Situation

A factory produces fire-resistive tiles for revetting chimneys of heating systems. Let us assume that the quality of the tiles depends on two factors: their dovetailing and their solidity (Figure 29.2).

1. Good dovetailing means: the tiles cling to each other as tightly as possible. Bad dovetailing means: the tiles are disjoint.

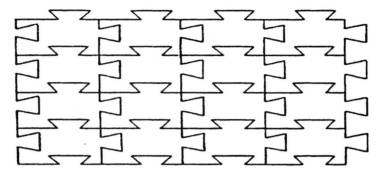

Figure 29.2   Dovetailed tiles.

2. Good solidity is indicated by a light gray color. The grades of solidity range from light gray to deep black, the latter indicating low
   quality. Unfortunately, it is not possible to produce tiles of equally
   high quality. Fluctuations in form and solidity are unavoidable.
   Therefore, an expert has to sort the tiles with respect to the different levels of quality.

Let us assume that in case of inexact dovetailing, the tiles will be fitted
by aid of cement. Exposed to great heat, the two materials will expand
differently. The better the solidity of the tile, the greater the difference of
tension that can be sustained, which means deficiencies in dovetailing
can be compensated by solidity. On the other hand, some lack of solidity
can be compensated by good form. To investigate this situation empirically, a similar task was outlined, slightly simplified for experimental purposes. Subjects were asked to rate the grade of fitting of wooden pates to
a given standard (Figure 29.3).

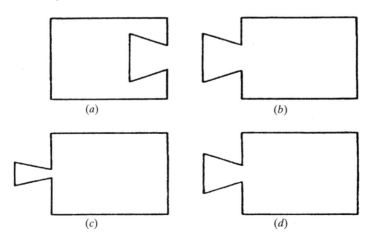

Figure 29.3   Standard (a) and three different tiles (b, c, d).

29.2.2. Stimuli

The collection of stimuli consisted of 24 "tiles" and one standard stimulus. The "solidity" ranged from light gray to deep black, the "good form" from exact dovetailing to bad dovetailing (i.e. the "tile" could easily be drawn out of the groove).

The two attributes can be assumed to be stochastically independent; that is, some magnitude of μ_S is not affected by some magnitude of μ_D and vice versa (S = "good solidity," D = "good dovetailing").

As it is not possible to offer all possible combinations of the attributes, we had to draw a sample of objects (see [19, p. 173]). Our procedure of selection had to guarantee:

- An even distribution of stimuli with respect to both attributes.

- The statistical independence of the two attributes. As an operational criterion, a correlation of zero was demanded: $r_{SD} = 0$.

29.2.3. Experimental Procedure

Sixty students served as unpaid subjects. Each of them was run individually through two experimental sessions, the first taking about 10 minutes, the second about 20 minutes. In order to avoid influences of memory, the interviews were performed in intervals of approximately three days. The subjects were instructed to give ratings between 0 and 100 percent according to the grade of fitting of the serial stimulus to the standard.

During the first interview, we asked for judgments concerning "ideal tile" (ideal with respect to both attributes). The subjects were asked to put themselves into the role of the expert and give a judgment concerning the overall quality of each tile. The stimuli were presented in an arbitrary sequence. As mentioned, we wanted the subjects to use their "own (latent) connectives." Therefore, we did not use the words "and" and "or" in connection with the two attributes.

In the second session, judgments concerning the single attributes ("good solidity," "good dovetailing") were requested; in order to control sequential effects, half the subjects first judged solidity, then form, and the other half, the opposite way round.

29.2.4. Analysis of Results

To determine the membership values, we computed the arithmetic mean of the judgments concerning the objects of each set. In accordance to our former studies, the three μ-scales were also determined by an indirect technique.

As each corresponding membership scale correlates at least according to (Pearson) 4 = 0.975, the correction of scale values based on the indirect method was dropped. The final membership scales for "good solidity," "good dovetailing," and "ideal tile" are shown in Table 29.1. First it had to

Table 29.1 Membership Scales
of "Good Solidity" (S), "Dovetailing" (D),
and "Ideal Tile" (I)

Stimulus	μ_S	μ_D	μ_I
1	0.426	0.241	0.215
2	0.352	0.662	0.427
3	0.109	0.352	0.221
4	0.630	0.052	0.212
5	0.484	0.496	0.486
6	0.000	0.000	0.000
7	0.270	0.403	0.274
8	0.156	0.130	0.119
9	0.790	0.284	0.407
10	0.725	0.193	0.261
11	1.000	1.000	1.000
12	0.330	0.912	0.632
13	0.949	0.020	0.247
14	0.202	0.826	0.500
15	0.744	0.551	0.555
16	0.572	0.691	0.585
17	0.041	0.975	0.355
18	0.534	0.873	0.661
19	0.674	0.587	0.570
20	0.440	0.450	0.418
21	0.909	0.750	0.789
22	0.856	0.091	0.303
23	0.974	0.164	0.515
24	0.073	0.788	0.324

be proven that the series of stimuli had been well selected with respect to the independence of the two attributes "good solidity" and "good dovetailing." As $r_{SD} = -0.147$ is not significantly different from zero (when $\alpha = 0.05$ and df = 22, then R = ± 0.432), the sample is accepted.

We can now predict the quality of an operator: Based on the observed membership values for "solidity" and "dovetailing," a "theoretical" value for the combined attribute "ideal tile" is obtained. These computed predictions can be compared with the corresponding empirical values for the "ideal tile." Table 29.2 shows the empirical scale together with the grades of membership computed by using the minimum, maximum, arithmetic mean, and geometric mean, respectively.

The following Figures (29.4, 29.5, 29.6, 29.7) show graphically the relationship between empirical and theoretical grades of membership. The straight diagonal line indicates locations of perfect prediction.

The four operators were chosen for the following reason: Minimum and maximum are the "extremal" operators corresponding to the "logical and" and the "inclusive or." They are computationally also very efficient. Today, they could be replaced by any other pair of t-norms and t-conorms. Arithmetic mean and geometric mean map pointwise between minimum and maximum of the membership functions considered. They average between the norms, that is model positive compensation. From the operators tested, the geometric mean obviously predicts the empiri-

Table 29.2 Predicted Membership Values for "Ideal Tile"
Using Different Operators

Stimulus	Empirical	Min	Max	Arithmetic mean	Geometric mean
1	0.215	0.241	0.426	0.334	0.321
2	0.427	0.352	0.662	0.507	0.483
3	0.221	0.109	0.352	0.230	0.195
4	0.212	0.052	0.630	0.341	0.182
5	0.486	0.484	0.496	0.490	0.490
6	0.000	0.000	0.000	0.000	0.000
7	0.274	0.270	0.403	0.337	0.330
8	0.119	0.130	0.156	0.143	0.141
9	0.407	0.284	0.790	0.537	0.473
10	0.261	0.193	0.725	0.459	0.374
11	1.000	1.000	1.000	1.000	1.000
12	0.632	0.330	0.912	0.621	0.549
13	0.247	0.020	0.949	0.485	0.138
14	0.500	0.202	0.826	0.514	0.409
15	0.555	0.551	0.744	0.648	0.640
16	0.585	0.572	0.691	0.632	0.628
17	0.355	0.041	0.975	0.508	0.200
18	0.661	0.534	0.873	0.704	0.683
19	0.570	0.587	0.674	0.631	0.629
20	0.418	0.440	0.450	0.445	0.445
21	0.789	0.750	0.909	0.830	0.826
22	0.303	0.091	0.856	0.474	0.279
23	0.515	0.164	0.974	0.569	0.400
24	0.324	0.073	0.788	0.431	0.241

cal data best. Therefore, with respect to the question whether or not people avoid the area between minimum and maximum we can state:

1. People use averaging operations when making judgments or evaluations resulting in membership values between minimum and maximum (Figure 29.8).

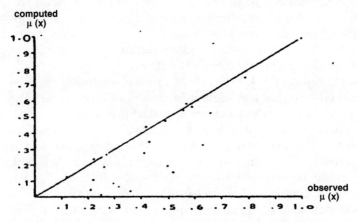

Figure 29.4 Min-operator: Observed versus computed grades of membership.

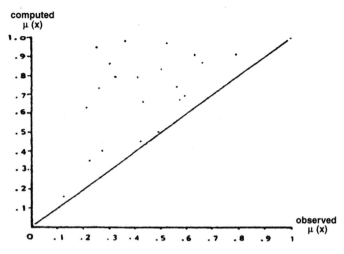

Figure 29.5 Max-operator: Observed versus computed grades of
membership.

2. The geometric mean is an adequate model for human aggregation
   of fuzzy sets when a compensatory effect exists.
3. People use still other connectives than "and" and "or."

29.3. A Concept of General Aggregation

Our experiment has shown that in the context modelled, the min-
operator and the max-operator are not sufficient to model human aggregating behavior. There are two directions in which one can proceed: On
can "soften" the logical "and" and "or" models of minimum and maxi-

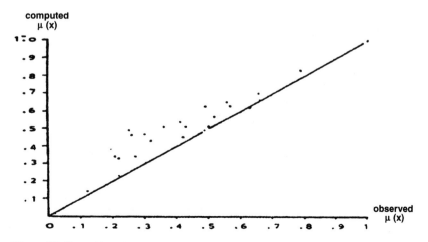

Figure 29.6 Arithmetic mean: Observed versus computed grades of membership.

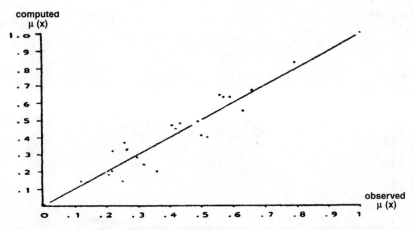

Figure 29.7   Geometric mean: Observed versus computed grades of membership.

mum but still keep two different models corresponding to the linguistic
"and" and the linguistic "or." This approach was suggested by Werners
[24] when introducing the "fuzzy and" and the "fuzzy or."

   Alternatively, one can try to introduce a "general" connective, which
maps between an extreme model of "and" and an extreme model of "or"
(for instance, between max $(0, a + b - 1)$ and min $(1, a + b)$).

   In both cases one can again try to design several nonparametric connectives or to choose a "family," that is, a general parametric model, for
all types of aggregation. We chose the last option and used as a hypothesis for experimentation a general connective, which maps between a t-
norm as the model for "and" and a t-conorm as the model for "or." (see
Figure 29.9).

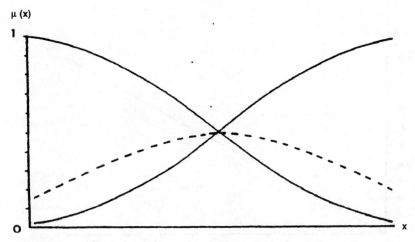

Figure 29.8   Aggregation of two membership functions by geometric means as depicted
by the dotted line.

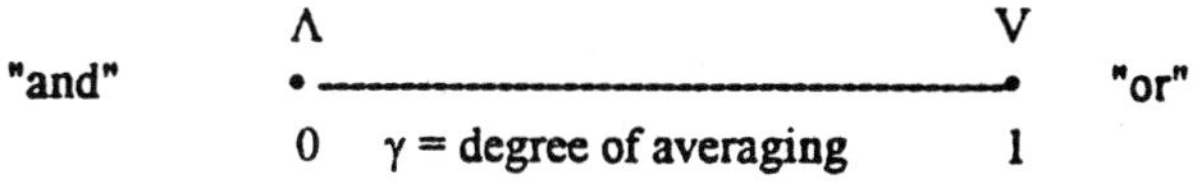

Figure 29.9 A general concept for aggregation.

If min and max are used as models for "and" and "or," respectively, then γ could also be interpreted as the "degree of positive compensation." If other t-norms and conorms are used, "negative" and "positive" compensation will occur for different ranges of γ. One can, of course, also choose different ways of linking the "and" with the "or." We start with a multiplicative coupling.

Thus we define:

$$\mu_{A\theta B} = \mu_{A\cap B}^{1-\gamma} * \mu_{A\cup B}^{\gamma}. \tag{1}$$

The membership of an object in the set $A\theta B$ equals the product of the weighted membership values for the intersection and the union.

If the intersection and the union are algebraically represented by the product and the algebraic sum, respectively, then (1) becomes:

$$\mu_\theta = \left(\prod_{i=1}^{m} \mu_i\right)^{1-\gamma} \left(1 - \prod_{i=1}^{m} (1-\mu_i)\right)^{\gamma}, 0 \le \mu \le 1, 0 \le \gamma \le 1 \tag{2}$$

$i = 1, 2, \ldots, m$, $m = $ number of sets to be connected.

If $\gamma = 0$, then:

$$\mu_\cap = \prod_{i=1}^{m} \mu_i, \gamma = 0. \tag{3}$$

This equals the product and provides the truth values for the connective "and." If $\gamma = 1$, then:

$$\mu_\cup = 1 - \prod_{i=1}^{m} (1-\mu_i), \gamma = 1. \tag{4}$$

This formula equals the generalized algebraic sum and provides the truth values for the connective "or" (see Figure 29.10).

If it is desired to introduce different weights for the sets in question, μ_i and $1 - \mu_i$ could for instance be replaced by:

$$\mu_i = \upsilon_i^{\delta_i}$$
$$1 - \mu_i = (1 - \upsilon_i)^{\delta_i} \tag{5}$$

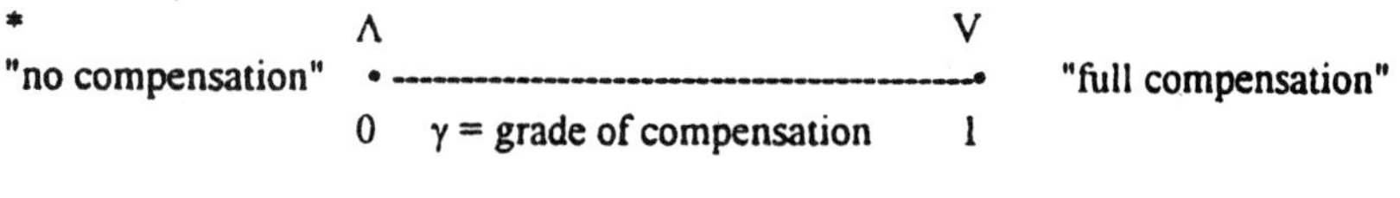

Figure 29.10 Generalized concept of connectives.

where υ_i are the (raw)membership values and δ_i their corresponding weights. In order to preserve the structure of our model, the sum of weights δ_i, should be equal to the number of sets connected.

$$\delta_i = m. \tag{6}$$

Using different weights may play an important role in modelling, for instance, preference structures. Since the weights essentially change, however, the membership functions that are considered in the aggregations procedure, the weighting procedure has to take care of the type of membership functions used (for instance, normalized or not, unimodal or not etc.) and the intended meaning of the weights.

The effects of the weights also depend on the connectives used and cannot be used independent of the aggregation procedure. Our experiment was designed on the basis of equal weight for the two set S and D (solidity and dovetailing):

$$\delta_S = \delta_D = 1.$$

In order to use this class of operators in a meaningful manner, an operational definition should, of course, be available for the empirical determination of γ. At present, such a definition is still missing. However, we can try to find out if there is any value of γ that enables us to predict our experiment data. If such a value does not exist, then the adequacy of the operator suggested must be doubted. On the other hand, if the operator works on the basis of some γ, then it seems reasonable to search for an operational definition as mentioned previously.

If (2) is solved for γ the result is:

$$\gamma = \frac{\log \mu_\theta - \log \prod_{i=1}^{m} \mu_i}{\log\left(1 - \prod_{i=1}^{m}(1-\mu_i)\right) - \log \prod_{i=1}^{m} \mu_i}, \tag{7}$$

$i = 1, 2, \ldots, m$ m = number of sets to be connected.

Naturally, γ will show some fluctuations because of some experimental error. We therefore used $\hat{\gamma}$ to find the results in Figure 29.11:

$$\hat{\gamma} = \frac{1}{n}\sum_{j=1}^{n} \gamma_j \tag{8}$$

where n is the number of experimental objects in each of the sets selected $(A, B, A\theta B)$.

On the basis of the data in Table 29.1 (omitting stimuli 6 and 11) the "grade of averaging" is:

$$\gamma_{SD} = 0.562. \tag{9}$$

Using this value of γ, our empirical data can be predicted sufficiently well (Figure 29.11).

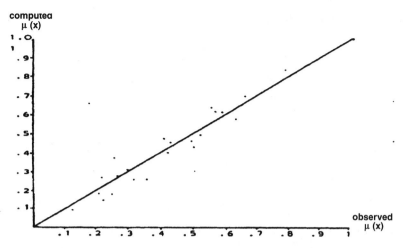

Figure 29.11 γ-operator: Observed versus computed grades of membership.

In addition it can be shown, that the γ-operator is pointwise injective, continuous, monotonous, commutative and in accordance with the truth tables of dual logic.

Other links between the norms are, of course, conceivable. For instance, the aggregation of two sets may be defined by:

$$\mu_{A\theta B} = (1-\gamma)\mu_{A\cap B} + \gamma\mu_{A\cup B}$$
$$= \mu_{A\cap B} + \gamma\,(\mu_{A\cup B} - \mu_{A\cap B}). \tag{10}$$

If the intersection and the union are represented by the product and the algebraic sum, respectively (10) becomes:

$$\mu_\theta = (1-\gamma)\prod_{i=1}^{m}\mu_i + \gamma\left(1 - \prod_{i=1}^{m}(1-\mu_i)\right). \tag{11}$$

Again, μ_i may be replaced by weighted membership values:

$$\mu_\theta = (1-\gamma)\prod_{i=1}^{m}\upsilon_i^{\delta_i} + \gamma\left(1 - \prod_{i=1}^{m}(1-\mu_i)^{\delta_i}\right)\ 0\le\upsilon\le 1, 0\le\gamma\le 1, \sum\delta_i = m \tag{12}$$

If $\gamma = 0$ and $\delta_i = 1$, then (12) becomes:

$$\mu_\cap = \prod_i\mu_i \tag{13}$$

If $\gamma = 1$ and $\delta_i = 1$, then (12) becomes:

$$\mu_\cup = 1 - \prod_i(1-\mu_i). \tag{14}$$

This class of operators is again in accordance with the truth tables of dual logic and allows the use of different weights. But its predictive quality is not sufficient with respect to our data.

29.4. Validation: A Field Study

The main concern of this field study was the performance of the γ-operator in real decision-making situations, in which several categories or criteria have to be aggregated. In this case, we chose a hierarchy of evaluation criteria. To model the situation the following paradigm was used.

29.4.1. Paradigm

Our paradigm assumes that people either learn or generate "evaluative concepts" or "subjective categories." These terms refer to two sides of one coin: the first refers to the intentional aspects of a set that can be described by a list of attributes, and the second stresses the accumulation of objects (extensional aspect of a set). We assume that human beings have such concepts or categories at their disposition and that they can relate them to each other. Attributes constituting a concept may be interpreted other than psychologically. They can be replaced by any mental information unit, for instance, the status of neural elements or the adjectives of a language. The relationships may actually be modelled by operators, connectives, rules, or others.

For our purposes we will limit our considerations to a specific type of amalgamation: We assume a hierarchy of concepts in which there are several levels of complexity (Figure 29.12).

The bottom level contains basic concepts that can be aggregated stepwise until the top concept of the hierarchy is attained. For reasons of practical relevance of the model we shall allow that:

- The subcategories are of unequal importance for the respective supercategory.

- The description of categories of each level may partly contain the same attributes.

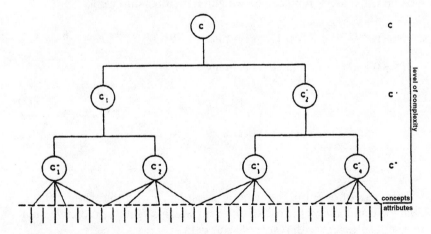

Figure 29.12 Hierarchy of concepts/categories.

29.4.2. Modelling Tools

The two essential aspects of the paradigm are the subjective categories and the connectives. Suitable format representations are given by fuzzy sets for the first and by connectives of fuzzy set theory for the second. As we want to support our suggestions by empirical evidence, we have to decide on methods to measure the degree of membership and to select suitable connectives for the prognostic power that has to be investigated. Furthermore, a situation has to be determined that is suitable for experimentation.

Finally, one or more methods for the design of a system of weights has to be examined with respect to its suitability for the evaluation hierarchy. These four problems will be discussed in detail in the following paragraphs.

From the viewpoint of measurement theory, the membership function maps an empirical relative $\langle X, S_1, \ldots, S_n \rangle$ with a set X and an n-tuple of relations $S_1, \ldots, S_n$ into a numerical one with elements of the interval $[0,1]$ and an n-tuple of relations $T_1, \ldots, T_n$:

$$\mu{:}\langle X, S_1, \ldots, S_n \rangle \rightarrow \langle [0,1], T_1, \ldots, T_n \rangle. \qquad (15)$$

This statement actually requires an axiomatic system [20], which would be the more useful the more axioms it contains that are empirically testable. Such an approach is not yet available in measurement theory. In order to have at least a workable tool available, we developed in one of the past projects the method ASI [19], which is an improved version of a classical scaling procedure, the method of successive intervals.

This method was modified to suit the empirical measurement of membership. ASI can be regarded as our operationalization of membership. Other proposals have been given by [16, 17, 2]. As a connective to aggregate the subjective categories of the lower levels, the γ-operator of (12) was used.

29.4.3. Decision Problem

Searching for an appropriate decision situation our choice fell on the rating of creditworthiness for the following reasons:

- This is a decision problem that is complex enough, though it is still relatively transparent and definable. In addition, this situation is highly standardized. Even though test subjects come from different organizations, similar evaluation schemes can be assessed.

- A sufficiently large number of decision makers is available who have about the same training background and similar levels of competence.

- The decision problem to be solved can be formulated and presented in a realistic manner with respect to contents and appearance.

In order to allow a weighting of the subcriteria as to their importance, the weighted γ-operator was used as a tool. The weighting scale should be at least a ratio scale. As no indirect technique is known that provides a scale of this level and seems properly applicable to our problem structure, we chose the direct way. However, this type of scaling poses greater demands on the subject as a measurement instrument. In order to avoid unnecessary risks, we tested three different procedures: constant sum, individual standard, and successive differentiation. The first method requires the highest experimental as well as computational effort. From the theoretical point of view, however, it is most satisfying, too.

Before beginning an empirical investigation it was necessary to explore whether a conceptual system on creditworthiness could be established. Three groups of six credit clerks were asked to design a hierarchical system of aspects for the evaluation of borrowers. Three sessions were arranged, each of which lasted five hours and was divided into three sections.

Session I: After an introductory discourse exposing the principal questions and intentions of the study, the participants' task was explained. Then four completed credit applications of fictitious borrowers had to be rated by "thinking loudly." Finally, each expert was asked to develop a concept hierarchy of creditworthiness on a piece of paper. On this basis, the group tried to find a first common criteria system, beginning from the top and going down successively to the lower levels.

Session II: The system arrived at so far was extended, refined, and modified by means of four more credit applications.

Session III: Clarification and agreement: superfluous aspects were eliminated, conceptual extensions were accepted only if the group consented by the majority. The final concept hierarchy has a symmetrical structure (Figure 29.13). Credit experts distinguish between the financial basis and the personality of an applicant. The financial basis comprises all realities, movables, assets, liquid funds, and others.

In order to evaluate the goodness of fit, the "prognostic error" was computed; it is defined as the distance between the empirical value and its theoretically expected counterpart. As a measure of fit, we used the squared deviation between observed values and computed ones:

$$d^2 = \frac{1}{2}(\mu_o - \mu_t)^2,$$

μ_o = observed μ-values, θ_t = theoretically expected μ-values.

The "average prognostic error" s_p^2 can now be defined by:

$$s_p^2 = \frac{\sum \frac{1}{2}(\mu_o - \mu_t)^2}{n-1} = \frac{\sum (\mu_o - \mu_t)^2}{2(n-1)}.$$

Tentatively, a level for rejection is introduced, the "intolerable error," which is fixed at $s_p^2 = 0.005$. At present, such a standard is somewhat arbi-

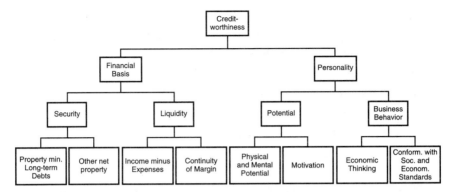

Figure 29.13 Concept hierarchy of creditworthiness.

trary. Principally, it should be fixed on the basis of general consent, external requirements, or experimental experience. Practically, it serves as a criterion of acceptance or rejection: If $s_p^2 < S_e^2$, then the model will be accepted. Therefore, if the ratio of variance $F_{comp} = s_c^2/s_p^2$ is greater than F_{crit} ($df_1 = df_2 = n - 1$) from the F-distribution, then the average prognostic error is regarded as "significantly less" than the intolerable error. Accordingly, the values of Table 29.3 are marked by two stars ($F_{crit} = 1.95$, $\alpha = 0.01$) or one star ($F_{crit} = 1.67$, $\alpha = 0.05$).

Table 29.3 shows some of the results, where CW-I means: The result Creditworthiness observed versus derived from the values or level I (Financial Basis and Personality), CW-II the same but derived from aggregating the respective values from level II (Security, Liquidity, Potential, and Business Behavior), and so on.

Surely, it would be interesting to include the credit amount as a variable into this investigation. But in order to receive a stable basis for scaling and interpretation, a serious enlargement of the sample of credit experts would be necessary. This, however, would have considerably exceeded our budget.

Forty-five credit clerks of the region of Aachen (West Germany) employed at five different banks participated in this investigation. Each subject got a test manual of 122 pages containing:

Table 29.3 Average Prognostic Error S_p^2 (* = $\alpha \leq 0.05$, ** = $\alpha \leq 0.01$)

	Min	Max	Geom. mean	γ-model	γ
CW-I	0.00092**	0.00209**	0.00101**	0.00087**	0.592
CW-II	0.00576	0.00917	0.00122**	0.00107**	0.782
CW-III	0.12631	0.00907	0.00349	0.00244**	0.903
FB-II	0.00761	0.00679	0.00182**	0.00160**	0.616
FB-III	0.12691	0.00510	0.00685	0.00117**	0.839
PE-II	0.00112**	0.00127**	0.00068**	0.00069**	0.597
PE-III	0.00467	0.00366	0.00133**	0.00137**	0.763
SE-III	0.12310	0.00260**	0.08228	0.00298*	0.978
LI-III	0.00123**	0.00122**	0.00066**	0.00051**	0.574
AP-III	0.00946**	0.00083**	0.00039**	0.00039**	0.551
BB-III	0.00340	0.00285*	0.00190**	0.00205**	0.547

- an explanatory introduction concerning the aims of the study,
- detailed instructions explaining the evaluation hierarchy of credit-worthiness together with practical definitions of the concepts,
- a description of the task,
- the 50 fictive credit applications,
- after the 20th, 30th, and 40th files one of the weighting tasks with separate instructions was inserted,
- the response sheet.

For processing the complete test materials a time of 12 hours was allowed. A second much less laborious poll was carried out using only the weighting procedure, which turned out to work most efficiently. It was intended to find out if the established weights hold in a larger geograph-ical area.

The weights of the subcriteria were determined based on an overall sample of 95 persons by the three methods mentioned. It turned out that the results of the three methods did not differ significantly, and the method of successive differentiation proved to be the most efficient computationally.

As mentioned, a necessary condition for the use of the ASI-method is the unidimensionality of the judgmental basis. This is examined by a fac-tor analysis of the subjects for each concept. According to the number of subjects, maximally 45 factors could be extracted.

There was a clear decrease of variance for each of the 15 criteria. While the first factor explained about 60 percent of the total variance, none of the subsequent factors kept more than 6 percent.

We, therefore believe that a single judgment dimension does exist for each concept. By application of the ASI-method to the data of each con-cept, 15 scales were obtained assigning a membership value to each of the 50 applicants.

29.4.4. Results

The predictive power of our model was then evaluated by comparing observed μ-grades with theoretical μ-grades. The latter were computed by aggregating the μ-grades of the lower-level μ-grades to arrive at the μ-grades of the higher-level μ-grades using the model of connectives to be tested.

The membership values for higher-level concepts should be predicted sufficiently well by any lower level of the corresponding branch. The quality of a model can be illustrated by a two-dimensional system, the axes of which represent the observed versus theoretical μ-values. Each applicant is represented by a point. In the case of exact prognoses, all points must be located on a straight diagonal line. As our data were collected empirically, there will be deviations from this ideal.

The evaluation of the economic situation depends on the actual securities, that is, the difference between property and debts, and on the liquidity, the continuous difference between income and expenses.

On the other hand, personality denotes the collection of traits by which a potent and serious person distinguishes him- or herself. The achievement potential bases on the mental and physical capacity as well as on the individual's motivation. The business conduct includes economical standards. While the former means setting of realistic goals, reasonable planning, and economic criteria success, the latter is directed toward the applicant's disposition to obey business laws and mutual agreements. Hence, a creditworthy person lives in secure circumstances and guarantees a successful profit-oriented cooperation.

29.4.5. Experimental Procedure

Testing the predictive quality of the proposed models required a suitable basis of stimuli, which were to rate with respect to the creditworthiness criteria and a weighting system that allowed a differentiated aggregation of these criteria.

The natural basis of information of evaluating creditworthiness is the credit file. Therefore, we would have liked to analyze original bank files. However, a selection of finished cases is always a biased sample since the initially rejected applicants are missing. Moreover, we wanted to avoid unnecessary troubles with the banking secrecy. Therefore, it was decided to prepare 50 fictitious applicants for credit.

A credit application form usually contains about 30 continuous or discrete attributes of applicants. If each variable were dichotomized, 2^{30} different borrowers could be produced. Clearly, one cannot realize all possible variations. Therefore, a sample was drawn that should satisfy the following two conditions. The 50 applicants (stimuli) should:

1. be distributed as evenly as possible along the continuum off each aspect,
2. be typical for consumer credits.

The files were produced in three stages:

1. 120 applications were completed randomly with respect to the grade of extension of the thirty attributers.
2. The resulting 30×120 data matrix was purged of 40 cases most unlikely and least typical. The remaining 80 files were completed using information of an inquiry agency (Schufa) and a short record of a conversation between the client concerned and a credit clerk.

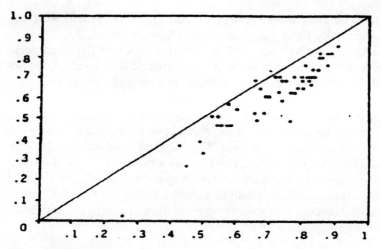

Figure 29.14   CW-II min-operator.

3. The applicants should represent the variability of the eight concepts. If each aspect is dichotomized into two classes ($\mu \leq 0.5 \Rightarrow 0, \mu$
   $> 0.5 \Rightarrow 1$), then the resulting $2^8 = 256$ patterns of evaluation can be
   put in a 16×16 matrix. By assistance of two credit experts, the 80
   credit files were placed into this tableau.

Finally, 30 files were eliminated in order to obtain equal frequencies
in rows and columns. We could now expect that the 50 applicants varied
rather evenly along each attribute and each criterium. Only one
attribute was constant: the credit amount was fixed at DM 8.000. This
because the judgment "creditworthy" is only meaningful with respect to

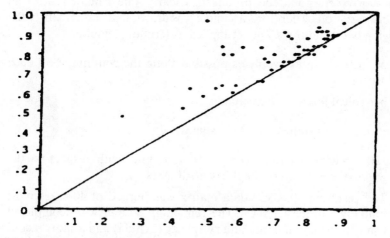

Figure 29.15   CW-II max-operator.

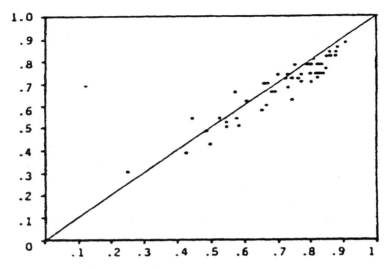

Figure 29.16   CW-II geometric mean-operator.

a certain amount. A borrower might be good for DM 8.000, but not for DM 15.000. Figures 29.14 to 29.20 illustrate selectively some of the results graphically.

Obviously, the minimum and maximum operators cannot be accepted as suitable connectives. Compensatory operators perform much better, but the geometric mean fails drastically for SE-II. In our view this is due to the fact that the model does not regard different grades of compensation.

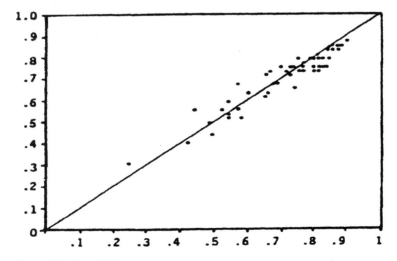

Figure 29.17   CW-II γ-operator.

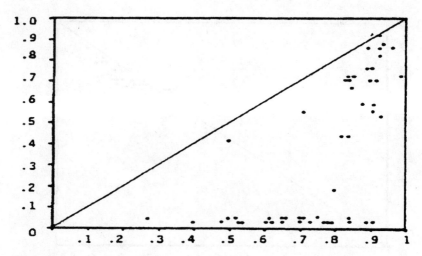

Figure 29.18   SE-II min-operator.

Finally, the complete hierarchy of creditworthiness is presented together with the elaborated weighting system and the γ-values for each level of aggregation (Figure 29.21).

Principally, it is possible to transform the system of weights. Clearly, the proportion of weights must not change. However, as ratio scales are invariant with respect to constant factors, the sum of weights might be modified. (For reasons of transparence we used $\sum \delta_i = m$.)

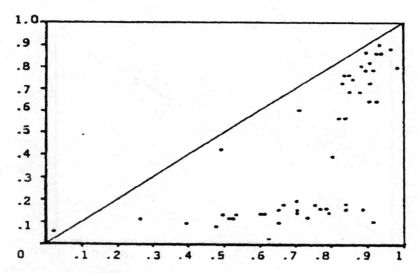

Figure 29.19   SE-III geometric mean-operator.

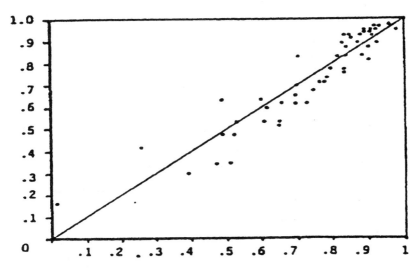

Figure 29.20 SE-III γ-operator.

29.5. Conclusion

Models of human decision making generally include the aggregation of criteria, which often are even modelled in a linguistic form. A large number of mathematical models have been proposed in the meantime and so have concepts of modelling linguistic descriptions by fuzzy sets. Most of these models, however, are formal in nature and it has never been proven empirically that they really correspond adequately to human aggregation behavior or to the meanings that human beings really attach to their linguistic expressions.

Our exemplary analysis of the process of rating creditworthiness yields a structure of criteria that is concept-oriented and self-explanatory. The γ-model, which was from the beginning designed to satisfy mathematical requirements as well as to describe human aggregation behavior, proved most adequate with respect to prognostic power. This class of operators is continuous, monotonic, injective, commutative, and in accordance with classical truth tables, which manifests their relationship to formal logic and set theory. The fact is that they aggregate partial judgments such that the formal result of the aggregation ought to make them attractive for empirically working scientists and useful for the practitioner.

Research verifying the validity of models of human communication and behavior is still pretty rare. Some results in this direction have, however, been published in the meantime. They mainly concern operators, linguistic approximation, and hedges or modifiers. It is hoped that in the future this type of research will grow, thus making our formal models better and proven images of human behavior and thinking.

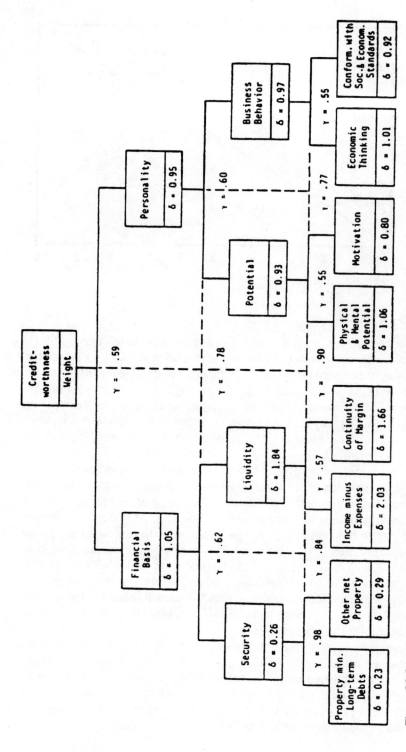

Figure 29.21 Concept hierarchy of creditworthiness together with individual weights δ and γ-values for each level of aggregation.

29.6. References

[1] Bellman, R., and L.A. Zadeh. "Decision-Making in a Fuzzy Environment." *Management Science,* Vol. 17 (1970), pp. 141–154.

[2] Beyth-Marom, R. "How Probable is Probable? A Numerical Translation of Verbal Probability Expressions." *Journal of Forecasting.* (1982), pp. 257–269.

[3] Bonissone, P.P., and K.S. Decker. "Selecting Uncertainty Calculi and Granularity: An Experiment in Trading off Precision and Complexity," in Kanal and Lemmer. pp. 217–247. 1986.

[4] Dishkant, H. "About Membership Function Estimation." *Fuzzy Sets and Systems,* Vol. 5 (1981), pp. 141–147.

[5] Dubois, D., and H. Prade. "Criteria Aggregation and Ranking of Alternatives in the Framework of Fuzzy Set Theory," in *Fuzzy Sets and Decision Analysis.* eds. H.J. Zimmerman, et al. pp. 209–240. Amsterdam: 1984.

[6] Dshrag, F., and E.H. Mamdani. "A General Approach to Linguistic Approximation." *International Journal of Man-Machine Studies,* Vol. 11 (1979), pp. 501–519.

[7] Hersh, H.M., and A.A. Caramazza. "A Fuzzy Set Approach to Modifiers and Vagueness in Natural Language." *Journal of Experimental Psychology,* Vol. 105 (1976), pp. 254–276.

[8] Hisdal, E. "Are Grades of Memberships Probabilities?" in *FSS,* (1988), pp. 325–348.

[9] Keeny, R., and W. Raiffa. *Decision Making with Multiple Objectives.* New York: John J. Wiley and Sons, 1976.

[10] Krantz, D.H., et al. *Foundations of Measurement.* New York: Academic Press, 1971.

[11] Norwich, A.M., and I.B. Turksen. "A Model for the Measurement of Membership and Consequences of its Empirical Implementations." *Fuzzy Sets and Systems,* Vol. 12 (1984), pp. 1–25.

[12] Murthy, C.A., et al. "Correlation between Two Fuzzy Membership Functions." *Fuzzy Sets and Systems,* Vol. 17 (1984), pp. 23–38.

[13] Oden, G.C. "Fuzziness in Semantic Memory, Choosing Exemplars of Subjective Categories." *Memory & Cognition,* Vol. 5 (1977), pp. 198–204.

[14] ———. "Integration of Fuzzy Linguistic Information in Language Comprehension." *Fuzzy Sets and Systems,* Vol. 14 (1984), pp. 29–41.

[15] Rapoport, A., et al. "Direct and Indirect Scaling of Membership Functions of Probability Phrases." *Mathematical Modeling,* Vol 9 (1987), pp. 397–418.

[16] Saaty, T.L. "Measuring the Fuzziness of Sets." *Journal of Cybernetics,* Vol. 4 (1974), pp. 43–61.

[17] Sticha, P.J., et al. *Evaluation and Integration of Imprecise Information.* Journal Supplement Abstract Service, American Psychological Association. Washington, D.C.: 1979.

[18] Spies, M. *Syllogistic Inference Under Uncertainty.* Munchen: 1989.

[19] Thole, U., et al. "On the Suitability of Minimum and Product Operators for the Intersection of Fuzzy Sets." *Fuzzy Sets and Systems,* Vol. 2 (1979), pp. 167–180.

[20] Torgerson, W.S. *Theory and Methods of Scaling.* New York: John J. Wiley and Sons, 1967.

[21] Turksen, I.B., et al. "Measurement of Fuzziness." *Proceedings, International Conference on Policy Analysis and Information Systems.* pp. 745–754. 1981.

[22] Turksen, I.B. "Measurement of Membership Functions and their Acquisition." *Fuzzy Sets and Systems,* Vol. 40. (1991), pp. 5–38.

[23] Wallsten, T.S, et al. "Measuring the Vague Meaning of Probability Terms." *Journal of Experimental Psychology,* Vol. 115 (1986), pp. 348–365.

[24] Werners, B. "Interaktive Entscheidungsunterstutzung durch ein Flexibles Mathematisches Programmierungssystem." Wirtschaftsinformatik und Quantitative Betriebswirtschaftslehre, Vol. 16 (1984).

[25] Yager, R.R. *On a General Class of Fuzzy Connectives. 4th European Meeting on Cybernetics and Systems Research.* Amsterdam: 1978.

[26] Zadeh, L.A. "A Fuzzy Algorithmic Approach to the Definition of Complex or Imprecise Concepts." *International Journal of Man-Machine Studies,* Vol. 8 (1976), pp. 249–291.

[27] Zimmer, A.C. "What Really is Turquoise? A Note on the Evolution of Color Terms."
      Psychology Research. (1982), pp. 213–230.
[28] Zimmerman, H.J., and P. Zysno. "Latent Connectives in Human Decision Making."
      Fuzzy Sets and Systems, Vol. 4 (1980), pp. 37–51.
[29] ————. "Decisions and Evaluations by Hierarchical Aggregation of Information."
      Fuzzy Sets and Systems, Vol. 10 (1983), pp. 243–260.
[30] Zimmerman, H.J. *Fuzzy Set Theory and Applications,* 3rd Rev. ed. Boston: Kluwer
      Academic Publishers, 1996.
[31] Zwick, R., et al. Measures of Similarity Among Fuzzy Concepts: A Comparative Anal-
      ysis." *International Journal of Approximate Reasoning.* (1987), pp. 221–242.

30 Use of a Fuzzy Decision-Making Method for a Large-Scale and Multiple Objectives Problem

Hiroshi Maeda, Shuta Murakami
Kyushu Institute of Technology-KIT

ABSTRACT: This chapter presents a practical use of a fuzzy decision-making method for a large-scale and multiple objectives problem, which is to decide what sort of computer system for research and education should be renewed in the Department of Computer Engineering, KIT. One member of a renewal committee appears as a decision maker. After describing the outline of the fuzzy decision-making method, the decision analysis process, objective hierarchy, identification of decision maker's preference, rating and ranking of alternatives are shown.

30.1. Introduction

When fuzzy set theory was presented, researchers regarded decision making as one of the most attractive application fields of the theory (Bellman and Zadeh [1]). Although many methods based on fuzzy set theory have been developed (Maeda and Murakami, Yager, Zimmermann, Zimmermann and Zysno [2], [4], [5], [6]), it seems that their applications are not satisfactory for a lack of scale and reality. In fact, there are a few applications (Siscos, Lochard and Lombard, Zimmermann, and Zysno [7], [8]) with large-scale and realistic merits. This chapter describes a real and large-scale application using a fuzzy decision-making method ([3]).

30.2. Decision Problem

In June 1987, the Department of Computer Engineering, KIT decided to renew an old computer system for research and education by April 1988. An investigating committee for renewal, which was a 17-member organization from faculties and staffs, was established. The committee decided on a fundamental policy for renewal as follows: the old system was a TSS system based on a host computer, but the new one should be formed by a distributed processing system using many engineering workstations (EWSs), which has four main merits: knowledge processing tools for AI, powerful image processing, a CAE system for computer architecture design, and a large-scale system simulation tool.

The committee asked four divisions in the department to present their demands for the new system, and then decided the detailed specifications for the new system by rearranging those demands. Next, the committee requested ten companies to propose new systems on the specifications. The working group of the committee selected four proposals as the final to be investigated. Only one representative decision maker (DM) who was the head of the working group, Dr. Masahiro Nagamatsu, will appear here, and his decision process will be described in detail with our fuzzy decision-making method. He pointed out two fuzzy aspects included in this problem: (1) To what degree will the present evaluation of CPU performance decrease in five years from now? (2) Which vender's EWS will obtain a large market share in near future?

30.3. Outline of the Fuzzy Decision-Making Method

The fuzzy decision-making method is summarized by the following five steps.

Step 1: Identification of a decision problem and construction of an objective hierarchy.

Step 2: Data collection by a questionnaire to identify a DM's preference structure.

Step 3: Identification of the parameters of preference models represented by three fuzzy operations of γ operation and its two extensions, and selection of one operation among the three as the optimum preference model.

Step 4: Assessment of the DM's evaluations on the lowest-level objectives for alternatives. If he/she cannot assess an unique value, fuzzy probability is applied.

Step 5. Aggregation of the evaluations on the lowest-level objectives and then ranking of the alternatives.

30.3.1. Definition

Let the sets of alternatives X and objectives C delineate as:

$$X = \{X_1, X_2, \cdots, X_n\}, C = \{C_1, C_2, \cdots, C_m\}.$$

The degrees to which the j-th objective and all the objectives are satisfied by the alternatives are given by the fuzzy sets, $C_j(X), D(X)$, respectively:

$$C_j(X) = \{\mu_{C_1}(X_1)/X_1, \mu_{C_2}(X_2)/X_2, \cdots, \mu_{C_n}(X_n)/X_n\},$$

$$D(X) = \{\mu_C(X_1)/X_1, \mu_C(X_2)/X_2, \cdots, \mu_C(X_n)/X_n\},$$

(1)

where

$$\mu_{C_j}:X \rightarrow [0,1], \mu_C(X_i) = f(\mu_{C_1}(X_i), \mu_{C_2}(X_i), \cdots \mu_{C_n}(X_i)).$$

The $f(\bullet)$ means an aggregation function that aggregates the degrees of satisfaction of all the objectives and represents a model of DM's preference structure. The best alternative is the one with maximum membership value in $D(X)$.

30.3.2. Objective Hierarchy

Most DMs confronted by complex decision problems often try to decompose a major objective into subobjectives. There are, however, some cases in which they could not clearly represent the objective itself or not suitably decompose the major objective. Our method allows the DM to describe the objectives in a vague or flexible way. However, the maximum number of decomposed subobjectives in a higher-level objective is restricted to three at most. This is because when extracting the DM's preference by a questionnaire, the number of objectives that he can fully consider simultaneously may be three or less.

30.3.3. Questionnaire Procedure

Now let the objective hierarchy of a DM be shown in Figure 30.1. Alternatives are evaluated on the attainment levels of the lowest-level objectives $C_i (i = 1,2)$ and $D_j (j = 1,2,3)$. Since it cannot be expected that the DM evaluates the five objectives precisely and simultaneously, the hierarchical evaluation as shown in Figure 30.1 can be employed. These

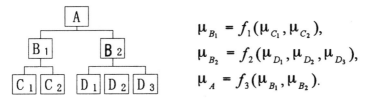

$$\mu_{B_1} = f_1(\mu_{C_1}, \mu_{C_2}),$$

$$\mu_{B_2} = f_2(\mu_{D_1}, \mu_{D_2}, \mu_{D_3}),$$

$$\mu_A = f_3(\mu_{B_1}, \mu_{B_2}).$$

Figure 30.1   An illustrative example of objective hierarchy.

aggregation functions show a DM's preference structure. Our method requires the DM to answer a questionnaire to identify each f. The questionnaire has two cases of two- or three-objectives aggregation. The DM is asked to evaluate each of the combinations on the three attainment levels (0.1=very unsatisfactory, 0.5=neutral, 0.9=very satisfactory) of objectives, as shown in Table 30.1 where the column on right-hand side shows the two-objectives case and the other columns show the three-objectives case. The DM can assess the synthesized evaluation by the 11 levels (from 0=completely unsatisfactory to 1.0=completely satisfactory).

30.3.4. Identification of Model Parameters

It is supposed that the model of a DM's preference is expressed by the following three operations:

1. γ-operation (Zimmermann [5])

$$\mu_C = \left[\prod_{j=1}^{m}(\mu_{C_j})^{\sigma j}\right]^{1-\gamma}\left[1 - \prod_{j=1}^{m}(1-\mu_{C_j})^{\sigma j}\right]^{\gamma},$$

$$\sum_{j=1}^{m}\sigma_j = m,\ \ 0 \le \sigma_j,\ \ 0 \le \gamma \le 1.$$

2. Extension 1 (Maeda and Murakami [2])

$$\mu_C = \left[\prod_{j=1}^{m}(\mu_{C_j})^{\sigma j}\right]^{1-\gamma(\mu)}\left[1 - \prod_{j=1}^{m}(1-\mu_{C_j})^{\sigma j}\right]^{\gamma(\mu)},$$

$$\sum_{j=1}^{m}\sigma_j = m,\ \ 0 \le \sigma_j,\ \ \gamma(\mu) = a_0 + \sum_{j=1}^{m}a_j\mu_{C_j},\ \ 0 \le \gamma(\mu) \le 1.$$

3. Extension 2 (Maeda and Murakami [2])

$$\mu_C = \left[\prod_{j=1}^{m}(\mu_{C_j})^{\sigma j(\mu)}\right]^{1-\gamma}\left[1 - \prod_{j=1}^{m}(1-\mu_{C_j})^{\sigma j(\mu)}\right]^{\gamma},$$

$$\sum_{j=1}^{m}\sigma_j(\mu) = m,\ \ 0 \le \sigma_j(\mu),\ \ \sigma_j(\mu) = b_{j0} + \sum_{k=1}^{m}b_{jk}\mu_{C_k},\ \ 0 \le \gamma \le 1.$$

Table 30.1 Combinations of Three Attainment Levels in the Questionnaire

(C_1, C_2, C_3)	(C_1, C_2, C_3)	(C_1, C_2, C_3)	(C_1, C_2)
(.1, .1, .1)	(.5, .1, .1)	(.9, .1, .1)	(.1, .1)
(.1, .1, .5)	(.5, .1, .5)	(.9, .1, .5)	(.1, .5)
(.1, .1, .9)	(.5, .1, .9)	(.9, .1, .9)	(.1, .9)
(.1, .5, .1)	(.5, .5, .1)	(.9, .5, .1)	(.5, .1)
(.1, .5, .5)	(.5, .5, .5)	(.9, .5, .5)	(.5, .5)
(.1, .5, .9)	(.5, .5, .9)	(.9, .5, .9)	(.5, .9)
(.1, .9, .1)	(.5, .9, .1)	(.9, .9, .1)	(.9, .1)
(.1, .9, .5)	(.5, .9, .5)	(.9, .9, .5)	(.9, .5)
(.1, .9, .9)	(.5, .9, .9)	(.9, .9, .9)	(.9, .9)

The number of estimated parameters for γ-operation, extension 1 and extension 2 are m, $2m$, and m^2 respectively, where m is the number of objectives. These parameters are identified by using the least-squares method. In this case, the sum of square errors for the questionnaire results is a nonlinear function. Thus a nonlinear optimization method known as the quasi-Newton projection method is applied here. After identifying parameters, the best preference model of the DM must be selected among three operations. For this purpose the following AIC criterion is employed:

$$AIC = N \log\{(1/N) \sum_{i=1}^{N} (\Phi_i - \hat{\Phi}_i)^2\} + 2m,$$

where Φ_i is the i-th datum (questionnaire result), $\hat{\Phi}_i$ is the estimated value of Φ_i, N is the number of data, and m is the number of parameters. The operation with less AIC value is statistically the better model.

30.3.5. Evaluation of Alternatives

First, the DM must assess the lowest-level objectives for all the alternatives by the previous 11 scale values. There is, however, the case where he/she cannot assess them uniquely, that is, there is branching. Our method employs fuzzy probability representation for this situation. Supposing probability independence, joint probability is calculated as follows:

$$\tilde{p}_i = \tilde{p}_i \otimes \tilde{q}_j, \quad \mu_{\tilde{p}ij}(P_{ij}) = \bigvee_{Pij = Pi \cdot Qj} (\mu_{\tilde{p}i}(P_i) \wedge \mu_{\tilde{q}j}(Q_j))$$

where the symbols $\sim$, $\otimes$, $\vee$, and $\wedge$ mean fuzzy set, product operation of fuzzy number, max operation, and min operation, respectively.

Next, fuzzy evaluations are calculated for the alternatives. If the evaluation for an alternative has branching, a fuzzy expected evaluation is introduced. This is a fuzzy set defined as:

$$\tilde{v}(x) = \sum_{i=1}^{i'} \oplus [\mu_c^i(x)\tilde{p}_i(x)], \sum_{i=1}^{i'} P_i = 1 \tag{2}$$

where the symbol $\sum\oplus$ means add operation of fuzzy numbers. The membership value of $\tilde{v}(x)$ can be obtained by using α-level sets (Maeda and Murakami [2]). Finally, the fuzzy expected evaluation is defuzzified with its centroid.

30.4.1. Alternatives and Objectives

The rough schemata and specifications of four alternatives are shown in Figure 30.2.

The alternatives are divided into two groups. One is a fully distributed system mainly using EWS's (systems A, B, and C). These systems have very similar architectures but different performance among EWSs. The

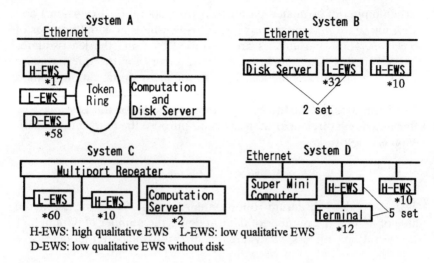

H-EWS: high qualitative EWS   L-EWS: low qualitative EWS
D-EWS: low qualitative EWS without disk

Figure 30.2   Rough schemata of four alternatives.

other is a hybrid system of host and distributed system (system D). The committee determined the objective hierarchy as shown in Figure 30.3. The major objectives are the following three aspects: performance of hardware, performance of software, and vender evaluation. Consequently, the total number of the lowest-level objectives is 34.

30.4.2. Preference Structure

The DM was asked to answer the questionnaire for drawing his preference structure. The questionnaire process was repeated 21 times according to the 21 clusters of the objective hierarchy shown in Figure 30.3. Two cases of the questionnaire results are shown in Table 30.2 (Objective: "Computer system" with three subobjectives, Objective: "Hardware" with two subobjectives). The results of identifying his preference structure in all the clusters are summarized in Table 30.3, where the left, the right, and underline show the sum of squared error, AIC value, and the least AIC value, respectively.

30.4.3. Evaluation of the Alternatives

The DM assessed each alternative with respect to the lowest-level objectives, as shown in Table 30.4. The symbol * indicates that the alternative with this symbol is higher than the other three alternatives. The fuzzy probability was used in two objectives, "CPU performance" and "Number of users." He judged that the evaluation of the two objectives depends on the two cases of initial and future consequences. Hence, he employed the fuzzy probability distribution on the two cases. As shown

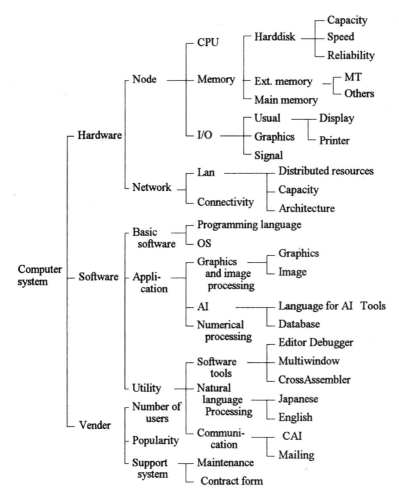

Figure 30.3 Objective hierarchy in a computer system.

Table 30.2 Example of Questionnaire Results

(C_1, C_2, C_3)	u c	(C_1, C_2, C_3)	u c	(C_1, C_2, C_3)	u c	(C_1, C_2)	u c
(.1, .1, .1)	0	(.5, .1, .1)	0	(.9, .1, .1)	0.1	(.1, .1)	0
(.1, .1, .5)	0	(.5, .1, .5)	0.1	(.9, .1, .5)	0.1	(.1, .5)	0
(.1, .1, .9)	0.1	(.5, .1, .9)	0.1	(.9, .1, .9)	0.1	(.1, .9)	0
(.1, .5, .1)	0	(.5, .5, .1)	0.2	(.9, .5, .1)	0.3	(.5, .1)	0.1
(.1, .5, .5)	0.1	(.5, .5, .5)	0.5	(.9, .5, .5)	0.6	(.5, .5)	0.5
(.1, .5, .9)	0.1	(.5, .5, .9)	0.6	(.9, .5, .9)	0.8	(.5, .9)	0.6
(.1, .9, .1)	0.1	(.5, .9, .1)	0.3	(.9, .9, .1)	0.5	(.9, .1)	0.6
(.1, .9, .5)	0.1	(.5, .9, .5)	0.6	(.9, .9, .5)	0.8	(.9, .5)	0.8
(.1, .9, .9)	0.1	(.5, .9, .9)	0.8	(.9, .9, .9)	0.9	(.9, .9)	0.9

C_1: Software, C_2: Software, C_3 Vender, C: Computer system, C_1: Node, C_2: Network, C: hardware

Table 30.3 Identification Results for Three Operations

Objective	γ-operation		Extension 1		Extension 2	
Computer system	.2343	−122.2	.1589	−126.7	.1540	−121.5
Hardware	.0625	−40.73	.0313	−42.95	.0468	−39.42
Node	.2044	−125.9	.1556	−127.2	.1445	−123.2
Memory	.1337	−137.3	.1159	−135.2	.0416	−156.9
Hard disk	.0757	−152.7	.0683	−149.4	.0713	−142.3
External memory	.0420	−44.30	.0355	−41.81	.0196	−47.19
I/O system	.1398	−136.1	.0930	−141.1	.1078	−131.1
Usual I/O	.0654	−40.32	.0452	−39.65	.0202	−46.90
Network	.0804	−38.46	.0597	−37.15	.0243	−45.23
LAN system	.0567	−160.5	.0153	−189.8	.0482	−152.8
Software	.6429	−94.91	.5221	−94.54	.5752	−85.92
Basic software	.0274	−48.17	.0242	−45.28	.0166	−48.69
Application	.1413	−135.8	.0619	−152.1	.1087	−130.9
Graphics	.0120	−55.58	.0099	−53.33	.0058	−58.18
AI environment	.1942	−127.2	.0842	−143.8	.1006	−133.0
Utility	.2887	−116.5	.0165	−125.7	.2641	−106.9
Software tools	.1028	−144.4	.0883	−142.5	.0927	−135.2
Natural language	.0654	−40.32	.0452	−39.65	.0203	−46.86
Communication	.0654	−40.32	.0452	−39.65	.0203	−46.86
Vender evaluation	.2929	−116.1	.2036	−120.0	.2341	−110.2
Support system	.1268	−34.36	.1040	−32.15	.0591	−37.23

in Table 30.4, the two objectives have two branches, and the upper and lower branch correspond to the future and the initial evaluation, respectively. The numbers with ~ show fuzzy probabilities. For expedience, he interpreted the two branches as if they were subobjectives, and thus used the fuzzy probabilities as fuzzy weights. According to the hierarchy aggregation in the manner of Figure 30.2, the fuzzy expected evaluation of equation (2) can be obtained as shown in Figure 30.4, where the numbers in the fuzzy sets show their centroids. Here we use

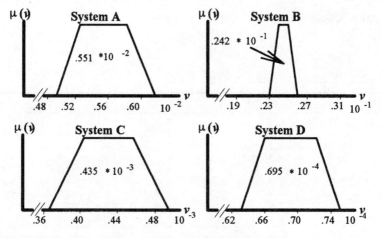

Figure 30.4 Fuzzy expected evaluations of four alternatives.

Table 30.4 Evaluation of the Lowest-Level Objectives

Objectives		Sys A	Sys B	Sys C	Sys D
1. CPU performance	0.6	0.4	0.5*	0.3	0.3
	0.4	0.6	0.6	0.5	0.4
2. Hard disk capacity		0.6	0.7*	0.6	0.2
3. Hard disk speed		0.5	0.5	0.5	0.5
4. Hard disk reliability		0.3	0.5	0.3	0.5
5. Magnetic tape		0.5	0.5	0.5	0.5
6. Other ext. memories		0.7*	0.5	0.5	0.5
7. Main memory		0.5	0.5	0.5	0.2
8. Display		0.5	0.5	0.5	0.5
9. Printer		0.5	0.5	0.3	0.2
10. Graphic I/O		0.5	0.5	0.3	0.3
11. Signal I/O		0.5	0.5	0.5	0.6*
12. Distributed resources		0.8*	0.5	0.3	0.3
13. Network capacity		0.6*	0.3	0.3	0.3
14. Network architecture		0.5	0.5	0.3	0.5
15. Connectivity to others		0.5	0.5	0.5	0.5
16. Programming language		0.6	0.8*	0.6	0.5
17. Operating system		0.6	0.6	0.4	0.4
18. Graphic application		0.6*	0.5	0.5	0.5
19. Image application		0.5	0.5	0.5	0.3
20. AI language		0.6	0.6	0.6	0.5
21. Expert system tool		0.6	0.6	0.6	0.5
22. Database		0.6	0.6	0.6	0.5
23. Numerical processing		0.6	0.8*	0.6	0.6
24. Editor and debugger		0.6	0.6	0.6	0.8*
25. Multiwindow		0.6	0.6	0.5	0.4
26. Cross environment		0.5	0.5	0.5	0.7
27. Japanese language		0.3	0.3	0.3	0.3
28. Foreign language		0.6	0.6	0.6	0.6
29. CAI		0.6*	0.3	0.3	0.3
30. Mailing		0.6	0.6	0.6	0.6
31. Number of users	0.7	0.2	0.9*	0.4	0.2
	0.3	0.4	0.8*	0.5	0.3
32. Popularity		0.4	0.8*	0.4	0.3
33. Maintenance system		0.2	0.3	0.3	0.3
34. Contract form		0.1	0.5	0.1	0.5

a trapezoid type membership function for the fuzzy probability. The evaluation by equation (1) is:

$$D(x) = \{.551 \times 10^{-2} / A, .242 \times 10^{-1} / B, .435 \times 10^{-3} / C, .695 \times 10^{-4} / D\}.$$

Hence, the ranking order of the alternatives is **B**, **A**, **C**, and **D**. The DM gives sys. **B** marked evaluation.

The fuzzy decision-making method can present more detailed information [3]; that is, a hierarchical decision process that presents evaluations for the alternatives at any clusters in the objectives hierarchy of Figure 30.3 and a sensitivity analysis that the sensitivity of the lowest-level objective is defined as increase in aggregated evaluation when the objective is rated up one level over the present evaluation. This information, however, is omitted here because of space limitations.

30.5. Conclusion

A fuzzy decision-making making method offered useful information; for instance, the clear difference of evaluation among the committee members. The evaluation was almost split two ways. One asserted the superiority of system A, and the other asserted the superiority of system B. The DM in this study was the latter.

30.6. References

[1] Bellman, R., and L.A. Zadeh. "Decision-Making in a Fuzzy Environment." *Management Science,* Vol. 17 (1970), pp. 146–164.

[2] Maeda, H., and S. Murakami. "A Fuzzy Decision-Making Method and its Application to a Company Choice Problem." *Information Science,* Vol. 45 (1988), pp. 331–346.

[3] ———. "The Use of a Fuzzy Decision-Making Method in a Large-Scale Computer System Choice Problem." *Fuzzy Sets and Systems,* Vol. 54 (1993), pp. 235–249.

[4] Yager, R.R. "Fuzzy Decision-Making Including Unequal Objectives." *Fuzzy Sets and Systems,* Vol. 1 (1978), pp. 87–95.

[5] Zimmerman, H.J., and P. Zysno. "Latent Connectives in Human Decision Making." *Fuzzy Sets and Systems,* Vol. 4 (1980), pp. 37–51.

[6] Siscos, J., et al. "A Multicriteria Decision-Making Methodology under Fuzziness," in *Fuzzy Sets and Decision Analysis, TIMS Studies 20.* eds. H.J. Zimmerman, et al. North Holland: 1984.

[7] Zimmerman, H.J., and P. Zysno. "Decisions and Evaluations by Hierarchical Aggregation of Information." *Fuzzy Sets and Systems,* Vol. 10 (1983), pp. 31–36.

31 Fuzzy Measures and Integrals: A Survey of Applications and Recent Issues

Michel Grabisch
Thomson-CSF, Central Research Laboratory
Domaine de Corbeville, 91404 Orsay Cedex, France

ABSTRACT: We introduce fuzzy measures and integrals as a very general way of representing importance of coalitions of elements in a decision problem. Depending on the problem, elements could be players (multiplayer game theory), criteria, (multicriteria decision making), attributes, expert's opinions, and so on. After presentation of necessary background in fuzzy measure theory, large classes of applications in several domains are detailed, such as multicriteria decision making, pattern classification and feature extraction, and image processing, illustrated with examples of practical applications. In every domain, issues concerning the identification of fuzzy measures in a real problem are dealt with. Finally, we indicate some promising new issues in the field of fuzzy measure theory.

31.1. Introduction

Since their introduction in 1974 by Sugeno [47], fuzzy measures and integrals have known an important development, either on a theoretical and applicative point of view, especially in Japan where the concept was originated. In fact, the idea of introducing monotonic nonadditive set functions—called fuzzy measures by Sugeno—has flourished in different domains around the seventies, or even before. One of the first apparitions can be found in the theory of capacities of Choquet [5], and cooperative game theory (see e.g. the works of Aumann [2], and Shapley [46]).

Later, nonadditive set functions were introduced to model uncertainty by Shafer [45] in 1976 (belief functions), and Zadeh [59] in 1978 (possibility measures). In the eighties, the community of expected utility theory became aware of the usefulness of *nonadditive probabilities* for making decision under uncertainty (see e.g. the works of Schmeidler [43, 44], Quiggin [42]).

Despite this growing interest, real applications of fuzzy measures and integrals have not yet emerged from some restricted small circles of people. Moreover, most of existing practical applications rely on a rather *ad hoc* methodology, ignoring the full potential of fuzzy measures—as well as their difficulties. The main reason for such a narrow dissemination seems to be due to a rather mathematical flavor emanating from the words "measure" and "integral," which sound so far from applications. The second reason is that there is a certain complexity in applying these tools, far beyond the well-known fuzzy control methodology.

The aim of this chapter is to give an updated state-of-the-art of the application of fuzzy measures and integrals in different domains, pointing out the advantages and the difficulties, and to give a clear vision of the high potential of this methodology.

From an application point of view, fuzzy measures can be used essentially in two ways: on the one hand a fuzzy measure is viewed as a more general uncertainty measure, whose typical representative is probability encompassing additive measures (probability), possibility measures, belief and plausibility functions, and so on. On the other hand, a fuzzy measure is viewed as a tool for representing weights (or importance) of coalitions (or groups) of elements, which could be players in a multiperson game, criteria in multicriteria decision making, experts or voters in a multiperson decision problem, and so forth.

The first interpretation has been used in decision making under uncertainty, in the framework of expected utility theory, and has lead to *nonadditive expected utility* models (see [43, 44]), which for example are able to take into account attitude toward risk: for example, the famous Ellsberg paradox [7] can be solved by introducing fuzzy measures (see e.g. [20] for the solution of the Ellsberg paradox, and main results along this line). To the author's knowledge, there are not yet real applications of nonadditive expected utility, and this subject will not be treated here.

As a consequence, we will concentrate in this chapter on applications relying on the second interpretation, that is, fuzzy measures as model of importance of coalitions. We will examine successively applications to multicriteria decision making, where elements are criteria, applications to pattern classification, where elements are features, and image processing, where elements are pixels. We will also give a quick survey of recent issues that could become new paradigms in fuzzy measure theory or give birth to new application areas.

Before entering into the main subject, we think it useful to mention that fuzzy measures, which can be said to be fairly apart from the main stream of fuzzy set theory (after all, fuzzy measures are not fuzzy at all, but should be rather named nonadditive measures or monotonic measures, on a mathematical point of view), have in fact very profound links to the fundamental concept of fuzzy set, more precisely to its membership function. Some authors, as Orlovski [40] and Nakamura [38], consider that vague categories can be described by a set of features, which are precise. In other words, the vagueness is caused by the fact that the category is multidimensional in essence (think for example of the category of beautiful women). A fuzzy measure is defined on this set of features, modelling the importance of every subset of features. Then for a particular element x of this category, its membership value in the category is the value of the fuzzy measure of the subset of features satisfied by x.

We begin by defining fundamental concepts. We will consider that the set of elements, on which we build coalitions and fuzzy measures, is finite, since this will be always the case in practice. Consequently, the definitions of fuzzy measures and fuzzy integrals will be adapted to this case, avoiding unnecessary mathematical complications. The reader is referred to the monographs of Denneberg [6], Grabisch *et al.* [20], Sugeno and Murofushi [52], and Wang and Klir [55] for a more complete treatment.

Throughout the chapter, *min* and *max* will be denoted by $\wedge$ and $\vee$ respectively.

31.2. Basic Definitions

Let us denote by $X = \{x_1, \ldots, x_n\}$ the set of elements, and $\mathcal{P}(X)$ the power set of X, that is, the set of all subsets of X.

Definition 1: *A* fuzzy measure *on X is a set function* $\mu\colon \mathcal{P}(X) \to [0,1]$*, satisfying the following axioms.*

(i) $\mu(\varnothing) = 0, \mu(X) = 1$.

(ii) $A \subset B \subset X$ *implies* $\mu(A) \le \mu(B)$.

In our framework, $\mu(A)$ represents the weight of importance of the coalition (or group of elements) A. Some particular cases are of interest:

- A fuzzy measure is said to be *additive* if $\mu(A \cup B) = \mu(A) + \mu(B)$ whenever $A \cap B = \varnothing$, *superadditive* (resp. *subadditive*) if $\mu(A \cup B) \ge \mu(A) + \mu(B)$ (resp. $\mu(A \cup B) \le \mu(A) + \mu(B)$) whenever $A \cap B = \varnothing$. An additive fuzzy measure is a probability measure.

- A λ-measure is a fuzzy measure satisfying for every disjoint A, B

$$\mu(A \cup B) = \mu(A) + \mu(B) + \lambda\mu(A)\mu(B)$$

  for a fixed $\lambda > -1$. Clearly, λ-measures are superadditive or subadditive depending on the sign of λ. The case of additivity is recovered when $\lambda = 0$.

Note that if a fuzzy measure is a λ-measure (*a fortiori* an additive measure), then it suffices to define the n coefficients (weights) $\mu(\{x_1\}), \ldots, \mu(\{x_n\})$ to define entirely the measure. In general, however, one needs to define the 2^n coefficients corresponding to the 2^n subsets of X, keeping in mind the monotonicity constraints $\mu(A) \le \mu(B)$ whenever $A \subset B$.

We introduce now the concept of fuzzy integral.

Definition 2: *Let μ be a fuzzy measure on X. The* Sugeno integral *of a function* $f : X \to [0, 1]$ *with respect to μ is defined by:*

$$(S) \int f \circ \mu := \bigvee_{i=1}^{n} (f(x_{(i)}) \wedge \mu(A_{(i)})) \tag{1}$$

where $\cdot_{(i)}$ indicates that the indices have been permuted so that $0 \le f(x_{(1)}) \le \ldots \le f(x_{(n)}) \le 1$, and $A_{(i)} := \{x_{(i)}, \ldots, x_{(n)}\}$.

We will denote sometimes $(S) \int f \circ \mu$ by using a connective-like notation $S_\mu(a_1, \ldots, a_n)$, with $a_i = f(x_i)$.

Another definition was proposed later by Murofushi and Sugeno [36], using a concept introduced by Choquet in capacity theory [5].

Definition 3: *Let μ be a fuzzy measure on X. The* Choquet integral *of a function $f : X \to \mathbb{R}$ with respect to μ is defined by:*

$$(C) \int f \, d\mu := \sum_{i=1}^{n} (f(x_{(i)}) - f(x_{(i-1)}))\mu(A_{(i)}) \tag{2}$$

with the same notations as above, and $f(x_{(0)}) = 0$.

As for the Sugeno integral, the Choquet integral will be sometimes denoted C_μ. The definition can be extended to real functions by the formula:

$$(C) \int f \, d\mu = (C) \int f^+ \, d\mu - (C) \int f^- \, d\mu$$

where f^+, f^- are the positive and negative parts of $f = f^+ - f^-$.

Sugeno and Choquet integrals are essentially different in nature, since the former is based on nonlinear operators (*min* and *max*), and the latter on usual linear operators. (However, see Imaoka [24] for a common representation of Sugeno and Choquet integrals, based on cumulative distribution functions.) In fact, the Choquet integral reduces to the usual Lebesgue integral when the measure is additive. Both compute a kind of distorted average of $f(x_1), \ldots, f(x_n)$. More general definitions exist but will not be considered here (see [20]).

Relying on the interpretation of a fuzzy measure, we could say that the importance of an element i is simply expressed by the value of μ_i alone. In fact, all values $\mu(A)$ such that $i \in A$ must also be taken into account. Shapley [46] has proposed a definition of a coefficient of importance, based on a set of reasonable axioms (see also [20]).

Definition 4: *Let* μ *be a fuzzy measure on X. The* Shapley index *for every i* $\in$ *X is defined by:*

$$v_i := \sum_{k=0}^{n-1} \gamma_k \sum_{K \subset X\backslash i, |K| = k} [\mu(K \cup \{i\}) - \mu(K)]$$

with

$$\gamma_k := \frac{(n-k-1)!k!}{n!}.$$

The Shapley value *of* μ *is the vector* $v(\mu) = [v_1 \ldots v_n]$.

The Shapley index v_i can be interpreted as a kind of average value of the contribution of element i alone in all coalitions. A basic property of the Shapley value is that $\sum_{i=1}^{n} v_i = 1$.

Another interesting concept is the one of interaction between elements. Taking two elements i, j, the value of μ_{ij} could be the sum of μ_i and μ_j. In this case, the individual importances are adding without interfering, and there is no interaction between i and j. If μ_{ij} is lower (resp. greater) than $\mu_i + \mu_j$, then i and j interfere in a negative (resp. positive) way. As for importance, a proper definition should consider not only μ_i, μ_j, μ_{ij} but also the measures of all subsets containing i and j. Murofushi and Soneda [35] (see also [20]) have proposed the following definition, borrowing concepts from multiattribute utility theory, which is very similar to the one of Shapley.

Definition 5: *Let* μ *be a fuzzy measure on X. The* interaction index *of elements i, j is defined by:*

$$I_{ij} := \sum_{k=0}^{n-2} \xi_k \sum_{K \subset X\backslash\{i,j\}, |K| = k} [\mu(K \cup \{i,j\}) - \mu(K \cup \{i\}) - \mu(K \cup \{j\}) + \mu(K)]$$

with

$$\xi_k := \frac{(n-k-2)!k!}{(n-1)!}.$$

The interaction index I_{ij} can be interpreted as a kind of average value of the *added value* given by putting i and j together, all coalitions being considered. When I_{ij} is positive (resp. negative), then the interaction is said to be positive (resp. negative). It is not difficult to show that the interaction index for a λ-measure takes the form:

$$I_{ij} = \lambda\mu(\{i\})\mu(\{j\}) \left[\sum_{k=0}^{n-2} \xi_k \sum_{K \subset X\backslash\{i,j\}, |K| = k} (1 + \lambda\mu(K)) \right].$$

Clearly, whatever the pair i, j of elements considered, I_{ij} is positive (resp. negative, zero) if and only if λ is positive (resp. negative, zero). This shows that a λ-measure is not able to represent mixed effects of interactions.

31.3. Application to Multicriteria Decision Making

31.3.1. Motivations and General Description

One of the fundamental steps in every multicriteria decision-making method is *aggregation*. There are now two main approaches of multicriteria decision making, namely multiattribute utility theory [27] and the preference modelling approach [8]. In multiattribute utility theory, each alternative is given an absolute score with respect to each criterion, and the global score, taking into account all the criteria, is obtained by aggregating all the (partial) scores. In preference modelling, a preference degree is assigned to every pair of alternatives, with respect to each criterion. Then, a global preference degree is obtained by aggregating all the (partial) preference degrees. In this approach, there is no total ordering on the alternatives: some alternatives may be incomparable each other.

The conclusion is that whatever the approach to be taken, a necessary step is aggregation, and quantities to be aggregated are either scores or preference degrees. We develop our explanation using the first approach for the sake of simplicity, but this is not limitative.

Referring to our previous notations, the set X of elements is here the set of criteria: a fuzzy measure μ on X will represent weights of importance on every coalition (or group) of criteria, and the fuzzy integral will perform a kind of average of all partial scores, taking into account the importance of all groups of criteria. More specifically, let us denote by a_i the score obtained by alternative a with respect to criterion i. We consider that it is a real number in $[0, 1]$. Then, the global score of alternative a is computed by $\mathcal{F}_\mu(a_1, \ldots, a_n)$, where $\mathcal{F}$ stands for "fuzzy integral," and could be either Choquet or Sugeno integral.

The question now is the legitimacy of such an aggregation method. The careful study of this point is beyond the scope of this chapter, and the reader is referred to detailed analyses done by the author (e.g. [15, 12], or [20] chapter 8). We will only give some indications here.

- Fuzzy integrals possess all desirable mathematical properties for aggregation, for example, idempotency, continuity, monotonicity, invariance to linear scale change (Choquet integral only).

- Usual aggregation operators are encompassed by fuzzy integrals. This is the case for the weighted sum, weighted minimum and maximum, OWA (Ordered Weighted Average) operators, the median and all order statistics, and others.

- Fuzzy integrals can range freely between minimum (conjunctive or intolerant aggregation) and maximum (disjunctive or tolerant aggregation).

- By the fuzzy measure, one can express not only importance of criteria, as does every weighted aggregation operator, but also interaction between criteria by defining weights on coalitions of criteria.

The Shapley value and the interaction index (see section 31.2) are quantities representing these notions, and are interpreted as follows:

> The Shapley index v_i measures the average importance of criterion i, and the more v_i is near to 1, the more criterion i is important.
>
> The interaction index I_{ij} is 0 if no interaction between criteria i and j exists. If i and j are *redundant* or *substitutive,* that is, if the importance of i and j taken together is not very different from the individual importances of i and j, then I_{ij} is negative. If, on the contrary, i and j have a *positive synergy* or are *complementary,* that is, if the combination of i and j is much more important than any of the importances of i and j, then I_{ij} is positive.

This ability to represent interaction is in fact the main originality of fuzzy integrals. For the difference between Choquet and Sugeno integrals, see [15, 12]. Roughly speaking, the Sugeno integral is more suitable for ordinal information, and the Choquet integral for cardinal information.

31.3.2. Some Practical Examples

We give a brief description of some real examples of applications, which have all been realized in Japan. More details can be found in the references (many of them in Japanese!), or in [20].

Prediction of wood strength (Ishii and Sugeno, 1985) [26]: The problem consists in predicting the ultimate bending strength of wood beams on the basis of some measurements, which are radii of curvature measured in different points under a uniform bending moment, density, grain angle, and moisture content. Experienced inspectors are able to predict quite accurately the wood strength from these measurements. Ishii and Sugeno applied the Sugeno integral to this four-criteria evaluation problem, and found a significant improvement compared to a linear model (i.e. weighted average). The identification of μ was performed by a heuristic learning algorithm of Ishii and Sugeno, and used 30 data for each type of wood.

Evaluation of printed color images (Tanaka and Sugeno, 1988) [54]. It is the first application of Choquet integral. Fifteen criteria were used to qualify proofs made from an original (color reversal film), such as contrast, transparency, feeling of volume, rendering of details, and so on, and pairwise comparison of proofs were performed. As the number of criteria is high, a factor analysis was performed in order to group the criteria into three main factors. A two-level model is then obtained, in which the Choquet integral was used, in both levels. Because of the linear character of the Choquet integral, quadratic programming and relaxation procedure was used to identify the fuzzy measure, by minimization of the squared error between data and the model.

Design of speakers (Mitsubishi Electric, 1991) [25]. This application concerns the design of a small audio speaker. Seven criteria were chosen, which are impression of lightness, of neatness, of precision, of the material, morphological characteristics, basic element, "plus alpha." The method used the Choquet integral with respect to a possibility and a necessity measure. The identification of the possibility density was performed by a possibilistic version of the AHP (Analytical Hierarchy Process) of Saaty. The Choquet integral with respect to a possibility measure behaves like a disjunctive operator, so that it favors speakers with high originality but with possible weak points, while the use of a necessity measure, which leads to a conjunctive behavior, tends to favor well-balanced speakers without weak points, intended to the average consumer.

Human reliability analysis (Mitsubishi Research Inst., 1992) [56]. Here, a human operator controls the coolant flow rate supplied to a water cooling tank, and this rather complex task is known to have a significant error operation rate. In order to improve the reliability, three options were proposed: (1) introduce a reliable automated control system so that the operator should just set the target flow rate, (2) introduce a plant simulator to train the operator, (3) employ an assistant operator. The human reliability of each option was evaluated by Sugeno integral, using five criteria (here called performance shaping factors) related to the situation recognition stage, the action judgment stage, and the manipulation stage. The fuzzy measure was identified through a questionnaire and simplifying assumptions on the fuzzy measure.

Modelling of public attitude toward use of nuclear energy (Onisawa et al., 1986) [39]. Formally, this is the converse of the problem of evaluation: we have *one* object and n persons $p_1, \ldots, p_n$ evaluating it with respect to m criteria. The global evaluation of the object by person p_i is again obtained by a fuzzy integral:

$$h(p_i) = S_\mu(h_1(p_i), \ldots, h_m(p_i)) \tag{3}$$

where $h_i(p_i)$ denotes individual evaluation. Here μ models the evaluation process of the persons concerning a particular object (the use of nuclear energy), in other words, a public attitude for a particular question. In the experiment, subjects were asked to give their opinion about 30 criteria (such as: improves standard of living, is harmful to future generations, provides a cheap energy source, leads to accidents that affect large number of peoples, etc), under a triplet form (evaluation: from bad to good, belief: from unlikely to likely, importance: from unimportant to important), and then an overall judgment, from unfavorable to favorable. The data came from three countries (Japan, Philippines, and Germany), and the data of each country were divided into the PRO group (positive favorability), and the CON group (negative favorability), thus leading to six distinct groups. Each group was then modelled by a different fuzzy measure. As in the example of color prints evaluation, a factor analysis was first performed to group the criteria into six factors, leading to a hierarchical model. The Sugeno integral was used in both levels, and the identification of the fuzzy measure was obtained by the learning algorithm of Ishii and Sugeno. The opinion of each group can be then analyzed using a semantical interpretation of the fuzzy measures.

Other applications. There are many other examples that can be cited, all developed in Japan. Among these, we can find:

- An evaluation of the taste of rice and coffee [31] by Satake Engineering. Recently, their data have been further processed and performance improved by Sugeno and Kwon [50].
- A diagnostic system for plant, build by Fuji Electric [11, 10].
- An evaluation of living environment in the area of Tokyo [37].

31.3.3. Identification of Fuzzy Measures

The main difficulty in applying fuzzy integrals is how to identify the fuzzy measure in a practical situation, that is, how to determine the 2^n coefficients of μ, taking into account the monotonicity relations between the coefficients. As it is a crucial point on an applicative point of view, we give some insights into this problem (see [20] chapter 10 for a full explanation of this topic). There are essentially three approaches.

31.3.3.1. Identification Based on the Semantics.   It consists of guessing the coefficients of μ, on the basis of semantical considerations. This could be for example:

Importance of criteria: This can be properly done by use of the Shapley value or by the value of $\mu(\{x_j\})$ alone.

Interaction between criteria: The interaction index (def. 5) is suitable for this. For $n \leq 3$, the sign of $\mu(\{x_i, x_j\}) - \mu(\{x_i\}) - \mu(\{x_j\})$ should be sufficient, although not equivalent to the interaction index.

Symmetric criteria: Two criteria x_i, x_j are symmetric if they can be exchanged without changing the aggregation mode. Then, $\mu(A \cup \{x_i\}) = \mu(A \cup \{x_j\}), \forall A \subset X - \{x_i, x_j\}$. This reduces the number of coefficients.

This approach is practicable only for low values of n, and above all, if one has at his or her disposal an expert or decision maker who is able to tell the relative importance of criteria, and the kind of interaction between them, if any. This could be the case, in application of design of new products, where the marketing "defines" what should be the ideal product, in terms of aggregation of criteria. As one can see, this approach is rather heuristic, and requires a non-negligible amount of experience.

31.3.3.2. Identification Based on Learning Data.   Considering the fuzzy integral model as a system, one can identify its parameters by minimizing an error criterion, provided that learning data are available. Suppose that (z_k, y_k), $k = 1, \ldots, l$ are learning data where $z_k = [z_{k1} \ldots z_{kn}]^t$ is an n dimensional input vector, containing the partial scores of object k with respect to criteria 1 to n, and y_k is the global score of object k. Then, one can try to identify the best fuzzy measure μ so that the squared error criterion is minimized.

$$E^2 = \sum_{k=1}^{l} (C_\mu(z_{k1}, \ldots, z_{kn}) - y_k)^2. \tag{4}$$

It can be shown [20] that (4) can be put under a quadratic program form, that is:

$$\text{minimize } \frac{1}{2}\mathbf{u}'\mathbf{D}\mathbf{u} + \mathbf{c}'\mathbf{u}$$

under the constraint $\mathbf{Au} + \mathbf{b} \geq \mathbf{0}$

where $\mathbf{u}$ is a $(2^n - 2)$ dimensional vector containing all the coefficients of the fuzzy measure μ (except $\mu(\varnothing)$ and $\mu(X)$ which are fixed), $\mathbf{D}$ is a $(2^n - 2)$ dimensional square matrix, $\mathbf{c}$ a $(2^n - 2)$ dimensional vector, $\mathbf{A}$ a $n(2^{n-1} - 1) \times (2^n - 2)$ matrix, and $\mathbf{b}$ a $n(2^{n-1} - 1)$ dimensional vector. This program can be solved by the Lemke method.

If there are too few learning data (there must be at least $n!/[(n/2)!]^2$ data: see [20] for details), matrices may be ill-conditioned. Moreover, the constraint matrix $\mathbf{A}$ is a sparse matrix, and becomes sparser as n grows, causing bad behavior of the algorithm. For all these reasons, including memory problems and time of convergence, the solution given by a quadratic program is not always reliable in practical situations.

Some authors have proposed alternatives to quadratic programming under the form of "heuristic" algorithms taking advantage of the peculiar structure of fuzzy measures, but often suboptimal. It seems that the best one in terms of performance, time, and memory is the one proposed recently by the author [16]. The basic idea is that, in the absence of any information, the most reasonable way of aggregation is the arithmetic mean (provided the problem is cardinal), that is, a Choquet integral with respect to an additive equidistributed fuzzy measure. Any input of information tends to move away the fuzzy measure from this equilibrium point. This means that, in case of few data, coefficients of the fuzzy measure that are not concerned with the data are kept as near as possible to the equilibrium point. This solves the problem of having too few data.

31.3.3.3. Combining Semantics and Learning Data. Obviously, the combination of semantical considerations, which are able to reduce the complexity and provide guidelines, with learning data should lead to more efficient algorithms. An attempt in this direction is given by Yoneda *et al.* [58]; (see also [20]). The basic ideas are the following:

- Objective: minimize the distance to the additive equidistributed fuzzy measure.

- Constraints: the usual constraints implied by the monotonicity of fuzzy measures, and constraints coming from semantical considerations. These could be about relative importance of criteria, redundancy, support between criteria, and so on.

The constraints being linear, this leads to a quadratic program as before, which can be solved by the Lemke method.

31.4. Application to Pattern Classification and Feature Extraction

31.4.1 Motivation and General Description

Consider samples or *patterns* $X_1, \ldots X_l$ that have to be classified in a set of predefined classes $C_1, \ldots, C_m$. There exists a considerable number of methods dealing with this problem, called *pattern classification* or *pattern recognition*, based on very different paradigms, such as probability theory, syntactical analysis, neural networks, fuzzy logic, and others. In the sole field of fuzzy logic, many methods have been proposed (see [3] for a compilation of works on pattern recognition), which are often generalization of existing methods (k nearest neighbors, perceptron, c-means, etc.).

A slightly different way of performing classification is the information fusion approach. Here, a decision to associate a pattern X to a class is made through the fusion of the information coming from several decision devices, which could be themselves classifiers—and in this case, we speak of a *multiclassifier* approach, or sensors measuring some feature of X and comparing the values with class prototypes, and then we speak of *multisensor* or *multiattribute* classification. In this context, a fuzzy integral can provide a powerful means of combining decisions.

The first papers using fuzzy integral in this way seems to be due to Keller and Qiu around 1986 [29, 41], and concerned image segmentation. Later, Tahani and Keller [53] published a paper using the Sugeno integral and λ-measures for classification of targets in FLIR images using a multiclassifier approach. The use of λ-measures simplifies the problem in the sense that only n coefficients have to be estimated for identifying a fuzzy measure, at the price of a much poorer aggregation tool: in particular, as it was shown in section 31.2, there is no flexibility in representing interactions since the sign of λ fixes the kind of interaction for all pairs of elements. Another weak point is that no well-established methodology exists to identify the coefficients of the λ-measure was given.

The use of the Choquet integral with respect to a general fuzzy measure, that is, not restricted to λ-measures, has been advocated by the author [23, 21], providing several learning methods for the identification of the fuzzy measure. These methods will be detailed in the section 31.4.2. Before that, we give a more formal description of the approach, in the multisensor case (the multiclassifier case is much the same). Let X° be an unknown pattern described by a n dimensional vector $[x_1^\circ \ldots x_n^\circ]$, whose coordinates are values of features measured by some sensors. We suppose that each sensor measures one feature, and has a decision device comparing a measured value with some prototype, which gives a degree of confidence of the statement "X° belongs to class C_j," on the basis of the observation. Let us denote by $\phi_k(C_j|X^\circ)$ the degree of confidence of sensor k about the class C_j.

The basis of the method is to take a kind of average of all these opinions by fuzzy integral, in a consensus-like manner. If we denote by $\Phi(C_j|X^\circ)$ the *global* degree of confidence in the statement "X° belongs to class C_j," this writes:

$$\Phi(C_j|X^\circ) = \mathcal{F}_{\mu^j}(\phi_1(C_j|X^\circ), \ldots, \phi_n(C_j|X^\circ)) \qquad (5)$$

where $\mathcal{F}_{\mu^j}$ indicates a fuzzy integral, either Sugeno or Choquet. μ_j is a fuzzy measure on the set of sensors, defined for class j. It expresses the degree of importance of each group of sensors for discriminating class j from the others (more on this in section 31.4.4). When $\Phi(C_j)$ has been computed for all classes, the simplest way to decide is to choose the class with the highest degree of confidence (however, see section 31.4.3 for an example of different procedure).

Our presentation has been done in the context of fusion of decisions. The approach can be as well presented as a general fuzzy pattern matching method—this point of view is adopted in [21], or as a Bayesian-like method using conditional densities (see [23] for this approach).

31.4.2. Learning of the Classifier

We suppose that the $\phi_k(C_j|X)$ have already been obtained by some parametric or nonparametric classical probability density estimation method, after suitable normalization: possibilistic histograms, Parzen windows, Gaussian densities, and so on. Then the learning of the classifier reduces to the learning of the parameters entering into $\mathcal{F}_{\mu^j}$, for $j = 1, \ldots, m$. Once the choice is made between the Sugeno and Choquet integral, it remains to learn the m fuzzy measures μ_j, that is, $m(2^n - 2)$ coefficients. Several approaches have been tried, consisting in the minimization of some criterion. We cite here the most relevant criteria, and state them in the two classes case ($m = 2$) for the sake of simplicity. Full details can be found in [21, 20]. We suppose to have $l = l_1 + l_2$ training samples labelled $X_1^j, X_2^j, \ldots, X_{l_j}^j$ for class $C_j, j = 1, 2$. The criteria are the following:

- The squared error (or quadratic) criterion; that is, minimize the quadratic error between expected output and actual output of the classifier. This takes the following form:

$$J = \sum_{k=1}^{l_1} (\Phi(C_1|X_k^1) - \Phi(C_2|X_k^1) - 1)^2 + \sum_{k=1}^{l_2} (\Phi(C_2|X_k^2) - \Phi(C_1|X_k^2) - 1)^2 \quad (6)$$

It can be shown that this reduces to a quadratic program with $2(2^n - 2)$ variables and $2n(2^{n-1} - 1)$ constraints in the case of Choquet integral.

- The generalized quadratic criterion. Let Ψ be any increasing function from $[-1, 1]$ to $[-1, 1]$:

$$J = \sum_{k=1}^{l_1} (\Psi\Phi(C_1|X_k^1) - \Phi(C_2|X_k^1)] - 1)^2 + \sum_{k=1}^{l_2} (\Psi\Phi(C_2|X_k^2) - \Phi(C_1|X_k^2)] - 1)^2$$

$$(7)$$

Ψ is typically a sigmoid type function $\Psi(t) = (1 - e^{-Kt})/(1 + e^{-Kt})$, $K > 0$. With suitable values of K, differences between good and bad classifications are enhanced. This is no more a quadratic program, but a constrained least mean squares problem, which can also be solved with standard optimization algorithms when the Choquet integral is used. In fact, this optimization problem requires huge memory and CPU time to be solved, and happens to be rather ill-conditioned since the matrix of constraints is sparse. For these reasons, the author has recently looked toward heuristic algorithms better adapted to the peculiar structure of the problem and less greedy [16]. A satisfying algorithm has been found, which although suboptimal, reduces the computing time by a factor 200.

Experimental results show that the generalized criterion works better than the quadratic criterion. Also, classical algorithms cannot be applied to Sugeno integrals because of nondifferentiability, and techniques such as simulated annealing have to be used.

31.4.3. Some Applications

We give here a list of existing real applications of this approach, with brief comments. In addition, the author has tested extensively the preceding approach with different learning criteria, on several well-known sets of data (iris, cancer, appendicitis), and obtained very good results, especially on cancer (see [21, 17, 13]).

Identification of targets on FLIR (Forward Looking InfraRed) images [53]: This is a two-classes problem (tank, APC), with four features. The Sugeno integral with respect to a λ-measure was used, and compared with a Bayesian classifier, and a Dempster-Shafer classifier. The fuzzy integral classifier gave the best results. A second step in this experiment was to combine the Bayesian classifier, a fuzzy two-means algorithm and the fuzzy integral classifier (feature-level) by a fuzzy integral, which improved the results.

Recognition of handwriting characters [4]: In this application, the Sugeno integral with respect to a λ-measure was used for combining three neural networks used as classifiers of handwritten characters. The results showed a significant improvement, compared to single classifiers, and other methods of aggregation (majority rule and Borda count).

Face recognition for image database [33, 34]: This application has been realized in the Japanese LIFE project. The Choquet integral was used for performing the recognition of components of the face at low and high levels of processing. In the same field of application, Arbuckle *et al.* realized a multiclassifier system based on the Choquet integral [1].

Customer segmentation for creditworthiness [32]: In this application, the Choquet integral with respect to a general fuzzy measure was applied to a difficult large size problem: 7 classes, 12 qualitative (non-numerical) features, and a recognition rate for the best statistical methods of around 50 percent. The fuzzy integral was not able to outperform the best classical method when the usual hard decision rule (i.e., choose the class with highest confidence value) was used. But, a significant improvement of around 10 percent to 15 percent over the best statistical method was obtained when a second choice was allowed in the case of a very small difference between the two highest confidence values.

31.4.4. Feature Extraction

As said before, the fuzzy measures μ_j contain all the information about the importance of all individual features (or sources) and all groups of features for distinguishing class C_j from the others. This information is well summarized into the Shapley value and the interaction index. This can be rephrased as follows:

- Feature i is more important than feature j for distinguishing class k from the others if $v_i > v_j$, where v denotes the Shapley value of measure μ_k.

- Feature i and j are independent for distinguishing class k from the others if $I_{ij} = 0$, where $_{ij}$ is the interaction index of measure μ_k. This means that both features bring their contribution.

- Feature i and j are redundant for distinguishing class k from the others if $I_{ij} < 0$. This means that it is sufficient to take one of the two.

- Feature i and j are complementary for distinguishing class k from the others if $I_{ij} > 0$. This means that the combination of the two is much more important than features i and j taken individually.

This provides useful guidelines for selecting a relevant subset of features for classification. The method has been tested on the iris data by the author [17] for analyzing fuzzy measures obtained by automatic learning. The results were in conformity with the intuition.

The converse can also be done: an expert may give information on importance and interaction, which can be translated in terms of Shapley values and interaction indexes. Then, it is possible to found the "simplest" fuzzy measures having precisely these Shapley values and interaction indexes. (In this case, the simplest fuzzy measure is a 2-order additive fuzzy measure. See definition in section 31.6.) Such an experiment, again on the iris data set, has been done by the author [13], with successful results: the recognition rate obtained with fuzzy measures constructed from information on importance and interaction of features was better than results obtained by automatic learning, especially with few learning data.

31.5. Application to Image Processing

In this section we will give a brief description of some applications in image processing. They can be divided into two categories:

- Applications where fuzzy integral is used as an aggregation operator, in a manner very similar to what was done in pattern classification. Such an approach has been used for segmentation.

- Applications where fuzzy integral is viewed as a new kind of filter, generalizing linear filters and order filters, and some operators of mathematical morphology. In particular, this approach has been used for texture recognition.

We will develop the two approaches in the next paragraphs.

31.5.1. Segmentation of Images

Segmentation of images is an operation consisting of partitioning an image into "homogeneous" zones, and is one of the most important steps in image processing, so that errors made at this stage could have a non-negligible impact on higher-level activities. Therefore, methods incorporating uncertainty degrees in region definition are desirable.

The algorithm of fuzzy c-means is well suited to this problem, since we have here a nonsupervised problem of classification, with usually an unknown number of clusters (here the number of uniform regions). However, fuzzy c-means applied to digital images is a time-consuming process, and Keller and Krishnapuram [28] suggested that an approach based on information fusion by fuzzy integral (or other operators) can be used here, in the same way it was used with pattern recognition problems. Information (at the decision level) can come from different sensors (e.g., color), different pattern recognition algorithms, different features, or a combination of image data with nonimage information (intelligence), and can be organized in a hierarchical structure. The structure of the aggregation network depends of course on the application considered.

As an illustration, we give two examples of segmentation by fuzzy integrals, by Keller *et al.*

Segmentation of FLIR images: Keller *et al.* [29] applied segmentation by fuzzy integral on gray-level images, essentially FLIR (Forward Looking InfraRed) images containing an APC (Armored Personnel Carrier) and two types of tank (this is in fact the same experiment as in section 31.4.3). Here segmentation consists of extracting the objects of interest (tanks) from the background, so there are two classes. The features used for doing this were gray level, average gray level, and local busy-ness (a simple texture measure). A Sugeno integral with respect to a λ-measure was used.

Segmentation of color images: This example concerns color images of natural scenes with road, trees, and sky [57, 28]. Using six features (intensity, excess green, difference, homogeneity texture, entropy texture, and position), the aim is to separate the three parts of the image, that is road, trees, and sky. The values of the $\phi_i(C_j)$ were provided by histograms. Good results were obtained using a Sugeno integral with respect to a possibility measure following the method described in [30]. Identification of the possibility measure was simply done by discretization and exhaustive search.

31.5.2. Choquet Integral Filters and Their Application to Texture Recognition

The idea of considering a fuzzy integral as a new class of filters is relatively recent, so that there are few applications at the moment, and the full potential of this approach is not yet known.

We begin with a short description of the idea (see more details in [14, 22]). Let us consider a two-dimensional gray-level image f that is a mapping from Z^2 in [0, 1]. A point $x \in Z^2$ is called a *pixel,* whose gray level is $f(x)$. A *window* W of size n is a subset of Z^2 containing n pixels (usually connected). A *filter* is a mapping transforming an image into another image, and is often associated with a window. Some examples of filters are:

- **Linear filters:** Let W be a window of size n, and $\alpha = [\alpha_1 \ldots \alpha_n]$ a vector of n real values such that $\sum_{i=1}^{n} \alpha_i = 1$. The output of the linear filter associated with α and W is:

$$LF_W^\alpha(f)(x) := \sum_{u_i \in W_x} \alpha_i f(u_i)$$

  where W_x indicates the translation of W by x.

- **Median filter and k order statistic filters:** Let W be a window of n pixels, and $1 \le k \le n$. The output of the k order statistic filter $OS_W^k(f)$

for pixel x is simply the kth value of $f(z), z \in W_x$, where the $f(z)$ are sorted in increasing values. When n is odd and $k = (n + 1)/2$, we have the *median filter.*

- **Order filters:** They are a generalization of order statistic filters. With the same notations as before, the output of the order filter associated with α and W is:

$$\mathrm{OF}_W^\alpha(f)(x) := \sum_{u_i \in W_x} \alpha_i f(u_{(i)})$$

where $._{(i)}$ indicates that indices have been permuted so that $f(u_{(1)}) \leq \cdots \leq f(u_{(n)})$.

- **Algebraic dilation and algebraic erosions:** An algebraic dilation (resp. erosion) is any filter ψ commuting with $\vee$ (resp. $\wedge$), i.e. $\psi(\vee_i f_i) = \vee_i \psi(f_i)$ and similarly for the erosion ($\wedge$). A simple example of algebraic dilation is the *morphological dilation* with respect to W defined by:

$$(f \oplus \breve{W})(x) := \bigvee_{u \in W_x} f(u)$$

and similarly for the *morphological erosion,* defined with $\wedge$.

Clearly, all these filters have the same form $\odot_{u \in W_x} f(u)$, and one can use the Choquet or Sugeno integral as well for the operation $\odot$. Moreover, it can be shown that linear filters and order filters are particular cases of Choquet integrals, while morphological dilations and erosions are recovered by both integrals. In addition, the class of all algebraic erosions and dilations among fuzzy integrals has been identified: these belong to the Sugeno type of integral [22]. An example of application of this special class of algebraic operators is given in [22].

There is another field where Choquet integral filters can be successfully applied, namely texture recognition. The basic idea is the following (see full details in [19]). A texture can be constructed by a more or less regular repetition of a given pattern, which may be binary (i.e., containing only black and white pixels) or gray level. Let us consider at first a binary pattern P containing n pixels denoted $x_1, \ldots, x_n$ being either black ($P(x_i) = 1$) or white ($P(x_i) = 0$). Then it is easy to see that for any (monotonic or not) fuzzy measure μ defined on the set of pixels in P, we have:

$$C_\mu(P(x_1), \ldots, P(x_n)) = \mu(\{x | x \in P, P(x) = 1\}). \tag{8}$$

Now define the *nonmonotonic* fuzzy measure μ_P by:

$$\mu_P(A) := \begin{cases} 1, \text{if } A = \{x | x \in P, P(x) = 1\} \\ 0, \text{otherwise.} \end{cases}$$

Then we define a Choquet integral filter with measure μ_P and window W identical to P in size and shape. From the definition of μ_P and (8) it is clear that the output of this filter will be always 0 except when W coincides exactly with P, where the output will be 1. Repeating the same operation for all possible arrangements of the pattern P with respect to the window W, we construct a nonmonotonic fuzzy measure μ_P which has learned the texture in the sense that the output of the Choquet integral filter with respect to μ_P will be 1 everywhere if and only if the texture is built from a perfectly regular repetition of the pattern P. In a sense, the fuzzy measure μ_P is a kind of coding of the texture. This basic idea can be extended to textures made of an irregular repetition of gray-level noisy patterns, even of size that can be much larger than the size of the window of the filter. This method has been tested on real natural textures, with excellent results.

31.6. Recent Issues

In this last section, we will indicate some recent topics, which seem to bring new promising developments in the field of fuzzy measures and integrals. They aim at solving the endless problem of reducing the exponential complexity of fuzzy measures without too much weakening of its potential. It has been seen that people often use λ-measure to avoid the complexity, but we have shown that this solution is a very poor one and should be avoided. The next two sections will present two promising tools for dealing with complexity.

31.6.1. Hierarchical Decomposition of Choquet Integral

The idea of decomposition of fuzzy measures comes from the following fact: if a fuzzy measure on a set of $2n$ elements requires 2^{2n} coefficients, two fuzzy measures on a set of n elements require only 2^{n+1} coefficients, so that we have an interest in dividing as much as possible the elements of the original set into subsets. Fujimoto *et al.* [9, 49, 48] have looked for conditions for a Choquet integral with respect to μ, a fuzzy measure defined on a set X of n elements, to be decomposed into several Choquet integrals with respect to fuzzy measures defined on subsets of X. More specifically, let μ be a given—eventually nonmonotonic—fuzzy measure on X. (Here, nonmonotonic fuzzy measures takes value in **R**, not in [0, 1].) Find a covering $C = \{C_1, \ldots, C_m\}$ of X, $C_i \subset X$, $\cup_{i=1}^{m} C_i = X$, find m (eventually nonmonotonic) fuzzy measures μ_i on C_i, find a (eventually nonmonotonic) fuzzy measure v on C such that:

$$(C) \int_X f \, d\mu = (C) \int_C f_M \, dv$$

with

$$f_M(C_i) = (C) \int_{C_i} f \, d\mu_i.$$

In particular, Fujimoto *et al.* have shown that, when μ is nonmonotonic, there exists an additive (nonmonotonic) measure *v*, nonmonotonic fuzzy measures μ_i on C_i if and only if *C* is an inclusion-exclusion covering (IEC) with respect to μ, that is satisfying:

$$\mu(A) = \sum_{I \subset \{1,\dots,n\}, I \neq \varnothing} (-1)^{|I|+1} \mu(\bigcap_{i \in I} C_i \cap A)$$

for every measurable *A*. This necessary and sufficient condition becomes much more complicated if μ and *v* are required to be monotonic fuzzy measures.

Sugeno and Kwon have tried to use the decomposition of Choquet integral in practical applications of multicriteria evaluation [50] and time series modelling [51]. They considered the case where *v* is simply additive, defined by $v(\{C_i\}) = 1$, $\forall i$, trying to find the best IEC in the sense of Akaike criterion. The search of the best IEC is a very combinatorial problem, which was solved by a branch and bound algorithm in [50] and by genetic algorithms in [51].

Experimental results on several real data sets showed an improvement of the proposed method compared to the usual Choquet integral model in the sense of the Akaike criterion (best trade-off between complexity and accuracy), but not for accuracy alone, where the usual Choquet integral model was still better. From a purely methodological point of view, it can be noticed that the equivalent μ is a *nonmonotonic* fuzzy measure: at least in multicriteria evaluation problems, this is questionable since the nonmonotonicity of fuzzy measure entails the nonmonotonicity of the integral, and one of the most basic requirements of an aggregation operator in such situations is monotonicity, in order to avoid inconsistent decisions.

31.6.2. *k*-Order Additive Fuzzy Measures

The introduction of *k*-order additive fuzzy measures stems from the following observation: additive measures (and related concepts such as decomposable measures) are easy to use but far too rudimentary; on the other hand, general fuzzy measures are very powerful but far too complicated. One can ask if there does not exist an intermediate concept, trading off richness against complexity. In fact, the answer is yes: such intermediate measures exist, and they are called *k-order additive fuzzy measures*. The definition is based on the concept of *pseudo-Boolean functions*, which are simply functions from $\{0, 1\}^n$ to $\mathcal{R}$. In fact, a pseudo-Boolean function is a concept more general than the one of fuzzy measure (even nonmonotonic). To see the correspondence, simply remark that for any $A \subset X$, *A* is equivalent to a point $(x_1, \dots, x_n)$ in $\{0, 1\}^n$ such that $x_i = 1$ iff $i \in A$. It can be shown that any pseudo-Boolean function can be put under a multilinear polynomial in *n* variables:

$$f(x) = \sum_{T \subset X} \left[a_T \prod_{i \in T} x_i \right] \tag{9}$$

with $a_T \in \mathcal{R}$ and $x = (x_1, \ldots, x_n) \in \{0, 1\}^n$. Remark that an additive measure has a multilinear extension reduced to a one degree polynomial. Then the following definition is natural [18].

> **Definition 6:** *A fuzzy measure μ defined on X is said to be k-order additive if its corresponding pseudo-Boolean function is a multilinear polynomial of degree k.*

In [18], the author has given three ways of representing k-order additive fuzzy measures, defining in particular interaction indexes for more than two elements, and has established all formulas to pass from one representation to another. A result that is of particular interest in applications is the following. Suppose we give a set of Shapley indexes $v_1, \ldots, v_n$ so that $\sum_{i=1}^n v_i = 1$, and a set of interaction indexes I_{ij} for all i, j. Then there exists a unique two-additive fuzzy measure whose Shapley and interactions indexes coincides precisely with all v_i and $_{ij}$. The multilinear extension $\sum_{i=1}^n a_i x_i + \sum_{i \neq j} a_{ij} x_i x_j$ of this measure is determined by:

$$a_i = v_i - \frac{1}{2} \sum_{j \in X \backslash i} I_{ij}, i = 1, \ldots, n \tag{10}$$

$$a_{ij} = I_{ij}, i, j \in X, i \neq j. \tag{11}$$

This result has been applied to pattern classification problems [13], as explained in section 31.4.4.

31.7. Conclusion

We have attempted in this chapter to bring as far as possible a clear and complete view of the applications of fuzzy measures and integrals, when fuzzy measures are considered as expressing importance of coalitions of elements.

Fuzzy measures appear to be a very rich tool for modelling importance of coalitions, but their potential is not completely explored, and their use not yet fully mastered. We believe that the recent concepts of hierarchical decomposition of Choquet integral and k-order additive measures are key issues that will shed light on unexplored domains of fuzzy measure theory.

We hope that the usefulness of fuzzy measures and integrals in many fields of application, not yet widely known, will become apparent and motivate further research and applications.

31.8. References

[1] Arbuckle, T., et al. "Fuzzy Information Fusion in a Face Recognitions System." *International Journal of Uncertainty, Fuzziness and Knowledge-based Systems,* Vol. 3, No. 3 (1995), pp. 217–246.

[2] Aumann, R.J., and L.S. Shapley. *Values of Non-Atomic Games.* Princeton: Princeton University Press, 1974.

[3] Bezdek, J.C., and S.K. Pal. Fuzzy Models for Pattern Recognition. IEEE Press, 1992.

[4] Cho, S.B., and J.H. Kim. "Combining Multiple Neural Networks by Fuzzy Integral for Robust Classification." *IEEE Transactions on Systems, Man, and Cybernetics,* Vol. 25, No. 2 (1995), pp. 380–384.

[5] Choquet, G. "Theory of Capacities." *Annales de l'Institut Fourier,* Vol. 5 (1953), pp. 131–295.

[6] Denneberg, D. *Non-Additive Measure and Integral.* Boston: Kluwer Academic Press, 1994.

[7] Ellsberg, D. "Risk, Ambiguity, and the Savage Axioms." *Quarterly Journal of Economics,* Vol. 75 (1961), pp. 643–669.

[8] Fodor, J.C., and M. Roubens. *Fuzzy Preference Modeling and Multicriteria Decision Aid.* Boston: Kluwer Academic Press, 1994.

[9] Fujimoto, K. "On Hierarchical Decomposition of Choquet Integral Model." Ph.D. Thesis, Tokyo Institute of Technology, 1995.

[10] Goto, K., et al. "Intelligent Alarm Method by Fuzzy Measure and its Application to Plant Abnormality Prediction." *International Joint Conference of the 4th IEEE International Conference on Fuzzy Systems and the 2nd International Fuzzy Engineering Symposium.* pp. 395–400. Yokohama, Japan: 1995.

[11] ———. "A Method of State Synthesis Evaluation for Plant-based on Fuzzy Memory-based Reasoning and Fuzzy Measure." *Journal of Japan Society for Fuzzy Theory and Systems,* Vol. 7, No. 2 (1995), pp. 390–401.

[12] Grabisch, M. "The Application of Fuzzy Integrals in Multicriteria Decision-Making," to appear, *European Journal of Operational Research.*

[13] ———. "The Representation of Importance and Interaction of Features by Fuzzy Measures." *Pattern Recognition Letters.*

[14] ———. *Fuzzy Integrals as a Generalized Class of Order Filters.* European Symposium on Satellite Remote Sensing. Roma, Italy: 1994.

[15] ———. "Fuzzy Integral in Multicriteria Decision-Making." *Fuzzy Sets and Systems,* Vol. 69 (1995), pp. 279–298.

[16] ———. "A New Algorithm for Identifying Fuzzy Measures and its Application to Pattern Recognition." *International Joint Conference of the 4th IEEE International Conference on Fuzzy Systems and the 2nd International Fuzzy Engineering Symposium.* pp. 145–150. Yokohama, Japan: 1995.

[17] ———. "Pattern Classification and Feature Extraction by Fuzzy Integral." *3rd European Congress on Intelligent Techniques and Soft Computing (EUFIT).* pp. 1465–1469. Aachen, Germany: 1995.

[18] ———. "k-Order Additive Fuzzy Measures." *6th International Conference on Information Processing and Management of Uncertainty in Knowledge-based Systems (IPMU).* Ganada, Spain: 1996.

[19] Grabisch, M., and F. Huet. "Texture Recognition by Choquet Integral Filters." *6th International Conference on Information Processing and Management of Uncertainty in Knowledge-based Systems (IPMU).* Granada, Spain: 1996.

[20] Grabisch, M., et al. *Fundamentals of Uncertainty Calculi with Applications to Fuzzy Inference.* Boston: Kluwer Academic Press, 1995.

[21] Grabisch, M., and J.M. Nicolas. "Classification by Fuzzy Integral—Performance and Tests." *Fuzzy Sets and Systems,* Vol. 65 (1994), pp. 255–271.

[22] Grabisch, M., and M. Schmitt. "Mathematical Morphology, Order Filters and Fuzzy Logic." *International Joint Conference of the 4th IEEE International Conference on*

Fuzzy Systems and the 2nd International Fuzzy Engineering Symposium. pp. 2103–2108. Yokohama, Japan: 1995.

[23] Grabisch, M., and M. Sugeno. "Multi-Attribute Classification using Fuzzy Integral." *1st IEEE International Conference on Fuzzy Systems.* pp. 47–54. San Diego, Calif.: 1992.

[24] Imaoka, H. "A Proposal of Opposite-Sugeno Integral and a Uniform Expression of Fuzzy Integrals." *International Joint Conference, 4th IEEE International Conference on Fuzzy Systems and 2nd International Fuzzy Engineering Symposium.* pp. 583–590. Yokohama, Japan: 1995.

[25] Inoue, K., and T. Anzai. "A Study on the Industrial Design Evaluation based upon Non-Additive Measures." *7th Fuzzy System Symposium.* (In Japanese). pp. 521–524. Nagoya, Japan: 1991.

[26] Ishii, K., and M. Sugeno. "A Model of Human Evaluation Process using Fuzzy Measure." *International Journal of Man-Machine Studies,* Vol. 22 (1985), pp. 19–38.

[27] Keeney, R.L., and H. Raiffa. *Decision with Multiple Objectives.* New York: John J. Wiley and Sons, 1976.

[28] Keller, J.M., and R. Krishnapuram. "Fuzzy Decision Models in Computer Vision," in *Fuzzy Sets, Neural Networks and Soft Computing.* eds. R.R. Yager and L.A. Zadeh.

[29] Keller, J.M., et al. The Fuzzy Integral and Image Segmentation. North American *Fuzzy Information Processing Society.* pp. 324–339. New Orleans, La.: 1986.

[30] Keller, J.M., and B. Yan. Possibility Expectation and its Decision-Making Algorithm. *1st IEEE International Conferency on Fuzzy Systems.* pp. 661–668. San Diego, Calif.: 1992.

[31] Matsuda, M., and T. Kameoka. Application of Fuzzy Measure, Fuzzy Integral and Neural Network to the System which Estimate Taste by using Industry Analysis. *2nd International Conference on Fuzzy Systems and Neural Networks.* pp. 601–606. Iizuka, Japan: 1992.

[32] Metellus, O., and M. Grabisch. "Une Approache de la Classification par Filtrage Flou—Methodologie et Performances sur un Probleme de Segmentation Clientele." *Proceedings Rencontres Francophones sur la Logique Floue et ses Applications (LFA).* Paris, France: 1995.

[33] Miyajima, K., and A. Ralescu. Fuzzy Logic Approach to Model-based Image Analysis. Technical Report TR-4K-004E, LIFE. Yokohama, Japan: 1992.

[34] ———. Modeling of Natural Objects including Fuzziness and Application to Image Understanding. 2nd Congress on Fuzzy Systems. pp. 1049–1054. San Francisco, Calif.: 1993.

[35] Murofushi, T., and S. Soneda. Techniques For Reading Fuzzy Measures (iii): Interaction Index. *9th Fuzzy System Symposium,* pp. 693–696. (In Japanese). Sapporo, Japan: 1993.

[36] Murofushi, T., and M. Sugeno. "A Theory of Fuzzy Measures. Representation, the Choquet Integral and Null Sets." *Journal of Mathematical Analysis Application,* Vol. 159, No. 2 (1991), pp. 532–549.

[37] Nakamori, Y., and N. Iwamoto. Analysis of Environmental Evaluation Structure by the Choquet Integral Model. *International Joint Conference of the 4th IEEE International Conference on Fuzzy Systems and the 2nd International Fuzzy Engineering Symposium.* pp. 695–700. Yokohama, Japan: 1995.

[38] Nakamura, K. On Semantic Structure of Vague Categories. *10th Fuzzy System Symposium.* pp. 325–326. (In Japanese). Osaka, Japan: 1994.

[39] Onisawa, T., et al. "Fuzzy Measure Analysis of Public Attitude Towards the Use of Nuclear Energy." *Fuzzy Sets and Systems,* Vol. 20 (1986), pp. 259–289.

[40] Orlovski, S.A. *Calculus of Decomposable Properties, Fuzzy Sets and Decisions.* Allerton Press, 1994.

[41] Qiu, H., and J.M. Keller. *Multiple Spectral Image Segmentation using Fuzzy Techniques.* Proceedings North American Fuzzy Information Processing Society. pp. 374–387. Purdue University. 1987.

[42] Quiggin, J. *Generalized Expected Utility Theory: The Rank Dependent Model.* Boston: Kluwer Academic Press, 1993.

[43] Schmeidler, D. "Integral Representation without Additivity." *Proceedings of the American Mathematical Society,* Vol. 97, No. 2 (1986), pp. 255–261.

[44] ———. "Subjective Probability and Expected Utility Without Additivity." *Econometrica,* Vol. 57, No. 3 (1989), pp. 571–587.

[45] Shafer, G. *A Mathematical Theory of Evidence.* Princeton. Princeton University Press, 1976.

[46] Shapley, L.S. "A Value for n-Person Games," in *Contributions to the Theory of Games,* Vol. II. eds. H.W. Kuhn and A.W. Tucker. pp. 307–317. Princeton: Princeton University Press, 1953.

[47] Sugeno, M. "Theory of Fuzzy Integrals and its Applications." Ph.D. Thesis, Tokyo Institute of Technology, 1974.

[48] Sugeno, M., et al. "A Hierarchical Decomposition of Choquet Integral Model." *International Journal of Uncertainty, Fuzziness and Knowledge-based Systems,* Vol. 3, No. 1 (1995), pp. 1–15.

[49] Sugeno, M., et al. Hierarchical Decomposition Theorems for Choquet Integral Models. *International Joint Conference 4th IEEE International Conference on Fuzzy Systems and 2nd International Fuzzy Engineering Symposium.* pp. 2245–2252. Yokohama, Japan: 1995.

[50] Sugeno, M., and S.H. Kwon. "A Clusterwise Regression-type Model for Subjective Evaluation." *Journal of Japan Society for Fuzzy Theory and Systems,* Vol. 7, No. 2 (1995), pp. 291–310.

[51] ———. A New Approach to Time Series Modeling with Fuzzy Measures and the Choquet Integral. *International Joint Conference of the 4th IEEE International Conference on Fuzzy Systems and the 2nd International Fuzzy Engineering Symposium.* pp. 799–804. Yokohama, Japan: 1995.

[52] Sugeno, M., and T. Murofushi. "Fuzzy Measure Theory." Course on Fuzzy Theory, Vol. 3, (in Japanese). Nikkan Kogyo. 1993.

[53] Tahani, H., and J.M. Keller. "Information Fusion in Computer Vision using the Fuzzy Integral." *IEEE Transactions on Systems, Man, and Cybernetics,* Vol. 20, No. 3 (1990), pp. 733–741.

[54] Tanaka, K., and M. Sugeno. A Study on Subjective Evaluations of Color Printing Images. *4th Fuzzy System Symposium.* pp. 229–234. (In Japanese). Tokyo, Japan: 1988.

[55] Wang, Z., and G.J. Klir. *Fuzzy Measure Theory.* New York: Plenum, 1992.

[56] Washio, T., et al. A Method for Supporting Decision-Making on Plant Operation-based on Human Reliability Analysis by Fuzzy Integral. *2nd International Conference on Fuzzy Logic and Neural Networks.* pp. 841–845. Iizuka, Japan: 1992.

[57] Yan, B., and J. Keller. *Conditional Fuzzy Measures and Image Segmentation.* NAFIPS Congress. pp. 32–36. University of Missouri at Columbia. 1991.

[58] Yoneda, M., et al. "Interactive Determination of a Utility Function Represented by a Fuzzy Integral." *Information Sciences,* Vol. 71 (1993), pp. 43–64.

[59] Zadeh, L.A. "Fuzzy Sets as a Basis for a Theory of Possibility." *Fuzzy Sets and Systems,* Vol. 1 (1978), pp. 3–28.

32 Risk Management with Imprecise Information

Kurt J. Engemann, Ronald R. Yager
Iona College

Holmes E. Miller
Muhlenberg College

ABSTRACT: This chapter is concerned with risk management in the practical situation in which we have imprecise information about the likelihood of the events that may occur. We propose and apply a general method of selecting an alternative under uncertainty to a real-world case involving risk management at one of the nation's largest banks.

32.1. Introduction

Risk management decisions are among the most conceptually difficult faced by managers. The difficulty arises because, by their very nature, such decisions must come to grips with uncertainties surrounding highly unlikely events with major potential adverse impact upon the operation of a business. Traditionally, decision alternatives are analyzed using the classical methodology of choosing the alternative that minimized the total expected cost. An underlying problem using the classical expected value approach is the softness of many of the probability estimates for specific events. We believe that in many real-world examples this is the case, and the decision analyst is forced to use numbers of questionable validity, even after conducting extensive sensitivity analyses. We have designed a methodology for decision making useful with imprecise information. In this chapter, we apply our proposed methodology to a real-world case involving risk management at one of the nation's largest banks.

32.2. Risk Management

Risk management identifies potentially catastrophic events and selects the best alternatives to deal with the risks. A risk management methodology provides a conceptual framework to aid a decision maker who must choose among decision alternatives in an environment characterized by risk. It integrates all the aspects influencing the decision including risk attitude.

An example of how a risk management methodology can be used occurs in developing a contingency plan for a bank's operations. Today, virtually all areas of bank operations depend upon computer processing and telecommunications. These operations are exposed to a variety of potential disasters, characterized by low-threat rates that manifest themselves in events causing potentially high losses. To control these risks, banks use contingency planning. Contingency planning involves implementing control alternatives that impact earnings and either reduce the rate of occurrence of a threat or mitigate losses if events occur.

The objective of contingency planning is to limit the impact of major disruptions to an acceptable level. In the first step, senior business managers identify the critical services that require contingency plans. Services will be disrupted if the resources required to deliver the services are unavailable. The loss of a resource can be due to disasters such as fire, flood, power outage, strike, civil disturbance, acts of nature, and acts of war. It may be short-term or long-term, depending on the time required to repair the damage incurred.

The loss of a resource for a definite time period is called an event. Identifying possible events involves reviewing all internal and external resources required to deliver services, and requires an understanding of transaction workflows, operations configurations, and utility services such as electricity, communications, water, air conditioning and heating.

Each event has a consequence associated with it. This consequence consists of asset loss, direct loss, and indirect loss. Asset loss includes the cost of equipment destroyed and site reconstruction. Direct loss contains the loss of fees during the outage as well as interest lost. Indirect losses are associated with loss of future business and contingent liability. Estimates of losses are obtained from extensive interviews with operations and business managers. The total loss from an event is the sum of the losses for all areas affected by the event and is adjusted to account for insurance recovery, future increases in insurance premiums, and additional expenditures required by the insurers.

In order to compare the impact of the alternatives, all costs and losses are expressed in terms of after-tax annualized earnings impact, derived, using a multiple-year project life and depreciation period.

The large consequence events, which are the subject of this study, are inherently rare—no bank could tolerate frequent occurrences of such magnitude. Thus, estimates of occurrence rates for these events must be extrapolated from occurrence rates for less serious events, or inferred from experiences outside the bank, and from engineering judgment. Moreover, since the events are often for specific outages in specific building locations, probability estimates must be adjusted to reflect specific duration and locations.

The probability of an event may be estimated after reviewing historical data, and through discussions with experts such as fire departments, weather bureaus, utility companies, police departments, building engineers, reliability engineers, and government agencies. A serious problem is that even after obtaining all the available data and making "best estimates," the resulting event probabilities are not very reliable and give the analysis a false sense of precision, even after sensitivity analysis.

32.3. Decision Making with Imprecise Information

Our method is useful in those situations where the decision maker does not know the underlying probability distribution for the specific outcomes. We propose a general formulation to the optimal alternative selection problem under uncertainty. The approach is based upon the OWA aggregation operators introduced by Yager [7], [8]. We provide a methodology for selecting the optimal alternative in situations in which our knowledge about the uncertainty is contained in a belief structure.

We define an ordered weighted averaging (OWA) operator of dimension n as the function F, that has associated with it a weighting vector W:

$$W = [w_1, w_2, \ldots, w_n]$$

such that: (1) $0 \leq w_j \leq 1$, and (2) $\Sigma_j w_j = 1$, and for any set of values $a_1, \ldots, a_n$:

$$F(a_1, \ldots, a_n) = \Sigma_j w_j b_j$$

where b_j is the jth largest element in the collection $a_1, \ldots, a_n$.

The OWA operators can be used to help in the selection of an optimal alternative in the face of uncertainty. In particular, we can use these operators to provide the aggregated value for each alternative. We can calculate $V_i = F(C_{i1}, \ldots, C_{in})$, where F is an OWA aggregation operator. We then select the alternative that has the highest V value.

The aggregation associated with each particular alternative can be seen as a kind of expected value. If $C_{i1}, C_{i2}, \ldots, C_{in}$ are payoffs corresponding to each state of nature under the selection of alternative A_i, then $b_{i1}, \ldots, b_{in}$ are the ordered set of these payoffs. Then if $w_1, \ldots, w_n$ are the OWA weights interpreted as probabilities of the jth best thing happening under any selection of alternative, we see:

$$V_i = \Sigma_j w_j b_{ij}$$

is the expected payoff in this case. In decision making under uncertainty, the weights are assigned not to a particular state of nature, but to the preference ordered position of the payoff, for example, to profit payoffs in descending order. Thus w_1 is the weight assigned to the best payoff and w_n is the weight assigned to the worst payoff. Using this interpretation we can see that the pessimistic strategy is effectively a situation in which a weight of 1 is assigned to the worst thing happening given any selection of alternative. In the optimistic approach we are assuming a weight of 1 is assigned to the best thing happening. In the normative case we are assigning equal weights for each of the preference positions. The Hurwicz strategy effectively assigns a weight α that the best thing will happen and weight $1-\alpha$ that the worst thing will happen.

A measure of optimism associated with these weights is defined as:

$$Opt(W) = \Sigma\ w_j h_n(j)$$

$$h_n(j) = (n-j)/(n-1).$$

A second measure associated with these weights is a measure of entropy or dispersion:

$$DISP(W) = -\Sigma_j\ w_j ln(w_j).$$

The larger the $DISP(W)$, the more the payoffs play a role in the determination of F.

A question that naturally arises is, how does a decision maker obtain the weights he or she is going to use in solving a particular problem? At the fundamental level, the answer is that he or she subjectively decides, just as he or she does in deciding to be pessimistic or optimistic or normative. The most straightforward way of obtaining the weights is for the decision maker to directly select the values of the weights. If he or she chooses to allocate more weight to the elements near the top of the vector, he or she can be seen as optimistic. If he or she allocates more weight to elements near the bottom he or she is pessimistic.

O'Hagan [5] suggested a method of selecting the weights. With this approach, the decision maker subjectively decides upon the coefficient of optimism α. He or she then inputs this value into a mathematical programming problem which is used to obtain the weights that have an appropriate degree of optimism while maximizing the dispersion. The mathematical programming problem (1) is:

$$\text{maximize} - \Sigma\ w_j ln(w_j)$$

Subject to:

$$\Sigma_j\ h_n(j)w_j = a$$

$$\Sigma_j w_j = 1$$

$$w_j \geq 0 \text{ for } j = 1, \dots, n.$$

One benefit of this approach is that for various cardinalities of OWA operators, we can consistently provide weights corresponding to a given α.

While the preceding approach incorporates the decision maker's subjectivity through the coefficient of optimism, Engemann, Filev, and Yager

[4] developed a related approach that modifies event probabilities using the decision maker's level of optimism.

32.4. The Study

The following case comes from an actual study done by Engemann and Miller [4] at a large money center bank. The study involves a risk management decision involving the selection of a contingency planning strategy. The data are realistic in our example, although for the sake of exposition we will make some simplifications. The study involves the threat of power failure to several critical services at the bank's operations center. Power outages may be confined to a few floors of the bank's operations building or extended to the entire building. Localized power outages will result from a disruption of the connection between the basement and particular floors. Power outages extending to the whole bank's operations building can result from outages from the electric utility company or from damage to the electrical system in the basement. These outages are discretized into events from 0 through 5 days.

The bank occupied the first 22 stories of a 50-story building. Key areas include:

Money Transfer Operations (floors 4 and 5)

Telecommunications (floor 4)

Letter of Credit (floor 6)

Demand Deposit Accounting (floor 7)

Check Processing (floors 9 and 10)

Money Transfer Data Center (floor 11)

Corporate Data Center (floor 11)

Treasury Operations Support (floor 12)

Operations and Corporate Staff Areas (floors 13–22)

The decision involved whether to purchase a generator and, if so, what size generator would be most cost efficient. In the study, six alternatives were considered, providing different levels of backup. They are:

- (A1) No Generator
- (A2) $2 MM Generator—Money Transfer Operations only
- (A3) $5 MM Generator—Money Transfer Operations and Data Center
- (A4) $10 MM Generator—All areas on floors 4, 5, and 11
- (A5) $15 MM Generator—All areas on floors 2 through 11
- (A6) $25 MM Generator—All areas on floors 2 through 22

The total costs include the cost of the generator plus all associated installation costs. In order to compare the alternatives, the one-time cost of the emergency generator was equated to an annualized earnings impact.

A set of events was developed to encompass the most likely power-outage scenarios, but as a practical matter other extremely unlikely events were dropped from the analysis. Since outages actually could be of any length, the continuous nature was "collapsed" into discrete outages of specific duration and location. Fifteen events were defined in addition to the sixteenth null event (i.e., no outage) yielding the following collection of mutually exclusive and collectively exhaustive events:

(BW1) Building-wide 1 day

(BW2) Building-wide 2 days

(BW3) Building-wide 3 days

(BW4) Building-wide 4 days

(BW5) Building-wide 5 days

(MT1) Money Transfer Operations 1 day

(MT2) Money Transfer Operations 2 days

(TC1) Telecommunications 1 day

(TC2) Telecommunications 2 days

(CP1) Check Processing 1 day

(CP2) Check Processing 2 days

(MD1) Money Transfer Data Center 1 day

(MD2) Money Transfer Data Center 2 days

(CD1) Corporate Data Center 1 day

(CD2) Corporate Data Center 2 days

Note that even though some departments share the same floor, they had different local circuits. Therefore, for example, a power outage could occur in Telecommunications while Money Transfer Operations continued.

The financial impact of each event is determined by estimating the resulting loss of assets, direct losses, indirect losses, and financial impact of insurance and taxes. Loss of assets results from damage to the equipment and premises or destruction of negotiable instruments. Direct losses include compensation losses, late money losses, losses resulting from overdraft/return items, and extra recovery losses. Indirect losses result from a loss of customers, that is, from a loss of balances and a loss of fees. Direct and indirect losses were obtained via analyzing product volumes, product prices, and penalty costs for missing daily processing deadlines, coupled with in-depth specific products impacted. All of these estimates were developed assuming that existing departmental contingency plans were in place, which mitigated the losses.

Table 32.1 contains the losses and annualized costs associated with each event, given that a particular strategy is in place.

Determining the probabilities associated with events is imprecise at best. In many instances, historical records do not exist and even when they do, history is often not a good predictor of the future. Detailed assumptions need to be made to specify probabilities for the events. It may be more appropriate to assign weights to broader events, with a belief structure tying previous events to these broader events.

We propose a more general framework for the representation of uncertainty using the Dempster-Shafer belief structure [1], [6]. The belief structure allows us to represent various forms of information a decision maker may have about the state of nature.

A basic probability assignment or belief structure, m, on the set Y consists of a collection of nonempty subsets of Y, B_k, and an associated set of weights, $m(B_k)$, such that:

$$m(B_k) > 0$$

$$\Sigma_k \, m(B_k) = 1.$$

The subsets B_k are called the focal elements of the belief structure. Our concern is the determination of which event within Y will occur.

More formally, we can see the Dempster-Shafer belief structure as arising in the following way. Let X and Y be two spaces. Assume we have a probability distribution P on X, such that:

$$P(x_k) = p_k$$

Table 32.1 Events, Strategies, Losses, and Annualized Costs of Strategies (in $ Millions)

EVENT	STRATEGY					
	A1	A2	A3	A4	A5	A6
BW1	4.69	1.60	0.59	0.11	0.06	0.00
BW2	12.37	2.63	1.37	0.22	0.12	0.00
BW3	28.10	4.00	2.60	0.40	0.24	0.00
BW4	47.50	8.00	5.20	0.80	0.48	0.00
BW5	96.66	16.00	10.40	1.60	0.96	0.00
MT1	4.10	0.00	0.00	0.00	0.00	0.00
MT2	11.00	0.00	0.00	0.00	0.00	0.00
TC1	1.10	0.00	0.00	0.00	0.00	0.00
TC2	2.80	0.00	0.00	0.00	0.00	0.00
CD1	0.05	0.05	0.05	0.05	0.00	0.00
CD2	0.10	0.10	0.10	0.10	0.00	0.00
MD1	0.47	0.47	0.00	0.00	0.00	0.00
MD2	1.26	1.26	0.00	0.00	0.00	0.00
CD1	0.48	0.48	0.48	0.00	0.00	0.00
CD2	1.15	1.15	1.15	0.00	0.00	0.00
NO	0.00	0.00	0.00	0.00	0.00	0.00
Cost	0.00	0.34	0.86	1.72	2.57	4.29

To each element x_k of X, let there be a subset B_k of Y in which it is known that the actual state of the world will occur. Then we can say that:

$$m(B_k) = p_k.$$

We note that p_k is the weight associated with B_k, it is $m(B_k)$.
   We consider the following focal elements:

(B_1) No power outage

(B_2) Power outage within building network A

(B_3) Power outage within building network B

(B_4) Power outage within building network C

(B_5) Regional network failure

(B_6) Major substation failure

(B_7) Minor substation failure

(B_8) No power to entire building.

Our rationale is that weights for the focal elements can be determined more easily and with more reliability than can probabilities for the specific events. There are fewer estimates to be made, there are fewer assumptions necessary, and the electric utility company and building engineers can provide more relevant data. Table 32.2 gives a belief structure consisting of eight focal elements and weights. A 1 indicates a specific event is included in the belief structure and a 0 indicates it is excluded. For example, focal element B_5 (regional network failure) is

Table 32.2   Belief Structure with Focal Elements and Weights

	FOCAL ELEMENTS							
EVENT	B_1	B_2	B_3	B_4	B_5	B_6	B_7	B_8
BW1	0	0	0	0	1	0	1	1
BW2	0	0	0	0	1	0	1	1
BW3	0	0	0	0	0	1	0	1
BW4	0	0	0	0	0	1	0	1
BW5	0	0	0	0	0	1	0	1
MT1	0	1	1	0	0	0	0	0
MT2	0	1	1	0	0	0	0	0
TC1	0	1	1	0	0	0	0	0
TC2	0	1	1	0	0	0	0	0
CP1	0	1	0	1	0	0	0	0
CP2	0	1	0	1	0	0	0	0
MD1	0	1	0	1	0	0	0	0
MD2	0	1	0	1	0	0	0	0
CD1	0	1	0	1	0	0	0	0
CD2	0	1	0	1	0	0	0	0
NO	1	0	0	0	0	0	0	0
WEIGHTS	.70	.03	.03	.03	.03	.06	.06	.06

comprised of the events: BW1 (building-wide outage 1 day) and BW2 (building-wide outage 2 days). Note that the outcomes for two different focal elements may be the same. For example, both B_5 (regional network failure) and B_7 (minor substation failure) induce the same outcomes: building-wide outages for 1 and 2 days (BW1 and BW2). However, the probabilities of the focal elements are different. The bottom row lists the weights associated with each focal element.

The following summarizes the methodology, assuming we have obtained the payoff matrix, the belief function m about the state of nature, and the decision makers degree of optimism, α.

1. Solve for each different cardinality of focal elements, mathematical programming problem (1) with the degree of optimism α. This gives us a collection of weights, w_j, to be used in the OWA aggregation function F.

2. Determine the payoff collection, M_{ik}, if we select alternative A_i and the focal element B_k occurs, for all values of i and k. Hence $M_{ik} = \{C_{ij} \mid S_j \in B_k\}$.

3. Determine the aggregated payoff, $V_{ik} = F(M_{ik})$, for all values of i and k.

4. For each alternative, calculate the generalized expected value, C_i, where $C_i = \Sigma_k V_{ik} m(B_k)$.

5. Select the alternative with the largest C_i as the optimal.

The procedure for the determination of the best alternative combines the schemes used for both decision making under risk and uncertainty. In a manner similar to decision making under risk, we obtain a generalized expected value, C_i, for each alternative A_i. To obtain this expected value, we use evidential knowledge by means of the weights associated with the focal elements. $m(B_k)$ is the probability that B_k will be the set that determines the state of nature.

V_{ik} is the payoff we expect when we select alternative A_i and focal element B_k occurs. The determination of the value V_{ik} can be seen as equivalent to the problem of decision making under uncertainty. In particular, for a given A_i and the knowledge that the state of nature lies in B_k, we have a collection of possible payoffs, M_{ik}. In this case, each element S_j in B_k contributes one element to M_{ik}, its payoff under S_j. In order to determine the value of V_{ik} from M_{ik}, we use the procedure developed for decision making under uncertainty using OWA operators.

We will illustrate the method of selecting an alternative assuming that the decision maker has a degree of optimism of 0.8. Solving the mathematical programming problem (1), we obtain the weights associated with the OWA operators for various numbers of arguments:

No.	w_1	w_2	w_3	w_4	w_5	w_6	w_7	w_8	w_9	w_{10}
1	1.0									
2	.80	.20								
3	.68	.24	.08							
4	.60	.25	.11	.04						
5	.53	.26	.12	.06	.03					
6	.48	.25	.14	.07	.04	.02				
10	.34	.23	.15	.10	.07	.04	.03	.02	.01	.01

We recall M_{ik} is the collection of payoffs that are possible if we select alternative A_i and the focal element B_k occurs. The sorted payoff collections, M_{ik}, are:

M_{11}	M_{21}	M_{31}	M_{41}	M_{51}	M_{61}
0.00	0.00	0.00	0.00	0.00	0.00

M_{12}	M_{22}	M_{32}	M_{42}	M_{52}	M_{62}
11.00	1.26	1.15	0.10	0.00	0.00
4.10	1.15	0.48	0.05	0.00	0.00
2.80	0.48	0.10	0.00	0.00	0.00
1.26	0.47	0.05	0.00	0.00	0.00
1.15	0.10	0.00	0.00	0.00	0.00
1.10	0.05	0.00	0.00	0.00	0.00
0.48	0.00	0.00	0.00	0.00	0.00
0.47	0.00	0.00	0.00	0.00	0.00
0.10	0.00	0.00	0.00	0.00	0.00
0.05	0.00	0.00	0.00	0.00	0.00

M_{13}	M_{23}	M_{33}	M_{43}	M_{53}	M_{63}
11.00	0.00	0.00	0.00	0.00	0.00
4.10	0.00	0.00	0.00	0.00	0.00
2.80	0.00	0.00	0.00	0.00	0.00
1.10	0.00	0.00	0.00	0.00	0.00

M_{14}	M_{24}	M_{34}	M_{44}	M_{54}	M_{64}
1.26	1.26	1.15	0.10	0.00	0.00
1.15	1.15	0.48	0.05	0.00	0.00
0.48	0.48	.010	0.00	0.00	0.00
0.47	0.47	0.05	0.00	0.00	0.00
0.10	0.10	0.00	0.00	0.00	0.00
0.05	0.05	0.00	0.00	0.00	0.00
0.22	0.22	0.06	0.00	0.00	0.00

M_{15}	M_{25}	M_{35}	M_{45}	M_{55}	M_{65}
12.37	2.63	1.37	0.22	0.12	0.00
4.69	1.60	0.59	0.11	0.06	0.00
6.23	1.81	0.75	0.13	0.07	0.00

M_{16}	M_{26}	M_{36}	M_{46}	M_{56}	M_{66}
96.66	16.00	10.40	1.60	0.96	0.00
47.50	8.00	5.20	0.80	0.48	0.00
28.10	4.00	2.60	0.40	0.24	0.00
38.30	5.93	3.85	0.59	0.36	0.00

M_{17}	M_{27}	M_{37}	M_{47}	M_{57}	M_{67}
12.37	2.63	1.37	0.22	0.12	0.00
4.69	1.60	0.59	0.11	0.06	0.00
6.23	1.81	0.75	0.13	0.07	0.00

M_{18}	M_{28}	M_{38}	M_{48}	M_{58}	M_{68}
96.66	16.00	10.40	1.60	0.96	0.00
47.50	8.00	5.20	0.80	0.48	0.00
28.10	4.00	2.60	0.40	0.24	0.00
12.37	2.63	1.37	0.22	0.12	0.00
4.69	1.60	0.59	0.11	0.06	0.00

Next we calculate V_{ik}, using the OWA weights. We recall that $V_{ik} = F(M_{ik})$.

An example will illustrate the calculation:

$$V_{26} = .68(4.00) + .24(8.00) + .08((16.00) = 5.92$$

Similarly: $V_{ik} =$

0.00	0.52	2.29	0.22	6.23	38.30	6.23	19.19
0.00	0.06	0.00	0.22	1.81	5.92	1.81	2.13
0.00	0.02	0.00	0.06	0.75	3.85	0.75	1.04
0.00	0.00	0.00	0.00	0.13	0.59	0.13	0.16
0.00	0.00	0.00	0.00	0.07	0.36	0.07	0.09
0.00	0.00	0.00	0.00	0.00	0.00	0.00	0.00

Finally, we use these values to obtain C_i, the generalized expected value for each alternative:

An example will illustrate the calculation:

$C_1 = .7(0) + .03(.52) + .03(2.29) + .03(.22) + .03(6.23)$

$$+.06(38.3) + .06(6.23) + .06(19.19) = 4.10$$

Similarly:

$$C_1 = 4.10, C_2 = 0.66, C_3 = 0.36, C_4 = 0.06, C_5 = 0.03, C_6 = 0.00.$$

Table 32.3 lists the generalized expected value for each alternative using a degree of optimism of .8. A2, the \$2MM generator is the most preferred.

Sensitivity analysis indicates that as long as $\alpha > .36$, the preferred alternative is A2 (\$2 MM Generator - Money Transfer Operations). If α is between .23 and .36 A3 (\$5 MM Generator - Money Transfer Operations and Money Transfer Data Center) is the preferred alternative. And if $\alpha <$

Table 32.3 Generalized Expected Values Obtained Using Belief Structure
Approach (in $ Millions)

| | STRATEGY | | | | | |
	A1	A2	A3	A4	A5	A6
EXPECTED LOSS	4.10	0.66	0.36	0.06	0.03	0.00
STRATEGY COST	0.00	0.34	0.86	1.72	2.57	4.29
TOTAL COST	4.10	1.00	1.22	1.78	2.60	4.29

.23 the preferred alternative is A4 ($10 MM Generator - All areas on
floors 4, 5, & 11). Alternative A2 was the actual choice made by bank
management.

32.5. Conclusion

Implementing a risk management methodology in a large organization
involves institutionalizing the methodology via policies and procedures.
The ultimate success of implementation is increased when the methodology is understandable, when the underlying data can be developed, and
when the results are grounded in a solid methodological base.

Applying the general approach that is introduced here to decision
making with imprecise information achieves these ends. The aggregation
operator and decision methodology presented possess certain desirable
rational properties as presented by Engemann, Miller, and Yager [3]. In
the example presented here, we used monetary value as a criteria,
although utility could have been used had it been appropriate.

32.6. References

[1] Dempster, A.P. "Upper and Lower Probabilities Induced by a Multi-Valued Mapping."
    Annals of Mathematical Statistics. (1967), pp. 325–339.
[2] Engemann, K., and H. Miller. "Risk Management at a Major Bank." *Interfaces,* Vol. 22,
    No. 6 (1992), pp. 140–149.
[3] Engemann, K., et al. "Decision-Making with Belief Structures: An Application in Risk
    Management," to appear. *International Journal of Uncertainty, Fuzziness, and Knowledge-
    based Systems.*
[4] Engemann, K., et al. "Modeling Decision-Making using Immediate Probabilities," to
    appear. *International Journal of General Systems.*
[5] O'Hagan, M. "Aggregating Template Rule Antecedents in Real-Time Expert Systems
    with Fuzzy Set Logic." *Proceedings, 22nd Annual IEEE Asilomar Conference on Sig-
    nals, Systems, and Computers.* Pacific Grove, Calif.: 1988.
[6] Shafer, G.A. *Mathematical Theory of Evidence.* Princeton: Princeton University Press,
    1976.
[7] Yager, R.R. "On Ordered Weighted Averaging Aggregation Operators in Multicriteria
    Decision-Making." *IEEE Transactions on Systems, Man, and Cybernetics,* Vol. 18
    (1988), pp. 83–190.
[8] ———. "Decision-Making under Dempster-Shafer Uncertainties." *International Jour-
    nal of General Systems,* Vol. 20 (1992), pp. 233–245.

33 Use of Possibility Theory to Measure Driver Anxiety During Signal Change Intervals

Shinya Kikuchi, Ph.D., P.E.
Professor
Civil Engineering Department
University of Delaware
Newark, Delaware

Vijaykumar Perincherry, Ph.D.
Parsons Brinckerhoff
Herndon, Virginia

ABSTRACT: Anxiety that a driver experiences at the onset of yellow while approaching a signalized intersection is analyzed. The driver's decision process is modelled as a fuzzy inference process determining either stopping or going. The input to the process is the information on the current condition that the driver perceives. Because both the rules and the perceived information are not clear, the decision is made under uncertainty. This uncertainty is quantified by possibility and necessity measures. Yager's anxiety measure is used to measure the driver's anxiety associated with making decisions under uncertainty, as a function of possibility and necessity measures for the conflicting actions. Anxiety is computed for both aggressive and conservative drivers. The measures for these two extreme types of drivers form the range; most drivers are believed to fall between the two. The model is used to estimate the degree of anxiety and its location on an actual intersection approach based on the field data. The proposed method should be useful to evaluate the accuracy and the type of information to be provided to the drivers. A concept of a neural network based model of a drive decision-aid system is proposed.

33.1. Introduction

Safety and efficiency of traffic flow depend largely on the perception and reaction of individual drivers. Most of the time, each driver determines the appropriate action by exercising a set of vague driving rules. One example of this is the case of driver's action when the signal changes to yellow as he or she is approaching the intersection. He or she experiences the state of indecision and anxiety because he or she must evaluate many parameters and decide either to go or to stop in a short time period.

This study proposes a decision model that evaluates the degree of anxiety that a driver experiences when he or she has to choose one of the conflicting actions at the onset of yellow indication. The method also identifies the zone on the approach where the driver experiences anxiety. An approach that uses a neural network to learn the driver decision pattern and issue appropriate advice to the driver at the time of signal change interval is proposed. The study is part of our effort to understand driver decision processes when the perceived information and decision rules are not clear, and also to understand how improved information helps a driver make decisions and reduces anxiety [Kikuchi et al., 5,6].

The present practice of determining the signal change interval is based on the idea that each driver has complete knowledge of the information needed for the decision. In reality, the driver does not have the complete information nor the rigid rules needed to make the correct decision. As a result, regardless how correct the setting of the interval of signal change (based on the existing standards) is, most drivers face a period of indecision and anxiety at the onset of the yellow indication.

Indecision and anxiety is caused by the lack of clear information and well-defined criteria to make the decision. Unclear information allows different interpretations of the decision parameters by the decision maker; two extremes are optimistic and pessimistic interpretations. The decision mechanism under uncertainty is usually based on the fuzzy inference rules, which are developed through the individual's attitude and experience. Thus, different decision outcomes emerge among drivers.

Recently developed uncertainty theory allows the measurement of anxiety as a function of optimistic and pessimistic interpretations of the perceived information and inference rules. In this chapter, the anxiety measure developed by Yager [15] is used to compute the degree of anxiety that a driver experiences at the onset of the yellow indication at at different locations along the approach. Further, the model is intended to help evaluate the features of a driver decision support system by examining how improved information and decision rules affect drivers' behavior and anxiety. This is a relevant issue for the IVHS implementation.

This chapter first presents the existing approaches to the model driver decision process during the signal change interval. It then explains the basic measures of uncertainty; the possibility measure and the necessity measure. By a combination of these two measures, the degree of anxiety associated with choosing one of the decision options is computed for the aggressive and conservative drivers.

33.2. Driver Anxiety and the Problem

The study of anxiety in the driver's mind requires understanding of the decision process, which takes place under imprecise rules and vaguely perceived information. This section discusses anxiety during a decision process and defines the need to develop a model that expresses anxiety in the mind of a driver.

33.2.1. Driver Anxiety

A driver has two alternative actions to choose from when the signal turns yellow while approaching an intersection. One is to go through before the signal turns red; and the other is to stop at the intersection. In order to make the decision, he or she requires a set of decision rules and information on the current condition.

Vagueness is embedded in these two factors in this decision process. One type of vagueness lies in the information available to the driver. He or she does not know, for example, how long the yellow will last nor the exact current location. Thus, he or she interprets the available information in the form of perception, which may take the form of linguistic expressions rather than numerical expressions.

Another type of vagueness is the one embedded in the decision rules. The rules are not based on the rigid mathematical functions; rather they constitute a fuzzy inference system, consisting of a set of if-then rules; for example, if the vehicle is traveling at high speed and is very close to the intersection when the light turns yellow, then clear the intersection; or, if the vehicle is far from the intersection and traveling at a low speed when the light turns yellow, then stop. Given the input, the match between the input and the anticident of a rule determines the degree of truth of the application of the rule. The input is the perceived information discussed previously.

Anxious feelings occur when one must take one of the choices based on imprecise information and decision rules in a very short time, in this case, either stop or go. The differences among drivers' behaviors emerge from the perception of information and application of the rules. Precise numerical information of distance, for example, may not be helpful unless he or she has the decision rules that use it. How one interprets and perceives the given state is critical in this process. If the range of possible interpretation increases, one's anxiety level should increase. If, on the other hand, rules are rigid and the information is precise, then an external command can substitute the driver's decision and no anxiety will be present.

33.2.2. The Problem

The problem of this study is to develop a model that represents the anxiety that a driver feels at the onset of yellow light. The model should be capable of measuring the degree of anxiety along the approach. It should also be capable of evaluating the effect of improving the quality of information and rules in the driver decision support system. Further, it should be capable of explaining the differences among driver behaviors (for example, conservative versus aggressive drivers) based on the difference in the interpretation and application of the rules.

The model will be helpful in addressing several important issues related to driver decision and its implication to traffic engineering: one, the driving attitude of the elderly; two, the perception and decision patterns of impaired drivers, such as drivers under the influence of alcohol or drugs; three, the effect of in-vehicle information system. Under ITS (Intelligent Transportation Systems), it is conceivable that the signal's yellow indication is transmitted to the vehicle, and with the information on the vehicle's speed and location, the on-board computer advises the driver about the appropriate action.

33.3. Existing Approaches Dealing with Driver's Dilemma

Driver decision and behavior during the signal change interval is a classic topic in the traffic engineering literature. Various approaches and models have been proposed to analyze the appropriate signal change intervals and the driver's decision process. They are grouped into two categories here: deterministic approach and statistical approach.

33.3.1. Deterministic Approach

The signal change interval is provided to warn drivers of the impending red signal. When a driver approaches an intersection, there exists a point (Point A) on the approach roadway before which it is impossible for him or her to clear the intersection during the signal change interval. Similarly, there exists a point (Point B) beyond which it is not possible for the driver to stop. If Point B is farther from the intersection than Point A, and if he or she is in the region between these two points, he or she can neither clear nor stop during the signal change interval. This zone is called the dilemma zone. Conversely, if Point A is farther from the intersection than Point B, an area called the option zone, where both the clearing and stopping maneuvers are possible, exists between points B and A. The sizes of the dilemma zone and the option zone can be controlled by the signal change interval.

Gazis et al. [4] developed equations for calculating the "clearing distance (D_g)," the "stopping distance, (D_s)," and the signal change interval (t) which prevents the creation of the dilemma zone. D_g is the distance measured from the intersection within which one can safely clear the intersection, and D_s is the distance measured from the intersection beyond which one can safely stop before the intersection. They are:

$$D_g = Vd - (w + 1) + a(t - d)^2/2 + V(t - d) \tag{1}$$

$$D_s = V^2/2b \stackrel{\cdot}{+} Vd \tag{2}$$

where V = speed of the vehicle(ft/sec)
      d = driver perception/reaction time(sec)
      t = signal change interval(sec)
      b = deceleration rate(ft/sec^2)
      l = vehicle length(ft)
      a = acceleration rate(ft/sec^2)
      w = intersection width(ft)

When $D_g \geq D_s$, the dilemma zone is eliminated; thus the value of t is

$$t \geq d + \frac{w + 1}{V} + \frac{V}{2b} \tag{3}$$

where acceleration during clearing is assumed to be zero.

In this approach, it is assumed that all drivers have accurate information to make the decision, and also that all the drivers behave in the same manner by evaluating the current location with respect to D_g and D_s. Normally, this is not the case. The information available to the drivers is neither precise nor complete; further, not all drivers travel at the same values of V, w, l, b, and a. As a result, regardless how correct the signal change interval for the design vehicle and driver, drivers experience anxiety and their decisions are different.

33.3.2. Statistical Approach

Many researchers have examined driver anxiety based on field observations of the frequency of the drivers who stop from different distances on the approach upon seeing the yellow light. The zone on the road where the "stopping probability" is between 10 percent and 90 percent has been assumed as the dilemma zone by many researchers. The percent of drivers who stopped was interpreted as the probability that an individual driver would stop. Plots of the cumulative probability function were developed by many. Among them are Zegeer and Deen [16], Olson and Rothery [12], May [10], Williams [14], and Chang et al. [1].

The preceding approach has been expanded to model the relationship between the actions of stopping (or going) and the distance. The dependent variable is a binary probability value (1 if the vehicle stops and 0 if the vehicle goes) and the independent variable is the distance from the intersection. A typically assumed cumulative probability function is a cumulative normal function (probit model). We review the probit model application and discuss its merits and limitations using the presentation of Sheffi and Mahmassani [9].

The probit model expresses the probability of stopping as a function of drivers' perceived time to reach the stop line, T. Considering variation among the drivers in perception and reaction time, T is assumed as a random variable of the following form:

$$T = t + \psi \tag{4}$$

where t is the time taken for a car to reach the stop line at a constant speed, and ψ is a random variable reflecting the differences in perception and reaction among the drivers. It is assumed that ψ is normally distributed, $\psi: N(0, \sigma^2_\psi)$.

It is hypothesized that, if T is less than a critical value T_{cr}, then the driver would choose to proceed through the intersection. The value of T_{cr} is also assumed to vary with the driver due to many factors, such as driving experience. Thus, the value of T_{cr} can also be assumed to follow the normal distribution:

$$T_{cr} = t_{cr} + \varepsilon \tag{5}$$

where t_{cr} is the mean critical time and ε is the disturbance term that is normally distributed $\varepsilon: N(O, \sigma^2_\varepsilon)$.

The probability that a driver would stop is then given by:

$$Pr(Stop) = Pr[T_{cr} < T] \tag{6}$$

The fundamental assumption in this model is that both values of T_{cr} and T follow a normal distribution. The probability of stopping is expressed by the probability that the driver perceives the value of T to be greater than the value of T_{cr}. This is perhaps a valid assumption if the model is to represent the variation in the behavior of the population. In other words, it is valid under the following: while each individual knows the values of T_{cr} and T clearly, and decides either to go or to stop with no hesitation, different persons assume different values of T_{cr} and T, and their values are distributed normally among the population. As such, the model is useful to explain the variation of decisions for the population as a whole statistically.

If this model is used to infer the *state of mind of an individual*, however, it implies that each driver's decision process is random, and on encountering the same situation he or she may react differently in a *random* manner. This contradicts with the understanding that he or she knows the values of T_{cr} and T.

33.3.3. Discussion on the Existing Approaches to Driver Anxiety

Both approaches discussed attempt to capture the process that the driver compares the current state (either in the distance from the intersection or in the time before the signal turns red) with his or her threshold values of decision. The deterministic approach considers that the driver knows both the current condition and the threshold values clearly, and all drivers' knowledges are the same. The statistical approach, on the other hand, considers that each driver has a different understanding of the current values and the threshold values. In this respect, the latter approach is more realistic, and it attempts to account for the variation in driver behavior.

When an individual interprets a value that is vague, his or her perception can be represented as possibility instead of probability. The possibility distribution, in short, represents the distribution of values based on the notion of "can be," while probability distribution represents the value based on the frequency of random outcomes.

Many have proposed that possibility, instead of probability, is a more appropriate form to represent the individual's choice under uncertainty. Among them are Shackle [13], Cohen [2], and Klir [7]. If the possibility distribution is used to represent the uncertainty in the assumed values of T_{cr} and T, then the choice of going should be based on the *possibility* that T is greater than T_{cr}, and the outcome of "can clear" or "cannot clear" is expressed by *possibility*.

The possibilistic approach is suited for analyzing the process of subjective inference and reasoning. It is also suited to express the degree of anxiety during the decision. Anxiety is caused by the vagueness of information provided to the decision maker. Thus, the possibilistic approach allows to assess how specific engineering measures are effective in mitigating driver anxiety.

33.4. Basic Measures of Uncertainty: Possibility and Necessity Measures and Anxiety

33.4.1 Possibility and Necessity Measures

Given the imprecise and uncertain information, one's perception can vary depending on the attitude in interpretation. The extreme cases are the possibility-based interpretation and the necessity-based interpretation. Possibility-based interpretation accounts for all non-negative evidence and draws a conclusion, while the necessity-based interpretation accounts for only positive evidence that supports the truth. It can be said that these two represent optimistic and pessimistic interpretations, respectively.

In our problem, given the current condition (which is characterized by vague information), the driver's judgment that the current condition indicates stopping or clearing action can be represented by these two measures. Each parameter that determines the stopping or clearing distance in equations (1) and (2) is perceived fuzzy by the driver; in other words, the values of both D_s and D_g are perceived as fuzzy numbers and are represented by membership functions. The driver compares the current location with the fuzzy values of D_s and D_g. The comparison can be performed either in a possibilistic- or necessity-based manner; the former represents optimistic and the latter pessimistic manner.

The difference between these two measures for an action signifies the degree of uncertainty that the driver has for executing the action successfully. These two measures are related to the attitude of the driver (aggressive and conservative). For most persons, however, the degree of uncertainty of taking an action A is a value between $Nec(A)$ and $Poss(A)$. Explanation and discussion on the $Poss$ and Nec measures are found in many books on fuzzy sets. They include Dubois and Prade [3], Klir [7], Kosko [8], and Zimmerman [17].

33.4.2. Measure of Anxiety

The uncertainties explained previously cause anxiety in the mind of the decision maker. Yager [15] has proposed an equation that expresses the degree of anxiety when making a choice from a set of conflicting actions. The equation proposed by him is:

$$Ax = 1 - \int_0^1 \frac{1}{|A_\alpha|} d\alpha \qquad (7)$$

where Ax is the degree of anxiety given information x,

A is the set of alternative decisions,

$|A_\alpha|$ is the number of alternatives whose possibility or necessity measurs are greater than α,

$\int_0^1 \frac{1}{|A_\alpha|} d\alpha$ is called the tranquility measure. (Ax is 1 minus the tranquility measure.)

Ax is used to represent the degree of anxiety that a driver experiences.

In the case of a two-choice situation, stop or go, Yager's model reduces to:

$$Ax = 1 - \max(m_G, m_S) + \frac{1}{2} [\min (m_G, m_S)] \qquad (8)$$

where, m_G and m_S correspond to the possibility and (or) necessity measures of go and stop, as will be explained later.

Figure 33.1 shows a plot of the anxiety measure as a function of m_G and m_S. The anxiety measure is the highest when both measures, m_G and m_S, are equal to 0; and it is equal to 0 when one of the two measures equal 1 and the other 0. This shows that anxiety is the highest when the possibility (or necessity) measure of the two conflicting actions are both 0, indicating that neither action is possible (yet one has to be chosen). It is the lowest when only one action is supported fully.

33.5. Modeling of Driver Characteristics and Behavior

This section defines the decision pattern of aggressive and conservative drivers and computes possibility and necessity measures for stopping and going actions of these drivers. These two types of drivers are assumed to

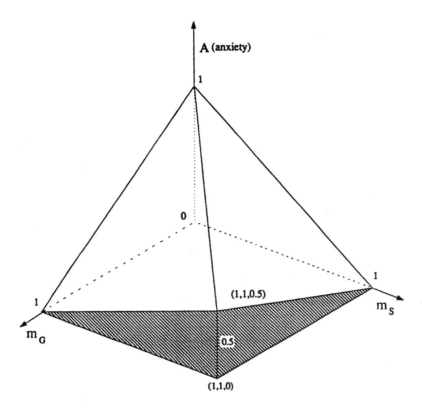

m_G : The possibility measure or the necessity measure for going

m_S : The possibility measure or the necessity measure for stopping

Figure 33.1   Measure of anxiety as a function of m_G and m_S.

define the range of behaviors of most drivers. These values are used to compute anxiety in the next section.

33.5.1. Definition of Aggressive and Conservative Drivers

An aggressive driver has the primary desire to reduce the travel time. Thus, his or her first choice is to go. He or she examines the possibility to go first at the onset of yellow. He or she stops only if it is impossible to clear. The decision rule of the aggressive driver is:

Go if possible; stop if necessary.

A conservative driver is safety conscious and resorts to a safe action. He or she goes only if it is impossible to stop. In other words, his or her first choice is to stop, and he or she will go only if it is necessary. The decision rule of the conservative driver is:

Stop if possible; go if necessary.

Between these two extreme types of drivers are some drivers who may act based on "go if possible and stop if possible."

33.5.2. Measures of Going and Stopping

Normally, a driver perceives information of the current speed, current location, and the current driving conditions as fuzzy quantities and applies these values to the general rules for stopping and going; and if the perceived current states match the antecedents of the rules completely, the corresponding action is undertaken. If the perceived states match the antecedents of the rules of both actions partially, anxiety is assumed to occur. Possibility and necessity measures are used to evaluate how the perceived states match the rules (for stopping and going).

The following notation is used to represent the possibility distribution of the current states: speed, $\pi(s)$; distance, $\pi(d)$; driving conditions, $\pi(z)$, where s is speed, d is distance, and z is an index of goodness of road/traffic conditions.

Possibility of going: The decision to go is based on the combination of the following criteria:

Criterion 1: The current speed is high.

Criterion 2: The current location is near the intersection (or distance is short).

Criterion 3: The current road/traffic condition index is high.

Given $\pi(s)$, $\pi(d)$ and $\pi(z)$, validity of each statement is evaluated by possibility measures.

For Criterion 1:

$$Poss(V_h) = Max\ Min\{\pi(s), \mu v_h(s)\} \qquad (9)$$

where v_h denotes the notion, "high speed," and $\mu v_h(s)$ denotes the membership grade of s in the fuzzy set of "high speed."

For Criterion 2:

$$Poss(D_s) = Max\ Min\{\pi(d), \mu D_s(d)\} \qquad (10)$$

where D_s denotes the notion, "short distance," and $\mu D_s(d)$ denotes the membership grade of d in the fuzzy set of "short distance."

For Criterion 3:

$$Poss(I_h) = Max\ Min\{\pi(z), \mu I_h(z)\} \qquad (11)$$

where I_h denotes the notion, "high index," and $\mu I_h(z)$ denotes the membership grade of z in the fuzzy set of "high index." A road/traffic index is introduced to account for all other environmental effects on driver decisions, such as road surface condition, traffic condition after the intersection, geometric design.

Going is possible only when all three criteria are satisfied; in other words, the possibilities that the current speed is high, *and* the current distance is small, *and* the current road/traffic condition index is high. Hence, the possibility of going under the current condition x can be computed as the minimum of the possibility measures of the three criteria:

$$Poss_x(Go) = Min\{Poss(v_h), Poss(D_s), Poss(I_h)\} \tag{12}$$

Possibility of stopping: The decision to stop is based on the following criteria:

Criterion 1: The current speed is low.

Criterion 2: The current distance is long.

Criterion 3: The current road/traffic index is low.

Given $\pi(s)$, $\pi(d)$ and $\pi(z)$, validity of each statement is evaluated by possibility measures, similar to the case explained previously.
Criterion 1:

$$Poss(V_l) = Max\ Min\{\pi(s), \mu V_l(s)\} \tag{13}$$

where V_1 denotes the notion, "low speed," and $\mu V_1(s)$ denotes the membership grade of s in the fuzzy set of "low speed."
Criterion 2:

$$Poss(D_l) = Max\ Min\{\pi(d), \mu D_l(d)\} \tag{14}$$

where D_1 denotes the notion, "long distance," and $\mu D_1(d)$ denotes the membership grade of d in the fuzzy set of "long distance."
Criterion 3:

$$Poss(I_l) = Max\ Min\{\pi(z), \mu I_l(z)\} \tag{15}$$

where I_1 denotes the notion, "low index," and $\mu I_1(z)$ denotes the membership grade of z in the fuzzy set of "low index."

Stopping is possible only when all three criteria are satisfied; in other words, the possibility that the current speed is low, *and* the current distance is long, *and* the possibility that the road/traffic condition index is low (not suitable for going). The possibility of stopping under the current condition x can be computed as a minimum of the possibility measure of the three criteria:

$$Poss_x(Stop) = Min\{Poss(V_l), Poss(D_l), Poss(I_l)\} \tag{16}$$

Necessity of going: The necessity of going is derived from the basic relationship between possibility and necessity measures:

$$Nec(Go) = 1 - Poss(Stop) \tag{17}$$

Using equation # (16), it can be shown that this is equivalent to:

$$Nec_x(Go) = Max\{Nec(V_h), Nec(D_s), Nec(I_h)\} \tag{18}$$

This expression means that going is necessary under the current condition x if the current speed is high, *or* the current distance is short, *or* the road/traffic condition index is high. The necessity to go is the maximum of all these necessity measures. In other words, if any one of these conditions is necessarily satisfied, one will decide to go.

Necessity of stopping: Similarly, the necessity of stopping is derived from the basic relationship between possibility and necessity measures as:

$$Nec(Stop) = 1 - Poss(Go) \tag{19}$$

It can be shown that this is equivalent to:

$$Nec_x(Stop) = Max\{Nec(V_l), Nec(D_l), Nec(I_l)\} \tag{20}$$

This shows that going is necessary under the current condition x only if any one of the three criteria is necessarily satisfied.

33.6. Anxiety and Influencing Factors

In this section, anxiety is expressed for aggressive and conservative drivers based on Yager's measure, and the factors that influence anxiety are discussed.

33.6.1. Anxiety for Aggressive and Conservative Drivers

The degree of anxiety is computed by introducing possibility and necessity measures developed in the previous section into equation # (8), separately for aggressive and conservative drivers.

The aggressive drivers utilize the rule of "go, if possible, and, stop, if necessary," hence, m_G and m_S in equation # (8) corresponds to $Poss_x(Go)$ and $Nec_x(Stop)$, respectively. Thus, the anxiety under the current condition x is calculated as:

$$Ax = 1 - Max[Poss_x(Go), Nec_x(Stop)] + \frac{1}{2} Min[Poss_x(Go), Nec_x(Stop)] \tag{21}$$

The conservative drivers utilize the rule of "stop, if possible, and, go, if necessary," hence, m_G and m_S in equation # (8) corresponds to $Poss_x(Stop)$ and $Nec_x(Go)$, respectively. Thus, anxiety under the current condition x is calculated as:

$$Ax = 1 - Max[Poss_x(Stop), Nec_x(Go)] + \frac{1}{2}Min[Poss_x(Stop), Nec_x(Go)] \quad (22)$$

These two types of drivers constitute the range of the driving population. For most drivers, anxiety should be computed for values of $Nec_x(Go)$ $\leq m_G \leq Poss_x(Go)$ and $Nec_x(Stop) \leq m_S \leq Poss_x(Stop)$ in equation # (8).

33.6.2. Effect of Perception on Anxiety

Vagueness in the perception of the parameters of the current condition x is represented by the shapes of the possibility distributions of the parameters $\pi(s)$, $\pi(d)$ and $\pi(z)$. Their shapes influence the values of $Poss_x(Go)$, $Poss_x(Stop)$, $Nec_x(Go)$, and $Nec_x(Stop)$.

The weakening of perception would result in possibility distributions with larger spread, and the sharpening of perception results in possibility distributions with smaller spread. For an aggressive driver, an increase in $Poss_x(Go)$ and, at the same time, a decrease in $Nec_x(Stop)$ in Eq(21) results in a lower degree of anxiety. Similarly, for a conservative driver, an increase in $Poss_x(Stop)$ and, at the same time, a decrease in $Nec_x(Go)$ results in a lower degree of anxiety. Consequently, under the weak perception, an aggressive driver may attempt to go from a distance too far from the intersection, or a conservative driver may attempt to stop from a point too close to the intersection, both with little feeling of anxiety. This may help explain the effects of impaired recognition on driving behavior, for example, driving under the influence of alcohol and drugs.

33.6.3. Effect of Driving Experience on Anxiety

As a driver travels on the same road and through the same intersection regularly, he or she tends to get an increasingly clear picture of which location is "too far" and which location is "too close" or what speed is "too high" and what speed is "too low" for the intersection. Hence, the experience sharpens his or her perception. This explains why drivers with high familiarity to the road and the intersection experience less anxiety than unfamiliar drivers. The reduction in anxiety brings about more uniformity among the behavior of the drivers.

33.7. Analysis Based on Field Data

In order to understand how much anxiety a driver experiences at the onset of a yellow light, a series of field surveys were conducted at an intersection in New Castle County, Delaware. The purpose of this survey was to measure the drivers' anxiety only through the observation of the final actions (stopping or going). Based on the data, necessity measures of stopping and going were derived and the corresponding possibility measures were calculated. Using these observed values, anxiety and the zone of anxiety were identified along the approach.

33.7.1. Survey Procedure

The selected intersection is located on a level terrain, and it has a good visibility and sufficient shoulder width. The speed limit on the approach roadway is 50 mph (=80 km/hr). The duration of yellow is 4 seconds. A video camera was placed on a pedestrian overpass at the intersection to record the following data at each instant of yellow indication:

- the location of the last vehicle that cleared the intersection,
- the location of the first vehicle that stopped at the intersection.

A total of 22 hours of survey were conducted and 1120 valid data points were collected. Most vehicles were approaching near the 50 mph (=80 km/hr) limit before the signal changes. Each data point represents evidence that is to be used as the basis for developing necessity measures.

33.7.2. Analysis

The data were used to perform the following:

- derivation of necessity measures and possibility measures for stopping and going,
- computation of the degree of anxiety,
- identification of the zone of anxiety.

It was assumed that the sampled drivers behaved rationally and consistently; in other words, if a driver decided to stop from a location when he or she saw the signal change, he or she would stop from any location farther than that location. Similarly, if he or she decided to go from a location when he or she saw the yellow signal, he or she would go from any location nearer than that location. Thus, the possibility and necessity measures were either monotonically increasing or decreasing function along the approach.

Computation of necessity measures of stopping and going: Necessity measures of stopping and going for the population are obtained from the proportion of data that supports the action *necessarily*. Thus, the necessity measure of stopping under a given condition x is an increasing function with respect to the distance from the intersection. $Nec_{300'} (Stop)$, for example, is the proportion of drivers who stopped at 300' (=91 m) or closer. Similarly, the necessity to go from 300' (=91 m), $Nec_{300'} (Go)$, is given by the proportion of drivers who went from 300' (=91 m) or farther. The necessity measures for stopping and going are plotted along the approach in Figures 33.2 and 33.3. *Nec(Stop)* is 1 at a location very far from the intersection, and it gradually decreases as the location becomes closer to the intersection. Conversely, the *Nec(Go)* is 1 near the intersection and decreases with increasing distance from the intersection.

Derivation of possibility measures of stopping and going: Given the necessity measures, the possibility measures for going and stopping are computed based on the relationship between possibility and necessity measures: $Poss_x(Go) = 1 - Nec_x(Stop)$; $Poss_x(Stop) = 1 - Nec_x(Go)$; for example, the possibilities of going and stopping from 300' (=91 m) are: $Poss_{300'}(Go) = 1 - Nec_{300'}(Stop)$, and $Poss_{300'}(Stop) = 1 - Nec_{300'}(Go)$. The possibility measures that are computed based on these relationships are also shown in Figure 33.2.

33.7.3. Degree of Anxiety

Using the possibility and necessity measures obtained previously, we compute the degree of anxiety that the aggressive and conservative drivers would experience according to equations # (21) and (22), respectively. The degrees of anxiety for these two types of drivers are shown in Figures 33.4 and 33.5. It is seen that in both cases the highest degree of anxiety occurs at the location where the measures of the two conflicting choices are equal; in other words, the intersection of *Poss(Go)* and *Nec(Stop)* for aggressive drivers and the intersection of *Poss(Stop)* and *Nec(Go)* for

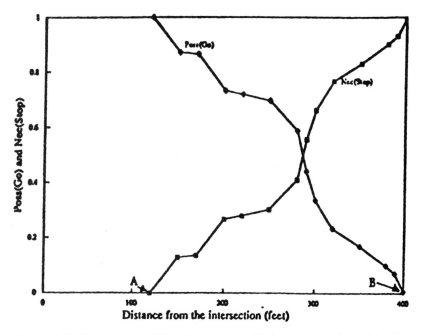

Figure 33.2 Distributions of Nec(Stop) and Poss(Go): Aggressive drivers' decision measures.

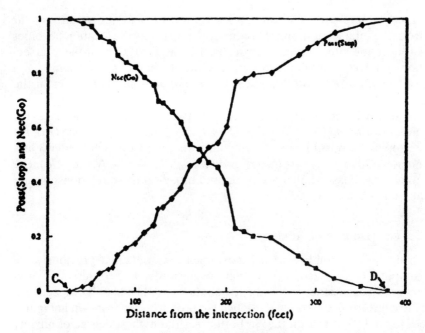

Figure 33.3 Distributions of Nec(Go) and Poss(Stop): Conservative drivers' decision measures.

conservative drivers. This confirms the notion that when the two conflicting choices are equally supported by the perception, one feels the maximum anxiety.

The aggressive and conservative drivers are two extreme types of drivers. Most drivers fall between these types, and their values of m_G and m_S in Eq(8) are perhaps between the Possibility and Necessity measures, that is, $Nec(Go) < m_G < Poss(Go)$, and $Nec(Stop) < m_S < Poss(Stop)$. To test the anxiety measures of this type of a driver, the values of m_G and m_S are taken as the middle values of their respective ranges; in other words, the assumed values are:

$$m(Go) = 0.5 \times (Nec(Go) + Poss(Go)),$$

$$m(Stop) = 0.5 \times (Nec(Stop) + Poss(Stop)).$$

The distributions of $m(Go)$ and $m(Stop)$ for this driver are derived using the values obtained in Figures 33.2 and 33.3, and they are shown in Figure 33.6. The corresponding anxiety measure is calculated by the following equation and shown in Figure 33.6.

$$Ax = 1 - Max[m(Go), m(Stop)] + \frac{1}{2} Min[m(Go), m(Stop)] \qquad (23)$$

When this anxiety measure is compared with those in Figure 33.2, the anxiety measure of Figure 33.7, is located between those of the aggres-

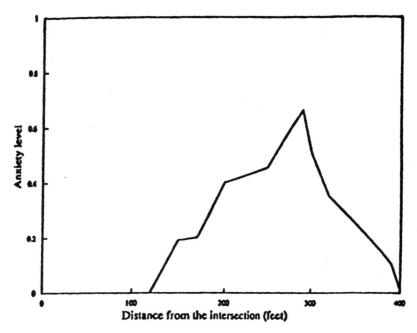

Figure 33.4   Anxiety level of aggressive drivers along the approach roadway.

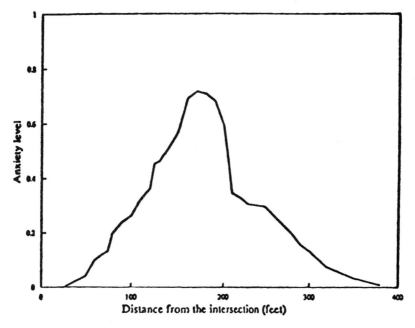

Figure 33.5   Anxiety level of conservative drivers along the approach roadway.

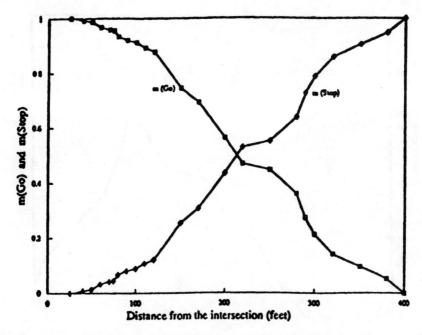

Figure 33.6   Distribution of m(Go) and m(Stop) along the approach roadway.

sive and conservative drivers. This indicates that the two extreme types of drivers help define the range of drivers' decision patterns.

33.7.4. Zone of Anxiety

The zones of anxiety for the aggressive and conservative drivers can now be identified in Figure 33.2. It is seen that the width of the anxiety zone for the two types of drivers are approximately same. But the location of the anxiety zone and the maximum anxiety for the conservative drivers occur closer to the intersection than the case for the aggressive drivers.

This can be explained by the following. The conservative driver's first choice is to stop. Therefore, he or she decides to stop at a location farther from the intersection with no hesitation, and decides to go only when he or she is very close to the intersection. Thus, his or her anxiety increases at a location closer to the intersection than that of the aggressive driver.

The previous research has identified the zone of driver indecision or dilemma based only on the observed data on the frequency of stopping; for example, the area where the probability of stopping is between 0.1 and 0.9. Our study suggests that not only the frequency of stopping but also the frequency of going must be counted to determine the area of dilemma.

The zone between A and B of Figure 33.2 corresponds to the area of indecision or dilemma according to the dilemma zone by the previous studies. Based on our analysis, however, this area corresponds to the anx-

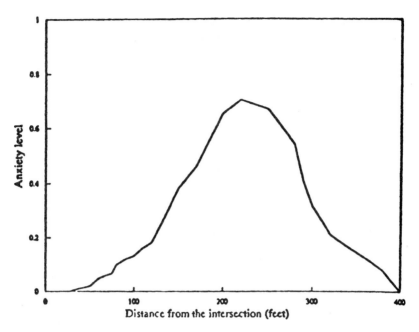

Figure 33.7 Anxiety level of drivers with m(Go) and m(Stop).

iety zone of the aggressive drivers. The anxiety of conservative drivers occurs in the area where both the Poss(Stop) and Nec(Go) are greater than 0 (the area between C and D of Figure 33.3). Hence, the zone of anxiety is actually C to B, which is greater than what was previously considered. This is because the anxiety of the drivers who decided to go has not been counted in defining the dilemma in the previous studies.

33.8. Framework for a Driver Decision-Aid System during Signal Change Interval

The zone of anxiety presents a potentially dangerous situation to a driver. Within this zone he or she is apt to make a decision that is not entirely objective. The state of anxiety may force him or her to behave in an inconsistent manner. A system to aid the driver's decision making would contribute significantly toward reducing the effects of anxiety and improving safety. In order to develop such a system and to ensure its effectiveness, certain requirements are to be satisfied. The most important characteristics of such a system are:

- Ability to gather information and to provide decisions very quickly.
- Ability to make decision consistent with the behavioral pattern of each driver.
- Ability to learn and update the decision-making pattern.

To meet these basic requirements, we propose a system that is supported by an on-board data-gathering device and a driver alert command delivery. The major elements of the system are:

- A device that detects the onset of an impending yellow signal phase.

- An on-board computer that houses the decision-aid system. This computer receives information from the various systems within the automobile and also from the previous device.

- A device that can alert the driver and deliver appropriate commands effectively.

33.8.1. Model Structure

A system is proposed that observes and learns the decision pattern of a driver and is properly "tuned" to the driver and can be installed on a vehicle to aid the driver. The system can be structured as a neural network with one input layer of neurons, one hidden layer, and one output layer. The network receives information on the vehicle dynamics, the driver and the driving conditions to the input layer, and issues appropriate advice to the driver according to the inferences that were developed by past experience. The current conditions and the past decision patterns are matched in the hidden layer.

The decision on the action is dependent upon the values of two measures, $\Pi(G)$ and $N(S)$. When one of these measures is much larger than the other, the choice is clear. It is when the values of these two measures have approximately the same value that confusion arises. Figure 33.8 shows the four zones that define appropriate actions for different values of $\Pi(G)$ and $N(S)$.

The four decision zones shown in the figure represent four clusters of points on the $\Pi(G) - N(S)$ plain. The boundaries of these four clusters vary from driver to driver. Hence, in order to model the behavior of a driver, the network must learn the driver's decision pattern in terms of the regions in Figure 33.8.

33.8.2. Principle of Learning

In the learning phase, the network forms the four clusters based on the behavior of the driver; in other words, the input vectors are grouped based on the actual event of stop or go. The pattern and the size of the clusters will change as more data are input. The input data are the travel speed, the distance to the intersection, and road condition, and they are mapped to the two measures $\Pi(G)$ and $N(S)$:

$$I_i = [\Pi_i(G), N_i(S)]. \tag{24}$$

where I_i is the ith data.

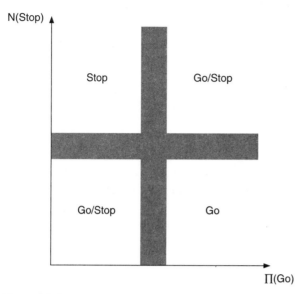

Figure 33.8 The four decision zones.

If the desired conclusion for this ith input is to "Go," then the size of the cluster characterizing "Go" is adjusted so as to include this input vector. Similarly, if another input vector I_j is desired to result in "Stop," the cluster characterizing "Stop" is adjusted to include I_j. The cluster is characterized by the cluster center and the distance to the farthest point in the cluster.

If the cluster center after n learning steps is (X_c, Y_c) and a new vector $(\Pi_{n+1}(G), N_{n+1}(S))$ is to be incorporated and the cluster modified, the new cluster center is computed using:

$$\acute{X}_c = \frac{nX_c + \Pi_{n+1}(G)}{n+1} \tag{25}$$

$$\acute{Y}_c = \frac{nY_c + N_{n+1}(S)}{n+1} \tag{26}$$

where (X_c, Y_c) is the cluster center prior to modification,
(X_c', Y_c') is the cluster center after modification,
$(\Pi_{n+1}(G), N_{ni+1}(S))$ is the $n+1$st input vector, and
n is the number of learning steps prior to modification.

If the input vectors during the learning phase cover a significant portion of the entire array of values of $\Pi(G)$ and $N(S)$, and there exists fairly distinct separations between stop and go, then learning is said to be completed.

33.8.3. The Application Phase

Once the level of learning is deemed adequate, the system makes decisions for the current input. The input layer receives the information regarding the current conditions (travel speed, distance to the intersection, and road condition) and the values of $\Pi(G)$ and $N(S)$. The system determines the cluster to which the vector representing the given conditions belongs by the following criteria:

1. The closeness of the cluster center to the current condition. It is computed as a function of the distance between the cluster center and the point representing the current condition.
2. The size of the cluster. It is expressed as a function of the distance between the cluster center and the farthest point in the cluster.

The distance between the vector (X_i, Y_i) and the cluster center (X_c, Y_c) is given by:

$$D_c = [(X_i - X_c)^2 + (Y_i - Y_c)^2)]^{1/2} \qquad (27)$$

If the size of the cluster is S_c, the parameter λ_c is given by:

$$\lambda_c = \frac{S_c}{D_c} \qquad (28)$$

Thus, for the current condition, depending on the value of λ_c, one of the following commands is issued.

The values of $\Pi(G)$ and $N(S)$ are computed for the input conditions of the travel speed, the distance from the intersection, and the driving conditions (congestion level). Given the computed values of $\Pi(G)$ and $N(S)$, the system responds in one of the following ways to aid the driver:

1. "You can definitely go."
2. "You can go if you speed up."
3. "You should not try to go."
4. "You must stop."

These four commands are the linguistic interpretations of the four decision zones discussed earlier.

The information on the travelling speed can be obtained easily. The change of signal to yellow may be detected by an electronic "eye" attached to the car, triggered possibly by the microwave from the signal. The distance from the car to the intersection can be determined through other electronic means. The congestion on the road can be determined in three ways: by the external congestion level information transmitted from the signal detectors, by a device on the vehicle that measures distance to the vehicle in front and rear, and by the general driving speed in relation to the design speed.

The system will emulate the past behavior of the driver; hence, once trained, it can aid a driver when he or she is in the condition of feeling weak perception and slow decision making, for example, at the time of fatigue. There are various other features in an automobile with which such a system can be utilized very effectively, for example, the braking mechanism for a collision avoidance system, in which the automobile maneuvering can be made compatible to the driver's attitude. The transmission gear change mechanism is another possibility. A system that can learn the behavioral patterns of the driver that operates the vehicle is a step toward the realization of the automobile that adjusts itself to the driver rather than the driver adjusting to the vehicle.

33.9. Conclusion

The driver's decision process during the signal change interval is modelled. The study treats the driver's decision mechanism as a fuzzy inference process, an interaction of imprecise information and vague inference rules. Uncertainty associated with the interpretation of information and feasibility of alternative actions are measured by possibility and necessity. The decision process is analyzed for two extreme types of drivers, conservative and aggressive. Yager's measure of anxiety is proposed to measure the drivers' anxiety.

A series of field surveys were conducted to collect data on the driver decision patterns. Applying the data to the model, we identified the degrees of anxiety and the zones of anxiety for the two types of drivers. The conservative drivers were found to experience anxiety closer to the intersection than the aggressive drivers. The zone of anxiety was found to be greater than what was previously considered, when the anxiety experienced by drivers who went as well as those who stopped were taken into account.

The models can be useful in understanding the effect of information on the decision process and behavior, and in evaluating the effectiveness of improving information and communications in reducing driver's anxiety. The study underscores the notion that regardless of how correct the timing of the yellow phase from the established standard standpoint, drivers still experience anxiety during signal change intervals. A possible way to alleviate the anxiety is by providing commands to the driver externally that are adjusted to individual driver's decision tendency. An idea of such a driver-aid system is also presented.

33.10. References

[1] Chang, M.S., et al. Timing Traffic Signal Change Intervals based on Driver Behavior. The National Research Council, Transportation Research Record 1027. pp. 20–30. Washington, D.C.: 1985.

[2] Cohen, L.J. *The Implications of Induction.* London: 1970.

[3] Dubois, D., and H. Prade. "Fuzzy Sets and Systems: Theory and Applications." *Mathematics in Science and Engineering,* Vol. 144. 1980.

[4] Gazis, D.C., et al. "The Problem of the Amber Signal Light in Traffic Flow." *Operations Research,* Vol. 8 (1960), pp. 112–132.

[5] Kikuchi, S., and J. Riegner. A Methodology to Analyze the Driver Decision Environment at a Signal Change Interval: Application of Fuzzy Set Theory. *Transportation Research Record,* No. 1368, pp. 49–71. 1993.

[6] Kikuchi, S., et al. Modeling of Driver Anxiety During Signal Change Intervals. *Transportation Research Record,* No. 1399. pp. 27–35. 1993.

[7] Klir, G.J., and T.A. Folger. *Fuzzy Sets, Uncertainty and Information.* Englewood Cliffs: Prentice Hall, 1988.

[8] Kosko, B. *Neural Networks and Fuzzy Systems.* Englewood Cliffs: Prentice Hall, 1991.

[9] Mahmassani, H.S. A Probit Model of Driver Behavior at High-Speed Isolated Signalized Intersections, CTS. Working Paper No. 79-10. MIT, 1979.

[10] May, A. A Study of Clearance Interval at Traffic Signals. University of California at Berkeley. ITTE Special Report. Berkeley: 1967.

[11] Miller, A.J. "Nine Estimators of Gap Acceptance Parameters," in Traffic Flow and Transportation." ed. G.F. Newell. *Proceedings, 5th International Symposium on the Theory of Traffic Flow and Transportation.* New York: American Elsevier, 1972.

[12] Olson, P.L., and R.W. Rothery. *Driver Response to Amber Phase of Traffic Signals.* Highway Research Board Bulletin No. 330. pp. 40–51. 1962.

[13] Shackle, G.L.S. *Decision, Order, and Time in Human Affairs.* Cambridge: Cambridge University Press, 1969.

[14] Williams, W.L. *Driver Behavior During the Yellow Interval.* National Research Council, Transportation Research Record 644. pp. 75–78. Washington, D.C.: 1977.

[15] Yager, R.R. "Measuring Tranquility and Anxiety in Decision-Making: An Application of Fuzzy Sets." *International Journal of General Systems,* Vol. 8 (1982), pp. 139–146.

[16] Zegeer, C., and R.C. Deen. "Green Extension Systems at High-Speed Intersections." *ITE Journal* (1978), pp. 19–23.

[17] Zimmerman, H.J. *Fuzzy Set Theory and its Applications.* Boston: Kluwer Academic Press, 1990.

34 An Interactive GDSS for Consensus Reaching Using Fuzzy Logic with Linguistic Quantifiers

Janusz Kacprzyk, Sławomir Zadrożny
Systems Research Institute, Polish Academy of Sciences

Mario Fedrizzi
University of Trento

ABSTRACT: We present an interactive user-friendly group decision support system (GDSS) for consensus reaching in a group of individuals (experts, decision makers, and so on) who present their testimonies (opinions) as individual fuzzy preference relations. Initially, these opinions are usually quite different; the group is far from consensus. Then, a moderator supervising the session tries to make the individuals change their testimonies by, for example, rational argument, bargaining, and so on to eventually get closer to consensus. For gauging and monitoring the process, Kacprzyk's (1987) and Kacprzyk and Fedrizzi's (1986, 1988, 1989) "soft" degrees (measures) of consensus are used, which determine to what degree, for instance, "most of the individuals agree as to almost all of the relevant options." A fuzzy logic-based calculus of linguistically quantified propositions is employed.

34.1. Introduction

Since today virtually all real-life problems concern diverse aspects and involve different actors with their diverse, often conflicting, value systems, a group decision-making (DM) framework may be appropriate and useful. A group may consist of individuals and some subgroups (e.g., institutions, agencies, departments,) if only they can be viewed uniform as to some aspect in question.

Group DM problems are difficult, and some group decision support systems (GDSS) can be useful; such GDSSs are widely advocated, developed, and employed (cf. DeSanctis and Gallupe, 1985; Gray, 1987 or Huber, 1984).

In this chapter we discuss a GDSS, in part for supporting consensus reaching which is a crucial part of group DM; the whole GDSS covers many more aspects of group DM, as we share a popular view (cf. Huber, 1984) that the greater the range of tasks supported by a GDSS, the more chance that it will be used.

The basic framework is: we have a set of *individuals* (experts, decision makers) who present their opinions (testimonies) concerning an issue in question, and a *moderator,* who is responsible for the session with the individuals. The individuals present their testimonies, possibly different to a large extent; that is, the group may be far from consensus (unanimous agreement, as traditionally meant). Then, the moderator—via some exchange of information, rational argument, bargaining—tries to persuade the individuals to change their opinions. If they are rationally committed to consensus, this usually occurs, and the group gets closer to consensus. This is continued until the group gets sufficiently close to consensus.

Clearly, if the number of individuals is high enough and the form of their opinions is complex enough, then it may be difficult for the moderator to assess how close to consensus the group is; hence, to efficiently run the session. Thus, he or she needs a *degree of consensus,* as well as some effective communication means with the system and individuals, both being user friendly and human consistent. This is attained, first, by defining a "soft" degree of consensus-using fuzzy logic with linguistic quantifiers, and, second, by allowing elements of natural language, computer graphics, interactive mode, and so on for communication.

We have therefore a set of options $S = \{s_1, \ldots, s_n\}$, and m individuals. The individual fuzzy preference relation of individual k is R_k such that its membership function's value $\mu_{R_k}(s_i,s_j) \in [0,1]$ yields the strength of preference of option s_i over option s_j as felt by individual k.

For assessing the similarity of individual fuzzy preference relations, that is, the closeness to consensus, we use Kacprzyk and Fedrizzi's (1986, 1988, 1989) new degrees of consensus meant to be the degree to which, for example, "most of the individuals agree as to their preferences concerning almost all of the relevant options"; "most" and "almost all" may be replaced by any suitable linguistic quantifier. This degree of consensus takes on its values in [0,1], from 0 for a complete lack of consensus (dissensus) to 1 for full consensus, through all intermediate values. These new degrees of consensus are derived and manipulated using Zadeh's (1983) fuzzy logic-based calculus of linguistically quantified propositions.

Recently, Fedrizzi, Kacprzyk, and Nurmi (1993) proposed the use of Yager's (1988) OWA operators. These tools and techniques are implemented in a PC-based GDSS.

34.2. Linguistically Quantified Propositions

A linguistically quantified proposition, for example "most experts are convinced," is generally written as "Qy's are F" where Q is a linguistic quantifier (e.g., most), $Y = \{y\}$ is a set of objects (e.g., experts), and F is a property (e.g., convinced). Importance B may also be introduced yielding "QBy's are F," e.g., "most (Q) of the important (B) experts (y's) are convinced (F)."

The problem is to find truth (Qy's are F) or truth (QBy's are F), respectively, knowing truth (y is F), $\forall\ y \in Y$ which is done here using Zadeh's (1983) fuzzy logic-based calculus of linguistically quantified propositions.

Property F and importance B are fuzzy sets in Y, and a (proportional, nondecreasing) linguistic quantifier Q is assumed to be a fuzzy set in $[0,1]$ as:

$$\mu_Q(x) = \begin{cases} 1 & \text{for } x \geq 0.8 \\ 2x - 0.6 & \text{for } 0.3 < x < 0.8 \\ 0 & \text{for } x \leq 0.3 \end{cases} \tag{1}$$

Then, due to Zadeh (1983):

$$\text{truth}(Qy\text{'s are } F) = \mu_Q\left[\frac{1}{n}\sum_{i=1}^{n}\mu_F(y_i)\right] \tag{2}$$

$$\text{truth}(QBy\text{'s are } F) = \mu_Q\left[\sum_{i=1}^{n}(\mu_B(y_i)\wedge\mu_F(y_i))\bigg/\sum_{i=1}^{n}\mu_B(y_i)\right] \tag{3}$$

34.3. A "Soft" Degree of Consensus

The new "soft" degree of consensus—proposed in Kacprzyk (1987), and then advanced in Kacprzyk and Fedrizzi (1986, 1988, 1989)—meant to overcome some "rigidness" of conventional degrees of consensus in which full consensus (=1) occurs only when "all the individuals agree as to all the issues." This may often be counterintuitive, hence that new degree can be 1, standing for full consensus, when, say, "most of the individuals agree as to almost all (of the relevant) issues."

This degree of consensus is derived sequentially. We start with the degree of strict agreement between individuals k_1 and k_2 as to their preferences between options s_i and s_j:

$$v_{ij}(k_1,k_2) = \begin{cases} 1 & \text{if } r_{ij}^{k_1} = r_{ij}^{k_2} \\ 0 & \text{otherwise} \end{cases} \tag{4}$$

where $k_1 = 1,\ldots,m-1; k_2 = k_1 + 1,\ldots,m; i = 1,\ldots,n-1; j = i+1,\ldots,n.$

Relevance of a pair of options is defined as $b_{ij}^B = 1/2[\mu_B(s_i) + \mu_B(s_j)]$, and similarly the importance of a pair of individuals, b_{k_1,k_2}^I.

The degree of agreement between individuals k_1 and k_2 as to their preferences between all the relevant pairs of options is:

$$v_B(k_1,k_2) = \sum_{i=1}^{n-1}\sum_{j=i+1}^{n}[v_{ij}(k_1,k_2)\wedge b_{ij}^B] / \sum_{i=1}^{n-1}\sum_{j=i+1}^{n} b_{ij}^B \qquad (5)$$

and then the degree of agreement between individuals k_1 and k_2 as to their preferences between Q_1 relevant pairs of options is:

$$v_{Q_1}^B(k_1,k_2) = \mu_{Q_1}[v_B(k_1,k_2)] \qquad (6)$$

while the degree of agreement of all the pairs of individuals as to their preferences between Q_1 relevant pairs of options is:

$$v_{Q_1}^{I,B} = \frac{2}{m(m-1)}\left[\frac{\sum_{k_1=1}^{m-1}\sum_{k_2=k_1+1}^{m}[v_{Q_1}^B(k_1,k_2)\wedge b_{k_1,k_2}^I]}{\sum_{k_1=1}^{m-1}\sum_{k_2=k_1+1}^{m} b_{k_1,k_2}^I}\right] \qquad (7)$$

and, finally, the degree of agreement of Q_2 pairs of individuals as to their preferences between Q_1 relevant pairs of options, called the *degree of $Q_2/Q_1/I/B$ – consensus*, is:

$$\mathrm{con}(Q_1,Q_2,I,B) = \mu_{Q_2}(v_{Q_1}^{I,B}) \qquad (8)$$

Since the strict agreement (4) may be viewed too rigid, we can use the degree of sufficient agreement (at least to a degree $T \in [0, 1]$), or even explicitly the strength of agreement, obtaining some additional degrees of consensus (cf. Kacprzyk, 1987 or Kacprzyk and Fedrizzi, 1986, 1988, 1989).

One can also define similarly degrees of consensus using Yager's (1988) OWA (ordered weighted averaging) operators—cf. Fedrizzi, Kacprzyk and Nurmi (1993).

34.4. An Interactive GDSS for Consensus Reaching

34.4.1 The Structure of the System

The structure of the GDSS proposed is portrayed in Figure 34.1. The *Data Elicitation Module* elicits from the moderator and the individuals data needed as, for example, individual fuzzy preference relations, relevance of options, fuzzy linguistic quantifiers, and so on. The *Managing Module* is an "operating system" for decoding the moderator's commands, the individuals' responses, and so on to: (1) control the data elicitation mode, (2) set appropriate parameters and types of algorithms, and (3) activate appropriate reporting facilities, for example, the display of the value of a consensus measure or of some "troublesome" options or individuals. The *Parameter Setup Module* determines necessary parameters and their values due to the moderator's commands decoded by the Managing Module.

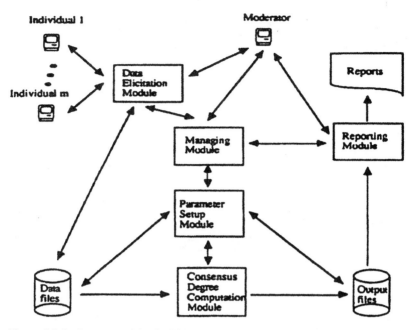

Figure 34.1   Structure of the GDSS for consensus reaching.

The Consensus Degree Computation Module calculates the value of a consensus degree and provides some additional information. The Reporting Module provides various reporting facilities such as display of the value of a degree of consensus and its temporal evolution, "troublesome" options and individuals, "history" of changes and updates, and more.

```
                          MEDIATOR
                         MAIN MENU
Do you want to:
       1        PREPARE DATA (PREFERENCE MATRICES)

       2        SET PROGRAM PARAMETERS

       3        DIAGNOSE GROUP'S PREFERENCES

       4        ANALYZE GROUP'S STRUCTURE

       5        DISPLAY INDIVIDUAL AND GROUP CHOICE

       6        GENERATE REPORT

       7        GET HELP

       8        QUIT THE SYSTEM

Press a key with a number of suitable item from the list
```

Figure 34.2   Main menu.

```
                          MEDIATOR
                    DATA PREPARING MENU
Do you want to:

      1       save data to a disk file

      2       restore data from the disk file

      3       enter/examine/correct data from the keyboard

      4       correct particular expert's preference matrix

      5       get help

      6       go back to the main menu


  Press a key with a number of suitable item from the list
```

Figure 34.3 Data Preparation menu.

34.4.2. Brief Description of Running the System

The system is menu-driven. The system's operation is governed by the Main Menu, shown in Figure 34.2, meant for the moderator for initializing, running, and quitting the session. The *Prepare Data* (*Preference Matrices*) option activates the *Data Preparation Menu* shown in Figure 34.3. The fuzzy preference matrices (relations) of the particular individuals are introduced as in Figure 34.4. The membership function values for fuzzy preference relations may be not only numbers from [0,1] but also linguistic values.

The *Set Parameters* option is quite complex. It should be chosen in the beginning of each session, and less frequently during it, to consecutively

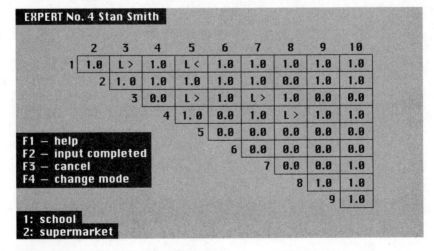

Figure 34.4 Preference matrix filling screen.

define the problem's parameters: name of the problem, number of individuals and options, importance coefficients of the particular options, and so on. The next group of parameters is input in a different way. First, by pressing keys F3 and F4 we define the fuzzy quantifiers Q_1 and Q_2, given by (1), by specifying two numbers by moving the cursor from 0 to 1 along the x-axis and stopping it at an appropriate point (value), and similarly for other parameters (cf. Figure 34.5).

Let us now present an example of a consensus-reaching session concerning the choice of an investment option in a small community.

Example 3: There are four options: school, movie theater, shopping center, and swimming pool. There are ten individuals who represent both the local and upper-level authorities, social and political organizations, some informal groups, a "man-in-the-street," and so on. Their (initial) individual fuzzy preference relations are given in Fedrizzi, Kacprzyk, and Zadrożny (1988); and to quote two:

$$R_1 = \begin{bmatrix} - & 0.9 & 0.9 & 1.0 \\ & - & 0.8 & 0.7 \\ & & - & 0.7 \\ & & & - \end{bmatrix} \cdots R_{10} = \begin{bmatrix} - & 1.0 & 0.6 & 1.0 \\ & - & 0.0 & 0.7 \\ & & - & 1.0 \\ & & & - \end{bmatrix}$$

and Q_1 and Q_2 are "most" given by (1). First, without any interaction with the individuals, we obtain $con(.) = 0.8069$. If, say, we diminish the importance of the shopping center, we obtain $con(.) = 0.934$, and so on, and these values can then be increased during the session to $con(.) = 1.0$ (cf. Fedrizzi, Kacprzyk and Zadrożny, 1988).

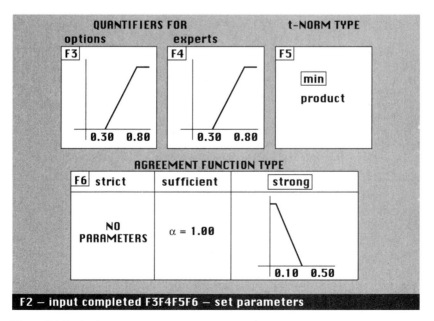

Figure 34.5   Setting parameters screen.

34.5. Conclusion

We sketched a GDSS for consensus reaching based on a "soft" human-consistent degree of consensus, and fuzzy logic with linguistic quantifiers. Some advanced tools for the clustering of preference profiles, specification of group choice, group member's and/or options' "contributions" to consensus, and more were also added in Fedrizzi, Kacprzyk, Owsínski and Zadrożny (1994).

34.6. References

[1] DeGroot, M.M., "Reaching a Consensus." *Journal American Statistical Association,* Vol. 69 (1974), pp. 118–121.

[2] DeSanctis, G., and B. Gallupe. "Group Decision Support Systems: A New Frontier." *Data Base* (1985), pp. 3–10.

[3] Fedrizzi, M., et al. "Consensus Degrees under Fuzzy Majorities and Fuzzy Preferences using OWA (Ordered Weight Average) Operators." *Control and Cybernetics,* Vol. 22 (1993), pp. 71–80.

[4] Fedrizzi, M., et al. "Consensus Reaching via a GDSS with Fuzzy Majority and Clustering of Preference Profiles." *Annals of Operational Research,* Vol. 51 (1994), pp. 127–139.

[5] French, S. "Consensus of Opinion." *European Journal of Operational Research,* Vol. 27 (1981), pp. 332–340.

[6] Gray, P. "Group Decision Support Systems." *Decision Support Systems,* Vol. 3 (1987), pp. 233–242.

[7] Huber, G.P. "Issues in the Design of Group Decision Support Systems." *MIS Quarterly,* Vol. 8 (1984), pp. 195–204.

[8] Kacprzyk, J. "Some Commonsense Solution Concepts in Group Decision-Making via Fuzzy Linguistic Quantifiers," in *Management Decision Support Systems using Fuzzy Sets and Possibility Theory.* eds. J. Kacprzyk and R.R. Yager. pp. 125–135. Cologne: 1985.

[9] ———. "Group Decision-Making with a Fuzzy Majority via Linguistic Quantifiers: Part I: A Consensory-like Pooling; Part II: A Competitive-like Pooling." *Cybernetics and Systems: An International Journal,* Vol. 16 (1985), pp. 119–129; pp. 131–144.

[10] ———. "Group Decision-Making with a Fuzzy Linguistic Majority." *Fuzzy Sets and Systems,* Vol. 18 (1986), pp. 105–118.

[11] ———. "On Some Fuzzy Cores and Soft Consensus Measures in Group Decision Making," in *The Analysis of Fuzzy Information.* ed. J.C. Bezdek. Vol. 2. pp. 119–130. Boca Raton: CRC Press, 1987.

[12] Kacprzyk, J., and M. Fedrizzi. "Soft Consensus Measures for Monitoring Real Consensus-Reaching Processes under Fuzzy Preferences." *Control and Cybernetics,* Vol. 15 (2986), pp. 309–323.

Exploiting Information

PART 2
Designing and Optimizing

GUIDING NOTE

Design is a field that has been very much affected by the advent of computers. Computer-aided design methods, very sophisticated ones, have been used in the industry. Typical of design is the existence of numerous design parameters, which at the beginning of the design process are not yet chosen and thus are ill known. An ill-known parameter can be represented by a fuzzy number and since the parameters are controllable (they are the designer's choice), membership functions represent preference profiles. Engineering design seems to be the field where fuzzy arithmetic is best fitted. Indeed, performing operations on fuzzy numbers comes down to a constraint propagation problem including preference propagation such that peak preferences on the performance evaluation indices are computed from peak preferences on the design parameters. Especially, knowing the overall performance level enables design parameters to be chosen accordingly. This methodology has been developed by Dubois in the early eighties for the problem of tuning the cutting conditions on a transfer line of machine tool. At the same time, Antonsson and Wood investigated the fuzzy arithmetic approach to engineering design on a larger scale, and, since then, have published numerous papers, one of which appears in this volume in an updated form.

In fact, the whole field of fuzzy optimization, of which fuzzy engineering design is a subfield, is an offspring of Bellman and Zadeh's seminal paper on the max-min approach to decision making under several objectives. Historically, the first application was linear programming, with the pioneering work of Zimmermann. His chapter indicates that fuzzy linear programming immediately gave rise to numerous applications in the field of operations research (here the choice of media for a publicity campaign). The uniqueness of the fuzzy max-min approach is to consider fuzzy specifications, goals, and so on, as flexible constraints where satisfiability or feasibility is a matter of degree, but no compensation is allowed. This implies that a single violated constraint is enough to make a solution infeasible. Another application of this constraint-based methodology to chemical process design is given. It lays bare the fact that an alternative approach to fuzzy optimization can be devised in terms of fuzzy decision rules. The particularity of this approach is that it naturally leads to greedy algorithms in the case of combinatorial problems as the one dealt with in the chapter by Djouad, Floquet, Domenech, and Pibouleau.

The three last contributions are typical of another important field of applications of fuzzy sets: scheduling, and especially, in the production research area. The first chapter by Fargier entirely focuses on a constraint-directed formulation of jobshop scheduling, and describes a branch and bound procedure. Its main merit is to show the contribution of preference modeling in the problem: computational experiments clearly indicate that the first solution found is much better when preferences are accounted for (as opposed to a crisp constraint formulation), and that computational efficiency is improved in a high proportion of cases dealt with. The two last chapters handle fuzzy objectives using a rule-based approach, and take advantage of the flexibility of fuzzy priority rules over nonfuzzy rules. Türksen uses a hierarchically arranged set of fuzzy rule-based systems for job selection, assignment of operations to machine, and positioning of operations in the machine queues. Decisions are made on the basis of selecting the best rule in the rule base. Grabot and Geneste more specially focus on dispatching rules and show that the introduction of fuzzy sets allow for building compromises between such priority rules. Moreover, such compromises are tuned using a neural network, thus achieving a compromise between expert scheduling knowledge (which is often very poor) and experimentally validated scheduling strategies. Fuzzy rules and fuzzy constraints seem to be two complementary approaches to decision support in areas of decision making such as production scheduling, and can be used conjointly.

35 Tuning the Cutting Conditions on a Machining Transfer Line Using Fuzzy Constraint Propagation

Didier Dubois
I.R.I.T., University of Toulouse III, France

ABSTRACT: The attractiveness of fuzzy set-based methods, and especially fuzzy arithmetic, is shown on a technological problem: that of tuning the feed and cutting speed of a machine-tool for the proper performance of metal-cutting operations. A method for simultaneous tuning of machine-tools in a synchronized transfer line is described. Fuzzy arithmetic makes it possible to delay as long as necessary the assignment of precise values to parameters. The feasibility analysis is carried out once for all, from fuzzy-valued cutting parameters reflecting subjective preferences. The procedure eventually converges to a trade-off between the quality of cutting and the consistency of the tool-replacement policy, under the synchronization constraint. The advantages of the proposed methodology are its computational efficiency and its ability for handling different sources of knowledge.

35.1. Introduction

Fuzzy sets were first suggested by Zadeh [11] as a convenient mathematical representation of incompletely or imprecisely defined quantities or concepts. The aim is to enable computers to process information pervaded with vagueness. The kind of imprecision that is modelled by fuzzy sets is typically that which any designer of complex systems encounters in the first stages of his or her task: he or she can only supply a rough description of what he or she is planning, an approximate appraisal of expected performance and characteristic parameter values. But such vague notions expressing preference are guiding the decisions of designers, until imprecision has entirely vanished. Proceeding further in the design process requires some verifications to be made in order to check the consistency of decisions. The corresponding computations are performed by arbitrarily assigning precise values to significant parameters, and modifying them until satisfactory tuning is obtained. Such a procedure is very often tedious. On the contrary, modelling the system as a fuzzy one, by integrating in the model the actual imprecision pervading specifications, obviates this blind search because it is possible to make computations out of fuzzy data. The designer is no longer obliged to supply precise values when he or she is unable to.

Clearly, the kind of fuzziness that is dealt with here is not related to random phenomena, and refers to preference. However, the system under design may be prone to random phenomena such as failures, wear, and so on.

To illustrate such considerations we consider a manufacturing system made of a machine-tool or a synchronized line of machine-tools, on which cutting conditions must be tuned. This problem has been studied at length in the literature, especially the single-machine case, for which optimization algorithms have been proposed. The transfer-line problem has been scarcely dealt with in the past. It is hard to solve because all the machine-tools must be simultaneously tuned under many constraints such as prescribed cycle times, synchronization of all stages, quality of cutting, and consistent replacement policy for worn tools. This task is very common in the industry, and is carried out by trained people using rules of thumb through a—sometimes long—iterative procedure. As indicated in this chapter, fuzzy arithmetic leads to speeding up this procedure which no longer has to be initialized by precise (and often infeasible) *a priori* specification of cutting parameters. The necessary background in fuzzy set theory and fuzzy arithmetic can be found in the books of Dubois and Prade [5], [7] or in the survey [6]. This chapter is a short version of a previously published article [3].

35.2. Results in Fuzzy Arithmetics

Let U be a set taken as a reference. A fuzzy set F on U is a subset of U whose elements are weighted by numbers conventionally in the unit interval [0,1]. The weight of element u is denoted $\mu_F(u)$ and called grade of membership of u in F. Crisp sets are obtained by restricting the range of membership grades to {0,1}. Grades of membership can be interpreted in various ways according to the context, such as preference grades, similarity indices, degrees of compatibility with a subjective category, upper probabilities, and others. In this chapter membership functions will express preference or feasibility, not uncertainty.

The membership function μ_F is interpreted as a possibility distribution restricting the values of a variable. Let S be a crisp subset of U. The *possibility* of selecting in S *some* element in accordance with (= belonging to) F is assessed by the quantity $\text{Pos}_F(S)$ such that [12]:

$$\text{Pos}_F(S) = \sup_{u \in S} \mu_F(u), \qquad (1)$$

That is, we search for the element in S that is most in accordance with F. When μ_F expresses preference, $\text{Pos}_F(S)$ is the degree of consistency of a constraint-satisfaction problem involving the fuzzy constraints F and the crisp constraint S. It presupposes that the variable x whose value is constrained by F and S is controllable and can be chosen as u* such that $\mu_F(u^*) = \text{Pos}_F(S)$.

Similarly, the extent to which S includes *all* feasible elements in the sense of F is viewed as the grade of impossibility of finding in the complement $\bar{S}$ some element belonging to F. The grade of *necessity* for all elements consistent with F to be in S is thus defined by [5], [13]:

$$\text{Nec}_F(S) = 1 - \text{Pos}_A(\bar{S}) = \inf_{u \in S} 1 - \mu_F(u). \qquad (2)$$

If S is a fuzzy event, that is, is a fuzzy set, equations (1) and (2) can be generalized. $\text{Nec}_F(S)$ is also the degree of certainty of satisfying a constraint S when all that is known about an uncontrollable variable x is that "x is F." Then μ_F expresses uncertainty and not preference. This situation will not be met here (see Dubois, Fargier and Prade [4] for fuzzy constraint satisfaction under uncertainty).

A fuzzy number M is a fuzzy set of real numbers clustered around some modal value. More specifically, the membership function μ_M is normalized and unimodal. Any level set of M, $M_\lambda = \{u \mid \mu_M(u) \geq \lambda\}, \forall \lambda \in {]0,1]}$ is a closed interval. The modal value can be extended to a closed interval $[m, \bar{m}]$. M is then called a fuzzy interval (see Figure 35.1). Any arithmetic real operation *, that is, any two-place mapping, can be extended to interval arguments;

$$[x_1, x_2] * [y_1, y_2] = \{x * y \mid x \in [x_1, x_2], y \in [y_1, y_1]\}; \qquad (3)$$

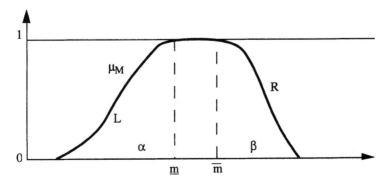

Figure 35.1   L-R type fuzzy interval.

582   FUZZY INFORMATION ENGINEERING

and, consistently, to fuzzy numbers or intervals as follows: if M and N are fuzzy intervals, M * M has the membership function:

$$\forall\, w \in \mathbb{R}, \mu_{M*N}(w) = \sup_{u,v} \min(\mu_M(u), \mu_N(v)) \qquad (4)$$

under the constraint u * v = w.

It can be seen that $\mu_{M*N}(w) = \text{Pos}_{M \times N}(\{u, v \mid u * v = w\})$, where $M \times N$ is the Cartesian product of M and N (translated via the minimum operator). In other words, (4) can be viewed as computing the degree of consistency of a constraint satisfaction problem involving variables x and y. It operates the propagation of preference from x, y to the range of variable $z = x * y$.

As soon as the supremum is reached in equation (4) (e.g., * is continuous, μ_M and μ_N upper semicontinuous), the λ-level set of M * N, say (M * N)$_\lambda$, can be obtained by combining the level sets M_λ and N_λ via equation (3). Consequently, as soon as equation (3) is easy to perform (e.g., * = addition, product), equation (4) becomes simple. It can become even simpler if we adopt the following representation of fuzzy intervals: M is said to be a LR-type fuzzy interval if it defined by:

- a range $[\underline{m}, \overline{m}]$ of values with membership grade 1,
- a support $\{u \mid \mu_M(u) > 0\} =]\underline{m} - \alpha, \overline{m} + \beta[$
- shape functions L and R $[0, +\infty) \to [0,1]$ with $L(0) = R(0) = 1; R(1) = L(1) = 0$, L and R are nonincreasing upper semicontinuous mappings.

μ_M is then defined by (see Figure 35.1)

$$\mu_M(u) = L\left(\frac{\underline{m} - u}{\alpha}\right); u \leq \underline{m}$$

$$= 1; u \in [\underline{m}, \overline{m}]$$

$$= R\left(\frac{u - \overline{m}}{\beta}\right); u \leq \overline{m}.$$

M is denoted $(\overline{m}, \underline{m}, \alpha, \beta)_{LR}$ or $(m, \alpha, \beta)_{LR}$ if it is a fuzzy number; α and β are called left and right spreads, respectively. The following results hold [5], [6]:

(a) if $M = (m, \alpha, \beta)_{LR}, N = (n, \gamma, \delta)_{LR}$, then
$$M \oplus N = (m + n, \alpha + \gamma, \beta + \delta)_{LR} \text{ (extended addition)};$$

(b) 1/M is defined by $\mu_{1/M}(w) = \mu_M\left(\frac{1}{w}\right);$

(c) $\forall\, a \in R, a \cdot M = (am, a\alpha, a\beta)_{LR} \ (a > 0)$
$$= (am, -a\beta, -a\alpha)_{LR}(a > 0) \text{ (scalar multiplication)};$$

(d) if $M = (m, \alpha, \beta)_{LR}; N = (n, \gamma, \delta)_{RL}$ (N is of the opposite type), then
$$M - N = (m - n, \alpha + \delta, \beta + \gamma)_{LR} \text{ (extended subtraction)};$$

(e)   if M and N have supports in $[0, +\infty)$, and both L – R typed, then

$$\mu_{M \cdot N}(w) = L\left(\frac{n\alpha + m\gamma - \sqrt{(m\gamma - n\alpha)^2 + 4\alpha\gamma w}}{2\alpha\gamma}\right), w \leq mn,$$

$$= R\left(\frac{n\beta + m\delta + \sqrt{(m\delta - n\beta)^2 + 4\beta\delta w}}{2\alpha\gamma}\right), w \geq mn \text{ (extended product)}.$$

A second-order approximation (small spreads) of the product formula is
$$M \cdot N \simeq (mn, m\gamma + n\alpha, m\delta + n\beta)_{LR}.$$

Other results and proofs are given by Dubois and Prade [5], [6]. Such simple formulae indicate that it is not too difficult to perform calculations with ill-defined quantities modelled by fuzzy numbers.

35.3. The Cutting Conditions Tuning Problem on a Transfer Line

Very often, the tuning of cutting conditions must be carried out on a group of machines rather than on an isolated one. It is sometimes crucial to achieve simultaneous tuning, take into account the dependence between several cutting operations. This is especially true on a synchronized transfer line. The methodology presented in this section has been developed in collaboration with a machine-tool company [1]. It was first outlined in [2].

35.3.1. Statement of the Problem

The transfer line is supposed to be made of a sequence of M workstations. At each station i, a sequence of K_i operations is performed. One operation may be the performance of several identical tasks in parallel (e.g., drills). Each operation j at station i is characterized by a cutting speed v_{ij} and a feed rate f_{ij}, limited by technological bounds such as the following constraints:

$$\underline{v} \leq v \leq \overline{v}, \tag{5}$$

$$\underline{f} \leq f \leq \overline{f}, \tag{6}$$

$$v \cdot f^{\beta f} \leq B, \tag{7}$$

$$f \cdot v^{\gamma v} \geq C_S, \tag{8}$$

where β_f and γ_v are technological coefficients. The upper bound on v is due to the maximum available spindle speed and temperature limitations; the upper bound on f is due to cutting force restrictions or surface finish requirements. Lower bounds on v and f, together with inequality (8) define the stable cutting region. Constraint (7) stems from the maximal available horsepower. Constant B also depends upon the depth of cut. Objectives are usually the minimization of machining cost and the maximization of production rate, metal removal rate, tool life, production between tool changes, and so on. When technological coefficients are assumed to be well-known, many techniques exist for the single objective optimization of the cutting operation. A classical survey is the one by Philipson and Ravindran [10], who also discuss explicit solving through differential calculus methods. Cutting speeds at each station are related via the spindle speed w_i:

$$\forall j, v_{ij} = \pi D_{ij} w_i, \tag{9}$$

where D_{ij} is the work-piece diameter. Hence, decision variables at each station are K_i feed rates and one spindle speed. The transfer line is synchronized in the sense that each station has the same cycle time t_c. If t_{ij} denotes the cutting time for operation j of stage i, then one must have:

$$t_c \geq \sum_{j=1, K_i} t_{ij} + \Delta t_i, \forall i = 1, M, \tag{10}$$

where Δt_i is a nonproductive setup time. Goals to be achieved are:

- Suitable machining times so that the cycle time, which defines the production rate, is respected.

- A good quality of cutting, expressed in terms of preferred speeds and feed rate ranges for each operation.

- A reasonable worn-tool replacement policy that allows a single replacement frequency and specifies a number N of produced parts without changing tools. For each operation j of stage i, the number of parts machined by the same tool, say N_{ij} should be of the form:

$$\begin{cases} N_{ij} = q_{ij} N + r_{ij} \\ r_{ij} \ll N_{ij}, \end{cases} \tag{11}$$

where q_{ij} = integer part of N_{ij}/N, i.e., tool (i,j) is changed every q_{ij} replacement stops of the linear; r_{ij} is the number of parts that could still have been safely machined by the replaced tool.

Optimizing the whole system at once may be quite challenging and leads to rigid procedures (e.g., maximizing N, minimizing t_c). Another approach consists in suboptimizing each operation. This has been done by Iwata et al. [9] and Hitomi [8] with single objectives (minimization of cost, maximization of production rate), and Philipson and Ravindran [10] with several objectives, by goal programming. Here the optimization will be performed at each station.

The spirit of the procedure described next is to provide an interactive design tool where consequence of cycle time constraint and cutting quality requirements are evaluated, but the final choice of cutting conditions is the designer's responsibility. The procedure will only guide the designer's choice so that goals are attained, including the tool-replacement policy. Basically, the methodology is based on fuzzy constraint propagation.

35.3.2. Outline of the Tuning Procedure

Usually, designers are compelled to resort to experience-guided search for good cutting conditions; that is, try, check, then modify, check again, and so on until a reasonable solution is reached. The main idea of the procedure described here is to avoid assigning precise values to cutting parameters immediately, but to perform suitable evaluations using as operands fuzzy numbers whose shapes account for the cutting quality requirements. Here the role of fuzzy arithmetics is to propagate preference.

More specifically, for each operation, the designer specifies ranges of permitted values for the cutting speed $[\underline{v}, \overline{v}]$ and feed rate $[\underline{f}, \overline{f}]$ (subscripts are dropped for simplicity); that is, $v \notin [\underline{v}, \overline{v}]$, $f \notin [\underline{f}, \overline{f}]$ is forbidden. Ranges of preferred values $[v_*, v^*]$, $[f_*, f^*]$ are also requested. Fuzzy intervals are thus obtained as shown in Figures 35.2 and 35.3; thus:

$$
\begin{cases}
\text{a fuzzy cutting speed } \tilde{v} = (v_*, v^*, v_* - \underline{v}, \overline{v} - v^*)_{LR} & (12) \\
\text{a fuzzy feed rate } \tilde{f} = (f_*, f^*, f_* - \underline{f}, \overline{f} - f^*)_{LR}; & (13)
\end{cases}
$$

according to the representation proposed in section 35.2. Here $L(u) = R(u) = \max(0, 1 - u)$; that is, linear membership functions are assumed. $\tilde{v}$ and $\tilde{f}$ may significantly vary according to the nature of the operation (e.g., rough or final cutting) of the tool or the processed part.

At a given station i, from the knowledge of $\{\tilde{v}_{ij}, \tilde{f}_{ij}, j = 1, K_i\}$, the following quantities can be computed, owing to the results presented in section 35.2 and expressions (9)–(11):

1. Fuzzy specifications $\tilde{w}_{ij}$ of spindle speeds whose consistency must be checked.

2. A fuzzy processing time at station i, to be compared with the required cycle time t_c.

3. A fuzzy specification $\tilde{N}_{ij}$ of the number of processed parts per tool. This fuzzy number will encompass the cycle time constraint and will also reflect the cutting quality specifications. $\tilde{N}_{ij}$ clearly pictures for the designer a range of possible choices regarding the operation under concern.

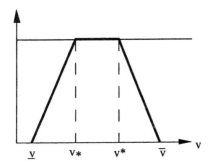
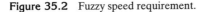
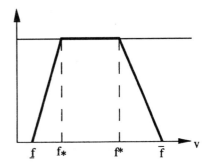

Figure 35.2 Fuzzy speed requirement.   **Figure 35.3** Fuzzy feed requirement.

Once the set of $\tilde{N}_{ij}$ values is known, the designer chooses crisp numbers of processed parts N_{ij} consistent with these fuzzy numbers [i.e., $\mu_{\tilde{N}_{ij}}(N_{ij})$ close enough to 1] so that the tool-replacement condition (11) is met. The computer is then able to determine the best corresponding cutting conditions $\hat{v}_{ij}, \hat{f}_{ij}$, maximizing $\min(\mu_{\tilde{v}_{ij}}, \mu_{\tilde{f}_{ij}})$, in accordance with the cycle time constraint. This is the final defuzzification step. The fuzzy Cartesian product $\tilde{f}_{ij} \times \tilde{v}_{ij}$ is thus supposed to be a reasonable approximation of the feasibility region described by constraints (5)–(8). In the following, the necessary calculations are detailed for single- and multi-operation stations.

35.3.3. Single-Operation Station

The cutting time at single-operation station i is:

$$t_i = \frac{l_i \pi D_i}{f_i v_i}, \tag{14}$$

where l_i = distance travelled by the tool in a pass. Let $G_i \triangleq l_i \pi D_i$ express the geometrical data.

The fuzzy cutting time $\tilde{t}_i$ is now obtained by calculating the fuzzy product $\tilde{f}_i \cdot \tilde{v}_i$, using the expressions provided in section 35.2 and the fuzzy intervals defined by equations (12) and (13), and we have:

$$\mu_{\tilde{t}_i}(\theta) = \mu_{\tilde{f}_i \cdot \tilde{v}_i}\left(\frac{G_i}{\theta}\right). \tag{15}$$

In the preceding, $\tilde{f}_i \cdot \tilde{v}_i$ is obtained by calculating a product of fuzzy intervals (see section 35.2) and $\tilde{t}_i$ is a fuzzy interval whose support is:

$$\left]\frac{G_i}{\overline{f_i}\overline{v_i}}, \frac{G_i}{\underline{f_i}\underline{v_i}}\right[\triangleq]\underline{t},\overline{t}[$$

and

$$\forall \theta \in \left[\frac{G_i}{f^*_i v^*_i}, \frac{G_i}{f_{i_*} v_{i_*}}\right] \triangleq [t_*, t^*], \mu_{\tilde{t}_i}(\theta) = 1.$$

$\tilde{t}_i$ must now be compared with the cutting time $\hat{t}$ induced from the cycle time constraints, that is:

$$\hat{t} = t_c - \Delta t_i. \tag{16}$$

The following situations may occur:

1. $\hat{t} > t^*$ and $\mu_{\tilde{t}_i}(\hat{t})$ is low. The station is underloaded whatever the cutting condition. It may be useful to add another operation to this station. Otherwise the cycle time constraint can be dropped.

2. $\hat{t} > t_*$ and $\mu_{\tilde{t}_i}(\hat{t})$ is 1 or close to 1. The stage is adapted to the cycle time constraint; cutting conditions can be chosen in the preferred ranges. If $\hat{t} < t^*$, then, for instance:

$$v_i \in [v_{i*}, v^*_i] \cap \left[\frac{G_i}{\hat{t}f^*_i}, \frac{G_i}{\hat{t}f_{i*}}\right]. \tag{17}$$

3. $\hat{t} < t^*$ and $\mu_{\tilde{t}_i}(\hat{t})$ close to 1. The best cutting conditions $(\hat{f}_i, \hat{f}_i)$ maximizing $\min(\mu_{\tilde{f}_i}(f_i), \mu_{\tilde{v}_i}(v_i))$ under the cycle time constraint are such that:

$$\mu_{\tilde{f}_i}(\hat{f}_i) = \mu_{\tilde{v}_i}(\hat{v}_i) = \mu_{\tilde{t}_i}(\hat{t}) \triangleq \alpha_i. \tag{18}$$

Since f_i and v_i are L-R fuzzy intervals, it can be checked that:

$$\left.\begin{aligned}\hat{f}_i &= f^*_i + (\bar{f}_i - f^*_i)R^{-1}(\alpha_i)\\ \hat{v}_i &= v^*_i + (\bar{v}_i - v^*_i)R^{-1}(\alpha_i).\end{aligned}\right\} \tag{19}$$

4. $\hat{t} < t^*$ and $\mu_{\tilde{t}_i}(\hat{t})$ is 0 or low. The station is overloaded and needs some modification.

The consequence of the cycle time constraint on the choice of cutting conditions can be calculated more generally, so as to encompass all cases (1–4). This is achieved via fuzzy constraint propagation. Consider the feed rate: it is restricted not only by $\tilde{f}_i$, but also by the fuzzy range:

$$\mu_{\tilde{f}_i}(\theta) = \mu_{\hat{t}_i \cdot \tilde{v}_i}\left(\frac{G_i}{\theta}\right). \tag{20}$$

thus:

$$\tilde{f}'_i = \frac{G_i}{[0,\hat{t}] \cdot \tilde{v}_i} \tag{21}$$

where $[0,\hat{t}]$ is viewed as a fuzzy interval with null spreads, and the fuzzy product:

$$[0,\hat{t}] \cdot \tilde{v}_i = (0, \hat{t}v^*, 0, \hat{t}(\bar{v} - v^*))_{LR}. \tag{22}$$

In other words, including the cycle time constraints leads to reduction of the fuzzy specification $\tilde{f}_i$ on the feed rate, to $\tilde{f}_i \cap \tilde{f}'_i$.

It can be checked that when the station is very much underloaded ($\hat{t} > \tilde{t}$), $\tilde{f}'_i \cap \tilde{f}_i = \tilde{f}_i$ [case (a)] or if the station is too much overloaded ($\hat{t} < \tilde{t}$), $\tilde{f}_i \cap \tilde{f}'_i = \varnothing$ [case (d)]. Otherwise $\tilde{f}'_i \cap \tilde{f}_i$ is as shown in Figure 35.4.

Note that $\sup \mu_{\tilde{f}_i \cap \tilde{f}'_i} = \alpha_i$ is attained for $f_i = \hat{f}_i$, as calculated in case (c). Similarly, $\tilde{v}_i$ can be changed into:

$$\tilde{v}_i \cap \tilde{v}'_i = \frac{G_i}{[0,\hat{t}] \cdot \tilde{f}_i}.$$

The fuzzy restriction on the number N_i of processed parts per tool can now be obtained from the restricted fuzzy cutting conditions, via Taylor's formula:

$$N_i = \frac{T}{t_i}, \text{ where } T = \frac{K}{v^\alpha f^\beta} \text{ is the tool life,}$$

$$= \frac{K}{G_i} \cdot v_i^{1-\alpha} \cdot f_i^{1-\beta}, \tag{23}$$

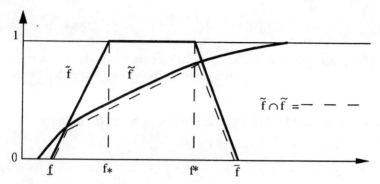

Figure 35.4 Fuzzy constraints on the feed.

where K depends upon the depth of cut and α and β are Taylor coefficients. When stage i is fully utilized $(t_i = \hat{t})$, N_i depends only upon, say the feed rate:

$$N_i = \frac{K}{G_i{}^\alpha} \cdot \frac{1}{\hat{t}^{1-\alpha}} f_i^{1-\beta}. \tag{24}$$

The fuzzy interval $\tilde{N}_i$ is obtained by substituting $\tilde{f}_i \cap \tilde{f}'_i$ in equation (24). $\tilde{N}_i$ is of the form $a \cdot M^p$, whose membership function is simply:

$$\mu_{a \cdot M^p}(n) = \mu_M\!\left(\frac{n^{1/p}}{a}\right).$$

When the station is definitely underloaded, $\tilde{N}_i$ has to be obtained via equation (23) and $\tilde{f}_i \cap \tilde{f}'_i, \tilde{v}_i \cap \tilde{v}'_i$; the calculation must then be performed through a level-set combination, or by means of an approximate formula, as given in section 35.2 or in Dubois and Prade [6], [7].

35.3.4. Multioperation Station

If K_i operations must be performed at station i, K_i fuzzy cutting speeds $\tilde{v}_{ij}$ are provided. $\tilde{v}_{ij}$ induces a fuzzy range of spindle speeds $\tilde{w}_{ij}$, such that:

$$\forall j, \forall w, \mu_{\tilde{w}_{ij}}(w) = \mu_{\tilde{v}_{ij}}(\pi D_i w). \tag{25}$$

Since only one spindle speed w_i need be determined, its corresponding range is the intersection $\cap_{j=1,K^i} \tilde{w}_{ij}$. Especially when the D_i values are somewhat different, this range may be very narrow. Moreover, the set of possible spindle speeds, say Ω, is discrete. Thus the (fuzzy) set of spindle speeds compatible with the fuzzy cutting speeds is usually very small. It is reasonable to choose w_i, which maximizes $\min_j \mu_{\tilde{w}_{ij}}(w)$. If no spindle speed can be found that is consistent with the quality of cutting, the station must be modified.

The cutting time at station i is now of the form:

$$\tilde{t}_i = \frac{1}{w_i} \sum_{j=1,K_i} \frac{l_{ij}}{\tilde{f}_{ij}}. \tag{26}$$

This fuzzy sum of inverses can be calculated by means of level sets, by L-R approximation formulae, or exactly, if $\tilde{f}_{ij}$ is defined such that $1/\tilde{f}_{ij}$ is of LR type. If the $\tilde{f}_{ij}$ are all equal to $\tilde{f}_i$, equation (26) becomes:

$$\tilde{t}_i = \frac{1}{w_i \cdot \tilde{f}_i} \sum_{j=1,K_i} l_{ij}. \tag{27}$$

The same argument for matching $\tilde{t}_i$ and $\hat{t}_i$ as in the previous section may be used. The calculation of the range of feed rates induced from the cycle-time constraint is carried out as follows: if t_i is the cutting time, then f_{ij} satisfies:

$$\frac{l_j}{f_{ij}} = w_i t_i - \sum_{k \neq j} \frac{l_k}{f_{ik}}. \tag{28}$$

The induced fuzzy range $\tilde{f}'_{ij}$ is obtained by changing t_i into $[0, \hat{t}_i]$ and f_{ik} into $\tilde{f}_{ik}$ $(k \neq j)$ in equation (28), similarly to equation (21).

For each operation j, the fuzzy number of processed parts per tool is, from equation (24):

$$\tilde{N}_{ij} = \frac{K}{l_i(w_i)^{\alpha - 1} \cdot (\pi D_i)^\alpha} (\tilde{f}_{ij} \cap \tilde{f}'_{ij})^{1 - \beta}. \tag{29}$$

35.3.5. The Tool-Replacement Policy

The fuzzy ranges $\tilde{N}_{ij}$ visualize the possible tool-replacement policies, and bottleneck tools are located; that is, tools (i,j) with smallest $\tilde{N}_{ij}$. Note that when optimum cutting conditions exist in the sense of equation (19), they correspond to a number $\hat{N}_{ij}$, which maximizes the membership function of $\tilde{N}_{ij}$.

The tool-replacement policy problem is now of the form: find an integer N maximizing the feasibility level $\alpha(N)$ under the constraints:

$$\begin{cases} N_{ij} = q_{ij} N & q_{ij} \text{ positive integer} \\ N = \min_{i,j} N_{ij} \\ \text{and} \\ \mu_{\tilde{N}_{ij}}(N_{ij}) \geq \alpha(N) & \forall i,j. \end{cases} \tag{30}$$

In other words, the transfer line stops every N produced parts, and tool (i,j) is replaced every q_{ij} stops. System (30) can be solved interactively, or a solution can be obtained by the computer. To ensure no $(N_{ij})_\alpha$ is empty, the threshold $\alpha(N)$ is obviously such that:

$$\alpha(N) \leq \hat{\alpha} = \max_{ij} \sup \mu_{\tilde{N}_{ij}}. \tag{31}$$

If system (30) has no solution for $\alpha = \hat{\alpha}$, then α must be decreased until a solution is found. The cutting conditions can then be retrieved in the following way:

- if $N_{ij} < \hat{N}_{ij}$, the optimal cutting conditions (19) are kept, provided tool (i,j) is not underutilized too much ($\hat{N}_{ij} - N_{ij}$ remain small).

- Otherwise, the knowledge of N_i and $t_i = \hat{t}_i$ on single-operation stages completely determines the cutting conditions. On multioperation stages, the knowledge of N_{ij} and w_i determines f_{ij}.

An algorithm for the calculation of the values N_{ij} solutions to system (30) can be the following. Let $A = \{\alpha \le \hat{\alpha} \mid \exists i,j,n \text{ s.t. } \mu_{\tilde{N}_{ij}}(n) = \alpha\} \triangleq \{\alpha^1 \ge \alpha^2 \ge \cdots \ge \alpha^p\}$, be the set of attained membership values. Let ε be a subutilization rate, such that a tool is allowed to be replaced when it has cut $N_{ij}(1 - \varepsilon)$ parts instead of N_{ij}. Let $(\tilde{N}_{ij})_\alpha = \{n \mid \mu_{\tilde{N}_{ij}}(n) \ge \alpha\}$. a $\leftarrow$ b means: assign to a the value of b.

Algorithm
For $k = 1$ to p
begin
    (1) $\alpha \leftarrow \alpha^k; \underline{N}_{ij} \leftarrow (1 - \varepsilon) \cdot \min(\tilde{N}_{ij})_\alpha; \overline{N}_{ij} \leftarrow \max(\tilde{N}_{ij})_\alpha; \forall ij$.
    (2) $\underline{N} \leftarrow \min_{ij} \underline{N}_{ij}; \overline{N} \leftarrow \overline{N}_{ij}$ s.t. $\underline{N}ij = \underline{N}$.
    (3) For $N = \overline{N}$ down to $\underline{N}$
        begin $q_{ij} \leftarrow \overline{N}_{ij}/N \; \forall i,j$ (Euclidean division)
                 $N_{ij} \leftarrow q_{ij}N \; \forall i,j$
                 If $\forall i,j, N_{ij} \ge \underline{N}_{ij}$ stops with success
    end
end; stop with failure.

35.3.6. Example

To illustrate the procedure, we consider a transfer line comprising three workstations:

Station 1: rough turning $l_1 = 200$ mm; $D_1 = 100$ mm; single-edge tool.

Station 2: final turning $l_2 = 200$ mm; $D_2 = 100$ mm; single-edge tool.

Station 3: turning $l_{31} = 200$ mm; $D_{31} = 210$ mm; two-edge tool levelling $l_{32} = 17$ mm; $D_{32} \in [166, 210]$mm; one-edge tool.

The cycle time is 1 min. $\Delta t_1 = \Delta t_2 = \Delta t_3 = 0.1$ min, i.e., $\hat{t} = 0.9$ min.

(a) Station 1
    Quality specifications: $\tilde{v}_1 = (80, 90, 10, 30)$ m/min ($L(x) = R(x) = \max(0, 1 - x)$); $\tilde{f}_1 = (0.4, 0.8, 0.2, 0.2)$ mm.
    Cutting time:

$$\mu_{\tilde{t}_i}(\theta) = \begin{cases} 1 - \dfrac{1}{4}\left(20 - \sqrt{144 + \dfrac{160\pi}{\theta}}\right), & \theta \ge 1.96 \text{ min}; \\[3mm] 1 - \dfrac{1}{12}\left(42 - \sqrt{36 + \dfrac{480\pi}{\theta}}\right), & \theta \ge 0.87 \text{ min}. \end{cases}$$

It can be checked that $\mu_{\tilde{t}_i}(\hat{t}) = 1$ ($\hat{t} = 0.9$ min); thus, this stage fits the cycle time.
    Fuzzy feed rate (including cycle time constraint) $f_1 \cap f'_1$: see Figure 35.5a. Fuzzy number of processed parts per tool $\tilde{N}_1$ [using equation (36)]:

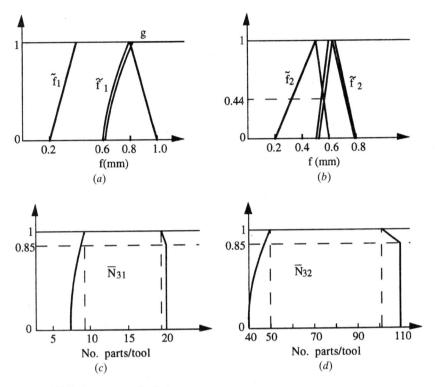

Figure 35.5 Fuzzy sets of solutions.

n	14	15	16	17	18	19	20	21	22	23
$\mu(n)$	0.2	0.4	0.62	0.82	1	0.9	0.69	0.47	0.25	0.03

(b) *Station 2*
   Quality specifications: $\tilde{v}_2 = (110, 120, 20, 10)$ m/min; $\tilde{f}_2 = (0.5, 0.5, 0.3, 0.1)$ mm.
   Cutting time:

$$\mu_{\tilde{t}_2}(\theta) = \begin{cases} 1 - \dfrac{1}{2}\left(17 - \sqrt{49 + \dfrac{80\pi}{\theta}}\right), \ \theta \geq 1.05 \text{ min}; \\ 1 - \dfrac{1}{12}\left(43 - \sqrt{549 + \dfrac{480\pi}{\theta}}\right), \ \theta \geq 1.14 \text{ min}. \end{cases}$$

It can be checked that $\mu_{\tilde{t}_2}(\hat{t}) = \mu_{\tilde{t}_2}(0.9) = 0.44$. This stage is slightly overloaded with respect to the best cutting conditions.
   Fuzzy feed rate (including cycle time constraint) $\tilde{f}_2 \cap \tilde{f}'_2$: as shown in Figure 35.5b the range of possible values has become quite narrow.
   The optimal cutting conditions are $\tilde{f}_2 = 0.555$ mm; $v_2 = 1255$ m/min. $\tilde{N}_2$ is a fuzzy singleton whose support is {13} and membership grade = 0.39.

(c) *Station 3*
   Quality specification: $\tilde{v}_3 = (80, 90, 10, 30)$ m/min for both operations; $\tilde{f}_3 = (0.4, 0.8, 0.2, 0.2)$ mm for both operations.

Table 35.1 Optimal Cutting Conditions and Tool Replacement Policy

Station	Operation	min($\bar{N}_{ij}$)$_\alpha$	$\bar{N}_{ij}$	$\underline{N}_{ij}$	N_{ij}	μ	f_{ij}(mm)	v_{ij}(m/min)	t_{ij}(min)	t_i(min)
1	1	15	21	12	20	0.69	0.861	81	0.9	0.9
2	2	13	13	10	10	0.39	0.555	125,5	0.9	0.9
3	3.1	8	19	6	10	1	0.739	99	0.3	0.58
3	3.2	43	109	33	100	1	0.406	[78,99]	0.28	

μ is the grade of membership of the cutting conditions

Spindle speed: $D_{31} = 210$ mm $\Rightarrow \tilde{w}_{31} = (121.3, 136.4, 15, 45)$ rev/min; $(D_{32})_{min} = 166$ mm $\Rightarrow \tilde{w}_{32} = (153.40, 172.5, 19, 57)$ rev/min; $(D_{32})_{max} = 210$ mm $\Rightarrow \tilde{w}'_{32} = \tilde{w}_{31}$. Range of spindle speeds $\Omega = \{50, 100, 150, 200 \ldots\}$ rev/min. The support of $\tilde{w}_{31} \cap \tilde{w}_{32}$ is included in $[134, 181]$; the highest membership grade $= 0.73$, for a spindle speed $w_3 = 148.3$ rev/min. Hence $w_3 = 150$ rev/min.

Cutting time: $\tilde{t}_3 = (l_{31} + 2l_{32})/2w_3 \tilde{a}_3$ (coefficient 2 comes from a two-edge tool). It can be checked that $\mu_{\tilde{t}_3}(\hat{t}) = \mu_{\tilde{t}_3}(0.9) = 0.85$, and the stage is slightly underloaded (the one-level cut is $(\tilde{t}_3)_1 = [0.42, 0.85]$min).

Fuzzy feed rates: $\tilde{f}'_{31} = \tilde{f}'_{32} = [(l_{31} + 2l_{32})/2\hat{t}w_3, +\infty) = [0, 37, +\infty)$ mm; thus, $\tilde{f}'_{31} = \tilde{f}'_{32} = \tilde{f}'_3$ is crisply truncated from below. $\tilde{N}_{31}$ and $\tilde{N}_{32}$ are shown in Figures 35.5c and 35.5d. $\tilde{N}_{32}$ is calculated from an average diameter (188 mm).

(d) *Tool-replacement policy:* $\hat{\alpha} = 0.39$ due to $\tilde{N}_2$. For $\alpha = 0.39, \varepsilon = 0.25$ we get the values shown in Table 35.1.

Note that the algorithm finds $\overline{N} = 13, \underline{N} = 10$, and finds nothing for $N = 13, 12, 11$. Station 2 tool is underutilized since v_2 and f_2 are the optimal cutting conditions; that is, the membership value is $\mu = 0.39$, which corresponds to $N_2 = 13$. The cutting conditions at Station 1 are revised in order to properly use the tool ($\mu = 0.69$).

35.4. Conclusion

The attractiveness of fuzzy sets for computer-aided design has been stressed in the machine-tool transfer-line case. We have described a procedure where, starting from fuzzy information describing subjective preferences, physical constraints are introduced little by little, in order to reduce fuzziness, until final decisions are made. This procedure may be useful for choosing the stages of a cutting process, namely, the clustering of machining operations into production stages corresponding to workstations.

35.5. References

[1] Dubois, D. *Determination des Conditions de Coupe sur Une Chaine Automatisee d'Usinage.* Centre d'Etudes et de Recherches de Toulouse. Technical Report CERT-DERA No. 1/7610. France: 1981.

[2] ———. "A Fuzzy Set-based Method for the Optimization of Machining Operations." *Proceedings, International Conference on Cybernetics and Society.* pp. 331–334. Atlanta, Ga.: 1981.

[3] ———. "An Application of Fuzzy Arithmetics to the Optimization of Industrial Machining Processes." *Mathematical Modeling,* Vol. 9 (1987), pp. 461–475.

[4] Dubois, D., et al. "Fuzzy Constraints in Job-Shop Scheduling." *Journal of Intelligent Manufacturing,* Vol. 6 (1995), pp. 215–234.

[5] Dubois, D., and H. Prade. *Fuzzy Sets and Systems—Theory and Applications.* New York: Academic Press, 1980.

[6] Dubois, D., and H. Prade. "Fuzzy Numbers: An Overview," in *The Analysis of Fuzzy Information, Vol. 1: Mathematics and Logic.* ed. J.C. Bezdek. pp. 3–39. Boca Raton: CRC Press, 1987.

[7] ———. *Possibility Theory—An Approach to Computerized Processing of Uncertainty.* New York: Plenum Press, 1988.

 [8] Hitomi, K. "Optimization of Multistage Machining Systems." *Journal Engineering Industry Transactions.* ASME 93. (1971), pp. 498–506.

 [9] Iwata, K., et al. "Optimum Machining Conditions for Flow-type Multistage Machining Systems." *Annals ICRP,* Vol. 23, No. 1 (1974).

[10] Philipson, R.H., and A. Ravindran. "Application of Mathematical Programming to Metal Cutting." *Mathematical Programming Studies,* Vol. 11 (1979), pp. 116–134.

[11] Zadeh, L.A. "Fuzzy Sets." *Information Control,* Vol. 8 (1965), pp. 338–353.

[12] ———. "Fuzzy Sets as a Basis for a Theory of Possibility." *Fuzzy Sets and Systems,* Vol. 1 (1978), pp. 3–28.

[13] ———. "Fuzzy Sets and Information Granularity," in *Advances in Fuzzy Set Theory and Applications.* eds. M.M. Gupta, et al. pp. 3–18. North Holland: 1979.

36 Media Selection and Other Applications of Fuzzy Linear Programming

Prof. Dr. H.-J. Zimmermann
Lehrstuhl für Unternehmensforschung (Operations Research),
RWTH Aachen, D-52062 Aachen, Federal Republic of Germany

ABSTRACT: Mathematical programming has been applied to a large number of problems in areas such as production, logistics, inventory control, and so on in which quantitative data are readily available. It has, however, also been applied to marketing, ecological engineering, and similar areas, which involve numerous subjective and not easily quantifiable factors and multiple criteria. In these applications, mathematical programming has often not performed satisfactory. This is even sometimes the case for problems of the former type.

In the meantime, fuzzy mathematical programming, which can accommodate many of these more subjective and vague relationships has been developed extensively and applied to a variety to problems. In this chapter, the basic principles of fuzzy linear programming are described. This method is then applied to the media selection problem. Other applications are briefly sketched and discussed.

36.1. Introduction

The main concern of this chapter are problems that do not have an entirely dichotomous structure, those in which in some parts it is not possible to distinguish clearly between feasible and unfeasible, in which parameters cannot really be modeled as real numbers but rather as fuzzy quantities, or in which the goals cannot be specified as the maximization or minimization of one objective function; that is, profit, cost, and so on.

Media planning is one of these problems that we shall first consider exemplarily: Media planning, media selection, or media scheduling has been a major concern in advertising. The media decision problem is generally defined as follows: given a media budget, a set of media alternatives and data describing the audiences and costs of media alternatives, decide on the media alternatives to use and the number of insertions in each and their timing such that the effect (measured in some appropriate way) of the media budget is maximized [6, 7, 21].

Media selection models can be classified into two major classes:

- Mathematical programming models
- Heuristic models

One of the major disadvantages of heuristic methods is that the quality of solution can often not be judged well enough. Mathematical programming models guarantee an optimal solution but also have serious shortcomings. Those models for which efficient algorithms are available, such as linear programming, do not approximate the real problem well enough, and for those models that approximate to the real problem quite well, the solution algorithms are too inefficient to find optimal solutions for problems of reasonable size.

As a point of departure let us consider existing LP-models for media selection: The first linear programming model intended for practical use in media planning was presented and discussed in November 1961 [1]. This model, referred to as LP I by Charnes et al. essentially optimized an appropriate unit of measurement, such as the sum of contacts of the spread-over, while observing budget restrictions for the entire media plan as well as for different media categories and restrictions for given limits of purchasing the different media.

This type of model has been criticized, because there was no consideration of:

(I) cumulative and duplication effects of contacts,

(II) frequencies and distributions of contacts,

(III) discounts of multiple purchases of media, and

(IV) timing of the advertisements.

An additional weakness of this model is the

(V) determination of weighting factors for the quality of contacts, which are rather hard to determine.

*A goal programming formulation of media selection: **LP II**.* This model was developed by Charnes et al. in 1968 [10] in order to improve the weak points of **LP I** as well as "... (a) to obtain a model which can be operationally implemented over a wide variety of situations in which optimally selected media plans are of interest and (b) to lay a foundation for continued assimilation of data and experience so that systematically we may on the one hand (I) improve the **LP II** model and on the other hand (II) provide a start toward an **LP III** and possibly even further new models as the necessary background materials are accumulated"[10].

This goal programming model offers, in comparison with **LP I**, considerable advantages. At first it can combine several criteria for optimization. Furthermore, cumulations and duplications are considered using a logarithmic approach. Deductions for multiple purchases of the same medium as well as requirements for certain distributions of contacts further improve this model.

On the other hand, weights are still used to evaluate the distances from various criteria to the "ideal point" according to the preference order imposed by the media planner. These weighted distances from the objective function are to be minimized under the condition that the criteria satisfy certain levels also imposed by the media planner. Nevertheless, the current model is based on the improvements created by **LP II**.

36.2. Fuzzy Linear Programming (FLP)

One of the shortcomings of the models mentioned in section 36.1 is that they try to map a problem that includes rather vague human evaluations and sentiments using precise mathematical methods which are based essentially on two-valued logic; thus a solution can be feasible or not feasible, optimal or not optimal and there is no "gray zone" in between. In human life, however, there exist many phenomena such as "satisfactory profits," "promising products," "qualified advertising," which can hardly be defined in these terms. The vagueness under discussion is obviously not due to randomness, otherwise probability theory would be a proper tool to model it.

Since 1965, when L. Zadeh [35] published his seminal paper on fuzzy sets, 16,000 to 18,000 publications have appeared in this area, and it would probably mean carrying coal to Newcastle, if one would introduce this area here. Readers that are not at all familiar with fuzzy sets are referred to introductionary literature, such as [41]. We focus on one special area here, namely fuzzy linear programming.

Fuzzy mathematical programming is not limited to fuzzy versions of linear programming models. Most publications, however, focus on linear [9, 19, 39] and integer mathematical programming models, which can, if required, be extended to other types of mathematical programming models with one or more objective functions without very serious difficulties. We, therefore, also focus on linear programming, that is, on the model,

$$\text{maximize } f(x) = z = \mathbf{c}^T \mathbf{x}$$

$$\text{such that} \qquad \mathbf{Ax} \leq \mathbf{b} \qquad \qquad (1)$$

$$\mathbf{x} \geq 0$$

with $\mathbf{c}, \mathbf{x} \in \mathbb{R}^n, \mathbf{b} \in \mathbb{R}^m, \mathbf{A} \in \mathbb{R}^{m \times n}$.

In this model, it is normally assumed that all coefficients of A, b, and c are real (crisp) numbers; that "cc" is meant in a crisp sense, and that "maximize" is a strict imperative. This also implies that the violation of any single constraint renders the solution unfeasible and that all constraints are of equal importance (weight). Strictly speaking, these are rather unrealistic assumptions, which are partly relaxed in "**F**uzzy **L**inear **P**rogramming" (FLP).

If we assume that the LP-decision has to be made in fuzzy environments, a number of possible modifications of (1) exist. First of all, the decision maker might not want to actually maximize or minimize the objective function. Rather he or she might want to reach some aspiration levels that might not even be definable crisply. Thus he or she might want to "improve the present cost situation considerably," and so on.

Secondly, the constraints might be vague in one of the following ways: The "≤" sign might not be meant in the strictly mathematical sense, but smaller violations might well be acceptable. This can happen if the constraints represent aspiration levels as mentioned or if, for instance, the constraints represent sensory requirements (taste, color, smell, etc.) which cannot adequately be approximated by a crisp constraint. Of course, the coefficients of the vectors b or c or of the matrix **A** themselves can have a fuzzy character either because they are fuzzy in nature or because perception of them is fuzzy.

Finally, the role of the constraints can be different from that in classical linear programming where all constraints are of equal weight. For the decision maker, constraints might be of different importance or possible violations of different constraints may be acceptable to different degrees. Fuzzy linear programming offers a number of ways to allow for all those types of vagueness and we discuss some of them.

Before we develop a specific model of linear programming in a fuzzy environment it should be clear that by contrast to classical linear programming fuzzy linear programming is not a uniquely defined type of model but that many variations are possible, depending on the assumptions or features of the real situation to be modeled.

Essentially two "families" of models can be distinguished: One interprets fuzzy mathematical programming as a specific decision-making environment to which Bellman and Zadeh's definition of a "decision in fuzzy environments" [3] can be applied. The other considers components of model (1) as fuzzy, makes certain assumptions, for instance, about the type of fuzzy sets, which as fuzzy numbers replace the crisp coefficients in **A**, **b**, or **c**, and then solve the resulting mathematical problem [11, 24]. The former approach seems to us the more application-oriented one. From experience in applications, a decision maker seems to find it much easier to describe fuzzy constraints or to establish aspiration levels for the objective(s) than to specify a large number of fuzzy numbers for **A**, **b**, or **c**.

In this chapter, we concentrate on the first approach, in which FLP is considered as a special case of a decision in a fuzzy environment. The basis in this case is the definition suggested by Bellman and Zadeh [3]:

Definition 1: Assume that we are given a fuzzy goal $\tilde{G}$ and a fuzzy constraint $\tilde{C}$ in a space of alternatives X. Then $\tilde{G}$ and $\tilde{C}$ combine to form a decision, $\tilde{D}$, which is a fuzzy set resulting from intersection of $\tilde{G}$ and $\tilde{C}$. In symbols, $\tilde{D} = \tilde{G} \cap \tilde{C}$, and correspondingly:

$$\mu_{\tilde{D}} = \wedge \{\mu_{\tilde{G}}, \mu_{\tilde{C}}\}.$$

More generally, suppose that we have n goals $\tilde{G}_1, \ldots, \tilde{G}_n$ and m constraints $\tilde{C}_1, \ldots, \tilde{C}_m$. Then, the resultant decision is the intersection of the given goals $\tilde{G}_1, \ldots, \tilde{G}_n$ and the given constraints $\tilde{C}_1, \ldots, \tilde{C}_m$. That is:

$$\tilde{D} = \tilde{G}_1 \cap \tilde{G}_2 \cap \ldots \cap \tilde{G}_n \cap \tilde{C}_1 \cap \tilde{C}_2 \cap \ldots \cap \tilde{C}_m$$

and correspondingly:

$$\mu_{\tilde{D}} = \min\{\mu_{\tilde{G}_1}, \mu_{\tilde{G}_2}, \ldots, \mu_{\tilde{G}_n}, \mu_{\tilde{C}_1}, \mu_{\tilde{C}_2}, \ldots, \mu_{\tilde{C}_m}\}$$

$$= \min\{\mu_{\tilde{G}_i}, \mu_{\tilde{C}_j}\} = \min\{\mu_i\}.$$

This definition implies:

1. The "and" connecting goals and constraints in the model corresponds to the "logical and."
2. The logical "and" corresponds to the set theoretic intersection.
3. The intersection of fuzzy sets is defined in the possibilistic sense by the min-operator.

For the time being, we accept these assumptions. An important feature of this model is also its symmetry, the fact that, eventually, it does not distinguish between constraints and objectives. This feature is not considered adequate by all authors (see, for instance, [4]). We feel, however, that this models well the real behavior of decision makers.

If we assume that the decision maker can establish in model (1) an aspiration level, z, of the objective function, which he or she wants to achieve as far as possible and if the constraints of this model can be slightly violated—without causing unfeasibility of the solution—then model (1) can be written as [38, 40]:

$$\text{Find } \mathbf{x}$$

$$\text{such that } \mathbf{c}^T\mathbf{x} \gtrsim z$$

$$\mathbf{Ax} \lesssim \mathbf{b} \tag{2}$$

$$\mathbf{x} \geq \mathbf{o}$$

Here, $\tilde{\leq}$ denotes the fuzzified version of $\leq$ and has the linguistic interpretation "essentially smaller than or equal." $\tilde{\geq}$ denotes the fuzzified version of $\geq$ and has the linguistic interpretation "essentially greater than or equal." The objective function in (2) might have to be written as a minimizing goal in order to consider z as an upper bound.

We see that (2) is fully symmetric with respect to objective function and constraints and we want to make that even more obvious by substituting $(^cA) = \mathbf{B}$ and $(^zb) = d$. Then (2) becomes:

$$\text{Find } \mathbf{x} \tag{3}$$

$$\text{such that } \mathbf{Bx} \tilde{\leq} \mathbf{d}$$

$$\mathbf{x} \geq 0$$

Each of the $(m+1)$ rows of (3) will now be represented by a fuzzy set, the membership functions of which are $\mu_i(x)$. The membership function of the fuzzy set "decision" of model (3) is:

$$\mu_{\tilde{D}}(X) = \min_i \{\mu_i(X)\} \tag{4}$$

$\mu_i(X)$ can be interpreted as the degree to which x fulfills (satisfies) the fuzzy inequality $B_i x \tilde{\leq} d_i$ (where $\mathbf{B_i}$ denotes the ith row of $\mathbf{B}$).

Assuming that the decision maker is interested not in a fuzzy set but in a crisp "optimal" solution, we could suggest the "maximizing solution" to (4), which is the solution to the possibly nonlinear programming problem:

$$\max_{x \geq o} \min_i \{\mu_i(x)\} = \max_{x \geq o} \mu_{\tilde{D}}(x) \tag{5}$$

Now we have to specify that the membership functions $\mu_i(x)$. $\mu_i(x)$ should be 0 if the constraints (including objective function) are strongly violated, and 1 if they are very well satisfied (i.e., satisfied in the crisp sense); and $\mu_i(x)$ should increase monotonously from 0 to 1; that is:

$$\mu_i(x) = \begin{cases} 1 & \text{if } B_i x \leq d_i \\ \in [0,1] & \text{if } d_i < B_i x \leq d_i + p_i \ i = 1, \dots m+1 \\ 0 & \text{if } B_i x > d_i + p_i \end{cases} \tag{6}$$

Here, $B_i x$ denotes the ith row of the system of linear inequalities.

Using the simplest type of membership function, we assume them to be linearly increasing over the "tolerance interval" p_i:

$$\mu_i(x) = \begin{cases} 1 & \text{if } B_i x \leq d_i \\ 1 - \dfrac{B_i x - d_i}{p_i} & \text{if } d_i < B_i x \leq d_i + p_i \ i = 1, \dots, m+1 \\ 0 & \text{if } B_i x > d_i + p_i \end{cases} \tag{7}$$

The p_i are subjectively chosen constants of admissible violations of the constraints and the objective function. Substituting (7) into (5) yields, after some rearrangements [38] and with some additional assumptions:

$$\max \min \left(1 - \frac{B_i x - d_i}{p_i} \right) \tag{8}$$

Introducing one new variable, λ, which corresponds essentially to (4), we arrive at:

$$\text{maximize} \quad \lambda$$

$$\text{such that} \quad \lambda p_i + B_i x \le d_i + p_i \quad i = 1, \ldots, m+1 \qquad (9)$$

$$x \ge 0$$

If the optimal solution to (9) is the vector (λ, x_0), the x_0 is the maximizing solution (5) of model (1) assuming membership functions as specified in (7). The reader should realize that this maximizing solution can be found by solving one standard (crisp) LP with only one more variable and one more constraint than model (3). This makes this approach computationally very efficient.

So far, the objective function as well as all constraints were considered fuzzy. If some of the constraints are crisp, $Dx \le b$, then these constraints can easily be added to formulation (9). Thus (9) would, for instance, become:

$$\text{maximize} \quad \lambda$$

$$\text{such that} \quad \lambda p_i + B_i x \le d_i + p_i \qquad (10)$$

$$Dx \le b$$

$$x, \lambda \ge 0$$

36.3. An FLP-Model for Media Selection

Two properties of this fuzzy linear programming approach are of particular interest for the later model:

1. Many objective functions can be taken into account simultaneously without having to specify special distance measures (such as in LP II) or explicit weights for combining the objective functions.

2. The parameters p_i, which determine in combination with the respective b_is the shape of the membership functions, are very well suited for interactively adapting the model to the decision maker's attitudes.

The problem-solving process could, for instance, comprise the following steps:

1. Define criteria (objective functions).

2. Define restrictions.

3. Determine aspiration levels for objective functions.

4. Choose "tolerance intervals" of the length p_i for the objective functions and for those constraints that do not have to be satisfied crisply.

5. Determine membership functions for all fuzzy objective functions and all fuzzy constants on the basis of steps (1)–(4).

6. Formulate and solve problem (7).

7. If the solution is satisfactory and sensible, stop. If the solution either does not satisfy the decision maker or is not plausible, consider variations in step (4) and process with step (5).

36.3.1. The Model

36.3.1.1. Objective functions (criteria).

Let $\quad x_{ij}(t) = j$th cumulative purchase of medium i in period t

with $\quad x_{ij}(t) = \begin{cases} 1 \text{ if cumulative purchase of medium } i \text{ in period } t \text{ equals } j \\ 0 \text{ otherwise} \end{cases}$

for $i = 1, \ldots, n; j = 1, \ldots, m_i$ and $t = 1, \ldots, T$.

1. *Criterion.* Maximize the gross audience obtained in period t; that is:

$$\max \sum_i \sum_j jd_{it}(t)x_{ij}(t),$$

with $d_{it}(t) = $ relative gross audience, obtained by 1 media i purchase in period t.

2. *Criterion.* Maximize the cumulative gross audience in period t; that is:

$$\max \sum_i \sum_i d_{ij}(t)x_{ij}(t).$$

The relationship between d_{ij} and d_{it} could, for instance, be:

$$d_{ij}(t) = \alpha_i d_{it}(t)^{\beta_{ij}} \text{ for } j = 2, \ldots, m.$$

3. *Criterion.* Maximize net audience or "reach" in period t; thus:

$$\max - \sum_i \sum_j \ln[1 - d_{it}(t)]x_{ij}(t),$$

where $\prod_i \prod_j [1 - d_{it}(t)]^{x_{ij}(t)}$ is the proportion of the "nonreach" audience.

4. *Criterion.* Maximize the combined "reach" in period t; thus:

$$\max - \sum_i \sum_j [1 - d_{ij}(t)]x_{ij}(t).$$

5. *Criterion.* Maximize the gross audience per reached person in period t:

$$\max \frac{\sum_i \sum_j jd_{it}(t)x_{ij}(t).}{-\sum_i \sum_j [1 - d_{ij}(t)]x_{ij}(t)}$$

36.3.1.2. Constraints.
In order to keep the model simple and clear enough, the decreasing effect of past contacts and seasonal fluctuation of

"reach" of different media should not be formulated functionally. Such aspects are introduced using the experience of the media planner who specifies minimum and maximum requirements for audience segments by period and by medium (see Figure 36.1).

For this purpose it is necessary to split the available media into l homogeneous media class (for instance: advertising on TV, on radio, in newspapers, etc.).

Constraints Type 1: Minimum requirements for gross audience per period and per media class:

$$\sum_{i \in n_r} \sum_j jd_{it}(t)x_{ij}(t) \geq D_r(t) \text{ for } r = 1, \ldots, l.$$

Constraints Type 2: Minimum requirements for the cumulative gross audience per period and media class:

$$\sum_{i \in n_r} \sum_j d_{ij}(t)x_{ij}(t) \geq \hat{D}_r(t) \text{ for } r = 1, \ldots, l.$$

Constraints Type 3: Minimum requirements for net audience or reach per period and class:

$$\sum_j \sum_{i \in n_r} \text{In}[1 - d_{i1}(t)]x_{ij}(t) \geq \text{In}[1 - R_r(t)] \text{ for } r = 1, \ldots, l.$$

Constraints Type 4: Minimum requirements for combined reach per period and class:

$$\sum_{i \in n_r} \sum_j \text{In}[1 - d_{ij}(t)]x_{ij}(t) \geq \text{In}[1 - \hat{R}_r(t)] \text{ for } r = 1, \ldots, l.$$

Constraints Type 5: Minimum requirements for average gross audience per reached person per period and class:

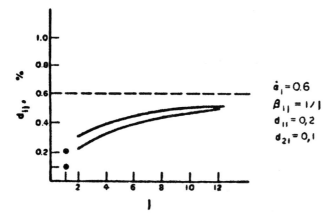

Figure 36.1   Functional relationship between gross audience and cumulative audience.

$$\frac{\sum\limits_{i \in n_r} \sum\limits_{j} jd_{it}(t)x_{ij}(t)}{-\sum\limits_{i \in n_r} \sum\limits_{j} \ln[1 - d_{ij}(z)]x_{ij}(t)} \geq \frac{D_r(t)}{-\ln[1 - \hat{R}_r(t)]} \quad \text{for } r = 1, \ldots, l.$$

Constraints Type 6: Minimum requirements for purchase per media class and period:

$$\sum\limits_{i \in n_r} \sum\limits_{j} jx_{ij}(t) \geq B_r(t) \text{ for } r = 1, \ldots, l.$$

Constraints Type 7: Maximum requirements for purchase per media class and period:

$$\sum\limits_{i \in n_r} \sum\limits_{j} jx_{ij}(t) \geq B_r(t) \text{ for } r = 1, \ldots, l.$$

Constraints Type 8: Maximum budgetary requirements for the entire planning horizon T:

$$\sum\limits_{t=1}^{r} \sum\limits_{i} \sum\limits_{j} c_{ij}(t)x_{ij}(t) \leq C(T).$$

where $c_{ij}(t)$ is the cost of purchasing one unit of medium i in period t (including discounts) and $C(T)$ is the total advertising budget for period T.

Constraints Type 9: Minimum requirements for allocation of funds per media class in period t:

$$\sum\limits_{i \in n_r} \sum\limits_{j} c_{ij}(t)x_{ij}(t) \geq \underline{C}_r(t) \text{ for } r = 1, \ldots, l.$$

Constraints Type 10: Maximum requirements for allocation of funds per media class in period t:

$$\sum\limits_{i \in n_r} \sum\limits_{j} c_{ij}(t)x_{ij}(t) \leq \overline{C}_r(t) \text{ for } r = 1, \ldots, l.$$

The type of membership function will primarily depend on the type of restriction it is supposed to characterize. For minimum requirements, membership functions of the type (5) are appropriate.

For equality constraints, the membership function will have the following shape:

$$f_i(x) = \begin{cases} 0 & \text{for} & (A'x)_i < b'_i - \underline{p}_i \\ 1 - \dfrac{b'_i(A'x)_i}{\underline{p}_i} & \text{for } b'_i - \underline{p}_i \leq (A'x)_i < b'_i \\ 1 & \text{for} & (A'x)_i = b'_i \\ 1 - \dfrac{(A'_x)_i - b'_i}{\overline{p}_i} & \text{for } b'_i \quad < (A'x)_i \leq b'_i + \overline{p}_i \\ 0 & \text{for } b'_i - \overline{p}_i < (A'x)_i, \end{cases}$$

where $\bar{p}_i$ and $\underline{p}_i$ are the selected upper and lower bounds, respectively, of the "acceptability range's" specified by the media planner. Membership functions for maximum requirements are estimated similarly.

36.3.2. Numerical Example

Consider the planning of a six-month advertising campaign for the introduction of a new product in a regionally limited submarket. The target group is: all female persons between 21 and 49 years of age who live in households of at least three persons in the target area, and the monthly gross income exceeds DM 2500. In the test market considered 1.2 million persons live with these properties. We consider as media one regional newspaper and three nonregional journals. The total budget for journal and newspaper advertising is DM 50,000. Each issue of a journal or newspaper can be used once at a maximum. All further information is contained in Table 36.1.

Because of the limited choice of media, it does not seem sensible to use the reach or net audience per period as a criterion. We also exclude as a criterion the maximum of the average gross audience because it would have induced a very high gross audience and a relatively small combined audience. The remaining plausible criteria are the maximization of gross audience, cumulative gross audience, and combined reach.

We also consider constraints concerning gross audience, cumulative reach, average gross audience, and minimum purchases for specified media and periods. The only maximum constraint considered concerns the total budget. The respective data are shown in Table 36.2.

For the three criteria, the media planners have specified levels, below which they are not satisfied at all $[f_i(x) = 0]$ and above which they are fully satisfied $[f_i(x) = 1]$, respectively (see Table 36.3). Thus we arrive at the following "equivalent" LP-formulation. The right-hand side is self-explanatory. The variables have the following interpretation:

$$\lambda \in [0,1] = \text{degree of "overall-satisfaction"}$$

$$\left.\begin{array}{l} x_{i1}(t) \\ x_{i3}(t) \\ x_{i6}(t) \\ x_{i9}(t) \\ x_{i12}(t) \end{array}\right\} \in \{0,1\} = 1, 3, 6, 9, \text{ or } 12 \text{ purchases of medium } i \text{ in period } t, (t = 1,2), (i = 1,2)$$

$$\left.\begin{array}{l} x_{31}(t) \\ x_{33}(t) \\ x_{36}(t) \end{array}\right\} \in \{0,1\} = 1, 3, \text{ or } 6 \text{ purchases of medium 3 in period } t, (t = 1,2)$$

$$\left.\begin{array}{l} x_{41}(t) \\ x_{43}(t) \end{array}\right\} \in \{0,1\} = 1 \text{ or } 3 \text{ purchases of medium 4 in period } t, (t = 1,2).$$

By contrast to LP-formulation (10), this LP problem is a mixed integer problem for which, however, exists the same equivalence relationships as

Table 36.1 Data for Media Selection

Planning period:	$i = 1$ (3 months)				$i = 2$ (3 months)			
Medium i: Criterion	1	2	3	4	1	2	3	4
Frequency per period	76	13	6	3	76	13	6	3
Relevant purchase in i	1, 3, 6, 9, 12	1, 3, 6, 9, 12	1, 3, 6	1, 3	1, 3, 6, 9, 12	1, 3, 6, 9, 12	1, 3, 6	1, 3
Reach for $j = 1$	120,000	80,000	100,000	90,000	100,000	80,000	80,000	90,000
Cum. reach								
$j = 3$	180,000	120,000	160,000	160,000	160,000	110,000	140,000	160,000
$j = 6$	210,000	150,000	180,000		200,000	140,000	150,000	
$j = 9$	230,000	170,000			220,000	160,000		
$j = 12$	240,000	180,000			230,000	170,000		
Medium Means	Newspaper Advert.	Weekly Suppl.	Magazine Suppl.	Journal Suppl.	Newspaper Advert.	Weekly Suppl.	Magazine Suppl.	Journal Suppl.
Cost per advert. (DM)	930	1300	1800	2000	930	1300	1800	2000
Discount per period	$j \geq 5 : 10\%$ $j \geq 10 : 15\%$	$j \geq 5 : 12\%$ $j \geq 10 : 18\%$	$j \geq 3 : 8\%$	$j \geq 3 : 10\%$	$j \geq 5 : 10\%$ $j \geq 10 : 15\%$	$j \geq 5 : 12\%$ $j \geq 10 : 18\%$	$j \geq 3 : 8\%$	$j \geq 3 : 10\%$

Table 36.2 Data for Constraints

Planning period:		$t = 1$				$t = 2$		
Media class:		$i = 1$		$i = 2$		$i = 1$		$i = 2$
Medium i:								
Restr. type	1	2	3	4	1	2	3	4
Total contacts			≥300,000				≥250,000	
Cum. reach			≥160,000				≥140,000	
≠ Contacts per reached person	$\geq \dfrac{800,000}{200,000} = 4$				$\geq \dfrac{600,000}{200,000} = 3$			
Min. purchases	≥10		≥3		≥10		≥3	
Tot. budget				≤50,000				

for problem (10). Table 36.4 shows the initial tableau, and Table 36.5 shows the optimal solutions of this problem. Due to the integer requirements, we obtain three different optimal solutions, which a λ value of 0.4924.

In order to select one out of these three solutions we shall perform a kind of sensitivity analysis. We first "fuzzify" the minimum requirements for gross audience and cumulative reach for media class 2, which so far constituted crisp constraints (rows ZE 04, 05, 06, 07), as shown in Table 36.6.

Table 36.7 shows the new solutions: the additional integer solution is not optimal and the remaining three optimal solutions are the same as in Table 36.5; that is, no differentiation of the three solutions with respect to gross audience or reach is possible.

If we calculate the costs for the three optimal solutions shown in Table 36.5 we find that solution 2 is DM 936 more expensive than the other two solutions (DM 48,996).

If money is very scarce and we can invest this amount profitably elsewhere, we might prefer solutions 1 and 3 to solution 2. If, however, money is not very scarce, we might want to "soften" the budget constraint. We will assume that the budget could be increased to DM 60,000 and therefore specify the following "tolerance-interval" for the budget constraint:

$$f_{22}(x) = \begin{cases} 0 \text{ for } (A'x)_{22} \geq 60.000 \\ 1 \text{ for } (A'x)_{22} \leq 50.000. \end{cases}$$

Table 36.8 shows the optimal solution under these circumstances.

The overall satisfaction λ has been increased from 0.4924 to 0.5508 at the expense of an increased cost to DM 54,492. The structure of the new optimal solution corresponds essentially to the structure of the third

Table 36.3 Data for Criteria

Planning period:	$T = 6$ months	
Criterion	$f_i(x) = 0$	$f_i(x) = 1$
Tot. contacts	≤1,400,000	≥8,000,000
Cum. reach	≤600,000	≥1,200,000
Comb. reach	≤200,000	≥600,000

Table 36.4 Initial Tableau of Media Selection Problem 1

	SP01 λ	SP02 $x_{11}(1)$	SP03 $x_{13}(1)$	SP04 $x_{16}(1)$	SP05 $x_{19}(1)$	SP06 $x_{112}(1)$	SP07 $x_{21}(1)$	SP08 $x_{23}(1)$	SP09 $x_{26}(1)$	SP10 $x_{29}(1)$	SP11 $x_{312}(1)$	SP12 $x_{31}(1)$	SP13 $x_{33}(1)$	SP14 $x_{36}(1)$	SP15 $x_{41}(1)$	SP16 $x_{43}(1)$
E 00	1															
E 01	-5.5	0.1	0.3	0.6	0.9	1.2	0.067	0.2	0.4	0.6	0.8	0.083	0.25	0.5	0.075	0.225
E 02	-0.5	0.1	0.15	0.175	0.192	0.2	0.067	0.1	0.125	0.142	0.15	0.083	0.133	0.15	0.075	0.133
E 03	-0.511	0.105	0.163	0.192	0.213	0.223	0.069	0.105	0.134	0.153	0.163	0.087	0.143	0.163	0.078	0.143
E 04												0.083	0.25	0.5	0.075	0.225
E 05																
E 06												0.083	0.133	0.15	0.075	0.133
E 07																
E 08		-0.283	-0.295	-0.101	0.123	0.386	-0.185	-0.183	-0.089	0.042	0.205					
E 09																
E 10		1	3	6	9	12	1	3	6	9	12					
E 11												1	3	6	1	3
E 12																
E 13																
E 14		1	1	1	1	1										
E 15							1	1	1	1	1					
E 16												1	1	1		
E 17															1	1
E 18																
E 19																
E 20																
E 21																
E 22		0.93	2.79	5.022	7.533	9.486	1.3	3.9	6.864	10.296	12.792	1.8	4.968	9.936	2.	5.4

Table 36.4 *Continued*

	SP17 $x_{11}(2)$	SP18 $x_{13}(2)$	SP19 $x_{16}(2)$	SP20 $x_{19}(2)$	SP21 $x_{112}(2)$	SP22 $x_{21}(2)$	SP23 $x_{33}(2)$	SP24 $x_{56}(2)$	SP25 $x_{39}(2)$	SP26 $x_{312}(2)$	SP27 $x_{31}(2)$	SP28 $x_{33}(2)$	SP29 $x_{36}(2)$	SP30 $x_{41}(2)$	SP31 $x_{43}(2)$	RH500 $b'+p$
E 00																
E 01	0.083	0.25	0.5	0.75	1	0.067	0.2	0.4	0.6	0.8	0.067	0.2	0.4	0.075	0.225	≥ 1.167
E 02	0.083	0.133	0.167	0.183	0.192	0.067	0.092	0.117	0.133	0.142	0.067	0.117	0.125	0.075	0.133	≥ 0.5
E 03	0.087	0.143	0.183	0.202	0.213	0.069	0.097	0.124	0.143	0.153	0.069	0.124	0.134	0.078	0.143	≥ 0.182
E 04																≥ 0.25
E 05											0.067	0.2	0.4	0.075	0.225	≥ 0.208
E 06																≥ 0.133
E 07											0.067	0.117	0.125	0.075	0.133	≥ 0.117
E 08																≥ 0.
E 09	-0.167	-0.161	-0.026	0.169	0.388	-0.131	-0.079	0.044	0.189	0.36						≥ 0.
E 10																≥ 10
E 11																≥ 3
E 12	1			9	12	1			9	12						≥ 10
E 13		3	6				3	6			1	3	6	1	3	≥ 1
E 14																≤ 1
E 15																≤ 1
E 16																≤ 1
E 17																≤ 1
E 18	1	1	1	1	1											≤ 1
E 19						1	1	1	1	1						≤ 1
E 20											1	1	1			≤ 1
E 21														1	1	≤ 1
E 22	0.93	2.79	5.022	7.533	9.486	1.3	3.9	6.864	10.296	12.792	1.8	4.968	9.936	2	5.4	≤ 50

Table 36.5 Optimal Solution for the Media Selection Problem 1

Node	33	46	18
Functional	0.4924	0.4924	0.4924
Estimation	Integer	Integer	Integer
SP06	1.0000	1.0000	1.0000
SP09	1.0000	—	—
SP10	—	1.0000	—
SP11	—	—	1.0000
SP13	1.0000	1.0000	1.0000
SP21	1.0000	1.0000	1.0000
SP24	—	—	1.0000
SP25	—	1.0000	—
SP26	1.0000	—	—
SP31	1.0000	1.0000	1.0000

Table 36.6 Tolerance Intervals for Constraints ZE 04-07

Planning period:	$t = 1$		$i = 2$	
Media Class	$l = 2$		$l = 2$	
	$f_i = 0$	$f_i = 1$	$f_i = 0$	$f_i = 1$
Tot. contacts	≤ 200,000	≥ 300,000	≤ 200,000	≥ 250,000
Cum. reach	≤ 120,000	≥ 160,000	≤ 100,000	≥ 140,000

Table 36.7 Optimal Solution for Problem 2

Node	27	45	63	52
Functional	0.4787	0.4924	0.4924	0.4924
Estimation	Integer	Integer	Integer	Integer
SP06	1.0000	1.0000	1.0000	1.0000
SP09	—	—	1.0000	—
SP10	—	1.0000	—	—
SP11	1.0000	—	—	1.0000
SP13	—	1.0000	1.0000	1.0000
SP14	1.0000	—	—	—
SP15	1.0000	—	—	—
SP21	1.0000	1.0000	1.0000	1.0000
SP24	—	—	—	1.0000
SP25	—	1.0000	—	—
SP26	—	—	1.0000	—
SP31	1.0000	1.0000	1.0000	1.0000

Table 36.8 Optimal Solution for
"SOFT" Budget Constraint

Node	8
Functional	0.5508
Estimation	Integer
SP06	1.0000
SP11	1.0000
SP13	1.0000
SP21	1.0000
SP26	1.0000
SP28	1.0000

solution of problem 1. From a budgetary point of view the following solutions can be suggested: (a) Budgetary constraint very stringent:

1. More purchases in first period:
   Solution: x_{112} (1), x_{212} (1), x_{33} (1)
   x_{112} (2), x_{26} (2), x_{43} (2)
   Degree of satisfaction: $\lambda = 0.4923$
   Total contacts: 4.650.000
   Cum. reach: 1.110.000
   Comb. reach: 762.500
   Cost: DM 48.996.

2. More purchases in second period:
   Solution: x_{112} (1), x_{26} (1), z_{33} (1)
   x_{112} (2), x_{212} (2), x_{43} (2)
   Degree of satisfaction: $\lambda = 0.4923$
   Total contacts: 4.650.000
   Cum. reach: 1.110.000
   Comb. reach: 762.500
   Cost: DM 48.996.

3. Purchases evenly spread:
   Solution: x_{112} (1), x_{29} (1), x_{33} (1)
   x_{112} (2), x_{29} (2), x_{43} (2)
   Degree of satisfaction: $\lambda = 0.4932$
   Total contacts: 4.650.000
   Cum. reach: 1.120.000
   Comb. reach: 766.400
   Cost: DM 49.923.
   Budgetary constraint "soft":
   Solution: x_{112} (1), x_{212} (1), x_{33} (1)
   x_{112} (2), x_{212} (2), x_{33} (2)
   Degree of satisfaction: $\lambda = 0.5508$
   Total contacts: 5.100.000
   Cum. reach: 1.120.000
   Comb. reach: 766.850
   Cost: DM 54.492

36.3.3. Conclusion

When Charnes et al. suggested their "LP II" as an operational approach to solve media planning problems, they already mentioned "... it is expected that further improvements and refinements will be effected in this model, from time to time, but that its main essentials will remain unaltered until, at some future date, it becomes with undertaking an LP III." The possible improvements of LP II envisaged by these authors concerned probably less the conceptual or formal modelling of media planning problems but more problems of adaptation of this model to real-world situation. We think that the theory of fuzzy sets offers one way of improving Charnes' model in this direction.

The main advantages of the approach put forward in this chapter are, to our mind:

1. The model considered many objective functions simultaneously without having to decide about rather demanding distance norms. Fuzzy phenomena that seem to be quite frequent in marketing can be taken account of in a rather natural way.

2. The model is well suited for interactive use by the media planner and therefore easily adaptable to real-world situations.

3. The method is very efficient in terms of computing time. It can be solved easily on any acceptable PC.

36.4. Other FLP Applications

It was already mentioned that FLP has in the meantime been applied to a variety of problems. Areas in which applications have become known include blending problems (such as the blending of chocolate stretch, champaign cuvees, paints, etc.) [42], in finance [11, 26], in logistics [5, 13, 25, 26, 30] and layout planning, and in production and quality control [8, 29]. Many examples can be found in ecological engineering and management [14, 15, 23, 26, 27, 28, 37] and in earthquake engineering [17, 18], but there are also examples in other management areas such as research and development planning [33].

It was also already mentioned, that FLP—by contrast to classical linear programming—is not represented by a single standard model, but, since there are many components in LP that can be fuzzified in a variety of ways, that there are different approaches to FLP. It would exceed the scope of this chapter to explain all or even many of them. Therefore, only two additional applications are described briefly and exemplarily. We shall start with an example in logistics by Ernst [13].

He suggests a fuzzy model for the determination of time schedules for container-ships, which can be solved by branch and bound, and a model for the scheduling of containers on container-ships, which results eventually in an LP. We only consider the last model (a real project).

The model contained in a realistic setting approximately 2,000 constraints and originally 21,000 variables, which could then be reduced to approximately 500 variables. Thus it could be handled adequately on a modern computer. It is obvious, however, that a description of this model in this book would not be possible. We therefore sketch the contents of the modelling verbally and then concentrate on the aspects that included fuzziness.

The system is the core of a decision support system for the purpose of scheduling properly the inventory, movement, and availability of containers, especially empty containers, in and between 15 harbors. The containers were shipped according to known time schedules on approximately 10 big container-ships worldwide on 40 routes. The demand for container space in the harbors was to a high extent stochastic. Thus the demand for empty containers in different harbors could either be satisfied by large inventories of empty containers in all harbors, causing high inventory costs, or they could be shipped from their locations to the locations where they were needed, causing high shipping costs and time delays.

Thus the system tries to control optimally primarily the movements and inventories of empty containers, the capacities of the ships, and the predetermined time schedule of the ships.

This problem was formulated as a large LP model. The objective function maximized profit (from shipping full containers) minus cost for moving empty containers minus inventory cost of empty containers. When comparing data of past periods with the model, it turned out that very often ships transported more containers than their specific maximum capacity. This, after further investigations, lead to a fuzzification of the ships' capacity constraints, which will be described in the next model.

Let:

$$z = \mathbf{c}^T\mathbf{x} \qquad \text{the net profit to be maximized}$$

$$\mathbf{Bx} \leq \mathbf{b} \qquad \text{the set of crisp constraints}$$

$$\mathbf{Ax} \lesssim \mathbf{d} \qquad \text{the set of capacity constraints for which a crisp formulation turned out to be inappropriate}$$

Then the problem to be solved is:

$$\text{maximize} \quad z = \mathbf{c}^T\mathbf{x} \qquad\qquad (11)$$

$$\text{such that } \mathbf{Ax} \lesssim \mathbf{d}$$

$$\mathbf{Bx} \leq \mathbf{b}$$

$$\mathbf{x} \geq 0$$

This corresponds to (2). Rather than using (9) to arrive at a crisp equivalent LP model, the following approach was used: The following membership functions were defined for those constraints that were fuzzy:

$$\mu_i(t_i) = \frac{t_i}{p_i - d_i} \quad 0 \leq t_i \leq p_i - d_i, i \in I,$$

$I =$ Index set of fuzzy constraints.

As the equivalent crisp model to (11), the following LP was used:

$$\text{maximize } z' = c^T - \sum_{i \in I} S_i(p_i - b_i)\mu_i(t_i) \tag{12}$$

such that $\mathbf{Ax} \leq \mathbf{d} + \mathbf{t}$

$\mathbf{Bx} \leq \mathbf{b}$

$\mathbf{t} \leq \mathbf{p} - \mathbf{b}$

$\mathbf{x, t} \geq 0$

where the s_i are problem-dependent scaling factors with penalty character.

Formulation (11) only makes sense if problem-dependent penalty terms s_i, which also have the required scaling property, can be found and justified. In this case, the following definitions performed successfully: First the crisp constraints $\mathbf{Bx} \leq \mathbf{b}$ were replaced by $\mathbf{Bx} \leq .9\mathbf{b}$, providing a 10 percent leeway of capacity, which was desirable for reasons of safety. Then "tolerance" variables t were introduced:

$$\mathbf{Bx} - \mathbf{t} \leq .9\mathbf{b}$$

$$\mathbf{t} \leq .1\mathbf{b}$$

The objective function became:

$$\text{maximize } z = \mathbf{c^t x} - \mathbf{s^t t}$$

s was defined to be:

$$s = \frac{\text{average profit of shipping a full container}}{\text{average number of time periods which elapsed}}$$
$$\text{between departure and arrival of a container}$$

By the use of this definition, more than 90 percent of the capacity of the ships was used only if and when very profitable full containers were available for shipping at the ports, a policy that seemed to be very desirable to the decision makers.

The final example is an application of FLP to forestry management in which again some hints as to the quality of the solution of the FLP, compared to others, is given. The problem is that of determining the optimal sequence and timing of timber harvests subject to continuity and other linear constraints. As described by the authors [26], public and private forest management organizations typically use harvest scheduling linear programs as the primary economic analysis tool for planning. Several conflicting goals must be incorporated into the model. Of articular interest are the goals of maximizing the present net value (PNV) and trying to achieve a stable flow of wood and fiber. These goals conflict with each other. The traditional procedure is to maximize PNV subject to a set of constraints which assure that planned harvests will never decline between any successive pair of cutting periods. This approach—choosing one of the goals as objective function and modelling the others as constraints—normally cause a severe reduction in the level of achieved PNV. The author used essentially approach (9) and applied it in a case study to the conversion of a nonregulated forest (a forest in which some age classes are more common than others) into a regulated forest with a predetermined rotation age. The model scheduled harvest of a 100,000 acre tract of planted slash pine in Florida over a planning horizon of 30 years.

Rather than looking at the model in detail, we regard the solutions of three different models: model 1 is the traditional model with PNV maximization subject to nondeclining yield constraints; model 2 is the FLP model that uses (9); model 3 maximizes PNV with no consideration of stable harvests. Table 36.9 shows the solutions of the three models (from [26]).

It can be observed from this table the solution to model 2 is superior to that of model 1 in terms of profit, total harvest, and smoothness of the harvest schedule. Whether it is preferable from the decision makers point of view is not known.

As conclusion to this chapter, one can probably state:

1. FLP is an approach to model problems, which contain gradual rather than crisp components better than with traditional LP.

2. The models described are generally computationally as efficient as classical LP, and they can also be solved using existing LP codes.

3. Sensitivity analysis and parametric programming play an even more important role in FLP than in crisp LP because in a sense they are the only way to determine the (fuzzy) decision.

Table 36.9   Solutions for Three Models

Model	1	2	3
Profit $	46 323 915	60 219 225	79 804 305
Total Harvest	7 452 748	7 799 460	7 613 033
Harvest Schedule:			
Time Period			
1	281 637	513 929	1 654 775
2	281 637	513 929	1 135 217
3	281 637	513 929	993 315
4	281 637	513 929	0
5	281 637	513 929	0
6	604 457	604 457	604 457
7	604 457	513 929	111 848
8	604 457	513 929	193 587
9	604 457	513 929	275 478
10	604 457	513 929	353 630
11	604 457	513 929	353 630
12	604 457	513 929	425 707
13	604 457	513 929	469 236
14	604 457	513 929	491 000
15	604 457	513 929	551 152

4. It is hard to establish the superiority of FLP over LP in general, because the benchmarks for a comparison, such as the optimal solution to the real problem, are normally not known.

36.5. References

[1] Mathematical Programming for Better Media Selection. American Association of Advertising Agencies. Regional Conventions, Group IV. 1961.

[2] Bardozzy, A., et al. "Fuzzy Composite Programming with a Water Resources Engineering Application." *Engineering.* (1991), pp. 13–16.

[3] Bellman, R., and L.A. Zadeh. "Decision-Making in a Fuzzy Environment." *Management Science,* Vol. 17 (1970), pp. B141–B164.

[4] Bit, A.K., et al. "Fuzzy Programming Approach to Multicriteria Decision-Making Transportation Problem." *Fuzzy Sets and Systems,* Vol. 50 (1992), pp. 135–141.

[5] Bit, A.K., et al. "Fuzzy Programming Approach to Multiobjective Solid Transportation Problem." *Fuzzy Sets and Systems,* Vol. 57 (1993), pp. 183–194.

[6] Brown, B. "A Practical Procedure for Media Selection." *Journal Marketing Research,* Vol. 4 (1967), pp. 262–269.

[7] Brown, D., and M.R. Warshaw. "Media Selection by Linear Programming," *Journal Marketing Research,* Vol. 2 (1965), pp. 83–88.

[8] Chakraborty, T.K. "A Class of Single Sampling Inspection Plans based on Possibilistic Programming Problem." *Fuzzy Sets and Systems,* Vol. 63 (1994), pp. 35–43.

[9] Chanas, St. "Fuzzy Programming in Multiobjective Linear Programming—A Parametric Approach." *Fuzzy Sets and Systems,* Vol. 29 (1989), pp. 303–313.

[10] Charnes, A., et al. "A Goal Programming Model for Media Planning." *Management Science,* Vol. 14 (1968) pp. B423–B430.

[11] Dias, O.P. "The R & D Project Selection Problem with Fuzzy Coefficients." *Fuzzy Sets and Systems,* Vol. 26 (1988), pp. 299–316.

[12] Dubois, D., and H. Prade. *Fuzzy Sets and Systems.* New York: 1980.

[13] Ernst, E. Fahrplanerstellung und Umlaufdisposition im Containerschiffsverkehr. Dissertation, RWTH Aachen.

[14] Esogbue, A.O., and K. Guo. "Optimization of Nonpoint Source Water Pollution Control Planning using Fuzzy Mathematical Programming." *Computer Management & Systems Science.* (1991), pp. 67–70.

[15] Esogbue, A.O., et al. "On the Application of Fuzzy Sets Theory to the Optimal Flood Control Problem Arising in Water Resources Systems." *Fuzzy Sets and Systems,* Vol. 48 (1992), pp. 155–172.

[16] Filev, D., and G. Sotirov. "An Application of FLP to the Ethanol Production." International Workshop on Fuzzy System Applications. pp. 27–28, 1988.

[17] Furuta, H., et al. "Application of Fuzzy Optimality Criterion to Earthquake-Resistant Design." *Analysis of Fuzzy Information—Vol. III Applications in Engineering.* (1987), pp. 17–27.

[18] Furuta, H., and N. Shiraishi. "Multi-Objective Formulation of Earthquake-Resistant Design of Buildings Structures." International Workshop on Fuzzy System Applications. (1988), pp. 165–166.

[19] Hamacher, H., et al. "Sensitivity Analysis in Fuzzy Linear Programming." *Fuzzy Sets and Systems,* Vol. 1 (1978), pp. 269–281.

[20] Hintz, G.W., and H.J. Zimmermann. "A Method to Control Flexible Manufacturing Systems." *European Journal of Operation Research,* Vol. 41 (1989), pp. 321–334.

[21] Kotler, P.H. "On Methods: Toward an Explicit Model for Media Selection." *Journal Advertising Research,* Vol. 4 (1964), pp. 34–41.

[22] Leberling, H. "On Finding Compromise Solutions in Multicriteria Problems using the Fuzzy Mini-Operator." *Fuzzy Sets and Systems,* Vol. 6 (1981), pp. 105–118.

[23] Ohno, K., and T. Kondo. "Inverse Analysis of Seepage through Earth Structures using Fuzzy Sets." *International Workshop on Fuzzy System Applications.* (1988), pp. 167–168.

[24] Okada, S., et al. "A Method for Solving Multiobjective Linear Programming Problems with Trapezoidal Fuzzy Coefficients." *Japanese Journal of Fuzzy Theory and Systems,* Vol. 5 (1993), pp. 15–27.

[25] Perincherry, V., and S. Kikuchi. "A Fuzzy Approach to the Transshipment Problem." *Uncertainty Modeling and Analysis.* (1990), pp. 330–335.

[26] Pickens, J.B., and J.G. Hof. "Fuzzy Goal Programming in Forestry: An Application with Special Solution Problems." *Fuzzy Sets and Systems,* Vol. 39 (1991), pp. 239–246.

[27] Slowinski, R. "A Multicriteria Fuzzy Linear Programming Method for Water Supply System Development Planning." *Fuzzy Sets and Systems,* Vol. 19 (1986), pp. 217–237.

[28] Sommer, G., and M.A. Pollatschek. "A Fuzzy Programming Approach to an Air Pollution Regulation Problem." *Progress in Cybernetics and Systems Research,* Vol. 3 (1978), pp. 303–313.

[29] Tamaki, F., et al. "A Fuzzy Design of Sampling Inspection Plans by Attributes." *Japanese Journal of Fuzzy Theory and Systems,* Vol. 3 (1991), pp. 315–327.

[30] Tao, C.W., et al. "A Fuzzy Approach to Multidimensional Target Tracking." *2nd IEEE International Conference on Fuzzy Systems.* pp. 1350–1355. San Francisco, Calif.: 1993.

[31] Tsai, C.C., et al. "Fuzzy Linear Programming Approach to Manufacturing Cell Formation." *3rd IEEE International Conference on Fuzzy Systems,* Vol. 2. (1994), pp. 1406–1411.

[32] Vasko, F.J., et al. "A Practical Solution to a Fuzzy Two-Dimensional Cutting Stock Problem." *Fuzzy Sets and Systems,* Vol. 29 (1989), pp. 259–275.

[33] Weber, R., et al. "Planning Models for Research and Development." *European Journal of Operational Research,* Vol. 48 (1990), pp. 175–188.

[34] Wiedey, G., and H.J. Zimmermann. "Media Selection and Fuzzy Linear Programming." *Journal of the Operational Society,* Vol. 29 (1978), pp. 1071–1084.

[35] Zadeh, L.A. "Fuzzy Sets." *Information & Control,* Vol. 8 (1965), pp. 338–353.

[36] Zhao, R., and R. Govind. "Symmetrical Fuzzy Linear Programming and its Application to Chemical Engineering Problems." *Uncertainty Modeling and Analysis.* (1990), pp. 500–505.

[37] Zhi-wei, W., et al. "Fuzzy Management Model for Ground Water." Preprints of 2nd IFSA Congress. pp. 341–344. 1987.

[38] Zimmermann, H.J. "Description and Optimization of Fuzzy Systems." *International Journal of General Systems,* Vol. 2 (1976), pp. 209–215.

[39] ———. "Fuzzy Programming and Linear Programming with Several Objective Functions." *Fuzzy Sets and Systems,* Vol. 1 (1978), pp. 45–55.

[40] ———. "The Use of Fuzzy LP and Approximate Reasoning in Production Scheduling." 3rd IFSA Congress. pp. 193–195. Washington, D.C.: 1989.

[41] ———. *Fuzzy Set Theory and its Applications.* 3rd Edition. Boston: Kluwer, 1996.

[42] ———. "Lack und Farbmischungen zu Minimalen Kosten." *Farbe & Lack,* Vol. 92 (1986), pp. 379–382.

37 Fuzzy Set Methods in Separation Process Synthesis

S. Djouad, P. Floquet, S. Domenech, and L. Pibouleau
Laboratoire de Génie Chimique, UMR 5503 CNRS
18 Chemin de la Loge 31078 Toulouse, France

ABSTRACT: The optimal synthesis and design of petroleum, chemical, pharmaceutical, and food industrial units are basic topics in the chemical engineering field. Among these material and energy transformation units, a suitable design of separation processes, specially continuous rectification, can lead to important money savings in this highly competitive engineering domain. We present, in this chapter, a new approach based on fuzzy set methods, for the synthesis and design of sharp separation sequences. The procedure enables to take into account unavoidable uncertainties arising in the synthesis data and ambiguities of the heuristic synthesis advises used to derive the best separation scheme.

37.1. Introduction

Among the separation processes, continuous rectification is widely used in industrial frameworks. Because of their large investment and operating costs (several millions $ per year), the distillation system design must be carried out in order to minimize a technico economical criterion.

The problem to be solved is the following: A multicomponent mixture, whose partial flowrates are not exactly known, is to be separated into specified pure products. The goal is to synthesize the structure of optimal or near-optimal (in terms of the total annual cost) separation units, and also to analyze the effect of uncertainties in this synthesis strategy.

Many published works have dealt with the synthesis of sharp separation sequences [1–2]. The methods proposed for solving this problem are commonly classified into three main categories: algorithmic methods, evolutionary strategies, and heuristic approaches. The procedure presented lies in the latter category, combined with fuzzy set methods to take into account both ambiguities of the linguistic expert rules and data uncertainties. The heuristic advises are based on the engineering practice and involves ambiguous linguistic terms. Furthermore, a set of conflicts can arise between these rules. The linguistic terms are represented by classical fuzzy sets, in order to avoid these conflicts. This representation also allows a gradual transition of the rule's truthfulness and provides an efficient tool for computer handling of such quantitative and imprecise expert knowledge in a systematic manner. Insofar as the synthesis data are often pervading with uncertainties, it seems also to be interesting to deal with a set of possible values, instead of a mean value that does not always represent the entire data description.

37.2. Problem Description

The problem to be addressed can be stated as follows: "Given a single multicomponent feed stream, whose characteristics may be imprecisely known (here, the flowrate compositions are imprecise, and the other characteristics of the feed—temperature, pressure or thermodynamical properties of the components—are assumed to be precisely known), systematically synthesize a process that can isolate the desired pure products from the feed with a minimal total annualized cost."

The main assumptions for this synthesis problem are the following:

a) Only simple (single feed, two product streams) straight distillation columns are considered without energy integration.

b) Each column operates at high recovery (≥98%), sloppy splits of key components (nonsharp separation) are not allowed.

c) Mixture or division of intermediate streams are prohibited.

d) Saturated liquid feeds each distillation column.

e) Component volatility order does not change in the sequence.

Let us roughly recall that a sharp continuous rectification operation allows the ordered separation of a multicomponent mixture, for example ABCD, in two submixtures called top stream (or distillate), for example AB, and bottom stream (or waste), like CD. Formally, this operation can be linked to an ordered list splitting, here [A, B, C, D], in two sublists [A, B] and [C, D]. A separation sequence corresponds to a set of separations of this type, until the initial list becomes entirely splitted. It is easy to notice [3] that the number of possible separation sequences, given by Catalan's number $S_n = (2(n - 1))!/n! \, (n - 1)!$, highly increases with the number n of components to be separated. We can illustrate this point by the five possible separation sequences of a four-component mixture ABCD, as shown in Figure 37.1.

The separation sequence synthesis problem addressed in this chapter consists in choosing, in terms of gain potentiality, the best structure of separation into the S_n possible sequences, and in technically designing this sequence, in an uncertain data environment.

37.3. Synthesis Advises Description

The synthesis algorithm is based on the application of expert rules, well suited for an economical design problem. From an extensive compilation of Aly et al.[4], four rules of thumb have been retained:

1. Favor the separation where the difference ΔT_b of boiling point temperatures between two adjacent key components is the most important.

2. Favor the separation at the point where the relative volatility $\alpha_{a,b}$ of two adjacent key components is the most important.

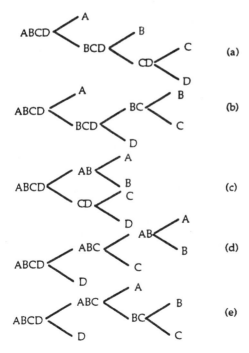

Figure 37.1 Possible separation sequences of a four-component mixture ABCD.

3. Favor equimolar separation between the distillate D and the bottom B. The ratio D/B or B/D must be as close as possible to one.

4. Favor the separation where the estimated mass load coefficient (EML) [5] is less important. This coefficient EML is the molar flowrate that has to be processed by all separation units in the downstream sequence. It is a linear function of molar fractions of each component in the mixture, and can be computed either in a recursive way [5] or in a nonrecursive form [6].

From a physical point of view, it can be observed that advises 1 and 2 partially overlap, because they both privilege the separation point where the physical properties exploited in the separation method are maximum, and consequently the cost minimum. Advises 3 and 4 are both related to the mass load to be separated. However, they are not totally redundant, insofar as the EML coefficient takes into account the total mass load to be separated from the current separation step up to the complete separation, when rule 3 is only related to the current separation step. These four rules incorporate the two well-known precepts in the synthesis of separation trains [7]: "The most delicate separations must be carried out last" and "separations that eliminate the most abundant components are preferable."

These four engineer's advises are expressed in vague and imprecise terms like "important" or "close to one." As mentioned by Dubois and Prade [8], the fuzzy set theory offers a general framework for representing uncertainty and vagueness. The advises are quantified by fuzzy quantities represented by the following membership functions.

$$\text{Advise 1} \quad \mu_1 = \begin{cases} 0 \text{ if } \Delta T_b < T_{\min} \\[2mm] \dfrac{\Delta T_b - T_{\min}}{T_{\max} - T_{\min}} \text{ if } T_{\min} \leq \Delta T_b \leq T_{\max} \\[2mm] 1 \text{ if } \Delta T_b > T_{\max} \end{cases}$$

$$\text{with } T_{\min} = \min(\Delta T_b) \text{ and } T_{\max} = \frac{\displaystyle\sum_{i=1}^{n-1} \Delta T_b}{(n-1)}$$

$$\text{Advise 2} \quad \mu_2 = \begin{cases} 0 \text{ if } \alpha_{a,b} < 1.1 \\[2mm] \dfrac{\alpha_{a,b} - 1.1}{0.9} \text{ if } 1.1 \leq \alpha_{a,b} \leq 2 \\[2mm] 1 \text{ if } \alpha_{a,b} > 2 \end{cases}$$

$$\text{Advise 3} \quad \mu_3 = \begin{cases} P \text{ if } 0 \leq P \leq 1 \\[2mm] (2 - P) \text{ if } 1 \leq P \leq 2 \\[2mm] 0 \text{ otherwise} \end{cases}$$

$$\text{where } P \text{ corresponds to the ratio } \frac{D}{B} \text{ or } \frac{B}{D}$$

Advise 4 $\mu_4 = \begin{cases} 0 \text{ if EML} < \text{EML}_{min} \\ \dfrac{\text{EML}_{max} - \text{EML}}{\text{EML}_{max} - \text{EML}_{min}} \text{ if EML}_{min} \leq \text{EML} \leq \text{EML}_{max} \\ 0 \text{ if EML} > \text{EML}_{max} \end{cases}$

37.4. Data Uncertainty Description

The other uncertainty parameter to be analyzed is the imprecision related to the feed stream to be separated. We have chosen to fuzzify the independent partial flowrates F_i ($i = 1$ to n) of the mixture, represented by classical trapezoidal fuzzy numbers (TrFN). This molar flowrate F_i of each component i is defined by the t-uple (a, b, c, d), where the interval [b, c] contains the modal values and the interval [a, d] is the support of the TrFN. Let us note that by fuzzifying the partial molar flowrates F_i, the molar fractions of each component $x_i = F_i / \sum_{i=1}^{n} F_i$ are also indirectly fuzzified, and, consequently, the relative volatilities $\alpha_{a,b}$ (nonlinear functions of x_i), the ratio D/B or B/D and the EML coefficients (linear relations of x_i).

37.5. Fuzzy Synthesis Procedure

The main steps of the fuzzy synthesis procedure are presented in Figure 37.2, and detailed next.

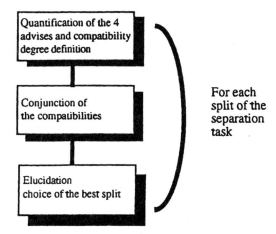

Figure 37.2   Fuzzy synthesis procedure principles.

Let us detail these three main steps:

1. In the first step, the advise quantification is carried out by fuzzy evaluation of the difference ΔT_b of boiling point temperatures, the relative adjacent key component volatilities $\alpha_{a,b}$, the ratio D/B and B/D, and the EML coefficients for each possible split, in terms of F_i fuzzy variables. The first value is independent of the fuzzy molar flowrates F_i, so it corresponds to a crisp value of the membership function μ_1. For the other values, an extended version of the vertex method of Dong and Shah [9] is implemented to compute the functions of fuzzy F_i. The second part of this step is the evaluation of grade of matching between imprecise data, $\Delta T_b - \alpha_{a,b} - D/B$ or B/D − EML, and linguistic advises. We have chosen to apply the extension principle [10] and to define a fuzzy compatibility degree between the data and the synthesis rule by:

$$\forall\, \alpha \in [0,1], \mu_{\text{ADVISE/DATA}}(\alpha) = \sup \{\, \Pi_{\text{DATA}}(u) \,/\, \mu_{\text{ADVISE}}(u) = \alpha \,\}$$

For the third value, the choice of the ratio closest to one is made by the choice of the greatest compatibility degree (the two ratio are ranked by the Liou and Wang method [11]).

2. The second step is the classical conjunction of fuzzy compatibility degrees. The membership function of the compatibility conjunction, for the separation point j, is done by:

$$\mu^j = \min(\max(\mu_{\text{ADVISE } i/\text{DATA}}, 1 - \omega_i)) \qquad i = 1 \text{ to } 4$$

where ω_i is a weighting factor that can be introduced on rule i, and min, max are extended min, max operators to fuzzy numbers [8].

3. The final step corresponds to the choice of the separation point. The operation is carried out by ranking all the compatibility conjunctions μ^j for all of the possible separations (there are $(n-1)$ possible separations of a mixture of n components) and by choosing the greatest. A number of methods have been proposed for ranking fuzzy numbers [12], but these various procedures do not always agree each other. The ranking procedures of fuzzy numbers can be divided in three classes:

   Use of probabilistic indices [13]: in the method, proposed by Lee and Li, generalized mean values of the fuzzy numbers are first calculated and then compared. It is evident that a problem arises when a fuzzy number and a real number are to be compared, which may occur in the synthesis procedure.

   Use of possibility indices: For comparing two fuzzy numbers, the authors [8] have introduced four indices (grade of possibility of dominance and of strict dominance, grade of necessity of dominance and of strict dominance). The advantage of this approach is that if one index cannot distinguish two alternatives, another can. But the problem is that the four indices do not always lead to the same ranking order. In these conditions, it may be difficult for the decision maker to conclude.

Use of an index of optimism, reflecting the decision's maker attitude [11]: Liou and Wang proposed a method for ranking fuzzy numbers by means of an integral value. The method overcomes the difficulties that may be encountered in the preceding approaches. We have retained it, with a value of optimism equal to 0.5 reflecting a moderate decision's maker optimism.

The three main steps of synthesis procedure are carried out until the complete separation of the mixture is achieved.

37.6. Detailed Numerical Example

Let us now illustrate this approach by a five-component mixture (feed flowrates are listed in Table 37.1) to be separated into pure components. The advises are of equal importance ($\omega_i = 1$).

Figure 37.3 shows the first part of the first step, that is, the advise quantification and the membership of each data. It can be noted that:

- For advise 1, the data ΔT_b is a crisp number (it is not a function of F_i).

- For advise 3, a choice must be made between the two ratio (B/D or D/B). The results are the following: D/B ratio is chosen for separation A/BCDE, AB/CDE, ABC/DE, and B/D ratio is chosen for separation ABCD/E because of their closeness to synthesis rule 3.

- For Figure 37.3d (advise 3 – ratio B/D), the data of A/BCDE separation is not represented because it is out of range (no compatibility with advise).

- For advise 4, because of the existence of two pairs of bounds on EML values [4], two graphs are represented.

The second part of the first step corresponds to the definition of the fuzzy compatibility degrees between each advise and each set of data. They are shown in Figure 37.4. It can be observed that fuzzy compatibil-

Table 37.1   Data for the Illustrative Example

Component	Boiling point temperature (K)	Fuzzy F_i (kmol.h^{-1})			
		a	b	c	d
A - Propane	231.1	2.5	4.9	6	7.5
B - i Butane	261.3	7.5	14.9	15.1	23
C - n Butane	272.7	12.5	24	29	38
D - i Pentane	301.0	10	16	20	30
E - n Pentane	309.2	17	32	36	52

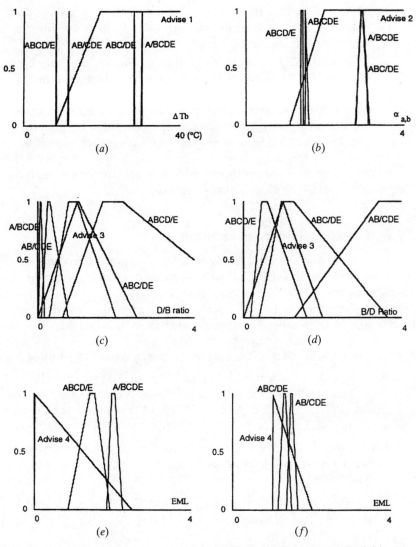

Figure 37.3 Quantification of advises and data description (detailed example) (a) advise 1; (b) advise 2; (c) advise 3 (D/B ratio) (d) advise 3 (B/D ratio); (e) and (f) advise 4.

ities are not always of trapezoidal form, even if data and advises are classical TrFNs. Finally, Figure 37.5 shows the conjunction of these compatibilities. It is easy to see that the final step of the first separation elucidation gives the separation ABC/DE as best separation of the five-component mixture. Our procedure, by the computation of Liou and Wang's integrals retrieves this result. The procedure is continued with the three-component mixture ABC to be separated. Finally, the optimal sequence is [ABC/DE; AB/C; A/B; D/E].

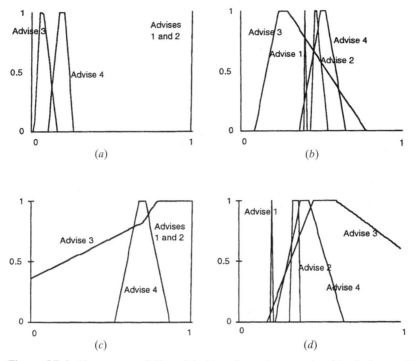

Figure 37.4 Fuzzy compatibility advise/data for each separation (detailed example) (a) A/BCDE; (b) AB/CDE; (c) ABC/DE; (d) ABCD/E.

37.7. Industrial Example and Uncertainty Analysis

Let us analyze the separation of an industrial seven-component mixture. Feed characteristics are given in Table 37.2.

For this seven-component separation, the best separation sequence resulting from the presented procedure (advises are equal importance) is [ABCD/EFG; ABC/D; AB/C; A/B; EF/G; E/F].

The influence of uncertainty on the choice of the first separation point is now discussed. The uncertainty analysis was carried out on various values of the bandwidth δ, where $(m - a) = (d - m) = \delta m$, with $m = c - b/2$ and $0 \le \delta \le 1$. We have plotted in Figure 37.6 the variations of the integral values of Liou and Wang [11], basic item leading to the separation point choice, versus the values of the bandwidth δ, that is, the percentage of data uncertainty.

It can be observed, for example, that the separation ABC/DEFG, which is the best one with precise data, becomes out of interest when the uncertainty increases. This is a basic point for the design of separation units, because it shows the relative stability of the engineer choice with data uncertainty, at the preliminary stage of a chemical unit elaboration. For this seven-component separation problem and for a large range of uncertainties in the feed flowrates, the best separation sequence resulting

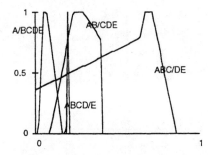

Figure 37.5 Conjunction of the compatibilities (detailed example).

from the synthesis procedure coupled with the uncertainty analysis is [ABCD/EFG; AB/CD; A/B; C/D; EF/G; E/F].

37.8. Fuzzy Design of Separation Sequences

Once the synthesis of separation sequences has occurred, a fuzzy technico-economical design can be carried out, with respect to data uncertainties. The current procedure generally used in chemical engineering consists in overdesign of each separation task in order to avoid data imprecision and uncertainties. We have chosen to get a fuzzy design of the plant, to obtain fuzzy technical characteristics of each separation (column heights and diameters) and fuzzy economical parameters (cost of each separation, total annual cost of the plant) by preserving data uncertainty description. The data uncertainties are the same as previously. The technico-economical criterion related to separation sequences has been evaluated, by using technical correlations given by the literature and by extending them to the fuzzy data case.

The design of each separation (distillation) column is made by a classical iterative shortcut method [14]: the distribution of the components in the distillate and the bottoms is computed by solving the Engstebeck and Geddes equations; the Fenske equation gives the minimum number of plates, and the minimum reflux ratio is calculated from nonlinear Underwood equation. Finally, the number of theoretical plates is computed

Table 37.2 Data for the Industrial Example

Component	Boiling point temperature (K)	Fuzzy F_i (kmol.h^{-1})			
		a	b	c	d
A - Propylene	225.4	42	70	115	168
B - Propane	231.1	44	76	110	170
C - i Butane	261.3	150	307	460	672
D - n Butane	272.7	100	192	288	420
E - i Pentane	301.0	78	150	228	333
F - n Pentane	309.2	150	320	480	700
G - Hexane	341.9	78	153	230	336

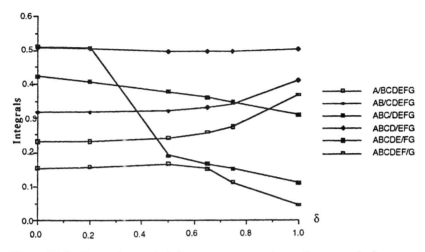

Figure 37.6 Uncertainty analysis (seven-component mixture, first separation).

from the Eduljee equation, and the feed plate location from the Kirk-bride correlation.

The investment cost of a distillation column is made up of three items: FOB (freight on board) costs of shell and trays; FOB costs of heat exchangers (reboiler and condenser) and direct and indirect costs of equipment installation and contingencies. The Mulet et al. [15] method is selected for estimating shell and trays FOB costs, as a function of the shell diameter, height tangent to tangent and weight. The heat exchanger FOB costs are computed with the method given by Woods et al. [16], the design parameter being the heat transfer area. The two previous costs, which are only base costs, are adjusted to FOB actual costs by means of corrective factors, relative to pressure, temperature, type of equipment, and number of plates. The equipment installation costs and contingencies are computed by the Guthrie's modular method [17].

Among the methods able to compute functions of fuzzy variables F_i, we have extended the vertex method of Dong and Shah [9]. For each α-cut, the solution of two nonlinear programming problems (NLP) gives the lower and upper bounds for the nonlinear function f (height of the column, diameter, cost) to be computed:

$$B_{\text{lower}}\left(f(F_i)\right) = \text{Min } f(F_i); \; B_{\text{upper}}\left(f(F_i)\right) = \text{Max } f(F_i)$$

with

$$F_{il} \le F_i \le F_{iu}, i = 1 \text{ to } n$$
(F_{il} and F_{iu} are lower and upper bounds of F_i for each α-cut)

An example of fuzzy cost, for the case of the five-component mixture above mentioned, is shown in Figure 37.7.

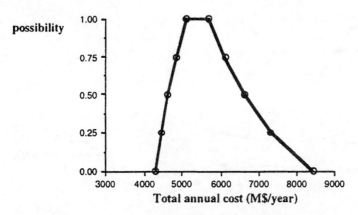

Figure 37.7   Total annual cost of the five-component separation
problem.

   This result takes into account the uncertainties of the flowrates mentioned. The engineer may either defuzzify this result, to obtain more classical cost estimation, or preserve this type of fuzzy result that gives a
more realistic cost estimation of the plant.

37.9. Conclusion

In this chapter, a new procedure for synthesizing, designing, and costing
separation sequences was presented. The main interests of this approach
are:

- The graduation of the design rules that avoids "crisp reasoning."
  Indeed, in many classical heuristic or evolutionary methods, the synthesis advises are implemented according to a predefined order.

- The use and propagation, in synthesis or costing procedures, of
  uncertainties on input data, instead of overestimating crisp output
  results.

- The uncertainty analysis that provides the engineer with significant
  information on reliability of the chosen separation sequence referring to the uncertainty of design data.

- The flexibility in the synthesis procedure due to the use of both
  fuzzy concepts in synthesis advises and data.

These points constitute a significant advance for real-world chemical
engineering problems.
   Works in progress on separation sequence synthesis aim at taking into
account other kinds of uncertainties that can arise (economical factors,
physico-chemical parameters, and others) in a complete fuzzy design

procedure. Another panel of works under development concerns the implementation of a backtracking procedure in the fuzzy branch and bound procedure.

37.10. References

[1] Nishida, N., et al. "A Review of Process Synthesis." *American Institute of Chemical Engineers Journal,* Vol. 27, No. 141. (1981).

[2] Floquet, P., et al. "Mathematical Programming Tools for Chemical Engineering Process Design Synthesis." *Chemical Engineering Process,* Vol. 23, No. 99. (1988).

[3] Floquet, P., et al. "Some Complements in Combinatorics of Sharp Separation Systems Synthesis." *American Institute of Chemical Engineers Journal,* Vol. 39, No. 6 (1993).

[4] Aly, S., et al. "Heuristic Approach for Designing Distillation Sequences." *AMSE Periodicals Modeling Measurements & Controls,* Vol. 36, No. 2 (1993).

[5] Lu, M.D., et al. "Computer-Aided Total Flowsheet Synthesis." *Institution of Chemical Engineers Symposium Series,* Vol. 74, No. 141. (1982).

[6] Floquet, P., et al. "Fuzzy Heuristic Approach for Sharp Separation Sequence Synthesis." *Computers and Chemical Engineering,* Vol. 18, No. 9 (1974).

[7] Thompson, R.W., and C.J. King. "Systematic Synthesis of Separation Schemes." *American Institute of Chemical Engineers Journal,* Vol. 8, No. 941 (1972).

[8] Dubois, D., and H. Prade. *Theorie des Possibilites.* Masson: 1988.

[9] Dong, W., and H.C. Shah. "Vertex Method for Computing Functions of Fuzzy Variables." *Fuzzy Sets and Systems,* Vol. 24, No. 65 (1987).

[10] Dubois, D., and H. Prade. *Fuzzy Sets and Systems, Theory and Applications.* New York: Academic Press, 1980.

[11] Liou, T.S., and M.J.J. Wang. "Ranking Fuzzy Numbers with Integral Value." *Fuzzy Sets and Systems,* Vol. 50, No. 247 (1992).

[12] Bortolan, G., and R. Degani. "A Review of Some Methods for Ranking Fuzzy Numbers." *Fuzzy Sets and Systems,* Vol. 15, No. 1 (1985).

[13] Lee, E.S., and R.J. Li. "Comparison of Fuzzy Numbers based on the Probability Measure of Fuzzy Events." *Computers and Mathematical Applications,* Vol. 15, No. 10 (1988).

[14] Pibouleau, L., and S. Domenech. "Discrete and Continuous Approaches to the Optimal Synthesis of Distillation Sequences." *Computers and Chemical Engineering,* Vol. 10, No. 5 (1986).

[15] Mulet, A., et al. "Estimation Costs of Distillation and Absorption Towers via Correlations." *Chemical Engineering,* Vol. 88, No. 26 (1981).

[16] Woods, D.R., et al. "Evaluation of Capital Cost Data: Heat Exchangers." *Canadian Journal of Chemical Engineering,* Vol. 54, No. 469 (1976).

[17] Guthrie, K.M. "Capital Cost Estimating." *Chemical Engineering,* Vol. 24, No. 114 (1969).

38 Improving Engineering Design with Fuzzy Sets

Erik K. Antonsson
Engineering Design Research Laboratory
Division of Engineering and Applied Science
California Institute of Technology

Kevin N. Otto
Department of Mechanical Engineering
Massachusetts Institute of Technology

ABSTRACT: The Method of Imprecision (M_OI) is a formal method, utilizing the mathematics of fuzzy sets, for incorporating the natural level of imprecision that occurs throughout the engineering design process. This chapter presents the details of the Level Interval Algorithm (LIA) used internally by the M_OI, and its extensions to permit application to engineering design problems in industry where monotonicity cannot be guaranteed, only discrete values may be available for some variables (and hence continuity must be relaxed), and engineering analyses are expensive and must be minimized.

Computation problems that reach beyond the scope of the LIA, such as singularities, are also examined, showing that the LIA behaves no worse than conventional calculations in the presence of these difficulties.

38.1. Introduction

Imprecision is an integral part of the engineering design process, not imprecision in thought or logic, but rather the intrinsic vagueness of a preliminary, incomplete description. Obtaining *precise* information upon which to base decisions is usually impossible, yet it is critical to make early engineering design decisions on a sound basis.

At the stage where concepts are being generated, the description of a design is nearly completely vague or imprecise (fuzzy). This imprecision is reduced during the design process until ultimately the final description is precise (crisp), except for tolerances, which represent the allowable limits on stochastic manufacturing and material variations.

The need for a methodology to represent and manipulate imprecision is greatest in the early, preliminary phases of engineering design, where the designer is most unsure of the final dimensions and shape, materials and properties, and performance of the completed design. Additionally, the most important decisions, those with the greatest effect on overall cost, are made in these early stages [12, 38, 41, 43].

Our work focuses on the development of methods for representing and manipulating imprecise descriptions of designs to permit the designer to compare alternatives during the preliminary design phase. Because design imprecision concerns the choice of design variable values used to describe an artifact or process, we use the designer's preference to quantify the imprecision with which design variables are known. Preference, as used here, denotes either subjective or objective information that may be quantified and included in the evaluation of design alternatives. We call our approach the *Method of Imprecision* (M_OI) [2, 20, 23, 24, 25, 26, 27, 36, 45, 46, 47, 48]. Other researchers have also recently contributed to this area: Diaz [6, 7], Hamburg [11, 13], Knosala and Pedrycz [18], Müller and Thärigen [22], Posthoff [29], Rao [30, 31, 32, 33, 34], Sakawa and Kato [35, 37], Thurston and Carnahan [39, 40], and Zimmermann and Sebastian [50, 51, 52]. The following sections present a brief review of how imprecision is used to facilitate decision making in engineering design using the M_OI, followed by a description of the calculation methods (and a few difficulties).

38.2. The Method of Imprecision

The M_OI begins with one or more design alternatives, at the concept level. The designer's preferences are then applied to each of the variables that (imprecisely) describe the design. Commonly, performance specifications will also be imprecisely described and can be elicited from customers through market surveys, and so on. The imprecise design variables are then *induced* onto the performance space, by use of the algorithm described in a moment. The design preferences induced onto the performance variables are compared to the specifications. At that point, decisions regarding the feasibility of each alternative concept can be made, and promising ranges of design variables can be identified.

Definitions and Notation: *Design variables* are denoted d_i, and the valid design variable values within the *design variable space* (DVS) form a subset X. The set of valid values for d_i is denoted X_i. The preference that a designer has for values of d_i, the ith design variable, is represented by a preference function on X_i, called the *design preference:* $\mu_d(d_i)$.

Performance variables are denoted p_j. For each performance variable p_j there must be a mapping f_j such that $p_j = f_j(\vec{d})$. The mappings f_j can be any calculation or procedure to measure the performance of a design, including closed-form equations (*e.g.*, for stress, weight, speed, cost, *etc.*), iterative solutions, heuristic methods, "black box" calculations, testing of prototypes, or consumer evaluations. The subset of valid performance variable values $\mathcal{Y}$ is mapped from X, and the set of valid values for p_js denoted $\mathcal{Y}_j$. The *performance variable space* (PVS) is the dependent set of performances evaluated for each design in the DVS. In order to compare design alternatives, design preferences are mapped onto the PVS via the extension principle [49], discussed shortly.

Specifications and requirements also embody design imprecision, even though most are written as if they were crisp; for example, "This device must have a range of at least 250 km." Such a requirement implies that given two designs arbitrarily close together, one with a range of 250 km and one just below, the first would be acceptable but not the second, as shown by the dashed line in Figure 38.1. Specifications and requirements in the real world are commonly fuzzy. Often the designer must ask questions to distinguish the underlying fuzzy constraint so that the final design will satisfy the customer's actual requirements even though it may violate the crisp constraint initially given. The fuzziness of constraints and the fuzziness of preliminary design variables are both forms of design imprecision and can be represented in exactly the same way. The customer's preference (requirements) for values of p_j, the jth performance variable, is represented by a preference function called the *functional requirement:* $\mu_p(p_j)$. The solid line in Figure 38.1 shows a fuzzy functional requirement.

Quantifying Imprecision: Utility and risk-aversion are quantified in utility theory via the lottery method [17]. Unfortunately, no such formal method exists for eliciting preference [4, 5, 9, 14, 15]. However, limits of acceptability for variable values, whether communicated formally or established informally by experience, are familiar to engineers in industry [42]. Such acceptable limits correspond to intervals over which preference is greater than zero. This suggests that rather than determine the

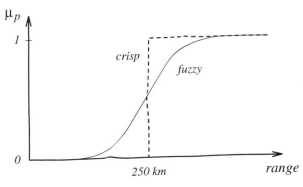

Figure 38.1 Example of imprecise functional requirement.

preference μ_d at each value of d, as shown in Figure 38.1, it may be more natural to determine the intervals in d, called α-cuts, over which μ_d equals or exceeds certain preference values α. The use of intervals encourages the passing of set-based design information between engineering groups early in the design process [42], and permits the early release of possible sets of design data from one engineering group to the next in advance of precise design information. This approach has many advantages over the traditional "point-by-point" design iteration. The M_OI can extend set-based concurrent design by providing preference information over the possible range of design data.

Imprecision Calculations: After specifying design preferences μ_{d_i} on X_i and functional requirements μ_{p_j} on Y_j (and an aggregation function [36, 23]), the next step is to determine the induced values of μ_{d_i} on $\mathcal{Y}$ (design preferences mapped onto the performances), given by Zadeh's *extension principle* [49]:

$$\mu_d(\overrightarrow{p}) = \sup_{\overrightarrow{d}:\overrightarrow{p}=\overrightarrow{f}(\overrightarrow{d})} [\mu_d(\overrightarrow{d})] \tag{1}$$

A simple one-dimensional example of Zadeh's extension principle is shown in Figure 38.2. The performance p achieved for each value of the design variable d is given by the function f, which is a curve in this simple example. The corresponding $\mu_d(d)$ can be mapped onto p, producing $\mu_d(p)$, the design preference mapped onto the performance space (as illustrated by the dashed lines in Figure 38.2). For higher-dimension design problems, each p will be a function of many d's, and each function f will be a hypersurface.

An algorithm to compute Zadeh's extension principle (and thus to calculate $\mu_d(\overrightarrow{p})$) is the *Level Interval Algorithm* (LIA), first proposed by

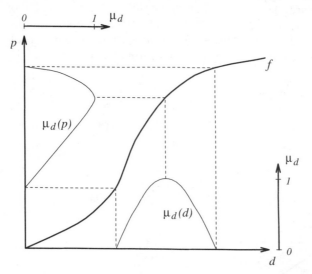

Figure 38.2   Zadeh's extension principle.

W. M. Dong and F. S. Wong [8] as the "Fuzzy Weighted Average" algorithm and also called the "Vertex Method." Note that in the simple example preceding f is nonlinear. Nonmonotonic and discrete functions can also be used, as introduced in [26, 48], and reviewed later here.

Once the imprecision on each design variable ($\mu_d(\overrightarrow{d}\,)$) is induced onto the PVS, the induced preferences are combined with the functional requirements ($\mu_p(\overrightarrow{p})$) to obtain an overall preference ($\mu_o(\overrightarrow{p})$). The point (or points) with the highest preference correspond to the performance of the overall most preferred design(s). The design problem is to find the corresponding set of design variables ($\overrightarrow{d}\,^*$) that produce the maximum overall preference ($\mu_o^*(\overrightarrow{d}\,^*)$). In the typical engineering design case, where the inverse mapping ($\overrightarrow{f}^{-1} : \mathcal{Y} \to \mathcal{X}$) doesn't exist, $\mu_o(\overrightarrow{d}\,)$ can still be obtained point by point [19].

38.3. The Computational Model for Design Imprecision

As indicated, one of the central elements of the procedure to represent and manipulate imprecision in engineering design developed by the authors, and briefly just described, is the algorithm to induce preferences from independent variables to dependent ones. The following sections describe the algorithm as originally presented in the literature and some of the extensions recently developed and implemented.

38.3.1. Computation of the Extension Principle

Kaufmann and Gupta [16, 44] describe an analytical method of calculating a fuzzy output (an application of Zadeh's extension principle) from imprecise inputs. This method is based on α-cuts [16] and interval arithmetic [21]. Although the method is straightforward in its approach, the manipulation of symbols and the solution of expressions that include high-order polynomials, both in the numerator and denominator (for extended division), make this method infeasible for computer-assisted design applications. This is compounded by the fact that the exact solution to the analytical application of the extension principle can be shown to be equivalent to an unwieldy nonlinear programming problem [3]. A discrete numerical approach is therefore necessary to meet the computational requirements for handling many design variables. The next section discusses useful numerical techniques.

38.3.1.1. The Level Interval Algorithm (LIA). Many discrete and analytical methods exist in the literature for carrying out extended operations with fuzzy sets (or fuzzy numbers). The Fuzzy Weighted Average (FWA) algorithm, as presented by W. M. Dong and F. S. Wong in [8], outlines a simple and efficient algorithm that is useful for carrying out engineering design calculations. This algorithm is extended here for generalized real functions of fuzzy variables, and the extended form is referred to as the *level interval algorithm* (LIA). Comparing the algorithm to the analytical method outlined in [16], LIA uses the interval analysis techniques as described; yet, LIA simplifies the process extensively by discretizing the membership functions of the input fuzzy numbers into a prescribed number of α-cuts. Performing interval analysis for each α-cut and combining the resultant intervals, the output is a discretized fuzzy set, the performance variable output of input preference functions for the case of a design calculation. Dong and Wong also include a combinatorial interval analysis technique in order to avoid the problems of the multiple occurrence of variables for division and multiplication in an algebraic equation expression. A condensed version of the algorithm from [8] has been provided (where the terminology has been changed to reflect the application to design calculations). Later sections describe the implementation and extension of this algorithm.

There are conditions that must be satisfied for application of the algorithm: the preference functions must satisfy the normality and convexity conditions and must be continuous over the design variables $(\tilde{d})$, no singularities of the functions can occur over $\tilde{d}$ (*i.e.*, no division by zero can occur, and no zero arguments can occur in $f_i(\overrightarrow{d})$ for each $\tilde{d}_i$ for the unary operations, such as the natural logarithm and the square root), and only monotonic regions of multivalued functions, for example, sine and cosine, are computed for a given $\tilde{d}_i$.

The algorithm is as follows: for N real imprecise design variables, $\tilde{d}_1, \ldots, \tilde{d}_N$, let d_i ($i \in [1,N]$) be an element of $\tilde{d}_i$. Given a performance variable represented by the mapping:

$$p = f(d_1, \ldots, d_N) \qquad d_i \in \tilde{d}_i,$$

let $\tilde{P}$ be the fuzzy output of the mapping. The following steps lead to the solution of $\tilde{P}$.

1. For each $\tilde{d}_i$, discretize the preference function into a number of α values, $\alpha_1, \ldots, \alpha_M$, where M is the number of steps in the discretization.

2. Determine the intervals for each variable $\tilde{d}_i$, $i = 1, \ldots, N$ at each α-cut, $\alpha_j, j = 1, \ldots, M$.

3. Using one end point from each of the N intervals for each α_j, combine the end points into an *N-ary* array such that 2^N distinct permutations exist for the array.

4. For each of the 2^N permutations, determine $p_k = f(d_1, \ldots, d_N)$, $k = 1, \ldots, 2^N$. The resultant interval for the α-cut, α_j, is then given by:

$$\tilde{P}^{\alpha_j} = [\min(p_k), \max(p_k)].$$

Figure 38.3 shows the results of the analytical application of the extension principle to the column-stress equation.

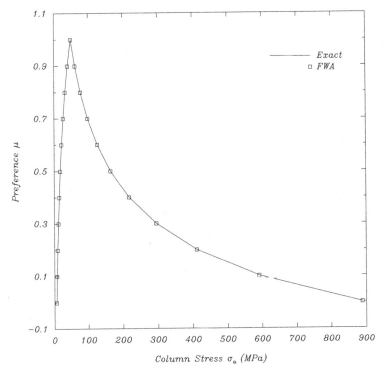

Figure 38.3 Example column calculation: Exact and LIA.

$$\sigma_a = \frac{\pi^2 E}{n\left(\dfrac{Kl}{r}\right)^2}. \tag{2}$$

The input variables for the maximum allowable stress σ_a are triangular preference functions as listed in Table 38.1.

38.3.1.2. Extending LIA for Internal Extrema.   The LIA is valid only for real-valued functions f, and corresponding interval extensions $F(X_0)$ that do not include internal bounded *extrema* for the intervals in question, $X \in X_0$. This is because only the end points (at a given α-cut) of the input variables $d_i \, i = 1, \ldots, N$ are used in the computation. An extension to the LIA will now be introduced to determine the correct bounds $P^{\alpha_j}(\overrightarrow{D}^{\alpha_j})$ for a given α-cut α_j with the following procedure:

Table 38.1   Design Variable Data for Column Equation

DPs (units)	$\alpha = 0$	$\alpha = 1$	$\alpha = 0$
n	1.0	3.0	5.0
l/r	60.0	100.0	160.0
E (GPa)	75.0	150.0	225.0
K (simply-supported)	1.0	1.0	1.0

1. For each α-cut α_j, determine if an internal extremum exists for the α-cut intervals of d_i, $i = 1, 2, \ldots, n$, $p = f(d_1, d_2, \ldots, d_n)$. This may be accomplished by either analytically or numerically solving:

$$\frac{\partial p}{\partial d_i} = 0$$

   for each d_i as a set of simultaneous equations. Section 38.3.2 introduces an additional extension to efficiently locate internal extrema by use of optimization methods [20].

2. Denote the extrema by ξ_l and the values of the d_i that make up a given ξ_l by $\varepsilon_{l,i}$. If none of the points $\varepsilon_{l,i}$ lies within X_0, the extrema can be ignored and the standard LIA applied as before.

3. If every $\varepsilon_{l,i}$ lies within the α-cut X_α, calculate $\xi_l = f(\varepsilon_{l,i})$.

4. If not every $\varepsilon_{l,i}$ lies within the α-cut, let q span those that do not, $\varepsilon_{l,q}$, and m span those that do, $\varepsilon_{l,m}$. Calculate all of the extrema values outside X_α (but within X_0) as $\xi_l = f(\varepsilon_m, d_q)$. This will be a two-factorial set across the end points of the α-cut for all $\tilde{d}_q$.

5. Continuing with the standard LIA, using one end point from each of the N intervals for each α_j, combine the end points into an N-ary array such that 2^N distinct permutations exist for the array. For each of the 2^N permutations, k determine $p_k = f(d_1, \ldots, d_N)$.

6. The resultant interval for the α-cut α_j is given by:

$$P^{\alpha_j} = [\min(p_k, \xi_l), \max(p_k, \xi_l)]$$

   over all k, l.

To illustrate the application of this algorithm, consider the function z: $\mathbb{R} \rightarrow \mathbb{R} \mid z(x) = 2.927x^3 - 1.927x$, which is a cubic equation passing through $(-1, -1)$, $(0, 0)$, and $(1, 1)$ with two local extremum, as shown in Figure 38.4. (The function z is to be interpreted as a performance variable p.)

Let $\tilde{X}$ be a triangular imprecise number with preference function $\mu(x|\tilde{X})$, where $\mu(x|\tilde{X})$ equals 0 outside $\{x | x \in (-1, 1)\}$, equals 1 at $x = 0$, and linearly increases to $\mu(0) = 1$ from the end points $\mu(-1) = 0$ and $\mu(1) = 0$. ($\tilde{X}$ is to interpreted as a design variable d.) Substituting $\tilde{X}$ and the equation for z into the LIA, the incorrect preference function for $\tilde{Z}$, shown in Figure 38.5, is obtained. The problem is the two local extrema in the function z. Hence the algorithm of section 38.3.1.2 must be applied.

Substituting $\tilde{X}$ and the equation for z into the extended LIA for functions with extrema, the correct preference function for $\tilde{Z}$, shown in Figure 38.6, is obtained. Jump discontinuities in preference occur at $z = \pm 0.602$. These result from the local extrema in the function z, shown in Figure 38.4 ($x = \pm 0.42$). At z values just above $z = 0.602$, only points in the neighborhood of $x = 0.926$ are in the preimage of these z; the map is one-to-one. But at z values just below $z = 0.602$, the preimage contains points in

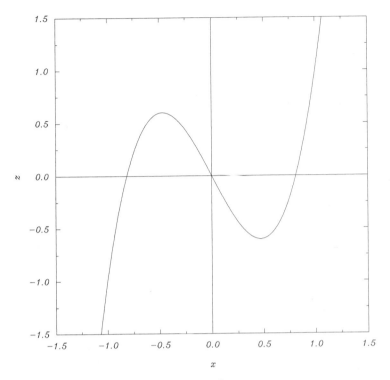

Figure 38.4 The cubic equation $z = 2.927x^3 - 1.927x$.

the neighborhood of both $x = -0.42$ and $x = 0.926$. Values of z below the local maximum in Figure 38.4 ($x = -0.42$, $z = 0.602$) have three points x in their preimage. Points in the neighborhood of $x = -0.42$ have higher preference than points in the neighborhood of $x = 0.926$, and hence at $z = 0.602$ there is a jump discontinuity in preference.

This type of discontinuity in output preference is easily understood; it arises from the multiplicity of points in the map's preimage (in this case, at most three points). The multiplicity here is finite, and can be dealt with using the extended LIA. Real concerns arise, however, when the output preference functions exhibit unboundedness, either in support or in the number of discontinuities. Representation and calculation of the imprecise preference functions then becomes difficult, as will be demonstrated in section 38.4.

38.3.2. Optimization

One of the major limitations of the LIA stems from the assumption that the extreme values of f_j will occur at the corner points of the D_{α_k} n-cube [20]. The algorithm may thus be improved by relaxing this assumption. The problem restated is to find:

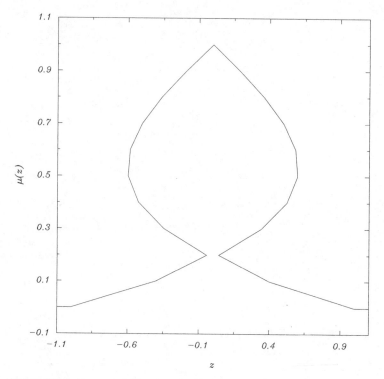

Figure 38.5 Incorrect LIA solution for $\mu(z|\tilde{Z})$.

$$p_{j\min}^{\alpha_k} = \min\{p_j = f_j(\vec{d}\,) \mid \vec{d} \in D_{\alpha_k}\}$$
$$p_{j\max}^{\alpha_k} = \max\{p_j = f_j(\vec{d}\,) \mid \vec{d} \in D_{\alpha_k}\}$$

(3)

Finding extrema within a subspace is a constrained optimization problem.

In choosing an optimization technique, a trade-off must be made between computational cost and robustness. Traditional calculus-based optimization methods converge in relatively few function evaluations but seek only local minima. Randomized search methods such as genetic algorithms offer greater robustness [10] but require more function evaluations. Where function evaluations are relatively expensive, as is common in engineering design, traditional optimization methods are a satisfying solution.

The traditional optimization algorithm utilized here is Powell's method, which begins as a one-at-a-time search. After each iteration, a heuristic determines whether to replace the direction of maximum decrease with the net direction moved during the last iteration. This allows minimization down valleys while avoiding linear dependence in the set of search directions [1].

An important feature for a practical computational tool is a means to trade off the number of function evaluations against accuracy. Such an adjustment enables the designer to use the same program to obtain quick

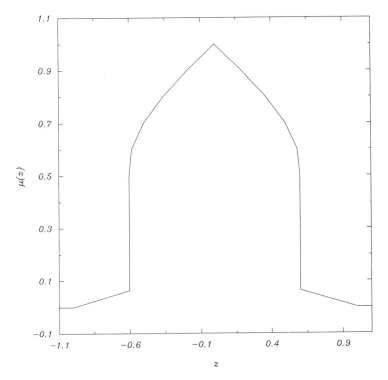

Figure 38.6 Output preference function $\mu(z|\tilde{}Z)$.

estimates as well as precise evaluations. This is implemented as a user-specified fractional precision that defines termination criteria for the optimization algorithm.

Suppose that it is necessary to incur the minimum number of function evaluations. A fractional precision of 1 would be specified, creating automatically satisfied termination criteria, and the optimization would proceed through exactly one iteration of a one-at-a-time search using the maximum step size. The algorithm begins at one corner of the search space D_{α_k}, and checks corners in each of the n directions given by $d_1, \ldots, d_n$, moving to the minimum each time. It expends $n + 1$ function evaluations to find each end point, and therefore $2n + 2$ per α-cut, as compared to 2^n per α-cut for the LIA. This is a substantial improvement, but the α-cut interval obtained is only correct if f_j is monotonic: none of the interior points of the D_{α_k} n-cube is evaluated. Minimizing function evaluations carries the cost of implicitly assuming monotonicity.

If f_j is known to be monotonic, $2n + 2$ is not the minimum number of function evaluations. The first pass of the optimization algorithm identifies the direction for each d_i in which f_j increases. Subsequent extrema can then be directly evaluated, without the need for searching. Hence, where f_j is monotonic, $n + 2$ function evaluations are required for the first α-cut and 2 for each subsequent α-cut. Experimental design methods [28] may also be used to identify design variables with near-linear effects, and remove those directions from the optimization search [20].

38.4. Anomalies in Imprecise Calculations

38.4.1. Introduction

The extended-operations algorithm (LIA) presented provides a basis for computing with sets of *imprecise* variables in preliminary engineering design. Even though the algorithm and extensions can be applied to standard computing functions, certain limitations apply. For the LIA without the optimization extension the preference functions must satisfy the normality and convexity conditions and must be continuous over $\tilde{}d$; no singularities of the functions can occur over $\tilde{}d$ and only monotonic regions of multivalued functions, for instance, sine and cosine, are computed for a given $\tilde{d}_i$. For the optimization extended algorithm, the continuity and monotonicity requirements are relaxed, though singularities must still be avoided. This section considers cases in which one or more of these conditions are violated.

38.4.2. Unbounded Preference Functions

Consider the possibility of functions that operate on well-formed imprecise numbers and create output preference functions whose support becomes unbounded. If such functions exist, they would fail when applying the methods of section 38.3.

Consider an imprecise number $\tilde{X}$ of "about 1/4, and possibly negative"; that is, let $\tilde{X}$ be a triangular imprecise number with preference function $\mu(x|\tilde{X})$, where $\mu(1/4) = 1$, and $\mu(x|\tilde{X}) = 0$ outside $\{x|x \in (1/4 - s, 1/4 + s)\}$, and s will be gradually increased to observe the variation in calculation results. Such an imprecise number will be expected to become ill-defined with inversion (when s becomes large enough to encompass zero), since the inverse of points in the neighborhood of zero become unbounded.

The imprecise variable $\tilde{}X$ centered at 1/4 was systematically increased in support to include negative numbers to observe the effects of inclusion of zero within the support. The effect on the output of the inverse function $z : \mathbb{R} \to \mathbb{R} \mid z(x) = 1/x$ was observed. Substituting $\tilde{}X$ and the equation for z into the extension principle, the equation for the preference of any z becomes:

$$\mu(z) = \mu(x), \text{ where } x : x = 1/z \tag{4}$$

since $z = f(x) = 1/x$ is one-to-one.

The results are shown in Figure 38.7. As s increases, the preference function for z begins to extend to include nonzero preference for unbounded values; all calculations are performed with the nominal $\tilde{X}$

remaining at 1/4. This is a case of a function that operates on a well-formed imprecise number and produces a preference function with unbounded support. This occurs because $\tilde{X}$ includes 0, a singularity of the function z. Hence the output preference includes $z(0) = 1/0 = \infty$. When the input preference function $\mu(x|\tilde{X})$ includes both positive and negative points in the neighborhood of zero, the output preference function $\mu(z)$ has support over both positive and negative values in the "neighborhood" of infinity. Therefore the output preference function will appear as shown in Figure 38.7.

The LIA will fail, of course, since zero is a singularity of z, and hence cannot occur in $\tilde{X}$. This result seems to indicate that using preference curves to represent designer uncertainty will sometimes fail. But consider what the result indicates when the preference function is interpreted as the degree of designer preference. The unbounded results on z are due to the preferences stated on x. The problem has been incorrectly formulated, and must be reformulated to hedge the preferences on x away from the singular point zero, just as the designer would have to do if imprecision were not used. This method warns the designer of the problem, whereas using crisp or single-valued calculations (in the example, just using $x = 1/4$) would not.

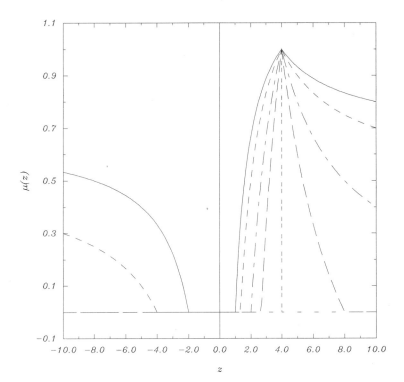

Figure 38.7 Output preference functions $\mu(z)$.

38.4.3. Singular Points and Preference Functions

Consider any function that operates on well-formed imprecise numbers and creates an output preference function requiring a limit process for evaluation. Such could be the case of a function with a singularity within the support of the design variable's preference. To demonstrate this, consider $z : \mathbb{R} \rightarrow [-1, 1] \subset \mathbb{R}$ such that:

$$z(x) = \begin{cases} \sin(1/x) & x \neq 0 \\ 0 & x = 0 \end{cases}$$

This function has a nonremovable singularity at $x = 0$ (multiplying by $(x - 0)^n$ will not create a locally regular function for any n). As $x \rightarrow 0$, $z(x)$ oscillates an unbounded number of times between -1 and 1 (refer to Figure 38.8). The question then arises as to the output preference behavior when the input imprecise number $\tilde{X}$ includes in its support the singular point $x = 0$.

Let $\tilde{X}$ be an imprecise number with preference function $\mu(x|\tilde{X})$, where $\mu(x|\tilde{X}) = 0$ outside $\{x | x \in (-\pi + s, \pi)\}$, $\mu(s/2) = 1$, and s is gradually decreased from $3/2\pi$ to 0 to observe the variation in calculation results. Figure 38.9 shows the corresponding output preference functions resulting from application of the extension principle to the imprecise numbers $\tilde{X}$.

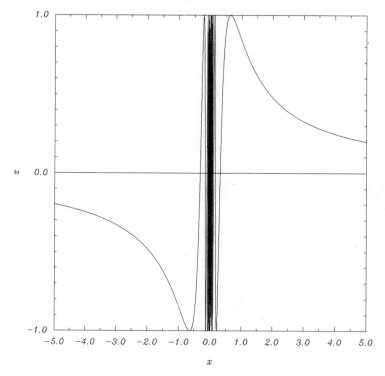

Figure 38.8 The function $z = \sin(1/x)$.

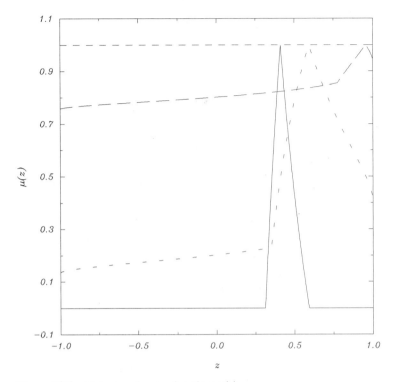

Figure 38.9   Output preference functions $\mu(z)$.

When the support for the input $\tilde{X}$ does not include the singular point 0 (*i.e.*, $s > \pi$), the output preference function remains perfectly well defined. When the input preference function does include the singular point for any support range, the output preference function would be expected to become not well defined, since the function z itself becomes oscillatory (unstable). But note that the output preference function remains well defined. This is due to the supremum in the extension principle definition, and the selected input preference function $\mu(x|\tilde{X})$. There is always a point x in each z value's preimage such that the preference of that x is greater than the singular point preference. Since this supremum preference is greater than the singular point preference, the preference for all z are well defined. Hence the preference $\mu(z)$ is well defined when $x = 0$ does not have the peak preference among all x. When $x = 0$ has the peak preference, the *sup* definition must be explicitly used, since the point with maximum preference in the preimage of any z does not exist; only a least upper bound exists. All values of z have in their preimage points x arbitrarily close to zero. In this case, the peak preference of $x = 0$ would be the least upper bound of preference for all z, *i.e.*, $\mu(z) = 1 \ \forall z$.

Calculation of the preference for $z = \sin(1/x)$ poses difficulty. There are numerous and possibly an infinite number of internal extrema within the support of the design variable (depending if $x = 0$ is in the support).

Hence the methods of section 38.3.1.2 are impractical as posed. They must be extended using a limiting process. That is, the support of $\mu(x)$ must be split into monotonic intervals of z between the zeros of the slope of z as discussed and solved in section 38.3.1.2. The difference here is that there are an unbounded number of such intervals. However, these intervals will become smaller in a limit as will their contribution to $\mu(z)$. The limiting process can be terminated with a convergence criterion.

Given that functions exist that exhibit such computational difficulty, a mechanism must be found to identify when the methods of section 38.3 will fail. This problem's key feature, which causes the real-time methods to fail, is the presence of the singularity of the function z in the design variable $\tilde{X}$'s support. The same can be said of the previous example involving unbounded support ($z = 1/x$). In both cases, the output preference functions are defined and exist, but they exhibit difficulty in representation or evaluation. These effects are a direct result of the singularity of the function being within the support of the design variable.

Note in the case of $z = \sin(1/x)$, the singularity requires particular care, in that $\mu(z)$ is defined, even though there is a singularity of z within $\tilde{X}$. Any conclusions drawn by a designer when observing such a resulting preference curve for z may be misleading. Failure to meet the criteria of the real-time techniques of section 38.3 indicates that the functions being considered (z) are incompatible with the specified design variable preference functions ($\mu(x|\tilde{X})$), and hence is a warning to the designer that the values desired for $\tilde{X}$ should be reconsidered.

38.5. Interpretability of Imprecision Results

Consider the possible existence of continuous functions $f : \mathcal{D} \to \mathcal{P}$ that operate on well-formed design variable preference functions and with them create output performance variable preference functions that oscillate in preference from 0 to 1 as the output z approaches a limit value $\bar{z}$. The existence of any such function would question the viability of the entire proposed method, since such a function would be an interpretable mapping from a design variable set, where the preferences are known, to an output set where the preferences are uninterpretable. Via construction, it will be shown (though not formally proven) that this is only possible for functions that are infinitely multivalued (have an infinite number of branches), but need not be singular. The existence of any such function that maps specified preferences into uninterpretable preferences is not due to the fuzzy extension principle, but rather to the multivalued character of the function itself.

Such a function z must convert a well-formed, convex input preference function $\mu(x|\tilde{X})$ into a preference function with a nonremovable singularity. Such a membership function might be of the form:

$$\mu(z) = 1/2 \sin(1/z) + 1/2,$$

or more simply behave like:

$$\mu(z) \sim \sin(1/z),$$

that is, behave uninterpretably in the neighborhood of $z = 0$. Denoting $z = f(x)$ the "equation" above can be inverted to derive:

$$f(x) = 1/\arcsin(\mu(z|\tilde{Z})).$$

Simplifying through the extension principle (equation 1), this can be equated to:

$$f(x) = 1/\arcsin(\mu(x|\tilde{X})).$$

Now define $\mu(x)$ as a convex function over all real values with range $[0, 1]$, such as e^{-x^2}. This construct:

$$z : \mathbb{R} \to \mathbb{R} \mid z = 1/\arcsin(e^{-x^2})$$

is based on $\mu(z)$ and $\mu(x)$. Using different functions that exhibit the same behavior as the chosen $\mu(z)$ and $\mu(x)$ will construct a similar z, though it may not be as easily expressible. The created z is defined over all x and contains no singularities. It is, however, multivalued (refer to Figure 38.10). Considering all of the branches, the preimage of each value z has either zero or two points x.

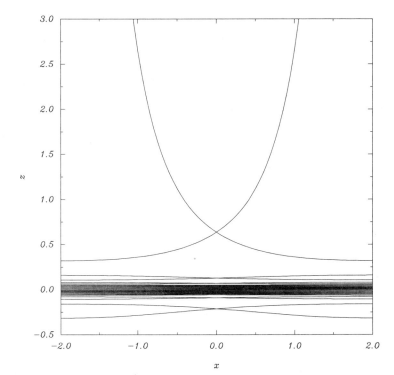

Figure 38.10 $z = \dfrac{1}{\arcsin(e^{-x^2})}$.

To observe the effects of z on an imprecise number $\tilde{X}$, consider $\tilde{X}$ where $\mu(x|\tilde{X}) = 0$ outside $\{x | x \in (-1, 1)\}$, $\mu(0) = 1$, and $\mu(x|\tilde{X})$ smoothly increases to the peak at 0 between -1 and 1. Substituting $\tilde{X}$ and the equation for z into the extension principle, the resulting $\mu(z)$ is shown in Figure 38.11.

Note that for z values in the neighborhood of zero, the preference function becomes arbitrary, from 0 through 1 in preference. That is, moving a small amount (δ) in the neighborhood of $z = 0$ will result in large changes in $\mu(z)$, from zero to one. Also note the intervals on z where the preference function is not mapped from any x (for example, all z values between $-\infty$ and $\sin(1/\pi)$). These z values require complex x; there are no real x in the preimage of these z. The number of such intervals in a neighborhood of z becomes unbounded as z approaches zero (and the length of the each interval approaches zero length). These intervals arise since f is not a surjection; that is, $Z = f(\mathbb{R}) \neq \mathbb{R}$, but $Z \subset \mathbb{R}$. According to the interpretation of preference used here, $\mu(z) \simeq 0$ for the values of z having no real points x in the preimage. Therefore $\mu(z) = 0$ for such points to define $\mu(z) \; \forall z$, as reflected in equation 1.

These results would suggest that a preference function could become uninterpretable, since this preference function became uninterpretable

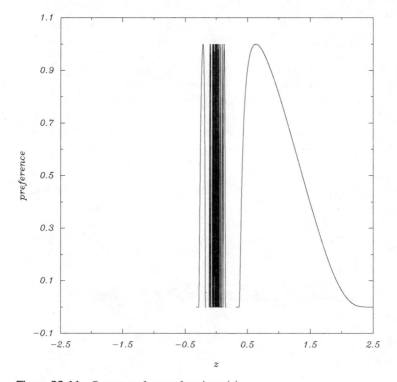

Figure 38.11   Output preference function $\mu(z)$.

as $z \rightarrow 0$. But this was entirely due to the unbounded number of branches considered in z: z is not a function. For any particular branch, however, the mapping is well defined. This result (infinitely many choices as $z \rightarrow 0$) exists using crisp numbers as well as imprecise numbers.

Note z was constructed based on the desired output function $\mu(z)$ being uninterpretable at a value. The only way to exhibit this behavior was with a multivalued function, where the multivalued character arose as a direct consequence of the desired uninterpretability. Thus the conclusion: only multivalued functions can lead to uninterpretability, entirely due to the indecision on which branch is being used in the function z itself, not in the fuzzy mathematics. Once a branch is selected, the problem reduces to a simple case that the methods of section 38.3 can accommodate. Replacing the specific *sine* used for $\mu(z)$ by any general periodic function and replacing the specific $\mu(x)$ by a general convex imprecise number in the construction would demonstrate the conclusion for the general case (though this is not a formal proof). Overall, if the performance expression is interpretable, then the use of the fuzzy mathematics in design calculations will also produce interpretable results.

38.6. Conclusion

Imprecision and uncertainty occur throughout the engineering design process. Many methods for incorporating uncertainty (*e.g.,* utility theory, probability methods, Taguchi's method, *etc.*) are in common use, but methods to represent imprecision in engineering design are few [2]. The Method of Imprecision (M_OI) is a formal method for incorporating the natural level of imprecision that occurs throughout the engineering design process. This chapter has presented the details of the Level Interval Algorithm (LIA) used internally by the M_OI and its extensions to permit application to engineering design problems in industry where monotonicity cannot be guaranteed; only discrete values may be available for some variables (and hence continuity must be relaxed), and engineering analyses are expensive and must be minimized.

Computation problems that reach beyond the scope of the LIA, such as singularities, have also been examined. It has been shown that the LIA behaves no worse than conventional calculations in the presence of these difficulties.

The approach embodied in the M_OI encourages the designer and customer to specify preferences on design and performance variables (specifications), and thus promotes design communication to evolve from individual "point" designs to (fuzzy) sets of designs. Since a range of possible design variable values can be communicated to downstream design processes earlier than a completed individual design, the M_OI can facilitate (fuzzy) set-based concurrent design.

38.7. References

[1] Adby, P., and M. Dempster. *Introduction to Optimization Methods.* London: Chapman and Hall, 1974.

[2] Antonsson, E.K., and K.N. Otto. "Imprecision in Engineering Design." *ASME Journal of Mechanical Design,* Vol. 117 (1995), pp. 25–32.

[3] Baas, S., and H. Kwakernaak. "Rating and Ranking of Multiple-Aspect Alternatives using Fuzzy Sets." *Automatica 13,* Vol. 13 (1977), pp. 47–48.

[4] Bandemer, H. *Modeling Uncertain Data.* 1st ed. Berlin: Akademie Verlag, 1993.

[5] Barrett, C.R., et al. "On Choosing Rationally when Preferences are Fuzzy." *Fuzzy Sets and Systems,* Vol. 34, No. 2 (1990), pp. 197–212.

[6] Diaz, A.R. "Fuzzy Sets-based Models in Design Optimization." *Advances in Design Automation.* ed. S.S. Rao. Vol. DE-14, ASME (1988), pp. 477–485.

[7] Diaz, A.R. *A Strategy for Optimal Design of Hierarchical Systems using Fuzzy Sets.* College of Engineering, University of Massachusetts at Amherst. The 1989 NSF Engineering Design Research Conference. ed. J.R. Dixon. pp. 537–547. June, 1989.

[8] Dong, W.M., and F.S. Wong. "Fuzzy Weighted Averages and Implementation of the Extension Principle." *Fuzzy Sets and Systems,* Vol. 21, No. 2 (1987), pp. 183–199.

[9] Dutta, B., et al. "Exact Choice and Fuzzy Preferences." *Mathematical Social Sciences,* Vol. 11 (1986), pp. 53–68.

[10] Goldberg, D.E. *Genetic Algorithms in Search, Optimization, and Machine Learning.* Reading: Addison Wesley, 1989.

[11] Hamburg, I., and P. Hamburg. "Fuzzy Logic: A User-Friendly Technology for the Management of Uncertain Knowledge in Engineering Design Process," in *Modeling Uncertain Data.* ed. H. Bandemer. pp. 153–157. Mathematical Research Series, Lectures from the GAMM Workshop. Vol. 68. (1992).

[12] Holmes, M.F. "Machine Dynamics, The Need for Greater Productivity," in *Research Needs in Mechanical Systems.* ed. K.N. Reid. pp. 140–159. New York: 1984.

[13] Hsu, Y.L., et al. "Engineering Design Optimization as a Fuzzy Control Process." *Proceedings, 4th IEEE International Conference on Fuzzy Systems (FUZZ-IEEE/IFES '95).* Vol. 4 (1995), pp. 2001–2008.

[14] Kacprzyk, J., and M. Fedrizzi. "Combining Fuzzy Imprecision with Probabilistic Uncertainty in Decision Making." *Lecture Notes in Economics and Mathematical Systems,* Vol. 310. New York: 1988.

[15] Kacprzyk, J., and M. Roubens. "Non-Conventional Preference Relations in Decision Making." *Lecture Notes in Economics and Mathematical Systems,* Vol. 301. New York: 1988.

[16] Kaufmann, A., and M.M. Gupta. "Introduction to Fuzzy Arithmetic: Theory and Applications." *Electrical/Computer Science and Engineering Series.* New York: Van Nostrand Reinhold Company, 1985.

[17] Keeney, R., and H. Raiffa. *Decisions with Multiple Objectives: Preference and Value Tradeoffs.* Cambridge: Cambridge University Press, 1993.

[18] Knosala, R., and W. Pedrycz. "Evaluation of Design Alternatives in Mechanical Engineering." *Fuzzy Sets and Systems,* Vol. 47, No. 3 (1992), pp. 269–280.

[19] Law, W.S., and E.K. Antonsson. "Implementing the Method of Imprecision: An Engineering Design Example." Proceedings, 3rd IEEE International Conference on Fuzzy Systems (*FUZZ-IEEE '94*). Vol. 1 (1994), pp. 358–363.

[20] ———. "Optimization Methods for Calculating Design Imprecision." *Advances in Design Automation,* Vol. 1 (1995), pp. 471–476.

[21] Moore, R.E. "Methods and Applications of Interval Analysis." *Society for Industrial and Applied Mathematics.* Philadelphia, Penn.: 1979.

[22] Muller, K., and M. Tharigen. "Applications of Fuzzy Hierarchies and Fuzzy Madm-Methods to Innovative System Design." *Proceedings, 3rd International Conference on Fuzzy Systems,* Vol. 1 (1994), pp. 364–367.

[23] Otto, K.N., and E.K. Antonsson. "Trade-Off Strategies in Engineering Design." *Research in Engineering Design,* Vol. 3, No. 2 (1991), pp. 87–104.

[24] ———. "Design Parameter Selection in the Presence of Noise." *Research in Engineering Design,* Vol. 6, No. 4 (1994), pp. 234–246.

[25] ———. "Modeling Imprecision in Product Design." *Proceedings, 3rd IEEE International Conference on Fuzzy Systems (FUZZ-IEEE June, 1994).* Vol. 1 (1994), pp. 346–351.

[26] Otto, K.N., et al. "Approximating α-cuts with the Vertex Method." *Fuzzy Sets and Systems,* Vol. 55, No. 1 (1993), pp. 43–50.

[27] Otto, K.N., et al. "Determining Optimal Points of Membership with Dependent Variables." *Fuzzy Sets and Systems,* Vol. 60, No. 1 (1993), pp. 19–24.

[28] Phadke, M. *Quality Engineering using Robust Design.* Englewood Cliffs: Prentice Hall, 1989.

[29] Posthoff, C., and M. Schlosser. "Learning from Examples for the Construction of Fuzzy Evaluations." *Proceedings, 3rd IEEE International Conference on Fuzzy Systems.* Vol. 1 (1994), pp. 368–371.

[30] Rao, S.S. "Description and Optimum Design of Fuzzy Mechanical Systems. *ASME Journal of Mechanisms, Transmissions, and Automation in Design,* Vol. 109 (1987), pp. 126–132.

[31] Rao, S.S., and A.K. Dhingra. "Integrated Optimal Design of Planar Mechanisms using Fuzzy Theories," in *Advances in Design Automation 1989.* Vol. DE-15-2, ASME. pp. 161–168. New York: 1989.

[32] ———. *Applications of Fuzzy Theories to Multiobjective System Optimization.* NASA Ames Research Center. NASA Contractor Report 177573. 1991.

[33] Rao, S.S., et al. *Nonlinear Membership Functions in the Fuzzy Optimization of Mechanical and Structural Systems.* AIAA. Technical Report 90-175-CP. New York: 1990.

[34] Rao, S.S., et al. "Multiobjective Fuzzy Optimization Techniques for Engineering Design." *Computers and Structures,* Vol. 42, No. 1 (1992), pp. 37–44.

[35] Sakawa, M., and K. Kato. "An Interactive Fuzzy Satisficing Methods for Large-Scale Multiobjective Linear Programs with Fuzzy Numbers." *Proceedings, 4th IEEE International Conference on Fuzzy Systems (FUZZ-IEEE/IFES '95),* Vol. 3 (1995), pp. 1155–1162.

[36] Scott, M.J., and E.K. Antonsson. "Aggregation Functions for Engineering Design Trade-Offs." *9th International Conference on Design Theory and Methodology,* Vol. 2, ASME, (1995), pp. 389–396.

[37] Shih, C.J., and R.A.S. Wangsawidjaja. "Multiobjective Fuzzy Optimization with Random Variables in a Mix of Fuzzy and Probabilistic Environment." *Proceedings, 4th IEEE International Conference on Fuzzy Systems (FUZZ-IEEE/IFES '95),* Vol. 3 (1995), pp. 1163–1170.

[38] Sullivan, L.P. "Quality Function Deployment." *Quality Progress.* pp. 39–50. June, 1986.

[39] Thurston, D.L., and J. Carnahan. "Fuzzy Ratings and Utility Analysis in Preliminary Design: Evaluation of Multiple Attributes." Submitted for review, *ASME Journal of Mechanical Design.* September, 1990.

[40] ———. "Fuzzy Ratings and Utility Analysis in Preliminary Design Evaluation of Multiple Attributes." *ASME Journal of Mechanical Design,* Vol. 114, No. 4 (1992), pp. 648–658.

[41] Ulrich, K.T., and S.A. Pearson. *Does Product Design Really Determine 80 Percent of Manufacturing Cost?* MIT Sloan School of Management, Working Paper MSA 3601-93. Cambridge, Mass.: 1993.

[42] Ward, A.C., et al. "Set-based Concurrent Engineering and Toyota." Design Theory and Methodology—DTM 1994, Vol. DE-68 (1994), pp. 79–90.

[43] Whitney, D.E. "Manufacturing by Design." *Harvard Business Review,* Vol. 66, No. 4 (1988), pp. 83–91.

[44] Wood, K.L. "A Method for Representing and Manipulating Uncertainties in Preliminary Engineering Design. Ph.D. Thesis, California Institute of Technology, Pasadena, Calif., 1989.

[45] Wood, K.L., and E.K. Antonsson. "Computations with Imprecise Parameters in Engineering Design: Background and Theory." *ASME Journal of Mechanisms, Transmissions, and Automation in Design,* Vol. 111, No. 4 (1989), pp. 616–625.

[46] ———. "Modeling Imprecision and Uncertainty in Preliminary Engineering Design." *Mechanism and Machine Theory,* Vol. 25, No. 3 (1990), pp. 305–324.

[47] Wood, K.L., et al. "Representing Imprecision in Engineering Design—Comparing Fuzzy and Probability Calculus." *Research in Engineering Design,* Vol. 1, No. 3/4 (1990), pp. 187–203.

[48] Wood, K.L., et al. "Engineering Design Calculations with Fuzzy Parameters." *Fuzzy Sets and Systems,* Vol. 52, No. 1 (1992), pp. 1–20.

[49] Zadeh, L.A. "Fuzzy Sets." *Information and Control,* Vol. 8 (1965), pp. 338–353.

[50] Zimmermann, H.J., and H.J. Sebastian. "Optimization and Fuzziness in Problems of Design and Configuration." *Proceedings, 2nd IEEE International Conference on Fuzzy Systems.* pp. 1237–1240. San Francisco, Calif.: Pergamon Press, 1993.

[51] ———. "Fuzzy Design—Integration of Fuzzy Theory with Knowledge-based System Design." *Proceedings, 3rd IEEE International Conference on Fuzzy Systems,* Vol. 1 (June, 1994), pp. 352–357.

[52] ———. "Intelligent System Design Support by Fuzzy Multicriteria Decision-Making and/or Evolutionary Algorithms." *Proceedings, 4th IEEE International Conference on Fuzzy Systems (FUZZ-IEEE/IFES '95),* Vol. 1 (March, 1995), pp. 367–374.

39 Fuzzy Scheduling: Principles and Experiments

Hélène Fargier
I.R.I.T., University of Toulouse III, France

ABSTRACT: A fuzzy model of job-shop scheduling problems is proposed, allowing the representation of flexible temporal constraints. The classical solving tools (e.g. constraint analysis rules, date propagation and incremental search) can easily be extended to this new formalism. These new solving paradigms have been implemented and experimented on real-size problems: it appears that handling the flexibility of a job-shop scheduling problem does not increase the computational cost and can even enhance the efficiency of the solving procedure.

39.1. Introduction

Scheduling over long horizons, considering temporal constraints, such as job release date and due date as compulsory, may lead to rejecting an efficient schedule even when the violation of these constraints is insignificant with regard to the precision of the realistic limits of predictability. Nevertheless, constraints often prove to be more or less relaxable or subject to preferences; this is typically true for due-date constraints in scheduling [1][2]. Fuzzy sets and possibility theory have appeared to be a suitable framework for the representation of flexible constraints [3][4][5][6][7].

Taking it a step further, we have proposed a fuzzy approach of flexible job shop problems that both allows the representation of flexible constraints and offers a suitable framework for uncertain parameters, such as uncertain durations [8][9]. Classical constraint propagation, search procedures, and constraint analysis schemes can be easily extended to this new framework. The worst-case complexity of these different algorithms does not change significantly; but, in order to provide real applications with an efficient approach, it is still necessary to study them from an experimental point of view. After recalling, in section 39.2, the definition of a fuzzy job shop scheduling problem and showing in section 39.3, how classical solving tools can be extended, this chapter is mainly devoted to the results of an experimental study of fuzzy scheduling (section 39.4).

39.2. The Fuzzily Constrained Scheduling Problem

A typical scheduling problem can be described as follows: a set of jobs must be performed by means of a set of resources. Each job j requires the scheduling of a set Ω_j of operations according to a process plan that specifies precedence constraints. Once started, operations cannot be interrupted. In the simplest situation, each operation O_i must be performed by a given resource and has a precise duration t_i. Capacity constraints between two operations requiring the same resource express that these two operations cannot overlap in time. Let s_i denote the starting time of O_i that the scheduling procedure must compute. Propagating the release dates and the due dates of job j over operations in Ω_j yields time windows $[r_i, d_i]$ within which each operation O_i must take place; r_i is its release date (earliest starting time) and d_i its due date (latest ending time). The different constraints that the starting times of each operation bear translate into linear inequalities of the type:

precedence constraints $P_{i \to k}$: $s_k - s_i \geq t_i$ (O_i before O_k)

capacity constraints $C_{i \leftrightarrow k}$: $s_k - s_i \geq t_i$ or $s_i - s_k \geq t_k$

release date constraints R_i: $s_i \geq r_i$

due date constraints D_i: $s_i + t_i \leq d_i$.

Of course, this is not the most general form of scheduling problem, but this one is quite often found in the literature, and is known to be very combinatorial. Solving a classical job-shop problem consists in searching for a consistent sequencing of operations on each machine, from which earliest and latest starting times can be computed.

39.2.1. Flexible Temporal Constraints

Release and due dates of jobs are often subject to preference. For instance job j must absolutely be completed at the latest completion date d_j^{sup} (e.g., the date after which the customer cancels an order) and it should preferably be completed before the due date d_j^{inf}, or as soon as possible after this due date. Similarly, it is better to start job j after its preferred release date r_j^{sup}, while it is impossible to start it before the earliest acceptable release date r_j^{inf} ($r_j^{inf} \leq r_j^{sup} < d_j^{inf} \leq d_j^{sup}$). The requirement about the release date (resp. due date) associated to job j is no longer crisp but can be modelled by a *fuzzy* number R(j) (resp. D(j)) (see Figure 39.1).

Namely, the membership function $\mu_{R(j)}$ (resp. $\mu_{D(j)}$) is increasing when r_j goes from r_j^{inf} to r_j^{sup} (resp. is decreasing when d_j goes from d_j^{inf} to d_j^{sup}). Hence, the temporal window in which the job must take place is the fuzzy interval [R(j),D(j)]. Taking into account the precedence constraints, temporal constraints attached to each job lead to define a fuzzy temporal window [R(i),D(i)] for each operation Oi [3][4].

39.2.2. Satisfaction Degree of a Flexible Temporal Constraint

When the knowledge about the release date of a job is fuzzy, the constraint $s_j \geq r_j$ is not necessarily violated or satisfied but its satisfaction can be matter of degree. Indeed, the coefficient:

$$\Pi(s_j \geq r_j) = \mu_{[R(j), +\infty)}(s_j)$$

can be understood as the satisfaction degree of the release date constraint for job j starting at time s_j. Similarly, when the requirement about the due date is fuzzy, the constraint $s_j + t_j \leq d_j$ is satisfied to degree:

$$\Pi(s_j + t_j \leq d_j) = \mu_{(-\infty, D(j)]}(s_j + t_j)$$

$\Pi(s_j + t_j \leq d_j)$ indicates to what extent there exists an acceptable value for d_j greater than $s_j + t_j$, given that d_j is restricted by D(j): it is equal to 1 if $d_j^{inf} \geq s_j + t_j$; that is to say if the job is completed before the preferred due date. If the job finishes after the latest acceptable completion date ($d_j^{sup} \leq s_j + t_j$), then $\mu_{(-\infty, D(j)]}(s_j + t_j) = 0$. Otherwise, the closer $s_j + t_j$ to the preferred due date, the higher $\mu_{(-\infty, D(j)]}(s_j + t_j)$: the due date constraint is a flexible constraint and the fuzzy set models how it can be relaxed from the customer's preferred due date to the latest acceptable completion date.

39.2.3. Feasible Schedules

As in the crisp case, a solution to a fuzzy scheduling problem is typically an assignment $(s_1, \ldots, s_n)$ of starting times of every operation. It must satisfy precedence constraints, capacity constraints, release, and due date constraints. While release and due dates are flexible, capacity and

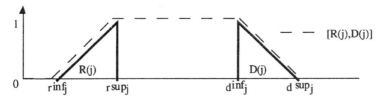

Figure 39.1 Fuzzy time horizon for job j.

precedence constraints remain crisp. An assignment satisfying precedence and capacity constraints satisfies the fuzzy scheduling problem insofar as it satisfies the least satisfied temporal constraint. The global satisfaction level depends on the chosen starting times for operations. It is defined as:

$$\text{Sat}(s_1, \ldots, s_n) = 0 \text{ if a capacity or a precedence constraint is violated}$$

$$= \min_{Oi}(\min \mu_{[R(i), +\infty)}(s_i), \mu_{(-\infty, D(i)]}(s_i + t_i)) \text{ otherwise}$$

Sat represents the minimal fraction of the flexibility ranges $d_i^{sup} - d_i^{inf}$ (resp. $r_i^{sup} - r_i^{inf}$) which are left between the completion times (resp. starting times) of the jobs and their latest acceptable completion times (resp. earliest release dates). Hence, the present approach is looking for a temporally safe schedule. The degrees of membership are not interpreted in terms of cost contrarily to [1][2]: a high degree of satisfaction for a constraint cannot counterbalance a low degree of satisfaction for another one. Here, satisfaction degrees should be interpreted in terms of safety ranges.

Hence, solutions are not equally preferred: satisfaction degrees induce a total ordering over the solutions of the problem defined by capacity and precedence constraints. A fuzzy job-shop scheduling problem is in fact a constrained optimization problem for which the best solutions are those requesting the least relaxation of release dates or due dates. In any case, the solutions violating any earliest release date or latest completion date are not acceptable (Sat = 0), whereas the solutions satisfying all preferred release and due dates (if they exist) are the best (Sat = 1). Otherwise, an implicit relaxation of flexible constraints is performed, achieving a trade-off between antagonistic constraints. This framework allows the treatment of partially inconsistent problems. In fact, the satisfaction degree of the best solution evaluates to what extent there is a solution satisfying every constraint. The feasibility degree of the problem can be defined as:

$$\text{Cons} = \max_{(s_1, \ldots, s_n)} \text{Sat}_{(s_1, \ldots, s_n)}.$$

39.2.4. Fuzzy Disjunctive Graph

The different types of constraints over the possible values of the starting times can be expressed by:

precedence constraints $P_{i \to k}$: $s_k - s_i \in [t_i, +\infty)$

capacity constraints $C_{i \leftrightarrow k}$: $s_k - s_i \in [t_i, +\infty)$ or $s_i - s_k \in [t_i, +\infty)$

release and due dates: $s_i \in [R(i), D(i) \ominus t_i]$

These fuzzy inequalities define a generalization to the fuzzy case of disjunctive graphs. Its nodes represent the operations. Precedence and temporal constraints define the conjunctive part of the graph: a fuzzy temporal window [R(i),D(i)] is associated to each node. Each conjunctive edge $P_{i \to k}$ represents a precedence constraint "O_i must precede O_k," by means of an inequality of the type $s_k - s_i \geq t_i$. Capacity constraints $C_{i \leftrightarrow k}$ define nonconjunctive edges ($s_k - s_i \geq t_i$ OR $s_i - s_k \geq t_i$), which represent conflicts of the type "O_i before O_k OR O_k before O_i."

This framework can also take into account flexible durations, which are under our control. Moreover, it is possible to integrate ill-known parameters, such as uncertain due dates (see [8][9]).

39.3. Solving Flexible Job-Shop Scheduling Problems

The solving approach consists in searching for a sequencing of operations on each machine, from which earliest and latest starting times can be computed: disjunctive constraints "O_i before O_k OR O_k before O_i" must be transformed into simple precedence constraints by the resolution procedure, which is based on three basic algorithms:

- a general search procedure that proceeds by managing new precedence constraints;

- a consistency enforcing procedure which propagates the effects of these decisions updating the precedence (conjunctive) graph;

- a constraint analysis procedure (or look-ahead heuristic) that determines which precedence decision to make next.

39.3.1. Consistency Enforcing

As soon as a new precedence constraint $P_{i \to k}$ is added to the conjunctive part of the graph, the fuzzy temporal window associated to O_k (resp. O_i) must be such that $r_k \geq r_i + t_i$ (resp. $d_i \leq d_k - t_k$). Hence, the temporal windows can be updated as follows:

$$r_k^{inf} := \max(r_k^{inf}, r_i^{inf} + t_i) \qquad r_k^{sup} := \max(r_k^{sup}, r_i^{sup} + t_i)$$
$$d_i^{inf} := \min(d_i^{inf}, d_k^{inf} - t_k) \qquad d_i^{sup} := \min(d_i^{sup}, d_k^{sup} - t_k)$$

The acyclicity of the graph can be exploited to produce an efficient ordering for updating the temporal windows. The R(k) are updated along precedence constraints, and the D(i) are updated backwards. A linear algorithm has been implemented that computes the fuzzy temporal windows according to the precedence constraints. It is an adaptation of classical shortest or longest path algorithms to fuzzy PERT-like networks.

It turns out that this method guarantees that the best among the earliest (resp. latest) starting times according to the precedence constraints can then be obtained when assigning to each s_i the lowest (resp. greatest) date among its best possible values, that is, values s^*_i with highest membership degree in the set $[R(i), D(i) \ominus t_i]$.

Hence, the consistency of the conjunctive part of the problem, which is the satisfaction degree of the best scheduling according to the precedence and limit date constraints, is given by:

$$\text{Cons(conjunctive part)} = \min_{i=1,n} \sup_{s_i} \min(\mu_{[R(i),+\infty)}(s_i), \min_{i=1,n} \mu_{(-\infty,D(i) \ominus ti]}(s_i))$$

Cons(conjunctive part) does not take into account the capacity constraints. It only yields an upper bound of the consistency of the global scheduling problem. However, Cons(conjunctive part) = 0 means that a contradiction is detected: constraints are totally inconsistent.

39.3.2. Search Procedure

The sequencing that is searched for is one of those having the best satisfaction degree. The search procedure is a classical Branch&Bound algorithm using a depth-first strategy. The nodes of the tree represent partial sequencing and its leaves complete sequences on machines: extending a node means choosing a disjunction and selecting one of its unexplored alternatives. This choice is done by the look-ahead procedure. The graph is then modified according to this decision (the corresponding linear inequality is substituted to the disjunction) and the consistency of the conjunctive part is enforced. Hence Cons(conjunctive part) is computed and associated to the node: this degree is an upper bound of the satisfaction of the best complete sequencing that can be reached from the node. A bound α represents the satisfaction degree of the best current complete sequencing (initialized to value 0). If the current node is such that Cons(conjunctive part) $\leq \alpha$, the algorithm backtracks to a node whose degree is greater than α. α is updated each time a complete sequencing is reached.

39.3.3. Look-Ahead Procedure (Constraint Analysis)

The efficiency of the search relies of course on the heuristic evaluation function that determines which disjunction to be instantiated next. For each disjunction, (O_i precedes O_k OR O_k precedes O_i), also called a conflict, an upper bound of the possibility of each alternative may be computed:

$$\Pi_{\sup}(O_i \text{ precedes } O_k) = \Pi((d_k - r_i) - (t_i + t_k) \geq 0) = \mu(-\infty, D(k) \ominus R(i)](t_i + t_k)$$

$\Pi_{\sup}(O_i$ precedes $O_k) = 0$ means that the decision "O_i precedes O_k" is inconsistent in the current search state according to O_i and O_k's temporal windows. Hence, decision "O_k precedes O_i" must be chosen (otherwise, the satisfaction degree of the sequencing will be 0). Note that the calculation $\Pi_{\sup}(O_i$ precedes $O_k)$ only gives an upper bound of $\Pi(O_i$ precedes $O_k)$.

Actually, $\min(\Pi_{\sup}(O_i$ precedes $O_k), \Pi_{\sup}(O_k$ precedes $O_i))$ estimates the degree to which the satisfaction will fall down if the best of the two alternatives is not chosen. The interest of choosing the best alternative between

$P_{i \to k}$ and $P_{k \to i}$, (i.e., the criticity of the conflict (O_i, O_k)) evaluates the degree of necessity that either O_i should precede O_k or O_k should precede O_i:

$$C(O_i, O_k) = 1 - \min(\Pi_{\sup}(O_i \text{ precedes } O_k), \Pi_{\sup}(O_k \text{ precedes } O_i))$$

If the dates are crisp, we recognize here the constraint analysis test proposed by Erschler [10].

Hence, the look-ahead procedure first computes the criticity of each conflict. Not all of the remaining conflicts are analyzed at each search state, but only those involving at least one operation whose fuzzy temporal window has been modified by the consistency-enforcing procedure while creating the search state. In order to keep the satisfaction degree as high as possible, a conflict whose criticity is maximal is then chosen to be instantiated by its most possible alternative.

39.4. Experiments

From a theoretical point of view, explicitly taking the flexibility of the problem into account does not significantly change the computational cost of the search procedure; the optimization problem we have to face is NP-hard since the crisp case defines a NP-complete problem. The search space we have to explore is basically the same. The theoretical cost of the constraint propagation procedure as well as those of the constraint analysis procedure has to be multiplied by 2: handling a fuzzy trapezoidal windows consists in handling two classical intervals, the first one representing the feasibility constraints (the support of the fuzzy window) and the second one the preference constraints (the core of the window).

In order to determine whether this approaches remain realistic from a practical point of view, we have built an experimental prototype (it has been implemented in Smalltalk) and a generator that provides the solver with randomly generated flexible job-shop problems.

39.4.1. The Problem Generator

The generator we used is basically this proposed in [2][11]; see [9] for more details. We first generate a crisp job-shop problem, where each job has a linear process routing specifying a sequence in which the job has to visit each machine. This sequence is randomly generated for each job, except for bottleneck resources, which were each visited after a fixed number of operations (to increase resource contention). The following parameters can be adjusted to cover different scheduling condition:

- Number of machines and number of jobs.

- Number (BK) and position in the sequence of the bottlenecks.

- Range parameter (RG). This parameter controls the release date and due date distributions in each problem. Due dates are randomly drawn from a uniform distribution $(1 + S)$ M $U(1 - RG, 1)$ where $U(a,b)$ represents a uniform probability distribution between a and b, M estimates the minimum makesplan and S is a slack parameter that has to be adjusted in order to keep demand for bottleneck resource(s) close to 100 percent; S is empirically set as $S = 0.1 \times (BK - 1) + RG$. Similarly release dates are drawn from a uniform distribution of the form $(1 + S)$ M $U(0, RG)$.

Following Sadeh [2], we have tested sets of problems involving one bottleneck, the durations of the operation ranging from 8 to 16 units on this machine. The durations of the other operations vary between 3 and 11 units.

This protocols generates classical, crisp scheduling problems, whose temporal windows can be flexibilized, given a flexibility rate. The flexibility rate of one temporal window is the proportion of the window that expresses ranges. Consider for instance a trapezoidal window defined by $(r^{inf}, r^{sup}, d^{inf}, d^{sup})$. Its flexibility rate (denoted Flex) is given by:

$$Flex = (L1 + L2) / L$$

where $\quad$ $L = d^{sup} - r^{inf}$
$\qquad$ $L1 = r^{sup} - r^{inf}$
$\qquad$ $L2 = d^{sup} - d^{inf}$

Hence, a crisp windows has its flexibility rate equal to 0 percent, and a triangular window is 100 percent flexible.

The next sections present our experimental results on a set of problems involving six jobs and five machines (hence, 30 operations, 75 conflicts and 24 precedence constraints). In this set, the average tightness of the windows (RG) ranges from −0.8 (very sparse problems) to 0.8 (very tight problems).

These problems are middle-sized. For a comparison, the biggest industrial examples presented in [12] for the Opal system involve about 90 operations and 260 conflicts.

Similar experiments were also realized for two other sets, the first one involving problems with eight jobs and five machines and the second one problems with six jobs and 10 machines. They led roughly to the same results [9].

39.4.2. Preliminary Study

Before studying the interest of the fuzzy model, let us present preliminary results considering only crisp problems. Each problem of a sample of 256 problems was solved with Ershler's (crisp) constraint analysis [10] and the cost of the resolution, that is, the number of nodes explored in the search three was measured (Figure 39.2).

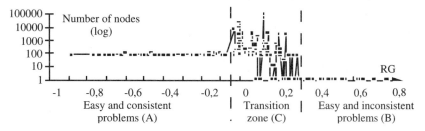

Figure 39.2 Nodes explored depending on the RG parameter (crisp resolution).

As in the experimental studies on CSP resolution, we can identify three zones:

- A: This zone contains sparse (RG ≤ −0.05) and consistent problems. The number of nodes explored before a solution is reached is optimal in most cases: 90 percent of the problems are backtrack-free (75 nodes explored); the cost of the 10 percent remaining is low: between 82 and 92 nodes (88 nodes in average).

- B: In this zone, the problems are very constrained (RG ≥ 0.3) and inconsistent. They are also very cheap: inconsistency is proved by constraint propagation without the need of node exploration.

- C: The intermediate zone corresponds to the complexity peak observed in all the experimental studies on constraint satisfaction. It is a transition zone between consistent and inconsistent problems (see Figure 39.3). In this zone, the resolution cost is extremely variable: 45 percent of the problems are solved in a minimal time (0 nodes for inconsistent problems, 75 nodes for consistent ones); 51 percent are rather cheap (less than 500 nodes); 10 percent are costly (500 to 5000 nodes); and 4 percent are extremely costly.

This preliminary experiment allows us to only consider, in the following experiments, problems whose RG varies from −0.8 to 0.3: it is useless to study the problems of zone C whose inconsistency is easily discovered by the propagation procedure. It is also useless to consider too loose

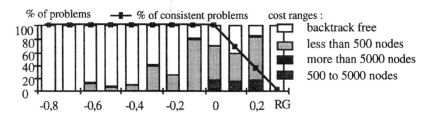

Figure 39.3 Rate of consistent problems and cost ranges (crisp problems).

problems, which are trivially easy. Moreover, it is necessary to have many problems in the C zone, where the resolution times are very variable.

39.4.3. Taking Preferences into Account

In order to determine whether taking the flexibility into account may enhance the resolution in terms of quality and/or in terms of resolution cost, we have "flexibilized" a sample of 169 problems using a flexibility rate of 90 percent (the fuzzy windows are quasi-triangular); in other terms, we have expressed preferences on each original crisp problem, considering that the original crisp problem describes the feasibility constraints. The quality (satisfaction degree) of the solution obtained by the classical (crisp) resolution procedure has been computed using the preferences. The corresponding flexible problem has then been solved using the fuzzy propagation procedure and the fuzzy constraint analysis, in order to determine the satisfaction degree and the resolution cost of the *first* solution reached by the resolution procedure. Then we have compared the solutions reached by the two approaches in terms of quality and resolution cost.

39.4.3.1. Quality of the First Solution Reached. Taking preferences into account during the resolution enhances clearly the quality of the first solution reached. Indeed, solving the crisp problems (i.e., neglecting the preferences during the resolution), we obtain very low satisfaction degrees (around Sat < 0,1 for 90 percent of the consistent problems). When the preferences are used by the resolution procedure, the quality of the first solution reached in much higher (Figure 39.4).

These encouraging results can be explained as follows: when the look-ahead heuristic considers flexible windows, it can motivate a decision as soon as a security range might be lowered. Hence, the tendency is to place the operations in the center of the windows. On the contrary, when preferences are neglected, the constraint analysis procedure takes a decision only when necessary; that is, when the windows of the operations are very tight: these operation may be at the limit of the feasibly window, therefore the low quality of the solution reached. The example of Figure 39.5 shows that the fuzzy constraint analysis can favor an alternative (here "O_i before O_j") while the crisp constraint analysis cannot settle the alternatives since it is limited to the supports of the windows.

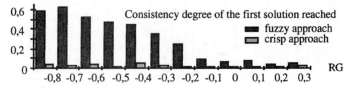

Figure 39.4   Average consistency degree of the first solutions reached.

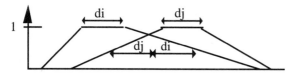

Figure 39.5 The fuzzy constraint analysis favors "O_i before O_j."

A further study of the productivity rate of the constraint analysis (we call "productivity rate" of the constraint analysis procedure the proportion of decisions in the search tree that are motivated by a conflict whose criticity is greater than the current inconsistency degree) corroborates this explanation (cf. Figure 39.6). Actually, on 93 percent of the consistent problems, the productivity rate is raised by the use of the fuzzy windows.

In summary, the quality of the first solution reached is greater or equal when taking the preferences into account in the resolution process. There is a great improvement on all the easy problems, i.e., where the constraint analysis procedure can only take few decisions if not using the information given by the security ranges (productivity rate of about 50%, against 80% for the fuzzy analysis).

39.4.3.2. Resolution Cost. Figure 39.7 shows, for the fuzzy approach, the proportion of problems in each cost range (refer to Figure 39.3 for the crisp case).

Taking flexibility into account gives very good results for all the easy problems ($RG \le -0.05$). In this zone, the fuzzy analysis is very productive, and allows to obtain a first solution without backtracking (although it is not systematically the case using the crisp procedure).

An interesting enhancement is also observed for very tight problems ($0.1 \le RG \le 0.2$): about 70 percent of the problems need a lower number of nodes; the number of problems solved using a minimal number of nodes reach 80 percent (against 20 percent only using the crisp approach).

In other terms, the peak zone is reduced to problems whose RG vary between −0.05 and 0.05. But the results are not so good in this latter zone: the average resolution cost remains stable, except for very constrained problems (for which we observe an enhancement). In fact, it decreases

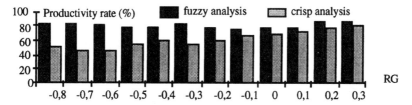

Figure 39.6 Productivity rates of the crisp and fuzzy constraint analysis.

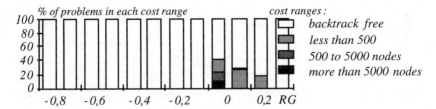

Figure 39.7 Percentages of more or less costly problems.

for some problems but increases for others: among the 61 problems of this zone, taking flexibility into account is an advantage in 42 percent of the cases but lead to a degradation of the performances in 34 percent of the cases. Nevertheless, it must be noticed that the proportion of problem solved in a minimal time increases (from 20 percent with the crisp approach to 40 percent in the fuzzy approach). In other terms, the peak zone in narrowed, but the resolution cost for the peak problems is not significantly changed in average.

39.4.4. Solving the Optimization Problem Completely

Considering this first experiment, it neither seems to be reasonable nor interesting to search for an optimal solution in the case of very constrained problems: the consistency degree is indubitably very low. Moreover, since we are in the peak, obtaining a first solution is extremely expensive; so is it to prove optimality.

This third study focus on sparse and average-constrained problems, for which reaching a first solution is quite cheap. We have worked on the sample of 18 problems whose RG vary from −0.7 to −0.1.

Figure 39.8 presents, the average consistency degree of the first and best solutions reached. Figure 39.9 presents the resolution costs for (1) reaching a first solution, (2) reaching an optimal solution, and (3) proving optimality.

It appears clearly that the first solution reached has a consistency degree close to those of the optimal solution. But, in the latter case, the resolution cost is much more expensive, and the search effort for the proof of optimality is prohibitive. For instance, for RG = −0.4, a first solution is reached in 75 nodes (i.e., backtrack-free) for a consistency degree

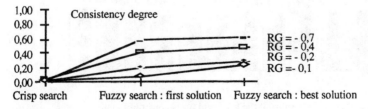

Figure 39.8 Consistency of the first and best solutions.

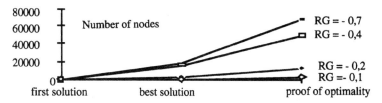

Figure 39.9   Resolution costs of first and best solutions.

equal to 0.42 in average; the best solution is reached after the exploration of 2369 nodes and has a consistency degree of 0.48 only; finally, 12000 nodes are necessary to prove optimality. In other terms, the first solution has a consistency degree that represents 85 percent of the optimal consistency degree but its effort represents only 3 percent of the resolution effort needed to reach the optimal solution and less than 1 percent of the effort needed to prove optimality.

Hence, for sparse problems, reaching a first solution is a very good compromise between quality and cost. Adopting an "anytime" point of view, the best approach should be to provide the Branch&Bound algorithm with a time limit, since reaching a first solution is really cheap; the search for optimality will stop as soon as the time limit is exceeded.

39.5. Conclusion

We have shown that fuzzy sets theory is a suitable tool for the representation of flexible temporal constraints in job-shop scheduling. This framework generalizes the notion of disjunctive graph and classical solving procedures like constraint propagation, constraint analysis, and incremental search. Moreover, it allows the handling of partial inconsistencies, for problems that are not totally inconsistent.

When scheduling over long horizons, this approach avoids considering temporal constraints as compulsory (which may lead to rejecting an efficient schedule even when the violation of these constraints is insignificant with regard to the precision of the realistic limits of predictability). Once having computed this first predictive schedule, the satisfaction degree may decrease if further information gives more precise constraints. Since our approach leads to search for a schedule fixing the operation in the center of their windows, the schedule might be robust, that is, still feasible even if the constraint become harder. This is not the case with crisp approaches of constraint satisfaction, which are perfectly contented with scheduling the operation near their limit dates.

Taking explicitly the flexibility into account does not significantly change the theoretical worst-case complexity of the algorithms. Moreover, we avoid a posteriori relaxation, which is often costly, difficult to formulate, and suboptimal.

Our experimental study shows that, for really costly problems, the fuzzy approach does not save time nor quality when compared to the crisp approach. But it does not degrade them either. However, it must be noticed that the peak is actually narrowed.

For sparse problems, taking flexibility into account is both a realistic and efficient approach. The fuzzy approach not only gets a first solution having a greater satisfaction degree than the crisp one (in fact, a degree not far from the optimal one) but also allows a decreasing of the resolution cost: the fuzzy constraint analysis detects a decreasing of the ranges before the arising of a potential contradiction (i.e., even if no conflicts are totally critical) by focusing the search procedure on the most constrained operations. This remark suggests that the fuzzy approach may be beneficial even for real problems that are not flexible in nature: flexibilizing the windows arbitrary will allow a more productive heuristic search, which can be understood as a range-preserving heuristic.

39.6. References

[1] Fox, M.S. *Constraint-Directed Search: A Case Study of Job-Shop Scheduling.* London: Pitman, 1987.

[2] Sadeh, N. *Look-ahead Techniques for Micro-Opportunistic Job-Shop Scheduling.* Carnegie Mellon University, Report of the School of Computer Science. CMU-CS. pp. 91–102. 1991.

[3] Dubois, D. "Fuzzy Knowledge in AI System for Job-Shop Scheduling," in *Applications of Fuzzy Set Methodologies in Industrial Engineering.* eds. Evan, Karwowsky and Wilhem. pp. 1989. Elsevier, 1989.

[4] Dubois, D., and H. Prade. "Processing Fuzzy Temporal Knowledge." *IEEE Transactions on Systems, Man, and Cybernetics,* Vol. 19, No. 4 (1989), pp. 729–744.

[5] Kerr, R., and R. Walker. "A Job-Shop Scheduling System based on Fuzzy Arithmetics." *Proceedings, 3rd International Conference on Expert Systems and the Leading Edge in Production and Operation Management.* pp. 433–450. Hilton Head Isl., South Car.: 1989.

[6] Slany, W. "Fuzzy Scheduling." Ph.D. Thesis, C. Doppler Laboratory for Expert Systems, Austria, 1995.

[7] Ishibuchi, H., et al. "Local Search Algorithms for Flow-Shop Scheduling with Fuzzy Due Date." *International Journal of Production Economic,* Vol. 33 (1994), pp. 53–66.

[8] Dubois, D., et al. "Fuzzy Constraints in Job-Shop Scheduling." *Journal of Intelligent Manufacturing,* Vol. 6 (1995), pp. 215–234.

[9] Fargier, H. "Problemes de Satisfaction de Contraintes Flexibles: Application a l'Ordonnancement de Production." (in French). Ph.D. Thesis, Universite Paul Sabatier, Toulouse, France, 1994.

[10] Erschler, J., et al. "Finding Some Essential Characteristics of the Feasible Solutions for a Scheduling Problem." *Operations Research,* Vol. 24 (1976), pp. 774–783.

[11] Ow, P.S. "Focused Scheduling in Proportionate Flow Shops." *Management Science,* Vol. 31 (1985), pp. 852–869.

[12] Bel, G., et al. "OPAL: A Multiknowledge-based System for Industrial Job-Shop Scheduling." *International Journal of Production Research,* Vol. 26, No. 5 (1988), pp. 795–819.

40 Scheduling System Design: Three Fuzzy Theory Approaches*

I. Burhan Türkşen
Department of Mechanical-Industrial Engineering
University of Toronto
Toronto, Ontario M5S 3G9,
Canada

ABSTRACT: Three distinct but progressively related scheduling system design approaches are reviewed with the implementation of fuzzy theory technologies. It is shown that in this evolutionary development, we were able to introduce more effective fuzzy theory technologies to the development of job-shop scheduling systems.

40.1. Introduction

Scheduling theory provides solutions for single machine, multiple machines, parallel machines, flow shops, and job shops where the priorities, processing times, due dates, slack times, and so on, all are deterministic. However, in most cases, we are faced with uncertain, imprecise, and vague information about priorities, processing times, due dates, and so on. Such imprecise and vague information can best be handled with the fuzzy theory and methodology.

In general, there are essentially four possible approaches where the fuzzy theory can be included in the development of a scheduling system. First, there are two ways in which the fuzzy knowledge and information can be extracted from and about a system. These are:

* Supported in part by the Natural Science and Engineering Council of Canada and the University of South Florida.

(i) subjective extraction of system behavior knowledge from the experts via protocol-based interviews; and

(ii) objective extraction of system behavior knowledge from input-output data via fuzzy cluster analysis, neural networks, and so on.

Secondly, beyond the two basic approaches of knowledge extraction and acquisition, there are also two basic design methodologies. These are:

(a) extension of an existing AI-based software such as **KEE, ART**, with the inclusion of the basic fuzzy tools;

(b) design of a software directly based on fuzzy theory for knowledge representation and inference with the inclusion of **AI**-based software tools where appropriate.

In this chapter, we discuss only three design approaches based on (i)-(a), (i)-(b) and (ii)-(b). In these design approaches, however, for the inclusion of a full fuzzy logic theory-based GMP, one needs to resort to the decomposition algorithms in order to reduce the computational complexity from exponential to polynomial in the number of antecedents of a fuzzy rule.

In the rest of this chapter, we first review the domain of scheduling theory as a background in section 40.2. In section 40.3, three different design approaches that we have developed will be discussed, and a real-life industrial problem will be analyzed. Comparison of results will be presented in section 40.4. Conclusions will be stated in section 40.5.

40.2. Scheduling Theory

Scheduling problems have been a challenge to researchers and manufacturers for a long time. With advances in technology, the associated difficulties tend to be more sophisticated. This creates an increasing need for improved usage of the costly machinery. Hence the methodologies for modelling a scheduling problem—representation and manipulation of scheduling information, gain a new importance.

There have been numerous studies by operations research and artificial intelligence researchers on the scheduling problem in manufacturing systems over the years. Research in scheduling has focused on understanding the variety of scheduling environments that exist, and constructing scheduling models specific to these particular cases. Several types of scheduling problems are distinguished in the literature. Among these are: a. single machine-single operations, parallel machines-single operations, flowshop, that is, series of machines-multiple operations, job shop, that is, network of machines-multiple operations. A job is defined as having one or more operations, a deterministic processing time for each operation, and a deterministic due date. The utility of a schedule is generally measured in terms of deterministic measures such as lateness, tardiness, flowtime, and makespan, and so on.

In most research papers, the scheduling problem has been considered a typical example of a constraint satisfaction problem that can optimally be solved by using mathematical programming methods. However, it is now clear that in many cases such scheduling problems are NP-hard, as shown by Lenstra and Rinooy Kan [12]. Thus it is recognized by scheduling researchers that in a real world of scheduling, the problem space expands so rapidly that the size of the search space for scheduling alternatives itself becomes an immediate problem. By the designation of implicit hierarchies, however, a complicated scheduling problem can be solved in various levels of abstraction. In such a situation, scheduling can proceed at the highest, least detailed level. At each level, a schedule generated can be used to constrain the scheduling activity at the next lower level, which addresses a more detailed problem in the scheduling domain. Thus, the search space can be pruned at each level.

There have been some applications of hierarchical structures in operations research. However, the idea of representing a problem space in terms of hierarchies and a set of constraints in artificial intelligence research has been around a long time (Simon [19], Sacerdoti [17], Erman et al. [6], Davis and Buchanan [5]).

A model that combines hierarchical search, constraint directed reasoning, and scheduling is ISIS, developed by Fox [7, 8] and Fox and Smith [9]. ISIS is one of the first successful applications of artificial intelligence to a production planning problem. In the design of our three different approaches to a scheduling system we have begun with ISIS as a "skeleton" in the initial approach. In our second and third approaches, however, we have only used real-life test case data used in ISIS in order to compare our results with each other.

40.2.1. Fuzzy Theory in Scheduling

In traditional scheduling theory literature, we find a common denominator in most of the approaches to the scheduling problem. That is, models are based on the assumption that the problem domain does not contain any imprecision, vagueness or subjectivity, and precise information is available for the model whenever required.

However, this assumption is strongly challenged in the implementation phase of such models by the fact that imprecision is inherent in almost all problem domains unless the system under consideration is totally mechanized, closed, and predictable, which seems to be valid only in laboratory environments used for prototyping. Modelling an imprecise problem domain using precise modelling tools not only results in unpredictable behavior of the model but total failure in many cases because of misrepresentation of the knowledge content.

In mechanistic problem domains that contain imprecision, a compromise cannot be reached by assuming that imprecision only leads to a deviation from the predicted behavior of the model. It is clearly articulated by Zadeh [37, 38, 39, 40] that an even larger problem of representation arises when the problem domain involves people, and hence the model must aim to represent a decision-making process that is "humanistic."

The recognition that knowledge, however imprecise, could be quite valuable leads to the exploration of methods that are able to deal with imprecision in a formal manner. Such methods are potential gateways to new approaches in mimicking the mind, which is the primary quest of computational intelligence studies.

There have been some studies in the recent literature that are located in the intersection of computational intelligence, fuzzy logic, and several scheduling problem domains. An example of such a model is the fuzzy train scheduling model developed by Fukumori [10]. The model uses a constraint-based approach to determine the arrival and departure times of trains at stations. This involves fuzzy times and hence fuzzy constraints. Another example is OPAL by Bensana, Bel, and Dubois [2], which is a short-term scheduling system designed in a modular fashion with constraint propagation and analysis modules in decision support of the model. A third example is an expert system approach to job shop scheduling by Bensana, Carrege, Bel, and Dubois [3], which describes two systems: one is related to a greedy algorithm, and the other is a knowledge-based approach used in [2].

A number of studies have been implemented by Turksen and Turksen et al. [21–35] where production planning and scheduling related problems are explored by the use of fuzzy logic and approximate reasoning. These studies are unique in the sense that they use fuzzy sets in representing imprecise knowledge, and fuzzy logic and inference for resolution of elastic constraints.

40.3. Design Approaches

Within the last decade or so, we have experimented with and built three different scheduling systems. Initially, we started out with a basic extension of the traditional scheduling theory constructs, in particular, the detail scheduling constructs. In this first approach, fuzzy theory elements such as fuzzy sets and logics components were introduced where appropriate. Furthermore, basic AI techniques along with a Knowledge Engineering Environment, KEE, software was used to integrate fuzzy theory, AI, and operations research concepts for the development of a scheduling system.

In the second approach, we began to deviate slightly from operations research constructs and developed a fuzzy expert system technology-based scheduling system. Later, we generalized this approach by the introduction of a windows-based user-friendly front end. Finally in the third approach, we introduced into the system design, fuzzy cluster analysis techniques for knowledge extraction of fuzzy set membership functions and rules of any scheduling system behavior. Whereas, in the first two approaches, the knowledge of the scheduling system was constructed with subjective methods of expert interviews, questionnaires, and so on. In the rest of this section we will briefly review each of these approaches.

40.3.1. First Approach

In an initial experiment, we designed a scheduling software by extending the capability of **KEE** by introducing to it a fuzzy toolbox and providing subjective knowledge, information, and rule extraction [28]. This model is designed to represent and generate alternative schedules for a job-shop production environment. A job order has a due date and a technological ordering of its operations at the time it is released into a shop, and a set

A_{11}:	IF the priority of the job is ___,
A_{12}:	AND the earliness of the due date of the job is ___,
B_1:	THEN suggested place for the job in the order of jobs is ___.
$B_1 = A_{21}$:	IF suggested place of job in the order of job is ___,
A_{22}:	AND likelihood of availability of resource for w/s(s) is ___,
B_2:	THEN suggested place of w/s(s) in the order of w/s(s) is ___.
$B_2 = A_{32}$:	IF suggested place of w/s(s) in the order of w/s's is ___,
A_{32}:	AND capability (cost of adjustment) of w/s(s) in meeting physical constraints of the operation is ___,
B_3:	THEN current suggested place of w/s(s) in the order of w/s(s) is ___.
$B_3 = A_{41}$:	IF suggested place of w/s(s) in the order of w/s(s) is ___,
A_{42}:	AND capability of w/s(s) in meeting quality requirements is ___,
B_4:	THEN current suggested place of w/s in the order of w/s(s) is ___.
$B_4 = A_{51}$:	IF current suggested place of w/s(s) is ___,
A_{52}:	AND WIP inventory cost due to position of operation in the queue arrangement of the w/s is ___,
B_5:	THEN suggested place of queue arrangement in the order of alternative queue arrangement is ___.

Figure 40.1 The structure of a hierarchical rule base.

of workstations required for the performance of operations. Workstations may be machines, operators, or a combination of these. The operations are to be assigned to the workstations. Each operation of a job has a set of workstation alternatives on which it can be performed. In addition, each workstation is defined as having a queue in which the prescheduled operations of jobs are positioned. Therefore, several feasible queue arrangement alternatives may exist at the time of assigning an operation of a job to workstation.

The scheduling activity then consists of a hierarchical set of decisions as follows: decision 1—choose a job to be scheduled from among the jobs to be scheduled in the job shop at a particular point in time; decision 2—choose a workstation for each operation in the operation sequence of the selected job; decision 3—choose a feasible queue arrangement for the operation of the selected job within the queues of the selected workstation.

The structure of the model for a hierarchical scheduling problem is described next, together with its rule base and descriptions of its linguistic variables. The model consists of five levels and a rule base for each level. Each level addresses a separate issue in the hierarchy of scheduling decisions. The rule bases are linked to each other in a chain-like manner in the sense that the consequent of one rule base constitutes a part of the antecedent of the next rule base. The constraints—that is, the criteria involved in the selection of alternatives—are represented as fuzzy rules with linguistic variables. The model is supported by a fuzzy knowledge-based system that uses approximate reasoning to schedule the jobs by fuzzy set representation and fuzzy logic inference at each level.

Within the context of the model, each rule base forms a decision constraint set regarding the scheduling activity. A common aim of all the decision constraint sets is to make a selection from among a set of alternatives. Through an approximate reasoning schema that is explained later, each rule base derives a "suggested selectability" for each element in the set of alternatives for the particular decision constraint set. The "suggested selectability" is a generalization of the consequent linguistic variable of each rule base, and it appears under a different name in each particular rule base. As a result, one or more of the elements that have the highest suggested selectability within the set of alternatives for the decision are then chosen by the model to proceed to the next decision level, which is represented by the next rule base in the chain of rule bases.

It must be noted that the policy regarding how many of the elements of a set of alternatives for a decision constraint set are chosen with high suggested selectability affects the breadth of the search for good schedules. Even if it is initially decided to use only the best alternative—that is, the alternative with the highest suggested selectability—the suggested selectability of each element in the set of alternatives may later be used in cases where there does not exist a feasible schedule for the selected element. Such situations cause backtracking in a depth-first search strategy.

The model is based on a set of assumptions that are specified through the detailed expressions of the rule bases and linguistic variables. It should be inferred from the details we have introduced in the prototype that there exist six basic factors of a scheduling problem in a five-level hierarchy where the consequent of each level becomes the linking antecedent in the next level. That is, we have an inference chain among the rule bases of each level as follows:

Level 1: A_{11} AND $A_{12} \rightarrow B_1$

Level 2: $(B_1 = A_{21})$ AND $A_{22} \rightarrow B_2$

Level 3: $(B_2 = A_{31})$ AND $A_{32} \rightarrow B_3$

Level 4: $(B_3 = A_{41})$ AND $A_{42} \rightarrow B_4$

Level 5: $(B_4 = A_{51})$ AND $A_{52} \rightarrow B_5$

where the six basic factors, $A_{11}, A_{12}, A_{22}, A_{32}, A_{42}$, and A_{52} represent:

1. the priority of a job, A_{11},
2. the earliness of the due date of a job, A_{12},
3. the likelihood of the availability of resources for the workstations, w/s(s), A_{22},
4. the capability of w/s(s) to meet physical constraints (cost of adjustment), A_{32},
5. the capability of w/s(s) to meet quality requirements, A_{42},
6. WIP inventory cost due to the position of operation in the queue arrangement of the w/s(s), A_{52}.

Five of these six factors, $A_{11}, A_{12}, A_{22}, A_{32}$, and A_{52}, take on one of the three linguistic terms LOW, MEDIUM, or HIGH within the context of their corresponding linguistic variables specified. A_{42} takes on the linguistic terms INSUFFICIENT, NEARLY SUFFICIENT, and SUFFICIENT (see Figure 40.2).

Furthermore, the five consequents B_1, B_2, B_3, B_4, and B_5, where four of these are the linking factors in the chain of reasoning, take on the linguistic terms NEAR THE END, NEAR THE MIDDLE, and NEAR THE FRONT within the context of their linguistic variables; that is:

1. the suggested place of a job in the order of jobs, B_1,
2. the suggested place of w/s(s) in the order of w/s(s), B_2,
3. the (current) suggested place of w/s(s) in the order of w/s(s), B_3,
4. the (next current) suggested place of w/s(s) in the order of w/s(s), B_4,
5. the suggested place of the queue arrangement in the order of alternative queue arrangements, B_5.

EARLINESS OF THE DUE DATE OF THE JOB

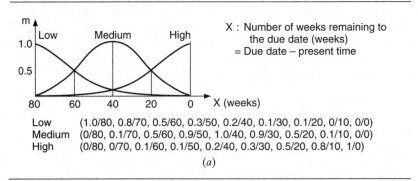

Low   (1.0/80, 0.8/70, 0.5/60, 0.3/50, 0.2/40, 0.1/30, 0.1/20, 0/10, 0/0)
Medium   (0/80, 0.1/70, 0.5/60, 0.9/50, 1.0/40, 0.9/30, 0.5/20, 0.1/10, 0/0)
High   (0/80, 0/70, 0.1/60, 0.1/50, 0.2/40, 0.3/30, 0.5/20, 0.8/10, 1/0)

(*a*)

CAPABILITY OF W/S IN MEETING QUALITY REQUIREMENTS

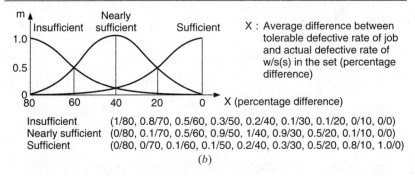

Insufficient   (1/80, 0.8/70, 0.5/60, 0.3/50, 0.2/40, 0.1/30, 0.1/20, 0/10, 0/0)
Nearly sufficient (0/80, 0.1/70, 0.5/60, 0.9/50, 1/40, 0.9/30, 0.5/20, 0.1/10, 0/0)
Sufficient   (0/80, 0/70, 0.1/60, 0.1/50, 0.2/40, 0.3/30, 0.5/20, 0.8/10, 1.0/0)

(*b*)

Figure 40.2 Examples of membership functions. (*a*) An example of membership functions for earliness of the due date of jobs. (*b*) An example of membership functions for the capability of w/s in meeting the quality requirements.

As can be seen from the details of this particular prototype, the scheduling problem can in general be very complicated and involves a large and dynamic set of constraints. Therefore, it is important to model such problems in a flexible fashion that lends itself to extensions in case additional aspects of scheduling need to be included in the model. In the design of the prototype, generality has been a main consideration. Thus, it is possible to modify the model, making use of its flexibility. There are two obvious extensions:

1. Addition of constraints: More constraints can be added to any level by adding linguistic variables to the antecedent of a rule in each of the five levels considered in our structure. This will, however, increase the number of rules in one or more of the rule bases, as the number of rules in a rule base is proportional to the number of linguistic variables in the antecedent of a rule. However, our results [29] on machine learning and self correction show that, at times, it is possible to reduce the number of rules in a rule base.

2. Addition of rule bases: Additional rule bases may be added if so desired. However, the more subrule bases added, the more detailed is the information related to the problem that will have to be used. Furthermore, the number of decisions that have to be derived by the expert system will increase with the addition of new rule bases. Note that a consistency check should be made before proceeding with the addition of any new rule base.

40.3.12. Fuzzy Knowledge-Based System

The structure of a hierarchical fuzzy knowledge-based system described here is independent of scheduling problems, and may be relevant to other applications, such as planning, design, and so on. In fact, it is at present being used for several operational research applications [23, 25, 31]. The system combines artificial intelligence technology to perform the knowledge organization and manipulation, with fuzzy representation and inference schemes to handle the underlying structure of the models. Modularity and generality have been two important considerations in the design of the system. The modular structure provides a flexible organization and ease of expansion whenever necessary. The generality results in flexibility in terms of applicability to various fields within the realm of knowledge-based systems.

The knowledge base is designed using the Knowledge Engineering Environment (KEE). An interface module provides the medium for the transfer of knowledge between the fuzzy knowledge base and the other modules. For each level in the hierarchy of the scheduling system, or any other planning, design, system, the fuzzy knowledge-based system prototype executes the following four steps: (1) the current system state is passed on to this level from the previous level of the five-level hierarchy and/or from the input state; (2) a rule that is closest to the particular current system state is sought and identified in this level's rule base; (3) a flexible decision is obtained by applying either the composition rule of inference (CRI) [37] or analogical reasoning (AR) [34, 35] to the current state and the chosen rule; (4) the decision is interpreted and the state of the system is updated. At this point, the fuzzy knowledge-based system prototype moves on to execute the next level; steps (1) to (4) are repeated again, and so forth.

Throughout the activity of the system, the knowledge base is constantly referred to, as well as the fuzzy toolbox, which contains a collection of modules that handle the fuzzy operators and modes of reasoning required in the calculations.

The frame-based structure of KEE is used for the representation of information and knowledge about the system. Since KEE is well known, we will not take space here to explain the meanings of *units, classes, slots, inheritance relations,* and so on, that are basic to an understanding of the knowledge engineering environment. It is sufficient to indicate that operations, workstations, and queue arrangements are represented in KEE with units.

40.3.13. Toolbox

The system contains a toolbox that handles basic fuzzy operations and operators. It is easy to add new options to the existing ones. Due to space limitation, we do not discuss these modules in detail. However, we point out our use of Type II fuzzy sets.

Most current application studies of fuzzy systems use *point valued,* Type I, membership functions to represent linguistic production rules in an attempt to capture the central tendency of an imprecise knowledge (Mamdani [13], Rinks [16], Whalen and Schott [36], Hosapple and Whinston [11]). However, in order to capture the dispersion of imprecise knowledge around its central tendency we need a *Type II fuzziness.* Type II fuzziness is second order fuzziness, a dispersion of imprecision around a point-valued fuzzy membership value. It may be possibilistic or probabilistic depending on the knowledge acquisition method used in extracting the membership values from experts [15, 18, 24]. The existence of Type II fuzziness was discovered in various measurement experiments by Norwich and Turksen [15] and Santamarina and Chameau [18]. An *interval valued* representation of membership functions is a special case of Type II fuzziness. It is defined as an extension of the disjunctive and conjunctive normal forms found in Boolean logic to Fuzzy Normal Forms [21, 27]. Details of these theoretical concerns are not included in this writing.

40.3.2. Second Approach

In this approach, we designed a knowledge representation and inference software with the assumption that fuzzy rule base, linguistic variables, and their terms (values) are to be given externally; and that they are extracted from the experts by subjective knowledge acquisition methods. The software included two aggregate modules: A fuzzy knowledge representation and inference module, and a simulation module. It is called FLES, Fuzzy Logic Expert System Scheduler. In fact, the detailed system architecture of FLES consists of five modules. These modules are: system setup module, knowledge base and inference reasoning module, schedule generation module, reports and statistics module, and order generation module.

40.3.2.1. System Setup Module. Throughout the system, it is assumed that a job shop consists of work centers, and that each work center has a user-defined number of identical machines. There are certain types of parts that are manufactured, and each part type consists of a sequence of operations, where each operation takes place in a unique work center. An operation can also have an alternate work center with an alternate unit processing time and setup time. Customer orders are for a specific part type. For each order, the system generates a lot with a lot size of the order quantity. Each lot is processed in a single machine; splitting of a lot between alternate machines in a work center is not allowed. In order to support these assumptions and simulate a real-life shop flow, the system setup module is examined in three sections:

- Job Shop Layout Representation: While a schedule is running, the flow of the lots between machines and the work center queues are displayed on the screen. The graphical model representation of the real shop floor and the display of each lot's movement enables the user to understand the behavior of the "decision engine" and increases his/her confidence in the scheduling model.

- Part Route Information: To represent part route information, the user enters the number of part types in the job shop and, for each part type, the number of operations. For each operation, the user enters the work center name, the unit processing time and the setup time for that operation. If the operation has an alternate work center, then alternate work center name, unit processing time, and setup time in the alternate work center are also entered.

- Order Information: Order information is composed of job ID, part ID, lot size, priority, requested start date (release date), and order due date for each order, (see Table 40.1).

40.3.2.2. Knowledge Base and Reasoning Module. The knowledge base and reasoning module is the heart of the system that makes this product different from other commercial scheduling software. The aim of FLES is to utilize user-defined scheduling rules to arrive at the best job release and dispatch decision. There are two types of scheduling decisions given by the module. These are lot releasing decisions (to decide which lot is to be released next to the job shop) and lot dispatching decisions (to decide which lot in a work center queue is to be assigned to the first next free machine in that work center).

To minimize the flow-time measure in a job shop, it is suggested that the Shortest Processing Time (SPT) which calls for dispatching in favor

Table 40.1 Sample Job Data

Job ID	Part ID	Lot Size	Priority	Requested Start Date	Due Date
1	1	144	VERY HIGH	25/Jun	26/Jun
2	6	109	HIGH	25/Jun	26/Jun
3	3	155	LOW	25/Jun	26/Jun
4	4	124	MEDIUM	25/Jun	26/Jun
5	2	111	SOMEWHAT-LOW	25/Jun	26/Jun
6	5	148	HIGH	25/Jun	26/Jun
:	:	:	:	:	:

of shortest available operation, be used [1]. Also, SPT sequencing is often effective at meeting due dates, even though it does not explicitly use due date information (thus it is good for tardiness measure as well). Due to its properties in favor of both flow time and tardiness criteria, SPT is selected to be one of the linguistic variable in the rule base.

There are also some due date-based scheduling rules for tardiness measure; slack time is one of them. However, unlike the flow time measure, the slack time measure yields an anti-SPT dispatching rule (at least among lots with similar due dates). Thus it works against the flow time measure. However, its dynamic treatment (being dependent on the current time and remaining operation time), makes it attractive, especially in dynamic scheduling systems.

The user specifies the Linguistic Variables and their Linguistic Values to be used for decision making. Currently, the system supports three linguistic variables in the left-hand side of a rule, and a defined number of linguistic values for each linguistic variable. The supported linguistic variables for job release decisions are *Priority, Slack Time,* and *Requested Start Date.* For job dispatching decisions, the variables are *Priority, Slack Time,* and *Remaining Processing Time* of the job. It's assumed that, for each linguistic variable, the same linguistic values are used. The default linguistic values are *Very Low, Low, Somewhat Low, Medium, Somewhat High, High,* and *Very High.* An example rule for job releasing decision is:

IF *priority is "high"* **AND** *slack time is "low"* **AND** *due date is "low,"*
THEN *selectability of this job for releasing is "very high."*

Default definitions for the Linguistic Variables, Linguistic Values and other parameters are provided internally.

There are parameters that can be changed by the user at any time. The supported menu functions in this module are:

- Fuzzy Sets Modification: The membership functions, also known as the fuzzy sets of each linguistic value of each linguistic variable, are graphically displayed on the screen. The user is prompted for new membership values. To optimize user-system interaction, the first one or two distinguishing letters of a linguistic variable and linguistic value with a set of membership values are entered on a single line. The new data is immediately plotted on the screen. The flexibility of the modification of the membership functions enables the user to easily analyze the effects of these functions on the scheduling decisions.

- Rule Base Modification: It's assumed that the same rule base for job releasing and dispatching decisions will be used. The rule base has all the possible combinations of the linguistic values. The entire rule base is displayed on the screen and user is prompted for a new rule. Each time a rule is modified, the effect of the new rule is immediately reflected on the screen. This feature enables the user to analyze the effects of the different rules on the schedule performance.

40.3.2.3. Schedule Generation Module. The inference engine that uses the Approximate Analogical Reasoning [34, 35] method combines an observation from the system with the rules and suggests a selectability measure for each job in the job queue. Then the job with the highest selectability may be assigned to the next available machine in the work center. This is how the jobs are released into the shop and also how the jobs are dispatched to the other work centers. (See Figure 40.3 for a snapshot of the shop floor display).

When the schedule is started, the system releases new lots to the shop floor. The lots move between machines and work center queues. Each lot is displayed with its order number in a color that represents the priority level. A description of priority colors is given at the bottom of the screen. There is a simulation clock in the top right corner of the screen, and this clock is updated each time a new event, such as loading or unloading of a machine, is generated. The maximum queue size of any work center is restricted by a user-defined parameter. The system gives appropriate error messages if any of these restrictions are violated.

While the schedule is running on the screen, the user can interactively migrate to different menus such as the Reports and Statistics menu to see the system statistics, machine utilizations, work center schedule Gantt

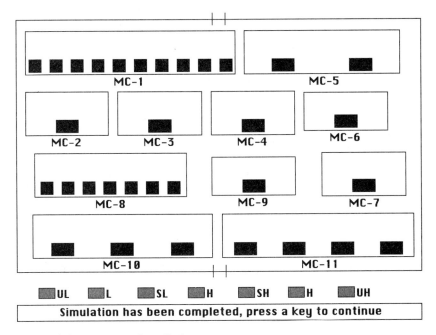

Figure 40.3 A job shop floor display.

charts, or queue statistics. The user can also use the Knowledge Base menu to modify membership functions and the rule base. It is possible to turn off the display flag to continue the schedule without the display. The user can specify a stopping point in the schedule, such as the number of scheduling days or the number of lots to be processed. The speed of the movements of the lots can also be controlled.

40.3.2.4. Reports and Statistics Module. While the schedule is running or after it's completed, the user can display generated schedules, statistical analysis of the schedule, machine utilizations, queue statistics, work center schedule Gantt charts, and lot schedule Gantt charts. The system supports two types of outputs, reports and graphical displays. Upon user request, the results are printed to a file in a report format, which can be sent to a printer. Reports and statistics module consists of six sections:

- Schedules: For each order, job ID, part ID, lot size, priority, requested start date, actual start date, due date, actual end date, and the tardiness are displayed in a report format. Using function keys, user can move backward and forward between pages.

- Statistical Analysis: This report gives a statistical analysis of the schedule. For each priority level, the number of orders, average flow time, average tardiness, and average setup time are displayed. Since the scheduling decisions are done according to an expert opinion, it is hard to measure the performance of the system with a unique performance criteria. Instead, a weighted sum of different measures are given to compare results between different simulation runs.

- Machine Utilizations: Average machine utilizations and amount of setup time used in each work center are given in both report format and a bar chart graphical display, (see Figure 40.4).

- Queue Statistics: Maximum queue size and average queue length of each work center are given in both report format and a bar chart graphical display.

- Work Center Schedule Gantt Charts: For each work center, detailed schedules at the machine level are given in a Gantt chart format. Through the use of function keys, these charts can be rolled backward or forward for different time intervals. The user can easily detect the usage of machines and the work load of the work centers during simulation time by using this menu entry. The setup time and the process time are displayed in two different colors. Schedules of different work centers can also be displayed through the function keys.

- Lot Schedule Gantt Charts: A detailed schedule for each lot is given by this menu entry via a Gantt chart representation. Through the use of function keys, Gantt charts for different lots are displayed. The

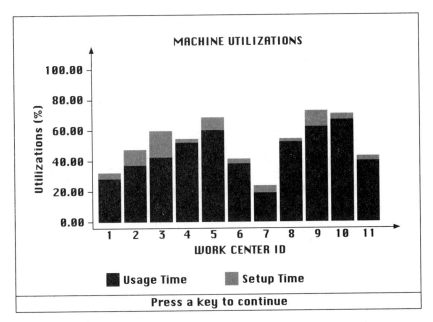

Figure 40.4 Machine utilization.

amount of time that is spent in the queues can be easily detected through this menu entry. (For work center and lot schedule Gantt charts see Figure 40.5).

40.3.2.5. Random Order Generation Module. The user can enter order data through an input file. If it is required, the system is designed to generate orders randomly. The behavior of the job-shop model under different conditions can be analyzed by running the scheduler with different data sets. The user can set part type, lot size, due date, requested start date, and priority distribution parameters, and generate different random order sets. The user is also able to define a time to start gathering statistical data to have system statistics at the steady state. Simulation end time and the number of orders are also set in this module. In the later versions of this approach, we introduced the windows technology with various pull-down menus. This improved system flexibility and user friendliness.

40.3.3. Third Approach

There are three reasons that suggest one to look into an objective fuzzy rule extraction approach via a fuzzy clustering techniques. a) The number of rules turn out to be generally very large in a subjective rule extraction approach; b) we have no clear idea which input factors really have a direct impact on the output performance measures; and c) we have no way to determine if some of the rules are redundant and/or not effective.

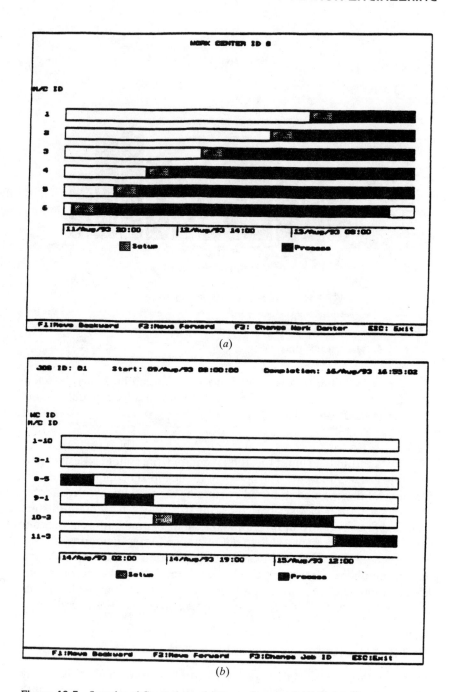

Figure 40.5   Samples of Gantt charts. (*a*) for work center 8 (*b*) for job #1.

40.3.3.1. Fuzzy Clustering Methods. It is known that a particularly important concern in practice is "the construction of membership functions from a *given set of data.*" When there are adequate data already collected and a model based on fuzzy sets is required to analyze the problem, the membership functions should be constructed from the available data.

In this regard, fuzzy clustering techniques [4, 20] are good tools for such an analysis. Usually the analysis proceeds as follows [14]:

- Apply clustering on the output data, then project it into the input data. Then generate clusters and select the variables associated with input-output relations. The clustering method determines clusters on the data space based on a selected norm, which is usually Euclidean norm.

- Divide the data into three subgroups. Use two groups in the model building for the selection of effective (important) variables and cross-validation for data set independence. The third group is used as the test data to validate the goodness of the model.

- Form the membership functions for the selected variables (i.e., determine the shape of the membership functions). There is a procedure [14] that lets one to select four parameters that completely characterizes trapezoidal membership functions.

40.3.3.2. A Minimal Set of Rules. In order to find a minimal set of effective operating rules, we have implemented a fuzzy c-means cluster analysis with its enhancements via the Sugeno method [14]. Our goal was (i) to extract hidden rules that dominate the behavior of the scheduling system from input-output data of that system; (ii) to see if the number of rules would be reduced drastically; and (iii) to find out if certain output performance measures are effected significantly by the third approach. The results of the third approach show that there are in fact seven fuzzy rules that are significant to control the behavior of this job-shop scheduling when we are concerned with tardiness measure (Figure 40.6). The structure of these rules is:

"IF the lot size is **A** AND the slack time is **B** AND the priority is **C**, THEN the lateness is **D**."

40.4. Comparisons

We have conducted three sets of comparisons for a job-shop model problem (Figure 40.7) with the same case study data of a real-life industrial scheduling problem: (i) between ISIS and our first approach, (ii) between ISIS and our second approach, and (iii) between our second and third

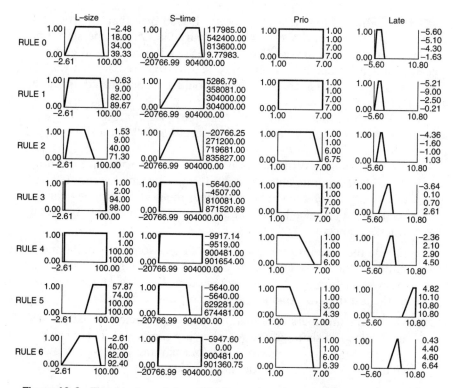

Figure 40.6   The objective rule base. The fuzzy rules extracted with fuzzy C-means cluster analysis.

approaches. A sample data set is shown in Table 40.1. Next we review these comparison results.

40.4.1. ISIS vs. First Approach

ISIS is a hierarchical job-shop scheduling model developed by Fox and Fox, et al. [7, 8, 9] using artificial intelligence technology. In the design of our first scheduling model, the structure of ISIS is taken as a framework in order to provide a structural basis for a comparison of performance of the two models.

ISIS represents the scheduling environment through constraints. Constraints are interrelated and linked to the components of the scheduling model using a variety of relationships. The method of constraint-directed search is used to generate schedules. Partial schedules are created for each state in the scheduling activity in a hierarchical manner. Each partial schedule is rated with respect to the constraints that affect that particular state in order to select the partial schedules that are to be considered for the next level in scheduling. The essential first step for every state in the scheduling activity is the presearch analysis where the relevant constraints for a search state are selected. The presearch analysis maintains the dynamic selection of constraints that influence the decisions at every level.

Although our framework of modelling the scheduling activity in our first approach is similar to ISIS, there are some conceptual differences in the designs of the two models. Our model is based on fuzzy set theory. Therefore, the representation and utilization of expertise is expressed in a qualitative manner with the representation of linguistic variables via membership values extracted from experts. Thus, in this approach, knowledge acquisition and representation are main concerns. The imprecise expertise regarding the scheduling environment is incorporated into the decision-making process through the use of fuzzy logic.

The scheduling environment of our model is again represented through constraints, which are in the form of fuzzy linguistic variables in

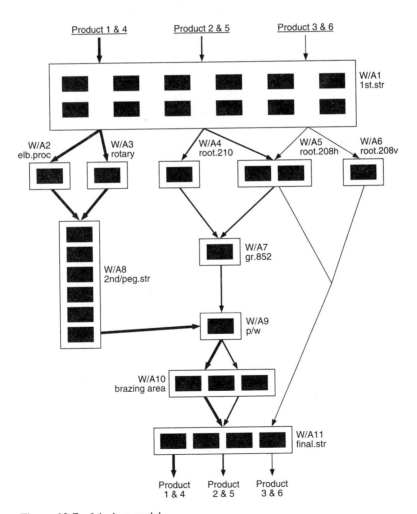

Figure 40.7 Job-shop model.

linguistic rules. The representation of the constraints using fuzzy linguistic variables has a smoothing effect on the constraints, resulting in "elastic constraints." A hierarchy of rule bases similar to that of ISIS is used to derive decisions at each step in the scheduling activity for this model. The constraints for each level of decision are acquired from the experts prior to the execution of the model and stored in the knowledge base in the form of linguistic rules.

The partial schedules are not rated with respect to discrete utility values for constraints, derived by the model, as in the case of ISIS. But the expertise regarding the current system states for each partial schedule is used in the approximate reasoning procedure, which produces qualitative decisions regarding each partial schedule. These decisions, which are in the form of fuzzy linguistic terms, determine the sequence of the partial schedules. This sequence is then used to select the partial schedules that are to be considered in the next level in the scheduling activity, and the pruning of the search space is handled in this manner.

40.4.2. The Tardiness Measure

The tardiness measure, which takes into account the start time, the setup time, and the processing time, which is the completion time minus the due date for those completion times that are beyond the due date; that is, completion time − due date > 0. It is found, as observed in rows (1) and (2) in Table 40.2, that the total tardiness, obtained from our first approach, which is known as FLAR, and hence average tardiness, is less than ISIS's total, and hence average, tardiness measures; thus, 132 vs. 135 and 1.1 vs. 1.25 respectively.

Finally, when we look at a comparison between FLAR's completion time and ISIS's completion time, we find, as shown, in Table 40.2 rows (3) and (4), that in the FLAR sequence more jobs finished later than ISIS, namely 24 jobs, with an average relative tardiness of 2.45, and 22 jobs finished earlier than ISIS, with an average relative earliness of 2.59. Furthermore, 72 jobs were completed at the same time in both sequences.

Table 40.2 Summary of the Comparison,
FLAR vs. ISIS

	Total difference	Average difference
(1)	132	1.1
(2)	135	1.125
(3)	+59 (24)*	+2.45
(4)	−57 (22)*	−2.59

(1) FLAR's tardiness.
(2) ISIS's tardiness.
(3) When FLAR's completion time > ISIS's completion time.
(4) When FLAR's completion < ISIS's completion time.
* The number of cases.

The difference, $2.59 - 2.45 = 0.14$, indicates a better relative earliness than tardiness for the FLAR sequence in comparison to ISIS.

Thus, on the basis of these comparisons, we conclude that our first approach, FLAR, produced a better schedule, in addition to being "user friendly" with the use of linguistic terms that capture expert's and operator's knowledge about system parameters. Therefore, it is reasonable to state that the fuzzy logic-based approximate reasoning model produces an improved schedule, and creates a communication ease between operators and users of such systems.

40.4.3. ISIS vs. Second Approach

In this comparison, 10 data sets from the real-life case study are used. The experiments are designed to focus on two scheduling objectives:

1. Minimize total tardiness of all orders.
2. Minimize the flow time of orders.

The ISIS sequence is taken as the sequence for job releasing and simulated through the job shop using first-in-first-out for job dispatching. The following results are obtained after comparing the output of our second approach, which is known as FLES, with ISIS:

1. The average tardiness times of FLES results, for all 10 data sets, are better than ISIS results.
2. FLES results for average flow time dominates ISIS results except for two data sets.

(For a detailed comparison of FLES with ISIS see Turksen [26]).

It is observed, further, that the schedules obtained from FLES can always be improved by defining a more appropriate rule base and fuzzy sets depending on the nature of the problem. For this purpose, we investigated our third approach.

40.4.4. Comparison between Second and Third Approaches

The comparison between our second and third approaches, again based on the same database, was implemented in order to find out whether subjective versus objective, that is, fuzzy cluster analysis, methods of knowledge base extraction made any difference at all. In this comparison it was found that:

1. The number of rules governing the behavior of this job shop is very few; 300 rules in the second approach versus 7 rules in the third approach.

2. While the priority and the slack time appears in the rule bases of both approaches, the requested start date and the remaining processing times only affect the rules of the second approach whereas the lot size affects only the rules of the third approach.

3. The consequence of the rules in the second approach is "selectability" whereas the consequence of the rules in the third approach is "lateness" measure.

Hence, we have a more direct relationship between the input factors and an output performance measure.

40.4.5. Second vs. Third Approach

In order to further compare the two design approaches, four data sets are *randomly* generated with 100 jobs each from the historical input output data set of the real-life problem. These are "jobsi.dat", i = 1, 2, 3, 4 (Table 40.3). With these four data sets, both software—our second and third approach softwares are executed and schedules are generated and "tardiness," "earliness" and "maximum lateness" and work-in-process measures—WIP are computed. For all these measures statistical **t**-tests are conducted in the following manner:

H0: Mean " . . . " measure generated by the second software is the same as the one generated by the third software.

H1: Mean " . . . " measure generated by the second software is not the same as the one generated by the third software.

where " . . . " stands for "tardiness" or "earliness" or "maximum lateness," and so on. In a similar manner, statistical **F**-test are also conducted. In all, the **t** and **F** tests at the 95 percent confidence level, it is found that there is no significant difference between the results of the performance measures obtained by the two softwares designed with two distinct approaches.

Table 40.3   A Summary Table of Experimental Results

	WIP		Earliness		Tard.		Max. Late	
	2nd	3rd	2nd	3rd	2nd	3rd	2nd	3rd
jobs1.dat	2.27	*2.11*	−1.98	−1.38	3.39	*2.56*	9.4	*7.5*
jobs2.dat	2.30	*1.97*	−1.48	−1.39	3.61	*2.07*	8.6	*5.5*
jobs3.dat	2.59	2.78	−5.4	−3.4	3.31	*3.14*	6.6	*6.1*
jobs4.dat	2.94	*2.83*	−2.3	*−2.8*	2.78	*2.51*	5.9	6.9
Average	2.525	*2.42*	−2.79	−2.24	3.27	*2.57*	7.63	6.5

(1) The numbers with bold and underline are the cases where the third design approach shows a better performance.
(2) 2nd and 3rd refers to second and third design approach-based software.
(3) All entries are average results related to 100 randomly selected jobs in each jobi.dat, i = 1, 2, 3, 4.

40.5. Conclusion

As a result of these investigations we found that the extension of classical approaches with fuzzy set theory in slight modifications, as it was done in the first approach, appears to be a good starting point. However, it is better to move to the second approach in order to fully implement the expressive powers of the fuzzy theory via fuzzy rule bases that are linguistic in nature. Finally, moving to the third approach really reflects the effective robustness of systems models generated via fuzzy cluster analysis. In this approach there are generally fewer rules and fewer variables that affect the behavior of a system.

In summary, it is reasonable to state that the third approach to the design of scheduling software—generation of a rule base via fuzzy c-means clustering approach—produces just as good or better results, as shown in Table 40.3, and based on statistical test of hypothesis, that is, **t** and **F** test. Furthermore, the third design approach has the benefit of a reduced set of significant rules, and it also brings to the surface certain variables that have a direct impact on the output measure of scheduling activity. For example, lot size was not thought to be significant by scheduling experts and systems designers in the first two approaches. But it surfaced with fuzzy-c means cluster analysis in the third approach. Furthermore, due date, which was part of the rules in the second approach, was eliminated from the left-hand side of the rules in the third approach. But both priority and slack time are selected to be important inputs for the determination of lateness as shown by the rules of the third approach. In conclusion, it appears that the third approach is the best design approach in the light of these experiments.

40.6. References

[1] Baker, K.R. "Sequencing Rules and Due Date Assignments in a Job Shop." *Management Science,* Vol. 30, No. 9 (1984), pp. 1093–1104.

[2] Bensana, E., et al. "OPAL: A Knowledge-based System for Industrial Job Shop Scheduling," in *Computer Integrated Manufacturing, Current Status and Changes.* ed. I.B. Turksen. pp. 295–330. Springer Verlag: 1988.

[3] Bensana, E., et al. "An Expert Systems Approach to Industrial Job Shop Scheduling." *Proceedings, IEEE Conference on Robotics and Automation.* pp. 1645–1650. San Francisco, Calif.: 1986.

[4] Bezdek, J.C., and J.D. Harris. "Convex Decompositions of Fuzzy Partitions." *Journal of Mathematical Analysis and Applications,* Vol. 6 (1979), pp. 490–512.

[5] Davis, R., and B. Buchanan. "Meta-Level Knowledge: Overview and Applications." 5th International Joint Conference on Artificial Intelligence. Cambridge, Mass.: 1977.

[6] Erman, L.D., et al. "The Hearsay-II Speech Understanding System: Integrating Knowledge to Resolve Uncertainty." *Computing Surveys,* Vol. 12, No. 2 (1980), pp. 213–253.

[7] Fox, M.S. Constraint Directed Search: A Case Study of Job Shop Scheduling. Robotics Institute, Carnegie-Mellon University, Technical Report. Pittsburgh, Penn.: 1983.

[8] ———. "Industrial Applications of Artificial Intelligence." *Robotics,* Vol. 2 (1986), pp. 301–311.

[9] Fox, M.S., and S.F. Smith. "ISIS: A Knowledge-based System for Factory Scheduling." *Expert Systems,* Vol. 1, No. 1 (1984), pp. 25–49.

[10] Fukumori, K. *Fundamental Scheme for Train Scheduling.* Artificial Intelligence Laboratory, MIT. MIT Al Memo No. 596. Cambridge, Mass.: 1980.

[11] Holsapple, C.W., and A.B. Whinston. *Managers' Guide to Expert Systems.* Irwin, Ill.: Dow-Jones, 1986.

[12] Lenstra, J.K., and A.H.G. Rinnooy Kan. *The Scheduling of Several Machines.* Department of Operational Research, Mathematical Center. Amsterdam: 1980.

[13] Mamdani, E.H. "Applications of Fuzzy Logic to Approximate Reasoning using Linguistic Systems." *IEEE Transactions Comput.,* Vol. 26 (1977), pp. 1182–1191.

[14] Nakanishi, H., et al. "A Review and Comparison of Six Reasoning Methods." *Fuzzy Sets and Systems,* Vol. 57 (1993), pp. 257–294.

[15] Norwich, A.M., and I.B. Turksen. "A Model for the Measurement of Membership and its Consequence on its Empirical Implementation." *Fuzzy Sets and Systems,* Vol. 12 (1984), pp. 1–25.

[16] Rinks, D.B. "A Heuristic Approach to Aggregate Production Scheduling using Linguistic Variables," in *Methodology and Applications in Fuzzy Sets and Possibility Theory, Recent Developments.* ed. R.R. Yager. pp. 562–581. New York: Pergamon Press, 1982.

[17] Sacerdoti, E.D. "Planning in a Hierarchy of Abstraction Spaces." *Artificial Intelligence,* Vol. 5, No. 2 (1974), pp. 115–135.

[18] Santamarina, J.C., and J.L. Chameau. "Membership Functions II: Trends in Fuzziness and Implications." *International Journal Approximate Reasoning,* Vol. 1 (1987), pp. 303–317.

[19] Simon, H.A. "Scientific Discovery and the Psychology of Problem Solving," in *Minds and Cosmos.* ed. Kolodny. 1962.

[20] Sugeno, M., and T. Yasukawa. "A Fuzzy Logic-based Approach to Qualitative Modeling." *IEEE Transactions of Fuzzy Systems,* Vol. 1, No. 1 (1993), pp. 1–24.

[21] Turksen, I.B. "Interval-valued Fuzzy Sets based on Normal Forms." *Fuzzy Sets and Systems,* Vol. 20 (1986), pp. 191–210.

[22] ———. "Approximate Reasoning with Interval-valued Fuzzy Sets." *Proceedings, 2nd IFSA Conference.* pp. 20–27. Tokyo, Japan: 1987.

[23] ———. "Approximate Reasoning for Production Planning." *Fuzzy Sets and Systems,* Vol. 26 (1988), pp. 1–15.

[24] ———. "Measurement of Membership Functions and their Acquisition." *Fuzzy Sets and Systems,* Vol. 40 (1991), pp. 5–38.

[25] ———. "Fuzzy Sets and their Applications in Production Research," in *Proceedings, ICPR, Toward the Factory of the Future.* eds. H.J. Bullinger and H.J. Warnecke. pp. 649–656. 1985.

[26] ———. "Fuzzy Expert Systems for IE/OR/MS." *Fuzzy Sets and Systems,* Vol. 51 (1992), pp. 1–27.

[27] ———. "Fuzzy Normal Forms." *Fuzzy Sets and Systems,* Vol. 69 (1995), pp. 319–346.

[28] Turksen, I.B., et al. "Hierarchical Scheduling based on Approximate Reasoning—A Comparison with ISIS." *Fuzzy Sets and Systems,* Vol. 46 (1992), pp. 349–371.

[29] Turksen, I.B., and H. Zhao. "Self-Correction of Fuzzy Knowledge Base." *Proceedings, NAFIPS 1990.* Vol. 1. pp. 145–148. Toronto, Canada: June, 1990.

[30] Turksen, I.B., and K. Demirli. "Rule Decomposition in CRI," in *Advances in Fuzzy Theory and Technology.* ed. P.P. Wang. Vol. 1 (1993), pp. 219–256.

[31] Turksen, I.B., and M. Berg. "An Expert System Prototype for Inventory Capacity Planning: An Approximate Reasoning Approach." *International Journal of Approximate Reasoning,* Vol. 5 (1991), pp. 223–250.

[32] Turksen, I.B., and T. Yurtsever. "Fuzzy Logic Expert System Scheduler." Proceedings, *2nd International Conference on Fuzzy Logic and Neural Networks.* pp. 371–374. Iizuka, Japan: 1992.

[33] Turksen, I.B., et al. "Fuzzy Expert System Shell for Scheduling." *Proceedings, SPIE 1993,* Vol. 2061, pp. 308–319. Boston, Mass.: 1993.

[34] Turksen, I.B., and Z. Zhong. "An Approximate Reasoning Approach based on Simi-larity Measures." *IEEE Transactions on Systems, Man, and Cybernetics,* Vol. 18, No. 6 (1987), pp. 1049–1056.

[35] ———. "An Approximate Analogical Reasoning Schema based on Similarity Measures and Interval-valued Fuzzy Sets." *Fuzzy Sets and Systems,* Vol. 34 (1990), pp. 323–346.

[36] Whalen, T., and B. Schott. "Alternative Logics for Approximate Reasoning in Expert Systems: A Comparative Study." *International Journal Man-Machine Studies,* Vol. 22 (1985), pp. 327–346.

[37] Zadeh, L.A. "Outline of a New Approach to the Analysis of Complex Systems and Decision Processes." *IEEE Transactions on Systems, Man, and Cybernetics,* Vol. 3, No. 1 (1973), pp. 28–44.

[38] ———. "The Concept of a Linguistic Variable and its Application to Approximate Reasoning I, II, III." *Information Science,* Vol. 8 (1975), pp. 199–249; pp. 301–357. Vol. 9 (1975), pp. 43–80.

[39] ———. "A Computational Approach to Fuzzy Quantifiers in Natural Languages." *Computer and Mathematical Applications,* Vol. 9 (1983), pp. 149–184.

[40] ———. "The Role of Fuzzy Logic in the Management of Uncertainty in Expert Systems." *Fuzzy Sets and Systems,* Vol. 11 (1983), pp. 199–227.

41 Tuning of Fuzzy Rules for Multiobjective Scheduling

Bernard Grabot, Laurent Geneste
Laboratoire Génie de Production, Ecole Nationale d'Ingénieurs de Tarbes

Arnaud Dupeux
Grai Productique S.A.

ABSTRACT: Most of the available industrial schedulers are based on a simulation approach using dispatching rules. An approach that allows to adapt compromises between rules to production objectives is set out in this chapter. Two ways to set up the compromises are compared: fuzzy expert system and neural network. These compromises can be implemented on each scheduler that uses a simulation approach. Tests have been made with an industrial scheduler called SIPAPLUS, the results of which are developed in this chapter.

41.1. Introduction

In a manufacturing system, the schedule is the precise allocation of shared resources to products through time. Most of the present industrial schedulers are based on a simulation approach; that is, the scheduler is a simulator that solves the conflicts chronologically: when an operation on a job has been performed, the job is supposed to use the resource necessary for its next operation, if this resource is available; if not, the job is put in a queue. When the resource is available, a dispatching rule decides which operation in the queue is performed first.

The quality of a schedule can be expressed according to many different criteria, such as lateness or tardiness minimization, work in progress minimization, or flow time minimization [1]. The numerous tested dispatching rules are known to be quite specialized in a single criterion, but the

objective of a workshop manager always consists of building a compromise between several criteria [2]. In order to build this compromise,
many works have been carried out about the definition of aggregated
rules that can provide intermediate results between the results of the elementary rules they are composed of (refer for example to [3] for a survey
of dispatching rules). One problem is that the result of the utilization of
a rule strongly depends òn the set of jobs to be scheduled. A solution can
be to analyze the characteristics of the jobs in order to choose the best
rule according to a given situation [4]. We suggest here to define compromises between rules thanks to fuzzy logic. This method has been
implemented, then tested on an experimental version of the industrial
scheduling software SIPAPLUS (GRAI Productique S.A.). The results
of the standard SIPAPLUS and of the fuzzy SIPAPLUS are compared in
this chapter.

41.2. Fuzzy Dispatching Rules in Scheduling

41.2.1. Choice of the Rules

Among the numerous dispatching rules defined in research, three are
very common in present scheduling software:

- Shortest Processing Time (SPT): The job with the shortest imminent
  operation is performed first. This rule allows to minimize the average waiting of the jobs.

- Slack time rule: If a routing contains n operations, and d_i denotes the
  duration of remaining operation i; if DD is the due date of the manufacturing order using this routing and t the current date, the slack
  time S can be defined as $S = (DD - t) - \sum d_i$.

- The Priority rule: Some jobs may be more significant than others,
  and it is not possible to prevent them from being tardy when the preceding rules are used; a subjective priority is therefore assigned to
  each job, and the job with the highest priority is chosen in a queue.

We focus in this chapter on compromises between these three rules
since these rules have very different advantages, which is why it may be
interesting to combine them in order to carry out a compromise between
these advantages. Moreover, they are representative of the other rules:
SPT is a "static" rule, the sorting criterion in a queue depends on static
data (here the duration of an operation); the slack time rule is
"dynamic," the value of the criteria depends on the date of the conflict;
the priority rule is based on a subjective criterion. However, the suggested method does not depend on the rules; it can be used whatever the
selected rules are.

41.2.2. Fuzzy Compromises between Rules

The combination of dispatching rules can be performed through the modelling of the following "good sense" linguistic proposition P: "IF the duration of the imminent operation is short and its slack time is low and its priority is high, THEN the job has a high global priority in the queue" (P).

Each elementary proposition of P can be modelled by a fuzzy set, the membership function μ_{spt}, μ_{slack} or $\mu_{priority}$ of which is given in Figure 41.1. The logical "and" connectors of P can be expressed through several mathematical operators (min, sum, product . . .); we have chosen the sum operator. If we wish to balance the influence of each rule, it is possible to weigh the corresponding membership degrees. Let w1, w2, and w3 be the weights of the three propositions. The matching of a job to the proposition (P) can be evaluated by the value v:

$$v = w_1 \cdot \mu_{spt}(a) + w_2 \cdot \mu_{slack}(b) + w_3 \cdot \mu_{priority}(c), \ w_i \ [0,1]$$

According to the proposition (P), the job with the highest value of v will be chosen in the queue.

A simulator has been designed in order to test many sets of jobs quickly [5]. It enabled us to make sure that the compromise between two rules gives intermediate results between the performances of each rule and showed that the use of weights allows to balance the respective influence of the rules and therefore to really adjust the result of the scheduling. Figure 41.2 shows the result obtained with a progressive increase in the slack time rule combined with the priority rule.

This method to define aggregations between rules has been used in an experimental version of the scheduler SIPAPLUS, which is implemented in more than 100 workshops in France and Spain. SIPAPLUS standard version includes these three rules: priority, slack time, priority then slack time.

The "quality" of the schedule resulting from the use of a rule strongly depends on the characteristics of the scheduled set of jobs and of the considered workshop [6]. Since it is not obvious to forecast which values of the weights provide the best results, several methods have been tested to provide a decision support for the tuning of these parameters.

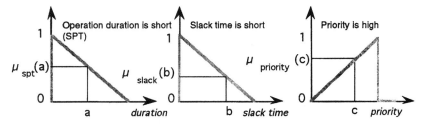

Figure 41.1   Membership functions of the propositions.

time units

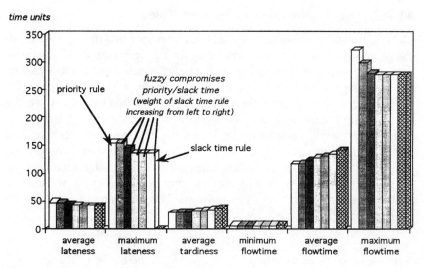

Figure 41.2   Influence of the weights on a compromise.

41.3. Tuning of the Balance between Rules

The first tested method was the experimental design method, using the Tagushi technique [7]. The performed tests have confirmed the interest of the compromises between rules [8], but the tuning of the balance between rules through the experimental design technique implies that new tests are made each time a set of jobs has to be scheduled. This is generally not possible in an industrial context. In order to avoid such tests, an expert system has been designed for the choice of the rule weights.

41.3.1. Fuzzy Expert System

The basic idea of the design of the expert system is to take into account the objectives of the workshop manager and the characteristics of the jobs in order to choose the different weights. Therefore, the premises of the production rules contain two kinds of propositions, describing the current objectives of the workshop and the applicability of a rule in accordance with the characteristics of the concerned jobs. We have chosen to represent the applicability of the rules according to the following basic characteristics of the jobs: the variation of the operation duration for SPT, the importance of the high-priority jobs for Priority, and tight or loose due dates for slack time rule.

The tests we made allowed to determine roughly the criteria that satisfy, or do not satisfy, the three rules. The results are consistent with those described in [3] and are summarized in Figure 41.3.

In order to avoid threshold effects [9], each parameter is calculated according to two fuzzy rules: one of them increases the value of the param-

criterion rule	average lateness	maximum lateness	average tardiness	average flowtime	maximum flowtime
SPT	average	poor	good	good	poor
priority	average	poor	good	good	poor
slack time	good	good	poor	poor	good

Figure 41.3 Rough appreciation of the performance of the rules.

eter, and the other decreases it. In the case of the SPT weight, these two rules are:

> IF (the variation of the duration is high) and (the minimization of the average tardiness and average flow time is important), THEN (the value of the SPT weight is high).

> IF (the variation of the duration is low) and (the minimization of the maximum lateness and the maximum flow time is important), THEN (the value of the SPT weight is low).

Each proposition is imprecise (through attributes such as "important" and "high") and defined by a fuzzy set. For a given set of jobs, the degree of satisfaction of the antecedent part of each rule is assessed and applied in the conclusion part of the rules to calculate the weights, with a method close to the fuzzy inference used in fuzzy control [10]. This method is shortly described hereafter.

Let us consider two production rules related to a particular dispatching rule k:

> Rule 1: if (x_1 is A_{11}) and (x_2 is A_{12}), then (w is low).

> Rule 2: if (x_1 is A_{21}) and x_3 is A_{22}), then (w is high).

Where the Aij are propositions containing fuzzy attributes, the xi are values of these attributes and w the weight of the dispatching rule. For a given input value, $x_1 = x_1°$, $x_2 = x_2°$ and $x_3 = x_3°$, we infer (fuzzification) a truth value for each rule by:

$$t1 = A11(x1°).A12(x2°) \qquad t2 = A21(x1°).A22(x3°)$$

where A is the membership degree of x to the fuzzy set A.

Each conclusion membership function is weighed by the corresponding truth value. An aggregated shape for all the rules is then derived by adding the modified conclusion membership functions of the two rules. The center of gravity w_g of this shape gives the weight attributed to the conclusion part of the rule (defuzzification):

$$w_g = \frac{t1 \cdot S1 \cdot Xg1 + t2 \cdot S2 \cdot Xg2}{t1 \cdot S1 + t2 \cdot S2}$$

where X_{gk} and S_k represent respectively the center of gravity and the surface of the conclusion membership function of rule k.

This expert system has been implemented on a Macintosh computer using the SuperCard environment. The rule weights calculated, thanks to this first version of fuzzy expert system, give better results than the SIPAPLUS standard rules in approximately 40 percent of the cases, and the same results in 10 percent of the cases. The best results are obtained for the minimization of the lateness and tardiness with improvements from 5 to 30 percent.

The improvement of the rule base is rather difficult. It is easy to find the best weights on a precise example, but the generalization of some examples through general production rules appears to be much more difficult. The influence of the workshop characteristics on the weights is, for instance, very difficult to express in rather simple production rules [6]. The neural network approach is an interesting alternative to the expert system in this case.

41.3.2. Neural Network

The basic idea of this method is to imitate the neural structure and connections with a computable model. A neural network is a set of interconnected neurons; the state of a neuron j depends on the value of $x_j = \sum w_{ij} \cdot y_i$ where y_i is the output of neuron i and the w_{ij} the weights of the connections between neuron i and neuron j (see Figure 41.4) [11]. The output value of neuron j y_j is given by $yj = 1/(1 + e^{-x_j})$, since the chosen transfer function for each neuron is a sigmoid.

The learning phase is performed through supervised learning; that is, it consists in showing examples to the neural network, along with their correct answers. The output values are compared with the expected result. Then, the error is back-propagated, which means that the values of the

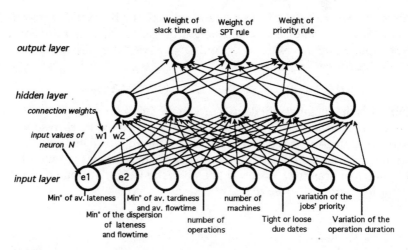

Figure 41.4 Neural network structure and inputs.

weights are successively modified, from the output layer to the input layer. At the end of the learning process, the network is able to find the correct answer to all the examples, but it can also generalize and find acceptable solutions to other cases. This property is of great interest in our study since we would like the network to interpolate results given a few typical examples.

We chose a network consisting of three layers, as shown in Figure 41.4. In order to define the input parameters, various research works led us to select the following points ([1], [3], [6] and [8]): dispersion of the priorities of the jobs, number of machines, number of operations per routing, dispersion of the operation duration, proximity of the due dates of the jobs. The output layer gives the attributed weights of the different rules. Three different kinds of objectives have been considered: minimization of the average lateness, minimization of the average tardiness and average flow time, minimization of the dispersion of the lateness. Eight different examples have then been defined, on the principle of the experimental design technique, and the optimal weights related to the three kinds of objectives have been searched. These 24 examples (eight examples scheduled with three different objectives) have then been presented to the neural network during the learning phase.

41.3.4. Results

Eighteen new representative examples have been designed in order to compare the results. The results of the neural network are better than those of the expert system: better solutions than those of the SIPAPLUS standard rules are obtained in more than 60 percent of the cases, and the neural network gives better results than the expert system in 75 percent of the cases. The performance of the neural network is quite good. Since the compromises suggested by the neural network give the best results on 11 experiments, and the benefit in comparison with the best rule of SIPAPLUS is more than 10 percent of the average value of the average lateness and average tardiness. In order to illustrate typical results, Figure 41.5 gives a comparison of the average lateness and average tardiness obtained on eight examples.

According to us, the essential point is that the neural network technique allows to take into account some characteristics of the workshops or jobs even if their influence is not clear; for instance, the number of machines and the number of operations per routing influence the result of the rules; however, we did not manage to express this influence through production rules. On the contrary, there was no problem with the neural network, because it was sufficient to add these characteristics to the examples. An improvement of the neural network only requires new examples, and not a better knowledge on the behavior of the rules as the expert system.

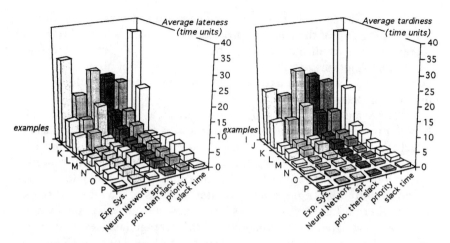

Figure 41.5   Comparison of the performances.

41.4. Conclusion

The optimization of the use of the manufacturing resources is an essential problem in workshops, which often requires the use of a scheduling software. Since the production context perpetually changes, there is a significant need in flexible scheduling tools that can be adapted to this context. The suggested fuzzy compromise between dispatching rules allows to take into account not only the current objectives of the workshop managers, but also the characteristics of the set of jobs and of the workshop. The adaptation of the dispatching rules to the production context sets the problem of their parametration. Different methods can be used in order to support decision in parameter tuning in complex cases. An important criterion of choice is the availability of "deep" knowledge on the process. Another criterion is the frequency of the tuning: an expert system or a neural network will not be designed for a few uses.

The design of a fuzzy expert system and the use of a neural network are considered in this chapter about the parameter tuning of fuzzy dispatching rules. Both solutions allow to use imprecise attributes for the description of a problem: it avoids to define many categories with all the implied threshold effects. As a general conclusion to these experiments, we can say that the fuzzy expert system approach allows to obtain a system ready to use very quickly when a strong expertise is available. The problem of the neural network is quite different: on one hand, much work can be required to find solutions to a sufficient set of problems, but on the other hand, there is no requirement of available "expertise" in order to improve the system.

Another point is that it is not directly possible to introduce the available *a priori* knowledge in the neural network. This is one of the reasons why combinations of fuzzy logic and neural networks may be of great interest: they allow to introduce a partial knowledge about the system, and therefore to shorten the learning phase even if this knowledge is not sufficient to design an expert system.

41.5. References

[1] Maccarthy, B.L., and J. Liu. "Addressing the Gap in Scheduling Research: A Review of Optimization and Heuristic Methods in Production Scheduling." *The International Journal of Production Research,* Vol. 1 (1993), pp. 59–79.

[2] Smith, S. "Knowledge-base Production Management: Approaches, Results and Prospectives." *Production Planning and Control,* Vol. 4 (1992), pp. 350–380.

[3] Montazeri, M., and L.N. Van Wassenhove. "Analysis of Scheduling Rules for a FMS." *International Journal of Production Research,* Vol. 4 (1990), pp. 785–802.

[4] Bel, G., et al. "Construction d'Ordonnancements Previsionnels: Un Compromis entre Approches Classiques et Systemes Experts." *APII,* Vol. 22 (1988), pp. 509–536.

[5] Grabot, B., et al. "Dispatching Rules in Scheduling: A Fuzzy Approach." *International Journal of Production Research,* Vol. 4 (1994), pp. 903–915.

[6] Boucon, D. Ordonnancement d'Atelier: Aide au Choix de Regles de Priorite. ENSAE, Ph.D. Thesis, Toulouse, 1991.

[7] Tagushi, G. *System of Experimental Design.* Unipub/Kraus International Publication, 1987.

[8] Grabot, B., et al. "A Multi-Heuristic Scheduling: Three Approaches to Tune Compromises." *Journal of Intelligent Manufacturing,* Vol. 5 (1994), pp. 303–313.

[9] Dubois, D., and H. Prade. *Possibility Theory, An Approach to Computerized Processing of Uncertainty.* New York: Plenum Press, 1988.

[10] Mizumoto, M. "Improvement Methods of Fuzzy Controls." *Proceedings, 3rd IFSA Congress.* pp. 60–62. 1989.

[11] Hertz, J., et al. *Introduction to the Theory of Neural Computation.* Addison-Wesley Publishing Company, 1991.

Index